RECREATIONAL SPORT PROGRAMMING

Fifth Edition

RICHARD F. MULL   **SCOTT A. FORRESTER**   **MARTHA L. BARNES**

SAGAMORE
PUBLISHING

©2013 Sagamore Publishing LLC

Publishers: Joseph J. Bannon and Peter L. Bannon
Director of Sales and Marketing: William A. Anderson
Director of Development and Production: Susan M. Davis
Technology Manager: Christopher Thompson
Production Coordinator: Amy S. Dagit

ISBN print edition: 978-1-57167-708-2
ISBN ebook: 978-1-57167-709-9
LCCN:2012952300

Sagamore Publishing LLC
1807 N. Federal Dr.
Urbana, IL 61801
www.sagamorepub.com

This fifth edition is dedicated to three previous authors who played essential roles in the development and evolution of this text's content. Special thanks and recognition go to:

Kathryn Bayless, *MS, Director, Campus Recreational Sports, Indiana University and Assistant Dean, School of Public Health (formerly School of Health, Physical Education and Recreation), Indiana University;*

Dr. Lynn Jamieson, *ReD, Professor, Department of Recreation, Park, and Tourism Studies, Indiana University; and*

Dr. Craig Ross, *ReD, Professor, Department of Recreation, Park, and Tourism Studies, Indiana University.*

Their contributions span over 30 years and integrate significant academic and practical knowledge of the recreational sport specialist and reflect their dedication to professional preparation and career development.

Contents

Preface

This text has been written to help current and future recreational sports leaders, or more specifically, programmers and specialists fulfill their role as professionals. The content will support and facilitate the learning concepts and facts as they relate to any management organization with the purpose to deliver sport as a leisure activity. With society becoming so health conscious and activity oriented, the role of sport is increasingly being recognized and supported as an integral part of everyday life for so many people. Hence, this text is designed to serve this interest and contributes to the professional preparation that takes place in sports management/kinesiology, recreation and leisure studies, and business. We will accomplish this by presenting recreational sports with its unique knowledge, key techniques and methods, leading to appreciation for it as a specialized field.

Part I, Foundations, addresses recreational sports as a theoretical and practical field of study. Chapter 1, Sports Identified; Chapter 2, Specialized Field; and Chapter 3, Management Model, each presents a logical frame of reference for complete insight to recreational sports.

In Part II, Values and Benefits, we review supporting research relevant to recreational sports and its critical role in today's society. Chapters 4 through 6 provide information on fitness and learning opportunities gained through sports participation as well as fun as a very popular outcome from participation.

In Part III, Program Delivery, we provide practical detail programming information that is relevant to any agency that wishes to deliver quality recreational sports experiences. Chapters 7 through 10 discuss traditional programming, which includes instructional sports, informal sports, intramural and extramural sports, and club sports, all of which represent the distinctive body of knowledge that recreational sport brings to an agency and its participants.

Being mindful of the academic interpretation of management and its overall role in curriculum and professional preparation, we will place emphasis on specific management areas and responsibilities that are judged critical and necessary to the recreational sports professional/programmer/specialist.

In Part IV, Resource Connection, we will look at the different resources and their impact on a specialist's role. In Chapter 11, Staffing, we examine the different personnel considerations and issues surrounding the supervision of paid and volunteer staff. In Chapter 12, Funding, we examine both income and expenditures along with pertinent budget and accounting information. Chapters 13 and 14 review key information and the significance for the existence and nature of facilities and equipment.

In Part V, Administrative Involvement, we provide select information where responsibilities can be integrated in any number of ways, but definitely part of everyday programming. In Chapter 15, Planning, we share the process of anticipating program details in order to assure the greatest possibilities for success! In Chapter 16, Marketing, we examine considerations that assess and then design efforts to attract participants. Chapter 17, Maintenance, creates awareness to details that could impact the recreational sports program delivery, an often behind the scenes function related to facilities and equipment. Chapter 18, Legal Concerns, addresses the need for security and safety measures to keep participants safe and reduce exposure to agency liability. Chapter 19, Career Implications, provides a closing that shares an overview of the nature and meaning as a recreational sport professional as well as career significance, options, and decisions.

Throughout the text we have updated the concept of career opportunities with the Shining Examples, helping the reader appreciate different agencies and the careers they offer. Also, at the beginning of each chapter, is a list of objectives and key concepts that signals the most important information in the chapter. Throughout the text, all Computer Tips have been updated. In addition, you will find examples of forms for use in daily programming operations.

Although changes have been incorporated into this edition of *Recreational Sports*, the basic premise has remained unchanged from the earlier editions. We have written the book for the specialist, providing information that will help the specialist initiate, maintain, and enhance the recreational experience for all participants. As in the prior four editions, the number one priority is to help professionals experience success in delivering recreational sports. We hope this text will contribute to the field's body of knowledge as well as the individual's ability to make a difference through recreational sports.

Acknowledgments

We are grateful for the assistance and contributions to this text from many people. In particular, special thanks to:

Donna Beyers for her editorial assistance, overall content preparation, and coordination of all the written material;

Evan Webb, graduate student at Brock University, St. Catharines, Ontario, Canada, for his research assistance and help with the shining examples and the instructor's guide for this text;

Bruce Hronek, Professor Emeritus, Department of Recreation, Park and Tourism Studies, Indiana University, who contributed to the chapter on legal concerns;

Kathryn Bayless, Director, Campus Recreational Sports, Indiana University, who developed the original content for the Informal and Club Sport chapters which is mostly maintained in this edition, and editing the content in this edition for the shining examples for Campus Recreational Sports and Club Sports;

Craig Ross, Professor, Department of Recreation, Park and Tourism Studies, Indiana University, who developed the original content for the Intramural and Extramural chapter, which is maintained in this edition, and the origination of the Computer Tips throughout the text;

Lynn Jamieson, Professor, Department of Recreation, Park and Tourism Studies, Indiana University, who developed the original concept and content for the shining examples; and

David Stewart, Indiana University Custom Publishing for providing distinct copies of selected figures in this text.

Our thanks also go to the following:

Vancouver Parks and Recreation

City of Welland Integrated Services - Recreation & Culture Division

City of Oakville Recreation and Culture Department

City of Reno-Parks, Recreation, and Community Services

In addition, thanks to all of the contributors of the shining examples who allowed us to share their successes in recreational sport programming.

Finally, we would like to acknowledge the millions of recreational sport participants—both active players and spectators. It is toward these individuals that all efforts in the text are directed, and it is our hope that the recreational sport specialists serving them will benefit from our experience and suggestions.

About the Authors

Richard F. Mull, MS, retired from Indiana University after 35 years of service. He served the School of Health, Physical Education, and Recreation (renamed the School of Public Health) in capacities as assistant professor (1972-2006); and as director of IU Campus Recreational Sports (1972-1992), HPER Auxiliary Operations; Center for Student Leadership Development; Tennis Center; and Outdoor Pool.

During his IU career, Mull created the Center for Student Leadership Development, a campus-wide leadership development concept that incorporated academic courses for student volunteers from various student organizations. He also created a student organization, Council for Advancing Student Leadership and was a significant influence with the development of the Student Recreational Sports Association, an active student voice in campus recreational sports.

His numerous professional contributions to the field led to his receipt of the 1989 Honor Award from the National Intramural-Recreational Sports Association (NIRSA). In 1994, he was inducted into the Professional Hall of Fame in the School of Sport and Physical Activity at West Virginia University. In 2006, Mull received the Office for Women's Affairs Athletic Award at Indiana University for his commitment to advancing opportunities for women in sport. Other awards included the Shoemaker Special Merit Award from the Division of Student Affairs, the Armstrong Ambassador Award from the IU Foundation, and the Student Recreational Sports Association Honor Award.

Mull has served as consultant and advisor in the field of recreational sports for more than 40 years. He also coauthored Recreation Facility Management, a current text used in the field of recreation and leisure studies. He also served as chairperson of the NIRSA's professional development committee, assistant chairperson of the NIRSA Standards Committee, and vice president of NIRSA. His contributions to this text include chapters 1-3, 13, 14, and 17. Throughout his career, Mull's special interests included professional preparation, student development, management, and leadership.

Scott Forrester, Ph.D., is an associate professor in the Department of Recreation and Leisure Studies at Brock University in St. Catharines, Ontario, Canada where he teaches courses in recreation programming, statistics, and campus recreation. He was previously an intramural graduate assistant and a doctoral research assistant in the Division of Recreational Sports at Indiana University while completing his master's degree in Recreational Sport Administration and his Ph.D. in Leisure Behaviour. He also briefly served as the interim Assistant Director for Club Sports at Indiana University. He is a lifetime member of NIRSA and currently serves on the editorial board for NIRSA's *Recreational Sports Journal* and is a member of NIRSA's Research and Assessment Committee. He has given numerous local, provincial, state, national, and international presentations on various topics related to recreational sports and has co-authored more than two dozen articles on the topic. His research examines the psycho-social determinants and benefits of participation in campus recreational sports and over the years his research has been recognized several times by NIRSA's President's RSJ Award for Outstanding Writing. His contributions to the text include chapters 4, 6-10, 15, and chapter 5, co-written with Dr. Barnes.

Martha Barnes, Ph.D., is an associate professor in the Department of Recreation and Leisure Studies at Brock University in St. Catharines, Ontario, Canada, where she teaches courses in community recreation, finance, and planning. Barnes received her Ph.D. in Recreation and Leisure Studies from the University of Waterloo. Previously, she worked as an assistant director at the Indiana University Tennis Center after the completion of her master's degree at Indiana University in Recreation Administration. Her research is focused on improving the delivery of sport and recreation in communities. Specific past projects have included understanding community partnerships, park use, sport councils, volunteer management, and networks among sport and recreation organizations. She has presented locally, regionally, nationally, and internationally for associations such as the National Recreation and Park Association, North American Society for Sport Management,

Canadian Association for Leisure Studies, and World Leisure on various topics related to community sport and recreation. Her work has also been published in several refereed, professional journals, related to recreation and sport management. Her contributions to the text include chapters 11, 12, 16, 19 and chapter 5, co-written with Dr. Forrester.

Part I

FOUNDATIONS

Part I introduces recreational sports as not only an academic field of study but a career opportunity as well. Key theories and concepts cover a variety of points, including a basic description of leisure and sport, a specialized field, and a comprehensive management model fundamental to all work-related responsibilities. The content is based on a logical and practical interpretation of very extensive and complicated historical information that hopefully will help the recreational sport specialist to have a sound, intellectual foundation to recreational sport.

CHAPTER 1

Identified and Realized

CHAPTER OBJECTIVES

After reading this chapter, the reader will be familiar with basic recreational sport terminology, understand the divisive and unifying aspects of sport, understand the leisure sport management model, and be able to describe the four sport management areas.

KEY CONCEPTS

Health	Playing	Activity
Leisure	Cooperation	Game form
Recreation	Competition	Leisure sport management model
Sport	Co-opetition	Sport management areas

Introduction

Fundamental to any subject is understanding and appreciating its meaning by learning relevant terms and concepts that support its entity. Recreational sport is a subject as well as a professional undertaking that requires a description because its identity and reality have encountered a moderately confused and diverse interpretation. Terms used to describe recreational sport include *physical activity, recreational programming, intramural sport, physical recreation,* and *athletics*; however, these terms do not adequately represent everything that recreational sport encompasses. In most settings, the definition of recreational sport lacks uniformity, consistency, and accuracy—all of which are necessary if recreational sport is to become a viable professional subject.

Consistent language that reflects the true nature of recreational sport is needed. Toward that end, this chapter presents past efforts to define sport, followed by a discussion of popular terms, including a variety of relevant concepts. Finally, a unified definition is presented, based on the four distinct sport management areas of the leisure sport management model.

This chapter is intended to help identify recreational sport as an important subject with both practical and academic substance.

Basic Concepts

To explore the foundation upon which recreational sport stands, it is necessary to take a close look at four key subjects: health, leisure, recreation, and sport. Each of these subjects has a social, cultural, and economic influence on society. Health, leisure, recreation, and sport are the foundation for recreational sport.

Health

Health is described as a state of physical, mental, and social well-being that might also include spiritual practices. Its discussion includes the mind and body, and its general condition can encompass a variety of positive and negative circumstances that can impact one's overall health.

More specifically, *mental health* is the measure of an individual's emotional and psychological well-being and how he or she is able to use cognitive and emotional capabilities to function in society. Central to this is the human brain at the helm of the central nervous system. On the other hand, *physical health* describes the status of bodily parts and functions that allow an individual to navigate his or her environment efficiently and effectively. It requires the seamless integration of all body parts and systems to function properly. Good health represents freedom from disease and abnormalities, hence the medical, education, and practical practice of fostering healthful living.

These definitions overlap and contribute to the overall concept of health and its integration into this text. Areas such as sleep, hygiene, nutrition, recreation, and exercise combine together to facilitate healthy living. Such activities involve one's personal care, practices, and use of leisure.

Leisure

Leisure can be categorized into two broad categories: qualitative and quantitative. The *qualitative* concept of leisure, exemplified by the early writings of Aristotle on the Greek upper class, perceives leisure as an expression of superior spiritual activities of the mind and body. This school of thought holds that leisure is a state of being in which people are free from biological or work constraints. The individual focuses on contemplation and reflection of activities once reserved for the highly educated, or the upper class. Today, education is no longer restricted to the upper class, so less emphasis is placed on leisure as a state of being.

The *quantitative* school of thought views leisure as discretionary use of time. Human functions are grouped into three types: personal care, work, and leisure. Personal care refers to time spent eating, sleeping, or attending to personal maintenance and bodily functions. Work is time spent training for a vocation and participating in gainful employment. Leisure is unobligated time spent participating in activities of personal interest. Its meaning is well documented, and it is a significant subject that is highly visible and easily recognizable. During leisure time individuals have the opportunity to choose to participate in an activity that ideally is positive, constructive, and healthy—recreation.

Recreation

Recreation is often defined as voluntary activity that creates a diversion from work. It is a reenergizing, socially acceptable use of leisure time. Recreation is a leisure-time experience during which the choices and expected outcomes of participation are left to the individual. The goal of recreational management is to provide participants with a variety of activities to choose from and to help participants have positive experiences.

People all over the world pursue a variety of leisure-time activities, making recreation a broad term. In addition, each leisure activity can have its own specialized areas of study. To move toward identifying recreational sport as a leisure-time activity, it is important to review the types of activities that recreation encompasses.

Social activity. Social activity is a broad category of recreation that fosters congenial, noncompetitive participation among people sharing a common interest. It emphasizes human interaction and often takes the form of parties, dances, conversation, dining, and other social activities.

Cultural activity. Cultural activities provide opportunities for individuality, creativity, and self-expression:

- *Art* focuses on creating aesthetic objects. Examples are painting, woodworking, sculpting, and crafts.
- *Dance*, such as folk, square, modern, or ballet, focuses on rhythmic patterns in movement.
- *Drama* is storytelling in a theatrical presentation.
- *Literary*, *mental*, and *linguistic* activities emphasize mental challenges and include reading, working puzzles, learning languages, and writing.
- *Music* involves vocal and instrumental expression of sound that possesses rhythm, melody, and harmony.

Outdoor activity. Any leisure activity experienced in the outdoors is considered an outdoor activity, but what distinguishes this type of activity is its emphasis on what the environment brings to the activity. The activities most often associated with outdoor leisure include hiking, camping, mountain climbing, spelunking, rafting, backpacking, cycling, boating, skiing, and snow sledding.

Garden activity. The garden is often seen as a place of peace and tranquility. Gardening activities focus on planning, implementing, and maintaining a plot where herbs, fruits, flowers, or vegetables are cultivated. Many participate in gardening activity for its therapeutic benefits of relaxation and distraction from work.

Fitness activity. Fitness activity involves activities whose main goal is to improve physical health. The list of fitness activities is seemingly endless with jogging, cycling, swimming, and walking being the most popular.

Faith-based activity. Many people spend a large portion of their leisure time engaged in faith-based activities. Faith-based activities are based on religious or spiritual practices. They often involve group participation in celebratory or service-oriented events, such as weekly worship services, choir practice, soup kitchens, and international mission trips. Faith-based activities also encompass individual activities such as prayer, meditation, and study.

Hobby activity. A hobby is a leisure activity involving a personal interest. Hobbies include collecting, constructing, or pursuing objects of special interest; examples are stamp and coin collecting, antiques, crafts, photography, bird-watching, and traveling. Hobbies are self-proclaimed areas of interest that often overlap with the other types of leisure activity.

Special-events activity. Special events is a catchall category that includes activities that involve a change of pace in a unique or nontraditional format. Special events may be short term, ongoing, or seasonal and include fairs, concerts, and open houses.

Sport activity. Sport is everywhere, reflecting many facets of the world's cultures. It ranges from a child's frolic and play to an athlete's vigilance in preparing for the Olympics to an executive creating a healthy lifestyle through sport participation to an adolescent watching sports on television. As a form of recreation, sport has been shaped by tradition, popularity, and potential for profit. It has evolved and prospered to the extent that it plays a major role in everyday life.

Figure 1.1 diagrams the health, leisure, recreation, and sport progression, or how basic human existence leads to sport activity as recreation. As this chapter continues, it will build a foundation of terms that describes sport and provides a solid framework for understanding sport as a healthy form of leisure activity.

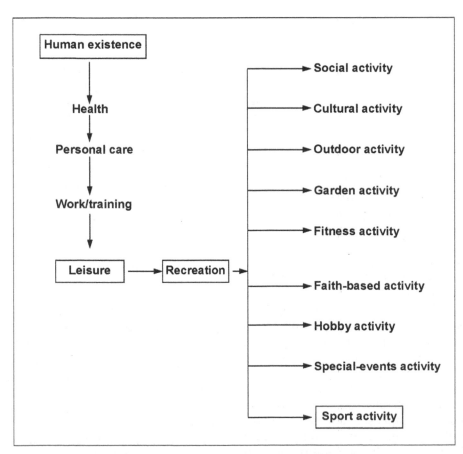

Figure 1.1. Establishing the Existence of Sport Activity

Exploring Sport

For decades, the definition of sport has been under debate, resulting in a variety of interpretations and professional and scholarly polarization. Scholars, schools, and agencies have staked out their particular intellectual territory by describing and applying sport as a means to some particular end. The subsequent confusion has resulted in linguistic and conceptual inconsistency as well as a myopic view of sport, and it has restricted the development of the recreational sport movement. The following material presents a unified management approach to all areas of sport and consistent terminology that provides a platform from which all factions can begin to work together.

Discerning Applications

Sport has been around since the beginning of recorded time. Countless books have been written on the history of sport, and it is a complete area of scholarly study. Unfortunately, as sport has evolved, its true meaning has been distorted because of varied forms of interpretations and inconsistent applications. It could be observed that only the gifted have the opportunity to fully benefit from the many ways sport promotes human growth and development. Less gifted participants often have been relegated to inferior programs that have poor or untrained leadership. There has been a growing emphasis on more inclusive sports programming for everyone, but these gains are minor compared to the benefits more talented athletes experience.

The predominance of the "sport for the athlete" mind-set has been fueled by both commercial and academic systems. Commercially, the demand for opportunities to watch athletes compete has encouraged administrators of these programs within sport to command resources (money, people, facilities, and equipment) and implement policies that set up elitism among participants. In the academic community, the recreational aspects of sport have been somewhat neglected in academic, participant, and professional preparation programs, while the educational and athletic aspects have prospered. Traditionally, physical education and recreation scholars have interpreted sport as activity for the skilled participant or the participant interested in learning how to develop sport skills, ignoring participants that do not fall into these two modes of involvement.

Recently, these scholars have begun to include sports management and exercise science in curricular development, but the emphasis remains upon the skilled participant, restricting both the development of sport as a discipline and the preparation of sport professionals. This situation evolved from the belief that the training of sport leaders should be grounded in physical science rather than management and business—a bias that limits the societal and cross-cultural potential of sport. This occurred because the physical education or sport teacher provided the scholarly leadership and also coached the athletic teams. It is a bias in the academic community that does not parallel society. While proponents in the United States have advanced this bias in favor of the elite athlete, most of the rest of the world has supported a recreational approach to sport that involves millions of people. There are some recreation agencies, training programs, and supervisory programs that attempt to advance recreational sport, but progress continues to be limited by a restricted vision of traditional physical education, now often referred to as kinesiology.

In light of this situation, a redefinition of sport that more accurately incorporates all its aspects is necessary in order to eliminate the biases and political influences that result in the inequities just described. This redefinition would have the potential to unify all areas of sport and advance its entire existence, thereby broadening the understanding of recreational sport around the world.

Varied Interpretations

Although many scholars have made admirable attempts to define sport, no single definition has encompassed the concept of sport in its entirety. To illustrate this dilemma, Figure 1.2 presents previously proposed definitions for sport. Each of these definitions contains limiting statements that necessitate sport as "competitive," "institutionalized," "physical in nature," or "organized according to a definite set of rules." These perspectives restrict sport to primarily the athletic and professional areas, and they leave out the recreational characteristics, such as mind, cooperation, and flexibility, out of many forms of sport. Such definitions limit unity among the different delivery areas of sport.

In contrast, the definition of sport in Figure 1.3 is too inclusive to be of practical value. It is too broad, encompassing delivery areas and time of activity.

Many of the authors quoted in Figures 1.2 and 1.3 openly admit to challenges in defining sport. Coakley (2008) suggests that definitions of sport are often limiting, placing too much emphasis on organized sport, thus the need for an alternative description. The definition of sport must be further developed by taking into consideration its true meaning, existence, and expansiveness. These considerations become critical as recreational sport looks to be incorporated into established management areas of sport such as athletics and professional sports.

- *Sport is a competitive physical activity, utilizing specialized equipment and facilities, with unique dimensions of time and space, in which the quest for records is of high significance.*
  (Vanderzwagg, 1988)

- *Any institutional game demanding the demonstration of physical prowess.*
  (Loy, McPherson, and Kenyon, 1978)

- *A competitive human physical activity that requires skill and exertion, governed by institutionalized rules.*
  (Snyder and Spreitzer, 1989)

- *A competitive form of play organized according to a definite set of rules and determinate boundaries of time and space.*
  (Martin and Miller, 1999)

- *Sports are institutionalized, competitive activities that involve rigorous physical exertion of the use of relatively complex physical skills by participants motivated by personal enjoyment and external rewards.*
  (Coakley, 2001)

Figure 1.2. Restrictive Definition of Sport

- **Sport is any activity, experience, or business enterprise focused on fitness, recreation, athletics, or leisure.**

  (Pitts, Fielding and Miller, 1994)

Figure 1.3. Broad Definition of Sport

A Unifying Description

Because this text is about how best to provide sport opportunities for everyone, it is logical for it to include a definition that describes sport in this light, incorporating all aspects of sport. The definition is this: Sport is playing cooperative–competitive activity in the game form. This definition liberates sport from the traditional, restrictive model that fails to recognize the depth and breadth of its diversity, management areas, and history. It is also a unifying description that encompasses each unique delivery area (education, recreation, athletics, and professional) of sport without one area taking on greater meaning. Careful consideration of this definition warrants breaking it into its components and explaining each one.

Playing

The first component, playing, describes the expectation that evolves out of human emotion in sport. Playing represents the state of mind or emotions that a person brings to and expects from sport participation. These emotions come from the challenge, risk, and chance that are inherent in sport. Challenge incorporates the excitement of the attempt and the struggle toward success and satisfaction, or failure and disappointment. Risk stirs one's mental state as it relates to danger, hazard, and the possibility of suffering harm. Chance is the unpredictability of sport that is enticing to so many. Figure 1.4 illustrates the emotional highs and lows associated with sport as well as the elements of play and the varied emotions that sport provokes.

The word *play* has been associated with all levels and forms of sport, as demonstrated by phrases such as playing professional football, playing in the backyard, playing on varsity teams, playing cards, playing golf, and so on. It is a word that represents the abstract emotions that come from all sorts of sport activity.

Cooperative–Competitive

This component of the unifying definition establishes the idea of involvement in sport as being cooperative and competitive. Both terms are part of all sport, although one may have greater emphasis at any given time. By placing these words at two extremes on a horizontal continuum, as shown in Figure 1.5, one can better understand their relationship. The left side of the continuum represents harmony and collaboration, while the right side represents struggle and conflict, with the extremes of the continuum being peace and war. Cooperation and competition are both integral to sport, which creates and reflects the potential for intensity in sport.

The sport intensity continuum also reflects the individual's interest as experienced through a wide array of levels of involvement. Involvement varies so greatly that cooperation and competition within sport can be integrated into a single concept: co-opetition. Sport involvement is never either cooperation or competition; it is a combination of both, with intensity of involvement taking shape through a person's level of commitment.

Activity

The word *activity* within this definition of sport represents the unique mental and physical process each person brings to sport, as shown in Figure 1.6. Sport is more than a physical process, it is a complicated union of the mind and body, otherwise known as the psychomotor process. Everyone has a certain level of ability in sport that is reflected through talent and effort. Ability either limits or enhances an individual's skill, and this information is used to determine an activity level for participation. Activity level can be structured as beginner, intermediate, or advanced as well as recreational, athletic, or professional.

Activity also represents a broader concept than sport. Several non-sport activities share many of the same mind–body characteristics as sport, including dance, drama, physical work, and music. Because activity is a general concept, it allows a person to bring the mind and body as a unified process.

Game Form

The final component of the definition, game form, describes the format, structure, and props (equipment that supports the activity) of sport. Game form has key considerations such as rules and regulations, strategies, facilities, and equipment, as illustrated in Figure 1.7.

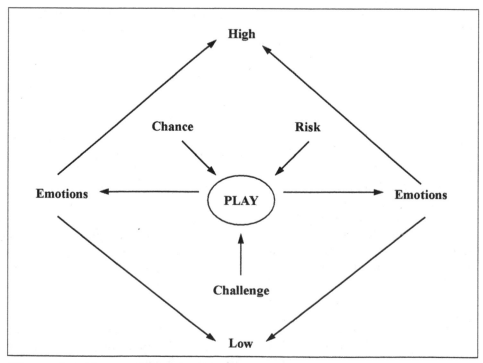

Figure 1.4. Play and Emotions in Sport

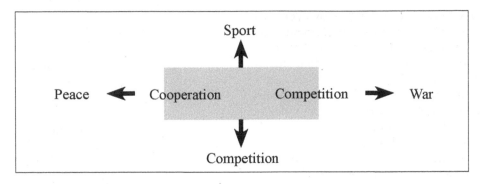

Figure 1.5. Sport Intensity Continuum

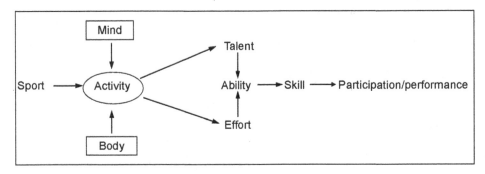

Figure 1.6. Unifying the Mind and Body in Sport

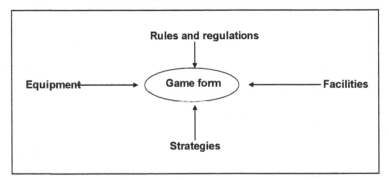

Figure 1.7. Key Sport Ingredients

Rules and regulations establish the procedures and governances necessary for sport to occur. They are the boundaries that control the action. Sport rules and regulations can vary greatly or be modified to fit different needs and interests, ranging from informal, casual participation to formal sponsorships and sanctioned events. Strategies are the plans and judgments that transpire to allow for any number of outcomes, incorporating all aspects of the sport effort and format. Facilities are the indoor or outdoor structures where sport occurs. Equipment includes the apparatus items, props, and objects that are used to facilitate the sport. Facilities and equipment enable the sport experience and represent tremendous diversity among sport.

The game form is what separates sport from other cooperative–competitive activities, such as dance, music, art, and drama. Such activities could be considered sport if conducted in a game form. For example, some auditions for musicals or theatrical productions incorporate characteristics of the game form, as do art exhibits that rank the work of contestants according to predetermined criteria. However, this interpretation is an extreme view of sport, mentioned only to describe the recreational potential of sport.

The game form also looks at interests that are not often recognized as sport but are popular as recreational activity, such as card games, gambling, board games, and video games. Each of these activities is different, but they all have game ingredients that allow them to fit into the world of sport.

What is important about this description of sport is that it embraces all of its elements, without a special interest, bias, or political system allowing one to have a dominant role over another. It allows sport to exist as an encompassing societal process, a broader area of study and research, and a diverse focus in management that views sport as a product for business, participation, and fun. It also creates a unified body of knowledge that is important for sport as an academic discipline or area of professional preparation.

Leisure Sport

With leisure defined as time away from work and personal care and sport defined as playing competitive–cooperative activity in the game form, it is time to show a system that illustrates how sport exists in society. Sport as it exists in leisure is complicated, especially because it has such diverse interests and applications. The purpose of the following model is to bring this diversity together, demonstrating recreational sport as a vital element of leisure.

Model

The leisure sport management model (Figure 1.8) incorporates all the management and organizational areas of sport, or the different fields that deliver sport as a product. The model is a hierarchy of sport, with its base representing the widest range of participation—educational and recreational sport. Participation decreases up the hierarchy to the apex, professional sport. At the apex, professional sport has fewer direct participants; however, there are more spectators. This model shows sport involvement as both direct participation (participant) and indirect participation (spectator). Both types of involvement can be considered as engaging in sport during leisure time.

The leisure sport management model also shows that the emphasis of sport as a product includes fun and fitness, two extremely popular outcomes of sport participation. These outcomes represent a complete philosophy and even a discipline unto itself by many scholarly interpretations. Equally popular as an end product is the enjoyment and diversion derived from spectatorship. Here, too, is a complete mind-set in the world of entertainment resulting from sport. All

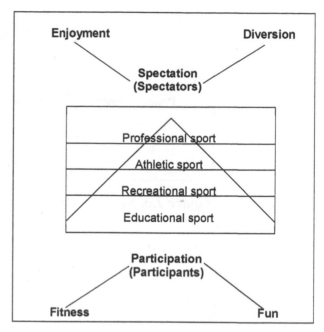

Figure 1.8. Leisure Sport Management Model

four categories of sport, as seen in the model, depict concepts that represent not only sport in leisure but also recreation and its basic beliefs. The terms represent fundamental societal interests that are real and easy to understand and appreciate.

Management Areas

Now that sport has been demonstrated as a viable aspect of society as reflected in the leisure sport management model, it is necessary to take the next step and describe each of the general management areas of sport. Each management area has a unique existence and history. The intent here is to further explain the leisure sport management model, providing specific descriptions that advance the meaning of sport in society and unify the different management areas.

Educational Sport

Educational sport management, or physical education, has been around since the beginning of institutional learning. It is part of an extremely broad, comprehensive system of education that includes subjects such as history, math, reading, and science. In this area of management, sport skills, strategies, and knowledge are taught in formal academic courses. Knowledge and skill are measured against a standard through planned and prescribed courses with professionally trained teachers. Educational sport occurs in public and private educational systems, including preschool, kindergarten, elementary school, junior high or middle school, high school, preparatory school, and college.

Recreational Sport

Although it has always been around, recreational sport has not been as well attended as other forms of sport management. It has evolved a great deal because people are naturally interested in its existence and applications. It has prospered largely through volunteer systems committed to the principle of sport for all and enthusiasm for sport participation in the pursuit of one's positive health.

Recreational sport includes the delivery of sport for the sake of fitness and fun. It is a diverse area that incorporates five program delivery areas: instructional sport, informal sport, intramural sport, extramural sport, and club sport. Each of the five areas represents a variety of participant ability levels and interests and is defined by its management interests, responsibilities, and principles of operation. They will be covered in detail in Chapters 7 through 10 of this text.

Athletic Sport

Historically, the most popular form of sport is athletic sport, which emphasizes rivalry, winning, and community bonding through participation and spectatorship. The contests and tournaments of athletic sport have brought it popularity and an institutional management system.

The basic premise of athletic sport includes directing individuals toward a margin of excellence in performance that can be identified as wanting and needing to win. The participant receives the best leadership, and this leadership emphasizes excellence in skill development. An athletic sport incorporates organizational sponsorship through junior varsity and varsity systems as well as through amateur systems and the Olympic system. Each athletic sport perpetuates itself because of spectator interest, enthusiasm for winning, and resource availability.

Professional Sport

The natural outgrowth of athletic sport is a system where the very best are brought together to compete at the highest level. This level includes marketing the athletes and sporting events with an emphasis on entertainment. It also involves financial gain to the highly skilled participants and management leadership. Participation occurs between pro athletes and different corporate sponsors, with the creation of income from spectators as a major consideration, because income affects the success of the sport franchise.

The world of professional sport takes many directions, which will be identified later. Much like recreational sport, professional sport has only recently progressed with professional preparation and studies.

All categories of the leisure sport management model support playing cooperative–competitive activity in the game form, allowing experts and scholars alike to place themselves into this structure to teach, manage, conduct research, and collaborate as colleagues while sharing a common, unifying meaning. The combination of health, leisure, recreation, and sport into a single entity can be challenging, but that does not mean it should not be unified as presented here. Unification works logically, supporting integration rather than discrimination, positing sport and leisure as two heathy and significant areas of society.

Conclusion

At this point, the full meaning of sport as well as how recreational sport fits into the scheme of leisure and recreation should be clear. Although this text's primary interest is recreational sport, it is important to respect the full meaning and depth of sport in the United States and throughout the world. Sport is real and carries tremendous value, and it deserves to have scholars and practitioners come together under a single definition and a cooperative spirit of knowing and appreciating sport.

The future of recreational sport will be determined by its positioning within the overall role of health, leisure services, and sport. How well the recreational sport specialist provides recreational services depends on his or her understanding of the basic makeup of recreational sport. Having a sound foundation accomplishes this and helps the recreational sport specialist reach the next level of awareness and career achievement. The basic knowledge of the identity and recognition of recreational sport should not be taken lightly because it is the cornerstone of the recreational sport specialist's career foundation.

Bibliography

Coakley, J. (2008). *Sports in society: Issues and controversies* (10th ed.). New York: McGraw-Hill.

Collins, M., & Kay, T. (2003). *Sport and social exclusion*. London: Taylor and Francis.

Cresswell, S., Hodge, K., & Kidmann, L. (2003). Intrinsic motivation in youth sport: Goal orientations and motivational climate. *Journal of Physical Education, 36*(1), 15-26.

Dawson, P., & Downward, P. (2011). Participation, spectatorship, and media coverage in sport: Some initial insights. In W. Andref (Ed.), *Contemporary issues in sports economics* (pp.15-42). Cheltenham, UK; Northampton, MA: Edward Elgar.

Dobbs, M. E. (2010). Co-opetition matrix for analyzing the cooperation competition mix in an industry: Examples from Major League Baseball. *Competition Forum, 8*(1), 35-43.

Eyles, J., & Williams, A. (2008). *Sense of place, health, and quality of life*. Hampshire, England: Ashgate Publishing.

Freeman, W. H. (2012). *Physical education and sport science in a changing society* (7th ed.). Sudbury, MA: Jones and Bartlett Learning.

Hall, A. E., Kuga, D. J., & Jones, D. F. (2002). A multivariate study of determinants of vigorous physical activity in a multicultural sample of college students. *Journal of Sports & Social Issues, 26*(1), 66-84.

Hammit, W. E., Backlund, E. A., Bixler, R. D. (2006). Place bonding for recreational places: Conceptual and empirical development. *Leisure Studies, 25*(1), 17-41.

Hosta, M. (2009). Play-sport culture. *Journal of Human Sport and Exercise, 4*(2), 72-77.

Jamieson, L., Ross, C., & Swartz, J. (1994). Research in recreational sports management: A content analysis approach. *National Intramural-Recreational Sports Association Journal, 19*(1), 12-14.

Jarvie, G. (2006). *Sport culture and society: An introduction*. New York, NY: Routledge.

Jowett, S. (2007). *Social psychology in sport*. Champaign, IL: Human Kinetics.

Kiger, J. R. (1997). *An examination of the determinants to the overall recreational sports participation among college students*. Eugene: University of Oregon Press.

Loy, J. W., McPherson, B. D., & Kenyon, G. S. (1978). *Sport and social systems: A guide to the analysis, problems, and literature*. Menlo Park, CA: Addison Wesley–Benjamin Cumming.

Martin, R., & Miller, T. (1999). *Sport cult*. Minneapolis: University of Minnesota Press.

Milne, G. R., & McDonald, M. A. (1999). *Sport marketing: Managing the exchange process*. Champaign, IL: Human Kinetics.

Mull, R. (1982). Toward a philosophical basis. In W. Holsberry, G. Lamke, and C. Vos Strache (Eds.), *Intramural–recreational sports: Its theory and practice* (p. 253). Corvallis, OR: National Intramural-Recreational Sports Association.

Mull, R. (1985). In support of calling things by their right names. *National Intramural–Recreational Sports Association Journal, 9*(2), 4-7.

Mull, R. (1986). Going beyond calling things by their right names. *National Intramural–Recreational Sports Association Journal, 10*(2), 3-4.

Parks, J., Quarterman, J., & Thibault, L. (2007). *Contemporary sport management*. Champaign, IL: Human Kinetics.

Pitts, B. G., Fielding, L. W., & Miller, L. K. (1994). Industry segmentation theory and the sport industry: Developing a sport industry segment model. *Sport Marketing Quarterly, 3*(1), 15-24.

Rohm, A. J., Milne, G. R., McDonald, M. A. (2006). A mixed-methods approach for developing market segmentation typologies in the sports industry. *Sport Marketing Quarterly, 15*, 29-39.

Ross, S. R., Rausch, M. K., & Canada, K. E. (2003). Competition and cooperation in the five factor model: Individual differences in achievement orientation. *The Journal of Psychology, 137*(4), 323-337.

Smith, E. (Ed.). (2010). *Sociology of sport and social theory*. Champaign, IL: Human Kinetics.

Smith, S. R., & Carron M. F. (1990). Comparison of competition and cooperation in intramural sport. *National Intramural–Recreational Sports Association Journal, 14*(2), 44-47.

Snyder, E. E., & Spreitzer, E. A. (1989). *Social aspects of sport* (3rd ed.). Englewood Cliffs, NJ: Prentice Hall.

Thomson, R. (2000). Physical activity through sport and leisure: Traditional versus 7 noncompetitive activities. *Journal of Physical Education, 33*(1), 34-39.

Vanderzwagg, H. J. (1998). Policy development in sport management (2nd ed.). Westport, CT: Praeger.

Weinberg, R. S., & Gould, D. (2011). *Foundations of sport and exercise psychology*. Champaign, IL: Human Kinetics.

Whannel, G. (2008). *Culture, politics, and sport: Blowing the whistle, revisited*. New York, NY: Routledge.

Williams, D. R. (2002). Leisure identities, globalization, and the politics of place. *Journal of Leisure Research, 34*(4), 351-368.

Zeigler, E. F. (1985). Guest editorial: Call things by their right names. *National Intramural– Recreational Sports Association Journal, 9*(2), 3.

Zeigler, E. F. (2002). The physical education and sport curriculum in the 21st century: Proposed common denominators. *Physical Educator, 59*(3), 114.

Zeigler, E. F. (2010). *Management theory and practice in physical activity education*. Victoria, BC: Trafford Publishing.

CHAPTER 2

A Specialized Field

CHAPTER OBJECTIVES

After reading this chapter, you will be familiar with the evolution of recreational sport; recognize the five program delivery areas of recreational sport; know the service and development purpose of recreational sport; comprehend the difference between active and passive participation; appreciate the broad audience of recreational sport; and be able to describe the 10 recreational sport settings and the significance that recreational sport offers to the individual, the community, the environment, and the economy.

KEY CONCEPTS

**National Intramural–Recreational
 Sport Association (NIRSA)**
Extracurricular activities
Community–society model
Delivery areas
Instructional sport

Informal sport
Intramural sport
Extramural sport
Club sport
Service
Development

Passive participation
Active participation
Audience
Delivery centers
Benefits

Introduction

The last chapter set the context for recreational sport as part of health, leisure, recreation, and sport. This chapter broadens that context to address recreational sport as a professional field. It covers topics such as the field's evolution, programming areas, underlying mission and goals, participation, different participants, settings and agencies, and its significance. From a theoretical perspective, recreational sport has been presented as a viable aspect of society, having a function unique from other areas of recreation and sport. Although scholarly and practical differences in the interpretation of sport result in varied approaches and opinions, this chapter provides substantial information that supports recreational sport as a specialized field.

Evolution

Recreational sport has evolved to unprecedented levels of participation. Almost everyone is involved in some form of recreational sport, such as working with a personal trainer, attending a sport clinic, participating in a tournament, learning to swim, climbing a mountain, watching professional sport, or playing sport video games. Such extensive leisure sport activity demonstrates not only its current significance but also its historical meaning.

Studies of the evolution of sport in the United States and other cultures have resulted in numerous texts on sport history, leisure, and recreation. Such documentation comes from teachers (the history of physical education) or coaches (the history of sport and athletics), and it often includes very little about the far-reaching implications of recreational sport, or, as it was once called, intramural sport. The recreation scholar almost always referred to sport as physical activity, recreation activity, athletics, and so on but hardly ever as described in this text. Although there was a national system that influences participation and involvement, its true meaning took the backseat to the primary mission that dominated such interests.

The mid-1970s saw the beginning of a new movement for recreational sport in society. A major development took place when a small national association adopted the name "recreational sport" to reflect the many types of sport activity they represented. The National Intramural–Recreational Sport Association professionalized the existence and meaning of recreational sport. Although this leisure activity existed, its real meaning as a specialization did not exist until then.

Progression

The documented origin of recreational sport can be observed as a progression in Figure 2.1. The existence of sport in the 1900s was characterized by an early school model that delivered sport in the form of physical education classes and extracurricular intramural and athletic sports. Sport offerings have since expanded to include a variety of sport agencies throughout the world. This is referred to as a community or society model because it takes into account modern delivery systems that transcend a specific agency and embrace all interest areas and levels of sport participation.

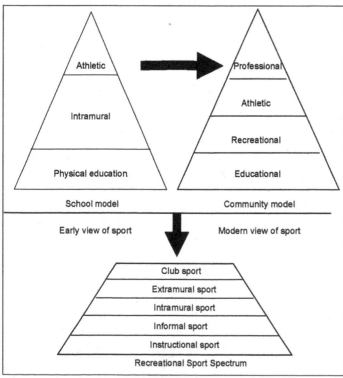

Figure 2.1. The Evolution of Sport

Within the progression of sport is a segment called the recreational sport spectrum. This spectrum is part of the leisure sport management model, and it identifies the different delivery areas of recreational sport. This spectrum emphasizes the participant's involvement in sport during leisure rather than the agency's involvement in delivering it.

Formal Beginnings

Although the concept of sport for everyone has been around for many years, the formalization or professionalization of the process regarding recreational sport as a specialization did not begin until the mid-1970s. Leaders and some scholars in the field incorporated various aspects of recreational sport or intramural sport in journals, articles, and conferences and presentations, but seldom did these definitions represent the full meaning of recreational sport in society. Two doctoral projects can be regarded as the formal beginning of the knowledge that represents recreational sport as a specialized field.

Competency analysis. In 1980, Lynn Jamieson completed her doctoral dissertation at Indiana University. Her dissertation recognized the need to conduct competency analyses in recreational sport. The study focused on management details involved with the administration and delivery of recreational sport in three different settings: community, military, and higher education. This information influenced the standards for collegiate recreational sport as well as other subsequent doctoral dissertations. Most recently in 2004, Bob Barcelona and Craig Ross continued to assess, verify, and develop competencies for the professional delivery of recreational sport programs. In order for a profession to exist, it must include competencies that reflect not only the work that is involved but also the values and meaning of its existence.

Percentage of sport. Realizing sport was growing in popularity, John Laws emphasized recreational sport in his 1986 doctoral dissertation. His study assessed the percentage of sport activity and programming in the community setting. The significance of sport activity was revealed in the budget data, which reflected far greater support of sport than of other recreational activities. This data not only shed light upon the extent to which resources were being used to support sport activity, but it also created awareness of the importance of addressing these areas as part of professional preparation.

In support of this percentage of sports, there was a survey 25 years ago by the National Sporting Goods Association (nsga.org) that assessed the fiscal aspect and participation in a variety of recreational sports. The purpose was to judge the extent of household expenditures on sporting equipment. In

2010, the same survey found continued and significant growth both economically and in participation. Such information also establishes the meaning and value of recreational sport in terms of its financial scope and participation at the national level, clearly indicating the significance of recreational sport as an academic discipline.

This formal beginning led to a body of knowledge that this entire text reflects. Although the idea of recreational sport or sport for everyone has been around for a long time, its interpretation was limited by the traditional physical education and athletic leadership. But with these various studies, the field saw the beginning and continuation of recreational sport as a field of study.

Extensiveness

Although not as well recorded as other areas of sport, it is still clear that, over time, recreational sport has been influenced by the heritage of a people and the desire for enjoyment, ritual, and competition between individuals and groups. Today, recreational sport is a major component of most individuals' lifestyle through either participation or sport spectation, with each individual benefiting from what sport brings. The following material points out just how extensive recreational sport has become.

Recreational sport delivery operations exist in literally thousands of agencies and businesses. Over 120 countries offer a nationally sponsored sport policy and program according to Jamieson and Pan (2000). In addition, within each leisure service delivery system, whether public or private, sport programming represents 60–80% of total recreational offerings. The demand for sport activity is part of what has fueled recent reports that recreation specialist positions are one of the top five employment opportunities available to college graduates. With sport as the dominant element in leisure service delivery, it represents a very strong job market. Commercial sport enterprises use the recreational sport concept to attract and maintain customers. These are merely a few of the values and meanings of recreational sport as a specialized field. This not only reflects the history of recreational sport but also demonstrates its great potential (DaCosta, Miragaya, & Tafisa, 2002).

Program Delivery Areas

To further explore recreational sport as a specialized field, it is necessary to take a closer look at the five different program delivery areas. Each area represents the principle of sport for all versus selection and representation as observed in athletic and professional sports. The recreational sport spectrum on page 14 shows the five unique opportunities for participation. The following section is a brief summary of the five areas. Each area is covered in greater detail in Part III.

Instructional Sport

Instructional sport is at the base of the spectrum because learning about different sports is fundamental to all forms of participation. Instructional sport is different from educational sport in that it is not taught for credit as part of an educational curriculum. Instructional sport is usually provided for a fee by instructors who teach participants sport-specific skills, techniques, strategies, rules, and regulations to help participants improve. Instruction can be given to individuals or groups through lessons, clinics, and workshops, with three levels of ability taken into consideration: beginner, intermediate, and advanced. Instructional sport occurs in a variety of settings, such as in the community, in the military, at a club, and at resorts. It often plays an important role in creating and maintaining interest in a particular sport. Instruction is a form of recreational activity that individuals may pursue as they aspire to improve their sport ability and performance.

Informal Sport

Often not recognized as "real" sport activity, informal sport has little to no structure and is completely self-directed. This program area acknowledges the participants' desire to meet their fitness needs and interests and to have fun, often with no predetermined goals. Informal sport requires minimal supervision and can maximize the capacity of sport space. Its application in some agencies is important and even critical to success, especially in the commercial and private sector, where agencies rely on the rental of sport space for income. Successful programming in informal sport means marketing sport facilities and services to attract individuals who will participate based on their personal schedule, willingness for involvement, and, in some cases, ability to pay.

Intramural Sport

The next area of recreational sport consists of sport contests, tournaments, leagues, and other events where participation is limited. Only those individuals within the setting (school, business, community, military base) may participate, and participation is almost always governed by written or understood eligibility rules and regulations. The participants themselves may mandate these restrictions through boards, committees, or councils. Most sport activities are structured into programs for males, females, or mixed participants, often taking into consideration ability and age. Participation in intramural sport is tremendous, ranging from youth programs and adult leagues in the community and YMCAs to college and university programs with tens of thousands of student participants.

Intramural systems can also be observed in facilities such as bowling centers with their various leagues, sport clubs with their championships, aquatic facilities with their swim meets, and so on. Intramural sport is a popular interest that continues to grow because sport contests bring positive involvement and many benefits to participants and the agency.

Extramural Sport

An extension of intramural sport, extramural sport usually involves intramural champions from different agencies competing to determine an overall winner. Other systems of participation that facilitate this type of recreational sport include sport extravaganzas, play days, and festivals that involve participants from any number of settings. Systems of selection are common in community sport programs, with program leadership picking an all-star team to play another all-star team. In recent years, extramural sport has expanded into youth sport, with children participating in contests of their sport almost year-round, often traveling long distances to compete. Such activity is almost always outside agency administration, leaving operational responsibilities to parents, sport enthusiasts, and sometimes sponsors.

Club Sport

At the top of the recreational sport spectrum is the least participatory form of involvement, club sport. This area serves as a bridge between the recreation and athletic concepts. Club sport systems are formed as the result of a common interest in sport. These systems are usually organized by individuals with a great deal of sport skills who are seeking an extension of intramural and extramural offerings. Participants and their leaders desire more than just having fun; they seek structured contests where winning is important to everyone who participates. Many members are so involved in their sport that they provide instruction to other members.

A club's existence is often the result of recruiting and retaining members who pay dues. In some cases, clubs solicit sponsorships. The club often goes beyond the sport itself, incorporating activities such as socials, group travel, and fund-raising. Members of clubs often form close bonds that focus on the club team and its success.

Each area of the recreational sport spectrum is its own area, defined by principle of operation, concept, policies, procedures, rules, regulations, and so on. Understanding each of these program delivery areas brings awareness of what recreational sport is all about, which is why Part III covers the details of each area.

Mission and Goals

As a field, recreational sport involves all walks of life and all levels of ability and interest. Delivering a quality product requires special skills. Considering all of the different program areas together reveals two fundamental missions that embody recreational sport: service and development.

Service

The primary mission of recreational sport is to provide quality service using available resources as best as possible. Service is greatly influenced by the agency offering recreational sport, reflecting the agency's leadership and commitment to participant satisfaction as it relates to fitness, learning, and fun. There are two general approaches that demonstrate the underlying goals of the service mission: positive experiences and profit.

Positive experience. Providing a positive experience is fundamental to each of the five areas of recreational sport; professionals are motivated by the desire to help participants benefit from their involvement in the sport. The importance of positive experiences can be observed in the allocation of state and federal funds to support programs that provide citizens with the opportunity to have a valuable experience by participating in sport activity. Centers and management systems that provide such services are public in nature and include educational, municipal, military, and correctional systems, among others. As a service, positive experiences are fundamental to the success of any delivery effort, often recorded statistically in evaluations and annual reports to substantiate fiscal support from tax-based management systems.

Profit. Another aspect of recreational sport as a service is the motivation to generate a profit. Fees are charged for services rendered and careful consideration is given to the marketing and service quality to sustain and expand participant involvement. Entire businesses perpetuate themselves using sport activity as their product for sale. Such service efforts are viable, putting the focus on management to prosper or fail based on capacity to generate income.

These two service approaches are not mutually exclusive; some agencies benefit from tax support as well as participant fees. Such agencies want to provide quality service and maximize participant enjoyment while generating income to help meet expenses. A legal conflict exists at this time over the fairness of the tax support allowed to some agencies, such as YMCAs, YWCAs, colleges, and universities. Although the purpose for service may vary, the program delivery systems are the same.

Human Development

A significant mission for recreational sport is to deliver sport activity in such a way as to foster developmental principles, giving the field professional meaning by making a significant contribution to society. This mission is accomplished by simply increasing involvement as well as creating leadership opportunities.

Involvement. Recreational sport participation creates a system of involvement that serves as a laboratory for human growth and development. Any number of situations can occur that help individuals, especially children, teenagers, and young adults, learn from what they experience. Sport can be seen as a miniature society where situations can be created and influenced, including winning and losing, cooperation and getting along, overcoming weaknesses, dealing with performance problems and adjustment, working on physical fitness, learning about sport and leisure, and realizing one's strengths and weaknesses. Basic involvement is a valuable part of recreational sport, and if applied properly, it can be formally structured to foster growth and development.

Leadership. Another outgrowth of recreational sport that fosters development is leadership opportunities, which, like involvement, can be structured. Structured leadership opportunities are another example of how the field can make a difference to participants, especially teenagers and young adults. No matter the form of participation, individual or self-leadership development occurs as people help themselves through self-assessment, motivation, problem solving, and so on. Also, some recreational sports are conducive to structuring organizational leadership opportunities. In these sports, individuals are able to assume roles where they can influence a group, such as serving as committee chairs, club presidents, and team captains. Structuring such leadership opportunities in recreational sport is covered in greater detail in Chapter 5.

Considering the fundamental meaning that its purpose brings, it is easy to see the importance of recreational sport. Such structured and well-delivered efforts have far-reaching potential for individual professionals and management teams, not to mention participants.

Participation

Participation plays a significant part in recreational sport. Describing participation is complex because individual values, standards, interests, and abilities are so different. An individual's decision to participate in a sport involves internal and external influences and motivations, which can vary widely from individual to individual. It is important to remember that varying degrees of involvement exist and can create challenges for the professional.

Participation in recreational sport is classified as either passive or active. Passive participation is the spectator aspect of sport, while active participation is more involved and requires trained leadership.

Passive

Although often unrecognized, watching sport is part of recreational sport. Any sport that an individual watches for enjoyment qualifies as recreation. People enjoy observing because they appreciate the skill of the players or because they are a participant in that sport and identify with the athlete they are watching. Spectation, or passive participation, is important to athletic and professional sport because of the income it generates, so the spectator should be understood, appreciated, and provided for as a recreational participant. Helping people find a greater appreciation for sport as spectators is a worthwhile goal for the recreational sport specialist, as enhancing spectators' knowledge of a sport can increase their enjoyment.

Active

Active participation in recreational sport is the heart of the field. Active participation involves such tremendous diversity of interest, ability, and spirit that negative situations can and do occur. On the positive side, recreational sport specialists are able to program sport activities to meet individual differences by modifying rules and regulations; placing emphasis on winning or not; and accommodating varying skill levels, physical sizes, and ages, from the elite to the physically and mentally challenged. Such adjustment can require creative thinking, but the effort is well worth it, as any leisure activity can create sport participation that brings fun and enjoyment. This is the unique quality that recreation brings to the sport world: Anything goes in reaching the goal to have fun, satisfying experiences. Figure 2.2 illustrates the varying degrees of active participation as they relate to some of the different elements involved in leisure sport. Flexibility can be crucial in meeting a setting's needs and individual interests in sport activity.

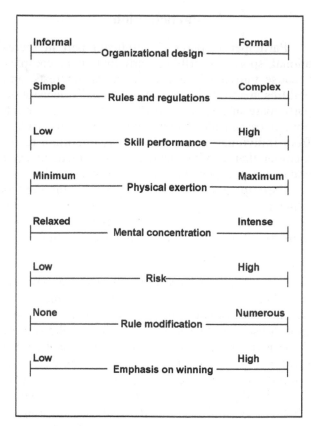

Informal   Formal
├──────── Organizational design ────────┤

Simple   Complex
├──────── Rules and regulations ────────┤

Low   High
├──────── Skill performance ────────┤

Minimum   Maximum
├──────── Physical exertion ────────┤

Relaxed   Intense
├──────── Mental concentration ────────┤

Low   High
├──────── Risk ────────┤

None   Numerous
├──────── Rule modification ────────┤

Low   High
├──────── Emphasis on winning ────────┤

Figure 2.2. Degrees of Recreational Sport Participation

Unfortunately, sport activity does not always bring about positive active participation, so being able to recognize and respond properly to negative developments is critical. This is one reason why trained, experienced recreational sport professionals are so important. Sport activity can create negative situations, including crowds that are out of control, bad officiating, stealing, forfeits and no-shows, maintenance problems, injuries, bad weather, verbal and physical abuse, hostile parents of youth participants, protests, damage to facilities and equipment, user dissatisfaction, and cheating. Anticipating and controlling such problems makes recreational sport specialists vital to the field.

Participation in recreational sport has been presented here as a broad area with many degrees of involvement and both positive and negative conditions that need to be managed. To a great extent, this is why sound leadership in program delivery is so important.

Participants

Recreational sport takes on a special role as it serves participants of all ages, experiences, or abilities. Even people with mental or physical disabilities are incorporated into the recreational sport spectrum, heightening their inclusion into mainstream society.

Recreational sport constitutes an important part of day-to-day activity for many, many people. Table 2.1 provides an overview of the types of active involvement in sport that are most common for specific age groups. Chapter 5 covers this subject in much greater detail; however, to demonstrate recreational sport as a specialization, the following brief discussion elaborates on the information in the table.

Children

From birth to age 5, children participate in activities centered in and around the home. Activity is unstructured frolic, and because children of this age have little organizational ability, their activity should be limited to low-level physical and mental effort. External leadership has little effect on actions that are exploratory and self-directed. Sometimes parents and other adults influence children's early sport-skill development in the attempt to improve later athletic performance. However, at this stage little emphasis should be placed on winning and high achievement.

Youth

Between ages 6 and 12, many young people learn about the world of sport. Participation often revolves around the school or community in the form of youth sport. Youth sport has grown tremendously in the past 30 years. For some, this is the beginning of an athletic sport career, and for others, it is simply recreation. This dichotomy involves conflicts in philosophy, but proper leadership helps provide a healthy, balanced experience.

Leaders in youth sport teach fundamental skills, strategies, rules, health, and well-being. In recent years, training programs for parents, coaches, and officials have come into being. Settings that sponsor such training efforts include the YMCA, the YWCA, Boys & Girls Clubs, schools, community or municipal recreation departments, and private clubs. Such training systems should be a high priority for the recreational sport specialist.

Table 2.1

Sport Participation by Age Groups

Participant Group	Age	Recreational					Athletic		Professional	
		Instructional	Informal	Intramural	Extramural	Club	Junior Varsity	Varsity	Minor	Major
Children	Birth - 5	X	X							
Youth	6 - 7	X	X	X						
	8 - 10	X	X	X	X					
	11 - 12	X	X	X	X	X				
Adolescents	13 - 14	X	X	X	X	X	X			
	15 - 17	X	X	X	X	X	X	X		
	18 - 19	X	X	X	X	X	X	X	X	X
Adults	20 - 30	X	X	X	X	X		X	X	X
	31 - 45	X	X	X	X	X			X	X
	46 - 65	X	X	X	X	X				
Seniors	65 - 75	X	X	X						
	76+	X	X							

Adolescents

The young person between ages 13 and 19 experiences a complex period of development leading to maturation, and involvement in sport may have a positive influence on this development. This is the stage when athletic sport receives its greatest emphasis, primarily in school settings. Unfortunately, recreational sport opportunities for the nonathlete barely exist in some settings. Adolescents unable to make an athletic team usually find themselves with few opportunities to participate in sport. These so-called nonathletes are often discriminated against because of their limited abilities or a different level of interest in sport.

Programs in settings outside of school, primarily in the community or commercial recreation agencies, do exist for adolescents. Unfortunately, the voluntary leadership support available at youth sport is not carried to the adolescent level, and emphasis on youth sport limits the availability of facilities and resources for adolescent recreational sport.

Adolescents not involved in structured sport may participate in other recreation activities on an individual, peer group, or family basis. Because sport may not be readily available, it is often the adolescents' responsibility to determine their own recreation needs and pursue them.

Adults

After age 19, sport interests can take any number of directions. Other than those with an athletic or professional sport career, adults usually participate in recreational sport based on educational or living areas as well as the workplace. Although dependent on what is available or affordable, adults have the most flexibility in choosing their recreational sport experience. Their degree of involvement usually has few or no limitations. Activities such as structured tournaments, self-directed sport activities, and leadership positions are all available to adults.

Seniors

One of the most rapidly growing areas in recreation is participation by the elderly. More and more senior citizens find enjoyment, satisfaction, and exercise through recreational sport. Their involvement depends on individual enthusiasm and physical and mental limitations. Although age may limit the degree of involvement, it does not prevent interest or enthusiasm. Retirees have more leisure time once they leave the workforce, and for most, recreational sport plays a major part in their lifestyle.

With such a wide audience of potential participants, it is easy to see the value of the recreational sport specialist's role. Such leadership should not be taken for granted.

Delivery Centers

The different delivery centers where leisure activities are produced also demonstrate the role of recreational sport as a specialization. For the purposes of this text, the delivery center incorporates the term *settings,* which refers to specific societal structures that incorporate separate agencies or management systems that share the same purpose. To visualize the relationship between settings and agencies, see Table 2.2, which illustrates different settings and related agencies.

Table 2.2

Settings and Agencies for Recreational Sport

Settings	Agencies
City or community	Chicago, IL New York, NY Denver, CO South Bend, IN Lawrence, KS
Educational	Publics schools Colleges and universities Private schools Military schools Community and junior colleges

(cont.)

Table 2.2 (cont.)

Settings	Agencies
Military	Army Navy Marines Air Force Coast Guard
Correctional	City and county jails Juvenile detention centers Federal penitentiaries State penitentiaries
Private club	Tennis clubs Country clubs Health clubs Boat clubs Riding clubs
Nonprofit	YMCAs YWCAs Boys & Girls Clubs Boys Scouts Girls Scouts Churches
Commercial	Tennis courts Golf courses Sky diving Riding stables Bowling centers Skiing
Corporation	IBM Coca-cola Caterpillar Inc. Procter and Gamble Microsoft Inc Ford Motor Company
Natural environment	Yellowwood State Forest Hoosier National Forest Yellowstone National Park Badlands National Park Everglades National Park Glacier National Park
Vacation	Hotels Resorts Theme parks Cruises

Because sport activity as a means of leisure enjoyment is so popular, recreational sport is an important aspect of these management settings and agencies. Specific agencies can have all kinds of resources to help meet that agency's needs and interests. Although there is great diversity among settings and agencies, much about recreational sport management is similar.

City or Community

A city or community setting is one of the best professional systems of management demonstrating great commitment to and involvement in recreational sport. Participation may involve family units, employment systems, and schools, all of which aim to promote a positive lifestyle through well-planned and well-delivered leisure activity. The city or community government provides the funds, facilities, equipment, and ultimate leadership for this type of recreation through a tax structure that incorporates many other public services. Recreational sport in these settings is usually limited to the residents of the area and provides opportunities for individuals of all ages.

Educational

All educational systems, whether they are public schools, private schools, or institutions of higher learning, put significant effort into teaching sport, providing sport opportunities as a recreational outlet or as an expression of athletic entertainment. Educational settings have always demonstrated commitment to the principle and philosophy of recreational sport as a leisure activity. They have done this primarily through physical education, where athletic and recreational sports are offered as extracurricular activities. Higher education is particularly invested in recreational sport; hundreds of colleges and universities make special efforts to bring sport activities to their students. These settings take campus recreational sport seriously, building elaborate facilities and fulfilling considerable operational responsibilities to meet the recreational needs of their students.

Military

The United States military is organized into five branches: Army, Navy, Air Force, Coast Guard, and Marines, each of which takes recreational sport seriously. Because personnel and families tend to stay within their military setting, recreational programs become a major part of their lives. Some of the finest indoor and outdoor sport complexes are on military bases. The idea of recreational sport meeting leisure needs, physical conditioning, and training is a high priority for military leadership. The field of recreational sport is significant in the overall scheme of military personnel management.

Correctional

The settings where individuals are incarcerated or taken out of society within the penal system are a viable area for recreational sport programming. These settings involve individuals who have demonstrated socially unacceptable behavior and thus need detention and separation from society. For people confined to correctional settings, one of the few benefits of the settings is recreational pursuit. Sport activity is popular in correctional facilities and in many instances is part of the rehabilitation effort to help inmates adjust when they reenter society.

Private Clubs

In the last few decades as recreational sport has become more and more popular, private clubs have seen a tremendous upsurge. Clubs provide a variety of recreational options for their members, and they usually limit membership based on a facility's capacity and one's ability to fit in financially. An example is a country club that offers recreational swimming, tennis, and golf along with dining and bar areas, creating a social atmosphere. The sport facilities are usually the primary attraction, and dues and supplemental user fees help maintain the club. The application of recreational sport in some private clubs may be very specialized, requiring certification from certain national organizations that provide special training for the leadership for such settings.

Nonprofit

Historically, organizations such as the YMCA and the YWCA, Boys & Girls Clubs, Boy Scouts and Girl Scouts, and large churches meet community needs by offering services such as short-term housing, social services, youth development, and recreation. As demands have increased, additional facilities such as gymnasiums, pools, and courts have been added, requiring qualified leadership to manage them. Many of these organizations have seen tremendous growth in sport and fitness activity. Activity in these settings is guided by the national organization or association, and a large percentage of such activity is sport, creating a significant role for the recreational sport specialist.

Commercial

Because of market demand for certain sport activity, entrepreneurs have established sole proprietorships, partnerships, and corporations to provide specific sports such as golf, racquetball, squash, tennis, swimming, bowling, boating, and fishing. Commercial settings have grown tremendously in the last 20 years. These businesses have evolved because, due to the ever-growing interest in recreational sport, money can be made by providing these sports.

Corporation

Many corporations that employ large numbers of people create special recreation opportunities. In this setting the recreational sport specialist can play a vital role, stimulating employee health, morale, and productivity. Most of these programs emphasize self-directed fitness through sport activity either at an on-site facility or through cooperation with the community and private clubs where special membership arrangements are made.

Natural Environment

Public lands such as forests, parks, and other areas owned by local, regional, state, and federal governments offer expansive settings for sport involvement in both informal and club activity. Extensive facilities accommodate activities such as skiing, boating, camping, hiking, swimming, and white-water rafting. These facilities are provided by the public agency or by commercial operations that are contracted by the agency to provide the service. The outdoor recreation field usually dominates these setting; however, training and competence in recreational sport is important as well.

Vacation

The last decade or so has seen tremendous growth in the tourism industry, including resorts and hotels. These settings often offer a variety of accommodations beyond lodging and food, including sport facilities, sport pro shops, and tours, all focused on the vacationer's need for leisure activity and enjoyment. For the recreational sport specialist, managing informal sports, structuring tournaments, and instructing vacationers is a huge opportunity. Such leadership makes a significant contribution to the setting's overall goal to satisfy the vacationer.

Significance

The physical and mental outcomes of recreational sport are well recognized, but the all-encompassing significance is often overlooked. The individual, the community, the environment, and the economy can all benefit through improved quality of life, increased family cohesion, reduced crime, enhanced environment, reduced health care expenses, increased work productivity, and increased property value (National Recreation and Park Association, 1998). The unique benefits that are realized in successful programming of recreational sport are an important part of its role in society.

Quality of Life

An improvement in overall satisfaction with life frequently occurs during leisure sport. This has been attributed to the proven positive effects that recreational activities have on psychological and physical health. Psychological benefits include feelings of increased self-esteem, security, and social belonging. Recreational sport involvement allows one to participate and interact instead of being alone and bored. In addition, recreational sport helps reduce the risk of stress-related diseases. Continued satisfaction with one's use of leisure time results in an elevated quality of life, and improvement in quality of life is often the goal of providing leisure opportunity.

Family Cohesion

Improved family cohesion, illustrated by the saying "A family that plays together stays together," is another benefit of recreational sport. Families often do not have a great deal of time to spend together, and involvement in sport can help them remain connected through either joint or individual accomplishment. Time spent together in sport can build family bonding as families pursue sport activity together, take sport vacations, and work together as volunteers to help with a sporting event.

Crime Reduction

Criminal activity is reduced when people participate in sport as a leisure activity. One reason is that participants are doing something productive during their free time. By providing such outlets, recreational sport reduces the occurrence of substance abuse, violence, and vandalism. Participation in common activities also helps individuals form positive social bonds. With increased social involvement comes an increased sense of community. The promotion of ethnic and cultural harmony results in increased community pride. For these reasons, negative social activity is less likely to happen when individuals pursue informal and formal sport activity.

Environmental Enhancement

A further benefit from leisure involvement in recreational sport is the enhancement of open spaces. The development of outdoor recreational facilities creates a human–environmental interface that in turn promotes environmental concern and education. Providing space for outdoor leisure activity often corresponds with providing habitat protection. The concept of parks and play space for healthy people includes providing healthy natural areas.

Health Care

Employee sickness, injury, and absenteeism are often problems for companies. When employees participate in sport, they have a reduced chance of health problems such as heart disease, back pain, depression, and other problems. Health care costs are reduced as a result of providing sport activities as part of the overall employee recreation program, thus reducing the cost of health care premiums for the business.

Work Productivity

Recreational sport can improve worker productivity by providing breaks to jobs that can be tedious and demanding. Studies have shown that participation in sport can improve employee morale, attitude, and ultimately productivity. Work attributes that are improved by participation in recreational sport include concentration, task persistence, mood, and analytical ability. A workplace that creates a balance between work and play by offering a sport program benefits everyone in the long run.

Property Value

Property values have increased in communities where active recreation, especially sport activity, is growing. This is the indirect result of the provision of areas for leisure involvement, which improves the quality of a community and makes it a place where people wish to live. Recent studies on livable cities cite the provision of active recreation as one of the attributes sought by those relocating to a different area. Recreational facilities increase tourism, generate revenue, and aid in business retention. As the community grows, in part due to investments in sport facilities, property values increase.

Recreational sport specialists must recognize the importance of the role they play in the delivery of these interrelated benefits to their community. These personal, social, environmental, and economic benefits can be realized in all agencies as they enhance lives by providing recreational sport activity.

Shining Example

Amateur Athletic Union of the United States, Inc.

The Amateur Athletic Union of the United States, Inc. (AAU) is the largest not-for-profit volunteer-driven multiple sport amateur athletic organization in the United States. AAU has a partnership with Walt Disney World Resort, and its national headquarters are located in Lake Buena Vista, Florida. Its mission is to offer a lifelong progression of amateur sports programs for persons of all ages, races, and creeds; to enhance the physical, mental, and moral development of amateur athletes; and to promote good sportsmanship, good citizenship, and safety.

Clientele:

The AAU registers over 500,000 members aged 19 years of age or younger each year, with a male-to-female ratio of approximately 55:45.

Facilities:

The AAU operates out of Disney's Wide World of Sports Complex in Lake Buena Vista, Florida.

Program Details:

The AAU sponsors both youth and adult sporting opportunities, including 34 different events (this does not include teams, clubs, or individuals). Along with the sports programs, the AAU also sponsors the AAU Junior Olympic Games, the AAU James E. Sullivan Memorial Award, AAU Complete Athlete Program and the President's Challenge Youth Physical Fitness Award Program.

Budget:

The budget for AAU is approximately $8 million per year

Marketing:

The AAU target market is focused on youth aged 6-19. The AAU uses radio and television Public Service Announcements, the *USA Today* Amateur Sports page, numerous brochures, press releases, and volunteer word of mouth. A Web site is also maintained: www.aausports.org. Social media is also utilized in their marketing approaches.

Jobs and Careers:

The AAU is divided into five departments: Sports operations, administration, association services, external relations, and finance. It has 40 employees and is run by five volunteer officers with assistance from a 35-member executive committee.

Salary:

The AAU is run primarily by volunteers.

Internships:

The AAU offers internships at its National Headquarters providing on-the-job learning experiences for college students. The departments of the AAU that offer internship positions include event operations, sports, AAU junior Olympic games, media / public relations, and information systems (web site development).

Affiliated Professional Organizations:

The AUU is affiliated with a number of other sport-related and public service organizations, including the National Collegiate Athletics Association (NCAA) and Covering Kids and Families (CKF), the United States Olympic Committee (USOC), and National Football League (NFL) Youth Partners.

Conclusion

From sport to fitness to simply having a good time, there is no question of the importance of the recreational sport specialist in any number of settings. It is a role that is vital, especially in serving such diverse participants and their unique needs and interests. The field may have had a slow start professionally, but with hundreds of millions of people pursuing such a vast array of sport experiences, the future looks bright. These needs can be met through well-planned and well-delivered sport programs that require expertise and special talents. Recreational sport specialists will create experiences with purpose and meaning that make a difference for everyone they serve. These responsibilities are crucial, and to realize this is to understand what recreational sport as a specialization is all about. This fundamental insight should help recreational sport specialists continue to build their understanding of and appreciation for their role in this worthy field.

Bibliography

Allison, M. T., & Hibbler, D. K. (2004). Organizational barriers to inclusion: Perspectives from the recreation professional. *Leisure Sciences, 26,* 261-280.

Barcelona, B., & Ross, C. (2004). An analysis of the perceived competencies of recreational sport administrators. *Journal of Park and Recreation Administration, 22*(4), 25-42.

Beggs, B. A., Elkins, D. J., & Powers, S. (2005). Overcoming barriers to participation in campus recreational sports. *Recreational Sports Journal, 29,* 143-155.

Biddle, S. J., & Mutrie, N. (2008). *Psychology of physical activity: Determinants, well-being, and interventions* (2nd ed.). London, England: Routledge.

Cushman, G., Veal, A. J., & Zuzanek, J. (2008). *Free time and leisure participation: International perspectives* (2nd ed.). Wallingford, United Kingdom: CABI.

DaCosta, L., Miragaya, A., & Tafisa, M. (2002). *Worldwide experiences and trends in sport for all.* Aachen, Germany: Meyer and Meyer Sport.

Dudenhoeffer, F. T. (1990). Genesis and evolution of the recreational sports profession. *National Intramural-Recreational Sports Association Journal, 14*(3), 12-13.

Eccles, J. S., Rodriguez, D., & Wigfield, A. (2003). Changing competence perceptions, changing values: Implications for youth sport. *Journal of Applied Sport Psychology, 15*(1), 67-81.

Gau, L., & Kim, J. (2011). The influence of cultural values on spectators' sports attitudes and team identification: An east–west perspective. *Social Behavior and Personality, 39*(5), 587-596.

Godbey, G., Crawford, D. W., & Shen, X. S. (2010). Assessing hierarchical leisure constraints theory after two decades. *Journal of Leisure Research, 42*(1), 111-134.

Holt, N. L., Kingsley, B. C., Tink, L. N., & Scherer, J. (2011). Benefits and challenges associated with sport participation by children and parents from low-income families. *Psychology of Sport and Exercise, 12*, 490-499.

Jamieson, L. M. (1980). *A competency analysis of recreational sports personnel in selected institutional settings* (Doctoral dissertation). Indiana University, Bloomington.

Jamieson, L.M., & Zhiwei, P. (2000). Government policies on Sport for All. *ICHPERSD Journal, 36*(4), 16-20.

Jackson, E., & Scott, D. (1999). Constraints to leisure. In E. Jackson & T. Burton (Eds.), *Leisure studies: Prospects for the twenty-first century* (pp. 299-321). State College, PA: Venture.

Jackson, E. L. (2005). *Constraints to leisure.* State College, PA: Venture.

Jensen, C. R., & Guthrie, S. P. (2006). *Outdoor recreation in America* (6th ed.). Champaign, IL: Human Kinetics.

Kelly, J. R., & Freysinger, V. J. (2004). *21st century leisure: Current issues* (2nd ed.). State College, PA: Venture.

Kirk, D., & MacPhail, A. (2003). Social positioning and the construction of a youth sports club. *International Review for the Sociology of Sport, 38*(1), 23-44.

Laws, J. R. (1986). *A study into the scope of sports within public recreation programming* (Doctoral dissertation). Indiana University, Bloomington.

Madrigal, R. (2003). Investigating an evolving leisure experience: Antecedents and consequences of spectator affect during a live sporting event. *Journal of Leisure Research, 35*(1), 23-49.

National Recreation and Park Association. (1998). *Benefits-based programming of recreation services.* Ashburn, VA: Author.

Rossman, J. R., & Schlatter, B. E. (2008). *Recreation programming: Designing leisure experiences* (5th ed.). Champaign, IL: Sagamore.

Russell, R.V., & Jamieson, L. M. (2007). *Leisure program planning and delivery.* Champaign, IL: Human Kinetics.

Schroeder, T. D. (1987). *Nonparticipants: Barriers to recreation participation.* Monticello, IL: Vance Bibliographies.

Shaw, G., & Veitch, C. (2011). Demographic drivers of change in tourism and the challenge of inclusive products. In D. Buhalis & S. Darcy (Eds.), *Accessible tourism: Concepts and issues* (pp. 160-173). Bristol, United Kingdom: Channel View Publications.

Shen, M. (2001). Considerations of community sport in China. *Journal of Beijing University of Physical Education, 24*(3), 313-314.

Sleap, M. (1998). *Social issues in sport.* New York: St. Martin's Press.

Tobar, D. A. (2006). Affect and purchase intentions of Super Bowl XL television spectators: Examining the influence of sport fandom, age, and gender. *Sport Marketing Quarterly, 15*, 243-252.

Tsiotsou, R. (1998). A survey of sport club programs. *National Intramural–Recreational Sports Association Journal, 22*(2), 40-41.

Wellner, A. S. (1997). *Americans at play: Demographics of outdoor recreation and travel.* Ithaca, NY: New Strategist.

Woods, R. B. (2011). *Social issues in sport* (2nd ed.). Champaign, IL: Human Kinetics.

CHAPTER 3

A Management Model

CHAPTER OBJECTIVES

After reading this chapter, you will understand the role of management in recreational sport, establish a frame of reference for defining recreational sport management, recognize the core product of recreational sport, identify the critical aspects of a management model, comprehend management terminology, be able to discuss administrative operations, be able to discuss delivery operations, know the resources of recreational sport, understand the role of marketing in recreational sport, and conceptualize the service and profit goals of recreational sport.

KEY CONCEPTS

Management	Administrative operations	Support
Core product	Planning	Auxiliaries
Core-product extensions	Organizing	Maintenance
Leadership	Directing	Resources
Management model	Controlling	Reach
Influence	Delivery operations	Goals
	Production	

Introduction

Now that recreational sport has been identified as a field, it is time to look at management. Without a doubt, *management* is a word that carries tremendous meaning in every individual's personal and professional lives. A recreational sport specialist should understand not only its descriptive meaning but also its specific concept. In many respects, a complete understanding of management can be complicated. In an effort to simplify and clarify, this chapter will focus on management's most basic identity: creating a model for information. This information brings practical meaning to the way management transcends and supports recreational sport's body of knowledge and practices. In the process, this chapter explains management's existence and provides a comprehensive definition and specific terms and concepts that give meaning to a management model for recreational sport professionals.

Description

The first step to describing management is recognizing that the term itself can have varied interpretations. Entire professions and fields have described management, often creating confusion and making it more complicated than necessary. It is important for the recreational sport specialist to have a frame of reference that does just the opposite: clarifying and simplifying what management is all about. To achieve this, it is necessary to look closely at the root of all management and then provide a definition that incorporates all the different elements that combine to create management.

Product

To fully appreciate management and its meaning, it is necessary to recognize that it represents a basic belief or a concept in action. In the process of management, the individual or group strives toward something fundamental to be accomplished. In a sense, management is a product that can be identified and even written about in mission statements, values, goals, and the objectives representing a plan on how it can be accomplished. The core product is the central focus of management and may include being successful, working for a profit, gaining satisfaction, or meeting set goals and objectives. In the field of recreational sport, the core product is providing sport to create fun, learning, and fitness opportunities for a particular population, as described in Chapters 1 and 2. Management does everything it can to provide such experiences as efficiently and effectively as possible.

Management often applies supplementary efforts that are beyond the core product; such efforts are called core-product extensions. These extended efforts reinforce the core product, adding to the overall success of the core product. Core-product extensions that are part of recreational sport management include parking, child care, food services, and locker rooms. Recognizing recreational sport management's core product and core-product extensions is just the beginning; the next step is an accurate description of management as it relates to product focus.

Definition

The term *management* is often confused, overused, and interchanged with words such as *administration, operations, business,* and *corporation.* What is needed is a logical way to define management that takes into account all these terms and their meanings. Management is also often misrepresented by placing the emphasis on taking charge and directing something to happen, an outdated definition. Modern management has taken a new direction with a slightly different meaning than in the past. In recent years, a concept has come to the forefront and made a valuable contribution to traditional management: leadership. Where in the past management has tended to be product- and goal-oriented, leadership places the emphasis on people. Management has become more aware of the human element, including individual and group feelings, attitudes, sensitivity to fairness, and cooperation in the attempt to accomplish something.

Taking management goals and the human element into consideration, this text presents a practical, encompassing definition for management. It is a simple definition, but one that works for all systems of management, including recreational sport: Management is influencing operational functions and resources to reach a goal. The remainder of this chapter discusses the ways this description incorporates all the elements of management, using Figure 3.1 as an illustration of the management model. Each term in Figure 3.1 and how it relates to recreational sport management will be explained in detail.

Influence

Influence is an important element of management. It incorporates the ideals of leadership, representing a modern interpretation of management as opposed to traditional descriptive terms such as *administer, direct,* and *control.* Influence means affecting a person, a course of events, or an outcome or change. It is a key description of all management systems.

There needs to be a way to make a satisfactory product, and there are two broad areas that influence this: administrative operations and delivery operations. These distinct systems of influence have different functions that bring about a desired result. The word *operation* works as a suggestive term because it means to act effectively and bring about a desired effect. The word *function* is applicable to supporting influence because it describes assigned duties or activities, or something closely related to another thing and dependent upon it for its existence. Having said that, take a closer look at administrative and delivery operations as the two components of management.

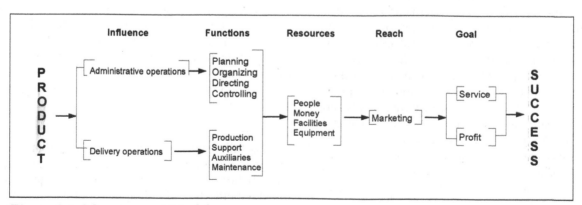

Figure 3.1. Management Model

Administrative Operations

All management starts with some type of authority, the person or system that is responsible for the product. The authority is the administrative operations, which can be described as the ultimate system or executive that applies functions that influence the desired outcome. Operations at this level represent several different functions that influence everything that happens. They will be presented here as concepts that are incorporated in management, particularly as they relate to the field of recreational sport. All of these operational functions are critical to sound management and are often observed to be omitted or poorly applied when management falls short.

Planning. Very little occurs without some degree of planning early in the effort. Planning can be short term, on a daily or weekly basis. Planning can also be a long-term, detailed process, also known as strategic or long-range planning. Such planning can be described as some degree of anticipation, and when appropriate, it documents all aspects that lead toward expected levels of success. Such planning can also be thought of as predetermined, theoretical thinking that is designed to accomplish set goals and objectives.

A number of areas reflect the importance of planning as an administrative function in recreational sport, including planning facility projects and renovations, creating emergency action and evacuation plans, planning equipment purchasing, maintenance, and budgeting. Planning specific to program delivery includes plans for personnel training, master planning, creating a calendar of sport activity, and so on. Because there is so much in recreational sport that should be properly planned, the list is virtually endless.

Organizing. The next administrative function is organizing, or identifying workers, areas, and space and then structuring employee responsibilities plus areas and space into a system that produces positive results. In organizing, specific steps are taken to create a system that allows understanding of all facets of what management wants to achieve. Organizing involves the actions that bring everything together, including specific tasks and responsibilities. Areas, materials, information, and so on can be categorized so that everyone knows where everything is and everyone knows what to do as they work with the product. Smooth flow with limited or no resistance is necessary so that activities may occur methodically and in a timely fashion.

In recreational sport, organizing involves tasks such as designating sport areas and space assignments, creating flow charts that illustrate authority, developing policies and procedures, establishing timetables, structuring program systems, and defining staff roles. Organizing creates an overall picture by putting all of the elements into a meaningful process whose goal is to improve success. It is a critical function because there are so many variables in recreational sport management.

Directing. Although all administrative functions are important, in today's world none takes on such significance as directing, which is the process of guiding individuals and groups as they pursue common goals. Leadership skills in directing help administrative efforts to influence tasks and responsibilities to create success. Proper directing also leads to recognition of performance. Influencing workers is a key for management to set up operations and keep them going.

As in other fields, recreational sport specialists should use sound directing principles, especially since proper, fair leadership is now recognized as paramount to success. This is essential in settings where management requirements are extensive, placing heavy demands on staff. To ensure success, recreational sport specialists should use the following directing techniques: sound leadership style, properly written and presented job descriptions, well-designed training systems, accurate delegation, sound communication, written performance standards, and manuals of operational details, to mention a few. The importance of directing cannot be overemphasized.

Controlling. The next function fundamental to administrative operations is controlling, which pertains to product success. In management, it is one thing to encourage people to fulfill designated job obligations, but the real challenge is making sure staff members do their work in a timely fashion and in a way that meets expectations. Controlling is the administrative process of assessing and correcting all resources and staff to improve chances of product success.

Control is important in management because, unfortunately, things often do not go smoothly. As in all fields, including recreational sport, things sometimes go awry and need to be attended to. Such negative developments can affect the sport activity, so they should be anticipated and dealt with using proper controlling techniques. In recreational sport, this means being alert for problems and then taking corrective action when they occur. Examples of control in recreational sport include reviewing staff performance, evaluating programmed activity, maintaining a preventive checklist, observing facilities and equipment regularly, recognizing and rewarding positive staff performance, using proper corrective techniques with staff, and so on. Later in this book, each of these examples will be elaborated on as they each relate to recreational sport.

As these examples show, influence is a function of management at the administrative level. However, this is only part of its significance. The following discussion will illustrate how the product actually moves forward to where it can be experienced by the consumer or participant.

Delivery Operations

Administrative operations initiate and oversee product creation by applying the different functions mentioned in the last section. However, once a product is created, it needs to be presented to potential users so that it may be experienced or purchased. This idea of bringing a product to a user or participant is the delivery operations aspect of management. Delivery options can be described as an integrating of the resource (employees, money, facilities, and equipment) and the administrative functions that create and maintain interest in a product, leading to use or purchase that affects the product's success. Delivery operations have four different functions and each makes a unique contribution to management.

Production. Probably the most important function of delivery operations is production. Production consists of the contact efforts, out-front activities, daily tasks, and responsibilities that create the product. Production is also the daily interaction with people who want to participate or make a purchase. It synthesizes all details, knowledge, and resources and is set in motion by the administration.

Another way of looking at production is to view it as concepts, methods, and systems that are learned in a variety of ways, such as through certification or degrees. Throughout this book, the production function, or programming, as it is more commonly known, is illustrated in the areas of instructional, informal, intramural, extramural, and club sports.

Support. Another element of delivery operations that affects overall management and especially production is support. Support consists of the activities that take place behind the scenes rather than in front where the product user can see them. Support is often not recognized as a contributing factor of product success, but it consists of activities that must take place and are critical to administrative and delivery operations. Some examples of support are clerical work (typing, filing, record keeping, appointment scheduling), payroll, communication systems (telephones, computers), work supplies and materials, employee insurance and benefits, and mail service.

The support function also includes outside assistance, such as legal advice, medical backup, accounting services, and special consultants. Such assistance is usually specialized in nature and not internally available. However, some large management systems do have such support functions as part of their internal operations. Such support activity is critical to recreational sport program delivery and success.

Auxiliaries. Management may need to consider products that are outside and contribute to the core product and its delivery. Such functions are auxiliaries, or core-product extensions, and they may only represent a small percentage of what is being delivered. They may be complementary or necessary in bringing about a complete experience within the total management system and important enough that their elimination could have a negative effect on overall product success.

There are many different auxiliary functions in recreational sport. One is parking, which can be critical to users' convenience. Another consideration is child care where users can leave their children while they use the facility. Food and beverage outlets such as vending machines, snack bars, and full-service restaurants are also auxiliary functions. Other auxiliaries that are almost always a part of recreational sport include equipment checkout and rental systems and locker and shower areas, all of which complement the core product or sport activity. Each management system has its own needs for auxiliary functions. These functions are often significant and sometimes even require their own production effort.

Maintenance. In delivery operation, keeping facilities and equipment in safe, functional condition is called maintenance, a type of support. Because maintenance is such a significant part of management, especially in recreational sport, it is singled out as a separate function. The scope of maintenance varies greatly, and as agencies grow, maintenance responsibilities increase proportionately. Such responsibilities vary from simple cleaning to a full system that incorporates preventative and cyclical maintenance. Maintenance activities include facility and equipment cleaning and repair, grass mowing, landscape and lawn watering, equipment and supplies inventory, electrical system control, and setup and takedown, to mention a few. Poor maintenance not only has a negative effect on management in the short term, but it also has serious long-term implications. Management should make maintenance a priority, especially where the safety of users and workers is involved.

Because product success is crucial, the functions of management's delivery operations are easy to include in the influencing portion of the definition. The product has to be brought forward, and the word *delivery* indicates just that. Delivery's functions, including production, support, auxiliaries, and maintenance, all influence the product's potential for success. Now it is time to identify the term *resources* and how it fits into the management model.

Resources

Administration influences product creation through information, theory, and documents. Delivery is the activity that helps to successfully bring forward a product to its intended audience. Influencing operations also incorporates critical resources, including employees, money, facilities, and equipment. Each of these resources makes a unique contribution to management, and proper use of these resources is management's greatest challenge. Management's capacity to influence these resources is crucial. While these topics will be discussed in greater detail later in this text, the following summarizes how each is part of management.

Employees

Management cannot take place without human involvement throughout the entire effort. It is critical for management to be able to influence employees to fulfill their obligations to a product's production and delivery. This process is called staffing, or the finding, hiring, and supervising of individuals who can fulfill a role necessary to the product's success. All efforts in management revolve around employees and the way they are hired, trained, assessed, corrected, and motivated. Employee management is important in recreational sport, particularly since its production revolves around staff who make things work properly. In management, having the right employees fulfilling the right responsibilities goes a long way to meeting management's expectations. Details on employees and staffing are covered in Chapter 11.

Money

No aspect of management can create such attentiveness as money, whether it is as an income or expense. The way money is earned and spent can make or break a management system. As a resource, the importance of money cannot be overemphasized. The use of money should be planned in advance through budgeting as well as recorded along the way through accounting.

Money is a complicated resource that has its own specialized application, especially as the agency or the volume of production increases. This is especially the case in recreational sport, with agencies having any number of money management requirements, including fees and charges, schedules, cost analyses, taxes, deposits, fund-raising, accounts receivable and payable, fiscal projections, and special seasonal charges, many of which are discussed in detail in Chapter 12. As a resource, money should always be a high priority.

Facilities

The greatest physical responsibility in management is the facility where the product is produced and delivered. Management's ability to recognize the nature and scope of facilities and their value is critical, as a properly functioning environment is an absolute necessity. Facilities can be indoor or outdoor structures, and they vary so greatly that each facility has its own unique existence. As a resource, facilities can be the most expensive aspect of a management scheme.

Managing indoor and outdoor recreational sport facilities can be a huge job. Responsibilities include coordination, scheduling, security, development, area and space utilization, control and supervision, maintenance, emergency and evacuation measures, accessibility, and temperature control. Facilities are incredibly involved, as will be discussed in Chapter 13.

Equipment

Equipment is a resource that enhances and facilitates everything that takes place in management. Equipment can be described as any item, mechanical or otherwise, that enhances operations. The ways to describe, categorize, and work with equipment will be presented in Chapter 14.

Especially in recreational sport, equipment is a diverse, extensive resource. Responsibilities include purchasing, receiving, inventorying, storing, distributing, and maintaining. Often management takes equipment for granted, yet it can be a big expense as well as a headache when it does not work as designed or expected. Management's ability to track and influence proper use and care of equipment can greatly contribute to the effectiveness of administration and delivery operations.

To summarize resources and their role in management is to simply describe what they represent: employees, money, equipment, and facilities. Product administration and delivery has to take place at some location, with people to do the work, with the necessary equipment, and with money complications being closely monitored. In many respects, operational functions and resources are synonymous, as each is dependent on the other.

Reach

No matter what the product is or how the resources are used, it is still necessary to bring the product to the potential benefactor. A system is required to help buyers or users become aware of and have an interest in the product. Management has to reach out and extend product potential, or market the product. This effort to reach out involves assessing a targeted population as well as creating a strategy that accomplishes product availability and success.

Marketing involves several methods and techniques and, in many respects, is a field unto itself. The four Ps of marketing—product, promotion, price, and place—are well known. Marketing also involves examining the demographic or statistical characteristics of a population in order to analyze a particular market. Lifestyles can be assessed to determine the logical or sociological influence of a product on a potential user. Marketing also attempts to reach the user or a particular segment of a population by recognizing their particular needs and interests. Marketing has proven to be extremely important to product delivery and thus is important to meeting management's overall goals.

In recreational sport, marketing creates product awareness in potential clients, customers, or members. Each program has unique marketable factors that can facilitate success. All such marketing considerations should be fully explored to determine what will bring the greatest success, as Chapter 16 discusses in more detail.

Goal

In the effort to provide a management model, this chapter has reviewed influencing functions, resources, and how to reach out or market to the potential user. No matter what the product is or how it is developed, management always wants to accomplish something, whether it is moving forward and finding success or simply meeting predetermined expectations. The desired outcome can be thought of in two ways: as a service goal that creates a positive situation or experience and as a profit goal that reaps financial reward. Both of these management goals are represented in any number of management settings, including the field of recreational sport.

Service

Service goals aim to provide a positive, meaningful experience for users or recipients without the incentive of making money. Federal, state, and local tax dollars support such service administrations and delivery operations. Employees are motivated by the idea that they are involved in a career that is a service to society. Such services are usually found within the public sector because they are necessary for society to function properly. Examples of service-oriented settings include educational, correctional, military, and community agencies. Settings with a service goal may charge fees to meet operational costs, but management's motivation is not to make money but to provide a public service, protect the public good, and contribute to the needs of society.

Profit

The second possible goal is profitability. Management with profitability motivation differs from service management and is found in the private sector. In private management, all efforts are focused on the bottom line; when all is said and done, the goal is a net profit. Products may be produced and delivered, but without profit or at least breaking even, the management system usually is unable to continue. Positive experiences and effective production efforts are necessary if a profit goal is to be accomplished. Whether the production is the sale of an item or the use of space or an area for a fee, the desired end result is generating a profit. Management systems of this nature include businesses, corporations, and franchises. Examples specific to recreational sport include clubs, fitness centers, country clubs, resorts, theme parks, and racquet clubs. Each system markets sport as a product with the intended goal of making money.

Goals are management's end result and is the last piece of the complete model. Goals may vary, but they can be modeled and systemized as shown in Figure 3.1, resulting in a sound management system.

Shining Example

Whiteface Mountain, Lake Placid, New York

Whiteface Mountain is located in Lake Placid, New York. At 4,876 ft., it is the fifth highest peak in the Adirondack Mountains. Its summit is accessible by hiking trails, and since the addition of the Veterans Memorial Highway in 1935, it is the only one of the high peaks accessible by vehicle. The ski resort at Whiteface opened in 1958 and was the venue for the alpine events of the 1980 Olympic Winter Games. Since that time, the mountain has offered a variety of competitive and family friendly activities year-round from skiing and snowboarding, to hiking, and even rides on the fastest gondola in North America.

Clientele:

Whiteface draws approximately 540,000 visitors per year

Facilities:

Whiteface Mountain hosts 86 ski trails with a longest run of 2.1 miles. It has 283 skiable acres and a lift-serviced 450 ft snowboarding pipe. It is serviced by 11 lifts including a high-speed eight-passenger gondola and offers two lodges (one at the base and one midway up the mountain) and a family center that offers dining, first aid, and restroom facilities. In addition, there is a ski shop and ski rental in the main lodge. For summer sports the mountain has several mountain bike trails.

Program Details:

Whiteface offers a variety of seasonal and year-round activities (both competitive and recreational) including alpine ski racing, freestyle skiing, snowboarding competitions, terrain park events, and tree skiing. Though it provides the majority of its programs during the winter ski season, during the summer months the mountain offers scenic gondola rides, downhill mountain biking, disc golf, interpretive hikes, and festivals. In addition to individual and club ski packages, Whiteface offers adult and youth ski and snowboarding lessons and workshops for all skill levels. One such program is Parallel From the Start, which offers an all-inclusive package for new skiers, including equipment rental, lift tickets, and a lesson. Other programs include a Ladies Ski and Ride Club and a Black Diamond Club.

Budget:

Whiteface Mountain operates on a portion of the $26 million annual budget used by the New York State Olympic Regional Development Authority (ORDA). However, it is a large contributor to the organization's revenue, generating approximately $11 million in 2010–2011.

Marketing:

As a part of ORDA, Whiteface employs a wide variety of marketing strategies including brochures and tourist information, a website (http://www.whiteface.com) as well as mentions in popular magazines such as *Ski*. Recently the marketing department has utilized "moving" billboards and social media to generate awareness and interest.

Jobs and Careers:

The staff at Whiteface include a venue manager, assistant venue manager, marketing positions, department heads, mid-level supervisors, ski instructors, ski patrol, snow makers, lift operators, equipment operators, laborers, ticket sellers, bus drivers, and night security.

Salary:

Salaries range from $40,000–$60,000 per year for the higher level management and from $25,000 to the upper $30,000 for marketing, depending upon years of service and level of responsibility. Salaries for department heads and mid-level supervisors range from $25,000–$35,000 per year. Ski Instructors earn $8–$15/hour, plus commission and tips, and Ski Patrol members earn $8–$15/hour, but without commission or tips. Laborers and Operators earn $8–$10/hour, depending upon responsibilities and years of experience. In addition, all full-time employees are able to ski free of charge.

Affiliated Professional Organizations:

Employees at Whiteface belong to a variety of national professional organizations, including the National Ski Patrol (NSP) and Professional Ski Instructors of America (PSIA).

Internships:

Due to housing restrictions, there are currently no internship positions.

Awards and Recognition:

Whiteface Mountain was voted by the readers of *Ski* magazine as the best ski mountain in the Eastern United States in 2001, 2002, and 2003 and second best in Eastern North America in 2003.

Conclusion

Management is a complete study in itself with many terms, theories, and practices. It would be naive to represent this chapter's brief snapshot of management as a comprehensive perspective. But it does provide a capsule view that addresses key areas of information, blending important points together in a complete model that accurately portrays management. Recreational sport specialists would be wise to learn these concepts and the overall outline of management as they move forward in developing an informational foundation.

Bibliography

Appenzeller, H., & Appenzeller, T. (2008). *Successful sports management* (3ʳᵈ ed.). Durham, NC: Carolina Academic Press.

Bright, A. D. (1997). Attitude-strength and support of recreation management. *Journal of Leisure Research, 29*(4), 363-380.

Casper, J. M., & Stellino, M. B. (2008). Demographic predictors of recreational tennis participant's sport commitment. *Journal of Park and Recreation Administration, 26*(3), 93-115.

Chelladurai, P. (2006). *Human resource management in sport and recreation* (2ⁿᵈ ed.). Champaign, IL: Human Kinetics.

Chelladurai, P. (2009). *Managing organizations for sport and physical activity: A systems perspective* (3ʳᵈ ed.). Scottsdale, AZ: Halcomb Hathaway.

Connaughton, D. P. (1998). The changing standard of care and the legal implications for recreational sports and fitness facility administrators. *Journal of the National Intramural–Recreational Sports Association, 22*(3), 20-22.

Green, P. (2002). Explaining continuity and change in the transition from compulsory competitive tendering to best value for sport and recreation management. *Managing Leisure, 7*(2), 124-139.

Greenwell, C. T., Fink, J. S., & Pastore, D. L. (2002). Perceptions of the service experience: Using demographic and psychographic variables to identify customer segments. *Sport Marketing Quarterly, 11*(4), 233-242.

Lamke, G. (1991). Human resource management in recreational sports. *Journal of the National Intramural–Recreational Sports Association, 16*(1), 42-45.

Lewis, G., & Appenzeller, H. (1985). *Successful sports management.* Charlottesville, VA: Michie.

Maas, G. M. (1992). Paradigms in recreational sports administration. *National Intramural– Recreational Sports Association Journal, 16*(3), 8-11.

Martens, R. (2001). *Directing youth sports programs.* Champaign, IL: Human Kinetics.

Maxwell, J. C. (2007). *The 21 indispensable qualities of a leader: Becoming that person that people will want to follow* (3ʳᵈ ed.). Nashville, TN: Thomas Nelson.

Nelson, J. P. (2001). Hard at play! The growth of recreation in consumer's budgets, 1959–1998. *Eastern Economic Journal, 27*(1), 35-54.

National Intramural–Recreational Sports Association. (2009). *Campus recreational sports facilities: Planning, design and construction guidelines.* Champaign, IL: Human Kinetics.

Parkhouse, B. L. (2004). *The management of sport: Its foundations and application* (4ᵗʰ ed.). New York, NY: McGraw-Hill.

Parks, J., Quarterman, J., & Thibault, L. (2007). *Contemporary sport management* (4ᵗʰ ed.). Champaign, IL: Human Kinetics.

Rohm, A. J., Milne, G. R., & McDonald, M.A. (2006). A mixed-methods approach for developing market segmentation typologies in the sports industry. *Sport Marketing Quarterly, 15*, 29-39.

Schneider, R. C., Stier, W. F., Kampf, S., Haines, S., & Gaskins, B. (2008). Factors affecting risk management of indoor campus recreation facilities. *Recreational Sports Journal, 32*, 114-133.

Shivers, J. S. (1987). *Introduction to recreational service administration.* Philadelphia: Lea and Febiger.

Spengler, J. O., Connaughton, D. P., & Pittman, A. T. (2006). *Risk management in sport and recreation.* Champaign, IL: Human Kinetics.

Torkilsen, G. (2005). *Leisure and recreation management* (5ᵗʰ ed.). New York, NY: Routledge.

Vanderzwagg, H. J. (1998). *Policy development in sport management* (2ⁿᵈ ed.). Westport, CT: Praeger.

Watt, D.C. (2003). *Sport management and administration* (2ⁿᵈ ed.). New York, NY: Routledge.

Young, S. J., Fields, S. K., & Powell, G. M. (2007). Risk perceptions versus legal realities in campus recreational sport programs. *Recreational Sports Journal, 31*, 131-145.

Part II

VALUES AND BENEFITS

Part II is a continuation of the foundations, placing emphasis on the very important and popular outcomes of sport participation. As recognized for decades, sport provides a means for people to live healthily, including both physical and mental fitness, life learning opportunities, and a positive fun experience. Such well-founded content will give sport specialists real meaning and purpose to their career and daily roles and responsibilities.

CHAPTER 4

Fitness

CHAPTER OBJECTIVES

After reading this chapter, you will understand the role of fitness in health and wellness, view participant fitness as a goal of recreational sport programming, and be able to identify components of fitness in recreational sport.

KEY CONCEPTS

Fitness
Wellness
Health
Healthy People 2020
Health-related components of fitness
Indirect fitness delivery

Performance-related components of fitness
Physical activity guidelines
Recreational sport contributions to fitness
Recreational sports over the life span
Sport and fitness outcomes

Introduction

This chapter identifies physical inactivity as a critical public health issue in the United States, discusses several physical activity initiatives, and outlines the physical activity guidelines for Americans. The chapter also touches on how fitness relates to health and wellness. Next, it discusses components of fitness, as understanding the health and performance components of fitness provides a foundation for understanding programming fitness indirectly through club, informal, instructional, and intra- and extramural sports.

Sedentary America

Physical inactivity is a critical public health issue for Americans as 1 in 4 Americans participates in no leisure-time physical activity (Mowen & Baker, 2009). According to the World Health Organization (WHO), physical inactivity is the fourth leading risk factor for global mortality (WHO, 2010). Globally, 6% of deaths are attributed to physical *inactivity*. Physical inactivity is also the main cause for approx-

imately 21–25% of breast and colon cancers, 27% of diabetes, and 30% of ischemic heart disease burden. Physical inactivity and sedentary lifestyles are also among the leading causes of obesity (Adderley-Kelly, 2007; Buckworth & Nigg, 2004; Fibkins, 2006; Gieck & Olsen, 2007; Kumanyika & Ross, 2007; Raine, 2004; WHO, 2000).

Obesity Epidemic

According to the WHO (2000), obesity represents a major chronological disease affecting people of all ages in all parts of the world. Moreover, obesity has become one of the greatest public health concerns, so much that it is now being classified as a global epidemic (WHO, 2000). Within North America, and especially the United States, obesity levels continue to rise at a rapid pace (Adderley-Kelly, 2007). It is estimated that 129.6 million (64%) Americans are overweight or obese (Adderley-Kelly, 2007). Furthermore, more than 17 million people have diabetes with another 16 million people having prediabetes, and about 90–95% of cases are type 2 diabetes, which is associated with obesity and physical inactivity (U.S. Department of Health and Human Services [USDHHS], 2002).

Overwhelming evidence exists that indicates obesity is a cause of many health problems afflicting North Americans, including type 2 diabetes (Kumanyika & Ross, 2007), asthma, hypertension, heart disease, cancer (Raine, 2004), osteoarthritis, sleep apnea, infertility, and premature death (Colditz & Stein, 2007). Other research indicates that obesity may also cause psychological problems such as increased risk of depression (Colditz & Stein, 2007), diminished social and emotional development via social discrimination (Raine, 2004), lower self-esteem, and increased risk of addiction to tobacco, alcohol, and pharmaceutical drugs (Fibkins, 2006).

Economic Consequences of Physical Inactivity

Physical inactivity and its associated health concerns, including obesity, have also been found to have profound economic consequences upon society (Colditz & Stein, 2007) and are creating an economic burden on the American health care system (USDHHS, 2002). The economic costs of obesity can be defined in terms of the direct and indirect costs, that is, money directly spent on the treatment and care of obese individuals and reductions in economic productivity resulting from illness caused by obesity (indirect costs) (Raine, 2004; Starky, 2005). U.S. expenditures on obesity are estimated to be roughly $117 billion per year (Colditz & Stein, 2007). The evidence regarding the detrimental effects of obesity on the individual and society is undeniable. Obesity represents a global epidemic that is not prejudiced toward age, gender, race, ethnicity, or socioeconomic status. Therefore, the need for widespread effective prevention strategies are sorely needed.

The Need for a Physically Active America—The Benefits of Physical Activity

Researchers agree that one of the most effective ways of treating and preventing obesity is through increasing the amount of time that an individual spends on daily physical activity, defined as bodily movement that enhances health (Adderley-Kelly, 2007; Buckworth & Nigg, 2004; Fibkins, 2006; Gieck & Olsen, 2007; Kumanyika & Ross, 2007; Raine, 2004; WHO, 2003). Studies by researchers at the Centers for Disease Control and Prevention found that physically active people had, on average, lower annual direct medical costs when compared to inactive people (Pratt, Macera, & Wang, 2000). The same study estimated that increasing regular moderate physical activity among the more than 88 million inactive Americans over age 15 could possibly reduce the yearly national direct medical costs by as much as $76.6 billion in year 2000 dollars.

In 1996, the U.S. Surgeon General published a landmark *Report on Physical Activity and Health* that documented in detail the medical benefits of physical activity on

- overall mortality;
- cardiovascular diseases;
- coronary heart disease;
- stroke;
- high blood pressure;
- cancer;
- colon cancer;
- breast cancer;
- noninsulin-dependent diabetes;
- osteoarthritis;
- osteoporosis;
- obesity;
- depression, anxiety, and mood; and
- psychological well-being.

Furthermore, the USDHHS (2010) found that

- moderate physical activity can substantially reduce the risk of developing heart disease, diabetes, colon cancer, and high blood pressure;
- regular physical activity helps maintain the functional independence of older adults and enhances quality of life for people of all ages;
- regular physical activity has been shown to improve muscle function, cardiovascular function, and physical performance;
- regular physical activity increases muscle and bone strength, helps decrease body fat, aids in weight control, and is a key part of any weight loss effort; and
- regular physical activity enhances psychological well-being and may even reduce the risk of developing depression; it appears to reduce symptoms of depression and anxiety and to improve mood.

Based on the mounting evidence, experts have grown increasingly aware that physical activity can make a real impact on the predicted rise in chronic diseases as the population ages.

Physical activity plays an important role in the fitness, health, and wellness of Americans. Many definitions exist for fitness, health, and wellness. There is not complete consensus on a single definition for each term, but most are adequate. This chapter uses the following definitions:

Fitness—The ability to meet the ordinary and usual demands of daily life without being overly fatigued and still have energy left for recreational sport participation.

Health—The state of complete positive well-being beyond the absence of illness and disease.

Wellness—The sustained, intentional effort to achieve optimal health and the highest potential for well-being in physical, emotional, mental, social, environmental, occupational, and spiritual dimensions of life.

Millions of Americans suffer from chronic illnesses that can be prevented or improved through regular physical activity (USDHHS, 2002). People who are physically active live longer, healthier lives. Regular physical activity helps to maintain a healthy body. Active people are more productive and more likely to avoid illness and injury. In general, the key benefits of regular physical activity include (Public Health Agency of Canada, n.d.)

- better health,
- improved fitness,
- better posture and balance,
- higher self-esteem,
- weight control,
- stronger muscles and bones,
- feeling more energetic,
- relaxation and reduced stress, and
- continued independent living in later life.

Physical activity also helps to promote healthy growth and development; prevent chronic diseases such as cancer, type 2 diabetes, and heart disease; make a person stronger; give a person energy; decrease stress; and prolong independence as a person gets older (Public Health Agency of Canada, n.d.). On average, people who are physically active outlive those who are inactive (USDHHS, 2002). An effective effort to mobilize this knowledge calls for the use of all the potential settings of health promotion, including communities, schools/universities, and workplaces.

Healthy People 2020

As part of the effort to create a national focus on health in the United States, the U.S. Department of Health and Human Services published *Healthy Peo-ple 2000: National Health Promotion and Diseases Prevention Objectives*. This document, updated as *Healthy People 2010*, and again as *Healthy People 2020*, sets public health goals for Americans that alleviate risk factors and promote healthy behaviors. Of the 10 leading health indicators, one is dedication to physical activity. The goal statement reads: "Improve health, fitness, and quality of life through daily physical activity" (USDHHS, 2010). The field of recreational sports can have an impact on the following objectives for 2020:

- reduce the proportion of adults who engage in no leisure-time physical activity;
- increase the proportion of adults who meet current federal physical activity guidelines for aerobic physical activity and for muscle-strengthening activity;
- increase the proportion of adolescents who meet current federal physical activity guidelines for aerobic physical activity and for muscle-strengthening activity;
- increase the proportion of the nation's public and private schools that provide access to their physical activity spaces and facilities for all persons outside of normal school hours (i.e., before and after the school day, on weekends, and during summer and other vacations);
- increase the proportion of physician office visits that include counseling or education related to physical activity;
- increase the proportion of employed adults who have access to and participate in employer-based exercise facilities and exercise programs; and
- increase legislative policies for the built environment that enhance access to and availability of physical activity opportunities.

The physical activity objectives for *Healthy People 2020* reflect the strength of the evidence supporting the health benefits of regular physical activity among youth and adults. These goals reflect the consensus that activity needs to increase to improve health and fitness, and recreational sport participation provides a key way for many Americans to meet these objectives.

Physical Activity Guidelines

In 1995, guidelines recommended by the Centers for Disease Control and Prevention and the American College of Sports Medicine for achieving health-related goals reflected a change in perspective on exercise, fitness, and physical activity by shifting the focus from intensive vigorous exercise to a broader range of health-enhancing physical activities. The 1995 recommendation stated that every adult should accumulate 30 minutes or more of moderate-intensity physical activity on most, preferably all, days of the week. In 1996, the U.S. Surgeon General's landmark *Report on Physical Activity and Health* supported the same recommendation (Pate et al., 1995).

In 2008, the USDHHS published the *2008 Physical Activity Guidelines for Americans* in a response to criticisms that previous guidelines were too specific and were not being met by Americans. More than 80% of adults do not meet the guidelines for both aerobic and muscle-strengthening activities. Similarly, more than 80% of adolescents do not do enough aerobic physical activity to meet the guidelines for youth (USDHHS, 2008). Furthermore, there is a lack of scientific evidence demonstrating whether or not the health benefits of 30 minutes of physical activity a day, 5 days a week, was any

different from the health benefits of 50 minutes of physical activity 3 days a week. Consequently, the new *Physical Activity Guidelines* allow a person to accumulate 150 minutes a week in a variety of ways.

The *Guidelines* are for Americans aged 6 and older and provide recommendations for three age groups: children and adolescents, adults, and older adults. The *Guidelines* divide the amount of aerobic physical activity an adult gets every week into four categories: inactive, low, medium, and high (see Table 4.1). The *Guidelines* include this classification because these categories provide a general rule of thumb in terms of how the total amount of aerobic physical activity is related to health benefits. Individuals that are inactive beyond baseline activities receive no benefit, low amounts of activity provide some benefits, medium amounts provide substantial benefits, and high amounts provide even greater benefits.

Table 4.1

Classification of Total Weekly Amounts of Aerobic Physical Activity Into Four Categories

Levels of Physical Activity	Range of Moderate-Intensity Minutes a Week	Summary of Overall Health Benefits	Comment
Inactive	No activity beyond baseline	None	Being inactive is unhealthy.
Low	Activity beyond baseline but fewer than 150 minutes a week	Some	Low levels of activity are clearly preferable to an inactive lifestyle.
Medium	150 minutes to 300 minutes a week	Substantial	Activity at the high end of this range has additional and mroe extensive health benefits than activity at the low end.
High	More than 300 minutes a week	Additional	Current science does not allow researchers to identify an upper limit of activity above which there are no additional health benefits.

U.S. Department of Health and Human Services. *2008 Physical Activity Guidelines for Americans.* Retrieved November 1, 2011 from http://www.health.gov/paguidelines.

Children and Adolescents

There is strong evidence that regular physical activity for children and adolescents improves cardiorespiratory and muscular fitness, bone health, and cardiovascular and metabolic health biomarkers and also contributes to favorable body composition. Moderate evidence exists indicating that regular physical activity reduces symptoms of depression (USDHHS, 2008).

Children and adolescents aged 6 to 17 should do 60 minutes or more of physical activity daily. This physical activity can be of three types: aerobic, muscle strengthening, and bone strengthening. Aerobic activities increase cardiorespiratory fitness and involve rhythmic movements of large muscles. Running, hopping, skipping, jumping rope, swimming, dancing, and bicycling are all examples of aerobic activities. Muscle-strengthening activities make muscles do more work than usual during normal daily activities and can be unstructured and part of play, such as playing on playground equipment, climbing trees, and playing tug-of-war. Bone-strengthening activities can also be aerobic and muscle strengthening and produce a force on the bones (commonly produced by impact with the ground) that promotes bone growth and strength. Running, jumping rope, basketball, tennis, and hopscotch are all examples of bone-strengthening activities. It is important for recreational sport specialists to encourage young people to participate in physical activities that are appropriate for their age, are enjoyable, and offer variety (USDHHS, 2008).

Active Adults

There is strong evidence that regular physical activity for active adults and older adults lowers the risk of early death, coronary heart disease, stroke, high blood pressure, adverse blood lipid profile, type 2 diabetes, metabolic syndrome, colon cancer, breast cancer, and weight gain and contributes to weight loss, improved cardiorespiratory and muscular fitness, prevention of falls, reduced depression, and better cognitive function (for older adults). There is moderate to strong evidence demonstrating that regular physical activity results in better functional health (for older adults) and reduced abdominal obesity. Moderate evidence exists indicating that regular physical activity for adults and older adults lowers the risk of hip fracture and lung and endometrial cancer and helps with weight maintenance after weight loss, increased bone density, and improved sleep quality (USDHHS, 2008).

The *Guidelines* for adults focus on two types of activity—aerobic and muscle strengthening—and recommend the following:

- For substantial health benefits, adults should do at least 150 minutes (2.5 hours) a week of moderate intensity or 75 minutes a week of vigorous intensity aerobic physical activity or an equivalent combination of moderate and vigorous intensity aerobic activity.

- For additional and more extensive health benefits, adults should increase their aerobic physical activity to 300 minutes (5 hours) a week of moderate intensity or 150 minutes a week of vigorous intensity aerobic physical activity or an equivalent combination of moderate and vigorous intensity activity.

- Adults should also do muscle-strengthening activities that are moderate or high intensity and involve all major muscle groups on two or more days a week, as these activities provide additional health benefits (USDHHS, 2008).

The *Guidelines* also recommend that all adults should avoid inactivity. Inactive adults, or those who don't yet do 150 minutes of physical activity a week, should gradually work to achieve this target. The initial amount of activity should be at a light or moderate intensity for short periods of time, with the sessions spread throughout the week. Research has found that some physical activity is better than none, and adults who participate in any amount of physical activity gain some health benefits (USDHHS, 2008).

Active Older Adults

The *Guidelines* for adults aged 65 years or older also focus on aerobic and muscle-strengthening physical activity and have the same recommendations outlined above for active adults. In addition, the *Guidelines* recommend the following:

- When older adults cannot do 150 minutes of moderate-intensity aerobic activity a week because of chronic conditions, they should be as physically active as their abilities and conditions allow.

- Older adults should do exercises that maintain or improve balance if they are at risk of falling.

- Older adults should determine their level of effort for physical activity relative to their level of fitness.

- Older adults with chronic conditions should understand whether and how their conditions affect their ability to do regular physical activity safely (USDHHS, 2008).

The *Guidelines* also offer numerous special considerations for each of the three age groups and provide real-life examples illustrating a variety of different ways to meet the physical activity guidelines. Furthermore, the *Guidelines* offer additional considerations for women during pregnancy and the postpartum period, people with disabilities, and people with chronic medical conditions.

Achieving the initiatives for a healthier America begins with increasing physical activity offerings in physical education programs, college and university recreational sport programs, workplace employee wellness and physical activity programs, and public agency and commercial fitness programs. Although the school system provides a large portion of physical activity and fitness education, the mission of recreational sport specialists is to recognize that, regardless of the setting, recreational sport goals underscore the need to improve healthy behaviors through participation in physical activity.

Recreational Sport Participation

Sport participation can represent a fundamental component of obesity prevention and reduction strategies (Kanters, Bocarro, Casper, & Forrester, 2008). Furthermore, children who participate in organized sport typically spend less time watching television (Kanters et al., 2008), which has been cited as a contributor to sedentary lifestyles (Buckworth & Nigg, 2004). Unfortunately, organized sport tends to be competitive, and greater emphasis is placed on winning and competition rather than on having fun and developing skills (Roberts, 1999). Therefore, competitive sports often marginalize those individuals who may seek to participate in sport, "forcing many to become sedentary spectators" (Kanters et al., 2008, p. 4).

In this and other ways, recreational sports contrast sharply with competitive sport. According to Kanters et al. (2008), recreational sports offer sport opportunities that are centered on motivations "to have fun, to stay in shape, to learn and improve skills and to play as part of a team" (p. 5). Typically, when asked why they participate in a recreational sport program, most people answer "to have fun" or "to get fit." Many individuals who list having fun as their reason for participating in a recreational sport program likely also believe they are reaping health and wellness rewards by doing so.

Recreational sport programs can provide opportunities for physical activity, fitness, and health. Involvement in physical activity leads to participation in a spectrum of sport programs. Through recreational sport, individuals can improve their health and help ward off illnesses that result from poor fitness and lifestyle choices. Approximately 25% of employee health care use is potentially preventable and linked with seven risk factors: obesity, sedentary lifestyle, smoking, stress, high blood sugar, depression, and high blood pressure (Anderson et al., 2000).

Corporations have designed employee wellness, sport, and fitness programs for the workplace to promote physical activity, fitness, and good health, which lead to

- lowered insurance premiums and health-related claims,

- improved morale and productivity,

- ensured health awareness and education, and

- improved recruitment of quality employees.

In fact, workplace employee fitness and wellness programs can reduce short-term sick leave by 6–3%, reduce health care costs by 20–55%, and increase productivity by 2–52% (USDHHS, 2002). According to the National Employee Services and Recreation Association (Mull, Bayless, & Jamieson, 2005), corporations and organizations develop sport programs around the goal of employee fitness, wellness, and health. These are also primary goals in military sport programs and in therapeutic recreation settings, and it is receiving heightened attention wherever recreational sport opportunities are available. Trends in YMCAs, health clubs, community centers, and at all levels of education attest that fitness, wellness, and health are now major goals of most recreational sport settings.

Components of Fitness

Recreational sport specialists must incorporate fitness and health basics into programming goals. The first step is understanding the components of total fitness: physical, emotional, and mental health. With this in mind, this section examines the physical aspects of fitness and then discusses how recreational sport programming can contribute to physical fitness.

Physical fitness. Physical fitness is commonly associated with performing exercises. While performing exercises is one means of enhancing physical fitness, it is important to begin with a broader understanding of the elements that make up physical fitness. Table 4.2 divides the elements of physical fitness into two groups, performance and health, and provides a list of sport programming options that supports the development of each group.

Table 4.2

Measurable Elements of Physical Fitness and Sport Programming Options

Components of Fitness	
Performance-related components of fitness	**Health-related components of fitness**
Agility	Cardiovascular endurance
Power	Muscular endurance
Coordination	Muscular strength
Speed	Flexibility
Reaction time	Body composition
Balance	

Types of Activities		
Performance-related fitness	**Both**	**Health-related fitness**
Archery	Basketball	Aerobic dance
Badminton	Handball	Backpacking
Baseball	Ice skating	Bicycling
Bowling	Racquetball	Calisthenics
Downhill skiing	Roller skating	Cross-country skiing
Fencing	Squash	Rope jumping
Football		Rowing
Golf		Running
Soccer		Snowshoeing
Table tennis		Stair climbing
Tennis		Swimming
Volleyball		Walking
		Weight lifting

Adapted from Caspersen, C. J., Powell, K. E., & Christenson, G. M. (1985). Physical activity, exercise, and physical fitness: Definitions and distinctions for health-related research. *Public Health Rep, 100,* 126-131.

Health-related components of fitness. Health-related components of physical fitness contribute to well-being by reducing the risk of degenerative diseases, increasing work efficiency, and improving quality of life. These components include cardiovascular and muscular endurance, strength, flexibility, and body composition.

Cardiovascular endurance refers to the efficiency of the heart, lungs, and blood vessels during vigorous muscular activity over time. Unless the heart, circulatory, and respiratory systems function efficiently, insufficient oxygen impairs activity.

Muscular endurance is the capacity of a muscle group to apply and sustain force over time. Muscle endurance helps individuals maintain good posture, resist fatigue, and avoid injuries.

Muscular strength refers to the maximum force a muscle or muscle group can exert against resistance. In athletes, strength has been a traditional symbol

of fitness. Although developing and maintaining muscular strength leads to an attractive physique, its major fitness benefits are protecting the joints and preventing injury.

Flexibility refers to the capability of the joints to move through a full range of movement. When the joints are not exercised often enough through a full range of motion, the surrounding connective tissues can't retain their normal length and flexibility. Lower back pain and postural misalignment are problems associated with inflexibility. Limited range of motion in a joint decreases the functional capabilities of the muscles around that joint. A reduced range of motion lowers performance level and may result in injury.

Body composition is also an important component of fitness. Most people use total body weight as a health indicator rather than the relationship between fat and lean body mass, but because muscle is denser than fat, body weight is a deceptive measure. It is the ratio of body fat to weight that reflects a healthy body. Having the recommended percentage of lean body fat improves performance and decreases problems associated with obesity, such as hypertension, diabetes mellitus, gallbladder disease, degenerative arthritis, digestive diseases, respiratory infections, kidney disease, and posture dysfunction.

Performance-related components of fitness. Performance-related components are the skills important for enjoyable participation in recreational sport, including agility, power, coordination, speed, reaction time, and balance.

Agility refers to the ability to rapidly change the direction of the body or body parts. Agility involves speed, accuracy, and control in making quick starts and stops; rapid changes of direction; and efficient footwork. Influenced by heredity, agility improves through training and instruction involving reaction time, strength, and coordination of large muscle groups.

Power is the ability to transfer energy into a fast rate of speed, combining strength with speed. Power is exhibited in activities such as shot putting, rowing, pitching, and punting.

Coordination is the smooth integration of muscular movements. Heredity tends to affect coordination, but it is possible to improve coordination through practice. However, progress is often task specific, so the recreational sport specialist should offer a range of recreational sport activities.

Speed is the ability to quickly move the body or body parts from one point to another. Speed is exemplified in activities such as running, boxing, swimming, skating, and lacrosse.

Reaction time is the time required to initiate a response to a stimulus. Individuals who have quick reaction times make fast starts in football, swimming, or running events; react quickly to a moving baseball or basketball; and move rapidly to dodge or defend against attacks in fencing or martial arts.

Balance is the ability to maintain body position. Static balance is the ability to maintain equilibrium while standing, and dynamic balance is the ability to maintain equilibrium while moving or performing a task. Three major principles affect balance:

- *Center of gravity*—The lower the center of gravity, the greater the balance and stability.

- *Base of support*—The larger the base of support, the greater the balance and stability.

- *Relationship between center of gravity and base of support*—The closer the center of gravity is to the center of the base of support, the greater the balance and stability.

Recreational Sport Contributions to Fitness

To maximize the benefits from health- and performance-related fitness, individuals need to know what activities contribute to each aspect of physical fitness. Table 4.3 lists health benefits of sports and other activities. Each sport is rated according to its contribution to health-related fitness. Health benefits from sport participation depend on the frequency, intensity, and duration of participation. The ratings in Table 4.3 require that the sport be performed regularly. Determining the relationship of sport or exercise to health-related fitness requires an understanding of the following:

- **Fitness training zone.** There is a range of participation from the minimum necessary to improve fitness to a maximum beyond which activity may be counterproductive. This continuum constitutes the fitness training zone.

- **Overload principle.** To improve an aspect of health-related fitness, engage in more than normal, or overload, participation.

- **Threshold of training.** Identify the minimum amount of participation that will improve each aspect of health-related fitness.

Table 4.3 lists the aspects of performance-related fitness that various sports require based on recreational participation. *Poor* means no skill is needed, *fair* means little skill is needed, *good* means some skill is needed, and *excellent* means much skill is required.

Physical fitness requires regular physical activity. The recreational sport specialist contributes to participant fitness by promoting physical activity opportunities. Sport and physical activity are the primary techniques of fitness programming. Physical activity involves vigorous or continuous physical activity. Physical activity is possible without participating in a sport, for example, riding a stationary bike. Most people engage in a physical activity program to attain a specific fitness outcome. Sport, on the other hand, is a broad category of activity that may or may not involve physical activity. Those who engage in sport may do so for fun and socialization, possibly with little regard for fitness. Because of differences in participant preferences and fitness benefits from sport activity, a recreational sport program should provide a variety of activities. Recreational sport specialists should make facilities, equipment, and playing partners accessible to facilitate participation. Fitness programs emphasizing the health-related components of fitness must recognize that results are affected by the type, frequency, duration, and progression of the workout. For example, strength conditioning with

Table 4.3

Health-Related Benefits of Sports

Health-related benefits	Develops cardiovascular fitness	Develops strength	Develops muscular endurance	Develops flexibility	Helps control body fat
Excellent	Rowing, crew[1] Cross-country skiing[1] Full-court Basketball[3] Soccer[3]	Gymnastics[1]	Gymnastics[1] Rowing, crew[1] BMX cycling[4]	Gymnastics[1]	Rowing, crew[1] Cross-country skiing[1] Full-court Basketball[3] Soccer[3]
Good	Handball/racquetball[2] BMX cycling[4] Mountain climbing[4]	Football[3] BMX cycling[4] Mountain climbing[4]	Cross-country skiing[1] Downhill skiing[1] Snowboarding[1] Handball/racquetball[2] Full-court Basketball[3] Soccer[3] Mountain climbing[4] Surfing[4] Waterskiing[4]		Handball/racquetball[2] BMX cycling[4] Mountain climbing[4]
Fair	Badminton[1] Golf (walking)[1] Gymnastics[1] Downhill skiing[1] Snowboarding[1] Half-court Basketball[3] Football[3] Volleyball[3] Canoeing[4] Surfing[4] Waterskiing[4]	Rowing, crew[1] Cross-country skiing[1] Downhill skiing[1] Snowboarding[1] Martial arts[2] Soccer[3] Volleyball[3] Waterskiing[4]	Badminton[1] Martial arts[2] Half-court Basketball[3] Football[3] Canoeing[4]	Badminton[1] Snowboarding[1] Martial arts[2] Soccer[3] BMX cycling[4] Surfing[4]	Badminton[1] Gymnastics[1] Downhill skiing[1] Snowboarding[1] Football[3] Volleyball[3] Canoeing[4] Surfing[4] Waterskiing[4]
Poor	Bowling[1] Martial arts[2] Table tennis[2] Baseball/ softball[3] Horseback riding[4] Sailing[4]	Badminton[1] Bowling[1] Golf (walking)[1] Handball/racquetball[2] Table tennis[2] Baseball/ softball[3] Half-court Basketball[3] Full-court Basketball[3] Canoeing[4] Horseback riding[4] Sailing[4] Surfing[4]	Bowling[1] Golf (walking)[1] Table tennis[2] Baseball/ softball[3] Volleyball[3] Horseback riding[4] Sailing[4]	Bowling[1] Golf (walking)[1] Rowing, crew[1] Cross-country skiing[1] Downhill skiing[1] Handball/racquetball[2] Table tennis[2] Baseball/ softball[3] Half-court Basketball[3] Full-court Basketball[3] Football[3] Volleyball[3] Canoeing[4] Horseback riding[4] Mountain climbing[4] Sailing[4] Waterskiing[4]	Bowling[1] Golf (walking)[1] Martial arts[2] Table tennis[2] Baseball/ softball[3] Half-court Basketball[3] Horseback riding[4] Sailing[4]

1 = Individual sport , 2 = Dual sport , 3 = Team sport , 4 = Outdoor/adventure sport
Adapted from C.B. Corbin and R. Lindsey (2005). *Fitness for life*. (5th ed). Champaign, IL: Human Kinetics.

weights may contribute very little to cardiorespiratory endurance and requires supplemental activity to stimulate the heart and lungs. Because people vary in fitness level, body structure, motivation, and fitness needs, an individual approach to assessment and physical activity may be more beneficial than a group approach.

Program Delivery

People of all ages, body types, and sport preferences are demonstrating interest in an active, healthy lifestyle. An awareness of the benefits of regular exercise and sport activity does not guarantee participation, however. People need encouragement and convenience to make time for regular involvement. Recreational sport specialists need to counter the sedentary patterns perpetuated by the rise of technology. They must program exercise and sport into current lifestyles and encourage participation as a lifetime pursuit. As Table 4.4 shows, fitness programming can be offered indirectly through instructional, informal, intramural, extramural, and club programming and directly through exercise consultation and supervision. Neither approach is better than the other, but they are different in application and purpose.

Indirect Delivery

This represents a recreation and leisure application and places fitness as a benefit of the recreational sport experience, not as a goal for staff to direct and monitor. In this process, the participant is motivated by fun, socialization, and the outcome of participation. The recreational sport specialist's role is to provide recreational sport experiences.

Indirect delivery through the recreational sport spectrum includes instructional, informal, intramural, extramural, and club sport. In this approach, people with a background in recreational sport management develop programs to meet the goals of fun and fitness. Recreational sport specialists retain responsibility for overall program management. The promotion of fitness indirectly will be covered later in the text in the respective recreational sport program chapters.

Direct Delivery

Direct delivery represents a physical education and kinesiology application that influences fitness outcomes through direct supervision. Trained and certified fitness specialists use the fitness techniques of testing, exercise consultation, monitoring, and supervising the participant during the activity.

Recreational Sports Over the Life Span

Research has shown that participation rates in sport and physical activity significantly decrease with age (Cordes & Ibrahim, 1999; Curtis, McTeer, & White, 1999; Vanreusel et al., 1997). However, there is a considerable body of evidence demonstrating a positive correlation between sport participation as a youth and later life participation (Bucher, 1974; Howell & McKenzie, 1987; Kelly, 1980; Malina, 1996; Montoye, Van Huss, & Zuidema, 1959; Morgan & Montoye, 1984; Paffenburger, Hyde, Wing, & Hsieh, 1986; Powell & Dysinger, 1987; Rees, Andres, & Howell, 1986; van Mechelen & Kemper, 1995; Vanreusel et al., 1997; Watkins, 1983; White & Curtis, 1990; Yang, 1997). Leisure repertoire theory can help explain how sport participation as a youth contributes to later life participation. Leisure repertoire refers to the number of different activities individuals engage in during their leisure. The leisure repertoire theory points to the importance of developing skills and personal resources during youth and adolescence in order to participate in a variety of recreational sport and leisure pursuits throughout life (Fache, 1987). Leisure repertoire theory is based on the assumption that people regularly participate in activities they feel they do well in, and this confidence in the activity leads to greater participation rates (Mobily et al., 1993). An individual's leisure "activities and relationships that have been cultivated and maintained over a long period of time in people's lives are the most likely to contribute to well-being and sense of integrity" (Mannell & Kleiber, 1997, p. 267).

As adults age, they become more conservative about their recreational sport and leisure lifestyle and tend to make leisure choices from their own repertoire of skilled activities (Iso-Ahola, 1980; Iso-Ahola, Jackson, & Dunn, 1994; Roberts, 1999). The greater the repertoire of choices, the more likely individuals will continue to participate when moving from adolescence to adulthood. Individuals with a background in recreational or noncompetitive sports are more likely to continue participating later in life when compared to those who are involved in competitive sport. In fact, "subjects with a recreational sport participation style appear to have better chances for continued sport involvement from youth to adulthood" (Vanreusel et al., 1997, p. 377). It is important for recreational sport specialists to help expand the number of different activities (repertoire) that individuals participate in and to develop skills and personal resources for participants during youth and adolescence in order to increase the likelihood that these individuals participate in a variety of recreational sports throughout life, in an effort to remain physically active in order to stay healthy.

Table 4.4

Skill-Related Benefits of Sports and Other Activities

Activity	Balance	Coordination	Reaction time	Agility	Power	Speed
Excellent	Bicycling Ballet dance Gymnastics Ice/roller skating Skiing, downhill	Badminton Baseball Basketball Bowling Ballet dance Golf (walking) Gymnastics Martial arts Racquetball/handball Skiing, cross-country Skiing, downhill Soccer Softball (fast pitch) Tennis Volleyball	Baseball Basketball Extreme sports Football Martial arts Softball (fast pitch)	Basketball Ballet dance Extreme sports Football Gymnastics Martial arts Racquetball/handball Skiing, downhill Soccer	Baseball Basketball Gymnastics Martial arts Skiing, cross-country	Football Martial arts
Good	Baseball Basketball Bowling Extreme sports Football Martial arts	Aerobic dance Extreme sports Football Ice/roller skating Rope jumping	Badminton Gymnastics Racquetball/handball Skiing, downhill Soccer Tennis Volleyball	Badminton Baseball Aerobic dance Fitness calisthenics Ice/roller skating Rope jumping Skiing, cross-country Softball (fast pitch) Swimming (laps) Tennis Volleyball	Circuit training Ballet dance Football Golf (walking) Skiing, downhill Soccer Softball (fast pitch) Tennis Weight training	Badminton Baseball Basketball Extreme sports Racquetball/handball Ice/roller skating Soccer Softball (fast pitch) Tennis
Fair	Badminton Circuit training Aerobic dance Fitness calisthenics Golf (walking) Interval training Racquetball/handball Rope jumping Skiing, cross-country Soccer Softball (fast pitch) Tennis Volleyball Weight training	Bicycling Circuit training Fitness calisthenics Interval training Weight training	Bicycling Aerobic dance Ballet dance Ice/roller skating Rope jumping Swimming (laps)	Bicycling Bowling Circuit training Golf (walking)	Badminton Fitness calisthenics Extreme sports Racquetball/handball Ice/roller skating Rope jumping Swimming (laps) Volleyball	Bicycling Bowling Circuit training Gymnastics Interval training Skiing, cross-country Volleyball
Poor	Jogging or walking Swimming (laps)	Jogging or walking	Bowling Circuit training Fitness calisthenics Golf (walking) Interval training Jogging or walking Skiing, cross-country Swimming (laps) Weight training	Interval training Jogging or walking Weight training	Bicycling Bowling Aerobic dance Interval training Jogging or walking	Aerobic dance Ballet dance Fitness calisthenics Golf (walking) Jogging or walking Rope jumping Skiing, downhill Swimming (laps) Weight training

Adapted from C.B. Corbin and R. Lindsey (2005). *Fitness for life.* (5th ed). Champaign, IL: Human Kinetics.

Shining Example

Health Fitness Corporation

Health Fitness Corporation is an award-winning provider of health-improvement management services. Established in 1975, HFC professionally manages nearly 400 programs in North America; offers a comprehensive health enhancement program; and provides consulting services to corporations, communities, universities, and property management companies. In 2009 Health Fitness became the largest provider of health management solutions.

Clientele:

HFC operates corporate health and fitness centers for over 300 corporate clients including many well known companies. It also operates community-based centers and occupational health centers across the country.

Facilities:

HFC operates nearly 400 facilities for various corporations, universities, and communities.

Program Details:

HFC provides an extensive range of program and services, including program development, facility consultation, professional management for fitness and wellness centers, group-exercise instruction, health screenings and education.

Budget:

HFC's budget is over $70 million per year.

Marketing:

HFC uses a variety of marketing strategies including, but not limited to, internet (www.hfit.com) and print campaigns, bulletin board displays, and special promotions.

Jobs and Careers:

HFC currently employs more than 4,000 in the U.S. Puerto Rico, Canada and South America. Positions include regional vice presidents; area manager (supervising the operation of several facilities), program manager (supervising programming activities at specific facilities), wellness coordinator, and Group Instructor.

Salary:

Salaries vary depending on experience, qualifications and location, but starting salaries average from the low $20,000 to mid $35,000.

Internships:

HFC has an intensive internship program that partners with colleges and universities to provide practicum experiences for college students and graduates wishing to go into the field of corporate health and fitness program management. This rigorous program includes students as part of on-site teams, and trains them in the wide range of managerial skills, safety certifications, and operational knowledge expected and required of professionals in the field.

Affiliated Professional Organizations:

HFC has earned awards and recognition from national and regional organizations such as Athletic Business, C. Evertt Koop, Club Industry, The Association for Worksite Health Promotion (AWHP), the Employee Services Management Association, the Governor's Council of Physical Fitness and Sports (in multiple states), and the Wellness Councils of America (WELCOA). In addition, the company has received numerous awards and special recognitions from its clients.

Conclusion

The role of fitness in recreational sport takes two directions—indirect fitness attainment through programming and direct fitness attainment through assessment and classes for follow-through on fitness assessment. The former is the concern of a recreational sport specialist, and the latter requires developing programs with a fitness specialist. In recreational sport, fitness is recognized as one of the goals of participation, along with enjoyment and diversion. Fitness from a wellness perspective involves more than physical fitness; however, the purpose of this chapter is to emphasize the attainment of physical fitness. Fitness delivery occurs through programmed recreational sport and through the recommendations resulting from fitness testing. With the *Healthy People 2020* goals and the *2008 Physical Activity Guidelines* from the U.S. Department of Health and Human Services, recreational sport programs can meet an individual's fitness goals, provide fun through sport and leisure, and enhance quality of life.

Bibliography

Adderley-Kelly, B. (2007). The prevalence of over-weight and obesity among undergraduate health science students. *The ABNJ Journal,18*(2), 46-50.

Anderson, D., Whitmer, R., Goetzel, R., Ozminkows-ki, R., Wasserman, R., & Serxner, S. (2000). The relationship between modifiable health risks and group-level health care expenditures. *American Journal of Health Promotion,* 15(1), 45-52.

Bocarro, J., Kanters, M., Casper, J., & Forrester, S. (2008). School physical education, extracurricular sports, and lifelong active living. *Journal of Teaching in Physical Education, 27,* 155-166.

Bucher, C. (1974). National adult fitness survey: Some implications. *Journal of Health, Physical Education and Recreation, 45,* 25-28.

Buckworth, J., & Nigg, C. (2004). Physical activity, exercise, and sedentary behaviour in college students. *Journal of American College Health, 53*(1), 28-34.

Carlson, S. A., Fulton, J. E., & Galuska, D. A. (2008). Prevalence of self-reported physically active adults—United States, 2007. *Morbidity & Mortality Weekly Report, 57,* 1297-1300.

Caspersen, C. J., Powell, K. E., & Christenson, G. M. (1985). Physical activity, exercise, and physical fitness: Definitions and distinctions for health-related research. *Public Health Report, 100,* 126-131.

Colditz, G. A., & Stein, C. (2007). Costs of obesity. In S. Kumanyika & C. B. Ross (Eds.), *Handbook of obesity prevention* (pp. 73-83). New York: Springer.

Corbin, C. B., & Lindsey, R. (2005). *Fitness for life.* (5th ed.). Champaign, IL: Human Kinetics.

Cordes, K. A., & Ibrahim, H. M. (1999). *Applications in recreation & leisure: For today and the future.* New York, NY: McGraw-Hill.

Curtis, J., McTeer, W., & White, P. (1999). Exploring effects of school sport experiences on sport participation in later life. *Sociology of Sport Journal, 16*(4), 348-365.

Fache, W. (1987). Making explicit objectives for leisure education. *European Journal of Education, 22*(3/4), 291-298.

Fibkins, L. W. (2006). *Teen obesity: How schools can be the number one solution to the problem.* Lanham, MD: Rowman & Littlefield Education.

Gieck, J. D., & Olsen, S. (2007). Holistic wellness as means to developing a lifestyle approach to health behaviour among college students. *Journal of American College Health, 56*(1), 29-35.

Howell, F., & McKenzie, J. (1987). High school athletics and adult sport-leisure activity: Gender variations across the lifecycle. *Sociology of Sport Journal, 9,* 403-422.

Iso-Ahola, S. E. (1980). *The social psychology of leisure and recreation.* Dubuque, IA: W. C. Brown.

Iso-Ahola, S. E., Jackson, E., & Dunn, E. (1994). Starting, ceasing and replacing leisure activities over the life-span. *Journal of Leisure Research, 26*(3), 227-249.

Kanters, M. A., Bocarro, J., Casper, J., & Forrester, S. (2008). Determinants of sport participation in middle school children and the impact of intramural sports. *Recreational Sports Journal, 32*(2), 134-151.

Kelly, J. (1980). Leisure and sport participation. In D. Smith & J. Macaulay (Eds.), *Participation in social and political activities* (pp. 170-176). San Francisco: Jossey-Bass.

Kumanyika, S., & Ross, C. B. (2007). Why obesity prevention? In S. Kumanyika & C. B. Ross (Eds.), *Handbook of obesity prevention* (pp. 1-23). New York: Springer.

Malina, R. M. (1996). Tracking of physical activity and physical fitness across the lifespan. *Research Quarterly for Exercise and Sport, 67*(Suppl. 3), 48-57.

Mannell, R. C., & Kleiber, D. A. (1997). *A social psychology of leisure.* State College, PA: Venture.

Mobily, K. E., Lemke, J. H., Ostiguy, L. J., Woodard, R. J., Griffee, T. J., & Pickens, C. C. (1993). Leisure repertoire in a sample of Midwestern elderly: The case for exercise. *Journal of Leisure Research, 25*(1), 84-99.

Montoye, H., Van Huss, W., & Zuidema, J. (1959). Sport activity of athletes and non-athletes in later life. *Physical Education, 16,* 48-51.

Morgan, W., & Montoye, H. (1984, July). *Quality of life and health status of aging athletes and non-athletes: A twenty-year longitudinal study.* Paper presented at the Olympic Scientific Congress, Eugene, OR.

Mowen, A. J., & Baker, B. L. (2009). Park, recreation, fitness, and sport sector recommendations for a more physically active America: A white paper for the United States National Physical Activity Plan. *Journal of Physical Activity and Health, 6*(Suppl. 2), S236-S244.

Mull, R., Bayless, K., & Jamieson, L. (2005). *Recreational sport management.* Champaign, IL: Human Kinetics.

Paffenburger, R. S., Hyde, R. T., Wing, A. L., & Hsieh, C. (1986). Physical activity, all causes mortality, and longevity of college alumni. *New England Journal of Medicine, 314,* 605-613.

Pate, R., Pratt, M., Blair, S., Haskell, W., Macera, C., Bouchard, C. (1995). Physical activity and public health: A recommendation from the Centers for Disease Control and Prevention and the American College of Sports Medicine. *Journal of the American Medical Association, 273*(5), 402-407.

Powell, K. E., & Dysinger, W. (1987). Childhood participation in organized school sports and physical education as precursors of adult physical activity. *American Journal of Prevention Medicine, 3,* 276-281.

Pratt, M., Macera, C. A., & Wang, G. (2000). Higher direct medical costs associated with physical inactivity. *The Physician and Sportsmedicine, 28,* 63-70.

Public Health Agency of Canada. (n.d.) The benefits of physical activity. Retrieved from http://www.phac-aspc.gc.ca/alw-vat/intro/key-cle-eng.php

Public Health Agency of Canada. (n.d.). Physical activity. Retrieved from http://www.phac-aspc.gc.ca/hp-ps/hl-mvs/pa-ap/index-eng.php

Raine, K. D. (2004). *Overweight and obesity in Canada: A population health perspective.* Ottawa, Canada: Canadian Institute for Health Information.

Rees, R. C., Andres, R. R., & Howell, F. M. (1986). On the trail of the "turkey trotters": The effects of previous sport involvement and attitudes on commitment to and skill of running. *Sociology of Sport Journal, 3,* 134-143.

Roberts, K. (1999). *Leisure in contemporary society.* Wallingford, United Kingdom: Cabi.

Starky, S. (2005). *The obesity epidemic in Canada.* Ottawa, Canada: Parliamentary Information and Research Service, Library of Parliament.

U.S. Department of Health and Human Services. (1996). *Physical activity and health: A report of the Surgeon General.* Atlanta, GA: Author.

U.S. Department of Health and Human Services. (2000). *Healthy People 2000: National Health Promotion and Diseases Prevention Objectives.* Retrieved from http://www.healthypeople.gov

U.S. Department of Health and Human Services. (2000). *Healthy People 2010: Objectives for improving health.* Retrieved from http://www.

healthypeople.gov

U.S. Department of Health and Human Services. (2002). *Physical activity fundamental to preventing disease.* Washington, DC: Office of the Assistant Secretary for Planning and Evaluation.

U.S. Department of Health and Human Services. (2008). *2008 Physical activity guidelines for Americans.* Retrieved from http://www.health.gov/paguidelines

U.S. Department of Health and Human Services. (2010). *Healthy People 2020.* Retrieved from http://www.healthypeople.gov

Van Mechelen, W., & Kemper, H. C. G. (1995). Habitual physical activity in longitudinal perspective. In H. C. G. Kemper (Ed.), *The Amsterdam Growth Study: A longitudinal analysis of health, fitness and lifestyle* (pp. 135-158). Champaign, IL. Human Kinetics.

Vanreusel, B., Renson, R., Beunen, G., Claessens, A. L., Lefevre, J., Lysens, R., & Vanden Eynde, B. (1997). A longitudinal study of youth sport participation and adherence to sport in adulthood. *International Review for the Sociology of Sport, 32*(4), 373-387.

Watkins, B. C. (1983). *Secondary schools and their effects on continuing participation in physical activity* (Unpublished doctoral dissertation). University of Oregon, Eugene.

White, P., & Curtis, J. (1990). English–French Canadian differences in types of sport participation: A test of the school socialization explanation. *Sociology of Sport Journal, 7,* 347-369.

World Health Organization. (2000). *Obesity. Preventing and managing the global epidemic* (WHO Technical Report Series 894). Geneva, Switzerland: Author.

World Health Organization. (2003). *Diet, nutrition, and the prevention of chronic diseases* (WHO Technical Report Series 916). Geneva, Switzerland: Author.

World Health Organization. (2010). *Global recommendations on physical activity for health.* Geneva, Switzerland: Author.

Yang, X. (1997). A multidisciplinary analysis of physical activity, sport participation and dropping out among youth Finns, a 12-year follow-up study. *Likes Research Report on Sport and Health, 103.*

CHAPTER 5

Learning

CHAPTER OBJECTIVES

After reading this chapter, you will recognize human characteristics as they relate to individual differences, understand the different learning outcomes associated with recreational sport participation, realize the potential for participant development through programming involvement, and appreciate how a recreational sport specialist can influence leadership development through individual experiences as well as group interaction and guidance.

KEY CONCEPTS

Human characteristics	**Age implications**
Taxonomy of learning	**Influencing Development**
Experiential learning	**Structuring Leadership**
Positive youth development	**Life skills**
Leadership skills	**Learning outcomes**

Introduction

One of the most rewarding aspects of being a recreational sport professional is providing developmental and learning opportunities to participants. Such an approach can create positive, meaningful experiences for participants, volunteers, and staff. The responsibilities involved in program delivery are initially challenging and can be time consuming, but they can also become routine. A commitment to providing opportunities for learning, personal growth, and development can add significance and satisfaction to the professional's role. Procedural knowledge alone, or knowledge used in activities such as setting up tournaments, overseeing facilities, scheduling personnel, training employees and volunteers, publicizing and advertising events, and judging and ruling on problems, does not contribute to learning and development unless it is based on the participants' characteristics and their potential for learning and development. This chapter will give the recreational sport specialist an appreciation for the significant impact that recreational sport can have on

development and learning by situating learning in the context of growth and development, presenting developmental characteristics of different age groups, highlighting key research findings documenting the impact of recreational sport on learning, and demonstrating ways to create learning and development opportunities through experiences in program involvement and leadership.

A Developmental Approach

A developmental approach to recreational sport programming is not new. Since the beginning of organized physical education, recreation, and intramural sport, educators have claimed that participation in sport contributes to physical, cognitive, emotional, and social development. These claims were based on theory, observation, and speculation rather than research. In the early 1960s, the human developmental potential of sport emerged as a major focus of research. The emphasis was on providing empirical evidence of the value of sport programs in order to demonstrate accountability to taxpayers and supporters. Sport programs that did not contribute to the goals of the setting or that were unable to support themselves financially were considered for cutbacks or elimination.

Through research, educators and practitioners sought to prove the contributions sport makes to the four areas of human development: physical, mental, emotional, and social. Although most inquiries have focused on interscholastic, intercollegiate sport activity, some studies apply to the recreational setting and its sport and fitness offerings. Physical activity has been shown to increase cardiovascular fitness and lung capacity; improve endurance; maintain or increase muscle mass; improve flexibility, balance, and coordination; and improve immune system functioning (Feldman, 1999). In the cognitive realm, physical activity decreases stress, anxiety, and depression and improves memory and problem solving (Mutrie, 1997). Emotionally, physical activity creates a sense of control over one's body and a sense of accomplishment (Brown, 1991; Gross, 1991). And without a doubt, participation in sport helps build social support systems. Understanding age-specific developmental tasks and needs contributes to the recreational sport professional's ability to facilitate activities that promote physical, cognitive, emotional, and social growth.

Table 5.1 presents developmental concepts as they apply to involvement in recreational sport. Included within the four domains of human development are major developmental tasks associated with each age category and ways to apply the developmental characteristics to program design and delivery. Based on recent research, a review of the literature, and professional experience, this table presents current knowledge about these characteristics and implications for providing recreational sport experiences.

Although some agencies sponsor programs for children under age 5 in sports such as swimming, soccer, and gymnastics, it is usually the family that provides recreational sport for this age group, emphasizing the structure and lead-up game of introductory skills and rules at a simple level. Because structured programs for children under age 5 are not prevalent in sport literature, this book does not include material on this age category. The best advice for recreational sport specialists is to follow guidelines established by the American Academy of Pediatrics, the American Red Cross aquatics programs, and similar developmental resources.

Age Implications

Keeping in mind the developmental characteristics of different age groups, the following section is a brief synopsis of each group, adding a few details to help the recreational sport specialist apply these principles to recreational sport programs. When considering such options, remember that programs can be structured so that they affect not only the participant but the volunteers and workers as well.

Ages 6 to 12. Participation is the main focus for this age group. A common approach is teaching techniques, as in traditional physical education classes. The emphasis is on skill development, participation, and fun. There is an increase in gross- and fine-motor coordination. There are few gender differences in strength and speed, and most activities can be offered coeducationally. Sports such as soccer and swimming offer opportunities for participation and exercise, while sports such as basketball and tennis may be too difficult for many children under age 12. Cognitively, children of this age are concrete thinkers, so they need to do things sequentially to understand. They may be able to apply some logic to understanding rules, but complicated or abstract activities may be frustrating. Often parents and/or coaches explicitly or implicitly emphasize winning, but good leadership can keep things in perspective. Building self-esteem is important for this age group. Self-esteem is based on a sense of support from parents and other adults and on doing well in the domains that are important to the person (Harter, 1990). For example, if swimming competitively is important to the child, but soccer is not, doing well at soccer but not doing well at swimming will not build self-esteem. This is true not only for children, but also for people of all ages.

Children usually progress rapidly in sport development if they are interested, whereas they drop out if they feel bored, left out, or do not experience success (Erikson, 1950). Often they need parental guidance and training by adult role models. This is an important age category because it is when children develop the attitude toward sport that they often maintain throughout life, so great care should be given to program delivery, especially keeping things such as winning in perspective.

Ages 13 to 19. "In no order of things is adolescence the simple time of life."—Jean Erskine Stewart

Adolescence is a time of rapid change in all areas of development. By adolescence, most physical activities are segregated by sex. Physically, boys become faster and stronger than girls, although their emotional development lags behind girls by about two years. Cognitive abilities expand to include abstract thinking and advanced logic, although adolescents rely more on emotional cognitive processing than do adults. Adolescence can be a tumultuous time socially and emotionally. Peer relationships are critical to psychological, cognitive, and social growth.

Table 5.1

Developmental Characteristics of the Five Age Groups

Age Group	Physical	Cognitive	Psychological	Social	Program Implications
Youth 6-12	44 to 62 in. 44 to 100 lb. Muscles are strong but immature Skeleton matures Heart grows slowly	Attention span lengthens Ability for reflective thinking increases Abstract thought develops Vocabulary develops Ability to discern right from wrong develops	Interactions with adults and peers serve as a base for self-concept Desire for achievement grows Preference for sex segregation develops Fears about personal safety decline Concern for personal competence develops	Comparisons of ideas, beliefs may change Internalizes cultural rules Develops awareness of others' intentions Attitudes toward ethnic groups in relation to those of parents develop Social values vary Peer pressure is significant Peer acceptance influences self-concept	Plan for skill development and create a social environment for bonding in sport interaction
Adolescence 13-19	Body grows rapidly Marked muscular growth occurs in boys, breasts develop in girls Lung capacity increases Onset of sexual maturity occurs Sebaceous glands cause acne Strength, reaction, and coordination improve	Mental perspective of past, present, and future develops Symbols, system coordination, factors used in problem solving Meaning of words in ideals and absolutes understood Inductive and deductive reasoning understood Ability to explain phenomena develops Sense of self-uniqueness develops	Old values are examined Stable self-concept develops General behavior is flexible Develops understanding of what is right or moral, independent of expectations Possibly prematurely accepts societal values Emotional independence begins	Peer group placement occurs Socializing with both sexes occurs Maximum impact of peer group pressure Peers become testing ground for new skills and behaviors Thoughts and feelings are shared Values are compared with what is popular Adults are looked to for role models	Be aware of the immense intensity of sport experiences and provide opportunities for leadership development
Early adulthood 20-39	Full height 21 years Peak muscles 25 to 30 Vision declines Reaction time stable Maximum physical potential Setting vertebrae Brain weight maximum Aging not uniform	Intellectual skills stable Ability for concepts gradually declining Formal reasoning improves	Is more defined Secure self-concept Absorption in interests Realistic perspective Sex role affect competence Integration of self with roles within society	Open and honest Less self-centered Occupied with career, family, community involvement Expand social relationships	Increased attention to programming sport for safety and time considerations New learning experiences can occur, and and greater responsibility is assumed by the participants

cont.

Table 5.1 (cont.)

Age Group	Physical	Cognitive	Psychological	Social	Program Implications
Middle adulthood 40-65	Hair goes gray Weight is gained Reaction time slows Some sensory function is lost Mobility declines Menopause occurs in women Chronic illnesses are prevalent	Brain physiology decreases Productivity and creativity peak Intelligence and cognitive skills at maximum	Stable self-concept Renewed self-awareness Potential for mid-life crisis Focus on ego maturity	Peak time for involvement occurs Leadership positions are pursued Responsibility for support of child and parents may occur Time is available for rest and own interests once child leaves home Become grandparents	Ongoing fitness needs become apparent; take greater care in the physiological aspects of programming as chance of injury increases
Later adulthood 65 and older	Risk of heart disease increases Balance and coordination decline Visual acuity declines Hearing loss occurs Teeth loss occurs Motor performance decreases	Some short-term memory is lost Verbal skills are retained and improved Time required for memory recall increases	Self-concept based on internal thoughts Activities important to individual are selected, less important activities may be dropped Sense of competence Sense of self-worth Traditional sex roles may reverse	May be influential in social interests Many are single women Prefer to live independently Time for married partner increases Remarriage hindered by physical concerns Affected by death of spouse	Provide greater education on the need for movement to prevent sedentary lifestyles

Sport and recreation can help with the development task of adolescence: finding one's own identity (Erikson, 1968). Participation in physical activity helps adolescents avoid drug and alcohol addiction, improves physical and psychological well-being, lessens ·anxiety and depression, and lessens behavioral problems (Kirkcaldy, Shephard, & Siefen, 2002). As young people continue in their chosen sports, they may become accomplished and thus experience satisfaction through success.

As adolescents struggle to discover who they are and how they fit into the world, they may "try on" a number of sports and activities, sometimes even dropping out of sports in which they are successful. Self-esteem tends to be lowest in early adolescence (Seidman, Allen, Aber, Mitchell, & Feinman, 1994) and may affect choice of activities. Young people may also experience disappointment in sports when better performers advance through the selection process. All efforts should be focused on creating positive rewards wherever possible.

Adolescence is an excellent time for participants to be given opportunities to be team leaders, organizers, and officers. Such opportunities allow them to practice the interpersonal and leadership skills that are important for success in adulthood.

Ages 20 to 39. In the last 20 years, the age group 20 to 39 emerged in a significant way in sport participation. In many sports, the early 20s are a time of peak performance for participants. Individuals in this age group are often interested in competitive opportunities to test their skills. On the other hand, the period from age 20 to 39 is the longest plateau of stable physical ability, and the few signs of aging that appear during these years may fool some individuals into thinking that physical ability is not important to maintaining health and fitness. The adoption of healthy lifestyle habits during this period is critical for a healthy old age. Programs that build lifelong skills and interest in sport will benefit participants and programs in the long run.

The "social clock," or involvement in new roles and responsibilities, ticks loudly during these years (Neugarten, 1968). Young adults become independent of their parents, choose whether to get married and have children, find jobs and build careers, and redefine friendships. Although all of these roles compete for an individual's time, sport is an important and perhaps necessary outlet for stress reduction. If young people fall short of their expectations during this period, they are prone to anxiety and depression. In fact, mental health problems are higher in this age group than in any other (Regier et al., 1988).

Besides participation, recreational sport specialists can offer young adults administrative opportunities in sport system organizations, volunteering, and group leadership. These roles offer opportunities for success outside of work and home, and they help build lifelong commitment to sport and recreation. It is during this period people make real commitments to sport and invest time, energy, and money. In many settings, this age group is a marketing segment that can make a big difference in the total operation of recreational sport.

Ages 40 to 65. The baby boomers who currently dominate this age group are redefining middle age (Dychtwald, 1999). The cohort that "discovered" jogging in the 1970s is now participating in sport and recreation in ways their parents would not have imagined. For many, middle age is a time of personal reevaluation. Marriage, career, and lifestyle all come under review. A new or renewed commitment to sport and fitness is often a hallmark of this period as individuals seek to redefine themselves for the better.

A number of studies point to the critical role exercise plays in physical health during midlife. A study of 17,321 Harvard graduates clearly demonstrates the link between lack of physical activity and increased likelihood of death. The more calories a man burned each week by engaging in any type of physical activity during his 30s, 40s, and 50s, the lower his mortality risk was over the next 25 years (Lee, Hsieh, & Paffenbarger, 1995). Everything possible should be done to create and maintain participants' interest in sport activity because it can literally save their lives.

During this period, the first signs of aging become visible. Those who have not maintained a healthy lifestyle are likely to begin to experience some physical limitations, increasing likelihood of injuries. Recreational sport specialists might consider rehabilitation programs for weekend athletes recovering from short-term disability as well as entry-level programs for deconditioned individuals.

While there is some decrease in social roles at midlife, most middle-aged adults are pressed for time. While parenting demands typically lessen, there may be a new need to care for aging parents. Work roles remain demanding, as the 40s and 50s are a time of peak career productivity. Recreational sport specialists should offer flexible scheduling and up-to-date programs to enhance participation from

this age group as middle-aged adults have many competing demands on their time.

While this age group may seem demanding in terms of service expectations, often reflecting an attitude about the quality of delivery operations, this is a peak time for involvement. Long-term commitment is common, and wherever there is interest, opportunities for leadership in program planning and delivery can meet these individuals' psychological need to mentor and help others, particularly younger generations (Kleiber & Ray, 1993).

Ages 65 and older. Life expectancy has increased dramatically over the last 100 years due to healthier lifestyles, nutrition, and medical advances. In developed countries, older adults are now the fastest growing population, and exercise and recreation programs for older adults have multiplied in recent years. Hundreds of studies on aging have shown that physical, cognitive, social, and emotional health are highly associated with sustained participation in physical activity (Pescatello, 1999; Swinburn & Sager, 2003).

Walking is the most common physical activity for older adults, and research shows that several daily bouts of moderate activity offer many of the same health and fitness benefits as more vigorous activity (Blair, Dunn, Marcus, Carpenter, & Jaret, 2001). Exercise leaders are also developing programs for older adults that offer fun challenges and opportunities for continued growth and development. The fastest growing exercises for those over 50 are water exercise, tai chi, yoga, and Pilates (Mitchell & Megan, 1998). Tai chi has been shown to be the most effective training regimen for improving balance and reducing falls (Taggart, 2001). An exercise program for older adults should offer cardiovascular, strength and endurance, flexibility, and balance and posture training (Cotton, 1998).

Recreational sport specialists must be enthusiastic and positive in guiding older adults, but at the same time they must be conscious of potential injury. Screening, assessment, physician approval, modifications, and careful monitoring will reassure participants that sport and recreation activity is age appropriate and not likely to result in injury. As with all age groups, staff should be taught what to do in an emergency situation.

The recreational sport specialist's awareness of age implications plays an important part in success. Being sensitive to the different age categories can enhance the participants' experience and contribute to their development. As the recreational sport specialist continues to discover the developmental opportunities that can be offered to different age groups, he or she will be faced with many options, each of which will require attention to individual differences and needs.

Influencing Development

Using this insight into the different age groups, it is time to explore how developmental concepts can be applied in recreational sport. Recreational sport specialists have two options for influencing the development of participants, volunteers, and paid workers. One is through the methods for providing active, experiential opportunities, and the other is through roles that foster leadership skills.

Experiential Learning

A developmental approach through experiential learning includes active sport participation as well as the total environment. For example, a common developmental experience in all sport participation is learning to handle winning and losing. Similarly, individuals learn how to handle competition, a valuable skill in many of life's situations. Controlling one's aggressiveness can also be learned in the sport environment. Knowledge awareness, another developmental consideration, occurs by having to learn and adjust to the rules and regulations that are part of sport information. All of these examples are common elements in the delivery of sport activity. The following material covers considerations for program delivery that create developmental experiences.

Staff influence. Staff members can have a positive influence on development when they are sensitive to and appreciative of those involved and provide quality programs based on participant needs and interests. Staff members should develop relationships with each other and participants by being accessible and using sound communication skills. They should offer an open door, allowing interaction in situations and conditions that come from sport activity. Such efforts encourage participants to behave appropriately and explore their potential. Recreational sport specialists will assume several roles in this process, including teacher, consultant, adviser, and evaluator. They should be sensitive to the appropriate time for assuming such roles and realize the importance of such roles as they interact and influence those with whom they come into contact.

Sport activity. A common goal for all recreational sport specialists is to provide suitable, well-balanced sport experiences. Because participants have diverse interests and skill levels, recreational sport specialists should provide a variety of sports, program areas, and special skills whenever possible.

Sports vary in the way they influence development. For example, table tennis offered as an intramural tournament provides different developmental opportunities than table tennis offered as a club sport. Along the same line, differences exist between team sport, dual sport, and individual sport. Classifying sport delivery into groups or divisions also affects development. Coed intramural sport participation may provide opportunities for males and females to appreciate gender differences as they relate to skills and interest levels. Also, systems that allow variations in ability and intensity can contribute to development, especially where success and gratification are part of the planned outcomes. Finally, social interaction, regardless of the sport or skill level, provides a number of experiences that contribute to individual awareness of self and others.

Rules and regulations. Rules and regulations that promote equity and satisfaction among participants contribute to development. When rules improve participants' chances of success, they encourage continued involvement and development. For example, most intramural programs use eligibility statements to counter unfair distinctions between participants. One of the most common eligibility requirements in intramural sport programs restricts or eliminates athletic and professional sports participants in a specific or related sport. This restriction indicates that domination by athletic and professional participants minimizes the chance for equitable participation by other players.

Still another example of reducing unbalanced experiences is special rules in youth sport programs that allow members of a team the opportunity to participate regardless of skill level. All participants have a chance to benefit in terms of self-esteem, acceptance, recognition, identity, and ability. Such rules recognize that development is contingent upon participation, a certain level of success, and a positive experience.

Rules and regulations also provide direction for behavior and participation. When a rule is enforced, individuals alter their thoughts and actions to comply with the rules, or else they face the consequences. This is an important developmental tool that has an effect in all sport activity.

Governance. Another type of developmental experience occurs when program participants are invited to serve on governance boards, committees, or councils. During deliberations over appeals made on staff rulings, for example, members are exposed to concepts such as fairness and precedence. Also, as part of a governing body, they learn personal responsibility for decision making, gain exposure to beliefs different from their own, and explore consistencies or inconsistencies among the values of board members, participants, and themselves. Guidance, not domination, is the key to objectivity in governance and its due process. The amount of responsibility granted to participants making governance decisions depends on their age, experience, and maturity. Decisions made by a governing body should not be overruled without good cause, otherwise the value of the developmental experience may be minimized. It takes special effort to create valid decision-making opportunities in governance, but the benefits far outweigh the effort.

Progression. A number of roles and responsibilities in program delivery can have a developmental influence upon those who are involved. Such roles include team captain, coach, instructor, club officer, official, personal trainer, lifeguard, and supervisor. The maturity and skills required to assume one of these positions can be placed in a sequence of progressive difficulty from one level to the next, creating greater responsibility and opportunities for learning. All roles or positions can be structured to create a hierarchy that inspires learning in order to achieve.

The goal for recreational sport specialists is to place individuals in positions commensurate with their experience and abilities while allowing them time and opportunity to develop so that they can assume a higher position in the hierarchies of responsibility in recreational sport programming.

Evaluation. Recreational sport involvement creates many opportunities for individuals to measure or judge their own abilities. The sport experience brings satisfaction or dissatisfaction, creating the opportunity to assess oneself as well as to be assessed by others. There are also avenues for participants to share opinions and feelings about their sport experiences through informal and formal evaluation systems. Evaluations, whether of personal participation or program effectiveness, lead to learning about oneself as well as one's involvement.

Recognition. Recognition can involve point systems, awards, and public awareness that foster development by encouraging participation. From a developmental standpoint, point systems may have a negative effect if they stimulate participation only for the sake of accumulating points. Although participation occurs and the individuals could have a positive experience, use of point systems is not always the best form of encouragement. However, points for achievement or progress in participation, sportsmanship, and cooperation can provide more positive reinforcement and learning.

Another form of recognition is awards, which may include certificates, trophies, medallions, apparel, or other objects. Awards usually reinforce positive and successful performance, which for some can be quite gratifying. However, awards may also be given that recognize types of effort that the recreational sport specialist would like to reinforce. The most important consideration in designing a recognition program is honoring accomplishments besides winning, such as leadership, honorable sporting behavior, and participation.

A final type of recognition is public notoriety, where positive and successful outcomes are recognized in special announcements, newsletters, local papers, and radio. Such recognition often reinforces participants' efforts, encouraging continued involvement and the sense of self-satisfaction that follows hard work and commitment.

When it comes to influencing development through program involvement, it is important to assess management interest in such a concept as well as potential benefit for the participant. Beyond mastering the technical aspects, basic awareness and willingness to apply the concept are necessary. Committing to this concept can bring professional satisfaction, not to mention the positive influence it has on program participants, volunteers, and paid workers. Now that the necessary background on participant/human development and actions the recreational sport specialist can take to influence that development have been provided, learning benefits of recreational sport—an idea that is becoming central to the work of many college administrators throughout the United States—can be examined.

Learning and Recreational Sports

Broadly speaking, there is much research that supports the notion that recreational sports are beneficial to learning. Recent research has found that physical activity is crucial to thinking and feeling (Ratey, 2008). Related to learning, aerobic exercise actually prepares the brain to learn, improves mood and attention, lowers stress and anxiety, and even reverses some of the effects of aging of the brain. The latest research has found that for the brain to be able to function at its peak levels, the body needs to move and be physically active. Exercise improves learning on three levels: First, it optimizes the mind-set to improve alertness, attention, and motivation; second, it prepares and encourages nerve cells to bind to one another, which is the cellular basis for logging in new information; third, it spurs the development of new nerve cells from stem cells in the hippocampus (Ratey, 2008). After a new fitness program was instituted in a school district in the state of Illinois (Ratey, 2008), the test scores of 19,000 students soared. In fact, students in this district scored first in the world in science and sixth in math. Given these findings, it seems there is tremendous potential for recreational sports to contribute to learning, both in terms of the benefits listed above and in terms of what individuals actually learn as a result of their participation. Before examining how this is most evident in youth sports and recreational sports in the collegiate setting, learning as a concept must first be understood.

When examining learning, the discussion seems to revolve around learning outcomes, so Fink's (2003) "taxonomy of significant learning" is a useful framework for this discussion. There are six parts, or six learning outcomes, that are identified by Fink, including foundational knowledge, application, integration, human dimension, caring, and learning how to learn (see Figure 5.1).

Each is described with a recreational sports example. Fink's original work was developed based on the learner being a student, but for the purpose of this text, a learner can be a recreational sport participant, a recreational sport official, club sport officer, front desk staff, or any number of other individuals found in a recreational sport setting.

Foundational knowledge. This refers to the basic concepts and understanding that are needed to perform an activity or complete a project. In recreational sports, the foundational knowledge needed for an individual participating in tennis is an understanding of the rules of the game (including scoring) as well as specific techniques such as the forehand swing, backhand swing, and serve. This knowledge is necessary for playing tennis and often taught to individuals through beginner lessons.

Application. Similar to all theories of learning, once a basic understanding of a concept is achieved, individuals need to be able to apply the knowledge they have gained. An ability to think critically aids with the application of any concept. For an intramural official, training occurs prior to any actual officiating during which different ideas and strategies (i.e., foundational knowledge) are presented. Each official then applies the knowledge he or she has gained when officiating intramural games. An official's ability to apply the knowledge will impact the experience of the participants. It should be noted that experience improves application.

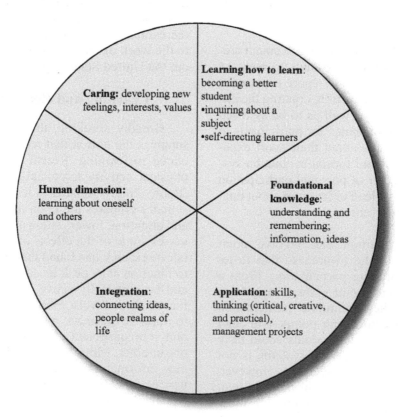

Figure 5.1. Taxonomy of Significant Learning

Integration. This category of learning relates to the idea of being able to make connections and links between various ideas that may otherwise not be associated. Clearly, a strong understanding of the concept is needed for this to occur. In recreational sports, a supervisor will need to integrate various ideas into overall programming such as risk, participant needs, facility amenities, funding, and staffing. A recreational sport specialist will draw upon his or her knowledge and experiences in integrating these concepts.

Human dimension. This is described as relating to learning about oneself as well as learning about interactions between others. In recreational sports, so much of what a person does occurs with other people, and it is therefore extremely important to understand how to work with others. For example, in a shared gym space, it is important that all participants learn to respect others and contribute to the type of environment that is open, safe, and respectful. Signs placed in various places throughout a gym can encourage this type of learning among participants as well as staff.

Caring. As a result of learning (i.e., participating in recreational sports), individuals can develop new interests, strengthen values, and exhibit a change in behavior. When recreational sport agencies operate in a socially responsible manner, their employees may develop a similar socially responsible interest. For example, a recreational sport agency may support a local food bank by encouraging participants and staff to donate canned goods at Christmas time. As an incentive, some agencies may offer a coupon or a discount in exchange for the food donation. This type of action will impact those involved in the agency and may lead to a more caring environment.

Learning how to learn. Once an individual knows the process involved in learning, he or she will be able to pursue learning throughout his or her lifetime. This is the ultimate benefit because learning can be a vehicle for so many opportunities in life. Recreational sports agencies can encourage staff members to become involved in professional associations that encourage lifelong learning.

As this previous list represents a classification of significant learning, it is important to recognize that there is no order given to the different learning outcomes and a sequence of learning outcomes or benefits is not required. Clearly recreational sports agencies are well positioned to offer experiences to staff, participants, and volunteers to enhance learning. Next, the discussion will focus on youth sport settings and collegiate sport settings.

Positive Youth Development and Learning Benefits

Many youth participate in sport during their childhood, with 90% of children taking part in some form of organized sport between ages 5 and 17 (Turman, 2007). Sports are "one of life's important growth experiences" (Margenau, 1990, p. 2), and organized sport is often viewed as a learning environment for acquiring values and work habits as much as sport skills (Humpries, 1991). Researchers have identified that youth sport has the potential to accomplish three important objectives in children's development (Cote & Fraser-Thomas, 2007). First, sport programs can provide youth with opportunities to be physically active, which in turn can lead to improved physical health. Second, youth sport programs have long been considered important to youth's psychosocial development, providing opportunities to learn important life skills such as cooperation, discipline, leadership, and self-control. Third, youth sport programs are critical for learning motor skills, which serve as a foundation for recreational adult sport participation (Cote, Strachan, & Fraser-Thomas, 2008).

This previous information on youth sport is embedded in a concept referred to as positive youth development, which has been used to describe optimal youth development. The National Research Council and Institute of Medicine (2002) outlines four key areas of youth development: physical, intellectual, psychological and emotional, and social. For each developmental area, several corresponding assets are recommended that contribute to positive youth development. For example, good health habits facilitate positive physical development; knowledge of decision-making and critical reasoning skills contribute to positive intellectual development; positive self-regard, coping skills, conflict resolution skills, sense of autonomy, moral character, and confidence contribute to youths' psychological and emotional development; and connectedness with parents, peers, and other adults are examples of assets facilitating youths' social development. The recreational sport specialist should also take note of the eight key features of settings that are most likely to foster these positive developmental assets as outlined by the NRCIM (2002) (Table 5.2).

Table 5.2

Key Features of Positive Development Settings as Outlined by NRCIM

1. Physical and psychological safety
2. Appropriate structure
3. Supportive relationships
4. Opportunities to belong
5. Positive social norms
6. Support for efficacy and mattering
7. Opportunities for skill building
8. Integration of family, school, and community efforts

Lerner, Fisher, and Weinberg (2000) provide another approach to understanding desired outcomes of youth development reflected in the five Cs of positive youth development: competence, character, connection, confidence, and caring and compassion. Lerner et al.'s Model of National Youth Policy (2000) suggests that policies must be developed to allow families and programs to foster and promote positive youth development. If this happens, then youth will ideally exhibit these five Cs of positive youth development, which should in turn lead to contribution—the sixth C of positive youth development that involves giving back to society. In so doing, youth will be promoting positive development to the next generation of youth.

Life Skills

Training life skills has also been recognized to have a positive impact on youth development. The World Health Organization (WHO, 1999) defines life skills as the abilities for adaptive and positive behavior that enable individuals to deal effectively with the demands and challenges of everyday life. Furthermore, the WHO advocates that teaching life skills is essential for the promotion of healthy child and adolescent development as well as for the preparation of young people for changing social circumstances. Life skills help youth succeed in the environments in which they live, whether it be at home, at school, at work, or just in their neighborhoods (Danish & Nellen, 1997). Life skills can be physical (e.g., taking a right posture), behavioral (e.g., communicating effectively with others), cognitive (e.g., making effective decisions),

interpersonal (being assertive), or intrapersonal (setting goals) (Danish, Pepitas, & Hale, 1993). Examples of programs that use youth sports to concurrently teach sport and life skills that promote personal, social, and sport development are the *First Tee* (http://www.thefirsttee.org) and *Right to Play* (http://www.righttoplay.com) programs, *Sports United to Promote Education and Recreation* (SUPER) (Danish, Fazio, Nellen, & Owens, 2002), and *Play It Smart* (Petitpas, Van Raalte, Cornelius, & Presbrey, 2004).

Life skills programs typically teach participants the physical skills related to a specific sport and life skills related to sports in general. The *First Tee* Program has nine core values (honesty, integrity, sportsmanship, respect, confidence, responsibility, perseverance, courtesy, and judgment) and nine healthy habits organized under three categories of physical, emotional, and social health. *Right to Play* uses the power of sport and play for development, health, and peace to improve the lives of children in some of the most disadvantaged areas of the world. *Right to Play's* eight values reflect the best practices of sport and play (cooperation, hope, integrity, leadership, dedication, respect, enthusiasm, and nurture). SUPER is a peer-led series of 18 20- to 30-minute modules or workshops that are taught like sport clinics (Danish, Forneris, Hodge, & Heke, 2004). In these workshops, youth learn the importance of having dreams for the future; setting goals and learning strategies to help them reach their goals and seeking help from others; using positive self-talk to relax, manage emotions, develop a healthy lifestyle and appreciate differences; having confidence and courage; focusing on personal performance; and identifying and building on their strengths.

Collegiate Recreational Sports and Learning Benefits

The traditional focus on student development in student affairs and collegiate recreational sports is being broadened to include a learning outcomes approach to the profession. This recognizes that learning is a complex, holistic activity that occurs throughout and across the college experience and is not just confined to traditional classroom learning. *Learning Re-considered 2: A Practical Guide to Implementing a Campus-Wide Focus on the Student Experience* (Keeling, 2006) provides a learning focus for collegiate recreational sports programs. In order to apply this approach in practice, the recreational sport specialist needs to be familiar with and be able to apply learning theory. Fink's (2003) taxonomy of significant learning provides one framework for implementing a learning focused approach to recreational sport programming. For a fairly comprehensive list of general learning outcomes for students in collegiate recreational sports refer to Table 5.3.

There have also been a number of studies within the field of collegiate recreational sports documenting the impact of participating in these programs on various learning outcomes. Several of these studies are summarized in the next section.

Table 5.3

General Learning Outcomes for Students in Collegiate Recreational Sports

---

- **Adaptability:** accepting and meeting others where they are; relating to a wide variety of different types of individuals and situations; making transitions fluidly; being flexible.
- **Assertiveness:** speaking for oneself confidently and authoritatively in a clear, direct, and constructive manner.
- **Attire:** ensuring that clothing is suitable and appropriate for the population with which you are working and the job being performed.
- **Civic engagement:** recognizing opportunities for making decisions with the community in mind.
- **Cognitive complexity/systems thinking:** demonstrating the ability to create standards of accountability for themselves and others and then holding themselves and others accountable for their actions.
- **Communication skills:** demonstrating the ability to express oneself in a variety of different ways and with clarity.
- **Comportment skills:** presenting oneself in a manner appropriate for a variety of different circumstances.
- **Confidentiality:** demonstrating the ability to be discrete when dealing with issues of liability, suitability, or other delicate or high-risk matters.
- **Critical thinking skills:** demonstrating the ability to gather, organize, and analyze information through the development of convincing arguments or strategies, critiquing ideas, or providing constructive feedback.
- **Customer service:** helping participants/customers reliably and responsively with any reasonable request they may present while using empathy and providing assurance.
- **Decision-making skills:** making appropriate judgments objectively and logically; taking responsibility for decisions.
- **Financial management skills:** planning, developing, implementing, monitoring and managing a budget.
- **Implementation:** planning and executing the steps and timeframes required to accomplish a task including the delegation tasks and managing resources.
- **Initiative:** being a self-starter, doing something without being told.
- **Integration and application:** being able to relate how information they are learning in a recreational sports context connects more broadly to their academic and life experiences.
- **Knowledge acquisition:** being able to comprehend information presented and relay it coherently.
- **Leadership:** effectively guiding or directing a group towards the accomplishment of a common goal.
- **Marketing:** effectively communicating information to a target audience.
- **Multicultural competence:** developing an appreciation for others without regard for individual differences such as race, ethnicity, religion, sexual orientation, or disability.
- **Organizational/planning skills:** developing informal and formal statements of purpose, planning potential uses of resources, identifying criteria for success in achieving goals; systematize and arrange priorities relevant to the achievement of a goal.

cont.

Table 5.3 (cont.)

- **Problem solving:** evaluating, assessing, diagnosing, generating alternatives, and anticipating needs.

- **Recruit:** actively engage and incorporate interested participants into your programs.

- **Reflection:** demonstrating the ability to assess where you are, where you're going, and where you would like to get to throughout the construction and implementation of initiatives.

- **Relationship building:** initiate, cultivate, and maintain professional contacts and interpersonal relations.

- **Self-awareness:** developing strategies to be more cognizant of their own behaviors while interacting with others in both social and professional settings.

- **Safety:** observing, applying and following approved precautions and procedures at all times.

- **Speech:** using language that is suitable and appropriate for the populations and settings in which you are working.

- **Team work:** working collaboratively toward a common goal with others.

- **Understanding group dynamics:** ability to solve problems effectively in a group context and make decisions benefitting a group.

Adapted from: Keeling, R. P. (Ed.). (2006). *Learning re-considered 2: A practical guide to implementing a campus-wide focus on the student experience.* Champaign, IL: Human Kinetics.

Officiating

Aside from participating in recreational sports, employment as an intramural official is a common experience for many college students and others involved with intramural and extramural sports. Schuh (1999) conducted a qualitative study involving four colleges (Drake University, Grinnel College, Iowa State University, and the University of Iowa) to determine what college students thought they had learned from their officiating experience. A total of 39 student officials (29 males, 10 females) were interviewed across the four colleges. The students found their experiences to be very important in their growth and development. While typically they began their work as officials for economic reasons or to stay close to sports, they reported that they developed a variety of skills from this experience, including improving their communication skills, becoming more self-confident and self-reliant, working better as a member of a team, understanding how to handle difficult situations more effectively, developing or having more self-control, developing leadership skills, and becoming better at making decisions.

Club Sport Participants

Haines and Fortman (2008) measured the impact of participating in club sports on student learning and development. The researchers used a proxy pretest–posttest design administered to 954 club sport participants and measured the perceived outcomes of participating in club sports using a 41-item survey. The main outcome domains included in this document were intellectual growth, effective communication, realistic self-appraisal, enhanced self-esteem, clarified values, career choices, leadership development, healthy behaviors, meaningful interpersonal relationships, independence, collaboration, social responsibility, satisfying and productive lifestyles, appreciation of diversity, spiritual awareness, and achievement of personal and educational goals. It was hypothesized that there would be significant differences between participants' ratings of their skills and abilities before and after participation. There was a significant increase in all of the outcomes items from *before* to *now*, and specific items in which participants demonstrated the greatest gains were travel planning skills, sense of belonging, time management, school pride, and overall leadership development. For a complete list of these outcomes, refer to Table 5.4.

In addition to studies that examine the impact of recreational sport participation on learning, there is also considerable research documenting additional academic benefits of recreational sport participation. Highlights from this research include the following:

- In Astin's (1993) research on persistence to complete a postsecondary education, he found support for the claim that participation in sports has a positive effect on persistence in school.

Table 5.4

Club Sports Participant Learning Outcomes

Travel planning skills	Inclination to not stereotype
Sense of belonging	Patience
Time management	Role modeling
School pride	Accountability
Overall leadership development	Tactful communication
Confidence in ability to lead	Ability to praise peers
Confidence you will succeed given a specific task	Expanded personal and educational goals
Self-esteem	Managing finances
Understanding the importance of managing finances	Problem solving skills
Ability to provide constructive criticism to peers	Ability to tactfully lose
Meaningful interpersonal relationships	Collaboration
Number of diversity experiences	Knowledge of diversity
Healthy behaviors	Punctuality
Ability to receive constructive criticism from peers	Understanding my values
Independence	Anger management
Extroversion	Critical thinking
Effective communication	Sportsmanship
Organization	Appreciation of diversity
Realistic self-appraisal	Humility
Satisfying and productive lifestyle	

- Another study examined the role of recreation and intramural participation in boosting freshman grade point average at a mid-sized public institution. The researchers found a strong positive association between freshman grade point average and participation in recreation. The authors concluded that investments in recreational opportunities for students are complementary to the institution's academic mission rather than a distraction from it (Gibbison, Henry, & Perkins-Brown, 2011).

- The results of a study conducted at a public university campus revealed that of the 11,076 freshmen entering school in fall 1993 to 1995, who used the Student Recreation Complex (SRC) "persisted at a greater rate after 1 semester and after 1 year than their counterparts who did not use the SRC" (Belch, Gebel, & Mass, 2001, p. 261).

- Intramurals are seen as a social outlet as well, and "students who become adequately integrated into the social and academic systems of their universities through participation in extracurricular activities, interaction with other students, and interactions with faculty develop or maintain strong commitments to attaining a college degree" (Christie & Dinham, 1991, p. 412–413).

- The National Intramural–Recreational Sport Association (NIRSA) hired the consulting firm Kerr and Downs Research to examine the value and contribution of recreational sports on college campuses. A representative sample of 2,673 students was selected from 16 different universities and colleges in the United States. The study found that participating in collegiate recreational sports benefited students academically by reducing their stress and helping them to manage their time and was an important part of their learning experience at college (NIRSA, 2003).

Leadership Skills

Beyond the numerous learning outcomes presented that occur as a result of recreational sport engagement, leadership skills represent an outcome that merits further discussion because of its natural association with recreational sports. Collegiate recreational sport programs provide a learning laboratory for students to gain leadership experience (Downs, 2003; Mull, Bayless, & Jamieson, 2005). Although the benefits of participating in recreational sport programs have been linked to a variety of leadership skills (Bryant, Banta, & Bradley, 1995; Cornelius, 1995; Downs, 2003; Haines, 2001), there is little empirical evidence documenting the leadership benefits of serving in various leadership roles typically associated with the provision of recreational sport programs. In addition to participating, there is a wide variety of ways to become involved with recreational sport programs such as officiating intramural or extramural contests, serving as an officer (president, vice president, treasurer, or secretary) of a club sport, or even volunteering on governance boards, committees, or councils. Therefore, the next several sections highlight research related to the leadership skills learned as a result of serving as a club sport officer and volunteering on a special event organizing committee.

Club Sport Officers

Club sports provide recreational, competitive, and social opportunities for participants, yet also emphasize the self-guided volunteer leadership nature of club sports (Matthews, 1987). Within this structure, significant responsibility is placed on elected officers of each club sport to run the organization (Matthews, 1987; Mull et al., 2005). A study by Hall-Yanessa and Forrester (2004) used a survey instrument called the Student Leadership Skills Inventory, which measures the leadership skill development of club sport officers. More specifically, the researchers examined differences in reported leadership skills both before and immediately following a 1-year leadership role serving as a president, vice president, treasurer, or secretary of a club sport in a collegiate setting. The top five leadership skills students reported after having served in the position for 1 year were as follows:

1. I respect the rights of others.
2. I am sensitive toward people who are different from me.
3. I understand the consequences of my actions.
4. I relate well to the opposite gender in a work-type situation.
5. I can identify my personal values.

The authors concluded that recreational sport professionals should focus on incorporating specific hands-on experiences as part of club sport officers training because students in this study tended to report gains in leadership skills from their experience, as opposed to intentional training sessions. As the amount and complexity of responsibilities for leaders in club sport organizations increase, so too will the leadership skills they obtain from these experiences.

Using the same data, Hall-Yanessa and Forrester (2005) examined the role that the adviser to the club sport had in the leadership development of the club sport officers. The researchers found that there were significant differences between the numbers of hours club sport officers consulted with their adviser and

- calculated risk taking,
- creative problem solving,
- critical thinking skills,
- facilitation of productive meetings,
- long-term goal setting,
- management of organization finances,
- time management,
- use of computer software,
- use of Internet technology, and
- written communication.

Hall-Yanessa and Forrester (2005) suggest that the frequency of time spent consulting with an adviser positively impacted the development of leadership skills. This is important for recreational sport specialists to consider when structuring club sports and identifying appropriate advisers for clubs as research has found they can play a pivotal role in the leadership skill development of the club's officers.

Volunteers

Within a typical collegiate recreational sports setting, there are several types of volunteer student leadership positions. Often there are governance boards, committees, councils, judicial boards, and club sport officers, all of which provide roles and responsibilities that can have a developmental influence on student leaders (Mull et al., 2005). Hall, Forrester, and Borsz (2008) explored the self-reported effects that leadership experiences have on students within the context of a collegiate recreational sport department. The researchers interviewed 21 student leaders, 13 females and eight males, who served on a planning committee for a major recreational sport special event. The researchers found that the experience had a considerable impact on the volunteers' leadership skill development in the areas of organizing, planning, and delegating; balancing academic, personal, and professional roles; mentor/role model and motivating others; problem solving and decision making; communication skills; working with others/diversity; and giving and receiving feedback. The researchers concluded that recreational sports professionals can support volunteers in these positions by providing additional resources to help with the challenging aspects of these roles. These challenges, such as balancing personal and professional lives; delegating, organizing, and planning; dealing with conflict, tense, or ethical situations; learning to delegate; giving and receiving feedback; and motivating others, can be discussed in one-on-one meetings, in council meetings, or at workshops. By understanding the areas in which volunteer leaders face challenges, recreational sport specialists can be more aware of issues as they arise and can be more prepared to discuss them with participants, officials, volunteers, employees, or club sport officers.

Structuring Leadership

Now that some background information/research has been provided regarding the learning outcomes of recreational sport engagement, it is time to examine how the recreational sport specialist can structure leadership experiences as part of program delivery. Any number of situations and positions can, if structured properly, enhance one's ability to become a better leader. Such an approach requires insight and commitment to planning, organizing, and watching for potential opportunities. Two general areas allow such development: situations that allow for individual self-leadership development and situations that allow an individual to influence or lead a group. Both concepts will be summarized, revealing basic points about leadership within recreational sport program delivery.

Self-Leadership Skills

Much about recreational sport enhances each participant's leadership potential. Often this learning is taken for granted, but the recreational sport specialist can help influence such development. Self-leadership development occurs as the participants, volunteers, and paid workers aspire to be involved and to be successful in their roles and responsibilities. There are two categories of self-leadership development: those that occur from within one's self and those that result from external influences.

Internal occurrences. Leadership begins as individuals work through daily life. Recreational sport is an excellent place for such development because in recreational sport individuals make a conscious choice to participate, they select their level of participation, and they are eager to experience what sport brings. These internal occurrences result from desires and abilities that exist within all individuals as they experience sport activity and what it brings to their own development.

One example of internal leadership is when individuals look critically at who they are, what they are doing, and the strengths and weaknesses in their sport participation. This self-assessment is a self-leadership skill that takes place with varying degrees of success and failure. Also, the idea of disciplining oneself and one's actions is another form of internal leadership. Disciplining oneself is a result of self-control, a valuable self-leadership skill. In addition,

recreational sport requires organizing how, when, and where things take place, contributing to time-management and organizational skills. Not only are these leadership skills valuable in recreational sport, but they also translate easily into the rest of life's many self-management responsibilities. Finally, self-motivation and the development of individual purpose in one's effort to perform and contribute is a form of internal self-leadership. Having a high level of inspiration and enthusiasm for accomplishing participation goals or work responsibilities can greatly improve one's success and satisfaction.

Each of these examples of internal self-leadership demonstrates the potential for self-leadership development. As the recreational sport specialist come to understand this concept, he or she will begin to recognize other self-leadership opportunities for participants.

External influences. Recreational sport can also structure opportunities that instill self-leadership through external influence, or situations originating outside the individual that affect how one functions. For example, sport activity requires an individual to receive external guidance and direction from a team captain, official, staff member, supervisor, coach, or club sport adviser. An individual's ability to accept this guidance and make the most of it is a valuable self-leadership skill. Another external influence is interaction with others. It is necessary to connect with others, which requires conveying and receiving information correctly. An individual needs to have reasonable listening and verbal skills, especially if connecting with others affects a critical sport or work situation. Group meetings can also help individuals realize their ability to connect with others.

Another external influence is the need to get along and work together. This is an excellent example of self-leadership that requires individuals to behave so that they are well received and contribute to the group's cohesiveness. A final example is the problems and difficulties that may occur in sport activity. Whether it is a group or personal problem, each individual has to deal with it, making it an excellent self-leadership experience.

To illustrate how recreational sport affects an individual, Figure 5.2 diagrams the three roles where internal and external experiences occur, developing specific skills that contribute to self-leadership. Figure 5.2 demonstrates how self-leadership exists and how it can be applied. The key to this concept is identifying the three roles and knowing that individuals in those roles are involved in their own self-leadership development.

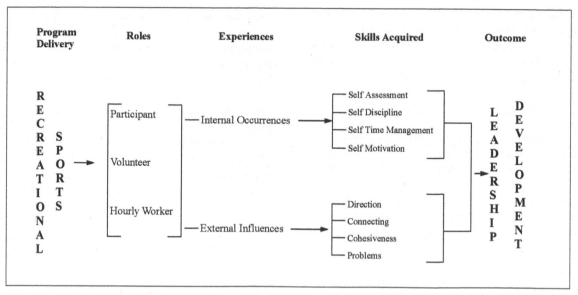

Figure 5.2. Self-Leadership Skill Development

Group Leadership Skills

The second part of structuring leadership development involves creating situations where participants and workers can influence a group to perform properly and progress. For this to occur, individuals need to have the responsibility of being in charge of a group. Such roles can be structured in all program delivery areas. They include roles such as head lifeguard, intramural unit manager, head volunteer, informal sport supervisor, intramural team captain, and club officer. Each of these positions creates excellent leadership experiences, which in turn yield specific beneficial skills. The following material touches on five different leadership experiences in recreational sport that can be structured to foster group leadership skills.

Getting started. The first example of group leadership is being in charge and helping a group get started. An individual in this position influences the group by judging strengths and weaknesses within the group. This effort also incorporates planning as the leader helps the group figure out where they are going and how they can best get there through specific goals and strategies. Getting started requires delegating responsibilities, a very important group leadership skill. Delegating tasks causes group members to invest themselves and support the group's goals. Finally, during this early stage, the leader needs to coordinate everything and everybody, making sure all parts come together in a cohesive group. No group can make progress unless individuals identify their responsibilities and perform them as planned.

It may be necessary for the recreational sport specialist to act in an advisory capacity in order to help a group leader get started in the right direction. However, it is equally important for recreational sport specialists to remove themselves from that initial effort so that the leader functions alone. The more a leader is able to influence the group, the more leadership skills they will acquire.

Forming relationships. Individuals in a group should become integrated by forming relationships and a sense of togetherness. Few clubs, teams, work groups, or committees can successfully work together or move forward if the group leader does not promote positive relationships within the group. This cohesiveness should facilitate a positive spirit and unity among members. Another critical group leadership skill is motivation, or building spirit and enthusiasm toward accomplishing a common goal. Motivation can be especially important as the leader aspires to set high standards and meet expectations. Networking, where the leader works outside the group to create recognition of the group and what they hope to accomplish, is another important group leadership skill.

The recreational sport specialist's role is to guide the group leader to promote positive relationships, which can be difficult because of individual and group dynamics. His or her experience and maturity should prove helpful as long as they make careful observations and help where necessary.

Sound communication. To a great extent, a group leader's capacity to effectively share information depends on skills such as speaking, listening, writing, and conducting meetings. These are critical skills in group leadership because the techniques a leader uses to convey information are critical to maintaining group support and making progress. Effective communication is vital, especially in this information age where such skill can significantly affect one's future.

Helping group leaders realize the strengths and weaknesses of their communication skills can be challenging, but where such advice is well received, improvement will be made. Communication skills can be especially important when group leaders need to convey information about management needs and interests.

Facing challenges. Facing challenges is another group leadership experience that takes place within the different roles found in recreational sport. Group leaders need to be creative in facing challenges, using fast thinking, alertness, flexibility, and sensitivity to others' input. Such creativity is critical to making progress, especially because of the varied interests that may be involved. Equally significant is the leader's ability to solve conflicts that result from individual differences in attitude and behavior. Any number of circumstances could require leadership in avoiding ongoing internal negativism. The group leadership skill of problem solving is similar but relates more to logistics and procedures rather than people. Addressing such situations as a group leader can be demanding, but it is essential to keep things moving smoothly.

For the recreational sport specialist, helping group leaders face their challenges is important. When the opportunity occurs, it is the recreational sport specialist's job to help them to be open-minded, fair, and consistent as they address conflicts and problems. When progress is made in spite of the challenges, group leaders experience great satisfaction.

Providing reinforcement. The final group leadership skill within recreational sport is reinforcement. This is accomplished when the person in charge shows support for what is taking place and recognizes group members for their work and contributions. Another aspect of reinforcement is the group leader serving as a mentor and role model by demonstrating leadership skills that positively reinforce progress.

The recreational sport specialist can demonstrate reinforcement by recognizing the group leader and group progress. This is an excellent technique for encouraging leaders to provide reinforcement to their group. It is vital to help group leaders realize their role as a positive mentor.

Structuring leadership opportunities as a group process in recreational sport should not be difficult to understand. As indicated, there are a number of roles where group leadership can be experienced and fostered. Figure 5.3 shows a list of the roles, experiences, and leadership skills that can be acquired in recreational sport.

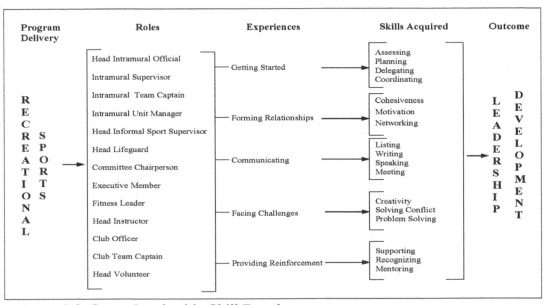

Figure 5.3. Group Leadership Skill Development

Shining Example

Indiana University Campus Recreational Sports

Indiana University Campus Recreational Sports serves the students, faculty, and staff of Indiana University as well as members of the surrounding community offering a wide variety of fitness, wellness, and recreational sport opportunities. With programming that goes back as far as 1918, the division has been recognized as one of the foremost programs in the country.

Clientele:

Campus Recreational Sports serves approximately 42,000 students attending Indiana University's Bloomington campus, as well as over 7,800 faculty and staff members, and a small number of individuals from the community.

Facilities:

Campus Recreational Sports operates two major indoor facilities on the Bloomington campus. The Wildermuth Intramural Center/School of Public Health complex consists of basketball and volleyball courts, racquetball courts, a free weight room, two strength-conditioning rooms, two pools and a diving well, and an indoor track. The Student Recreational Sports Center (SRSC) consists of basketball/volleyball courts, two multipurpose gymnasiums, an Olympic-sized pool and diving well, four strength and conditioning spaces, an indoor track, squash courts, and racquetball courts. Additional facilities on campus include an outdoor pool, an indoor tennis facility and outdoor tennis courts, a lighted outdoor complex, and two other large sports fields.

Program Details:

Campus Recreational Sports consists of four primary program areas: club sports, fitness and wellness, informal sports, and intramural sports. Auxiliary program areas include aquatics, special events, and outreach programs. There are nearly 50 student-run club sports, ranging from cycling to martial arts to soccer, all of which offer student leadership opportunities. In addition to facilities for individual cardio and strength training there are more than 80 group exercise sessions offered each week. Certified personal trainers and sessions for Yoga and Pilates are also available. The facilities for informal (self-directed) sport activities are open 362 days out of the year. There are typically fourteen different intramural sports tournaments with competitive and recreational divisions available for men's, women's, and co-intramural participation.

Budget:

The budget is approximately $7.1 million per year. Budget areas include personnel, supplies and expenses, equipment replacement and capital improvement. Revenue is generated through mandatory student activity fees, registration fees, memberships and state appropriated funds.

Marketing:

A marketing and design team produces and distributes a variety of materials every year, including flyers and advertising for each of the various program areas, an annual guide to Campus Recreational Sports campaigns to highlight specific program opportunities. These materials are distributed to the residence halls, Greek housing, off-campus living centers, and various locations around campus. In addition, they utilize ongoing social media, text notifications as well as an interactive website (www.iurecsports. org), where students and clients can access up to date information on facilities, schedules, activities, programs, tournaments, and events.

Jobs and Careers:

Campus Recreational Sports is the second largest hourly wage employer on the Bloomington campus. It employs over 900 student employees, 50 professional staff, and is comprised of a director, an associate director, 4 Program Directors, 6 service directors, 10 assistant directors, and 10 graduate assistants. In addition, there is 13 full-time support staff, over 300 sport officials, 200 supervisors, 75 lifeguards, 50 fitness/wellness instructors, 12 tennis instructors, and a variety of other part-time positions. It also offers over 600 leadership and volunteer opportunities through its many special events and advisory boards, program participant advisory councils and committees.

Salary:

The salary ranges vary based upon position and experience. For the director and associate director, the range is approximately $85,000-$135,000 per year; for program/service directors, it is approximately $55,000-$70,000 per year; and for program/ service assistant directors, the range is approximately $33,000-$48,000 per year.

Affiliated Professional Organizations:

Some personnel belong to national level professional organizations such as the National Intramural and Recreational Sports Association (NIRSA), as well as state and regional associations.

Awards and Recognition:

Campus Recreational Sports at Indiana University was ranked by Sports Illustrated on Campus as the best program of its kind in the nation.

Conclusion

You should now have a basic understanding of a developmental approach to recreational sport, helping you grasp the significance the field brings to various settings and society in general. Although there are some agencies where such an approach is not as important, in some settings it is critical to apply this information as best as possible. Contributing to the discussion of a developmental approach was the learning outcomes of recreational sport engagement. What is most rewarding about understanding both the developmental approach and learning outcomes is the satisfaction and reward it brings you as a professional. Not only will you see individuals change in a positive fashion, but also you will gain lifetime friends because of their appreciation for your assistance with program delivery as well as their leadership development.

This chapter presented an overview of a developmental approach to recreational sport. If this chapter has sparked your interest in such an approach, the bibliography lists readings that further develop the various concepts presented in this chapter. A developmental approach would be well served by a review of such literature and an application of its knowledge in your day-to-day responsibilities.

Bibliography

Astin, A. W. (1993). *What matters in college? Four critical years revisited*. San Francisco, CA: Jossey-Bass.

Bee, H. (1998). *Lifespan development*. New York, NY: Longman.

Belch, H. A., Gebel, M., & Mass, G. M. (2001). Relationship between student recreation complex use, academic performance, and persistence of first-time freshmen. *NASPA Journal, 38*(2), 254-269.

Blair, S. N., Dunn, A. L., Marcus, B. H., Carpenter, R. A., & Jaret, P. (2001). *Active living every day: 20 steps to lifelong vitality*. Champaign, IL: Human Kinetics.

Brown, J. D. (1991). Staying fit and staying well: Physical fitness as a moderator of life stress. *Journal of Personality and Social Psychology, 70*, 368-375.

Bryant, J. A., Banta, T. W., & Bradley, J. L. (1995). Assessment provides insight into the impact and effectiveness of campus recreation programs. *NASPA Journal, 32*(2), 153-160.

Christie, N. G., & Dinham, S. M. (1991). Institutional and external influences on social integration in the freshman year. *Journal of Higher Education, 62*(4), 412-436.

Cote, J. (1999). The influence of the family in the development of talent in sport. *The Sport Psychologist, 13*, 395-417.

Cote, J., & Fraser-Thomas, J. (2007). Youth involvement in sport. In P. Crocker (Ed.), *Sport psychology: A Canadian perspective* (pp. 270-298). Toronto, Canada: Pearson.

Cote, J., & Hay, J. (2002). Children's involvement in sport: A developmental perspective. In J. M. Silva & D. E. Stevens (Eds.), *Psychological foundations of sport* (pp. 484-502). Boston, MA: Allyn & Bacon.

Cote, J., Strachan, L., & Fraser-Thomas, J. (2008). Participation, personal development, and performance through youth sport. In N. L. Holt (Ed.), *Positive youth development through sport* (pp. 34-45). New York, NY: Routledge.

Cornelius, A. (1995). The relationship between athletic identity, peer and faculty socialization, and college student development. *Journal of College Student Development, 36*(6), 560-573.

Cotton, R. (1998). *Exercise for older adults: ACE's guide for fitness professionals*. Champaign, IL: Human Kinetics.

Danish, S. J., Fazio, R., Nellen, V. C., & Owens, S. (2002). Community-based life skills programs: Using sport to teach life skills to adolescents. In J. V. Raalte & B. Brewer (Eds.), *Exploring sport and exercise psychology* (2nd ed.) (pp. 269 -288). Washington, DC: American Psychological Association.

Danish, S. J., Forneris, T., Hodge, K., & Heke, I. (2004). Enhancing youth development through sport. *World Leisure, 46*(3), 38-49.

Danish, S. J., & Nellen, V. C. (1997). New roles for sport psychologists: Teaching life skills through sport to at risk youth. *Quest, 49*, 100-113.

Danish, S. J., Petitpas, A. J., & Hale, B. D. (1993). Life development intervention for athletes: Life skills through sports. *The Counseling Psychologist, 21*, 352-385.

Downs, P. E. (2003). Value of recreational sports on college campuses. *Recreational Sports Journal, 27*(1), 5-64.

Dychtwald, K. (1999). *AgePower: How the 21st century will be ruled by the new old*. New York: Tarcher/Putnam.

Erikson, E. H. (1950). *Childhood and society*. New York: W. W. Norton.

Erikson, E. H. (1968). *Identity: Youth and crisis*. New York: W. W. Norton.

Ettinger, W. H., Mitchell, B. S., & Blair, S. N. (1996). *Fitness after 50: It's never too late to start*. St. Louis, MO: Beverly Crocum.

Feldman, R. S. (1999). *Development across the lifespan* (2nd ed.). Upper Saddle River, NJ: Prentice Hall.

Fink, D. (2003). *Creating significant learning experiences*. San Francisco, CA: Jossey-Bass.

Fraser-Thomas, J., Côté, J., & Deakin, J. (2008). Understanding dropout and prolonged engagement in adolescent competitive sport. *Psychology of Sport & Exercise, 9*(5), 645-662.

Geller, W. W. (1976). *Student development in intramural sports* (Doctoral dissertation). Indiana University, Bloomington.

Gibbison, G. A., Henry, T. L., & Perkins-Brown, J. (2011). The chicken soup effect: The role of recreation and intramural participation in boosting freshman grade point average. *Economics of Education Review, 30*, 247-257.

Gross, P. A. (1991). *Managing your health: Strategies for lifelong good health*. Yonkers, NY: Consumer Report Books.

Haines, D. J. (2001). Undergraduate student benefits from university recreation. *NIRSA Journal, 25*(1), 25-33.

Haines, D. J., & Fortman, T. (2008). The college recreational sports learning environment. *Recreational Sports Journal, 32*(1), 52-61.

Hall-Yanessa, S., & Forrester, S. (2004). Differences in leadership development of club sports officers. *Recreational Sports Journal, 28*(1), 7-18.

Hall-Yanessa, S., & Forrester, S. (2005). Impact of advisor interaction on the development of leadership skills in club sports' officers. *Recreational Sports Journal, 29*(1), 9-21.

Hall, S., Forrester, S., & Borsz, M. (2008). A constructivist case study examining the leadership development of undergraduate students in campus recreational sports. *Journal of College Student Development, 49*(2), 125-140.

Harter, S. (1990). Processing underlying adolescent self-concept formation. In R. Montemayor, G. R. Adams, & R. P. Gulotta (Eds.), *From childhood to adolescence: A transitional period?* Newbury Park, CA: Sage Publications.

Humpries, C. (1991). Opinions of participants and non-participants toward youth sport. *Physical Educator, 48*(1), 44.

Keeling, R.P. (Ed.). (2006). *Learning re-considered 2: A practical guide to implementing a campus-wide focus on the student experience*. Champaign, IL: Human Kinetics.

Kirkcaldy, B. D., Shephard, R. J., & Siefen, R. G. (2002). The relationship between physical activity and self-image and problem behavior among adolescents. *Social Psychiatry and Psychiatric Epidemiology, 37*(11), 544-553.

Kleiber, D., & Ray, R. (1993). Leisure and generativity. In J. Kelly (Ed.), *Activity and aging: Staying involved in later life*. Newbury Park, CA: Sage Publications.

Komives, S., Lucas, N., & McMahon, T. R. (1998). *Exploring leadership: For college students who want to make a difference*. San Francisco, CA: Jossey-Bass.

Lee, I. M., Hsieh, C., & Paffenbarger, R. S. (1995). Exercise intensity and longevity in men. *Journal of the American Medical Association, 273*, 1179-1184.

Lerner, R.M., Fisher, C.B., & Weinberg, R.A. (2000). Toward a science for and of the people: Promoting civil society through the application of developmental science. *Child Development, 71*, 11-20.

Matthews, D. O. (1987). *Managing collegiate sport clubs*. Champaign, IL: Human Kinetics.

Margenau, E. (1990). *Sports without pressure: A guide for parents and coaches of young athletes*. New York, NY: Gardner Press.

Martin, D. (1997). Interscholastic sport participation: Reasons for maintaining or terminating participation. *Journal of Sport Behavior, 20*(1), 94.

Maxwell, J. C. (1993). *Developing the leader within you*. Nashville, TN: Thomas Nelson.

Maxwell, J. C. (1995). *Developing the leaders around you*. Nashville, TN: Thomas Nelson.

Maxwell, J. C. (1999). *The 21 indispensable qualities of a leader: Becoming that person that people will want to follow*. Nashville, TN: Thomas Nelson.

Mitchell, E., & Megan, R. (1998, November 30). Life stretchers: Yoga, qi gong, pilates and a new wave of water exercises are fast becoming the post-50 generation's choice workouts. *Time, 152*(22), 128.

Morrison, E. K. (1994). *Leadership skills: Developing volunteers for organizational success*. Tucson, AZ: Fisher Books.

Mull, R. (2002). *Organizational leadership development for students making a difference* (2nd ed.). Unpublished manuscript, Indiana University, Bloomington.

Mull, R., & Barnes, M. (1998). *Participant leadership development for students who will make a difference*. Unpublished manuscript, Indiana University, Bloomington.

Mull, R. F., Bayless, K. G., & Jamieson, L. M. (2005). *Recreational sport management* (4th ed.). Champaign, IL: Human Kinetics.

Mutrie, N. (1997). The therapeutic effect of exercise on the self. In K. R. Fox (Ed.), *The physical self: From motivation to well being*. Champaign, IL: Human Kinetics.

National Intramural–Recreational Sports Association. (2003). *Value of recreational sports in higher education*. Champaign, IL: Human Kinetics.

National Research Council and Institute of Medicine. (2002). *Community programs to promote youth development*. Washington, DC: National Academy Press.

Neugarten, B. L. (1968). The awareness of middle age. In B. L. Neugarten (Ed.), *Middle age and aging*. Chicago: University of Chicago Press.

Pescatello, L. S. (1999). Physical activity, cardiometabolic health and older adults: Recent findings. *Sports Medicine, 28*(5), 315-323.

Petitpas, A. J., Van Raalte, J. L., Cornelius, A. E., & Presbrey, J. (2004). A life skills development program for high school student athletes. *Journal of Primary Prevention, 24*, 325-334.

Pinto, B. M., Clark, M. M., Maruyama, N. C., & Felder, S. I. (2003). Psychological and fitness changes associated with exercise participation among women with breast cancer. *Psycho-Oncology, 12*(2), 118-126.

Ratey, J. J. (2008). *Spark: The revolutionary new science of exercise and the brain*. New York, NY: Little, Brown and Company.

Regier, D. A., Boyd, J. H., Burke, J. D., Rae, D. S., Myers, J. K., Kramer, M., . . . Locke, B. A. (1988). One-month prevalence of mental disorders in the United States. *Archives of General Psychiatry, 45*, 977-986.

Rikli, R. E., & Jones, C. J. (2001). *Senior fitness test kit–NTSC*. Champaign, IL: Human Kinetics.

Roggenbuck, J., Loomis, R., & Dagostino, J. (1990). The learning benefits of leisure. *Journal of Leisure Research, 22*(2), 112-124.

Russell, R. (2001). *Leadership in recreation*. New York, NY: McGraw-Hill.

Schuh, J. H. (1999). Student learning and growth resulting from service as an intramural official. *Recreational Sports Journal, 23*(2), 51-61.

Seidman, E., Allen, L., Aber, J. L., Mitchell, C., & Feinman, J. (1994). The impact of school transitions in early adolescence on the self-system and perceived social context of poor urban youth. *Child Development, 65*, 507-522.

Shertzer, J. E., & Schuh, J. H. (2004). College student perceptions of leadership: Empowering and constraining beliefs. *NASPA Journal, 42*(1), 111-131.

Spears, L. C. (1998). *Insights on leadership*. New York: John Wiley and Sons.

Swinburn, B., & Sager, R. (2003). Promotion of exercise prescriptions in general practice for older populations. *Geriatrics and Aging, 6*(7), 20-23.

Taggart, H. (2001). Self-reported benefits of tai chi practice by older women. *Journal of Holistic Nursing, 19*(3), 223-232.

Thoms, J. R. (1977). *Youth sports guide for coaches and parents*. Washington, DC: AAHPER Publications.

Turman, P. (2007). Parental sport involvement: Parental influence to encourage young athlete continued sport participation. *Journal of Family Communication, 7*(3), 151-175.

Yaffe, K. (2001). Women with higher levels of physical activity less likely to develop mental decline. *Archives of Internal Medicine, 161*, 1703-1708.

World Health Organization. (1999). *Partners in life-skills education* (Technical Report Series 916). Geneva, Switzerland: Author.

Yang, X. (1997). A multidisciplinary analysis of physical activity, sport participation and dropping out among youth Finns, a 12-year follow-up study. *Likes Research Report on Sport and Health, 103*.

CHAPTER 6

Fun

CHAPTER OBJECTIVES

After reading this chapter, you will be able to define fun and enjoyment, realize how fun and enjoyment are interrelated, understand the links between fun and numerous concepts from developmental sport and exercise psychology, and become familiar with different strategies to facilitate fun and enjoyable recreational sport experiences.

KEY CONCEPTS

Achievement goal theory
Competence
Ego orientation
Enjoyment
Flow
Fun

Intrinsic motivation
Motivation
Motivational climate
Optimal challenge
Self-determination
Task orientation

Introduction

Common sense suggests that when people have a choice, they participate in activities because they anticipate they will be fun or enjoyable. Having fun is often what is thought of when considering participating in recreational sports; almost everyone wants to have fun. Moreover, research has consistently found that people continue participating in an activity when they find it fun or personally worthwhile. Additionally, scholars believe that participants must find sport fun and enjoyable if they are to get any of the benefits of physical activity, sport, and recreation. But what is it that makes recreational sports fun?

Having fun is both an important determinant and outcome of recreational sport participation. One of the distinguishing qualities of recreational sport organizations is the goal of providing fun and enjoyable recreational sport experiences to participants. While this section of the text and the preceding two chapters have focused on physical fitness and participant development and learning, recreational sport specialists should not forget that the benefits they

provide are still at the core of what makes recreational sport unique and valuable when compared to other social services in the community—they facilitate fun and provide enjoyable experiences! Recreational sport specialists should remember the importance of play for the sake of fun and make sure that fun is a central component of recreational sport.

Intramural sports programming in the nation's junior and senior high schools has, by and large, "been predicated on the maxim that programs should be 'fun for everyone'" (Karabetsos, 1988, p. 34). Common beliefs held among recreational sport specialists that their programs should provide activities that lead to fun and enjoyable experiences are reflected in how recreational sport programs are promoted through mission statements or slogans. For example, the slogan for the Office of Recreational Sports at the University of Notre Dame is "Sports, Fun, and Fitness for the Notre Dame campus community" (http://recsports.nd.edu/). Similarly, the Recreation Department at the University of California, Santa Barbara strives to "provide a positive experience whether one chooses recreational sports for fun, fitness, friendship, or all of the above" (http://recreation.sa.ucsb.edu/). Regardless of the setting (education, community, etc.) recreational sport should be fun, first and foremost.

The emphasis on promoting fun and enjoyment is consistent with research that has consistently shown that (a) having fun is one of the most important motives young participants give for taking part in sport, (b) lack of fun is one of the reasons that youth often cite for withdrawing from sport, and (c) fun and enjoyment in organized youth sport are highly correlated with the desire and resolve to continue sport participation (Bengoechea, Stream, & Williams, 2004; Scanlan, Carpenter, Schmidt, Simons, & Keeler, 1993; Scanlan, Stein, & Ravizza, 1989; Weiss, Kimmel, & Smith, 2001; Wiersma, 2001). Furthermore, during the sampling years (ages 6 to 12), children and adolescents participate in a variety of sports primarily focused on deliberate play activities designed to maximize enjoyment that is important because "these years are considered essential building blocks for recreational sport participation" (Cote, Strachan, & Fraser-Thomas, 2008, p. 35).

However, simplistic notions of having fun are often devalued in a work-based and economically oriented society where recreational sport experiences are thought to be more purposefully developmental. By learning definitions of fun and understanding how fun is linked to a number of concepts from developmental sport and exercise psychology (see Weiss, 2004), recreational sport specialists can develop a better understanding of the importance of fun and its centrality to the mission of recreational sport agencies and organizations.

Defining Fun

While an individual knows what fun means, especially as it relates to his or her own recreational sport participation, it is actually a difficult term to operationally define. In his classic book, *Homo Ludens*, that advanced the idea that play is the civilizing force in human experience, Huizinga (1950) stated, "the fun of playing...resists all analysis, all logical interpretation" (p. 3). Although fun is difficult to define, each individual has his or her own preconceived notions of what fun is. Henderson, Glancy, and Little (1999) described fun as "the positively stimulating sensation of having a good time. Fun might occur through diversion, amusing oneself, merriment, and being playful" (p. 44). Aspects of fun included "being involved in an experience that draws our attention because we can imagine something of a special personal value that is challenging, not boring or threatening" (Henderson et al., 1999, p. 44). Today, *Merriam*

Webster Dictionary defines fun as "what provides amusement or enjoyment," "a mood for finding or making amusement," and "amusement, enjoyment." Fun usually implies laughter or gaiety but may imply merely a lack of serious or ulterior purpose (http://www.merriam-webster.com/).

Implicit in this definition of fun is enjoyment. Enjoyment is defined as something that provides keen satisfaction (http://www.merriam-webster.com/). Within the context of sport, enjoyment has been described as a "positive affective response to the sport experience that reflects generalized feelings such as pleasure, liking, and fun. It is considered an attractive variable and an important motivator in sport" (Scanlan, Carpenter, Schmidt, et al., 1993, p. 6). Research has examined how fun and enjoyment have played into participation in organized youth sports. Individuals identified a number of personal qualities that made sports' fun, including displaying humor and calmness and enjoying what they were doing (Holt, Garcia, & Strean, 2001). Given the similarity between the two terms—fun and enjoyment—they will be used interchangeably throughout this chapter.

Why Having Fun Is so Important: Understanding Motivation and Attrition

More than 20 million children register each year for youth hockey, football, baseball, soccer, and other competitive sports (The National Alliance for Youth Sports [NAYS], n.d.). However, 70% of these children quit playing league organized sports by age 13. Furthermore, 95% of youth sport participants drop out of at least one sport before 10th grade (Butcher, Lindner, & Johns, 2002). With figures such as these, it's time to rethink how recreational sport is presented to youth.

According to Michael Pfahl, executive director of the National Youth Sports Coaches Association (life.familyeducation.com/sports/behavior/29512.html), the number one reason why youth quit playing sports is that it stopped being fun. Taking away the fun aspects can be harmful for children and sour them on recreational sports. Repeated findings have identified the desire for enjoyment or fun as a major reason youngsters give for their participation in sport, while a lack of fun and enjoyment has been associated with quitting (Butcher et al., 2002; Ewing & Seefeldt, 1989; Gould & Horn, 1984).

Unpleasant Experiences = Less Fun = Drop Out

Understanding withdrawal reasons can be further enhanced by knowledge of what motivates children and adolescents to participate in sports. Weiss

(2000) and Weiss and Williams (2004) highlight three major motives for participation: (a) the desire to develop and demonstrate physical competence; (b) gaining social acceptance and support from peers and significant adults, including parents; and (c) fun and enjoyment. By understanding the main motivations to participate in recreational sport and the main reasons why so many youth stop participating, the recreational sport specialist will develop a better understanding as to why having fun is so important and should be at the core of recreational sport organizations' philosophies.

These authors found that the motivations related to enjoyment are fun, excitement, challenge, movement sensations, arousal, stress seeking, energy release, action, and access to equipment. Participant motivations for engagement in sport have been found to differ based on three developmental stages. In the sampling stage (ages 6–12), an athlete's primary motivation to engage in sport is to have fun, and participants this age generally do not have a desire to win or to be competitive (Fraser-Thomas, Cote, & Deakin, 2008; Turman, 2007).

Specifically related to recreational sport, and in this case intramural sport, Leppke and Tenoschok (2003), in a study of 3,626 middle school students from Georgia, found that the most important reason for participating in intramurals and sports was to have fun (72.3%), and the second most important reason students stopped playing a sport (or never started playing organized sports) was that they were not having fun (22.3%). Enjoyment, "or the lack thereof, apparently are primary reasons for participation and dropout, respectively" (Boyd & Yin, 1996, p. 384). Therefore, recreational sport programs should not focus on solely providing opportunities for developing athletic and physical fitness but should focus on games and play activities that foster fun and enjoyment (Wall & Cote, 2007).

Similarly, as part of an international World Health Organization study on health behavior in school-aged children, nationwide surveys on health behavior and lifestyle in 11- to 15-year-old school children were carried out in Finland, Norway, and Sweden. The findings revealed that social, fun, and health motives were the main motivations for sport participation. Experiencing competition and personal achievement were not rated as important reasons for liking sport, with older students attaching more importance to sport being fun. Winning and achieving better skills in sport also appeared to decrease in importance as participants grew older (Wold & Kannas, 1993). These findings imply that when developing programs aimed at increasing the level of physical activity among this age group, the recreational sport specialist should design these programs with

pro-social objectives in mind, emphasizing cooperation, fun, and sharing. Next, an overview of the four ways that recreational sport can facilitate fun and enjoyable experiences is provided.

Four Ways Recreational Sport Facilitates Fun Experiences

Four ways that recreational sport can facilitate fun and enjoyable experiences are discussed below.

Provision of Space

Recreational sport organizations often provide structures and facilities for fun and enjoyment. They construct and manage facilities that enable the leisure experience, including recreation centers; swimming pools; gymnasiums; fitness centers; ice rinks; bowling centers; golf courses; ski hills; tennis, racquetball, squash, and basketball courts; soccer, baseball, and football fields; and so on.

Participation

Recreational sports create opportunities for individuals who are brought closer together to share a common time of joy.

Working, Volunteering, Officiating

In addition to participating, there is a wide variety of ways to become involved with recreational sport programs, such as officiating intramural or extramural contests; serving as an officer (president, vice president, treasurer, or secretary) of a club sport; volunteering to serve on governance boards, committees, or councils; or helping with special events or other programs and activities.

Providing Spectator Experiences

Recreational sports produce many experiences that are enjoyable and fun to watch. An individual does not have to participate to have fun; many individuals have fun just watching recreational sports.

While there are a number of ways that recreational sport provides fun and enjoyable experiences, the focus of this chapter is on the experience of the participant and subsequently what recreational sport specialists need to know in order to provide fun and enjoyable experiences for participants in their programs.

Fun and Enjoyment – Links with Other Sport and Exercise Psychology Concepts

Research has found that fun is related to a number of other concepts from developmental sport and exercise psychology, all of which are important for the recreational sport specialist to understand in order to ensure the provision of fun and enjoyable experiences for participants. The following examples highlight some of these relationships:

- "Fun and enjoyment experienced through sport participation during the sampling years may be critical to the development of intrinsic motivation" (Cote, Baker, & Abernethy, 2003, p. 85–86).

- In a study of the components of fun in physical education classes, organized sport programs and a developmentally based physical activity program, researchers found fun to be greater when participants experienced flow and was highly correlated with desire to continue participation and other intrinsic variables (Mandigo & Couture, 1996).

- Furthermore, in a study that investigated the experience of fun in youth sport involvement over the first 12 games of a season, researchers found that postgame positive affect, how well one played, and challenge were the best predictors of fun (Wankel & Sefton, 1989). The authors further concluded that "fun in youth sports seems to be a positive mood state largely determined by perception of personal achievement and the matching of skills against a realistic challenge. Results are consistent with the theoretical perspectives of Csikszentmihalyi (1975) and Nicholls (1984, 1989)" (p. 355).

- Enjoyment has generally been discussed with regard to intrinsic motivation. Deci and Ryan (1985) posit that enjoyment is derived from achievement behavior, which is intrinsically motivating and provides perceptions of competence and self-determination.

- Research has also found that significant sources of sport enjoyment include task orientation, perceived competence, learned helpless affect, and years of participation in organized sport (Boyd & Yin, 1996).

- Self-derived perceptions of competence and the excitement of competition have also been found to be related to fun and enjoyment (Wiersma, 2001).

Clearly fun and enjoyment is much more complex than initially thought, and in order to understand how to provide fun and enjoyable recreational sport experiences, the recreational sport specialist needs to comprehend the different concepts related to fun and enjoyment. The rest of this chapter provides an overview of these concepts and offers considerations for the recreational sport specialist on how to make recreational sport experiences fun and enjoyable.

Enjoyment

Individuals generally do what they enjoy based on choice and intrinsic motivation. Choice centers on their perceptions of fun, enjoyment, and a sense of flow that results from their recreational sport participation. Enjoyment "often occurs when the outcome is purely for oneself, such as having fun or acting spontaneously…letting go of performance expectations often makes fun and enjoyment possible" (Henderson et al., 1999, p. 44).

Sport researchers have become increasingly interested in positive emotional experiences such as enjoyment (Crocker, Hoar, McDonough, Kowalski, & Niefer, 2004). Enjoyment has been recognized as a key motivator and factor in continuing participation in youth sport (Scanlan, Carpenter, Schmidt, et al., 1993; Scanlan & Simons, 1992; Weiss, Kimmel, & Smith, 2001). Enjoyment is also a component of most major sport motivation theories such as achievement goal theory (Nicholls, 1989), competence motivation theory (Harter, 1978, 1981), the sport commitment model (Scanlan, Carpenter, Schmidt, et al., 1993), flow (Csikszentmihalyi, 1975, 1997, 2000), and self-determination theory (Deci & Ryan, 1985). Understanding the various contributors to enjoyment in general, and recreational sport enjoyment in particular, is important for the recreational sport specialist in order to develop a comprehensive understanding of positive affect and its relation to continued recreational sport participation.

Sport Enjoyment

In a study of the predictors and enjoyment for male youth sport participants, Scanlan and Lewthwaite (1986) developed a two-dimensional model of sport enjoyment. As illustrated in Figure 6.1, they conceptualized achievement–nonachievement predictors of sport enjoyment vertically and intrinsic–extrinsic predictors of sport enjoyment horizontally to create four categories of sport enjoyment.

- **Quadrant I (Achievement-Intrinsic).** Predictors related to personal perceptions of competence and control such as the attainment of mastery goals and perceived ability.

- **Quadrant II (Achievement-Extrinsic).** Predictors related to personal perceptions of competence and control that are derived from other people such as positive social evaluation and social recognition of sport achievement.

- **Quadrant III (Nonachievement-Intrinsic).** Predictors related to (a) physical activity and movement such as sensations, tension release, action, and exhilaration and (b) competition such as excitement.

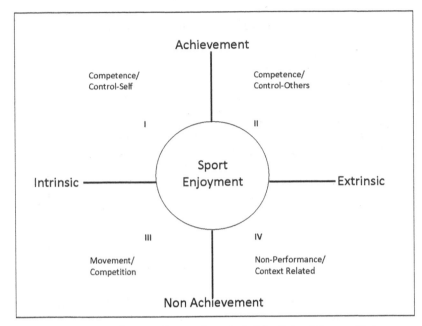

Figure 6.1. Scanlan and Lewthwaite's Model of Sport Enjoyment (1986). *Note:* Roman numerals represent the four quadrants of the model. Source: Scanlan, T.K., & Lewthwaite, R. (1986). Social psychological aspects of competition for male youth sport participants: IV. Predictors of enjoyment. *Journal of Sport and Exercise Psychology, 15,* 1-15.

- **Quadrant IV (Nonachievement-Extrinsic).** Predictors related to nonperformance aspects of sport such as affiliating with peers and having positive interactions with adults that revolve around the mutually shared sport experience.

In a qualitative study of sport enjoyment in the sampling years of sport participation, McCarthy and Jones (2007) examined the sources of enjoyment and non-enjoyment between younger and older children (aged 7–12). The researchers found that both younger and older children reported sources of enjoyment such as perceived competence, social involvement and friendships, psychosocial support, and a mastery-oriented learning environment (see Figure 6.2). Conversely, non-enjoyment sources included inappropriate psychosocial support, an increase in competitive orientation, negative feedback and reinforcement, injuries, pain, and a demonstrated lack of competence (McCarthy & Jones, 2007) (see Figure 6.3). Younger children reported movement sensations as a source of enjoyment and punishment for skill errors and low informational support as sources of non-enjoyment, whereas older children reported social recognition of competence, encouragement, excitement, and challenge as sources of enjoyment with rivalry, overtraining, and high standards as non-

enjoyment sources (McCarthy & Jones, 2007). These differences underscore the importance of tailoring recreational sport in the sampling years to the needs of the participants.

In an effort to understand what makes sport enjoyable, Wankel and Kreisel (1985) examined factors underlying enjoyment among male team-sport participants (aged 7 to 14). The relative importance of enjoyment factors across both sport and age groups was noticeably consistent. Specifically, intrinsic factors (e.g., excitement of the sport, personal accomplishments, and improving one's skills) were rated most important, with social factors (e.g., being with friends) of intermediate importance and extrinsic or outcome-related factors (e.g., winning the game and pleasing others) rated least important. Therefore, recreational sport specialists should focus on opportunities for improving one's skills and personal accomplishments while minimizing the focus on winning and pleasing others.

In a study of former elite figure skaters, Scanlan et al. (1989) asked why they had enjoyed their competition in the sport. Although it is not a recreational sport, some parallels between their findings and aspects of the recreational sport experience that can be fun and enjoyable are as follows:

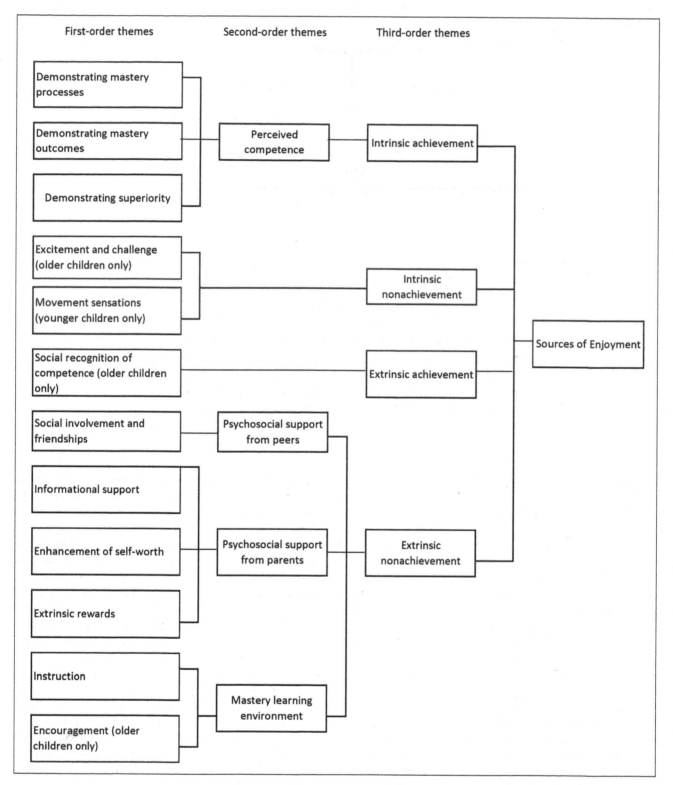

Figure 6.2. Sources of Enjoyment for Younger and Older Children. *Source:* McCarthy, P. J., & Jones, M. V. (2007). A qualitative study of sport enjoyment in the sampling years. *The Sport Psychologist, 21,* 400-416.

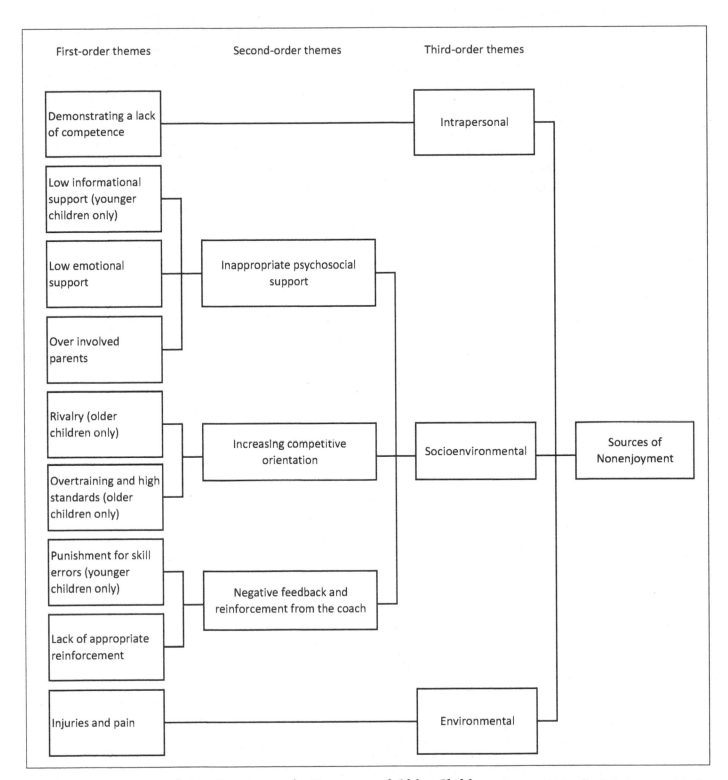

Figure 6.3. Sources of Non-Enjoyment for Younger and Older Children. *Source:* McCarthy, P. J., & Jones, M. V. (2007). A qualitative study of sport enjoyment in the sampling years. *The Sport Psychologist, 21,* 400-416.

- **Athleticism**—becoming physically fit, releasing tension because of the physically strenuous nature of participation.

- **Competitive achievement**—when socially and physically compared to others, the skater felt happy when winning or placing high.

- **Coping through skating**—feeling competent and therefore able to escape from other problems in life, gaining control of one's life within a highly controlled environment.

- **Demonstrating athletic ability**—becoming better than peers at a sport.

- **Achieving flow and some peak experiences**—feeling mastery and the sense of a perfect performance that in turns produces an intense and memorable sensory experience.

- **Building friendships**—making friends with other participants, and sharing common experiences while participating.

- **Achieving mastery**—individual achievement through learning skills and techniques and meeting challenges; mastery outcomes involving a sense of accomplishment.

- **Movement sensations when participating**—feeling of exhilaration and tactile and kinesthetic feeling during participation.

- **Travel experiences**—pleasure derived from going to tournaments or competitions including touring and meeting people in new and interesting places from various cultures.

- **Self-expression/creativity**—communicating one's individuality through participation.

It is important for recreational sport specialists to develop and provide enjoyable recreational sport experiences because research has found that sport enjoyment is associated with positive outcomes. For example, enjoyment involves an investment of attention and effort on behalf of the participant that results in psychological growth (Csikszentmihalyi, 1990). Also, when children and youth enjoy sport, they are more likely to stay in sport, have high expectancies for continued participation, and show greater sport commitment (Weiss & Raedeke, 2004). Sport enjoyment has also been found to be related to involvement in challenging skills, social involvement, friendships, extrinsic rewards, high activity levels, low parental pressure, positive emotional involvement of parents, mastery-focused teaching environment, pleasing of significant adults such as parents and coaches, and skill development (Weiss & Raedeke, 2004).

Enjoyment is an important motivational construct that is central to the recreational sport experience. Its potential sources are numerous and varied, and it affects both reasons for participation in recreational sport and reasons for discontinued involvement. Research has also indicated that fun and enjoyment are related to a number of concepts from sport psychology such as flow and optimal challenge, intrinsic motivation and self-determination, achievement goal orientations, motivational climates, and perceptions of competence. These concepts are discussed throughout the rest of the chapter in an effort to equip the recreational sport specialist with the necessary information to help facilitate fun and enjoyable experiences for recreational sport participants.

Flow and Optimal Challenge

The idea of "flow" (Csikszentmihalyi, 1975, 1982, 1990) is useful in understanding fun and enjoyment when participating in recreational sports. Enjoyment involves an investment of attention and effort and results in psychological growth (see Jackson, 2000). In this regard, enjoyment comes from being fully involved and in control of a challenging situation so that positive outcomes are created by personal effort. This implies that having a fun and enjoyable experience is highly individual, which intuitively makes sense (i.e., what might be construed as fun or enjoyable for one person may not be for another). Thus, the recreational sport specialist must depend on the participant to become a coproducer of a fun-filled experience. No matter what a recreational sport specialist does to provide choices, eliminate competition, encourage creativity and spontaneity, or even teach about the fun and enjoyment to be discovered in activities through instructional sports, "if the participants do not choose to focus their mental, emotional, and physical energy in the activity for their own reasons, fun is unlikely to occur" (Henderson et al., 1999, p. 45).

Csikszentmihalyi's Flow Theory proposed a state of being or autotelic experience in which an individual becomes so involved in an activity that nothing else seems to matter. Flow is defined as a deep and fulfilling personal enjoyment associated with engaging in an activity to which an individual feels their skills or abilities match the challenge of the activity (Csikszentmihalyi, 1990). Optimal challenge occurs when there is flow, or a harmony between the skill of the individual and the challenge of the task (Mandigo & Holt, 2002). Optimal challenge is usually accompanied by feelings of intense concentration, loss of self-consciousness, and loss of sense of time.

Over the years, Csikszentmihalyi has identified a number of elements associated with flow experiences. More recently, Csikszentmihalyi (2000) subdivided these elements into *conditions* and *characteristics* of the flow experience. Conditions refer to the circumstances and environments assumed to be conducive to facilitating flow experiences such as (a) balance between perceived challenge and perceived skill and (b) clear goals and immediate feedback. Characteristics refer to the experiential nature of flow, that is, how people experience flow or what they feel while having flow experiences. Characteristics of the flow experience include (a) a merging of action and awareness, (b) sense of control, (c) loss of self-consciousness, and (d) a transformation of time. Being able to differentiate between these conditions and characteristics of the flow experience is helpful for recreational sport specialists who seek to provide fun and enjoyable experiences by facilitating flow because they can affect or enhance opportunities to experience flow (characteristics) by managing aspects of the recreational sport environment (conditions) (Voelkl, Ellis, & Walker, 2003).

Numerous studies have investigated flow in recreation and sport programs (see Voelkl et al., 2003). These studies have consistently found that flow does indeed occur during these planned and organized activities. In a study comparing flow states between participants in recreational versus competitive sports, findings suggested that flow for the recreational sport participants was significantly more important in determining their satisfaction with participation when compared to the competitive sport participants (Walker, 2002). Understanding the conditions of recreational sport environments that may be conducive to flow experiences can provide helpful information to the recreational sport specialist for making programmatic decisions regarding the structure, content, and interactions between leaders and participants (Voelkl et al., 2003). The following are suggestions adapted from Voelkl et al. and Mandigo and Holt (2002) to promote flow experiences by providing optimal challenge in recreational sport programs:

- Provide a variety of skill level opportunities to participate in order to ensure an optimal match between participants' perceived skill levels and the perceived challenge required of the activity.

- Create recreational sport programs that minimize distractions and support participants' full involvement so that they can concentrate on the task at hand.

- Support expectations and an attitude that fosters engagement and reengagement in a flow activity.

- Consider the consequences of promoting excessive competition that focuses on outcomes such as winning and losing, and instead focus on task mastery.

- When planning recreational sport programs and activities for individuals, be sure to consider how these experiences relate to things that individuals value about themselves.

When participants experience flow and feel optimally challenged while participating in recreational sports, they are more likely to have fun and experience enjoyment and be intrinsically motivated to participate in the future.

Motivation

This chapter established the significance of fun and enjoyment to recreational sport because these are both important reasons why so many people participate as well as withdraw from recreational sports. As such, it is important for the recreational sport specialist to understand the concepts of intrinsic motivation and self-determination in terms of facilitating fun and enjoyable experiences for their participants.

Intrinsic Motivation and Self-Determination

It is important for the recreational sport specialist to also understand that sport enjoyment shares a common base with the construct of intrinsic motivation (Scanlan & Lewthwaite, 1986). This shared base involves the underlying perceptions of personal competence and control (self-determination), which are necessary conditions for both enjoyment and intrinsic motivation (see Deci & Ryan, 1985, 2000, 2002, 2008 for an elaboration of these perceptions and their relationships to intrinsic motivation). Intrinsic motivation is characterized by engagement in an activity for the sake of the activity itself rather than for external reasons. Experiencing interest, enjoyment, excitement, and challenge are examples of intrinsic motivations (Deci & Ryan, 1985; Kilpatrick, Hebert, & Jacobsen, 2002).

Self-Determination Theory (SDT) is an organismic theory that attempts to understand human motivation and personality (Deci & Ryan, 2002). SDT is based on the assumption that there are three innate psychological needs—the need for competence, autonomy, and relatedness (Deci & Ryan, 2008). Autonomy is characterized by an internal locus of control where individuals have a sense of freedom in choosing activities. Competence involves experiencing a sense of mastery and feeling that one is good at an activity. Relatedness refers to feeling a sense of connectedness with others. Satisfying these needs can bring about different forces or types of motivation, which SDT organizes along a continuum. This continuum ranges from completely self-determined (intrinsic motivation) to completely non-determined or amotivated forms of motivation (Deci & Ryan, 1985). Research in various life contexts, including sport, has found that the most positive outcomes result from the most self-determined forms of motivation (Vallerand & Bissonnette, 1992; Vallerand & Losier, 1999).

Research has also found that the degree of autonomy or freedom in the environment directly impacts participants' motivation and the satisfaction of psychological needs (Lundberg, 2007). There are a number of suggestions for the recreational sport specialist when trying to apply self-determination theory to develop guidelines for recreational sport programs. These suggestions are offered in an effort to facilitate increased participation through the provision of fun and enjoyable experiences that ultimately foster self-determined forms of participation that are likely to create adherence to a physically active lifestyle (Kilpatrick et al., 2002). Some suggestions for recreational sport programs are the following (Kilpatrick et al., 2002; Lundberg, 2007):

- Give positive feedback regarding some aspect of performance.

- Promote process goals that allow for success to be measured by improvement.

- Promote moderately difficult goals that are somewhere between "too easy" and "too difficult."

- Provide choice of recreational sport activities by offering several activities or formats from which to choose.

- Provide a rationale for activities explaining why the activity was selected.

- Promote the development of social relationships by encouraging the formation of social connectedness.

- Utilize rewards carefully and sparingly to develop new behaviors but not to sustain existing ones.

The extent to which the recreational sport specialist is able to apply these suggestions when designing and implementing various recreational sport programs from instructional, informal, intramural or extramural, and club sports will determine how successful these recreational sport experiences are at satisfying the psychological needs of autonomy, competence, and relatedness and ultimately providing fun and enjoyable experiences for participants. Refer to Table 6.1 for a checklist that recreational sport specialists can use to help provide autonomy supportive environments. Further related to facilitating fun and enjoyable recreational sport experiences is achievement goal theory, which is discussed next.

Achievement Goal Orientations

In order for the recreational sport specialist to understand the relationship between enjoyment and perceived competence, he or she needs to look at achievement goal theory (AGT) (Nicholls, 1978, 1984, 1989). One of the most consistent findings in research on goals and enjoyment in sport is the positive relationship between task orientation and enjoyment of sport (see Duda, 1996). This result seems to hold, regardless of the level of competition or age of the participants. Task or ego achievement orientation have been further found to impact the criteria individuals use to construe competence and also influence subsequent achievement behavior including task choice, persistence, and performance (Nicholls & Miller, 1984). According to AGT, individuals strive to demonstrate success through displaying competence. AGT identifies two basic dispositions individuals can have to varying degrees in achievement situations: task and ego goal orientation. Task orientation defines success in terms of getting better and trying hard, whereas ego orientation defines success in terms of winning and outperforming others (McCarthy, Jones, & Clark-Carter, 2008).

A task orientation involves focusing on mastery and self-improvement. Recreational sport participants who perform at their best or beyond their personal expectations provide perceptions of competence for those who are task involved (Boyd & Yin, 1996). An ego orientation, on the other hand, would be reflective of recreational sport participants who tend to dwell on social comparisons of their abilities and outcomes, such as outperforming others (Nicholls, 1989). For recreational sport participants who are ego involved, demonstrating greater ability than others provides competence perceptions especially when greater effort must be exerted by others (Jagacinski & Nicholls, 1987).

Within team sports, previous research has found that athletes who perceived their team atmosphere to be more task involving tended to report greater enjoyment in basketball, and this held true regardless of the team's record during the season (Seifriz, Duda, & Chi, 1992). Furthermore, this same study found that perceptions of a task-involving climate were also positively associated with the belief that hard work and cooperation with teammates lead to success in basketball. Motivational climates have also been differentiated based on task versus ego orientation and are described next.

Table 6.1

Recreational Sport Specialist's Checklist for Creating Autonomy Supportive Climates

As a recreational sport specialist, if you can answer yes to the following questions, you may be well on your way to providing an autonomy supportive motivational climate. Answering no to the following questions may also help you identify areas for improvement. Do you or your staff do the following:

- Help facilitate decision making by the recreational sport participant?

- Give participants a good rationale when requesting that a task or activity be done a certain way?

- Try to take the perspective of the participant?

- Express an understanding of the participant's feelings?

- Provide feedback that is directed toward accomplishment of tasks and personal improvement?

- Seek to diminish external pressures and demands?

- Help encourage initiative on the part of the recreational sport participant?

- Provide opportunities for individual choice and autonomy instead of requiring all participants to conform to the same activity expectation?

- Develop a sense of teamwork and mutual support?

- Emphasize the importance of effort over outcome?

- Focus on personal improvement and contributions to the team?

- Reduce the focus on "winning at all costs"?

Adapted from Lundberg, N. (2007). Research update: Creating motivational climates. *Parks and Recreation,* 22-26.

Motivational Climate

The concept of motivational climate is another important factor for the recreational sport specialist to understand as it has been found to influence participation in sport (Balaguer, Duda, & Crespo, 1999; Duda & Balaguer, 2007; Smith, Smoll, & Cumming, 2007). Like AGT, motivational climates have been described as either task or ego and reflect an individual's perception of the recreational sport setting. The recreational sport specialist creates a task climate when the focus is on personal skill development regardless of how others perform. Conditions where instructional sport instructors, club sport coaches, teammates, peers, and/or recreational sport staff encourage participants to give their best effort in attaining challenging but realistic goals help to facilitate a task oriented climate. Conversely, an ego climate is formed when the recreational sport specialist focuses on creating programs or environments in which participants can demonstrate superior ability over others (Smith et al., 2007). In general, research on motivational climate suggests that a task climate has a positive effect on participants, while an ego climate typically results in negative sport experiences (Duda & Balaguer, 2007).

Creating Motivational Recreational Sport Climates to Enhance Fun and Enjoyment

Recreational sport specialists can use the acronym TARGET, which has been used to identify effective strategies for structuring a master motivational climate (Weiss & Williams, 2004). TARGET stands for Task, Authority, Recognition, Grouping, Evaluation, and Time. Each is described briefly below:

- **Task**—use of task variety and optimal challenges.

- **Authority**—locus of decision making; some opportunities for choice and shared decision making are key to developing self-regulation and enhancing motivation toward the activity.

- **Recognition**—focuses upon effort and self-improvement rather than peer comparison and competitive outcomes; fosters competence beliefs, task orientation, enjoyment, and increased effort and persistence.

- **Grouping**—heterogeneous partner and small-group problem-solving tasks, rather than ability grouping; emphasizes cooperative learning and success and de-emphasizes interpersonal competition and rivalry.

- **Evaluation**—emphasizes self-referenced standards such as learning, effort, and individual progress; reinforces an intrinsic motivational orientation.

- **Time**—adequate time for learning and mastering skills increases the probability of being successful at optimal challenges and ensuing feelings of competence, pleasure, and desire to continue mastery attempts in the future.

In summary, these six elements define the ingredients for maximizing a mastery motivational climate and help ensure that recreational sport experiences are fun and enjoyable. In addition to trying to develop mastery motivational climates, recreational sport specialists also need to understand the implications of participants' skill level, ability, and perceptions of competence on providing fun and enjoyable recreational sport experiences, which is discussed next.

Importance of Skill Level, Ability, and Perceptions of Competence to Fun and Enjoyment

When a participant's skill level or ability in recreational sport, often referred to as competence, is perceived to be high, positive feelings of self-worth typically occur (Scanlan & Lewthwaite, 1986). Positive affect about the self should be associated with greater enjoyment of the activity that fosters this positive self-regard (Scanlan & Lewthwaite, 1986). Consistent with this contention are findings that show that ability-related factors such as the learning, testing, and improvement of skills are important to sport participation and enjoyment (Scanlan & Lewthwaite, 1986).

According to competence motivation theory (Harter, 1978, 1981), individuals have a natural desire to experience feelings of competence, and these feelings might be attained through mastery experiences in various achievement domains such as recreational sport. Enjoyment is associated with these feelings of mastery, which in turn increases motiva-

tion (Harter, 1978, 1981). Perceived competence can be defined as experiencing a sense of mastery and the perception of being effective in one's interactions with their environment while having the opportunity to exercise and express one's capacities (Kilpatrick et al., 2002; Deci & Ryan, 2002). Research has consistently found competence as a source of sport enjoyment (see Boyd & Yin, 1996). Those who perceive themselves to be more competent in sport and those who self-report more task orientation in sport tend to express greater levels of sport enjoyment (Boyd & Yin, 1996). These findings underscore the importance of the development of recreational sport competence and corroborate earlier research also reporting perceived ability to be intimately associated with enjoyment in sport (Scanlan & Lewthwaite, 1986; Wankel & Kreisel, 1985).

There are a number of considerations when developing competence for recreational sport participants. Instructional sport provides the foundation for the development of competence as these programs are designed to teach the knowledge and skills required by different sports. Informal sports programs could allow participants to search for activity partners based on ability level, offer ladder play to help facilitate this, or designate different basketball courts for pickup basketball based on ability or skill level during peak times. Intramural and extramural sport can foster positive perceptions of competence among participants by offering different leagues of competitive play based on skill level. Finally, club sports can foster perceptions of competence by allowing anyone to be members of the club but have tryouts for the travel or tournament team.

In summary, Weiss and Williams (2004) recommend five strategies for enhancing perceptions of competence, enjoyment, task orientation, and social support that in turn should help create an intrinsic motivational orientation and result in positive behaviors such as choice, effort, and persistence. Briefly stated, these are to

- provide optimal challenges,

- make sure the recreational sports experiences are fun,

- create a mastery motivational climate,

- maximize social support, and

- help participants help themselves.

When providing optimal challenges, the recreational sport specialist helps to ensure that there is a balance between the perceived skill on behalf of the participants and the skill level required of the activity. This in turn helps to produce flow experiences that are fun and enjoyable for participants. Task involved goals uniquely provide individuals of all ability levels with the opportunity to construe competence perceptions and the accompanying enjoyment affect. Furthermore, creating mastery motivational climates, where competence is construed in regard to self-referenced, internally generated perceived ability, would induce intrinsic motivation and further help the recreational sport specialist facilitate fun and enjoyable experiences.

Providing fun and enjoyable recreational sport experiences is probably not easy. In order to do so, the recreational sport specialist needs to develop an understanding of the numerous developmental sport and exercise psychology concepts previously presented in this chapter. Now that these concepts have been covered, the chapter's focus turns to providing some age-specific considerations to facilitating fun and enjoyable recreational sport experiences for different developmental age groups.

Age Level Considerations for Providing Fun/ Enjoyable Recreational Sport Experiences

Before providing age-specific considerations for facilitating fun and enjoyable recreational sport experiences for participants, there are a number of general considerations for the recreational sport specialist when providing these experiences to children:

- Introduce children to recreational sports appropriate for their interests. A beginning sport should get children moving and using their bodies, and the equipment should be easy to handle.

- Don't focus on rules, keeping score, or competition for preschool children.

- School-aged children enjoy games with rules and are concerned about how they are judged by others. Teamwork helps them master skills and learn about cooperation, taking turns, and respecting their peers. For adolescents, recreational sport provides further opportunities to use their abilities in communication, negotiation, and leadership.

- Encourage children to try a number of sports (i.e., generalize versus specialize), and consider not offering competitive recreational sport opportunities until middle school.

- Ideally, the best recreational sport programs for children, starting at about age 10, would be one dual or individual sport and one team sport per academic year.

- Be sure the physical requirements of the sport are within the capabilities of the children participating. Early specialization and too much practice

and play may result in injuries due to overuse of certain parts of the body.

- Remember, organized intramural and extramural and club team sports are not for all children. Other dual or individual recreational sport options such as bowling, golf, swimming, tennis, gymnastics, fencing, or martial arts could be encouraged instead.

- Don't provide recreational sport programs that allow children to specialize in a single sport before adolescence. The National Association for Sport and Physical Education (2004) recommends that children under age 15 should participate in multiple sports and informal activities rather than specializing. This can help children develop skills in more than one activity.

- Provide opportunities for children to play informally through unstructured playtime (i.e., informal sports) when they decide what they want to do and make up their own rules.

- When providing recreational sport opportunities for children remember that overzealous parents and coaches can take the fun out of the experience, which may push children away from recreational sport. Recreational sport specialists should consult the variety of sport parent education programs available such as Fun First from the National Recreation and Park Association or the Parents Association for Youth Sports Parent's Code of Ethics, which provides a parental handbook and code of ethics that adults must sign before each competitive season. This is a helpful tool to guide parents in their interaction with young participants.

Now that general guidelines have been outlined for recreational sport programs for children, following are key points to consider when providing recreational sport programs for participants of different ages.

Preschool

Recreational sport specialists should focus on the element of play and try to make every recreational sport activity fun. They should de-emphasize competition, keeping score, and rules. Rather, they should focus on getting preschool children running, kicking, throwing, catching, laughing, and having a good time. Appropriate equipment suitable for the child's body size, coordination, and skill level (i.e., toss a beanbag instead of a ball) should be used. Recreational sport specialists should also adapt games according to preschooler's ability levels and offer support and encouragement.

Elementary School

For elementary school students, Wolff (1997) recommends that it is important for children this age to develop a passion for the sport. At this age, it is important for the recreational sport specialist to be aware of what children can accomplish at their differing developmental levels—physically, intellectually, emotionally, and socially.

Middle School

This is the age when children start dropping out of organized sports at alarming rates. Playing sports loses its enjoyment for them, and fun takes a backseat to winning. Recreational sport specialists should facilitate pickup games through informal sports and encourage just playing for fun. The key at this vulnerable stage is to keep children playing the sports they enjoy, if not on school or youth sport teams, then informally with friends. Some middle school children may have to find other pleasurable ways to continue enjoying playing sports if they are not part of an organized team, and it is up to recreational sport specialists to provide these experiences.

High School

By high school, it's usually the competitive athletes who play both school sports and outside competitive organized sports. As spaces on these teams are limited, some adolescents who may still really enjoy playing sports can't because of their demanding academic, social, and work schedules. In these situations, recreational sport specialists need to provide an outlet for this competition through unstructured informal sports in which individuals can participate when their busy schedules permit. For those with less constraining schedules, intramural and extramural sport with different leagues for different skill levels (i.e., competitive A, competitive B, or recreational) and club sports may be appropriate.

College/University

For college/university students, a mix of programming areas is important, as are different competitive levels for previous athletes in a particular sport seeking competition versus those new to the sport seeking to play recreationally. Team sport may not be fun or enjoyable for some, so individual or dual sports are also important to offer. Coeducational opportunities in which males and females participate together are fun for this group as is being exposed to nontraditional sports such as broomball (similar to field hockey but on ice with no skates), innertube waterpolo, walleyball, or quidditch (from Harry Potter), to name a few.

Adults

Often comprised of recent college graduates, these young professionals likely have relocated to a new city and are seeking socialization opportunities to make new friends. Many adult social clubs and sport organizations use recreational sport programming to facilitate this socialization and stress the social benefits of participating as being fun. Age-appropriate programming, such as over-35 leagues, is also important in facilitating fun and enjoyable experiences for adults (http://life.familyeducation.com/sportsmanship/sports-parents/57495.html).

Shining Example

Monroe County YMCA Family Fitness Center

The Monroe County YMCA is a not-for-profit organization governed by YMCA USA, whose philosophy is to promote wellness through a healthy mind, body, and spirit. Extensive facilities allow it to offer a wide variety of programs, which serve families, adults, and youth throughout the community of Bloomington, Indiana. Over the past two decades, the Monroe County YMCA has expanded its facilities in order to meet the demands of the community, and instated programs such as a volunteer-run scholarship program that raises $65,000 each year for youth who cannot afford the membership and program fees.

Clientele:

The Monroe County YMCA serves approximately 11,500 members each year. Its 5200 memberships are broken into several categories, including adult (37%), family (28%), two adult same household (21%), single parent household (8%), and Youth (6%).

Facilities:

The YMCA is located in a 95,000 sq. ft. building on 17 acres of land. It includes a 25 meter lap pool, an instructional pool, two whirlpools, weight rooms, men's and women's locker rooms, a dance studio, racquetball courts, two gyms, and a soccer field. In addition, it also boasts a recently renovated wellness center (with a stretch/cardio/weight room), a yoga room, and a new preschool room.

Program Details:

The Monroe County YMCA offers over 200 programs for all ages and abilities, including an exercise program for cancer patients, swim lessons, lifeguard training, weight training and fitness, wellness classes, and a youth summer camp.

Budget:

The Monroe Country YMCA's budget is approximately $2.8 million per year.

Marketing:

The YMCA uses a variety of marketing techniques, including printed materials and television ads. In addition, the Monroe County YMCA maintains an internet Web site (www.monroecountyymca.org).

Jobs and Careers:

The Monroe County YMCA is a not-for-profit organization, run by a board of directors comprised of up to 30 members who focus on policy making. There is also an 18-member leadership team, which includes an executive director in charge of board relations, community relations, fiscal budget and fundraising, and the facility; an associate executive director in charge of the facility supervision, staff training and motivation, corporate fitness and special events, and the building supervisors; and eight directors in charge of other areas of the organization. The facility itself employs 250 staff, 22 of which are full-time. In addition, the Monroe County YMCA uses the services of 400 volunteers every year.

Salary:

Salary is based upon level and area of expertise. The Monroe County YMCA stays competitive with other not-for-profit businesses within the community.

Internship:

There are some non-paid internships available to university students every semester.

Affiliated Professional Organizations:

The Monroe County YMCA encourages its employees to participate in Leadership Bloomington, a community leadership program. In addition, it requires all of its employees to hold a variety of health and safety certifications.

Conclusion

While fun and enjoyment seem like simple terms to define and operationalize when developing recreational sport activities and programs, this chapter has hopefully conveyed just how complex these terms are and how much time and effort sport psychologists have spent studying these terms in the context of sport. These findings, and the information provided in this chapter, provide the recreational sport specialist with a foundation to guide recreational sport programs. Remember that in order to truly understand how to facilitate fun and enjoyable recreational sport experiences, the recreational sport specialist also needs to comprehend the links between fun and enjoyment and flow and optimal challenge, intrinsic motivation and self-determination, achievement goal orientations, motivational climates, and individual perceptions of competence. If recreational sport activities and programs are not fun and enjoyable, then we may have drastically distorted their original meanings. The recreational sport specialist must focus on how to make recreational sport experiences more like play than work if participants are to experience the fun and enjoyment that will motivate them to continue participating. Even though notions of fun and enjoyment are personal, recreational sport specialists can focus on how to facilitate conditions whereby activities can be fun and enjoyable; without fun and enjoyment, recreational sport is just another community social service.

Bibliography

Balaguer, I., Duda, J. L., & Crespo, M. (1999). Motivational climate and goal orientations as predictors of perceptions of improvement, satisfaction and coach ratings among tennis players. *Scandinavian Journal of Medicine & Science in Sport, 9,* 381-388.

Bengoechea, E.G., Stream, W.B., & Williams, D.J. (2004). Understanding and promoting fun in youth sport: Coaches' perspectives. *Physical education and sport pedagogy, 9*(2), 197-214.

Boyd, M. P., & Yin, Z. (1996). Cognitive-affective sources of sport enjoyment in adolescent sport participants. *Adolescence, 31,* 383-395.

Butcher, J., Lindner, K. J., & Johns, D. P. (2002). Withdrawal from competitive youth sport: A retrospective ten-year study. *Journal of Sport Behaviour, 25*(2), 145-163.

Cote, J., Baker, J., & Abernethy, B. (2003). From play to practice: A developmental framework for the acquisition of expertise in team sport. In J. Starkes & K. A. Ericsson (Eds.), *Expert performance in sports: Advances in research* on sport expertise (pp. 89-114). Champaign, IL: Human Kinetics.

Cote, J., Strachan, L., & Fraser-Thomas, J. (2008). Participation, personal development, and performance through youth sport. In N. L. Holt (Ed.), *Positive youth development through sport* (pp. 34-46). New York, NY: Routledge.

Crocker, P., Hoar, S., McDonough, M., Kowalski, K., & Niefer, C. (2004). Emotional experience in youth sport. In M. Weiss (Ed.), *Developmental sport and exercise psychology: A lifespan perspective* (pp. 197-221). Morgantown, WV: Fitness Information Technology.

Csikszentmihalyi, M. (2000). *Beyond boredom and anxiety.* San Francisco, CA: Jossey-Bass.

Csikszentmihalyi, M. (1997). *Finding flow: The psychology of engagement with everyday life.* New York: Basic Books.

Csikszentmihalyi, M. (1990). *Flow: The psychology of optimal experience.* New York, NY: Harper & Row.

Csikszentmihalyi, M. (1982). The value of sports. In J. T. Partington, T. Orlick, & J. H. Salmela (Eds.), *Sport in perspective* (pp. 122-127). Ottawa: Coaching Association of Canada.

Deci, E.L., & Ryan, R.M. (1985). *Intrinsic motivation and self-determination in human behaviour.* New York, NY: Plenum Press.

Deci, E. L., & Ryan, R. M. (2000). The 'what' and 'why' of goal pursuits: Human needs and the self-determination of behavior. *Psychological Inquiry, 11,* 227-268.

Deci, E. L., & Ryan, R. M. (2002). Chapter 19: Self-determination research: Reflections and future directions. In E. L. Deci & R. M. Ryan (Eds.), *Handbook of self-determination research,* (pp. 431-439). Rochester, NY: University of Rochester Press.

Deci, E. L., & Ryan, R. M. (2008). Self-determination theory: A macrotheory of human motivation, development and health. *Canadian Psychology, 49*(3), 182-185.

Duda, J. L. (1996). Maximizing motivation in sport and physical education among children and adolescents: The case for greater task involvement. *Quest, 48*(3), 290-302.

Duda, J. L. & Balaguer, I. (2007). The coach-created motivational climate. In D. Lavalee & S. Jowett (Eds.), *Social psychology of sport* (pp. 117-138). Champaign, IL: Human Kinetics.

Ewing, M., & Seefeldt, V. (1989). *Participation and attrition patterns in American agency-sponsored and interscholastic sports.* North Palm Beach, FL: Sporting Goods Manufacturers Association.

Fraser-Thomas, J. L., Cote, J., & Deakin, J. (2008). Youth sport programs: An avenue to foster positive youth development. *Physical Education and Sport Pedagogy, 10,* 19-40.

Gould, D., & Horn, T, (1984). Participation motivation in young athletes. In J. M. Silva & R .S. Weinberg (Eds.), *Psychological foundations of sport* (pp. 359-370). Champaign, IL: Human Kinetics.

Harter, S. (1981). *A model of intrinsic mastery motivation in children: Individual differences and developmental change.* Minnesota symposia on child psychology. Vol. 14. Hillsdale, N.J.

Harter, S. (1978). Effectance motivation reconsidered. Toward a developmental model. *Human Development, 21,* 34-64.

Hedstrom, R., & Gould, D. (2004). Research in youth sports: Critical issues status. Retrieved from http://hollistonsoccer.net/image/web/coaches/CriticalIssuesYouthSports%20(2).pdf

Henderson, K. A., Glancy, M., & Little, S. (1999). Putting the fun into physical activity. *Parks and Recreation, 70*(8), 43-45, 49.

Holt, N. L., Garcia, E., & Strean, W. B. (2001). Play, games, and fun in physical activity: Perceptions of instructors. *Research Quarterly for Exercise and Sport, 72,* 66.

Huizinga, J. (1950). *Homo ludens: A study of the play element in culture.* Boston, MA: Beacon.

Jackson, S. A. (2000). Joy, fun, and flow state in sport. In Y. L. Hanin (Ed.), *Emotions in sport* (pp. 135-155). Champaign, IL: Human Kinetics.

Jagacinski, C.M., & Nicholls, J.G. (1987). Competence and affect in task involvement and ego involvement: The impact of social comparison information. *Journal of Educational Psychology, 79*(2), 107-114.

Karabetsos, J. D. (1988). Where does the walking giant belong? *National Intramural–Recreational Sports Association Journal, 12*(1), 34-36.

Kilpatrick, M., Hebert, E., & Jacobsen, D. (2002). Physical activity motivation: A practitioner's guide to self-determination theory. *Journal of Physical Education, Recreation and Dance, 73*(4), 36-41.

Leppke, A., & Tenoschok, M. (2003). Social factors affecting intramural and sports participation in middle schools. *Teaching Elementary Physical Education,* 29-30.

Lindner, K. J., Johns, D. P., & Butcher, J. (1991). Factors in withdrawal from youth sport: A proposed model. *Journal of Sport Behaviour, 14*(1), 3-18.

Lundberg, N. (2007, January). Creating motivational climates. *Parks and recreation,* 22-26.

Mandigo, J., & Couture, R. T. (1996). An overview of the components of fun in physical education, organized sport and physical activity programs. *AVANTE, 2*(3), 56-72.

Mandigo, J. L., & Holt, N. L. (2002). Putting theory into practice: Enhancing motivation through OPTIMAL strategies. *AVANTE, 8*(3), 21-29.

McCarthy, P. J., & Jones, M. V. (2007). A qualitative study of sport enjoyment in the sampling years. *The Sport Psychologist, 21*, 400-416.

McCarthy, P. J., Jones, M. V., & Clark-Carter, D. (2008). Understanding enjoyment in youth sport: A developmental perspective. *Psychology of Sport and Exercise, 9*, 142-156.

National Association for Sport and Physical Education. (2004). *Physical activity for children: A statement of guidelines for children ages 5-12.* Reston, VA: National Association for Sport and Physical Education.

New York University School of Medicine. (2005, April). Sports: More than just fun. *About our kids: A letter for parents by the NYU Child Study Center, 3*(8), 1-2.

Nicholls, J. G. (1978). The development of the concepts of effort and ability, perception of own attainment, and the understanding that difficult tasks require more ability. *Child Development, 49*, 800-814.

Nicholls, J. G. (1984). Achievement motivation: Conceptions of ability, subjective experience, task choice, and performance. *Psychological Review, 91*(3), 328-346.

Nicholls, J. G. (1989). *The competitive ethos and democratic education.* Boston, MA: Harvard University Press.

Nicholls, J. G., & Miller, A. T. (1984). Development and its discontents: The differentiation of the concept of ability. *Advances in motivation and achievement: A research annual, 3*, 185-218.

Scanlan, T. K., Carpenter, P. J., Schmidt, G. W., Simons, J. P., & Keeler, B. (1993). An introduction to the sport commitment model. *Journal of Sport and Exercise Psychology, 15*, 1-15.

Scanlan, T. K., Carpenter, P. J., Simons, J. P., Schmidt, G. W., & Keeler, B. (1993). The sport commitment model: Measurement development for the youth-sport domain. *Journal of Sport and Exercise Psychology, 15*, 16-38.

Scanlan, T. K., & Lewthwaite, R. (1986). Social psychological aspects of competition for male youth sport participants: IV. Predictors of enjoyment. *Journal of Sport and Exercise Psychology, 15*, 1-15.

Scanlan, T. K., & Simons, J. P. (1992). The construct of sport enjoyment. In Glyn C. Roberts (Ed.), *Motivation in sport and exercise.* Champaign, IL: Human Kinetics.

Scanlan, T. K., Stein, G. L., & Ravizza, K. (1989). An in-depth study of former elite figure skaters: II. Source of enjoyment. *Journal of Sport and Exercise Psychology, 11*, 65-83.

Seifriz, J., Duda, J. L., & Chi, L. (1992). The relationship of perceived motivational climate to intrinsic motivation and beliefs about success in basketball. *Journal of Sport and Exercise Psychology, 14*, 375-391.

Smith, R. E., Smoll, F. L., & Cumming, S. P. (2007). Effects of a motivational climate intervention for coaches on young athletes' sport performance anxiety. *Journal of Sport & Exercise Psychology, 29*, 39-59.

The National Alliance for Youth Sports. (n.d.). Retrieved from http://www.nays.org

Turman, P. D. (2007). Parental sport involvement: Parental influence to encourage young athlete continued sport participation. *Journal of Family Communication, 7*(3), 151-175.

Vallerand, R. J., & Bissonnette, R. (1992). Intrinsic, extrinsic, and amotivational styles as predictors of behavior: A prospective study. *Journal of Personality, 60*(3), 599-619.

Vallerand, R. J., & Losier, G. F. (1999). An integrative analysis of intrinsic and extrinsic motivation in sport. *Journal of Applied Sport Psychology, 11*, 142-169.

Voelkl, J., Ellis, G., & Walker, J. (2003, August). Go with the flow: How to help people have optimal recreation experiences. *Parks and Recreation, 38*, 20-28.

Walker, J. (2002). *Exploring the influence of the individual's ability to experience flow while participating in a group-dependent activity on individual satisfaction with a group's performance.* Unpublished doctoral dissertation, Clemson University, Clemson, South Carolina.

Wall, M., & Cote, J. (2007). Developmental activities that lead to dropout and investment in sport. *Physical Education and Sport Pedagogy, 12*(1), 77-87.

Wankel, L. M., & Berger, B. G. (1991). The personal and social benefits of sport and physical activity. In B. L. Driver, P. J. Brown, & G. L. Peterson (Eds.), *Benefits of leisure* (pp. 121-144). State College, PA: Venture.

Wankel, L. M., & Kreisel, P. S. (1985). Factors underlying enjoyment of youth sports: Sport and age group comparisons. *Journal of Sport Psychology, 7*, 51-64.

Wankel, L. M., & Sefton, J. M. (1989). A season-long investigation of fun in youth sports. *Journal of Sport and Exercise Psychology, 11*(4), 355-366.

Weiss, M. (2004). *Developmental sport and exercise psychology: A lifespan perspective.* Morgantown, WV: Fitness Information Technology.

Weiss, M. R. (2000). *Motivating kids in physical activity.* Washington, DC: President's Council on Physical Fitness and Sports.

Weiss, M. R., Kimmel, L. A., & Smith, A. L. (2001). Determinants of sport commitment among junior tennis players: Enjoyment as a mediating variable. *Pediatric Exercise Science, 13,* 131–144.

Weiss, M., & Raedeke, T. (2004). Developmental sport and exercise psychology: Research status on youth and directions toward a lifespan perspective. In M. Weiss (Ed.), *Developmental sport and exercise psychology: A lifespan perspective* (pp. 1-26). Morgantown, WV: Fitness Information Technology.

Weiss, M., & Williams, L. (2004). The why of youth sport involvement: A developmental perspective on motivational processes. In M. Weiss (Ed.), *Developmental sport and exercise psychology: A lifespan perspective* (pp. 223-268). Morgantown, WV: Fitness Information Technology.

Wiersma, L. D. (2001). Conceptualization and development of the Sources of Enjoyment in Youth Sport Questionnaire. *Measurement in Physical Education and Exercise Science, 5,* 153–177.

Wold, B., & Kannas, L. (1993). Sport motivation among young adolescents in Finland, Norway and Sweden. *Scandinavian Journal of Medicine & Science in Sports, 3,* 283-291.

Wolff, R. (1997). *Good sports: The concerned parent's guide to competitive youth sports.* Champaign, IL: Coaches Choice.

Part III

PROGRAM DELIVERY

Part III focuses on sport program design and delivery. In doing so, sport serves as a product that is put into production in order to provide participants with a positive and developmental experience. This is accomplished through four distinct program delivery systems: instructional sports, which enhance one's skill; casual and self-directed informal sports; structured tournaments in both intramural and extramural sports; and group organizations, such as club sports. This portion of the text provides detailed methods and techniques significant to successful program delivery, which represents the key information to the success of the recreational sport specialist.

CHAPTER 7

Instructional Sport

CHAPTER OBJECTIVES

After reading this chapter, you will understand the systems that deliver instructional sport, be familiar with popular instructional delivery options, know the criteria for critiquing an instructional sport instructor, identify ways to assess instructional sport credentials, be aware of predelivery instructional sport considerations, understand methods of instruction, be able to identify key motivators in instructional sport, appreciate the support that instructional aids provide, and gain insight into the evaluation of sport instruction.

KEY CONCEPTS

Instructional systems
Instructional options
Instructor criteria
Credential assessment
Predelivery preparations

Methods
Motivators
Instructional aids
Evaluation

Introduction

Instructional sport is the area of recreational sport that provides knowledge and skills that lead to positive participation. Instructional sport begins in the home, and family members provide introductory opportunities to develop lifetime sport participation. Outside the home, the most important occurrence in instructional sport has been the development of instructional sport programs in communities, private clubs, YMCAs, YWCAs, Boys and Girls Clubs, commercial and industrial agencies, the military, resorts, and country clubs. As interest in sport learning increased, instructional sport programs expanded into these noneducational settings to supplement existing recreational activities. A quality instructional sport program serves as a natural springboard to ongoing participation in recreational sport. Recreational sport specialists need to recognize this potential and learn how to develop and deliver instructional sport programs.

Systems of Delivery

The roots of all sport participation, whether recreational, athletic, or professional, lie in some type of instruction. The delivery of instructional sport is influenced not only by participant needs but also by instructional sport's purpose and the systems that provide ways to learn about sport. These systems are educational, recreational, athletic, and professional.

Educational
The educational approach to learning about sport relies on the formal academic process. This is the delivery used in elementary schools, preparatory and secondary schools, and colleges and universities. Within these formal educational settings, sport is taught under the same premise as subjects such as history, math, and English. These programs are called classes and are taught by educated, certified teachers. Classes usually have many students with varied backgrounds. The teacher chooses the content of the course based on the growth and development patterns

of the students, their ages, and their capabilities. Various sport skill levels are taught according to progress in ability. The teacher sets the guidelines for delivering the material and measuring the students' progress in skill and knowledge. Formal grading reflects the learning achieved by students.

When teaching recreational sport in this context, instructors should take into account the National Association for Sport and Physical Education's (NASPE, http://www.aahperd.org/naspe/standards/nationalstandards/pestandards.cfm) national standards for physical education. These standards encourage the development of physically educated individuals who have the knowledge, skills, and confidence to enjoy a lifetime of healthful physical activity as the goal of physical education. More specifically, NASPE outlines six standards that specify a physically educated person should do the following:

- demonstrate competency in motor skills and movement patterns needed to perform a variety of physical activities;

- demonstrate understanding of movement concepts, principles, strategies, and tactics as they apply to the learning and performance of physical activities;

- participate regularly in physical activity;

- achieve and maintain a health-enhancing level of physical fitness;

- exhibit responsible personal and social behavior that respects self and others in physical activity settings; and

- value physical activity for health, enjoyment, challenge, self-expression, and/or social interaction.

While some of these standards may be more applicable to physical activity or physical education in general, the recreational sport specialist should consider these as broader goals when taking an educational approach to instructing recreational sport.

Recreational

Instructional sport delivered in nonacademic settings developed when people outside schools began to desire recreational outlets through sport. The recreational approach to instructional sport is present in private clubs, YMCAs and YWCAs, Boys and Girls Clubs, military bases, municipal centers, churches, and industrial and commercial recreational facilities. Instructional sport in these settings is more informal than in educational settings. Although learning about a sport is important, emphasis is also on enjoying the experience and gaining satisfaction while improving knowledge and skills.

Instructional sport programs are referred to as lessons, clinics, or workshops. The length of sessions can vary from one to two hours per week for private lessons to six to eight weeks for large groups. Programs may be coed or gender-specific and may involve a variety of ages. Instructional sport programs are usually conducted at local sport sites such as gymnasiums, fields, and courts and are scheduled for times when people are most likely to attend.

Athletic

The athletic approach to instructional sport focuses on the margin of excellence, or participants "being the best that they can be." Participants associated with a school varsity team, an industrial sport team, a club sport, or an Amateur Athletic Union (AAU) team often pursue this margin of excellence. It is also pursued by individuals who challenge themselves to succeed athletically, such as someone who wishes to complete a marathon or a bicycle trip with high expectations.

In this type of system, the athlete's goal is to gain as much skill and knowledge as possible. Performance is crucial because success is often measured by wins and losses or other standards of performance. Because success is such a large part of the athletic approach, all schools, club teams, and AAU teams use coaches. These coaches make the decisions about delivery and instruction; thus, most of the team's success or failure comes from the coach's abilities as an instructor. Emphasis is on personal performance as well as team performance. Only a select number of participants, usually the best performers, become involved in an athletic instructional program. The coach as instructor influences all aspects of mental and physical training in an attempt to create the optimal conditions for success.

Professional

The professional approach to learning sport is probably the most visible system. Almost every major city in the United States supports professional sport, whether it is football, baseball, hockey, basketball, tennis, or soccer. In professional sport, the bottom line is to influence the athletes' margin of excellence through instruction so that the athletes gain enough success to generate a profit for the organization. Professional sport organizations are corporations, with owners, presidents, and executive board members making decisions. Coaches and athletes are often paid large amounts of money for their involvement. Instruction for its own sake receives less emphasis because professional athletes already know how to perform. Most practice time is devoted to maintaining and refining skills.

Coaches in professional systems are often former professional athletes. Former professional athletes are also employed as instructors in individual sports such as tennis, golf, and bowling. These individuals are teaching professionals who instruct sport for a profit, most often at places such as a golf course, racquetball club, tennis club, martial arts studio, country club, or resort. These teaching professionals are usually certified by the governing bodies or specialty organizations of their respective sport. As in the recreational approach, lessons are given to one person at a time or to a large group. These individual instructors play a major role in generating income that is fundamental to the success of the business.

Types of Instruction

In the recreational world, there are three types of instruction sessions where sport is delivered as a learning experience. Each type is a unique approach to attracting participants based on their individual needs and interests in their sport, which is often influenced by what they can afford. Such instruction is not the same as the instruction that takes place in a formal class because it is not an academic delivery of sport in an educational setting. For this text's purpose, the single instructional meeting or structured learning experience is called a session, which is then organized into three types of delivery: lesson, clinic, and workshop.

Lesson

Lessons are one of the most popular types of instructional sport and are delivered in all settings by certified teaching professionals. Such lessons are geared toward individuals or small groups and take the form of private and semiprivate sessions. These sessions are usually scheduled in advance at a time that works well for both the participant and the instructor. They can also be arranged in packages of a certain number of sessions over a designated period of time. Private lessons provide individual attention, which allows for uninterrupted instruction regarding problems and weaknesses. They can be taken by individuals of any ability level; however, such specialized instruction can be costly. Semiprivate lessons incorporate a few more people and cost less than private lessons.

The instructing and learning can become vital to the success and satisfaction of all involved in lessons. Lessons create a special relationship between instructor and participant to the point where there may be great dependency on the instructor's ability to enhance performance. For this reason, lessons in all sports are widespread and continue to multiply wherever sport enthusiasts seek to improve their ability.

Clinic

The next type of instruction entails systems that allow a large number of individuals to learn about a sport. The number of participants depends on the instructor's ability and resources available (staff, facilities, and equipment) to meet the demand. Such an effort is usually planned and promoted with the intent to attract many participants. Because of the large number of participants, there may be more than one instructor involved. All instructors must be coordinated to contribute to the learning experience. Coordination requires presession planning along with anticipation of details such as techniques and methods to be applied. To offer the complete learning experience, the primary instructor should have experience not only in the sport but also in managing a large group. How well each session is organized and produced can be critical to participant satisfaction. Clinics are usually scheduled to meet once or twice a week for an hour or so over four to eight weeks. Clinic fees are usually lower than private or small group lessons, while large numbers can provide an excellent source of income for management.

Workshop

A workshop is similar to a clinic but is usually a one-time experience. Workshops can last from an hour up to a full day. Participants experience instruction on a particular area of a sport or an entire sport. Workshops can be promoted by focusing on participants who have a particular need, weakness, or problem area in their sport performance or to generate an interest in a particular sport. Specialized workshops could also include skilled performance areas, rules and regulations, strategies, equipment, and so on. Workshops can take any number of approaches to facilitate the learning experience. Certain popular sports as well as instructors can attract large numbers of participants, creating a meaningful way to learn about sport as well as a significant means of income for management.

Levels of Instruction

All instructional sport programs must determine in advance the level of instruction to be offered. Such decisions are influenced by the sport, participant age, and, most important, ability. For program delivery purposes, the participation can be generally broken down into three levels: beginner, intermediate, and advanced. These levels can be integrated, depending on the sport and participant circumstances.

Beginner

All sports undertake varying degrees of complexity beginning with more information than most realize. One's ability to grasp this information can be reflected in his or her ability to comprehend and perform. Learning begins with the basic knowledge of sport skills, hence the beginner. Basic information about a sport is fundamental and necessary to learn. Individuals starting a sport from the very beginning must learn the basic fundamentals. Often participants can be confused or lack the ability to grasp what is being taught. It is the instructor's ability and desire to provide help and assistance that bridges the gap between knowing nothing to making positive progress. Beginners usually have to dedicate themselves to extensive practice and trial and error in order to see success. Instruction at this level is demanding but very rewarding because participants' achievements and objectives can be very positive.

Intermediate

Once participants have grasped certain sport skills, rules and regulations, and experience, they may be determined as intermediate, or able to participate with a good amount of satisfaction. At this point, some learning can get into more complex options for success at the sport. Practice and training become more intense and even enjoyable. Sport competition is necessary to create the needed experience and learning. Usually at this point, participants are quite motivated and looking for greater challenges in their sport. Instructing is unique because the participant may not be motivated to be the best but instead be satisfied to just participate and have fun. Learning and making progress can be more important than winning.

Advanced

At the advanced level, the sport athlete often cannot get enough of his or her sport and looks forward to the next competition. Lessons refine skills, enhance overall ability, and deal with sport details at the highest level. The participant's ability is truly tested, and winning and losing become very important. When a loss occurs, it reverts back to the instructor to analyze and discuss what went wrong and then work at improving for the next contest. Training and practice is concentrated and regular, taking up a lot of time in one day. Instruction is at its highest level with the most knowledgeable and qualified person to get the job done.

Selecting Instructors

The inclusion of instructional sport within recreational sport is based on several factors, including the interests of the target population, funding, facility and equipment availability, and instructor ability. Of these factors, qualified instructors are critical because the instructor makes direct contact with the participant and is primarily responsible for designing and delivering a meaningful learning experience.

The recreational sport specialist is usually not responsible for instructing but is involved in hiring and supervising the instructors. Because instructional sport occurs within a recreational agency, the requirements for instruction may vary, and the recreational sport specialist must be able to find an individual who meets such requirements.

An absence of guidelines for personnel selection opens the door for criticism and suggests that the recreational sport specialist has an unprofessional attitude. A lack of criteria, however, does not necessarily stem from indifference but from inexperience in hiring and supervising instructional sport personnel. Therefore, the purpose of this section is to explore how to select instructors within the context of a recreational setting. See Chapter 11 for more details on hiring personnel.

Training and Background

Two main avenues exist for finding instructors. The first avenue is soliciting individuals with formal training in instructional sport. The second is finding individuals with an informal background in instructional sport.

The instructor with formal training typically carries certification that verifies training and experience in a sport. In many instances, certification also specifies a ranking, which indicates the person's level of expertise. The certification process is customarily handled by national sport associations or similar organizations recognized as sport governing bodies. Establishing contact with these organizations is one way of identifying local individuals to contact about becoming instructors.

Another formal certification process is physical education teaching programs. Individuals who complete degree programs are usually certified for specific age groups and focus on one or two sports. These individuals are highly qualified in the academic approach to sport. Such individuals can be recruited from college and university placement offices and conferences. Quite often, securing instructors with formal preparation can be costly and difficult to justify in a recreation agency. The goal, however, should always be to select the most qualified yet affordable instructor.

The recreational sport specialist often deals with instructors who have informal preparation. Although they carry no formal credentials or certifications, they may have considerable knowledge, skill, and experience from investing many hours in a sport. People in this category may not pursue instructional sport as a career but prefer concentrating on one or two sports and becoming involved as time and opportunity permit. Their sport interest also may not have a national organization or certification program through which they can pursue formal training.

Some instructors with informal preparation come from athletic or professional sport and lack certification from a national organization. The absence of such credentials means that the recreational sport specialist has to decide whether personality and experience make the person a qualified instructor. The person may have had enough practice and study time in a sport to parallel or exceed the requirements of any certification program. Noncertified individuals may also have a reputation that reflects positively on their ability to be an instructor.

Hiring personnel with informal preparation, although not acceptable by some standards, is better than hiring personnel with little or no preparation at all. If using a noncertified instructor, the recreational sport specialist must assume greater responsibility in the design and control of the instructional sport program until the ability of the person can be fully ascertained.

Planning

In the early stages of instructor recruitment, the recreational sport specialist should use systematic planning to ensure that he or she anticipates the position's requirements in order to find the best instructors. Determining the number of instructors depends on the number of programs offered and the potential income and expenses involved. The recreational sport specialist should compare the advantages and disadvantages of using a single full-time instructor to teach many lessons versus using several part-time instructors. Plan the program based on an ideal schedule and potential. After planning, cut back as the instructor resource pool becomes identified and structured as best as possible to meet the participant's interest.

Another planning consideration is choosing criteria for the abilities of each instructor. A recreational sport specialist could face a dilemma if instructors from an athletic or professional background have excellent sport skills and complete understanding of their sport's strategies but cannot deliver their knowledge to participants, especially beginners. Instructors from informal backgrounds may have exceptional skills but may not have the necessary technical knowledge of instructional methodology and techniques. When setting these standards, focus first on sport knowledge and skill, then on ability to instruct. An individual can always be taught how to instruct.

Announcement

The next step is to develop a job description, including what the position requires. Design the job description as an announcement that describes the responsibilities of the position. The announcement content will vary depending on the form of solicitation used. After completing the announcement, decide how to solicit applicants. The announcement can be shared through school newspapers, job fairs, word of mouth, employment offices, physical education departments, national organizations, club sport members, and various media. Which of these outlets works best depends on prior experience and the sport to be taught. In addition, the recreational sport specialist could seek advice from colleagues or look at what other agencies have done. Other options include classified ads, display ads, the Internet, information packets, and flyers.

Application

No matter how people learn about an instructional opportunity, they need to be aware of the job requirements. Required items could include a completed application, letter of interest, telephone call of interest, letters of reference, results from skill and knowledge tests, academic transcripts, copy of certification, and résumé. Include minimum requirements in the job announcement. Stating minimum requirements saves time for both the applicant and the recreational sport specialist. Some points to consider when determining minimum requirements include certification levels, letters of recommendation, high school or college degrees, types of experience, and minimum physical effort. The recreational sport specialist can determine most of these considerations ahead of time with staff or advisory committee members involved with the instructional sport program.

Assessing Credentials

Screening applicants may be time consuming. Whether screening is completed by individuals or by a committee, it should be taken seriously because instructors play a major role in the success of a program. Set aside some uninterrupted time for reviewing applicants. Take notes, especially if there are a large number of applicants, and create a checklist of factors important for the position (see Figure 7.1). This can become a rating system for each applicant.

After reviewing the application and background of all applicants, the recreational sport specialist can conduct a careful review of credentials. Judging the appropriateness of credentials and other applicant attributes is essential to make the best possible selection. Gather basic information on each candidate from the application forms, including the following areas. Each area pertains to applicants with formal or informal preparation.

EMPLOYMENT SCREENING FORM: TENNIS INSTRUCTORS

Candidate's name _____ Date _____ Time _____

Category	Points	Category	Points
Position		Tournament experience	
Head pro	12	High school	4
Assistant pro	10	Sanctioned	6
Staff pro	6	State	9
Total	_____	Regional	12
		Total	_____
Certification			
USPTA	12	Facility worked at	
USPTR	12	Indoor	10
Total	_____	Outdoor	10
		Outdoor lighted	5
Coaching		Hard court	5
Juniors	6	Hard true or clay	5
High school	8	*Total*	_____
College	10		
Pro	12	Tournament scheduling	9
Travel team	8	*Total*	_____
Total	_____		
		Eligibility	7
Instructing		*Total*	_____
Children	5		
Juniors	8	Computer knowledge	8
Adults	12	*Total*	_____
Handicapped	12		
Total	_____	Promotions	8
		Total	_____
Level			
Beginner	5	Public relations	8
Intermediate	8	*Total*	_____
Advanced	10		
Total	_____	Professional development	8
		Total	_____
Played as			
Junior	3	Recommendation letter	10
High school	7	*Total*	_____
Total	_____		
College degree	15		
Total	_____	GRAND TOTAL	_____

Figure 7.1. Employment Screening Form for Tennis Instructors. From *Recreational Sport Management* by Richard F. Mull, Kathryn G. Bayless, & Lynn M. Jamieson, 2005, Champaign, IL: Human Kinetics.

Knowledge and Skill

Ascertain what the person knows about a sport in terms of rules, regulations, strategy, facilities, equipment, and skill development. In addition, take into account how much the person knows about instructional methods, communication techniques, teaching techniques, and instructional aids. Inquire about qualifications for working with different skill levels and ages. In essence, solicit information that reveals the extent of the individual's knowledge of how to deliver instruction. Later, this chapter discusses the instructional process and sport content to assist the recreational sport specialist in designing questions to critique an individual's knowledge and skills for instructional sport.

Willingness

The first indication that the recreational sport specialist should not create an instructional sport program is when he or she cannot find good instructors. Some sports are so popular that it is easy to secure instructors, while it may be much more difficult to find qualified instructors in sports that are less common. In either case, the recreational sport specialist should not resort to pleading for instructors. Low pay or volunteer services by the instructors can easily result in a lack of willingness or a morale problem that damages the quality of the program.

Volunteers should have high interest and motivation because by nature volunteering stems from a desire to serve. Paid personnel may or may not be as motivated or as willing as volunteers; however, they will probably maintain interest because they are being paid. In practice, there is no guaranteed means to determine whether a volunteer or paid position is the best approach in terms of willingness. The recreational sport specialist simply has to assess candidates through interaction. One thing is certain: Knowledge and skill are useless unless the instructor is willing and self-motivated.

Reputation

Experience handling personnel interviews or reviewing credentials does not guarantee the ability to accurately judge character or potential behavior. Unless the recreational sport specialist pays thorough attention to reputation, he or she may select individuals based on a good interview only to find out later that they are less capable or qualified than they initially appeared. This risk is minimized by carefully evaluating the reputation of an applicant as an individual and instructor.

Information concerning reputation is most commonly obtained through the applicant's references. Whenever possible, confirm these references and cross-check them with additional sources provided by the applicant.

Experience

Background can provide insight into what an instructor can accomplish. Critique experience by looking at age, maturity, and time involved with the sport. Some of this information can be quantified by years, months, weeks, or hours. Additional areas of experience include lecture or speaking ability and involvement with particular age groups or skill levels. Experience can be hard to determine for potential instructors who are seeking their first opportunity at instructional sport. In such cases, concentrate on other areas besides experience. Do not automatically disregard these applicants unless the nature of the position requires previous experience. Thoroughly check the background of an applicant who lists a multitude of positions to determine if there is some history of difficulty in holding a position.

Enthusiasm

To some extent, the recreational sport specialist can judge enthusiasm by learning about the candidate's previous experience. Boundless energy is not necessarily a good sign, while commitment to working with sport participants goes a long way. It is a good sign when a candidate has a special interest in positively extending and providing the learning process. Enthusiasm for the sport and teaching can often compensate for a less-than-desirable environment or secondhand equipment. Enthusiasm can help an instructor withstand the redundancy of teaching the same routine, which is often necessary in sport skill development. Instructional sport often involves long, tedious hours, and sometimes the enthusiasm of the instructor makes all the difference in participant satisfaction. Assessing the instructor's interest, spirit, and excitement for the sport and for instructing can be critical.

Predelivery Considerations

Familiarity with various considerations involved in preparing for instructional sport before delivery will help the recreational sport specialist supervise and improve the quality of instructional sport programs. Such predelivery considerations include planning, orientation, on-site review, participant assessment, format development, and content.

Planning

An instructor must plan each phase of the program and the content of each session. The instructor identifies general and specific topics as outlines for the overall delivery, polishing lesson delivery to eliminate an off-the-cuff instructional method. Sound planning is essential in anticipating problems and identifying alternative strategies for unexpected situations. Good planning is the primary way to ensure that the instructional process meets the desired objectives.

Orientation

Create an opportunity for the instructor and potential participants to meet in an orientation session before starting an instructional sport program. During the orientation meeting, review the topics and goals of the program. Highlight the expected benefits for the participants, and discuss procedural matters such as fees, attendance, safety, lockers, dressing facilities, showers, and equipment.

An orientation session provides an opportunity for participants to ask questions about the program. By answering their questions before the program begins, the instructor can avoid misunderstandings. The instructor uses the meeting to learn the concerns and personalities of the participants, and, accordingly, can adapt teaching methods to the individuals. Orientation meetings should be used to motivate, reassure, enlighten, and challenge participants to become involved.

On-Site Review

The environment of an instructional session can affect how well participants learn and can influence their attitude toward the overall program. Inspect the location and double-check its availability before the scheduled start for a program. Verify that the location is free from noise and distractions. Check the size to make sure it can accommodate the number of participants scheduled. Also, if relevant, consider seating capacity, equipment availability, parking, concessions, and locker and shower facilities.

When reviewing the environment, consider it from the point of view of the participant. Participants in a limited space will perceive a situation differently than a group with adequate space. The size of the group in relation to the available space and equipment influences instruction method and delivery. Another aspect of the environment is whether the instruction is outdoors. Try to minimize distractions and plan for weather conditions. Similarly, unpredictable situations can happen at indoor sites, so be prepared to adjust accordingly.

Participants

Focus on individual capabilities and needs when designing and implementing any instructional sport program. Homogeneous grouping of individuals by age, sex, skill, and ability is common within instructional sport, but the recreational sport specialist should organize a program only after reviewing current participants and allowing for exceptions. What works for one individual or group may not work for others. Consider similarities and differences, ages and maturity, interests, socioeconomic backgrounds, and learning readiness before finishing instruction plans.

Format

Along with the content for the instructional sport program, the recreational sport specialist needs to develop the format for each session. In planning individual lessons consider attendance, announcements, warm-up or lead-up activities, skill or knowledge information, demonstrations, active participation or practice, reminders, questions, and dismissal. The time allotted for each topic will vary depending on participant characteristics, skill level, and instructor effectiveness. Generally, schedule active participation and synthesis of knowledge and skill for the beginning of the lesson. Use instruction methods that make learning easier, not only to improve effectiveness as an instructor but also to encourage continued participation.

Content

Content is the information and skill instruction that defines a lesson. Because each sport is unique, the lesson or session content is often varied and complex. Factors such as number of participants; motivation; purpose of the sport; whether it is an individual, dual, or team sport; skill requirements; fitness level; age and maturity; and readiness to learn all affect content.

Two issues to consider when developing content are the participants' mental and physical characteristics and safety. Some participants learn more easily than others. Some participants are more coordinated, more flexible, faster, have better timing, have better judgment, and have a wider range of motor skills than others. Safety involves keeping the participants free of injury and protected at all times. Participants have to be kept within their physiological limits. Site temperature, exhaustion levels, and the state of protective equipment and facilities all affect participants' safety.

Emphasize safety precautions with instructors of high-risk sports such as weight lifting, wrestling, rugby, football, archery, mountain climbing, martial arts, and gymnastics. Instructors of high-risk sport can be inattentive to risk factors due to inexperience with injuries. It is difficult to see the potential for injury when it has never happened before. The only way to keep instructors aware of safety is to remind them of their responsibility in this area.

Although instructional content can include a variety of information, the general categories are history, rules and regulations, skills, facilities, equipment, strategy, and factors such as supervision and officiating that affect the control of participation in the sport.

During instructional sport programs, participants spend most of the time on basic sport knowledge and drills. However, as their abilities improve, they may spend more time on rules and regulations, strategy, and officiating. The main consideration when designing content is the knowledge and ability of participants, or whether they are beginner, intermediate, or advanced in the sport.

Methods of Instruction

Instructional methods depend on the instructors' abilities and experience. They also vary from agency to agency according to how the instructional process is perceived. The recreational sport specialist needs to know these methods to assist instructors and monitor their performance. The methods discussed here are lecture, discussion, demonstration, part and whole, drills, and game and play experience.

Lecture

Of all instruction methods, the lecture is the most common. Lectures can be problem centered, argumentative, or knowledge based. Perhaps the biggest advantage of the lecture method is that it can present a large amount of information to many people at once.

However, the lecture method is impractical for skill acquisition because most skill learning occurs through active, two-way communication. Lecturing on sport information such as history, rules, regulations, strategies, and skill is useful, but learning skills requires practice.

Discussion

The discussion method is participant centered and works well for problem solving. It allows feedback and understanding of a participant's view. The discussion method works best in small groups because it allows everyone to pool their ideas. This method is used most often in seminars, clinics, workshops, debates, case studies, and role playing. While the discussion method has a place in instructional sport, it should be limited to specific, topical situations. This method is best used in the educational and recreational approaches to instructional sport.

Demonstration

Unlike the previous instruction methods, demonstration provides a visual image of the skill. There are two ways to use this method. The first is choosing an individual from the group to perform the skill so that the instructor can offer information on the observer's performance. If there is no suitable group member, the instructor can perform the demonstration. The second option is to bring in an expert to demonstrate skills. Well-known athletes who have devoted years to developing their skills and who demonstrate enthusiasm for sharing their competence are excellent choices for demonstrations. Having this person demonstrate skills for one or two sessions can be more meaningful toward helping participants appreciate the sport. This type of demonstration can require preparation and coordination; however, the outcome is worthwhile, especially if the athlete is respected and well known.

Part and Whole

A popular way to teach sport is the part-and-whole method. In this method, skills are broken down into parts and then brought back together as a whole.

Learning how to perform in most sports is complicated and difficult, especially for beginners. When the instructor teaches some aspect and builds on it in a meaningful progression, learning progresses faster and with more satisfaction. The method instructors use to break down a sport into parts is a function of the instructor's background and knowledge. A recreational sport specialist needs to observe the instructor's ability in delivering these methods. Different instructors may have unique ways of presenting the various parts of a sport.

There are thousands of examples of breaking down skills into parts. This method allows the easier or basic elements of a sport to be learned first, leading to the more difficult skills. This progression results in greater participant satisfaction and appreciation for the sport.

Drills

The instructional sport process must lead to active participation to maintain participant interest. Drills enable all participants to practice specific aspects of a sport at the same time. Depending on what skill is being learned, practice drills can be individual, partner, or group. The instructor has the option to participate in the drill or to move from one person to another, critiquing individual performance. One common type of drill is the mimic drill. In this drill, the instructor demonstrates a skill. The participants then copy the performance of the role model until they attain competency for that skill.

Drills should be designed so that the learning is progressive, moving from the simple to the complex. Usually, the instructor scans the performance of the entire group, focusing on individuals' strengths and weaknesses. In this way, some one-on-one instruction transpires with the instructor analyzing and correcting performance. Continual encouragement from the instructor during drills is necessary.

An instructor can also organize drills by stations so that certain sport skills are practiced at different areas, usually with selected equipment and group leaders. At each station, the participants repeatedly perform the skill and analyze it themselves, although the instructor may still comment on strengths and weaknesses. At the completion of the session, a signal for rotation occurs, and the participant moves to another station to practice another skill. This type of drill enables large groups to all be active and practice several skills within a sport.

Game Experience

Game simulation of the sport or a portion of the sport requires the participants to use acquired skills and knowledge. It is best to employ this method after the participants have learned the fundamentals of the sport. Without some ability, the participants will not be able to play the game with enjoyment, which may result in frustration and discouragement from further participation.

Game situations should be within the ability of the participants yet challenging enough for them to demonstrate what they have learned. Game situations require participants to draw on their knowledge of the sport and formulate strategies for playing. Throughout this method, the instructor observes the performance of participants as if in a drill. This allows the instructor to recognize individual weaknesses for practice and correction in later sessions.

Participant Motivation

Throughout the instructional sport program, attention should be given to maintaining the participant's commitment and interest. The ability to motivate participants requires knowledge about the sport as well as refined teaching skills. Some participants come to an instructional sport program highly motivated to learn, others come motivated but lose their motivation after a while, and others come with some degree of anxiety or reluctance. In each instance, the instructor must be able to detect the level of motivation and develop or maintain the participant's positive involvement and eagerness to learn. Successful motivational techniques should make learning easier and add to participant satisfaction, so this section presents elements for motivating participants in the learning process of instructional sport.

The Instructor

Perhaps the most important factor in motivating participants is the instructor's delivery style and personality. When the instructor believes in the benefits of participation in a sport, it is conveyed to the participants. Participants easily notice an instructor's friendliness, attentiveness, and interest in the class. Similarly, an unenthusiastic personality can discourage participants. The recreational sport specialist should make every attempt to gauge an instructor's personality before hiring. Although personality is not a substitute for knowledge about the sport or how to instruct, it is an important ingredient that adds to participant satisfaction and learning.

The Sport

The choice of sport for the instructional program, if based on participants' expressed needs and interests, is a motivational technique in itself. Too often recreational sport specialists rely on their own opinions instead of assessing a population and its needs and interests. Such an assessment identifies which sport activities are most popular with the participants. Additional information can be obtained from the assessment such as participant skill level, ideal time spans, and participant schedules. After de-

termining these specifics, the recreational sport specialist can select an appropriate sport and format to create the necessary motivation.

Benefits

Individuals pursue sport involvement for many reasons. Some seek an opportunity for social contacts or a change of pace. Others want to improve their sport performance or their personal fitness. Because the reasons for involvement are varied and because participants may not know the potential benefits, benefits need to be reviewed at some point. It is often helpful to indicate potential benefits in the publicity for the program to help persuade individuals to sign up. Once individuals become involved, the recreational sport specialist may cover potential benefits in depth. When individuals feel that their commitment will result in benefits, they are more motivated to learn.

One principal area of interest that motivates participation in sport is enjoyment. Many individuals are interested in sport because they feel it will be enjoyable. This expectation may be based on experience, spectatorship, or observation of other participants. On the other hand, some individuals are deterred from participating when they have negative experiences or are exposed to negative attitudes about participation. Take precautions when structuring the program to minimize situations that can hinder enjoyment, such as skill progression that is too fast and too much play without enough skill.

The other main benefit of sport participation is fitness. Not all sports improve overall fitness. However, with proper planning, instructional sport programs can maximize contributions to fitness. Share information about supplemental activities that enhance fitness, and point out the misconceptions associated with the sport and its potential fitness benefits. Fitness is a form of motivation when it is incorporated into instructional sport.

Reinforcement

Inherent within instructional sport is the need to provide participants with feedback on their performance. As individuals develop their knowledge and skills, they require a frame of reference to measure progress and correct mistakes. The manner in which this feedback is provided can either be motivating or discouraging.

People are motivated by positive reinforcement of their efforts. Instructors should praise accomplishments before commenting on weaknesses or mistakes. This approach helps the instructor establish rapport with participants and shows that the instructor is interested in their development as opposed to embarrassing or ridiculing them. All positive statements should be based on actual progress and effort. False, insincere, or deceptive statements are transparent and ruin the instructor's credibility. In addition, recognition should not be used in place of correction. The purpose of instructional sport is to guide individuals through learning and skill development. This can only be done by correcting mistakes. Quality instructors provide encouragement and focus on the positive even when correcting mistakes, contributing to the participants' motivation.

Incentives

On some occasions the instructor can use incentives to encourage participants. This is an out-of-the-ordinary approach to influencing participant learning. Incentives can provide novelty and stimulate interest. Types of incentives are not standardized but are the result of the instructor's imagination. Incentives can include prizes for the best performance of the day, point systems for achievements, ladder tournaments that rank participants, and novelty drills and games. The instructor should use care in selecting these incentives so that they have an effect but do not become the focus of the participants' development.

Instructional Aids

Instructional aids are devices that an instructor uses to demonstrate and communicate sport information. They include bulletin boards, audio and video players and recorders, DVDs, handouts, task cards, special equipment, websites, electronic learning management systems, and artificial or simulated environments. These aids are not a substitute for instruction; however, they can make learning easier as well as more interesting for participants. Instructional aids are excellent for speeding up learning through audio and visual stimulation. Instructional sport personnel need to be familiar with aids that can enhance their delivery of sport information. This section presents instructional aids, giving the recreational sport specialist an idea of the different options available.

Bulletin Boards

Bulletin boards can serve as an aid to both instructors and participants. They should be placed in a highly visible location near the area where the sport is taught. Boards should be at eye level for easy reading. Diagrams, drawings, graphs, charts, pictures, or pictures in sequence can provide sport instructional information. In addition to electronic bulletin boards, permanent boards such as chalk boards, flannel boards, and magnetic boards can be written on or used to post messages. These boards are often overlooked by sport instructors, but they merit consideration, especially when instructors are creative and willing to develop and maintain them.

Audio and Video Players and Recorders

Instructors can use numerous audio and video players and recorders, including DVD players, MP3 players (e.g., iPods), digital video recorders or cameras, or even smart phones. One way a recorder can help is in recording a presentation for review when participants are unable to attend a session. When using drills for a sport, the instructor can play audio files with the verbal information while moving around the area observing participants. Digital cameras and even some smart phones provide instructors with very small portable ways to video record participants and provide instantaneous feedback, allowing participants to observe their strengths and weaknesses. Viewing one's self on video allows self-analysis that is extremely helpful at all skill levels. Using videos for instruction enhances learning and serves as a valuable form of motivation. MP3 players can also be used to play audio (MP3) or video (MP4) files for students, or the instructor can also download instructional podcasts for a variety of sports from iTunes.

DVDs

Instructors can also use DVDs that have been commercially produced or developed by the instructor or a professional. There are a multitude of instructional sports DVDs for sale that enhance learning of sport skills (see www.sportsnationvideo.com).

Many commercially produced DVDs are available for almost all sports. These instructional aids are an excellent option, especially when there are limited instructors.

Handouts

Handouts are printed informational material given to participants. Handouts sometimes act as reminders for what has been taught. Other forms of information that can be printed are rules and regulations; facility diagrams; performance tips; strategy information; safety information; content not covered during sessions; and lists of related books, articles, or radio or television programs.

Task Cards

Task cards are often used as instructional aids to teach new skills. Instructors can use task cards to enhance task execution by providing simple instructions on a technique or drill by means of text, illustrations, or pictures. These cards can provide prompts, important cues, and directions to be followed by the participant as well as the number of exercises or repetitions for the participant to perform. Task cards can also enhance task-oriented behavior by providing checklists for peers to assess each other's performance. There is even a task card app available for iPads from iTunes (http://itunes.apple.com/ca/app/

task-cards/id382006709?mt=8) that instructors could use in place of traditional paper task cards.

Special Equipment

Because sport is so popular and so many people want to learn sport skills, devices and gimmicks to assist in learning skills have been developed. The purpose of these devices is to help individuals improve a specific sport skill. Examples of such equipment are rubber molded grips for tennis and golf, stroke developers for tennis, putting mats for golf, air mats for karate, and automatic pitching machines for various sports. Specialized equipment can help participants gain skill when they might not be improving or might be having trouble with a skill. Every sport has specialty equipment that enhances skill development, and instructors should be encouraged to learn about and use such aids.

Websites

Nowadays there are a multitude of sport-specific websites dedicated to the practice and instruction of numerous sports. Conducting searches through Google can help the recreational sport specialist find useful websites for instructing just about any sport. Also, websites such as YouTube contain a variety of helpful demonstration videos for learning different sports and sports skills. Regardless of the sport or skill, recreational sport specialists can use the Web to find helpful instructional aids to demonstrate and communicate sport information.

Electronic Learning Management Systems

Electronic Learning Management Systems (ELMS), such as Blackboard, eCollege, Whiteboard, or Moodle, have been widely used within higher education in a variety of disciplines for years now but are also starting to be used for instructional physical activity and sports classes as well. ELMS allow learning to happen anywhere at any time. It supplements in-class activities with Internet sites, slide presentations, audio lectures, videos, and live chats or blogs (forums). ELMS provide a multidimensional platform, allowing instructors to train, store data or files online available for students to download, and communicate with clients.

Artificial or Simulated Environments

Applications of simulation technologies have long been used for sporting activities via the development of synthetic surfaces. Synthetic sport surfaces have been developed for a wide range of sports including skiing, bowling greens, tennis, basketball, cricket, handball, volleyball, hockey, ice skating, golf, soccer, and football. In addition to numerous sports

being commonly played and practiced on synthetic surfaces, many outdoor environments and experiences have also been simulated as there are now artificial indoor rock climbing walls, indoor golf simulators, artificial human-made white-water rivers, indoor ski slopes, artificial wave slopes, and indoor miniature oceans in stadium-like facilities with real waves for surfing. These settings may be more accessible to the recreational sport specialist depending upon the sport being instructed, are controllable, and are often safer for participants first learning one of these sports. Recreational sport specialists should be cautioned that while these settings may serve as an instructional aid and be useful to introducing participants to a sport, there are often considerable differences between artificial and real settings when participating in a sport. This should be taken into consideration when demonstrating and communicating sport information.

Evaluation

Feedback on instructional effort is essential for an instructional sport program to have an ongoing positive effect. Evaluations communicate whether a program is being received as intended, and they provide feedback about the instructor. There are a variety of evaluation systems, but some of the most common are checklists, specific questions, rankings of key points, short answers, and computerized forms. Figure 7.2 is a sample evaluation form that contains specific points of information that should be considered when creating an evaluation. Each of these areas can be expanded depending on the instructor, the sport, the age of the participants, and the degree of administrative interest. Regardless, some form of evaluation is necessary. Too often, this final step is avoided or taken for granted. Such feedback can prove critical, especially when an instructional program affects agency income.

Session Delivery
　　Participant control
　　Session organization
　　Safety
　　Diagnosis and correction
　　Skill progression
　　Drills
　　Demonstrations
　　Lecture content
　　Discussion opportunities
　　Facilities
　　Equipment

INSTRUCTION EVALUATION FORM

Instructor's name _____   Date _____

Sport _____   Number in session _____

Respond to each statement in terms of your agreement or disagreement, with 1 meaning "strongly disagree" and 7 meaning "strongly agree."

1. The session always started on time.	1	2	3	4	5	6	7
2. The sessions were well organized.	1	2	3	4	5	6	7
3. The instructor was well prepared.	1	2	3	4	5	6	7
4. My learning experience was outstanding.	1	2	3	4	5	6	7
5. The instructor explained information well.	1	2	3	4	5	6	7
6. The instructor was enthusiastic.	1	2	3	4	5	6	7
7. The instructor demonstrated skills well.	1	2	3	4	5	6	7
8. The instructor was knowledgeable about the sport.	1	2	3	4	5	6	7
9. The instructor was always neat in appearance.	1	2	3	4	5	6	7
10. The instructor had a positive attitude about the sport.	1	2	3	4	5	6	7
11. The instructor communicated well verbally.	1	2	3	4	5	6	7
12. The progression of skill was easy to follow.	1	2	3	4	5	6	7
13. The environment was safe at all times.	1	2	3	4	5	6	7
14. The instructor was patient.	1	2	3	4	5	6	7
15. Skill diagnosis and correction were always helpful.	1	2	3	4	5	6	7
16. The facility was adequate.	1	2	3	4	5	6	7
17. Instructional aides were helpful.	1	2	3	4	5	6	7

Comments _____

_____

_____

_____

(Optional) Evaluator's name _____

Figure 7.2. Group Evaluation Form. From *Recreational Sport Management* by Richard F. Mull, Kathryn G. Bayless, & Lynn J. Jamieson, 2005, Champaign, IL: Human Kinetics.

Instructor Ability
 Communication skills
 Sport knowledge
 Interest in participant learning
 Overall performance as instructor
 Rapport with participants
 Organization of session and program
 Attitude
 Appearance

There are three types of evaluations: instructor evaluation, group evaluation, and specialist evaluation. The instructor evaluation is a self-assessment. While this method may not always be the best way to gain feedback, it is reasonable when an instructor is highly sensitive about being evaluated or when there is limited time for evaluation. Self-assessment evaluations force instructors to think about their effort and how the participants may have perceived their experience. Such an effort could be written up based on a predetermined outline of expected information.

The group evaluation is the most common technique for soliciting participant opinion about the program and the instructor. The instructor distributes a questionnaire that covers the effectiveness of the program for the participant. This is an objective form of evaluation. Figure 7.2 is a general evaluation form that could be adapted to most instructional sport programs.

The recreational sport specialist is part of the instructional sport programs and as such has predetermined instructional objectives that should be shared with the instructor. From these objectives, an evaluation form such as Figure 7.3 can be developed. Figure 7.3 assesses a tennis instructor's ability to teach the different tennis strokes. It also assesses other considerations that relate to session delivery. Such an observation and recording could be supplemented with notes and possibly interviews with participants to obtain feedback. It is recommended that the recreational sport specialist share these findings with the instructor so that the instructor understands the evaluation and can make the necessary adjustments.

Use whatever evaluation system is necessary to improve the instructional sport program. Failure to evaluate outcomes can be counterproductive, especially when instruction is popular and well received. Good instructors still need to be evaluated. Participants are also owed a positive experience and the option to express satisfaction or dissatisfaction.

TENNIS INSTRUCTOR EVALUATION

Instructor's name _____ Date _____ Time _____

Session title _____ Lesson level _____

Circle the number that represents assessment, with 1 being "very poor" and 7 being "excellent."

Stroke knowledge   **Comments**

Forehand	1	2	3	4	5	6	7	_____
Backhand	1	2	3	4	5	6	7	_____
Serve	1	2	3	4	5	6	7	_____
Volley	1	2	3	4	5	6	7	_____
Lob	1	2	3	4	5	6	7	_____
Overhead	1	2	3	4	5	6	7	_____
Drop	1	2	3	4	5	6	7	_____
Shot	1	2	3	4	5	6	7	_____

Specialty shots

_____	1	2	3	4	5	6	7	_____
_____	1	2	3	4	5	6	7	_____

Session delivery

Demonstration	1	2	3	4	5	6	7	_____
Diagnosis and correction	1	2	3	4	5	6	7	_____
Progression	1	2	3	4	5	6	7	_____
Safety	1	2	3	4	5	6	7	_____
Drills	1	2	3	4	5	6	7	_____
Aids	1	2	3	4	5	6	7	_____

Instructor

Organization	1	2	3	4	5	6	7	_____
Control	1	2	3	4	5	6	7	_____
Safety	1	2	3	4	5	6	7	_____
Patience	1	2	3	4	5	6	7	_____
Enthusiasm	1	2	3	4	5	6	7	_____
Appearance	1	2	3	4	5	6	7	_____
Attitude	1	2	3	4	5	6	7	_____
Overall	**1**	**2**	**3**	**4**	**5**	**6**	**7**	_____

Evaluator _____ Date _____

Figure 7.3. Specialist Evaluation. From *Recreational Sport Management* by Richard F. Mull, Kathryn G. Bayless, & Lynn J. Jamieson, 2005, Champaign, IL: Human Kinetics.

Shining Example

City of Henderson Parks and Recreation Department

The Parks and Recreation Department of Henderson, Nevada, serves one of the fastest-growing communities in the United States. Keeping pace with rapidly changing demographics and community needs, the Henderson Parks and Recreation Department (HPRD) has grown and adjusted with the city. It offers a variety of recreation and cultural enrichment programs as well as numerous sport and fitness facilities.

Clientele:

The HPRD serves the citizens of Henderson, Nevada, a city of 277,502 located approximately 7 miles from the Las Vegas strip.

Facilities:

The HPRD is made up of seven recreation facilities that include fitness centers, aquatic facilities, indoor climbing walls, indoor tracks, Kids Corners, and an outdoor performing arts facility. The facilities offer activities including basketball, aerobics, volleyball racquetball, wallyball, and even a games room. The department boasts 52 parks as well as tennis courts, walking courses, dog parks, skate parks, splash pads, and lighted sport areas. It also has over 50 miles of trails, and a system of bicycle, fitness, and equestrian trails. More recreational areas, parks, trails, and a bird viewing preserves are under development.

Program Details:

The HPRD sponsors over 600 recreation and enrichment programs for youths and adults of all ages, including excursions for teens and families, sports programs, therapeutic recreation programs, and educational forums.

Budget:

The HPRD received a percentage of the overall operation budget for the City of Henderson, which totaled $172.6 million for the 2011 fiscal year.

Marketing:

The HPRD uses a variety of marketing strategies, including a quarterly direct mailing of program brochures, as well as newspaper advertising. In addition, the department maintains an internet website (http://www.cityofhenderson.com/parks/index.php).

Jobs and Careers:

The HPRD's staff is made up of 195 full-time employees and 1,011 part-time employees.

Salary:

Salary ranges are not available at this time.

Internship:

Internships are offered on a competitive basis to college students majoring in fields concerning recreation and leisure, human/social services, education, health sciences, landscaping and business. Tasks could involve assisting in the work performed by the department, participating in special research studies, performing specialized duties within the department, routine office support, and providing additional manpower for the department.

Affiliated Professional Organizations:

The City of Henderson is a member of the Nevada Recreation and Parks Society and the National Recreation and Parks Association.

Awards and Recognition:

In addition to accreditation by the National Recreation and Park Association since 2001, the City of Henderson Parks and Recreation Department received the 1999 National Gold Medal for Excellence in Park and Recreation Administration. It was also named Sports Illustrated's 50th Anniversary Sportstown for Nevada.

► **Computer Tip**

....

Recreation Registration Software

Recreation registration software assists with recreational sport program registration. The software enables recreational sport specialists to disseminate information more effectively and efficiently to participants, instructors, facility managers, registration clerks, and other staff members. Most commercial packages are fully integrated with other recreation modules and offer menu-driven, easy-to-use programs that are adaptable to a wide variety of recreational sport agencies.

Automated recreation registration software streamlines the process of registering individuals and groups for all types of recreational sport programs, classes, trips, seminars, and memberships, regardless of the setting. A computerized registration system should include the features discussed below.

1. **Program brochure or catalog generator**
- Allows formatting and previewing of various program-catalog styles and produces copy for program brochures or catalogs, including activity description, dates, times, facility location, fees, instructor, and any other information pertinent to the brochure.

2. **Mass-mailing list management**
- Produces mailing labels or e-mail addresses of all current and past enrollees for follow-up postcards and other correspondence.

3. **Activity or class management**
- Tracks activity or class enrollment totals. Allows instructors to view enrollment and track attendance.
- Handles waiting lists and roster change, and supports lottery enrollments and enrollment transfers.
- Tracks activity or class prerequisites, insurance forms, age limitations, equipment, and supplies for each activity or class.
- Automatically displays open and closed activities or classes.
- Allows for preregistration as well as mail-in, phone-in, walk-in, and Web-based registrations.
- Carries over activity information from season to season, eliminating the need to re-enter similar information.
- Provides an enrollment history for each participant.
- Places enrollments on a prioritized waiting list when an activity is closed; calculates second-choice activities for any participants placed on a waiting list.

4. **Membership management**
- Manages membership entries and sales totals.
- Tracks enrollment for individuals or families.
- Develops financial and membership reports.

5. **Facility reservation system**
- Performs facility searches by user-defined criteria.
- Processes activity or class facility requests.
- Checks availability of a desired facility with activity or class usage demands and automatically reserves facility.
- Prints facility calendar and daily reservations.

6. **Instructor management**
- Calculates multiple pay rates based on hourly, percentage, or flat-fee rates for multiple instructors assigned to any given activity. Calculates total hours of instruction provided by each instructor.
- Tracks personnel information such as job descriptions and performance appraisals.
- Prints teaching assignments.
- Produces instructor contracts or agreements.
- Allows unlimited number of teaching assignments per instructor.
- Maintains enough flexibility to have multiple instructors assigned to any given activity.

7. **Reports**
- Prints registration receipts for participants.
- Prints activity or class rosters.

8. **Fiscal management**
- Manages refunds, activity or class transfers, and other modifications.
- Produces end-of-the-day and end-of-the-period financial reports.
- Calculates income, expense, and net revenue.
- Performs basic cost analysis.
- Allows for cancellations with full or partial refund processing.
- Tracks balances of individual membership dues and automatically updates the remaining amount due and the date due.

Computerized recreation registration systems are a tremendous tool for the recreational sport specialist. An effective system consolidates several functions of the manual registration process into one streamlined, automated process. This system enables you to maintain accurate and detailed information on all recreation programs and instructors, thus creating an effective information and communication network. An automated registration system will improve your department's service by offering greater capacity, speed, and accuracy as well as up-to-the-minute rosters and comprehensive record keeping.

Conclusion

Over the years, there has been tremendous interest in enhancing sport performance through instruction. With proper marketing, an instructional sport program can provide a valuable service as well as generate income for management. Critical to any instructional sport program is the ability of an instructor to provide the participant with a meaningful, satisfactory experience. This begins with an understanding of the different instructional systems so that the participants' varied interests in sport can be understood and met. The instructor selection process is the key to finding the best person for the job.

The process does not end with finding the instructor. A recreational sport specialist has to ensure that the instruction is delivered to the participants' satisfaction. The method of delivery has to be chosen and applied along with the different motivational techniques that enhance the learning experience. Finally, any instructional program must be sensitive to the participant's level of satisfaction, and an evaluation should be conducted to gain that insight.

Creating an effective instructional sport program requires a recreational sport manager with special interest in this program area. Nothing can be more rewarding than making a difference in sport participation because of a well-organized and well-delivered lesson or clinic in sport instruction.

Bibliography

Blunt, G. H., & King, K. M. (2011). Developing a fitness center-based, self-guided instructional program using MP4 player technology. *Recreational Sports Journal, 35*, 61-68.

Carey, D. (1998). Evaluating instructional programs. *Journal of the National Intramural–Recreational Sports Association, 22*(2), 52-54.

Coulson, M. (2007). *The fitness instructors handbook*. London, United Kingdom: A & C Black.

Howley, E., & Franks, B. (2003). *Health fitness instructor's handbook* (4th ed.). Champaign, IL: Human Kinetics.

Iserbyt, P., Madou, B., Vergauwen, L., & Behets, D. (2011). Effects of peer mediated instruction with task cards on motor skill acquisition in tennis. *Journal of Teaching in Physical Education, 30*, 31-50.

Laios, A., Theodorakis, N., & Gargalianos, D. (2003). The importance of internal and external motivation factors in physical education and sport. *International Journal of Physical Education, 40*(1), 21-26.

Lane, D. A. (2009). Does coaching psychology need the concept of formulation? *International Coaching Psychology Review, 4*(2), 195-208.

Leonida, M. (1986). Planning strategies for a non-credit instruction program. *National Intramural–Recreational Sports Association Journal, 10*(2), 38-48.

Melton, B., & Burdette, T. (2011). Utilizing technology to improve the administration of instructional physical activity programs in higher education. *Journal of Physical Education, Recreation, and Dance, 82*(4), 27-32.

National Association for Sport and Physical Education. (n.d.). *National standards for physical education*. Retrieved from http://www.aahperd.org/naspe/standards/nationalstandards/pestandards.cfm

Rapp, N. L. (1991). Instructional programs in campus recreation. *National Intramural–Recreational Sports Association Journal, 15*(3), 15-16.

Sherman, C. (1997). Instructional sport psychology: A re-conceptualization of sports coaching as sport instruction. *International Journal of Sport Psychology, 28*(2), 103-125.

Silverman, S., & Ennis, C. (2003). *Student learning in physical education: Applying research to enhance instruction* (2nd ed.). Champaign, IL: Human Kinetics.

Spittle, M., & Byrne, K. (2009). The influence of sport education on student motivation in physical education. *Physical Education and Sport Pedagogy, 14*(3), 253-266.

Spitzer, T. (1986). Non-credit recreational instruction: Safe aerobic dance classes. *National Intramural-Recreational Sports Association Journal, 10*(2), 42-43.

Sproule, J., Ollis, S., Gray, S., Thorburn, M., Allison, P., & Horton, P. (2011). Promoting perseverance and challenge in physical education: The missing ingredient for improved games teaching. *Sport, Education and Society, 16*(5), 665-684.

Tsangaridou, N., & O'Sullivan, M. (2003). Physical education teachers' theories of action and theories-in-use. *Journal of Teaching in Physical Education, 22*(2), 132-153.

CHAPTER 8

Informal Sport

CHAPTER OBJECTIVES

After reading this chapter, you will understand the purpose and nature of informal sport, recognize the program development characteristics of informal sport, and be able to identify program delivery requirements for a sound informal sport program.

KEY CONCEPTS

Informal sport
Program considerations
Facility availability
Conveniences
Fees

Eligibility
Conduct
Facility reservations
Facility policies
Personnel duties

Introduction

Although some individuals seek leisure enjoyment in structured programs, others prefer participation without imposed design or direction. Informal sport is self-directed participation in cooperative or competitive play activity that uses sport facilities that are not scheduled for short-term events or ongoing structured programs. In its broadest context, informal sport encompasses traditional and nontraditional activities and facilities (e.g., backyard volleyball games, card games, skiing, target shooting, wind surfing, and basketball games with friends). Participants determine the type of sport and place for participation as well as the length of their involvement.

Informal sport could be regarded as a precursor to the more structured instructional, intramural, extramural, club, athletic, and professional sports. Consider intramural team members who meet at the gymnasium for a pickup basketball game, the beginning tennis player who practices strokes with a friend before a lesson, the karate club member who finds an open spot in the gym to practice moves, or

the varsity football player who runs track to improve endurance. Each needs access to a facility free from structured events and ongoing programs. It is not surprising that informal sport involves the largest number of participants of all recreational sport.

Informal sport has not received adequate recognition as a program area requiring planning to meet an important need. Its identity has developed through interest in personal fitness and increasing public enthusiasm for recreational sport participation by all ages. The growth of commercial and private sport facilities demonstrates the popularity of self-directed sport activity. Indeed, the primary type of participation in commercial facilities is self-directed. Wherever sport facilities exist, an informal sport program is possible. Informal sport requires as much planning as structured sport programs to allow adequate time and space for participants who prefer self-directed activity. This chapter covers program development with an emphasis on facilities, participants, conveniences, personnel, and fees. It also covers the major components of program delivery including policies and procedures, reporting, and personnel.

Program Development

Even though the informal sport program is less structured, participants are still members of a program. When developing an informal sport program, the recreational sport specialist should concentrate on facilitating participation. A positive experience in informal sport often leads to involvement in more structured programs. Incentives to participation can include spontaneous structured events, facility tours, recognition, and fun, all of which encourage a sense of camaraderie among participants. The highest programming priority is creating a positive, satisfying experience, an elusive goal because the quality of the experience is a matter of personal interpretation. Although ways to attain this goal vary from setting to setting, some universal program considerations include facility availability, seasonal factors, scheduling, conveniences, cleanliness, supervising personnel, and fees.

Facility Availability

Perhaps the most important consideration in informal program development is maximizing facility availability for self-directed use. Examine the following considerations to help determine the type and number of facilities needed to satisfy participant interest:

Variety of sports. A quality informal sport program recognizes the diversity of participant interest and abilities by providing an adequate number and variety of sport facilities. Begin this process by analyzing participant interest. Common ways to do this include creating surveys and comment cards to gather participant feedback and analyzing participant use of facilities. Consider the following checklist:

- What needs are being expressed for additional activities or space?

- What are current participation patterns? Are some facilities underused or at capacity?

- Where demand for participation is greater than availability of facilities, is it possible to share facilities with another agency?

- Are facilities in good enough condition to support demand for use, or are repair and renovations needed?

If facilities are not already in place, what factors need to be considered to determine whether to provide facilities? For instance, a commercial skiing developer would carefully scrutinize terrain, weather, transportation, economy, and participant interest before committing resources to constructing and operating a ski lodge.

Accessibility of facilities. Maximizing facility availability means doing everything possible to make facilities as accessible as possible, including the elimination or minimization of barriers to participation. This involves providing facilities that accommodate persons with disabilities as outlined in the Americans with Disabilities Act. Accessibility also means placing facilities as close to as many participants as possible. Weigh the advantages and disadvantages of having primary facility locations or satellite locations. When possible, locate facilities close to residential areas to improve accessibility for children, individuals with disabilities, the elderly, and others with transportation limitations. Another variable is keeping costs within reach of users. Interest in using facilities is meaningless if use is not affordable. Finally, find out what times of the day and what days of the week are most convenient for participants, and schedule facilities accordingly.

Participant differences. Facilities should serve all age groups. Create facility schedules that coincide with the free time of target groups. For example, retirees may prefer facility use from 8 a.m. to 5 p.m., career executives 6 a.m. to 8 a.m. or noon to 1:30 p.m., and high school students 3:30 p.m. to 5:30 p.m. Also take into account differences in experience, ability, and confidence by setting up certain spaces or times exclusively for beginners or other target populations. Similarly, recognize special needs. Where facility design poses obstacles for people with disabilities, recommend the necessary renovations. For example, gender-neutral restrooms and changing rooms facilitate friends in helping persons with disabilities or adults helping children or assisting injured family members.

Seasonal Factors

Many recreational sport activities, such as basketball, racquetball, waterskiing, soccer, snowmobiling, softball, snow skiing, tennis, volleyball, and hunting, are associated with a particular season or time of the year. Anticipate increased participation in sports that are in season and keep facilities available as much as possible. Sometimes fees are higher during peak season than in the off-season. Maintenance requirements and supervision can also change based on seasonal usage. When possible, find multiple uses for facilities to extend availability. For example, during summer months, convert portions of snow-ski areas to accommodate an in-line skate park.

Scheduling

Because convenience is a major factor in informal sport participation, facility scheduling is critical. Here are a few considerations for enhancing participation and user satisfaction. Actual scheduling methods are addressed in Chapter 13.

Background factors. Before determining scheduling policies and methods, take into account factors such as participant age and interests, time required for participation, needs of other programs using the same facilities, budget constraints, personnel needs, and popularity of a sport. An effective communication plan should inform participants about the location of facilities and the times they are available. In addition to a schedule printed for mass distribution or posted on a website, a daily notice should be posted at each facility communicating temporary changes. Additionally, tracking facility use is essential for making future scheduling decisions.

Challenges. One of the most difficult challenges in facility scheduling is protecting time. Keeping facilities reserved for self-directed use is difficult because demand for structured programs often affects the time available for informal sport use. For example, when scheduling a new intramural sport event, it is more tempting to see the informal sport time as available than it is to look at a time where, for example, a yoga class is scheduled because with self-directed participation there is no guarantee that participants will be present consistently. Although scheduling specific percentages or blocks of time to protect facilities for informal sport use is not yet common, this practice could become more popular with increasing demand for informal sport participation.

Use this practice where demand for participation is typically greatest, such as basketball courts and strength and conditioning areas. Other techniques for protecting informal sport facility use include short-term reservations and specified times for groups such as children, women, senior citizens, faculty, and so on. A related challenge is monitoring scheduled use to ensure that the facility schedule does not become so structured that self-directed use is compromised. This is particularly important when facilities are limited, in high demand, and shared by different agencies.

Conveniences

Individuals interested in using a facility for informal sport are attracted to conveniences that add to the enjoyment of their recreational experience. Their decision to choose a program will often depend on what conveniences are present. Here are some ideas to consider.

Equipment and accessories. Availability of sport equipment and accessories is a bonus to individuals interested in trying a new sport. Other individuals who own equipment often do not have a convenient way to transport or store it. Examine the costs and benefits of providing an equipment checkout service by incorporating costs into membership fees or a daily rental fee. In addition, keep equipment clean and in working order and keep abreast of changes in equipment technology. For example, weight lifting and cardiorespiratory equipment is now available with television and Internet-access features. Many machines also have software applications where participants can create an individualized workout program. Where income generation is a priority, consider operating a pro shop where participants may purchase equipment, sport and fitness supplies, toiletries, and apparel. Other appealing conveniences include lounge or specialty areas with ATM machines, magazines and journals, public computer workstations, high-speed wireless Internet connectivity (Wi-Fi), water fountains, and courtesy telephones.

Shower and locker rooms. Another convenience that promotes participation is locker and shower rooms. The size of the rooms, number of showers, and amenities such as towel service, swimsuit wringers, and sauna and steam rooms can go a long way toward attracting participants. Most participants appreciate the convenience of storing their clothing and equipment at the site and the luxury of showering after a workout. When participants live at or close to the facilities, as in a college, military, or correctional setting, some of these services are unnecessary. Closely supervise shower and locker rooms for participant safety.

Transportation and parking. Participants are easily frustrated when it is difficult to use public transportation to access facilities or find adequate parking for personal vehicles. Examine whether additional public-transit routes are needed, whether parking lots require access control to facilitate turnover, or whether expansion of parking space is in order. Provide bike racks and pathways to encourage alternatives to motor vehicles. Quality programs and facilities are useless unless it is easy for participants to access them.

Child care. Offering quality child care on a short-term or day-care basis may distinguish one provider from other providers. However, while child care may provide a competitive advantage, it is rarely profitable. Some recreational sport specialists offset financial concerns with play and activity programs specifically targeted toward children in their care. Ensuring the safety of children under the care of others is also a significant challenge. Many settings now require background checks on volunteers or employees responsible for the care and supervision of children and youth. Additionally, the recreational sport specialist must also be able to select staff capable of working with children.

Food and vending. Food and beverage options range from vending machines to full-service restaurants. Vending machines reflect either low need by participants or low resource commitment by the agency. Conversely, a full-service restaurant may be warranted when there is high demand and when significant financial and operational resources are available. Consider hiring a consultant for food and beverage service extending beyond vending machines. Consultants can help create a market analysis to determine need and interest as well as ensure industry standards are met for food preparation, handling, and service. Also, restrict junk food and provide healthy food, snack, and beverage choices.

Spa services. Once considered luxuries, spa services are becoming more common. They attract a broad range of participants due to the relaxation and stress-reduction benefits attributed to these services. Possible services for skin care and body care are extensive. Examples of skin care include facials (cleansing, moisturizing, glycolic peels, aromatherapy), waxing, and makeup consultations. Body care includes massages (shiatsu, Swedish, sport, aromatherapy, reflexology), loofah scrubs, wraps (herbal, mud, seaweed), and salt rubs. Some locations have expanded into hair and nail salon services as well.

Cleanliness

Clean, attractive facilities positively influence any program's image. Although a facility may not be extensive or modern, it can still be a well-maintained and attractive space. If resources are unavailable to fund major facility repairs and renovations, emphasize both internal and external facility cleanliness.

Internal cleanliness. Attend to details such as picking up trash, maintaining attractive bulletin boards and signs, sweeping and mopping floors, keeping lights functional, replacing broken or bent basketball rims, using nets without rips, keeping water fountains clean and unobstructed, replacing worn or torn mats or safety padding, cleaning glass doors and windows, dusting furniture and fixtures, and so on. Pay special attention to keeping restrooms, locker rooms, showers, and pool decks clean and sanitary.

External cleanliness. Since participants often form their first impression of an agency by the outside appearance of the grounds and facility, keep these areas landscaped, maintained, and well lit. Strategically place trash receptacles along walkways, bike paths, and parking areas, and keep them emptied.

Personnel

Even the most attractive, well-maintained recreational sport facility will not attain the greatest use or provide maximum participant enjoyment if the on-site supervising personnel do not act appropriately. Informal sport personnel should not only be congenial, helpful, and knowledgeable about the facility but also capable of minimizing safety hazards, facility misuse, and disciplinary problems. Personnel must employ effective communication and conflict resolution skills with maturity and tact. Another important factor affecting participant satisfaction is the reliability of information provided to participants. All personnel must know the current schedules, policies, and procedures and communicate the correct information to avoid inconveniencing the participants. Additional information about personnel management is addressed later in this chapter.

Fees

Fees, which characterize commercial sport operations, have begun to affect informal sport programs. Commercial sport facilities that provide racquetball, ice-skating, tennis, swimming, skiing, bowling, and so forth rely on individuals paying a fee to pursue their sport. Noncommercial settings dependent on local, state, or federal funding are experiencing cutbacks and have turned to fees to offset operating costs for informal sport. Such revenue can expand services and facilities and enhance informal sport opportunities, but the cost of informal sport facility use can also decrease use. The following are fees common to informal sport programs.

Annual membership fees. These fees allow unlimited access to sport facilities for informal use. A common practice is to provide payment options whereby members pay membership fees on a monthly or seasonal basis. In some cases, particularly in commercial settings, an additional user fee is charged for a specific activity. For example, most tennis clubs charge an annual fee for membership plus a daily fee or reservation fee for court time.

Daily user fees. These fees are charged for unlimited facility use during a given day. Examples include a greens fee, a day pass to a swimming pool, a ski-lift ticket, or admission to an ice rink. The daily user fee can accommodate guests or serve as a backup for individuals who cannot provide the proper identification to show they are members.

Reservation fees. These fees are for access to specific space for a specific time period. Some examples include reservations for basketball courts, shelter houses, or tennis courts. Reservation or walk-in arrangements and fee adjustments encourage use during times that are less popular.

Rental fees. These fees guarantee exclusive use of a facility or equipment. Rental fees are typically based upon a one-hour time block. Discounted fees may be offered for multiple hours of reserved time. The user may enjoy all the advantages of use as long as the facility or equipment is not destroyed, damaged, or lost. A rental fee is usually applied when informal sport facilities or equipment are available during low-use times of the day, week, or month.

License and permit fees. These are fees for the right to participate in government-monitored activities such as hunting, fishing, or flying. During these sports, the participant usually has few restrictions except the written laws.

Program Delivery

Since the recreational sport specialist does not structure or direct the actual participation experience in informal sport, it may be easy to overlook important programming elements. Informal sport programs have the largest participation base within recreational sport, and these participants have high expectations for quality service, so carefully consider policies and procedures, personnel, and reporting.

Policies and Procedures

Policy statements outline the conditions for participation, and procedures direct the manner in which these policies are enforced. Customary topics include eligibility, fees collection, facility reservations, accident and emergency procedures, conduct, and facility use and control. The policy and procedure statements for an informal program often take the form of a participant manual. See Figure 8.1 for tips on how to create a participant manual.

A manual for an informal sport program is an excellent means to help employees and participants understand the program and follow its policies and procedures. A program will be more inviting and more effectively delivered if its policies and procedures are in writing. The manual should cover the topics listed in the following outline. In fact, the outline can easily be converted into the table of contents for a manual.

I.   Introduction
II.   Informal sport advisory council
III. List of facilities and services
IV.   Availability schedule
V.   User policies
    A.   Eligibility
    B.   Fees and charges
    C.   Facility use
    D.   Conduct
    E.   Dress
    F.   Concessions

VI.   Procedures
    A. Fee collection
    B. Locker room
    C. Equipment
    D. Facility reservations
    E. Accident, injury, and emergency procedures
    F. Lost and found
    G. Complaints and suggestions
VII. Emergency phone list
VIII. Staff directory
IX.   Map

The manual can be produced as a hard copy or created as an online version for Internet access by employees and participants. Regardless of the format, make sure this useful material is distributed to all participants and on-site staff.

Figure 8.1. Creating a Sport Participant Manual

Eligibility. Eligibility statements specify who is permitted to use the sport facilities, most often in terms of individual or group eligibility. Examples are student, faculty, staff, and alumni; employee and executive; inmate and guard; resident and nonresident; and member and guest. Group eligibility statements may specify age groups (children, teens, adults, senior citizens), social or civic groups (Lions Club, Girl Scouts, Boy Scouts), living units (dormitory, fraternity, sorority, married housing), or affiliation with the agency or setting (residents, nonresidents). Settings may prohibit certain categories of individuals from facility access, or they may restrict access to specific days, times, or activities. A private swimming club may limit guest pool use to certain hours during the week; a university may prohibit nonaffiliates from facility access; a military base may confine the dependents of active-duty personnel to facility access during evenings and weekends; and a corporation may designate special hours for executive staff access to a weight room.

Eligibility statements describe the intended user of a program. As eligibility requirements become more stringent, the informal sport specialist will need a monitoring system to prevent ineligible participation. The most common procedures for verifying eligibility are photo identification cards, a roster, or a database of names and personal information.

Developing eligibility statements involves the following considerations:

- Who is being served?
- What can the facilities handle?
- Are there certain facilities or times that require restricted use?
- What personnel are available or necessary to monitor facility use?
- What financial resources are available to support monitoring and control systems?
- What effect will eligibility statements have on public relations?
- Are there any legal considerations that affect eligibility?
- How will participants prove they are legitimate users of the facility?

Fee collection. Fees require a collection, deposit, and security system. They may involve an identification system that enables the user to verify payment for facility use. Determine procedures for fee collection and identification well in advance and consider questions such as the following: Are adjusted fees available for low-income participants? Can fees be prorated? Are credit cards, debit cards, or money orders acceptable? Are charge accounts available? Is there a penalty for bad checks or delinquent accounts? Can fees be paid online?

Facility reservations. The priorities for facility use determine the amount of time available for informal sport. Find out when participants prefer access to facilities and their activity preferences in order to protect blocks of time for self-directed use; otherwise, times may become dedicated to structured programs at the expense of the informal sport program. Keep in mind that facility availability and easy access are the fundamental components of informal sport participation. Once these priorities are finalized in a written policy, the recreational sport specialist can establish short-term facility reservation policies and procedures so participants will know how to reserve facilities for their favorite self-directed activities.

The most prevalent reservation technique is the court or field reservation. This technique accommodates a large number of participants and is useful for handball, racquetball, squash, tennis, basketball, and softball facilities. The following are common reservation practices:

- Reservations may be made in person or by computer.
- One in-person or phone-in reservation is accepted.
- A valid identification card or user pass is required to make a reservation.
- Only one reservation per day is permitted.
- Reservations may be made only for same-day use.
- Reservations may be made several days in advance.
- Cancellations must be made in person with proper identification.
- Cancellations must be made 24 hours in advance, or a no-show penalty will be imposed.
- Persons absent 10 minutes past the reserved playing time forfeit their reservation.

Programs that prohibit phone-in reservations or cancellations may do so because they have no way to verify user eligibility, they require a user fee, or they rely on the phone for other uses. Programs that accept phone-ins check eligibility at the facility when they collect fees. The major advantage of accepting phone calls is it accommodates participants with legitimate scheduling conflicts. A disadvantage of phone-in cancellations is the potential for tampering with reservations by an imposter posing as the participant who made the reservation. To avoid this problem, require some form of identification known only by the person making the original reservation.

Reservations reflect demand, use patterns, and staff availability. Publicize written reservation policy and include information on eligibility, reservation procedures, court availability, and fees. Also, post a reservation chart (see Figure 8.2) so users know what times are available.

Facility usage. Because participation in informal sport is self-directed rather than staff directed, the recreational sport specialist must find multiple ways to communicate the policies and procedures that guide participation. As noted previously, one avenue of communication is a participant manual. Others include posting signs throughout the facility and scheduling on-site supervisors to monitor facility use. Finding the most effective avenues for communicating policies, procedures, and program updates is one of the greatest challenges for the recreational sport specialist because participation patterns within informal sport are so varied.

Accident and incident prevention and reporting. The risk of injury is a concern for all informal sport specialists, as are incidents posing risk to personal safety and property, such as theft, vandalism, fighting, and verbal abuse. To protect participants and personnel and minimize the potential for legal action resulting from these concerns, develop a comprehensive plan for accident and incident prevention, first aid, and reporting. Focus efforts on facility and equipment inspection, hazard control, risk management, staff training, supervision, emergency medical procedures, and participant awareness.

Policies for informal sport participation must convey information on safety awareness and procedures for handling accidents and incidents. Printed statements on membership applications supported by notices at activity sites and staff supervision help ensure proper facility use and participant behavior. These statements should describe how and where to obtain assistance for an accident, injury, or incident. Common practices include having on-site personnel wear clearly marked apparel that identifies them as supervisors as well as having a prominent, designated location where participants obtain information and assistance. Finally, policy statements should inform participants whether the facility carries insurance to cover injuries sustained at the site. If the facility requires outside insurance or a medical examination before participation, the staff may be responsible for ensuring participant compliance.

Handball, Racquetball, and Squash Court Reservations

Day _____ Date _____

	4:00 P.M.	5:00 P.M.	6:00 P.M.	7:00 P.M.	8:00 P.M.	9:00 P.M.	10:00 P.M.
Court 1							
Court 2							
Court 3							
Court 4							
Court 5							
Court 6							
Court 7							
Court 8							
Court 9							
Court 10							
Court 11							
Court 12							

Note: A valid ID must be shown when making reservations. Only one court time per day, per ID will be allowed.

Figure 8.2. Informal Sport Reservation Form

Participants must also be aware of their responsibility to provide the necessary information for accident and incident reports. Accurate, complete forms are essential for hazard and injury analysis, insurance claims, and possible legal action. Accident reporting begins at the scene as soon as it is possible to communicate with the victim. Unnecessary delays may result in incomplete or inaccurate information.

Emergencies. Risks other than accidents and incidents also merit attention. Fires, tornadoes, electrical failures, chemical leaks, avalanches, explosions, and bomb threats necessitate an emergency plan, despite the unlikelihood of their occurrence. An emergency plan includes provisions for training personnel and informing the public of their responsibilities during emergency situations. Post evacuation plans, procedures, and safety codes prominently at facility sites. In an emergency, staff should be ready to take charge and execute the emergency plan. In general, duties include notifying the appropriate authorities (police, fire, or medical personnel), redirecting or evacuating participants and other endangered personnel, posting warnings, securing facilities, providing first aid, and documenting the incident.

Children. The presence of children and young adults often requires specific policies governing their participation. This group lacks the maturity, safety consciousness, and awareness of other participants. Rules for informal sport participation by children and young adults should

- require that children be directly supervised by a parent or adult,

- designate times for children to use facilities, and

- require parents or guardians to sign statements acknowledging potential risks of youth activities and awareness of user policies and procedures.

Participant conduct. One of the most demanding responsibilities in informal sport is observing, controlling, and reporting participant conduct. Policies that encourage appropriate conduct should include the following:

- where to dispose of litter;

- where food and beverages can be purchased and consumed;

- where spitting receptacles and fountains are located;

- where to obtain assistance with accidents, incidents, emergencies, or questions;

- recommended or required clothing and footwear;

- pet restrictions (mandated by some states);

- expectations for fair play, positive social interaction, and conflict resolution; and

- consequences of and process for addressing policy violations.

Specialized policies. Most settings establish policies for individual facilities either because the topics need to be addressed in greater detail or because the information needs to be tailored to the particular facility. For example, most strength and conditioning rooms require that participants wear closed-toe shoes, while few programs permit street shoes of any kind on indoor pool decks. The key to public acceptance of policy statements is justifying their existence, enforcing them consistently, and being sensitive to public relations. If personnel are overly aggressive in policy interpretation or enforcement, they will provoke negative participant reaction.

Participant acceptance of facility policy is heightened by participant involvement in the decision-making process. The recreational sport specialist can accomplish this through informal conversations, surveys, focus group sessions, and advisory councils.

Another technique is the development of policies to facilitate equitable participation access for the majority of users or to provide special consideration of target populations. This approach can be tailored to a setting's unique needs, providing various ways to address problems or build relations. Common practices include the following:

- establishing challenge courts whereby the winners of a self-directed basketball game are challenged by a new team of players;

- establishing an on-site queuing area for participants waiting to use facilities in order to avoid confusion over who has access next;

- putting time limits on use of facilities or equipment to accommodate demand;

- setting up designated spaces or times for practicing elements of sports (i.e., basketball shooting courts, tennis backboards, lap swim lanes);

- establishing procedures to provide women's priority on basketball courts, family swim hours, strength training for cardiac rehabilitation, and so on; and

- providing bulletin boards and posting ladder tournaments at courts for racket sports.

Control. Facility personnel need to be trained how to handle situations involving participant abuse of facilities, employees, and others. Having written policies and procedures that address these problems is a start, but the responsibility for maintaining a safe, enjoyable environment rests with the on-site personnel responsible for seeing that policies and procedures are followed. Handling problems professionally, fairly, and consistently builds a positive reputation for a program and builds personnel morale. When a problem arises, determine first whether current program or personnel practices contributed to the problem so that policy or procedure can be modified as necessary. It is also essential to document each occurrence for objective review to determine if disciplinary action is warranted. The goal is to minimize or eliminate problems by being proactive. Participants simply will not use facilities if they are concerned about their safety, health, convenience, and comfort.

The following guidelines are suggested to minimize problems:

- Provide attractive, well-lit, well-maintained facilities.

- Facilitate participant access to facilities and services by minimizing red tape.

- Hire committed, conscientious, and diplomatic personnel.

- Replace or repair vandalized equipment.

- Provide adequate personnel for monitoring participation and identifying maintenance needs.

- Enforce policies consistently.

Effective control also involves keeping participants and staff informed about conduct expectations, including the consequences of policy violation and the procedure for resolving problems. Policy statements need written administrative approval before implementation; otherwise, recreational sport specialists may be put in an embarrassing situation if their decision is overruled or disregarded. To ensure fair, thorough control practices, the following principles are recommended:

- Record the situation as soon as possible.

- Obtain statements from the involved parties, employees, and witnesses.

- Conduct an investigation and review the facts with all involved parties.

- Establish a ruling based on incident severity and precedent.

- Provide an appeals process.

Personnel

Because of the casual, self-directed nature of informal sport participation, on-site supervisory personnel do not have as prominent a role in program delivery as do personnel in other areas of recreational sport, such as officials, group exercise leaders, swim instructors, and personal trainers who guide the participant's experience in a direct way. Subsequently, supervisory personnel have a unique challenge in finding ways to connect with participants.

Responsibilities. While informal sport personnel do not facilitate the actual participation of individuals or groups, they have three responsibilities as supervisors of participants and facilities: safety, security, and public relations.

Safety. Personnel who supervise participants must be trained how to respond to injuries. This typically means training in and ongoing practice with cardiopulmonary resuscitation (CPR), basic first aid, and preventing disease transmission. Personnel must also be capable of addressing safety hazards, facility misuse, and disciplinary problems. Emphasize being proactive and preventing problems before they occur. For example, provide tools for conducting facility and equipment inspections to report needed repairs or take on-the-spot corrective action. Teach supervisors how to intervene in participant disputes before personal injury or property damage results. Participants will quickly come to appreciate efforts to create a safe environment.

Security. Closely related to safety is keeping facilities secure. This is particularly important for high-risk areas such as swimming pools, gymnastic studios, and chemical storage rooms. Security also involves establishing procedures for contacting the police or other specially trained personnel in the event of a significant conduct problem or incident where participants are at risk. Similarly, staff must know protocols for addressing security needs in the event facilities have to be evacuated. Also be sure that personnel enforce eligibility policies consistently. This can be critical when it comes to having a reliable way to identify participants who may be involved in incidents such as vandalism, theft, fights, voyeurism, and so on. See Chapter 13 for more on facility security.

Public relations. Informal sport personnel need to be congenial, helpful, and knowledgeable about the facility and have strong communication and interpersonal skills. Help them view their role as facilitating an enjoyable experience for the participant versus existing only to enforce rules. Perhaps certain positions can be created to provide facility tours or explain proper use of equipment. Personnel must also provide reliable information to participants. It is vital that all personnel communicate the most current schedules, maintenance plans, policies, and procedures in order to avoid inconveniencing participants.

Personnel positions. Informal sport activities typically require the services of door checkers, cashiers, equipment room and pro shop personnel, locker room attendants, supervisors, lifeguards, customer service personnel, facility managers, and custodians. The recreational sport specialist should determine what jobs are necessary for program delivery and supervision. State laws may guide some of these decisions. For example, state law establishes the number of lifeguards needed to supervise public swimming facilities. Another commonly followed standard of care is requiring certification in CPR for individuals supervising participation. Take care to identify experience levels or specialty certifications that are prerequisites for working. Standards of care are shaped largely by court rulings following liability lawsuits. The recreational sport specialist must maintain up-to-date knowledge about standards of care for use in making personnel management decisions such as determining job descriptions and training and scheduling personnel.

Job descriptions specify the tasks personnel are expected to perform. They form the basis for job training and performance evaluations. Even though a written description explains job qualifications and performance expectations, the recreational sport specialist can orally present and discuss specific responsibilities common to all jobs and specific responsibilities to a job. An employee manual is an effective tool for informing personnel about responsibilities. Topics commonly include job descriptions, program philosophy, organizational structure, employment and payroll procedures, benefits, performance expectations and assessments, communication and customer service skills, dress code, reasons for termination, liability concerns, financial accountability, grievance procedures, program policies, incentives and recognition, and facility maps.

Scheduling supervision is also heavily influenced by legal liability. Scheduling typically falls into one of two categories: indirect (general) or direct (specific) supervision. When the risk of injury, harm, or loss to participants or property is low, the indirect supervision approach is taken. This means that fewer employees are scheduled to supervise participants. It may also mean that knowledge, skill, and experience requirements of the supervisors are not as stringent. When the direct supervision approach is used, the ratio of supervisors to participants is smaller than in the indirect approach. For example, it would be appropriate to use the indirect approach and schedule a single supervisor to monitor adults using a six-field soccer complex. However, if the participants were 8 years old, the direct approach would be required, with one supervisor scheduled per field.

Motivation. Unlike the other program areas of recreational sport where participants depend upon on-site personnel (officials, instructors, coaches, personal trainers, group leaders) for directing participation, informal sport personnel have little direct involvement with service delivery. Interaction with participants is sporadic and brief, so tasks often become routine and unchallenging. To avoid personnel apathy, inconsistent job performance, and resentment, the following tips are suggested:

- Develop a regular system for monitoring performance frequently.

- Train and coach preventive action and quality customer service practices.

- Keep work shifts short, especially for tasks that are less desirable.

- Develop avenues for participants to provide on-site feedback on personnel job performance to share with personnel.

- Cross-train personnel and use job rotation during shifts.

- Know the personalities of the staff and match them up with the demands of the job.

- Use a sequential pay scale that increases with the demands of each job.

- Develop a job classification system that provides upward mobility and uses top performers as role models in the training or monitoring of others.

- Seek recommendations from personnel for improving job conditions.

- Take disciplinary action as warranted.

- Recognize and reward quality job performance.

Reporting

The recreational sport specialist is responsible for recognizing, reporting, and reviewing daily operations within the informal sport environment. A communication network can facilitate this responsibility, including on-site supervisors and participants who are familiar with the reporting process. One of the primary reasons for using personnel and participants is the impossibility of having professional staff at each facility site during all hours of operation. Using volunteers, employees, or participants already on-site increases the likelihood that important items will be reported because everyone has a stake in making improvements and can add new perspectives to situations.

Although reporting related to safety, participant conduct, and risk management are covered in other chapters, reports that have particular relevance for the informal sport program include facility usage reports and financial summary reports.

Facility usage reports. Profit and nonprofit informal sport programs can obtain useful information through facility usage reports. Regular monitoring reveals user trends in terms of increased or decreased participation, popularity of facilities and activities, and peak or low times for use. Further analysis specifies the type or age group of users, such as male, female, senior citizen, student, resident, officer, or executive. Facility usage reports (as in Figure 8.3) aid in planning and evaluating informal sport participation. Data can suggest a demand for additional facilities, a change in the number of supervisors needed, alterna-

tives for the hours a facility is available, strategies for improving use of certain facilities, and cost-efficient methods of operating facilities.

Financial summaries. Financial transactions require keeping records to satisfy legal requirements, safeguard assets, and control operations. Transactions that commonly involve informal sport personnel include sales of membership passes, season passes, concessions, clothing, and equipment and rental of equipment, lockers, and towels. Although accounting procedures are covered in more detail in Chapter 12, here are some guidelines for transactions handled by informal sport personnel:

Tennis Court Usage Report

Day _____   Date _____

Time	South battery	North battery	Waiting to play	Total	Initial
12:15 P.M.					
12:45 P.M.					
1:15 P.M.					
1:45 P.M.					
2:15 P.M.					
2:45 P.M.					
3:15 P.M.					
3:45 P.M.					
4:15 P.M.					
4:45 P.M.					
5:15 P.M.					
5:45 P.M.					
6:15 P.M.					
6:45 P.M.					
7:15 P.M.					
7:45 P.M.					
8:15 P.M.					
8:45 P.M.					
9:15 P.M.					
9:45 P.M.					
Total					

Count everyone using and waiting to use the facility for informal tennis. Do not count spectators, classes, intramurals, club sport, athletics, or reserved time.

The supervisor taking count should add the row total and then initial it.

After the final count, supervisors should add the columns.

Figure 8.3. Facility Usage Report

- Provide each person responsible for cash with a separate, fixed change fund and a safe depository.

- When cashiers use the same cash drawer, have the incoming replacement verify the amount left before the shift exchange. Record discrepancies and include the signature of each party.

- Use written receipts for all income.

- Keep a daily record of revenue and deposits.

- Regularly compare sales to inventory or merchandise.

▶ **Computer Tip**

Club Management Software

The club management software that is on the market today ranges from simple membership tracking modules to complex, expandable turnkey management systems designed exclusively for your club.

Clubs vary in design, purpose, operation, and membership, so it is important when purchasing a club management system to know what features are necessary to accomplish the goals of your particular club. Analyze your club's operational system and make a list of features that are essential. Eliminate those features that you do not need or use.

Club management software generally has two major categories of features: accounting features and club management features. Accounting features normally include

- collection of delinquent bills;

- electronic fund transfer for credit card transactions;

- credit card verification (especially helpful for pro-shop sales);

- food and beverage management and needs associated with food service;

- payment coupon books for mass mailing;

- automated statement billing for dues and other charges;

- point of sale designed for built-in cash registers; and

- integration of accounting software programs for general ledger, accounts payable, accounts receivable, payroll, and inventory.

Club management features, which help you manage membership and track club usage, usually include

- front desk check-in system that monitors comprehensive membership information records;

- member check-in that works with bar code readers, magnetic card readers, and biometric scanners;

- user tracking;

- guest registration;

- marketing system that solicits new members;

- facility and equipment rental management;

- usage reports that analyze and evaluate time, day, and actual use of the facility; and

- locker and towel rental.

Using club management software is an excellent way to monitor accuracy and to maintain control over club operations. Whether yours is a small, large, or multiple-site operation, automated management systems can be designed to meet management needs.

Conclusion

Unlike structured sport programs, the informal sport program emphasizes facility management, supervision, and customer service more than activity design and supervision. Although informal sport participants determine the activity and format for involvement, they depend on the recreational sport specialist for access to facilities and services. Considering the variety of participant interests that require facility access, the recreational sport specialist faces a major challenge in providing sufficient facilities to meet these interests.

The recreational sport specialist has a further responsibility to make the facilities and participation opportunities as attractive as possible. A quality informal sport program involves more than providing enough facilities and making them available for self-directed use. It entails establishing effective operating policies, providing capable supervision, responding to participant feedback, and maintaining facilities properly to increase their usefulness.

Bibliography

Bach, L. (1993). Sports without facilities: The use of urban spaces by informal sports. *International Review for the Sociology of Sport, 28*(2/3), 281-297.

Chalip, L., Csikszentmihalyi, M., Kleiber, D., & Larson, R. (1984). Variations of experience in formal and informal sport. *Research Quarterly for Exercise and Sport, 55*(2), 109-116.

Gaskins, D. A. (1993). Order on the court: Effective participant management in informal sports. *National Intramural–Recreational Sports Association Journal, 17*(3), 10, 12-13.

Lamke, G. (1985). Facility supervision: A vital function in overall facility management. *National Intramural–Recreational Sports Association Journal, 9*(3), 42-46.

Meagher, J. (1990). 43 steps to a successful facility. *Athletic Business, 14*(8), 41-43.

Scheele, K., & Hernbloom, T. (1990). Campus recreation supervisors: A comparison. *National Intramural–Recreational Sports Association Journal, 14*(2), 38-43.

Skirta, N. (2011). The value of informal and formal sports to youth development. *Soccer Journal, 56*(4), 54-55.

Resources

Athletic Business Magazine
www.athleticbusiness.com

Athletic Business Magazine is a business magazine for athletic, recreational, and fitness professionals. It covers facility design, construction, and management trends and provides a buyer's guide and product information on equipment and supplies. Details on the annual conference and exhibit are also included along with industry links.

Club Industry Magazine
www.clubindustry.com

Club Industry Magazine is a business magazine for health and fitness facility management. It covers issues that facility managers might encounter, such as public-wellness awareness, legal issues, trends in fitness programs, ways to target specific client populations, and equipment maintenance and retention.

International Health, Racquet, and Sportsclub Association (IHRSA)
www.ihrsa.org

The International Health, Racquet, and Sportsclub Association (IHRSA) is a not-for-profit trade association representing health and fitness facilities, gyms, spas, sport clubs, and suppliers worldwide. The mission of IHRSA is to grow, protect, and promote the industry and to provide its members with benefits that will help them be more successful.

National Intramural–Recreational Sports Association (NIRSA)
www.nirsa.org

The National Intramural–Recreational Sports Association (NIRSA) is a not-for-profit organization for institutions, professionals, and students dedicated to intramural and recreational sport, club sport, and fitness and wellness programs. It provides resources and networking opportunities as well as career services, support, and endorsement for programs and events.

CHAPTER 9

Intramural and Extramural Sport

CHAPTER OBJECTIVES

After reading this chapter, you will be able to identify the programming factors necessary for a successful intramural or extramural tournament, understand how to organize intramural and extramural sport events, and understand the roles and responsibilities of officials and supervisors.

KEY CONCEPTS

Intramural sport	**Elimination tournaments**
Extramural sport	**Round-robin tournaments**
Participant considerations	**Consolation tournaments**
Types of events	**Challenge tournaments**
Unit of participation	**Meets**
Eligibility	**Officials**
Protests	**Supervisors**
Disciplinary action	**Facility policies**
Forfeit	**Personnel duties**

Introduction

Historically, the term *intramural sport* has referred to collegiate recreational sport, but by 1975, the popularity of informal sport programs, club sport, extramural sport, and other programming areas required an expansion in terminology. Thus the term *recreational sport* surfaced, with intramural sport becoming one of its programming areas. The intramural principles originally documented by Dr. Elmer Mitchell at the University of Michigan (1926) are relatively unchanged. This new term, recreational sport, represents the diverse recreational interests of participants and pertains to both theory and practice.

An interpretation of intramural sport outside of the collegiate setting occurred at the turn of the 20th century, when municipal and community recreation departments, churches, elementary and secondary schools, industries, and private clubs began to offer a variety of sport events. Although programs within

these settings have not been traditionally considered to be intramural sport, they meet the definition as presented in the following material.

The word *intramural* is a combination of the Latin words *intra*, meaning "within," and *muralis*, meaning "wall." When used as an adjective with *sport*, it refers to sport events for members within the walls or jurisdiction of a setting. Intramural sport is structured sport participation that requires design and leadership. The term *intramural sport* may be used in any recreational sport setting, for example, a sport tournament sponsored by a community parks and recreation department, Boys Club, or YWCA. Youth sport is more appropriately termed *youth intramural sport*. Extramural sport is an extension of intramural sport. In extramural sport, participants, usually champions of intramural tournaments, compete against champions from other institutions. Extramural sport tournaments are often held outside the location where the intramural tournament champions live. Extramural events include sport days, play days, and other structured events conducted without a season-long schedule, league competition, or championship.

A quality intramural or extramural sport program encourages participation in voluntary sport activities for all. Equal opportunities in sport should be available to all interested individuals regardless of age, sex, race, religion, creed, employment, or economic status. The motto *sport for everyone* represents the philosophy of intramural and extramural sport. Such sport provides a natural outlet for competition and challenge.

This chapter covers participant characteristics, types of events, units of participation, rules and regulations, policies and procedures, tournaments, and personnel.

Program Development

Developing a program of events is an important ingredient in intramural and extramural sport delivery. Although many activities are possible, a successful program incorporates those best suited to the most participants. It is better to offer a few well-chosen sport activities than several poorly administered ones.

Participant Considerations

There are a number of considerations to take into account when determining optimal program offerings. Take time to plan and gather as much information as possible about participants and available resources; otherwise, participants may not receive the full benefit of the sport experience or be attracted to participate. The following principles may aid in developing program offerings.

Needs, interests, and preferences of participants. Develop the program content with participant input and an understanding of participant demographics. When conducting interest surveys ask questions that determine what people do now, what they would like added or changed to the current program, what skills they possess, and what activity they would participate in if offered. A good start would be to offer traditional tournaments that have wide appeal based on programs offered by similar agencies. Modify the content as new input indicates or as participant demographics change.

Balance of offerings. Individuals have different sport interests and skill levels. Consequently, offer a balance of individual, dual, and team sport; nontraditional tournaments, special events, and meets; indoor and outdoor sport; competitive and casual emphasis;

and strenuous and less strenuous events. Also, examine the number of tournaments offered during a season, session, or term to avoid too much overlap or concurrent tournaments. Balanced offerings also account for differences in age and health.

Flexibility. Keep an open mind in selecting events to meet the demands of the participants. What is appropriate one year changes the next. Factors affecting program selection include the following:

- age,
- number of events,
- gender,
- time availability,
- skill levels,
- climate and season,
- levels of competition,
- budget,
- physical capacity,
- area and facility availability,
- safety,
- equipment,
- number of participants, and
- leadership and supervisors.

These factors may not apply to every recreational sport setting because institutions have unique restrictions or limitations. The effective recreational sport specialist seeks to offer well-conducted tournaments serving the majority of clientele.

Types of Events

The delivery of events in the intramural sport program can be designed in many ways. Variety is encouraged in order to create a program with the greatest appeal to as many participants as possible. Variety of events is also essential for maximizing developmental opportunities for participants. Types of events include the following:

- Individual sports, such as swimming, golf, bowling, and archery, allow the individual to participate alone.
- Dual sports, such as table tennis, racquetball, badminton, or handball, require a partner.
- Group sports, such as relays, allow groups of various sizes to participate.
- Team sports, such as flag football, basketball, or soccer, require a specified number of players who play as a unit or organized team.

- Meets are organized competitions that include separate events and are usually completed within a specified time ranging from several hours to several days. Swimming, track and field, and wrestling are examples of meets.

- Special events consist of nontraditional tournaments that are not usually practiced for by the participants. Special events are an excellent way to promote positive public relations and introduce new activities.

- Co-intramural sport, applicable to many tournament designs, offers an avenue for fun, team spirit, and social interaction with members of both sexes.

Units of Participation

Units of participation categorize participants for intramural or extramural play. These units are essential for a well-balanced program. Consider the following two approaches to establishing units of participation.

Individual factors. The recreational sport specialist may prefer designating units of participation based on factors such as age, skill, or desired outcome of participation (i.e., skill development, competition, socialization). This approach helps participants connect with others who share similar interests and attributes. For example, a tennis tournament can be set up for participants who over 50 years old, and units can be subdivided by skill level for beginner, intermediate, and advanced players.

Group factors. This approach involves setting up units according to a common social grouping. Units of participation may be housing units, organizations, facilities, precincts, residential zones, and work shifts, among others. For example, in a military setting, units of participation are commonly established by squadron or barrack assignment. Individuals from a particular squadron or barrack enter tournaments as representatives of that unit. If a tournament objective is to improve internal socialization and group cohesion, the participants are typically placed in the same tournament brackets. However, if the goal is to facilitate interaction between units, then participants from different units are mixed within the tournament brackets.

Make every effort to develop units that will foster enthusiasm, enhance socialization, and maintain tradition in a wholesome, competitive atmosphere. Regardless of the setting, participation units should be equitable in size for the system to function effectively and fairly.

Rules and Regulations

Almost any activity for which there are participant interest and the necessary resources can be offered as an intramural or extramural sport. One of the key responsibilities of the recreational sport specialist is to select rules and regulations that direct the manner in which the sports are played. Rules may be chosen from a sanctioning body or modified to suit specific circumstances.

Sanctioned rules. A number of sources offer rules and regulations. Examples include the National Federation of State High School Associations, the Amateur Athletic Union, the National Collegiate Athletic Association, the National Intramural–Recreational Sports Association, and the National Youth Sports Association. One of the benefits of sanctioned rules is that they are standardized and participants tend to be familiar with them. Rule familiarity may reduce the amount of time required to teach rules, and participants may feel more comfortable getting involved when they've already had some experience with the rules of a sport tournament.

Modified rules. Recreational sport specialists may modify sanctioned rules and regulations to tailor the activity to satisfy participant interests, meet special needs, or address resource limitations and safety concerns. Common modifications include adjusting the number of players required for participation, changing timing regulations, altering the size and nature of the facilities, modifying the size or shape of the equipment, and changing the rules themselves. These adaptations may also help attract participants who are bored with or intimidated by the traditional rules.

Either way, selecting or modifying the rules and regulations provides tremendous opportunity for the recreational sport specialist to be creative and intentional in stimulating participant interest and building program satisfaction.

Program Delivery

Once the types of events have been finalized and the rules and regulations have been determined, the recreational sport specialist can make several important decisions related to program delivery, in particular operating policies and procedures, tournament formats, and personnel.

Program Policies and Procedures

The policies and procedures of the intramural and extramural sport programs should be clearly stated and available to all participants before the sport event. Some recreational sport specialists have found it helpful to prepare these statements in the form of a printed guide to participation or a page of a website about the intramural or extramural sport programs. Whenever possible, discuss the most pertinent information with participants, perhaps at a meeting for participants or team captains before play is scheduled.

Eligibility. Develop and enforce eligibility rules for intramural and extramural sport to ensure fair competition and eliminate controversy at the event. Theoretically, everyone should be able to participate; realistically, the recreational sport specialist must establish regulations governing individual and organizational eligibility. Refer to Figure 9.1 below on eligibility policy when setting policies.

The recreational sport specialist should provide all participants with good competition and a fair opportunity to win. The following outline is an example of commonly accepted eligibility requirements:

(a) A person is considered a member of a collegiate team if he or she has practiced 3 weeks before the first regularly scheduled athletic contest.

(b) Athletic coaches are considered members of their teams and are therefore restricted from participation.

(c) If an individual practices with a collegiate team for 1 year and does not letter, but is dropped from the team the following year 3 weeks before the first regularly scheduled athletic contest, he or she should be ineligible to compete in that sport and its counterpart in the intramural sport program during that year.

I. Individual eligibility

A. An individual may play for only one team per sport or contest. The team first represented should be the sole team for which a person may play for the remainder of the sport or contest.

B. Declare any player using an assumed name ineligible. The team involved should forfeit any contest in which the individual played under the assumed name.

C. Only individuals living, working, or attending a specified unit of participation should be allowed to play for that unit. Examples of this eligibility requirement are employment for a company or industry, regular attendance at a church, or union membership.

II. Skill-level eligibility

A. Professional eligibility

1. Any person established as a professional in any sport should be ineligible in that intramural sport or its counterpart.

2. A professional is any person recognized by a national governing body such as the United States Lawn Tennis Association, Professional Golf Association, National Collegiate Athletic Association; a professional member of the National Football League, Canadian Football League, National Basketball Association, major or minor league baseball; or a member of any other professional or semiprofessional organization.

B. Intercollegiate athletic eligibility

1. A person who has won a collegiate letter or award (i.e., trophy, plaque, jewelry, certificate, jacket) in a sport should not be eligible to compete in that sport or its counterpart for a 3-year period.

2. Only one varsity letter-winner is eligible to compete for a team in the sport or its related counterpart.

3. A person who has received an athletic scholarship or is a member of an intercollegiate athletic team, but did not receive a collegiate letter or award, should not be allowed to compete in that sport for 1 year following competition.

Figure 9.1. Eligibility Policy Guidelines *(cont.)*

C. Club sport eligibility

1. Club sport members may participate in their specific or related sport. Only one past or present club sport member may compete per team during a game to prevent domination by the club.

2. A club sport member is any individual who registers, pays dues, or practices with the club within three weeks of the first game or match of the club season.

3. At the end of 1 year, a past club member should return to a regular status for that specific or related sport.

D. Related sport

1. Professionals, intercollegiate athletes, and club sport members are ineligible for counterparts of their sports. The following is a list of sports and their counterparts that refers to professional, intercollegiate athletics, and club sport eligibility.

Professional, Athletic, Club Sport	*Intramural Sport*
Badminton	Badminton
Baseball	Softball
Basketball	Basketball (free throw, super shoot, one-on-one)
Billiards	Billiards
Bowling	Bowling
Cross country	Cross country, track, jogging
Diving	Diving
Field events	Field events
Football	Flag football, touch football
Frisbee	Frisbee
Golf	Golf, miniature golf
Handball	Handball
Judo	Judo
Racquetball	Racquetball
Soccer	Soccer
Softball	Softball, wiffleball, baseball
Swimming	Swimming, water polo
Table tennis	Table tennis
Track	Track, cross country, jogging
Volleyball	Volleyball, cageball, wallyball
Water polo	Water polo, swimming
Weight lifting	Weight lifting
Wrestling	Wrestling

III. Organizational eligibility

A. Individuals belonging to one or more teams should declare membership with only one team before the event. Individuals who change teams during the event should have the option of completing the schedule with their original team if they have participated in an event before moving.

B. Before participation, list team participants on the official entry form or score sheet in the sport office.

C. Only affiliated members are eligible to compete for an organization. Others may participate in any open division in the program.

Figure 9.1. cont.

Protests. Inevitably, there will be times when participants feel an official has made a mistake, a team has used an ineligible player, or some other situation occurs that seems unfair and warrants a verbal protest. The recreational sport specialist should have a procedure for receiving, documenting, and reviewing protests. Accept protests, but do not encourage them whenever someone feels a wrong has been committed. Regardless of the ruling, the recreational sport specialist can review the program and personnel objectively to reveal their strengths and weaknesses. A protest process brings the recreational sport specialist into direct contact with participants and provides an opportunity to establish a better understanding with them.

Protests may be made when an ineligible player has participated, there has been an improper interpretation of the rules, or a rule has been improperly enforced. Protests about a sport official's judgment calls are usually not accepted. In some situations, protests arise from judgment calls as a way to break the action. This permits the participants to let off steam by writing out a grievance instead of directing emotion toward an official. Although the recreational sport specialist generally does not accept protests on judgment calls, a review of the protest and discussion with participants may reveal a need to work more closely with officials on their mechanics or some other aspect of performance.

Any team or individual protesting the eligibility of a player should provide evidence that the player is ineligible. Such evidence may consist of the following:

- written and signed testimony of a witness;

- days, dates, and times validating illegal participation; and

- pictures, rosters, and other depictions of ineligibility.

Usually this evidence must be filed by a deadline designated by the sport staff. Protests not involving eligibility, on the other hand, should occur on the field of play and should be noted by the sport officials or supervisors on duty at the time of the incident. The protesting team should make sure that the officials or supervisors note the time of the contest, score, and particulars of the play in question before resuming play. The protesting team can accomplish this by filing a protest form during the game so that all pertinent information is obtained (see Figure 9.2). If the protest is sustained, replay the contest from the point of protest.

PROTEST FORM

Teams Involved

Protesting

Team A _____	Team A _____
Team captain _____	Team captain _____
Phone _____	Phone _____
Time-outs remaining _____	Time-outs remaining _____
Score _____	Score _____

Details

Period _____ Game (volleyball) _____ Inning (softball) _____

Time remaining _____

Team in possession _____

At bat (softball) _____

Explanation of protest and what occurred _____

_____

_____

How and where is ball to be put into play? _____

_____

_____

Protesting team captain _____
(Signature)

Officials

Referee _____	Phone/e-mail _____
Umpire _____	Phone/e-mail _____
Officials' comments _____	
Supervisor _____	Phone/e-mail _____
Sport _____	Date _____

Figure 9.2. Intramural Sport Protest. *Source: Recreational Sport Management* by Richard F. Mull, Kathryn G. Bayless, and Lynn Jamieson, 2005, Champaign, IL: Human Kinetics.

All protests should be verified in writing by the participant and submitted to the sport staff in a timely fashion. In many intramural and extramural programs, a protest sincerity fee must accompany each protest. This fee is returned to the protesting team if the protest is sustained. Otherwise, the department retains it. Such a fee discourages many unwarranted protests.

When a written protest and documentation of evidence have been received, the staff should further investigate the complaint, though staff should always have the authority to investigate an alleged violation of policy without a formal protest by a participant. After reviewing all materials, an appropriate staff member should make a decision. If the staff member makes an invalid protest ruling, the participant should have the right to appeal the decision to an appeals or governing board. This board serves as a hearing board for all intramural or extramural sport programs. In making their final decision, the board should be governed by the same rules and regulations adopted by the program. To reach its decision, the board may request any staff, sport official, supervisor, witness, or representative from the teams to attend a meeting or hearing. All decisions rendered by this board are final and not subject to appeal.

Disciplinary action. Individuals participating in sport may encounter disappointments or frustrations that are difficult for them to handle. The recreational sport specialist must have an objective, consistent procedure for dealing with negative behavior as well as properly trained personnel who can implement this procedure. Otherwise, participants may lose interest in the program, and the recreational sport specialist may encounter problems securing officials. Effective control of negative behavior is a major factor in the enjoyment of participants and personnel.

If an individual or spectator acts in an unsporting manner during intramural or extramural competition, the game official has authority to take action as necessary to keep control of the game. Depending on the severity of the incident, an official may take the following action: issue the offender a warning, eject the offender from the game, eject the offender from the area, or suspend the game. Game officials should report all incidents to the intramural supervisor and document them for the investigation. The staff should investigate all incidents that indicate unsporting conduct (using an ineligible player; theft or damage to facilities or equipment; physical or verbal abuse toward officials, supervisors, players, or spectators). They should question the individuals or teams involved and require a written statement of the incident due on the day following the incident. Staff should also obtain written statements from the officials and supervisors on duty in addition to an incident form. At the conclusion of the investigation, the staff rule on the individuals and teams involved. Penalties could include suspension from a game, games, or season; temporary or permanent probation; or suspension from the sport program for a period of time. Only action relating to the intramural or extramural sport program should be taken; however, refer any serious incident to the appropriate law enforcement office.

Forfeits

Forfeits have a detrimental effect on intramural and extramural sport programs and are frustrating to the individuals or teams who are ready to play but have no opponent. To minimize forfeits, schedule events at the most convenient times for participants, communicate schedules to participants in advance, categorize participants by skill level or age, and remind participants of their scheduled event.

All contests should be played on the scheduled date and hour. A team not ready to play within a specified period, usually 5 minutes after the scheduled time, is charged with a forfeit, subject to the discretion of the officials, supervisor, or staff. Games lost by forfeit are not rescheduled.

If a team leaves before an official or supervisor notes the forfeit, both teams should be charged with a forfeit. The team present at a forfeit must have the full complement of players required for that sport, or both teams are given a forfeit.

If one team does not have the required number of players, the other team's captain or manager should have the option to agree to play the game if provided for by the rules of that sport. It would then become a legal game and could not be protested on the grounds that an illegal team was fielded. If both teams and the staff agree to play the game after the scheduled starting time has elapsed, no protest based on the starting time is considered. Policies to discourage forfeits include the following:

- One forfeit results in the elimination of an individual or team from playoff competition in that sport.

- Two forfeits result in the elimination of an individual or team from all further competition in that sport.

- Forfeit fees are assessed to the individual or team.

- A forfeit means losing a certain number of league or tournament points if a point system is in effect.

- A team is allowed to play with a reduced number of players if the opponent agrees and if there are no safety concerns.

Regardless of forfeit procedures and policies, communication plays a vital role. Improve communication by posting the game schedule where it is accessible at all times. When a forfeit occurs, notify the forfeiting individual or team and the opponent immediately with a phone call, e-mail, or forfeit letter. Figures 9.3 and 9.4 are examples of effective forfeit notices. They are brief, restate the forfeit rules and policies, and encourage the participant to take action in case a clerical error has occurred.

This personal approach might eliminate future forfeits and demonstrate to participants the recreational sport specialist's desire to provide the best possible program.

Dear Mr. Smith:

According to our records, your flag football team, Smith's Team, has forfeited one of its regular season games. The rules governing intramural play state that any team forfeiting one game during regular season play will be disqualified from postseason play, and a team forfeiting two regular season games will lose all entry points and be dropped from further competition.

Forfeits are disruptive to our program and frustrating to those teams who are ready to play and receive the forfeit. Therefore, please make every effort to play the remaining games on your regular season schedule. If you think your team will not be able to play your remaining games or if our records are in error, please contact us as soon as possible so we can make the necessary arrangements.

Sincerely,

Figure 9.3. First Sample Forfeit Notice

Dear Mr. Smith:

According to our records, your flag football team, Smith's Team, has forfeited two of its regular season games. The rules governing intramural play state that any team forfeiting two games during regular season play will lose all entry points and be dropped from further competition.

If our records are in error, please contact us as soon as possible so we can make the necessary arrangements.

Sincerely,

Figure 9.4. Second Sample Forfeit Notice

Postponement and rescheduling. All sport events should be played at the scheduled time unless major problems occur that affect most participants. Inform teams that they should have enough players on their roster that the teams can still play in case several members have schedule conflicts.

If rescheduling is necessary, postpone a scheduled contest only with the consent of the opposing participants and the staff. Present a reschedule request form (Figure 9.5), providing all pertinent information to the staff at least 24 hours before the originally scheduled contest so all participants and game officials can be notified of the cancellation. Postponements may occur because of poor playing conditions due to inclement weather. In that case, intramural staff should notify all affected participants, if possible. A number of electronic methods of notification are popular, including 24-hour recorded telephone messages, voice mail messages, and e-mail updates. The obvious advantage to these modes of communication is they provide up-to-date game schedules and postponement or rescheduling information after regular office hours, which is when most intramural and extramural programs are conducted.

If participants have not received notification of postponement due to inclement weather before the scheduled contest, it is their responsibility to be present for the game or contact the sport office for a ruling. Always reschedule instead of canceling any games postponed by the staff.

Medical clearance. Urge all participants to obtain a physical examination before participating in the intramural and extramural sport program. Because most programs are voluntary, participants are responsible for knowing their physiological limitations before competition and are accountable for their involvement in the program. However, the recreational sport specialist is responsible for informing participants of the risks of participation and where financial responsibility for medical care rests. When participants are minors, have parents or guardians sign a statement indicating approval for their participation. If medical examinations are required before participation, the recreational sport specialist may need to keep a copy of the exam on file for future verification.

Structuring Tournaments

Deciding on and successfully implementing a tournament design is perhaps the most fundamental of all skills required of a recreational sport specialist. Although presented in this chapter because of their prevalence in intramural sport, these are tools applied throughout recreational sport programs. There are several possible structures for tournament competition, but there are three main categories: round-robin, elimination, and challenge. One of the most difficult aspects of tournament scheduling is providing accurate, consistent schedules and brackets.

RESCHEDULE REQUEST

Directions

1. All games will be played at the scheduled time unless *major* problems are present. Teams should anticipate having a player or players unavailable for a game or games due to conflicts with other activities and should have an ample number of players on their team roster.

2. If rescheduling is necessary, a scheduled contest may be postponed only with the consent of both team captains and the intramural staff.

3. This form must be completed and signed by both team captains and returned to the recreational sport office by 5:00 p.m. the day before the contest.

Team initiating request _____

Reason for rescheduling _____

The team of _____ and _____ agree to reschedule
                 (Team name)   *(Team name)*

their _____ game originally scheduled for _____, _____, at _____,
       (Sport)   *(Day)*   *(Date)*   *(Time)*

on _____, to a time to be decided by the intramural sport staff.
      (Field or court)

_____   _____   _____
     (Team)   *(Team captain or manager)*   *(Phone)*

_____   _____   _____
     (Team)   *(Team captain or manager)*   *(Phone)*

*For Office Use Only

League # _____

The above game has been *rescheduled* to

_____, _____, at _____, on _____
 (Day)   *(Date)*   *(Time)*   *(Field or court)*

Figure 9.5. Reschedule Request. Source: *Recreational Sport Management* by Richard F. Mull, Kathryn G. Bayless, and Lynn M. Jamieson, 2005, Champaign, IL: Human Kinetics.

Determining Factors

Selecting the best tournament design for the desired outcomes requires understanding of participant needs and interests, a solid grasp of the technical details of tournament design, and exceptional attention to detail and accuracy. To determine the most appropriate tournament plan, consider the following seven factors.

1.   Tournament objectives
- Determine a winner quickly
- Provide maximum participation
- Encourage social interaction
- Determine a true champion
- Emphasize the element of competition
- Motivate participants
- Improve participant sport skills
- Provide an equal number of matches per entry
- Rank all entries according to ability

2.   Participant characteristics
- Age group (child, youth, adolescent, adult, senior)
- Sex (male, female, coed)
- Playing ability (beginner, intermediate, advanced)
- Interest (level of participant interest in the sport)
- Attention span (young people generally have shorter attention spans than adults)
- Intensity of competition (competitive or informal)

3.   Facilities and equipment
- Policy for facility reservation
- Number of available facilities and equipment
- Availability of fields or courts
- Facility condition and costs of preparing the facility
- Accessibility to locker rooms
- Provisions for equipment rental and checkout
- Efficient maintenance staff

4.   Time parameters
- Length of time available to complete the tournament
- Dates, days, and hours available
- Provisions for inclement weather, rescheduled games, and championship play-offs

5.   Type of event
- Individual sport
- Dual sport
- Group sport
- Team sport
- Meet
- Special event
- Co-intramural

6.   Personnel
- Number of sport officials and supervisors
- Coaches' qualifications
- Administrative personnel requirements
- Medical supervision
- Funding for personnel

7.   Other factors
- Budget restrictions
- Publicity and promotion
- Program control
- Governance procedures
- Spectator (crowd) control

All tournaments have advantages and disadvantages; each format serves different objectives. Understanding these differences as well as the tools for tournament structure is essential to successful sport programming. The following pages present five tournament structures: round-robin tournaments, elimination tournaments, consolation tournaments, challenge tournaments, and meets. Each has its own schematic, advantages, disadvantages, applicable formulas, and programming procedures.

Round-Robin Tournaments

The round-robin tournament (see Figure 9.6), the most popular tournament format, allows for maximum participation because each entry plays against the other entries an equal number of times. The winner of the round-robin tournament is usually determined by a win–loss percentage. Table 9.1 illustrates the differences in round-robin, single elimination, and double elimination tournaments in terms of the number of games, rounds, and first-round games.

The advantages of round-robin tournaments include the following:

- They are easily organized and administered.
- They allow complete prescheduling of entries.
- Participants easily understand them.
- They are effective for outdoor sport programming

when weather is a concern because postponed games can be played later in the tournament.

- Participants know opponents and game times in advance.
- Emphasis is on maximum participation for an extended time.

Teams entered	Rounds							Total games per team
	1	2	3	4	5	6	7	
	Bye–7	Bye–6	Bye–5	Bye–4	Bye–3	Bye–2	Bye–1	
	1–6	7–5	6–4	5–3	4–2	3–1	2–7	
7	2–5	1–4	7–3	6–2	5–1	4–7	3–6	6
	3–4	2–3	1–2	7–1	6–7	5–6	4–5	

Figure 9.6. Round-robin Tournament Schematic

Table 9.1

Differences in Round-Robin, Single Elimination, and Double Elimination Tournaments

	ROUND ROBIN		SINGLE ELIMINATION			DOUBLE ELIMINATION	
Number of entries	Number of games	Number of rounds	Number of games	Number of rounds	Number of 1st round games	Number of games	Number of rounds
2	1	1	1	1	1	2	5
3	2	3	2	2	1	4	5
4	6	3	3	2	2	6	5
5	10	5	4	3	1	8	8
6	15	5	5	3	2	10	8
7	21	7	6	3	3	12	8
8	28	7	7	3	4	14	8
9	36	9	8	4	1	16	11
10	45	9	9	4	2	18	11
11	55	11	10	4	3	20	11
12	66	11	11	4	4	22	11
13	78	13	12	4	5	24	11
14	91	13	13	4	6	26	11
15	105	15	14	4	7	28	11
16	120	15	15	4	8	30	11
17			16	5	1	32	14
18			17	5	2	34	14
19			18	5	3	36	14
20			19	5	4	38	14
21			20	5	5	40	14
22			21	5	6	42	14
23			22	5	7	44	14
24			23	5	8	46	14
25			24	5	9	48	14
26			25	5	10	50	14
27			26	5	11	52	14
28			27	5	12	54	14
29			28	5	13	56	14
30			29	5	14	58	14
31			30	5	15	60	14
32			31	5	16	62	14

- Each entry competes against the others on a scheduled basis regardless of win–loss record.
- A single round-robin produces the true champion.
- Entries can be ranked at the end of the tournament.
- Although preferred, it is not necessary for rounds to be played consecutively.
- Participants can get acquainted because of the extended season.

The disadvantages of round-robin tournaments include the following:

- They are the most time consuming of all tournaments.
- They require a lot of facility usage.
- They do not provide an instant winner.
- Forfeits may occur in last rounds when entrants realize they have no chance of winning the league championship.

- With more than eight entries, participant interest is hard to maintain.
- If a large number of entries are divided into smaller leagues, several winners result with no true champion, thus an elimination tournament must be held to determine a single winner.
- It is possible for a league to end in a tie, which requires extra contests to decide a winner.

Formulas for round-robin tournaments. The following formulas have been developed to guide the design of round-robin tournaments. These formulas help the recreational sport specialist make decisions regarding the facilities, equipment, and personnel needed to complete the tournament.

With N = total number of entries, use the formulas below:

Examples Where N = 7

A. Number of games per league

$$\frac{N(N-1)}{2} = \frac{7(7-1)}{2} = \frac{42}{2} = 21 \text{ games}$$

B. Number of games per entry

$$N - 1 = 7 - 1 = 6 \text{ games}$$

C. Number of rounds
Even number of entries $\quad N - 1$
Odd number of entries $\quad N \qquad 7 = 7 \text{ rounds}$

D. Number of games per round
Even number of entries $\quad \dfrac{N}{2}$

Odd number of entries

$$\frac{(N-1)}{2} = \frac{7-1}{2} = \frac{6}{2} = 3 \text{ games per round}$$

E. Determining percentages
Games won / games played

$$\frac{5}{6} = .8333$$

Note: Ties should count as a half game won and a half game lost.

F. Number of games behind

$$\frac{(W_a - W_b) + (L_b - L_a)}{2}$$

W = Number of wins
L = Number of losses
a = First place entry
b = Specific entry in question

Standings

	Won	Loss
Lee	0	6
Al	6	0
Jeff	4	2
Rob	2	4

Number of games Rob is behind?

$$\frac{(6-2) + (4-0)}{2} = \frac{4+4}{2} = 4$$

Round-robin procedures. Construct pairings for the tournament by arranging all entries by name or assigned number into two vertical columns. List them consecutively down the first column and continue up to the second. When an odd number of entries are scheduled, place a bye in the fixed upper left position. This means that the entry scheduled against the bye is *standing by* and has no game in that round:

7 entries	8 entries
Bye–7	1–8
1–6	2–7
2–5	3–6
3–4	4–5

To obtain pairings for subsequent rounds, rotate the names or numbers *counterclockwise* around the participant located in the upper left position of the column.

Round 1	Round 2	Round 3	Round 4
Bye–7	Bye–6	Bye–5	Bye–4
1–6	7–5	6–4	5–3
2–5	1–4	7–3	6–2
3–4	2–3	1–2	7–1

Round 5	Round 6	Round 7
Bye–3	Bye–2	Bye–1
4–2	3–1	2–7
5–1	4–7	3–6
6–7	5–6	4–5

Record keeping for round-robin tournaments. A simple chart for notifying participants of the tournament progression is shown in Figure 9.7. List all entries in the league at both the top and left side of the chart. At the end of a contest, record the date and score in the appropriate boxes. Read the chart horizontally with the score of the horizontal team recorded first. The examples in Figure 9.7 read as follows:

- All-Stars defeated Heroes by the score of 1-0 (forfeit) on November 8.

- Rejects lost to Sluggers by the score of 2-12 on November 1.

- *F* represents a forfeit.

Write wins and losses in different colors for distinction. Once all rounds have been completed, determine the league champion. If two or more entries have an identical win–loss record at the end of the tournament, the recreational sport specialist may choose from several methods to determine the winner:

- Have a single elimination play-off between the tied entries.

- Declare the winner of the contest between the tied entries during league play the tournament champion.

- Allow the tie to stand and call them co-champions.

- Use a point differential system in which the points each entry allowed to its opponents are subtracted from the entry's total points scored. The entry with the largest total is the champion.

Round-robin tournament programming. The following are suggestions for programming round-robin tournaments:

- The most desirable number of entries per league ranges between four and eight. Divide a larger number of entries into several smaller leagues.

- If several entries have similar time conflicts, group those entries together for easier scheduling.

- Try to schedule each entry to play at least once a week.

- Designate several open dates for rescheduling.

- Double-check all work!

A variation of the traditional round-robin tournament is the Lombard tournament. In this type of round-robin, the entire tournament is completed in several hours. The entries play in an abbreviated time frame that is a fraction of the regular game. For example, if the regulation time for volleyball was 40 minutes and eight teams entered, there would be eight 5-minute games. Record each entry's scores, and at the conclusion of 40 minutes the entry with the largest total is the winner. The Lombard tournament usually works best when there are at least six and no more than 12 entries and when two or three courts are used at once.

Name of team	All-Stars	Sluggers	Rejects	Batboys	Heroes
All-Stars					Nov 8 1-0 W [F]
Sluggers			Nov 1 12-2 W		
Rejects		Nov 1 2-12 L			
Batboys					
Heroes	Nov 8 0-1 L [F]				

Figure 9.7. League Record-Keeping Chart

Round-robin tournament scheduling. After selecting the appropriate tournament design, proceed with the tournament scheduling. The first step is to develop a master tournament calendar that illustrates when the tournament will take place. After assigning dates, designate times that will not be played for various reasons (i.e., holidays, team captain's meetings, other sport conflicts). If specific dates for practice are assigned, include these on the calendar as well. Because postponements are inevitable, allocate extra playing dates for rescheduled games, league tie-breakers, and play-offs. Figure 9.8 is a sample master tournament calendar.

After creating the tournament calendar, develop a facility schedule (Figure 9.9) indicating 1 week of playing times for each court or field. The example in Figure 9.9 indicates there are 36 game openings per day, or 144 game openings in 1 week of 4 playing days. In other words, 288 teams could participate in one game each during the first week of the tournament. This type of schedule indicates the maximum number of entries that the tournament could accommodate.

Once the recreational sport specialist receives the entries, he or she should sort them into appropriate participation units. For example, an initial step is to separate all men, women, and coed entries into groups. Then divide each group into smaller sub-units, such as advanced, intermediate, and novice classes. Continue this process until all entries are in small units, grouping entries with special scheduling requests as much as possible. Now that the entries are sorted, the recreational sport specialist can assign them into leagues (round-robin) or place them into elimination brackets. League assignment plays a major role in the success of a tournament, so the recreational sport specialist must have a thorough knowledge of the requirements of each event, the availability of facilities, and the interest level of the participants. For example, if 28 teams signed up for a basketball tournament but only five-team round-robin leagues are wanted, in what ways could the recreational sport specialist create the leagues?

- Five 5-team leagues plus one 3-team league
- Three 6-team leagues plus two 5-team leagues
- Four 5-team leagues plus two 4-team leagues

The solution should be based on the number of available facilities and their operating hours, the time required for each event, and the days participants have conflicts. Creative planning must be used when developing league structure. Equal playing opportunities for all entries should be offered as much as possible.

Month _____ *May* _____

Sunday	Monday	Tuesday	Wednesday	Thursday	Friday	Saturday
1	2	3	4	5	6 No games	7 No games
8	9	10	11	12 Religious holiday; no games 5:00-8:00 p.m.	13 No games	14 No games
15	16	17	18	19	20 No games	21 No games
22	23	24	25	26	27 No games	28 No games
29 Hold for rescheduling	30 Hold for rescheduling	31 No games; team captain's meeting for play-offs				

Figure 9.8. Master Tournament Calendar

After the leagues are formed, each league's entries can be attached to a scheduling worksheet. On the cover of the worksheet, write the league number, division, entry names, and any special scheduling requests. Once this task is completed for all leagues and entries, construct a master schedule. The process of scheduling each league's round-robin contests is simple if schedulers use care and accuracy. As one scheduler reads aloud the league number and two corresponding team numbers, a recorder transcribes these figures on a master schedule and responds aloud with the date, time, and field or court assignment for that contest. In the example shown in Figure 9.10, at 5:00 PM on court 1, teams 1 and 2 from league 1 will play. At 6:00 PM on court 2, teams 3 and 4 from league 2 will play.

This process continues until all entries and contests are scheduled. Whenever possible, schedule all leagues on the same days and times throughout the tournament. Also, when scheduling several units, such as men's, women's, and coed, develop special codes for each or use different colored pencils.

With the completion of the rough draft, double-check all work for accuracy. A single error may cause great confusion for the scheduler. Once finalized, type the league schedules, duplicate them, and distribute them to the participants by handing out hard copies, sending e-mails, or posting them on a website.

An alternative to this process is instant scheduling. Instant scheduling is a method in which team captains or participants have scheduling responsibilities. After following a specified entry procedure, the participants schedule themselves into a league. League scheduling forms with playing days and game times are posted on a bulletin board, usually outside the sport office or on a website. Individuals look for openings in leagues where they can play. Once a suitable league is found, individuals write their name or the team name in the opening and copy down the playing date, time, and facility location. This process can also be completed through a website. Either way, participants have a copy of the league schedule without it being provided by a staff member.

Maas (1979) suggests several advantages and disadvantages of instant scheduling. Advantages of this system include the following:

- Responsibility for scheduling shifts from the intramural sport specialist to the team captain or participant.

- Participants may select from a variety of available times, and their schedule will be consistent from week to week for the entire season.

- Participants select alternative playing times if the preferred time is not available.

FACILITY SCHEDULE

Month		Date		Day	

Time/field	A	B	C	D	E	F
5:00						
6:00						
7:00						
8:00						
9:00						
10:00						

Month		Date		Day	

Time/field	A	B	C	D	E	F
5:00						
6:00						
7:00						
8:00						
9:00						
10:00						

Month		Date		Day	

Time/field	A	B	C	D	E	F
5:00						
6:00						
7:00						
8:00						
9:00						
10:00						

Month		Date		Day	

Time/field	A	B	C	D	E	F
5:00						
6:00						
7:00						
8:00						
9:00						
10:00						

Figure 9.9. Facility Schedule. Source: *Recreational Sport Management* by Richard F. Mull, Kathryn G. Bayless, and Lynn M. Jamieson, 2005, Champaign, IL: Human Kinetics).

	Court 1	Court 2
5:00 P.M.	League 1 1–2	League 2 1–2
6:00 P.M.	League 1 3–4	League 2 3–4

Figure 9.10. Master Tournament Schedule

- The system encourages entries well before the deadline.

- Participants do not need to be contacted again until play-offs, unless there is a schedule change.

- Programming time is reduced substantially and scheduling is finished on the deadline date except for late entries.

- Schedules do not need to be typed and copied for the participants.

The disadvantages of instant scheduling include the following:

- The recreational sport specialist needs to predict the breakdown of leagues in each classification or else be flexible about changing league designations if an imbalance occurs.

- A physical setting is needed for signing up (hallway, large room, bulletin board) that accommodates a large number of people.

- There may be problems until participants become familiar with the procedure.

Instant scheduling is a unique option in tournament scheduling. Although this method may not be applicable for all sport settings, the recreational sport specialist should keep it in mind as an option.

Single Elimination Tournaments

Single elimination tournaments are well known and easy to design (see Figure 9.11). All entries compete in the first round, but only the winners of each round compete in the subsequent rounds, with the winner of the final contest becoming the champion. Often there is a drawing for position placement in the tournament schedule with the best entries being seeded to separate the stronger entries so they will not compete against each other until the later rounds. This schedule sheet is often referred to as a draw. Byes are awarded in the first round of the draw if the number of entries is not equal to a power of 2 (2, 4, 8, 16, 32, 64, and so on).

The advantages of single elimination tournaments include the following:

- The participants understand them easily.

- They are the simplest tournament to conduct.

- They are useful in determining a champion for preliminary tournaments. For example, after teams participate in a round-robin league, a single elimination tournament can be used to determine a winner to advance to regional competition.

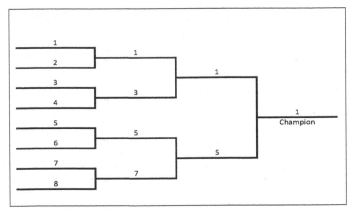

Figure 9.11. Single Elimination Tournament Schematic

- They determine the champion in the shortest amount of time of all tournaments.

- They can be conducted with limited facilities.

- They can accommodate a large number of entrants.

- They are interesting for spectators.

- They are the best format for a 1-day event.

- They are economical.

The disadvantages of single elimination tournaments include the following:

- They involve minimal participation.

- They place maximal emphasis on winning.

- The champion and runner-up may not be the best team or player.

- They do not allow for participants to have an off-day (i.e., perform at less than their best).

- They provide the least flexibility for the participant.

- Competition may become too intense because the entrant must win every contest, or they face elimination.

- Weather-related postponements can cause scheduling problems for outdoor sport programs because contests must be played sequentially.

Formulas for single elimination tournaments. The design of a single elimination tournament depends on the number of entries. A tournament schedule or bracket arrangement cannot be completed until all entries are received.

With N = total number of entries, use the following formulas:

Examples Where N = 13

A.   Number of tournament games   N - 1 = 13 - 1 = 12 games

B.   Power of 2—number of times 2 has to be multiplied to equal or exceed the number of entries

  $2 \times 2 = 4$ or (2^2)

  $2 \times 2 \times 2 = 8$ or (2^3)

  $2 \times 2 \times 2 \times 2 = 16$ or (2^4)

  $2 \times 2 \times 2 \times 2 \times 2 = 32$ or (2^5)

C.   Number of byes   (power of 2) - N = 16 - 13 = 3 byes

D.   Number of rounds—the power to which 2 must be raised (2^4) or 4 rounds

E.   Number of first-round games   N - (next lower power of 2) = 13 - (8) = 5 games

  or $\dfrac{N - byes}{2} = \dfrac{13 - (3)}{2} = \dfrac{10}{2} = 5$ games

Procedures for single elimination tournaments. The following is a guide for developing a single elimination draw:

1.   Check and recheck that all names are correctly spelled on the entry form and that units of participation, divisions, and affiliations are correct. Misspelling or overlooking entries is inexcusable.

2.   Select the draw sheet of the appropriate size (4, 8, 16, 32, 64, and so on).

3.   Determine the seeds. Separate the stronger entries so they will not compete against each other until the later rounds by distributing strength throughout the draw. Although seeding is not required, it ensures a fairer tournament when the superior players meet in the final rounds. The rule for the number of seeds is no more than one seed for every four entries. Place the top seed, chosen by ability, previous performance, and ranking, in the top of the upper bracket and the second seed at the bottom of the lower bracket (see Figure 9.12).

To check the draw placement of seeds, those at the extreme of each bracket should equal a consistent number when totaled. For example, in a 32-entry draw, place seeds so that each of the eight quarters of the bracket equals 17 (1 + 16, 9 + 8, 5 + 12, 13 + 4, 3 + 14, 11 + 6, 7 + 10, 15 + 2). An alternative method is to place the first seeded entry on the top line of the upper bracket and the second on the bottom line of the lower bracket. Place the third seed at the bottom of the upper bracket, the fourth at the top of the lower bracket, and so on (see Figure 9.13).

Don't attempt to equalize the upper or lower brackets. If the seeding procedures rank entries according to ability, it would be advantageous to require the first seed to play a weaker opponent (i.e., fourth seed instead of third seed).

4.   Determine the number of byes. When the number of entries is not an exact power of 2, the first round should have byes to avoid an uneven number of contestants remaining in the final round. All byes must be played in the first round. The number of byes should ensure that the number of contestants equals a power of 2 (full brackets) in the second round.

5.   Place the byes. Distribute all byes evenly between the upper and lower brackets. Grant seeded entries byes in order of ranking: First seed receives first bye, second seed receives second bye, and so on. In other words, the placement of byes should complement the placement of seeded entries.

6.   Number the games. The numbering of games should progress by round in sequential order. If the recreational sport specialist is using several bracket sheets simultaneously, he or she should number all games in the first round on each sheet before proceeding to the second round. Place game numbers where the winner's name will appear. Figure 9.14 illustrates the placement of game numbers and the even distribution of byes.

List the date, time, and location of the game on the bracket sheet. An alternative to placing the game information on the bracket sheet is to attach an additional sheet that contains only this information.

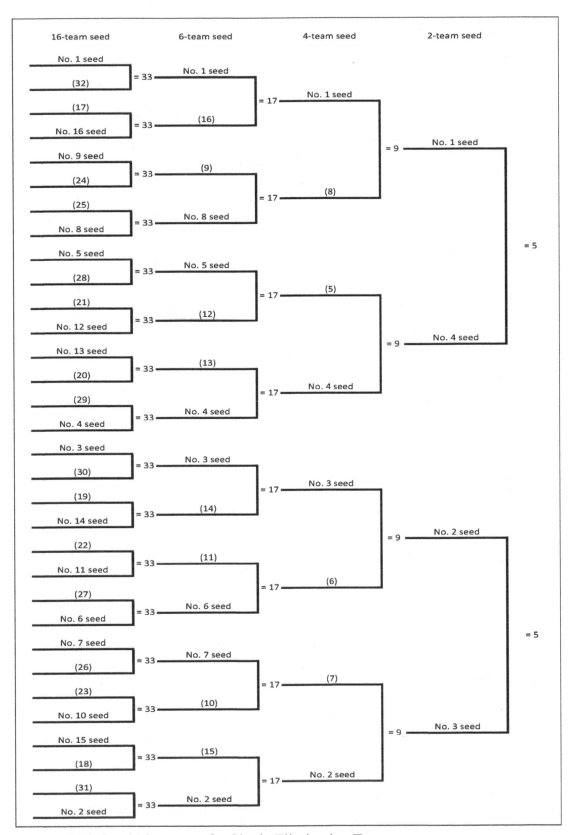

Figure 9.12. Seed Placement for Single Elimination Tournaments

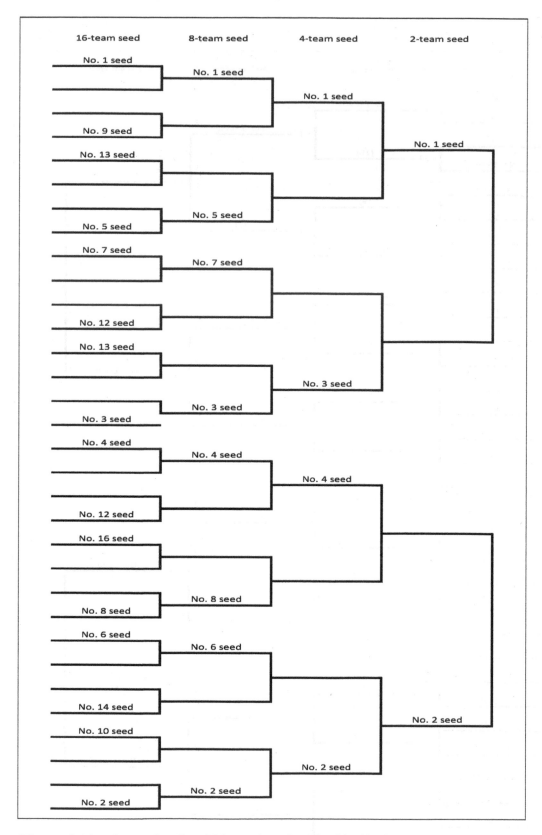

Figure 9.13. Alternative Seed Placement for Single Elimination Tournaments

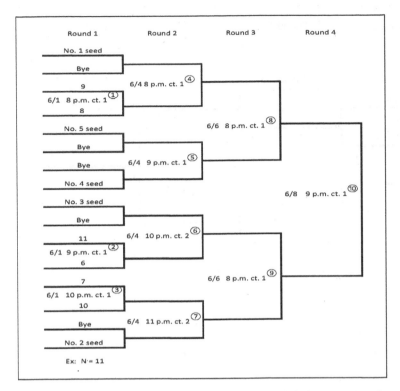

Figure 9.14. Bye Placement and Sequential Game Numbering for 11-team Single Elimination Tournaments with Seeds

Single elimination tournament programming.
The following are suggestions for programming single elimination tournaments:

- Indicate the appropriate round on the bracket
sheet for scheduling purposes. Remember, complete round 1 before progressing to round 2.

- Rather than indicating bye games, have implied
byes or blank spaces replace the first round bye
and have only second-round games appear (see
Figure 9.15).

- The placement of byes starts at the extremes and
moves toward the center.

- When the number of entries is only a few over
the number on a draw sheet (power of 2), such
as 17, it is less confusing to add one game to a
16-entry draw than it is to have several byes listed on a 32-entry draw. To accomplish this, start
at the center of the bracket and create two-line
pairings until there are as many lines as there are
entries.

- Determine position assignments on the bracket
sheet at random, by known ability (seeding), or
in the order the entries were received.

Double Elimination Tournaments

The double elimination tournament (see Figure
9.16), also known as the two loss and out tournament,
is basically a single elimination tournament with consolation format. No contestant is eliminated until two
losses occur. An entry that loses in the championship
or winners bracket is scheduled to play other losers
in a losers bracket or second-elimination tournament.
Play continues until there is a winner of the championship bracket and a winner of the losers bracket.
These two winners compete to determine an overall
winner. If the champion of the losers bracket defeats
the champion of the winners bracket, an additional
contest is required because both have only one loss.
The advantages of double elimination tournaments
include the following:

- They are one of the fairest types of tournaments
because each entry must be defeated twice before
being eliminated from the tournament.

- They allow twice as much participation as the
single elimination tournament.

- They hold participant interest for a longer
time than the single elimination or consolation
tournament.

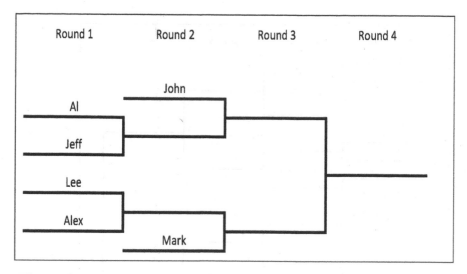

Figure 9.15. Implied Bye Schematic

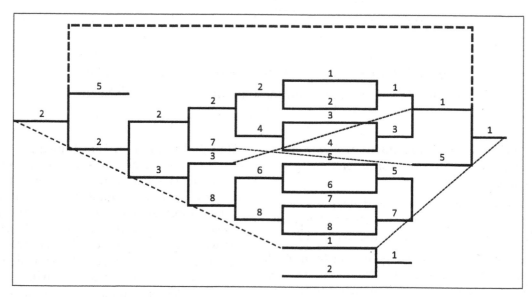

Figure 9.16. Double Elimination Tournament Schedule

- They allow entrants who have had an off-day or received a poor pairing a chance to win the losers bracket and play for the championship.

In addition to those disadvantages associated with a single elimination tournament, double elimination tournaments have the following disadvantages:

- They are complicated to show graphically because the loser rounds keep adding new contestants as teams lose in the winners rounds.

- They are confusing to participants who have difficulty understanding the tournament format.

- They are more time consuming than a single elimination tournament.

Formulas for double elimination tournaments. These formulas are used to set up a double elimination tournament schedule.

With N = total number of entries, use the following formulas:

Examples Where N = 13

A. Number of games

Minimum = 2N - 2 = 2(13) - 2 = 26 - 2 = 24 minimum games

Maximum = 2N - 1 = 2(13) - 1 = 26 - 1 = 25 maximum games

Note: The maximum number of games occurs when the champion of the losers' bracket defeats the champion of the winners' bracket, thus creating an extra game.

B. Number of rounds

Twice the power to which 2 must be raised to equal or exceed the number of entries, plus an additional round if an extra contest is required.

$= 2(2^2)$,

$= 2(4)$

$= 8$ rounds

Procedures for double elimination tournaments. The procedures of a single elimination tournament apply to the winners bracket of the double elimination tournament. However, procedures for the losers bracket are more involved. Arrange byes so that a second bye is not given to an entry that has already had a bye. Give special attention to crossing losers from the top and bottom halves of the winners bracket. This prevents entries who played each other in the winners bracket from playing each other a second time in the losers bracket until the latest possible opportunity. Achieve this crossing by using either of the following two scheduling methods. Regardless of the method, the results of the brackets are the same.

1. **Back-to-back.** The winners and the losers brackets are arranged side by side, with the winners progressing to the right and the losers following the broken lines to the left. This ensures that two previous opponents will not meet again until late in the losers bracket.

2. **Over–under.** This method arranges the losers bracket under the winners bracket and eliminates the broken lines. An example of this bracket may be seen in Figure 9.17. In the losers' bracket, the line of the pairings is indicated by a consecutive listing of respective letters. Each pairing of the winners bracket includes the words "Loser to" followed by the letter of the team. This method is the simplest for participants, spectators, and tournament directors to read and understand.

Semi-double elimination tournament. A variation of the double elimination format is the semi-double elimination tournament. An example of this bracket is in Figure 9.18.

This tournament is similar to the double elimination tournament in that all first-round losers and those entries scheduled a first-round bye who lost in the second round are placed in the losers bracket. From this point on, both the winners and the losers brackets continue on a straight single elimination basis with the winners of each bracket playing for the championship. In other words, each entry is guaranteed a minimum of two contests but not necessarily two losses.

Double elimination tournament programming. The following are suggestions for programming double elimination tournaments:

- In the losers brackets, after the first round each additional round must have two contests.

- Number contests consecutively as much as possible depending on facility limitations and playing times.

- List the times, locations, and game numbers of each contest on the bracket. This lessens the possibility of a participant losing additional sheets of information.

- In numbering the contests, make sure an entry is never scheduled to play two games in succession.

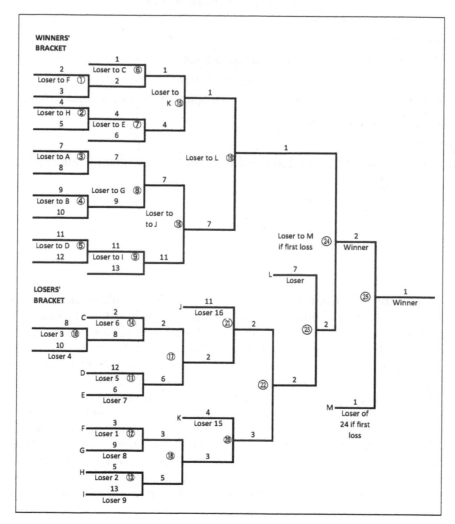

Figure 9.17. Double Elimination Over-Under Bracket

Consolation Tournaments

These elimination tournaments are superior to single elimination tournaments in that they permit each entry to participate in at least two contests. This tournament produces two winners: the champion of the elimination bracket and the winner of the consolation bracket. There are two types of consolation tournaments, type A and type B (see Figure 9.19). In type A, or simple consolation, all losers in the first round or those who lose in the second round after drawing a bye in the first play another single elimination tournament. The winner of the second single elimination tournament is the consolation winner.

Type B consolation tournaments, also called second-place consolations, provide an opportunity for any loser to win the consolation championship, regardless of the round in which the loss occurred. This is similar to double elimination tournaments, except the winner of the consolation tournament is the third-place finisher and does not play the champion of the winners bracket.

The advantages of consolation tournaments include the following:

- Each entry is guaranteed at least two contests.

- More participation is possible than in single elimination tournaments.

The disadvantages of consolation tournaments include the following:

- Interest sometimes wanes if there is no chance for winning the championship.

- There are more forfeits than in single elimination tournaments.

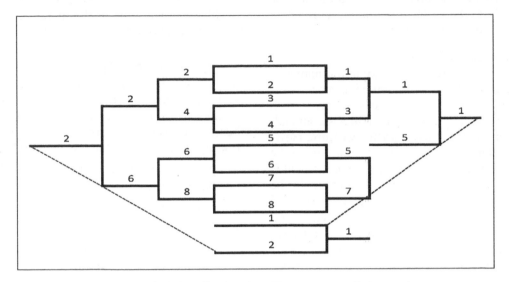

Figure 9.18. Semi-Double Elimination Tournament Schematic

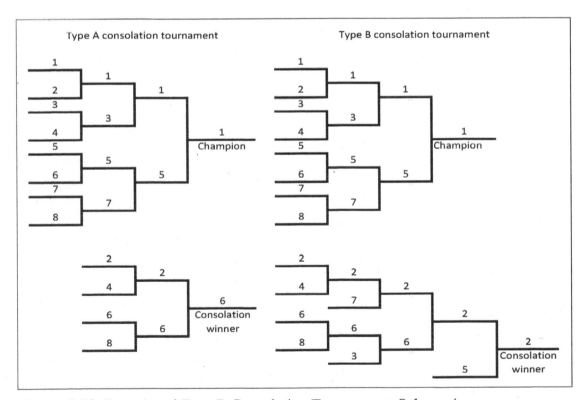

Figure 9.19. Type A and Type B Consolation Tournaments Schematics

Procedures for consolation tournaments. The rules that apply to the single elimination tournament also apply to a consolation tournament.

Challenge Tournaments

Challenge tournaments, or ongoing tournaments, emphasize participation rather than winning. Contestants issue and accept challenge matches from each other with the goal of winning all challenges and advancing to the top of the tournament structure. However, all contestants continue to play regardless of the outcome of the challenge. This type of tournament is used primarily in individual and dual sport but can be used in team sport as well. Commercial recreational institutions often use challenge tournaments, and they have proven to be an excellent format for individuals with busy and irregular schedules.

The advantages of challenge tournaments include the following:

- They are easily organized and programmed.
- They need minimal supervision.
- They don't eliminate participants.
- They encourage participants to choose opponents and engage in social interaction.
- They are useful for ranking participants.
- Win–loss records do not need to be maintained.
- Winning is not a requirement for continued participation.
- Participants play at their convenience.
- Each contest is self-programmed.
- No formal scheduling is required.
- All ages and skill levels may be involved.
- Participation is informal.
- The recreational sport specialist may end tournaments at any time.
- Formulas are not required.

The disadvantages of challenge tournaments include the following:

- They lack challenge for some participants.
- They are more suited for a small number of entries.
- They may appear complicated to participants.
- They often need external awards or incentives to maintain interest and participation.
- Some security is required in operating the challenge board.

- Participants must contact each other to arrange the date and time of the match. Communication can be a problem.

Procedures for challenge tournaments. A challenge tournament begins by transferring all names and telephone numbers from the entry forms to cards, circular discs, or other material that fit into slots or hang on hooks. There are several methods for positioning the players on the tournament board:

- positioning according to order in which participants entered or registered;
- random drawing;
- ranking according to ability, with the top player at the bottom of the tournament structure; and
- ranking derived from other tournaments.

Once placement is determined, conduct the tournament using a series of challenges issued by the participants. The objective for participants is to advance to the top of the structure and remain there. Movement to the top occurs when a participant issues a challenge to a participant on a higher level, defeats that individual, and changes positions.

In conducting a challenge tournament, establish rules and regulations before the competition and share them with the participants. Although the rules may vary according to the design of the tournament, the following seven principles apply:

1. Use sanctioned rules governing play, modified as necessary to meet local needs.

2. Use these challenge rules:

   a) Participants initiate their own challenges.

   b) All challenges must be accepted and played within or at an agreed-upon time (usually three to five days).

   c) Options for participants include challenging only those one level above; challenging those one or two levels above; challenging anyone in the tournament (not recommended); or challenging someone at the same level, with a win necessary before challenging a level above.

   d) If the challenger wins, the participants exchange positions in the tournament structure. If the challenger loses, both participants remain in their original position. However, the loser usually may not challenge the winner again until a designated time passes or until the loser has played at least one other match.

e) It is the winner's responsibility to update the tournament board.

f) Challenges may not be refused and should be met in the order that they were issued.

g) If a challenge has been accepted and one of the contestants fails to appear, a forfeit is declared and positions exchanged.

3. Keep each entry's position up-to-date so challenges can be arranged at any time.

4. Add late entries to the lowest level.

5. Establish a minimum and maximum number of contests that may be played during any given period.

6. Announce a definite date for the end of the tournament before the start of play.

7. Rank all players at the conclusion of the tournament to determine the winner.

Challenge tournament programming. The following are suggestions for programming challenge tournaments:

• Construct a challenge board from wood, cardboard, peg board, or similar sturdy material. Arrange small nails or eye hooks to suit the design of the tournament, with wooden tongue depressors (ladder) or circular price tags or discs (pyramid, crown) to record the name and telephone number of each participant. Instead of using nails or eye hooks, card holders can be used. Insert the participants' name cards in the card holder and move them as players change places in the tournament.

• If several skill levels are evident, set up two challenge tournaments, one for beginners and another for more skilled players.

• Give awards for top player, player with the most wins, and player who issued the most challenges.

• Use a message board located adjacent to the challenge board as a communication device.

Ladder, Pyramid, King or Crown, and Funnel Challenge Tournament Variations

Challenge tournaments can follow any number of schemes. The most popular challenge tournament formats are ladder, pyramid, king or crown, funnel, spiderweb, round the clock, bump board, progressive bridge, and tombstone. These tournaments are prevalent in commercial settings and are commonly used with racket sports. Details on the ladder, pyramid, king or crown, and funnel tournaments are provided in this section, while information on the rest of the tournaments is available in the bibliography.

Ladder Tournament

The ladder tournament (see Figures 9.20 and 9.21) is probably the most popular format for a challenge tournament.

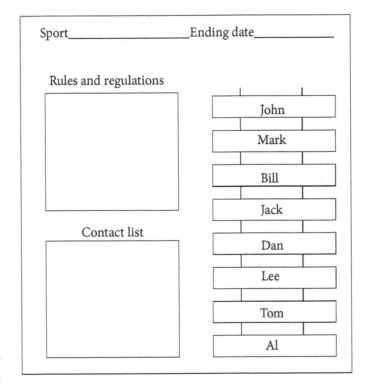

Figure 9.20. Ladder Tournament Schematic

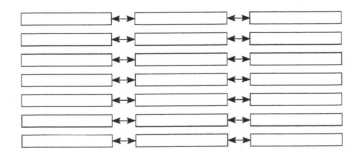

Figure 9.21. Ladder Tournament

List the entries on horizontal rungs and place them in a vertical column, with the best player at the bottom. As in climbing a ladder, use the rungs to advance players from one position to another according to challenge procedures previously outlined. The winner of the tournament is the participant at the top rung of the ladder when play is stopped. When there are a lot of entries, group the entries into several smaller tournaments that provide for both horizontal and vertical movement. At the end of the tournament, each ladder winner may participate in a play-off to determine the champion.

Pyramid Tournament

The pyramid design (Figure 9.22) permits more participation and greater freedom to challenge than the ladder format.

Arrange the names in rows, with one in the top row, two in the second row, and so on, with the number of rows depending on the number of entries. This design allows an infinite number of entries by adding additional levels to the pyramid. However, the recreational sport specialist should determine a realistic number based on the time available to complete the tournament and to allow the base-level entry the opportunity to reach the top.

King or Crown Tournament

This variation of the pyramid tournament is suitable when there are a large number of entries. Group entries into three smaller pyramids, each of which is a different level. After individuals reach the top of the lower units, they may challenge horizontally into a higher unit, then vertically again to advance to the crown or first position. As in the ladder tournament, several smaller tournaments may be appropriate.

Funnel Tournament

The funnel tournament (see Figures 9.23 and 9.24) is a combination of the ladder and the pyramid tournaments. The top seven positions are played as a ladder tournament, while the bottom positions follow the rules of a pyramid tournament. Place any additional entries on the bottom row of the pyramid. This tournament allows a large number of entries as well as a ranking of the top seven individuals.

Meets

The intramural or extramural meet is an organized competition in which individuals participate in separate events conducted in several sessions, usually over one to four days, which is a more concentrated time span than tournament formats. A meet can be a championship after months of training, a season-long program, or an informal play day. Meets lend themselves to a variety of sport settings.

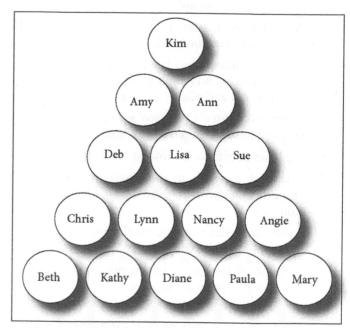

Figure 9.22. Pyramid Tournament Art

There are two types of participation in a meet, individual and team. A contestant who enters an event with no team affiliation participates as an individual. In team participation, teams have an equal number of participants who win points for placing in specific events. The team accumulating the most points is the meet champion. The following are common meets that can be used in a recreational sport program:

Meets With Several Events

- Track and field
- Swimming and diving
- Wrestling
- Gymnastics
- Ice skating
- Skiing
- Play day
- Martial arts
- Triathlon

Meets With One Event

- Cross country
- Golf
- Surfing

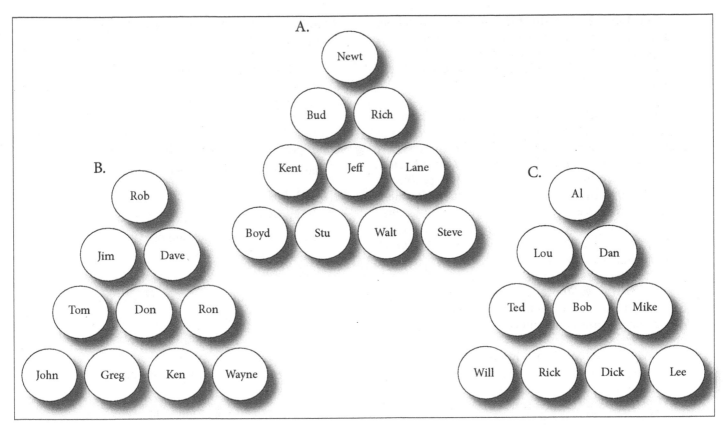

Figure 9.23. Funnel Tournament

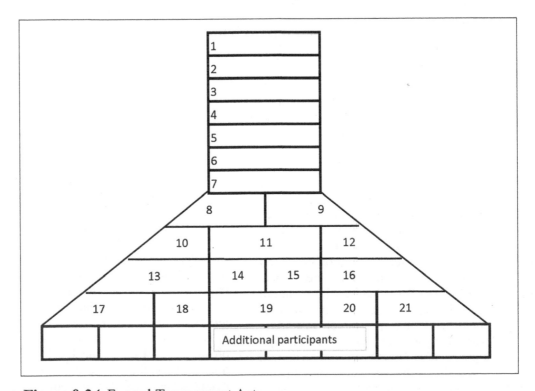

Figure 9.24. Funnel Tournament Art

Develop meets to suit the interests, population, and resources of the setting. This section discusses the programming areas common to all meets, accompanied by a detailed example using a track and field meet.

Meet organization. Before organizing the meet, review every facet of the event, from personnel to vehicle parking. Probably 80% of the recreational sport specialist's efforts take place before the meet begins. This process eliminates many potential problems. Once the type of meet has been selected, determine the program of events based on the following factors:

Age. For young children, fun events are more suitable than strength or endurance events. Relays and unusual events using game skills are popular with the youngest age group.

Physical capabilities. Events such as the discus, hammer throw, or javelin throw would not be appropriate for a community meet because they require unique physical skills.

Level of competition. A highly competitive meet with official sanction may require prior approval from an appropriate governing body.

Class groupings. If several groupings are used, each class should compete at intervals so that no participant must compete in consecutive events.

Time. Determine the time required to complete each event by estimating the approximate number of entries. If these variables are decided on in advance, it is possible to determine the total number and the order of events. Conduct as many events simultaneously as possible. Meets can result in undue fatigue and stress if a participant must remain at the site for several hours before participating in an event. Consequently, the recreational sport specialist must carefully schedule meet events to avoid delays or back-to-back participations, each of which could pose a threat to safe, enjoyable participation.

Facilities and equipment. Facilities that are suitable for the events and big enough to accommodate the number of participants are essential to a successful meet. Carefully prepare all facilities for each event. For example, in a track and field meet, properly mark running lanes and the start and finish lines; be sure the jumping and vaulting pits are in good condition and the locations for the field events are clearly designated before the meet. Quality signs should indicate locations for meet activities and stations for the participants and meet personnel. Providing spectator and participant seating is important if a large crowd is anticipated. It is customary to distribute a map of the facility that indicates where participants are to report for registration, an outline of the course

(if applicable), the location of spectator seating, and other pertinent information.

Conducting a meet. Once the program of events and the meet location is chosen, two or three weeks before the meet a meet entry form (see Figure 9.25) and a participant information announcement can be distributed or posted on a website. The entry form should provide the following information:

- date and place of the meet,
- entry fee,
- eligibility restrictions,
- required meeting dates and places for participants to review meet details,
- entry deadline,
- brief rules governing the specific events,
- list of events, and
- roster of team members.

The participant information sheet may cover the following items:

- participant entrance to the facility;
- reporting time;
- location of registration table, first aid station, and awards or recognition table;
- location of locker rooms;
- schedule and order of events;
- brief explanation of the rules and regulations for each event;
- scoring method;
- eligibility rules;
- equipment policies; and
- parking information.

After accepting entries, place individual names on a heat result form that will be used during and after each event (see Figure 9.26).

Meet personnel. The success of any meet depends on the quality of the meet personnel and their leadership ability. Each person should be familiar with the rules that govern their events, fulfill their specific functions, and anticipate problems. The number and type of officials or employees depends on the type of meet, the level of involvement, and the events on the program. In general, the following personnel are necessary to conduct a successful meet.

TRACK AND FIELD MEET ENTRY FORM

Sport	Men's and women's track and field
Entry deadline	Thursday, March 7, 2005, 4:00 p.m.
Entry Fee	$5.00 per team (See minimum numbers under eligibility.)
	$1.00 per individual
Competition	Individuals are limited to three events, including the relays. No more than two field events may be entered by an individual. No team may enter more than two individuals per event. An organization may only enter one team per relay.
Eligibility	To be eligible for team competition and points at the divisional level or the all-meet championship, a team must be composed of the following:

Minimum number
A—6 members
B—6 members
C—5 members
D—6 members

Mandatory Meeting	Intramural sport office, room 119, 7:00 p.m., Wednesday, March 6.
Dates and Places	Tuesday, March 12, 7:00 p.m.
	Divisional track preliminaries
	Men's and women's
	Wednesday, March 13, 7:00 p.m.
	Divisional field finals
	Men's and women's
	The one-mile and two-mile events will be run on this day.
	Thursday, March 14, 7:00 p.m.
	Final track events
	Men's and women's
Further Information	855-8359 or 855-2371

• Entry Form

☐ Team entries only   ☐ Individual entries only

Team _____   Individual _____

Manager _____   Address _____

Address _____   Phone number _____

Phone number _____

Program   Division
☐ Men   ☐
A
☐ Women   ☐
B
                                       ☐ C
                                       ☐ D

Eligibility Statement
This certifies that I know and understand the intramural sport eligibility rules and have completely checked the eligibility of all participants listed on the reverse side. If there is any discrepancy, I will assume full responsibility. I understand that failure to comply with these rules will result in disciplinary action as outlined in the guidelines to participation.

_____   _____
(Individual or manager signature)   (Date)

Figure 9.25. Meet Entry Form. From *Recreational Sport Management* by Richard F. Mull, Kathryn G. Bayless, and Lynn M. Jamieson, 2005, Champaign, IL: Human Kinetics.

OFFICIAL HEAT RESULTS FORM

Event _____   Division _____   Heat _____

Lane	Place	Division points	Final points
___	___	___	___
___	___	___	___
___	___	___	___
___	___	___	___
___	___	___	___
___	___	___	___

Figure 9.26. Heat Results Form. From *Recreational Sport Management* by Richard F. Mull, Kathryn G. Bayless, and Lynn M. Jamieson, 2005, Champaign, IL: Human Kinetics.

- The meet committee is responsible for supervising the meet, including the following:
  - forming heats;
  - determining number of contestants;
  - deciding on order of events;
  - ruling on appeals; and
  - suspending the meet because of weather, poor facility conditions, and so on.
- The meet coordinator monitors the organization and implementation of the meet and supervises personnel. If there is no meet committee, the meet director usually assumes all administrative and organizational duties.
- The referee is in charge of overseeing activities during the meet, assigning officials to specific duties, and explaining officials' responsibilities to them.
- The starter controls the start of each event.
- The clerk of the course is responsible for recording the name and number of each contestant and assigning contestants to proper heat and starting positions. The clerk is also responsible for giving instructions about rules for each event.
- Other personnel include clerical staff, judges, scorers, announcers, marshals, timers, inspectors, press stewards, runners, and supervisors.

Once the recreational sport specialist has identified and instructed meet personnel about their responsibilities, the meet can start. At a designated time before the meet, all contestants in the first event must report to the clerk of the course. The clerk verifies each entrant and informs them of heat and lane assignments. At this time, an event card should be completed for each participant (see Figure 9.27). While the first event is being conducted, the announcer announces the second event so contestants can receive their assignments and the event can follow promptly. Allow participants to warm up in a designated area before their event starts. Assign appropriate personnel to set up and remove equipment, such as hurdles, barriers, mats, and standards, as soon as possible. Arrange for the press steward or runner to promptly record the results of each event for the participants and the meet announcer.

EVENT CARD

Men _____   Women _____

Division   A   B   C   D

Track event   60 m hurdles   100 m dash   Mile run   400 m dash   800 m run
                  200 m dash   800 m relay   Mile relay   2 mile relay

Name(s) _____

Name(s) _____

Team name _____

_____

Timer 1 _____   Official time _____

Timer 2 _____   Place _____

Heat _____   Lane _____   Race _____

Recorded by _____

Figure 9.27. Meet Event Card. From *Recreational Sport Management* by Richard F. Mull, Kathryn G. Bayless, and Lynn M. Jamieson, 2005, Champaign, IL: Human Kinetics.

Scoring a meet. There are two types of scoring systems for meets. The first type is event scoring, in which each event is assigned a scoring system to indicate the points awarded for overall placement. For example, for the long jump, the scoring system might be based on the 12 best places within each division, as shown in Figure 9.28. The second type of scoring is divisional scoring, in which points are assigned for performance during preliminary and final events and totaled to determine final placement.

After the final event, the meet committee or coordinator should make sure that the following details have been attended to:

All score sheets have been collected.

- Tabulations of results have been made official.

- Awards have been distributed.

- Press releases announcing winners and other items of interest have been prepared.

- All equipment and supplies have been collected and returned.

- The facility has been cleaned and equipment put away.

Meet programming. Meets encompass a variety of events according to the characteristics of the participants. The possibilities for arranging and conducting a meet are limitless and depend primarily on the setting. The recreational sport specialist should ensure that every meet contributes to the enjoyment of the participants and spectators. Preliminary planning, competent personnel, a suitable facility, and necessary equipment ensure a successful meet.

Extramural Sport Program Delivery

Although extramural sport is similar to intramural sport in terms of programming policies or procedures, the extramural program is distinctive in many ways. Extramural sport may be defined as an extension of the intramural program because intramural champions from various institutions compete against each other to determine an extramural champion. Participation in extramural sport can be informal, emphasizing a fun and social interaction, or formal, stressing winning and championship.

Extramural sport has tremendous potential for providing visibility for the host institution and recognition for the participants. Traditionally, extramural sport programming has received minimal attention within recreational sport, in part because of the time, resources, and planning required in hosting participants from outside the setting and sending participants to extramural events in other settings. Recreational sport specialists discourage extramural sport events when participation by the few who are highly skilled is more expensive than events that provide opportunities for many individuals with varying skill levels. Although this principle is a good guideline, the recreational sport specialist should explore alternative sources of funding, perhaps donations or commercial sponsorship, to provide for extramural sport. A quality extramural sport event may be valuable for generating public awareness about recreational sport and facilitating positive relations with other settings.

Many aspects of extramural sport tournaments are similar to intramural sport tournaments. The actual tournament design tools are the same as those used in intramural sport. However, the following information covers aspects specific to extramural sport.

Organizing Events

Because extramural sport tournaments comprise participants from various geographic locations, the recreational sport specialist must schedule the extramural sport event as far in advance as possible in order to obtain housing accommodations suitable for the number of participants expected. When reviewing facility availability, make plans to schedule the facility for practice times before the tournament. Investigate any conflicting events scheduled in the proposed time to prevent problems. Once preliminary approval of dates, times, and facilities are secured, begin developing entry forms and invitations to distribute one or two months before the established date. Develop an effective publicity campaign to secure participant and spectator interest in the event. The host institution or agency, with assistance from participating institutions, is responsible for coordinating all pertinent details of the event, including the following:

Place:	1	2	3	4	5	6	7	8	9	10	11	12
Points:	15	12	10	9	8	7	6	5	4	3	2	1

Figure 9.28. Scoring System for a Track and Field Meet

- events to be held;
- number of participants allowed per team;
- eligibility rules;
- modified rules of the sport, if applicable;
- type of participation;
- number of institutions invited;
- housing accommodations, transportation, and hospitality;
- liability insurance;
- personnel requirements;
- finance and budgeting;
- equipment needs;
- registration procedure;
- recognition; and
- promotion and publicity.

Because extramural sport is an extension of the intramural sport program, tournament scheduling, seeding, bye placement, officiating, and facility supervision are the same as in intramural sport programming.

Invitation and entry forms. Invitations and entry forms should include all pertinent information to minimize confusion and the need for follow-up communication:

- type of event and specific activities to be conducted;
- date, time, place, and duration of the event;
- eligibility requirements;
- expected entry fee and other costs;
- approximate costs for housing accommodations, including travel to the facility;
- insurance coverage, if applicable;
- travel information concerning planes, trains, and buses as well as road directions and parking options;
- facilities for the event and practice;
- clothing or personal sport equipment and supplies needed for each event; and
- entry deadline date and the return address or e-mail address.

In addition to an entry form, request the name, e-mail address, and phone number of the agency's event coordinator and a signed affidavit verifying participant eligibility.

Follow-up letter. After an agency accepts the invitation to the extramural event and forwards the completed entry form, send a follow-up letter or e-mail. This correspondence provides specific details:

- registration time and location;
- tentative schedule of activities;
- appropriate attire for social events;
- parking arrangements and costs;
- restaurant information, including approximate prices; and
- city and facility maps.

Finance. Organize a finance committee to handle the expenses and income of the event. Here are some examples of financial transactions requiring attention:

Income

- Entry fees for team or participants
- Sponsor contributions
- Donations
- Gate receipts
- Business advertising in the program
- Concessions

Expenses

- Office supplies, mailing expenses
- Copies and duplicating materials
- Facility rental
- Equipment and supplies
- Maintenance
- Personnel (supervisors and officials)
- Insurance
- Awards
- Publicity
- Hospitality functions, including a banquet

Participants generally attend an extramural event at their own expense, unless a sponsor has provided some financial support.

Event Officials

The number of officials will vary from sport to sport, but the customary number used for an intramural event should suffice. The host institution or agency is responsible for securing officials; however, it is not unusual for each institution to provide one or more qualified officials.

Facilities and Equipment

Official regulation facilities should be available for the event. Make arrangements at the facility site for a registration table or tent, locker rooms, shower facilities, restrooms, a concession stand, a lounge area for officials, and spectator seating. Equipment will also need to be secured before the event, such as a scorer's table, standards, timing devices, or a public-address system.

Rules and Regulations

Whenever the recreational sport specialist organizes an extramural sport event, he or she should establish the rules and regulations early on and communicate them to potential participants when invitations and entry forms are sent. When the event is an outgrowth of intramural sport tournaments, pay special attention to rules and regulations to see if participating teams or individuals will need to be made aware of any modifications. Unless differences are communicated early, participants will not have time to adapt to different rules and regulations, placing pressure on participants and officials and resulting in possible disciplinary problems. This also makes the tournament less than fair and reflects negatively on the host agency.

Travel and Liability

If a host agency or an agency sending a representative is providing travel funding, the recreational sport specialist should know of any liability associated with this assistance. For example, if participants have access to a vehicle through an agency, what precautions need to be taken about insurance, adult supervision, and counseling for proper use? The host agency should also carefully review liability concerns about facility and equipment use and the handling of injuries.

Recognition

Design recognition and awards to highlight achievement. Extramural awards can be similar to those distributed at an intramural event. Although the focus of extramural sport should be participation, the events lend themselves to a recognition ceremony at the end of participation. This type of ceremony may recognize tournament finalists as well as the agency with the most participants, the most valuable players from each agency, an all-star team, outstanding officials, and so forth. Finally, the ceremony can recognize people responsible for organizing or contributing to the event.

Personnel Considerations

Leadership, paid or volunteer, is an important factor in the success of an intramural or extramural sport program. The term *leadership* suggests a range of responsibilities within the sport program, including four distinct leadership levels: functional, supervisory, administrative, and executive. Discussion in this chapter will focus on functional leadership, or the employees and volunteers who deal directly with the participants. Leadership implies that an individual has job responsibilities involving the authority to influence participants' habits or attitudes. A person achieves this authority in two ways. First, the person is placed in a leadership position and given thorough job training. Second, the person demonstrates competence on the job, gaining the respect, trust, and admiration of the participant. The two most important leaders in the intramural or extramural sport program are sport officials and sport event supervisors.

Sport Officials

Officiating is one of the most difficult leadership positions in sport. Some people consider it a thankless task, and others feel it is a personal challenge that results in the satisfaction of ensuring participants abide by the rules. Good officials extend their influence on the participants without being noticed. In Figure 9.29 on the next page, Schafer (1977) illustrates several points in officiating. To this extent, officiating is an art. Good officials possess the following attributes:

Quick reaction time. An official must make split-second decisions, as the tempo of most games allows little time to make a decision.

Confidence. An official can portray confidence in ways such as speaking in a firm voice, making positive motions when announcing decisions, or blowing a sharp and loud whistle.

Emotional control. By using poise, calm, and control, an official has a relaxing effect on participants and spectators.

Consistency. One of the most important attributes of a good official, consistency ensures that calls or decisions are the same regardless of participants or circumstances.

Integrity. An official should be honest at all times.

The following checklist, developed by Schafer (1977), illustrates several points in officiating:

- **Be competitive.** The players give maximum effort; so should you. Tell yourself, "I'm not going to let this game get away from me; I am better than that." You are hired to make the calls that control the game. Make them!

- **Have your head on right.** Don't think your striped shirt grants you immunity from having to take a little criticism. It's part of officiating. Plan on it. Successful officials know how much to take. Ask one when you get the chance.

- **Don't be a tough guy.** If a coach or team captain is on your back but not enough to warrant a penalty, then stay away from that person. This is especially true during time-outs. Standing near an unhappy coach just to show him will only lead to further tension. Some officials develop irritating characteristics. Don't be one of them.

- **Get into the flow of the game.** Each game is different. Good officials can feel this difference. Concentrate on the reactions of the players. Take note if the tempo of the game changes. A ragged game calls for a different style of officiating from a smooth game.

- **Don't bark.** If you don't like to be shouted at, don't shout at someone else. Be firm but use a normal, relaxed voice. This technique will do wonders in helping you reduce the pressure. Shouting indicates you have lost control, not only of yourself, but also of the game.

- **Show confidence.** Cockiness has no place in officiating. You want to inspire confidence. Your presence should command respect from the participants. As in any walk of life, appearance, manner, and voice determine how you are accepted. Try to present the proper image.

- **Forget the fans.** As a group, fans usually exhibit three characteristics: ignorance of the rules, highly emotional partisanship, and delight in antagonizing the officials. Accepting this fact will help you ignore the fans, unless they interrupt the game or stand in the way of you doing your job.

- **Answer reasonable questions.** Treat coaches and players in a courteous way. If they ask you reasonably, answer them in a polite way. If they get your ear by saying, "Hey, ref, I want to ask you something," then start telling you off, interrupt and remind them of the reason for the discussion. Be firm but relaxed.

- **Choose your words wisely.** Don't obviously threaten a coach or player. This will only put them on the defensive, and you will have placed yourself on the spot. If you feel a situation is serious enough to warrant a threat, then it is serious enough to penalize without invoking a threat. Obviously some things you say will be a form of threat, but using the proper words can make it subtle.

- **Stay cool.** Your purpose is to establish a calm environment for the game. Fans, coaches, and players easily spot nervous or edgy officials. Avidly chewing gum, pacing, or displaying a range of emotions before or during a game will make you seem vulnerable to the pressure.

Figure 9.29. Officials' Checklist.

Knowledge of the rules. An official must understand the rules of the game, the mechanics of the job, and the human-relation aspects of officiating before refereeing sport at any level.

Recruiting. Recruiting competent sport officials may be a taxing yet satisfying experience. Finding individuals for leadership positions requires the recreational sport specialist to know how many sport officials are needed and to have a job description explaining position requirements. Distribute and post position announcements. Ads placed in local newspapers can attract new officials. Recruit officials from among participants. Another good practice is to have an applicant complete an official's information card (Figure 9.30) indicating sports desired, daily availability, and hours desired per week. These cards provide a quick reference once the season begins.

OFFICIAL'S INFORMATION CARD

Name _____

          (Last)   (First)   (Middle)

Address _____

Phone _____ Registered official _____ Yes _____ No

Sports Desired

Men	**Women**	**Co-intramural**
_____ Basketball	_____ Basketball	_____ Basketball
_____ Flag football	_____ Cageball	_____ Inner tube
_____ Soccer	_____ Flag football	_____ Water polo
_____ Softball	_____ Kickball	_____ Softball
_____ Volleyball	_____ Inner tube	_____ Volleyball
_____ Water polo	_____ Water polo	
	_____ Volleyball	

Availability

Monday	**Tuesday**	**Wednesday**	**Thursday**	**Sunday**
_____ 5-8 p.m.	_____ 5-8 p.m.	_____ 5-8 p.m.	_____ 5-8 p.m.	_____ 1-4 p.m.
_____ 8-11 p.m.	_____ 8-11 p.m.	_____ 8-11 p.m.	_____ 8-11 p.m.	_____ 4-7 p.m.
_____ Either	_____ Either	_____ Either	_____ Either	_____ 7-10 p.m.
				_____ Any

Approximate number of hours per week desired _____

Date _____

Figure 9.30. Official's Information Card. From *Recreational Sport Management* by Richard F. Mull, Kathryn G. Bayless, and Lynn M. Jamieson, 2005, Champaign, IL: Human Kinetics.

In-service training. After recruitment, the selected applicants should attend an in-service training program to become familiar with policies, procedures, and rules relevant to their job.

Hold several meetings with the new officials, beginning with an orientation meeting. At this meeting, discuss the agency's goals, philosophy, benefits, conduct expectations, uniforms, safety, scheduling, and other pertinent information. This is also an ideal time to complete any necessary payroll or personnel forms. Hold a second meeting to review rule interpretation, mechanics, and positioning using slides, films, or other audiovisual aids. This meeting is vital to the success of the program because it ensures that all officials are familiar with specific interpretations and enforce them consistently during games. After this meeting, provide an on-field or on-court practical clinic in which the potential sport official officiates a practice game, working on floor, hand, and verbal mechanics. As instructors, experienced or senior officials can provide leadership and strengthen the relationship between new and veteran officials. Following these meetings, give all officials written and practical knowledge tests developed by the intramural staff or by a state or national officials' association. Require passing scores on proficiency and knowledge tests before scheduling officials; provide individual counseling for those scoring below the minimum.

After the tournament or season has begun, schedule periodic in-service sessions for the officials. The purpose of these sessions is to strengthen skills, build on what the officials have learned through experience, and review any persistent problems in rule interpretation.

Whatever method the recreational sport specialist uses, in-service training is necessary to ensure a quality officiating program. More agencies are deciding not to conduct these training sessions because of time and budget limitations. However, the dividends in reinforcement, morale, and positive public relations are more valuable than the cost. In-service training is a worthwhile investment.

Scheduling. Methods of assigning officials vary among institutions. Several methods are discussed in Chapter 11. Whatever method the recreational sport specialist chooses, he or she needs a carefully developed assignment plan.

Once the master schedule is complete, attach a daily list of scheduled officials (see Figure 9.31) to the sport supervisor's clipboard, indicating assigned course and shifts at the facility site. Later transfer the officials' names and hours worked from this form to a master payroll form.

Evaluation. Evaluating officials is a difficult task that occurs continually throughout the season. View evaluations with a positive attitude. When officials and administrators look on the evaluation process as an aid instead of a threat to employment, the quality of the program is enhanced. Presenting positive solutions and suggestions rather than reprimands and criticisms is important.

A popular evaluation method in intramural sport is the written evaluation form. Figure 9.32 is one example of a grouped officials evaluation form. This form may be adapted for individual evaluations in order to ensure confidentiality. Fellow officials, sport supervisors, participants, or teams may complete evaluations. It is a good practice to employ quality, experienced officials as daily evaluators. Whatever evaluation method is chosen, the official should have the opportunity for positive feedback and a chance to examine the report.

Sport Supervisors

Although the characteristics of competent sport officials also apply to sport supervisors, supervisors need several additional qualifications and have distinctive attributes.

Figure 9.31. Daily Official's Schedule. From *Recreational Sport Management* by Richard F. Mull, Kathryn G. Bayless, and Lynn M. Jamieson, 2005, Champaign, IL: Human Kinetics.

BASKETBALL OFFICIALS' EVALUATION

Date _____

Evaluator _____

Circle the appropriate rating

7 = excellent   6 = very good   5 = good   4 = average   3 = fair   2 = poor   1 = bad

Officials' names	Smith	Jones
I. Attitude		
Enthusiasm	7 6 5 4 3 2 1	7 6 5 4 3 2 1
Hustles	7 6 5 4 3 2 1	7 6 5 4 3 2 1
II. Rapport with participants		
Courteous	7 6 5 4 3 2 1	7 6 5 4 3 2 1
Takes criticism	7 6 5 4 3 2 1	7 6 5 4 3 2 1
Self-control	7 6 5 4 3 2 1	7 6 5 4 3 2 1
III. Mechanics		
Position as lead official	7 6 5 4 3 2 1	7 6 5 4 3 2 1
Position as trail official	7 6 5 4 3 2 1	7 6 5 4 3 2 1
Jump-ball administration	7 6 5 4 3 2 1	7 6 5 4 3 2 1
Free-throw administration	7 6 5 4 3 2 1	7 6 5 4 3 2 1
Throw-in administration	7 6 5 4 3 2 1	7 6 5 4 3 2 1
Call and report fouls	7 6 5 4 3 2 1	7 6 5 4 3 2 1
Switching at dead balls	7 6 5 4 3 2 1	7 6 5 4 3 2 1
Use of signals	7 6 5 4 3 2 1	7 6 5 4 3 2 1
Whistle	7 6 5 4 3 2 1	7 6 5 4 3 2 1
Eye contact with partner	7 6 5 4 3 2 1	7 6 5 4 3 2 1
IV. Consistency		
Calls both ways	7 6 5 4 3 2 1	7 6 5 4 3 2 1
No hesitation in calls	7 6 5 4 3 2 1	7 6 5 4 3 2 1

Total

V. Comments

_____

_____

_____

Figure 9.32. Officials' Evaluation. From *Recreational Sport Management* by Richard F. Mull, Kathryn G. Bayless, and Lynn M. Jamieson, 2005, Champaign, IL: Human Kinetics.

insist that the individual not participate. Report any problem to the sport office. When unfavorable weather occurs after the games have begun, play should not continue if it becomes too dangerous. Supervisors must exhibit good judgment in these cases.

Supervisors are also responsible for improving the quality of officiating and working with the officials to develop proficiency. In rating the officials, supervisors must use the evaluation form accurately.

Supervisors should prevent the misuse of any sport facility. If participants are misusing a facility, the supervisor should inform them of the proper use. If they fail to comply with the supervisor's instruction, the assistance of law enforcement should be requested. If a protest occurs while the supervisor is on duty, the supervisor should complete a protest form (Figure 9.2) on the field or court and return it to the sport office.

Sport supervisor's postgame responsibilities. The supervisor makes sure each official signs the completed game score sheet. If there are numerous games, the supervisor should collect score sheets after each game is completed. The supervisor should report all cases of unsporting conduct by a team or individual to the proper authority, submitting a written report to the sport office to document such behavior.

Supervisors should complete sign-out forms when equipment is checked out and file forms properly. Supervisors should also complete a maintenance repair form reporting facilities in need of repair. Without the help of the supervisors, maintenance problems will increase.

▶ **Computer Tip**

Sport Scheduling Software

The greatest computer need expressed by recreational sport specialists is for sport scheduling software, which includes league and tournament scheduling programs. Scheduling programs currently on the market range in price from free for basic and pricing per module to thousands of dollars. The wide range of prices reflects the diversity and complexity of the available features.

When considering the purchase of sport scheduling software, a number of key features should be considered:

- Team capacity—How many teams, leagues, divisions, and facility sites can the program handle?

- League formation—Is there flexibility in the program's selection of teams and the creation of leagues and divisions? That is, do you have the option of using either an automatic random selection by the computer or a selection based on a set of staff-defined criteria? Does the program permit online registration and provide a format where individual players can connect with teams looking for players? Can it produce e-mail distribution lists of all team captains and participants? Can it track and restrict registration of players unless a waiver is signed?

- Scheduling conflicts—Can the program identify scheduling overlaps and reschedule game dates as necessary? Can schedules be linked to the Internet and updated in real time? Does the program have an application available to send scheduling updates to cell phones or other electronic devices? Can the program track individuals and teams who are ineligible to play?

- Scheduling formats—Does the program appropriately seed teams when scheduling various tournament formats, such as round-robin, double round-robin, single elimination, double elimination, challenge, and meets?

- Master schedule—Can the program create master schedules that can be viewed in advance for a particular date, facility, league, or team? Does the program offer maps to a facility location?

- Team schedules—Does program scheduling include on-screen viewing, hard-copy or disk-file creation, editing capability, and rotating home and visitor assignments? Can the program track which teams are eligible for playoffs? Does it allow you to manually adjust the schedules?

- Reports—The design and printouts of reports and team schedules are the most important components of the scheduling program. To avoid participant confusion, game times should be printed in standard A.M.–P.M. time rather than military time, and dates should include the day of the week. Facility sites should be represented by the name of the facility rather than a code. Printing individual score sheets is also beneficial. Facility schedules are useful when managing tournaments if they are arranged by specific sites, by court or field, or by a range of dates, times, divisions, or leagues.

- Team rosters—Will the program list teams and rosters by sport, division, and league? Will the program generate an alphabetical phone and address list of team captains for use in a mail merge?

- Standings—Can the program generate league standings with win–loss records and games-behind calculations?

An effective computerized sport scheduling system can save many hours of tedious work and can eliminate the human mistakes that are an inevitable aspect of scheduling.

Conclusion

The recreational sport specialist plays a significant role in the success of the intramural and extramural sport program. A sound philosophy is a prerequisite for effective programming. The recreational sport specialist should have abilities in human relations, decision making, and conflict resolution and know rules and regulations, methods for scheduling tournaments, and program policies and procedures. Above all, the recreational sport specialist must have a genuine interest in intramural sport. Each institution has its own programming approach. Consider the information and tips offered in this chapter as tools for programming. It is up to the recreational sport specialist to apply these tools to daily situations. Intramural and extramural sport tournaments are rewarding aspects of program delivery for both the recreational sport specialist and the participant. Both disciplines offer wholesome competition and cooperation regardless of the skill and interest level of the participant.

Bibliography

Brown, E., Smith, S., & Bartley, T. (1989). Expanding all campus play-off opportunities without quality deterioration. *National Intramural–Recreational Sports Association Journal, 14*(1), 14-15.

Burwell, P., & Yeagle, S. (1990). Developing potential: The extramural sport clubs conference. In National Intramural Recreational Sports Association (Ed.), *Management strategies in recreational sports* (pp. 207-213). Corvallis, OR: National Intramural–Recreational Sports Association.

Byl, J. (1990). Formalizing a ladder tournament: Revisiting Rokosz proposal. *National Intramural–Recreational Sports Association Journal, 15*(1), 41.

Byl, J. (1999). *Organizing successful tournaments: Your complete guide for team and individual sports competition* (2nd ed.). Champaign, IL: Human Kinetics.

Byl, J. (2002). *Intramural recreation: A step-by-step guide to creating an effective program.* Champaign, IL: Human Kinetics.

Gaskins, D. A. (1994). Can Jennifer come out and play? *National Intramural–Recreational Sports Association Journal, 18*(3), 12-14.

Gaskins, D. A., & McCollum, T. B. (1990). Energizing officiating programs through extramural sports. *National Intramural–Recreational Sports Association Journal, 15*(1), 16.

Goodwin, J., & Flatt, D. (1990). Improve intramural programs through officiating. *National Intramural–Recreational Sports Association Journal, 14*(3), 46-47.

Haderlie, B., & Ross, C. (1993, March). Computerized sports league scheduling: Is it right for you? *Employee Services Management—A Journal of Employee Recreation, Health and Education,* 12-15.

Hall, D. (1990). Encouraging good sportsmanship: A behavior modification tool approved by East Carolina University intramural participants. *National Intramural–Recreational Sports Association Journal, 15*(1), 8.

Maas, G. (1979, December). *Instant scheduling for intramural sports.* Paper presented at the Big Ten Recreational Sports Directors' Conference, Chicago, IL.

Mull, Richard F., Bayless, Kathryn G., Ross, Craig M., & Jamieson, Lynn M. (1997). *Recreational sport management* (3rd ed.) pp. 93-145. Champaign, IL: Human Kinetics.

Rokosz, F. M. (1998). *Procedures for structuring and scheduling sports tournaments: Elimination, consolation, placement, and round robin design* (2nd ed.). Springfield, IL: Charles C. Thomas.

Ross, C., & Vaughn, T. (1995). Recruitment and retention of quality intramural sports officials. *National Intramural–Recreational Sports Association Journal, 19*(3), 17-22.

Ross, C., & Wolter, S. (1995, April). On schedule. *Athletic Business,* 47-52.

Ross, C., Wolter, S., & Handel, C. (1994, October). Computers in sport scheduling: Features of available software. *Employee Services Management: A Journal of Employee Recreation, Health and Education,* 6-14.

Schafer, R. C. (1977, January/February). Thinking right. *Referee,* 20.

Wade, G. (1991). The intramural sports officiating dilemma: Is self-officiating a viable solution? *National Intramural–Recreational Sports Association Journal, 15*(3), 45.

CHAPTER 10

Club Sport

CHAPTER OBJECTIVES

After reading this chapter, you will be able to differentiate the three purposes of club sport, understand financial and administrative patterns in club sport, and be able to identify control techniques for club sport.

KEY CONCEPTS

Club sport
Club types
Conservative (formal) administrative philosophy
Liberal (informal) administrative philosophy
Organizational structure
Operational guidelines
Officers

Constitution
Classification systems
Eligibility
Affiliation
Allocation
Control

Introduction

Club sport is a major program area within recreational sport. Clubs are special interest groups that organize because of a common interest in a sport. Self-administration and self-regulation are characteristics common to all clubs, whether they involve bridge, chess, sailing, hot-air ballooning, track, rugby, or spelunking. Those who desire club sport membership seek regular participation in one sport under a more continuous design than that found in informal, intramural, or extramural programs.

Club sport in the United States can be traced to the strong community club sport tradition that still exists in Europe and Australia. In both of these continents, clubs provide the main opportunities for sport participation and instruction for all ages, interests, and skill levels. These clubs are self-governed by volunteer, elected, or paid personnel, and members customarily participate with or compete in the sport against those representing other communities.

Club systems in the United States vary depending on their setting. For example, in municipal settings they are organized by age group, while military

settings parallel athletic sport by sponsoring the most skilled participants to compete against those from other military bases. Clubs in a commercial setting may incorporate more than one sport, such as racquetball and squash. These clubs are privately owned and operate for profit through membership fees and charges for facility use. Within a correctional setting, clubs operate on a single site with restricted or no opportunity for travel. Clubs are at educational settings (i.e., high schools and colleges) on a limited basis. Perhaps the biggest reason for the diversity of club sport in America is that sport programs were developed independently through educational or municipal settings.

Club sport organizations determine their own activities, leadership, and internal operating policies. Self-determination, unity, and common interest distinguish club sport from informal, intramural, and extramural sport. Additional features of club sport may include opportunities for sport participation unavailable elsewhere, opportunities to engage in the sport of one's choice, opportunities for community, and extramural opportunities distinct from those offered in intramural sport programs. This chapter covers information that helps the recreational sport specialist understand different types of club sport as well as external and internal organizational structure and operational guidelines of club sport.

Club Types

As club members pursue their sport interests, they participate in tournament competition, socialization, instruction and skill development, or a combination of the three. Club type is determined by traditions of the sport, member interests and abilities, capabilities of the leadership, facility and equipment availability, financial support, and the proximity of opponents.

Athletic

Clubs interested in scheduling and hosting tournaments, leagues, and structured events operate like athletic or professional sport teams. Club members tend to be goal oriented and enjoy the competition of structured tournaments. Consequently, clubs hold regular practice sessions, often hire coaches, and maintain an organized tournament schedule. Sometimes clubs hold tryouts to select a traveling team or individuals to compete against others of a similar skill level. In some instances, club-sponsored teams or members participate in structured events through the National Intramural–Recreational Sports Association (NIRSA), National Collegiate Athletics Association (NCAA), National Association of Inter-Collegiate Athletes (NAIA), Association of American Universities (AAU), American College Unions-International (ACU-I), and Olympic Games. However, to maintain the recreational sport philosophy, membership should not be denied if the participant does not have the interest or ability to play at a high skill level.

The biggest difference between athletic clubs and athletic sport is the degree of administrative support and complexity of the regulations governing their operations. Clubs are responsible for generating income and managing their finances, developing leadership, and determining guidelines and activities. If these functions were being performed for the club, it would more closely resemble athletic sport. In community youth programs such as soccer and basketball, traveling teams are often selected, coached, and financially supported to participate in scheduled tournaments. Similarly, commercial racquet clubs may sponsor individual members to participate in tournaments on behalf of the club.

Because involvement in scheduled activity requires fund-raising to handle the costs of entry fees, uniforms, equipment, travel and lodging, officials' and judges' fees, and so on, club members should

work together to decide how to use club resources to meet expenses.

Instructional

Another popular type of club concentrates on sharing knowledge and experience to improve skills. Although some teaching takes place in every club, in instructional clubs learning is not left to chance. Instructional clubs recruit qualified personnel to structure lessons or clinics appropriate for the interests and abilities of their members. Some clubs design tests and in-house tournaments so members can see what they have learned and what they need to improve. Other avenues for displaying newly acquired or polished skills include demonstrations, clinics, and extramural events. An instructional club may meet its financial needs through membership fees, lesson charges, and fines. The biggest expenses are instructors' wages and equipment purchases. Fund-raising may be necessary if a club wants to rent a facility or support members or a team in tournaments.

Social

In social clubs, participants seek membership to meet others who enjoy the same sport. Participation is more a means for socializing than for skill development, fitness, or tournament play. The fun of participation may diminish if too much structure and competitive rivalry are present, although some clubs hold regular intramural tournaments to encourage social interaction. Other social club activities include sponsoring clinics and giving demonstrations. Members of social clubs commonly provide their own equipment and support their activities through membership dues.

Program Development

For a club to develop and operate, it must maintain its resources. Changes in membership levels, interest, funding, facility availability, and leadership will influence its longevity. Consequently, an external support system may reinforce the club's internal leadership, helping provide continuity, organization, and programming assistance.

External administration for a club should be centralized under one board, department, unit, or agency. Preferably, the administration should be housed with the other recreational sport programming areas. A central approach maintains continuity, standardizes operational procedures, establishes equitable access to resources, allows assessment of needs, and permits evaluation of the program. Although external support is not always vital to the continuation of a club, it may make valuable contributions to the club's stability and quality.

The extent of external administration and services depends on the philosophy of the institution, agency, or board assuming administrative responsibility as well as the potential of the setting to provide program resources. The higher administrative levels decide the extent of support and communicate this to the club programming staff as policy or procedure, but the programming staff should have an opportunity to influence these administrative decisions.

While determining the type and extent of program leadership and scope of services to offer, consider legal liabilities. Who hires instructors or coaches, the club or the administration? Who owns equipment used by club members? Can clubs use motor vehicles owned by the administrative agency for club travel? What emergency first aid requirements have to be satisfied? At a minimum, there should be a staff member who investigates the legal aspects of working with clubs within a particular setting and helps solve problems for the club sport program. Additional services that can be provided to clubs include partial or total financial support, instructional or coaching personnel, equipment, facilities, travel, office space, storage space, telephone access, computer access, e-mail accounts, clerical assistance, and publicity.

Because services provided to clubs vary, there are no established requirements for programming a club sport. However, there are two philosophical models to club programming: conservative and liberal.

Conservative Administrative Philosophy

The major principle of the conservative, or formal, model is that club members have little or no discretion in determining operational procedures. Characteristics of this model include the following:

- Financial support is provided by the institution or agency having administrative responsibility.

- Schedules and activities must receive administrative approval.

- Travel must be approved. Properly insured vehicles must be used for travel, and approved supervisors must accompany the club.

- The club must have an approved adviser or coach.

- A formal document such as a constitution or guidelines must be maintained.

- Members must have insurance coverage and a medical examination.

- Financial transactions and purchases must be approved by a person within the administrative structure or a program staff person.

- Medical or athletic training supervision may be provided at club events.

Liberal Administrative Philosophy

The major principle of the liberal, or informed, model is that club members have greater latitude for determining operational procedures. Common characteristics of the liberal approach include the following:

- Members control operations, such as funding, travel, scheduling, and purchasing.

- Minimal or no external assistance is provided for funding, equipment, facilities scheduling, office use, or medical supervision.

- Members are responsible for their own insurance coverage and for knowing their own physiological limitations.

Club sport programs may flourish under either model. Agencies that provide partial or complete funding and adequate staff supervision usually follow the conservative model. The greater the financial support, the greater the external involvement in the club. The liberal model is most frequently used when funding and staffing are limited or unavailable. It relies heavily on volunteer leadership and voluntary assumption of risk, and it is more limited in the program services it offers. When selecting a programming model, make a firm decision to go in one direction or the other. Those who combine models may face legal liability because of indecisive or inconsistent administrative decision making. In the liberal model, because members are responsible for themselves and all club activities, the external administrative unit can't be held legally responsible. In the conservative model, the external administrative unit requires precautions such as medical exams, approval of expenditures, and liability insurance.

Program Delivery

After considering administrative philosophy, the next step is making operating decisions for program delivery. The first step is to identify the organizational framework, followed by determining specific operating practices.

Organizational Structure

The organizational structure within which the club operates usually exists at two levels. One is external and identifies the relationship of the club to its setting. The other is internal and describes the roles and responsibilities of club officers and members.

External structure. Sound external organizational structure involves documenting the policies of the setting that influence club operations, identifying supervisors and coordinators for the club sports, and specifying the services available to clubs, including the procedures for providing access to services.

Most club sport programs operating under a conservative model have a supervisor who enforces operational policy; advises club leadership and employees; serves as a liaison between the clubs and administrative personnel, shareholders, or groups within the setting; oversees services provided; handles disciplinary problems; maintains documentation; and works to meet the clubs' needs. When the need exists and resources permit, additional full- or part-time personnel may be involved on a paid or volunteer basis.

A number of programs use a club sport council, federation, or board to shape and implement operational policy. Made up of a representative from each club, the council and its executive officers play an active role in policy development, club leadership, and club governance, usually in conjunction with a liberal administrative approach. Under a conservative approach, the council may advise the programming personnel in charge of club sport. Regardless of the involvement of the council leadership and governance functions, the format allows for systematic input from each club. It keeps programming personnel aware of club needs, develops a sense of unity, provides representative input for decision making, facilitates the acceptance of policy, and serves as a forum for communication and problem solving.

Internal structure. Most clubs elect officers because they recognize the need for leadership; they know that certain tasks must be accomplished for the club to function. Under a conservative model, clubs must maintain elected officers. To an extent, the club sport staff dictates and supervises election procedures, which reflects a desire to structure stability and establish accountability to the club sport staff. The most common positions include president, vice president, secretary, and treasurer. The general responsibilities of the officers include the following:

- Convene regular club meetings for communication and business purposes.

- Be familiar with an approved code of parliamentary procedure.

- Monitor compliance with club policies.

- Maintain necessary records.

- Recruit new members.

- Initiate financial transactions.

- Prepare budget requests and annual reports.

- Serve as a liaison to the external administrative structure.

- Know agency policies and procedures affecting clubs.

- Know legal parameters affecting club operations.

- Know safety precautions and procedures for reporting accidents.

Specific duties for each club officer include the following:

President

- Organize and conduct all club meetings.

- Appoint necessary chairpersons and committees.

- Serve as an ex officio member of all committees.

- Coordinate and schedule all club activities.

- Supervise elections.

- Maintain contact with club officers and committee members.

- Call for oral and written reports as necessary.

- Represent the club to the national or regional governing body.

- Represent the club to the agency or setting.

Vice President

- Assume duties of the president in the president's absence.

- Oversee club equipment and purchase requests.

- Oversee all club committees.

- Assist the president as required.

Secretary

- Notify members of meetings.

- Record minutes of meetings.

- Handle club correspondence.

- Maintain club membership roster.

- Maintain club records and files.

- Prepare club annual report for approval.

Treasurer

- Maintain accurate financial records, salary schedules, and payroll.

- Prepare purchase requests for approval.

- Collect membership dues.
- Prepare club budget requests and annual financial reports.
- Pay all club bills.
- Report club financial status to general membership on request.

Other possible leadership positions in clubs include the following:
- Club adviser—Approves club activities and advises club members.
- Safety officer—Checks equipment and facilities for hazardous conditions and handles accident situations.
- Coach—Schedules and coaches practice sessions and contests.
- Instructor—Designs structured learning experiences for club sport members.
- Publicity manager—Initiates and implements all club publicity.

All club members should play a significant role in the success of the club. Without member involvement, a club may grow stale despite the enthusiasm of its officers. Each club member should attend meetings; participate in decision making; help shape the club constitution, bylaws, membership requirements, and dues structure; have a say in selecting club officers; and uphold club and agency policies.

Each club should put its operations in writing, which provides continuity when leadership and members change. A conservative administrative approach may require a constitution and bylaws. Once a document has been prepared, it usually needs to be approved by club sport staff. In some instances, constitutions may need approval by the administration. A staff member may need to provide assistance in the preparation of this type of document. Figure 10.1 shows a possible format for a club constitution and bylaws.

Operational Guidelines

Guidelines provided by the board or agency should be as comprehensive as possible but not so complex or strict that clubs are discouraged from organizing. Put guidelines in a manual, CD-ROM, or website available to the officers of each club. Because adherence to guidelines is important, review their content with the officers of each club. Make personal contact with the officers and emphasize that guidelines exist to encourage the success of the club, not to obstruct enjoyment. This section discusses concepts necessary to develop successful club guidelines.

Classification systems. In many agencies, the club sport program operates under a simple classification system in which all clubs follow the same policies and procedures. Regardless of the club's organization, programming skills, membership size, fund-raising, and financial needs, all clubs receive the same benefits. However, in agencies where there is a diverse offering of club sport, clubs might exist on both extremes of the spectrum. Some clubs will have a long history, high membership, and a number of events, and other clubs may have informal organization, few members, and little programming. Because all clubs are unique, classification systems afford equity among the clubs, especially in dividing the agency's resources among the clubs. A classification system also provides tangible goals for clubs to pursue as well as reinforcement for clubs successful in meeting the requirements. Classification systems may be developed according to risk (I, II, III) or organization level (A, B, C). The following is an example of classifying clubs by assigning risk levels to activities.

Level I—Activities at this risk level involve deliberate physical contact. Examples include martial arts (aikido, kung fu, hapkido, judo, karate, taekwondo), lacrosse, equestrian, fencing, gymnastics, ice hockey, water polo, riflery, rugby, scuba, self-defense, snow skiing, water skiing, and wrestling.

Level II—The risks associated with these activities often pertain to their setting. These sports may take place far away from a hospital and emergency personnel. Examples include bass fishing, common adventure, field hockey, cycling, racquetball, roller hockey, rowing, soccer, tennis, and ultimate Frisbee.

Level III—These sports normally don't have a high prevalence of injury or severe injuries. Examples include badminton, dance, table tennis, and billiards.

Table 10.1 illustrates categories based on organization level. Clubs are placed in one of three categories: A, B, or C. Once a club is in a category, it must abide by the requirements of that category or be lowered to the next category. Clubs that fulfill their responsibilities should receive comparable benefits as outlined in Table 10.2. For the strongest incentive, choose benefits that are closely related to the clubs' needs.

Constructing a constitution for a club team is one way to show the host facility that club members are serious about their endeavor. It might also indicate that club members will be good custodians of the host agency's facilities. Following is an effective outline for a club constitution.

Preamble

States the purpose and aims of the group.

Article I Name

States the name adopted by the organization. This section might also state whether the organization is incorporated and, if so, under what name or names.

Article II Membership

States the requirements for admission to the club and size limitations.

Article III Officers

Contains the list of officers and their terms of office.

Article IV Executive Committee

States the makeup of the executive committee (or board or council), the method of selection, and terms of office. A section under this article may include provisions for officer vacancies.

Article V Meetings

States the regular meeting time and provisions for calling special meetings. If meetings cannot be held regularly, indicates authority to call meetings.

Article VI Amendment Process

Details the constitutional amendment process. A constitutional amendment requires previous notification and a two-thirds or three-fourths affirmative vote of the membership for its adoption.

Article VII Ratification

Provision for ratifying the constitution. If ratification demands more than a simple majority of the voting members present at the time of ratification, this article must indicate so.

Bylaws

The bylaws may involve the following:

- details on membership, such as rights, duties, and procedures for resignation and expulsion;
- provisions for initiation fees, dues, and other assessments, along with a procedure for payment delinquency;
- date and method of electing officers;
- duties, authority, and responsibilities of an executive committee;
- names of the standing committees, the method of choosing committee chairs and membership, and the duties of each committee;
- provision for use of accepted parliamentary manual (e.g., Robert's Rules of Order, Newly Revised);
- percentage of members constituting a quorum;
- provision for honorary members and honorary officers; and
- method for amending the bylaws (usually accomplished through a simple majority vote).

The constitution and bylaws should be reviewed annually to keep them current. An annual review keeps a club aware of its operating code.

Figure 10.1 Club Constitution

Table 10.1

Classification of Club Sport by Level of Organization

Programming (home and away)	Category A	Category B	Category C
Competitions Special events Clinics Demos Socials Community service	10 2 2 2 6 2	5 1 1 1 3 1	Total of 3 activities of the programming categories (for example, 1 special event and 2 demonstrations)
Instruction	Beg-Int-Adv	Beg-Int-Adv	Beg-Int
Minimum active membership	30 members	20 members	10 members
Fund-raising	30% of total budget	20% of total budget	10% of total budget
Organization	Provide an instructor or coach	Provide an instructor or coach	-
	4 executive committee positions (promotion, fund-raiser)	4 executive committee positions	2 executive positions
	Serve on Club Sport Federation (CSF) subcommittees (allocation and classification)	Serve on allocation or classification committee	Serving on a committee is optional
	Develop and implement promotional materials (ads, flyers, newsletters)	Develop and implement promotional materials (ads, flyers, newsletters)	-

Affiliation. Establish a procedure for club sport use of the agency's name to associate the club with the setting. Investigate what, if any, legal responsibility exists for the agency and to what extent official approval is needed for the clubs to exist within the setting. This review should consider activities within the home setting (community, campus, military base) as well as activities outside the setting.

If the club and the agency establish a legal tie, the club automatically becomes subject to the policies, rules, and regulations governing the agency, giving the agency more control in managing a club program. On the other hand, the stipulations may hinder adherence. A large number of stipulations may discourage clubs from organizing, so choose only those necessary to protect the safety and welfare of participants and eliminate legal problems for the agency.

Application. Use a step-by-step application process for each group seeking approval to operate as a club. Settings where a legal bond exists between a club and sponsoring agency require formal application before approval; otherwise, effort and resources may be wasted on groups that lack proper leadership or understanding of the requirements for club operation. Additional requirements that assist the recreational sport specialist in assessing the viability of the club and developing a relationship with club leaders may include the following:

- a meeting with the club sport staff to review requirements, guidelines for operation, and application (see Figure 10.2);

- a club constitution and bylaws submitted for approval;

Table 10.2

Responsibilities by Category of Club

	Category A	Category B	Category C
Services	Duplicating	Duplicating	Duplicating
	Long-distance telephone calls	Long-distance telephone calls	Long-distance telephone calls
	Mail service	Mail service	Mail service
	Chalking the field dimensions	Chalking the field dimensions	N/A
	Help in obtaining officials, supervisors, lifeguards	Help in obtaining officials, supervisors, lifeguards	Help in obtaining officials, supervisors, lifeguards
Facilities	Primetime (practice, special events)	Prime time, non-prime time	Non-prime time
	Storage space	Storage space if available	Limited space for storage if available
	Obtain off-campus facilities	Obtain off-campus facilities	Obtain off-campus facilities
Programming	Professional staff assistance with all programming	Professional staff assistance as needed	Professional staff assistance as needed
	Office assistance	Office assistance	Office assistance
	Arranging for facility and equipment needs	Arranging for facility and equipment needs	Arranging for facility and equipment needs

- an officers' list and membership roster (facilitate this process by having forms available for club use; see Figures 10.3 and 10.4);

- a facility reservation request submitted for approval (sometimes unavailability of facility space prohibits a club from functioning);

- a formal statement of approval or disapproval for club status (this step may require the endorsement of an administrative unit); and

- a meeting with the club staff to review club status and discuss club responsibilities.

Active status. Once a club receives approval to function within the agency, it may encounter difficulties that jeopardize its ability to remain active. Operational guidelines should explain the conditions under which a club may become inactive as well as how it may be reactivated. For example, a club may become inactive due to disciplinary action. Other situations that may result in inactive status are loss of interest and inability to sustain operations. If this happens, plan to secure any leftover funds. If the club remains inactive for an indefinite time, establish a date when the money is to be moved into a general fund for club sport programming. If the club is able to regenerate, the funds are customarily returned to the club.

Membership eligibility. The primary responsibility for determining membership and officer eligibility rests with the club, though in some cases system-wide eligibility statements are necessary to maintain the philosophy and purpose of the program. Eligibility statements may limit membership to certain segments of a population or may specify the percentage of membership permissible for that segment. Settings that may warrant special eligibility statements include the following:

CLUB SPORT STATUS APPLICATION

Date _____

Name of club _____   Sport _____

I. Status desired

New club _____   Approved _____

Maintain status _____   Rejected _____

Reactivate _____   Date _____

II. Purpose(s) of club

_____

_____

_____

III. Facility request

Location 1st _____   2nd _____

Day(s) 1st _____   2nd _____

Time(s) 1st _____   2nd _____

_____

_____

_____

_____

IV. Officers' list

	Name	Address	Phone	E-mail
President	_____	_____	_____	_____
Vice president	_____	_____	_____	_____
Secretary	_____	_____	_____	_____
Treasurer	_____	_____	_____	_____

V. Constitution and bylaws

Approved _____   Date _____

Rejected _____   Date _____

Staff signature _____

Figure 10.2. Club Sport Application. From *Recreational Sport Management* by Richard F. Mull, Kathryn G. Bayless, and Lynn M. Jamieson, 2005, Champaign, IL: Human Kinetics.

CLUB SPORT OFFICER LIST

1. This information is to be completed by the club president and returned to the club sport office by the club's first meeting.

2. Any changes in officers or addresses and phone numbers must be recorded within one week of the change.

Club _____

Date officers elected _____

Date of term expiration _____

Date of next election _____

Officers	Name	Local address	Phone	E-mail
President				
Vice president				
Secretary				
Treasurer				
Advisers				

Change of officers

Date	Office	New officer	Local address	Phone	E-mail

I acknowledge that all information is accurate.

_____
(President's signature)

Figure 10.3. Club Sport Officer List. From *Recreational Sport Management* by Richard F. Mull, Kathryn G. Bayless, and Lynn M. Jamieson, 2005, Champaign, IL: Human Kinetics.

CLUB SPORT MEMBERSHIP REPORT

This form must be completed, kept up-to-date, and kept on file in the club sport office by the first meeting of the club. Any additional members must be added before the next scheduled practice or meeting.

Club _____

Identification Number Acknowledgment

	Name (last, first)	Number	Address	Phone	E-mail
1.					
2.					
3.					
4.					
5.					
6.					
7.					
8.					
9.					
10.					
11.					
12.					
13.					
14.					
15.					
16.					
17.					
18.					
19.					
20.					

Figure 10.4. Club Sport Roster. From *Recreational Sport Management* by Richard F. Mull, Kathryn G. Bayless, and Lynn M. Jamieson, 2005, Champaign, IL: Human Kinetics.

- military (off-base personnel, officers, noncommissioned officers, enlisted personnel, families),
- community (citizens of the community, age groups, skill levels),
- college (nonuniversity affiliates, faculty, staff, students, alumni), and
  correctional (staff, visitors, inmates).

Another mandatory eligibility requirement might be a medical exam and clearance. All eligibility requirements should be in writing and available to potential members. The document must acknowledge a commitment to nondiscriminatory membership practices regarding sex, race, religion, and age.

Meetings. Require periodic club business meetings to facilitate communication within each club and to keep officers accountable to the members. Review a copy of club minutes from each meeting to stay informed about each club. Good records of club functions help decision making. To ensure useful club minutes, secretaries should follow a prescribed format (see Figure 10.5).

CLUB MEETING MINUTES

Club _____

Date _____   Location _____

Time meeting started _____   Time meeting adjourned _____

Number of members present _____   Number absent _____

Report submitted by _____   Office _____

Items discussed

A.

B.

C.

D.

Motions made and voted upon

A.

B.

Figure 10.5. Club Meeting Minutes. From *Recreational Sport Management* by Richard F. Mull, Kathryn G. Bayless, and Lynn M. Jamieson, 2005, Champaign, IL: Human Kinetics.

Safety. The safety and well-being of club members must be the primary concern of club officers and program staff, or else the program will not satisfy moral and legal requirements. Mechanisms to ensure safety depend on resources, legal requirements, and age groups involved. An examination of the following options may assist in choosing safety mechanisms suitable for local conditions.

Medical examination. Club sport programs using the conservative model require medical examinations before participants are eligible to join. The exam may be given by a local doctor or by physicians employed by the agency. Time spans for updating exams vary from program to program.

After the examination, the physician should note any participation limitations on the individual's health record. In some programs, members must show officers a health-clearance card from a physician before participation. Other programs require that program staff verify this documentation. If a program requires a medical exam, the staff is responsible for preventing participation without the proper clearance.

A more liberal approach to medical eligibility places the responsibility for determining health status with the participant. Because participation in club sport is voluntary, individuals are expected to understand the risks involved and participate within their physiological limitations. Program staff should inform all prospective members of the policy and record the policy in writing. Additionally, some programs require participants to sign a statement (such as Figure 10.6) acknowledging the policy. With high-risk activities, the statement should include specific risks associated with participation. When a minor desires club membership, a parent or guardian must sign the form. The use of such a form does not release the staff or agency from liability for negligence.

CLUB SPORT MEMBERSHIP ACKNOWLEDGMENT OF PARTICIPATION STATEMENT AND CONSENT

I, _____, as a current member of the _____ club, a recognized organization and member of the club sport council at _____, affirm that I am aware of my physical condition, that I am voluntarily participating as a member of the aforementioned club, that I am aware that such participation may result in possible injury because of the nature of the sport, and that I am assuming any risk that may be involved in this sport.

I further acknowledge that I am aware of insurance policies that are available to me through private or institutional means, that I know and understand club and agency policies and procedures, and that I will represent the club and agency in the manner that is expected. I have read and understand the above statements and will carry them out to the best of my ability.

Signature _____   Date _____

Printed name _____

Address _____

Birth date _____ Phone _____ E-mail _____

If club member is under 18 years old, a parent or guardian must sign below.

Parent or guardian signature _____

Printed name _____

Figure 10.6. Acknowledgment Statement. From *Recreational Sport Management* by Richard F. Mull, Kathryn G. Bayless, and Lynn M. Jamieson, 2005, Champaign, IL: Human Kinetics.

Safety plan. The best way to control accidents and hazardous conditions is to use facilities and equipment properly, providing adequate supervision and requiring individual physical conditioning. Each club program should develop an action plan for safety designed to prevent and manage problems effectively. The plan requires regular inspection of facilities and equipment performed by the administrative staff, maintenance personnel, custodial staff, facility supervisor, or a club member designated as safety officer. Cost and storage problems make it difficult for many programs to care for personal equipment. Club members' personal equipment may be less protective and lower quality. An officer or appointed member should inspect personal equipment at each club function. A staff member organizes and performs the inspection of facilities and equipment using maintenance checklists. Club officers should know the procedures for reporting problems and initiating requests for repair or replacement. If a hazard remains, cancel or postpone the club activity.

Safe conduct. A safe environment requires safe conduct. Developing safety awareness among club members may be difficult. Work through the officers of the club or a club safety officer to raise awareness of the attitudes and behaviors that may lead to accidents. Selecting officials and other event personnel to prevent unsafe conduct is important. Some programs use the club member responsible for inspecting facilities and equipment as the on-site supervisor to monitor activity and handle unsafe conduct. Safety involves encouraging physical conditioning of club members. Because club participation is voluntary, there is no way to know whether a club member identifies with the values of conditioning or understands how to implement a conditioning program. Club sport staff should familiarize clubs with the need for conditioning by identifying medically approved literature; announcing or offering presentations, lectures, clinics, and workshops on fitness and related topics; designing conditioning programs specific to each club sport; and informing clubs of fitness and conditioning opportunities provided through approved sources. If the club staff chooses to sponsor or design conditioning programs, seek approval by qualified medical, exercise physiology, or sports medicine personnel.

Injuries and emergencies. Although accidents and injuries can be reduced, they cannot be completely eliminated. Each safety plan must specify a procedure for managing emergencies. Club officers should appoint safety members (see Figure 10.7) who understand that when they assume responsibility for handling accidents and injuries, they must know how to contact qualified help. They are also responsible for recording accident information for club sport staff.

The conservative model requires that someone with first aid and CPR–AED (cardiopulmonary resuscitation–automated external defibrillator) training attend each club practice or event. This individual could be an athletic trainer, physician, facility supervisor, or club member. This person should review procedures for handling the problem at the scene, securing additional help or transportation, and documenting the incident on required forms. To avoid misinterpretation, written accident procedures should be available. Other liability safeguards include maintaining a record of each person's first aid, CPR, or water safety instructor (WSI) certification; obtaining the signature of safety personnel agreeing to the responsibilities of the position; and denying club access to facilities until emergency aid personnel have been identified (see Figure 10.8).

Facility arrangements. Most recreational settings strain to meet the demand for facilities by clubs. Facilities are often used by many programs. For example, athletic and physical education programs may share facilities at colleges. Within the community, instructional programs, social programs, cultural programs, and public school programs may share a facility. In a military setting, instructional programs and physical fitness and training programs use common space. Facilities in a correctional or industrial setting may house instructional programs, social programs, and cultural programs. The demand for facilities requires standardized scheduling procedures. Information about the facility's reservation policy should include how, when, and where to reserve the facility; the amount of rental fees (if any); eligibility requirements; and rules governing proper use of the facilities. A policy statement should establish a maximum amount of time a club may request for regular practices. This helps equitably distribute facility access and reduce suspicion of preferential treatment. When developing this policy consider the number of club members, the type of facility and present demand for its use, the number of clubs seeking access to the facility, the nature of the sport, and the minimum time needed to conduct a practice. Allocated time should be based on growth in membership or availability of equipment.

When a club wants to conduct an event other than a regular practice, it needs to make a separate facility reservation request. Establish a deadline for submitting a reservation request, such as two weeks to one month before the desired time. This allows the recreational sport specialist to coordinate maximal use of facilities and avoid scheduling conflicts. It

---

CLUB SPORT MEMBER SAFETY

Club _____

The following people have been designated as individuals responsible for the safety of facilities and equipment. It is understood that at least one of these individuals must be present at all club functions.

Name	Phone	E-mail
_____	_____	_____
_____	_____	_____
_____	_____	_____
_____	_____	_____
_____	_____	_____
_____	_____	_____
_____	_____	_____
_____	_____	_____
_____	_____	_____
_____	_____	_____

Submitted by

_____
(Signature)

Office _____

Date _____

Figure 10.7. Member Safety Form. From *Recreational Sport Management* by Richard F. Mull, Kathryn G. Bayless, and Lynn M. Jamieson, 2005, Champaign, IL: Human Kinetics.

also allows time to counsel club officers on proper use of the facility, responsibilities of supervising the facility, and procedures for reporting accidents or maintenance problems. After the counseling session, have a club officer sign a statement accepting the conditions for facility use.

Once the club officers fully accept their role in protecting facilities, their members will take pride in caring for the facility and anticipating and identifying maintenance problems. See Chapter 13 for more on facility care.

Equipment. Club members provide their own equipment, use what is available at the agency, or purchase equipment through the club. Equipment concerns for program staff are purchasing, care and storage, and inventory and maintenance. Neglect results in waste, theft, loss, and possibly injury, so equipment purchased with club funds is considered agency equipment reserved for club use. In this way, equipment is protected until it is no longer serviceable. Another safeguard that protects equipment and provides the best value for the money is channeling purchase requests through the staff. First, determine the appropriateness of the request. Then, whenever possible, identify three potential vendors and compare quality and cost. After ordering equipment, keep

CLUB MEMBERS CERTIFIED IN EMERGENCY FIRST AID

Below are club members who have current certification in the indicated column. It is understood that at least one of these members will be present at all club functions. Copies of certification cards will be on file in the club sport office.

Name	CPR	First aid	*PDT	*WSI	Other (specify)
_____	_____	_____	_____	_____	_____
_____	_____	_____	_____	_____	_____
_____	_____	_____	_____	_____	_____
_____	_____	_____	_____	_____	_____
_____	_____	_____	_____	_____	_____
_____	_____	_____	_____	_____	_____
_____	_____	_____	_____	_____	_____

Submitted by

_____
(Signature)

Office _____

Date _____

Figure 10.8. Emergency Aid Personnel Form. From *Recreational Sport Management* by Richard F. Mull, Kathryn G. Bayless, and Lynn M. Jamieson, 2005, Champaign, IL: Human Kinetics.

a copy of the request and check the order when it arrives. On delivery, have the equipment marked, coded or engraved, inventoried, and checked out to the club. This keeps staff members aware of club needs and equipment costs, provides an opportunity to develop positive business relationships with vendors, and facilitates discussion regarding proper care and storage for equipment.

An up-to-date inventory is useful for fostering accountability for equipment and for familiarizing new officers or staff about club resources. The club should conduct an inventory that documents the number and types of equipment, purchase dates, and present condition. Such information is useful when considering additional purchase requests and evaluating merchandise quality. Proper care and storage allow maximum use. If the staff cannot handle this function, the responsibility rests with the club. The staff may influence proper care by withholding funds, imposing fines, denying purchase requests, or restricting facility use when a club demonstrates improper handling of equipment.

If the club needs storage space for its equipment, keep a record of its location and who is responsible for its security. Obtain a signed statement from any individual accepting this responsibility. Finally, a checkout system may reduce damage, theft, and loss by placing financial responsibility on the user. A checkout system may be appropriate when different programs use equipment and it is dispensed from a central location or when the club issues equipment to its members for the year. Although equipment procedures may be time consuming, systems that protect the lifespan of equipment have economic advantages. See Chapter 14 for more insight on properly caring for equipment.

Insurance. Agencies may carry blanket health, accident, and liability insurance for club participation. Other agencies may require club members to have personal coverage, require each club to carry group coverage, or encourage clubs and members to carry voluntary coverage. If clubs or members must provide their own coverage, a system of verification is necessary. If clubs don't need to carry personal or group coverage, each member must sign a consent statement releasing the agency from responsibility for personal injury sustained while participating in a club function. When minors are involved, a parent or guardian must sign the statement. This places responsibility for health, liability, and accident coverage on the individual. Insurance should be taken seriously. Carefully examine several alternatives to be sure the club has adequate coverage.

Travel. When clubs receive funding from a board, agency, or institution, their travel is governed by policies addressing approval, funding, or vehicle use. The most common requirements for club travel under a conservative model include the following:

- application for travel approval (see Figure 10.9),
- roster of people traveling,
- supervisor who accompanies the club,
- personnel certified in first aid and CPR–AED who accompany the club, and
- use of agency vehicles that carry adequate liability insurance (see Figure 10.10).

Ideally, club transportation should involve commercially bonded vehicles or vehicles owned and insured by the agency. Clubs may use privately owned vehicles. Some club programs permit agency money to cover travel, but others prohibit this practice due to liability concerns and the increased work of monitoring club travel. Whenever possible, encourage clubs to limit travel to nearby areas to reduce expenses and accident potential. Restrictions on distance and number of trips may limit access to vehicles owned by the agency. This stipulation typically occurs when the demand for travel exceeds the supply of vehicles or when the volume of requests hinders proper management.

Event management. Clubs in leagues or tournaments schedule regular opportunities for participation. Facility availability, proximity, finances, skill level, conference regulations, and travel regulations influence the scheduling of activities with other clubs or teams. Program staff may need to help with scheduling when there are limited resources, such as facility space and finances, or when clubs are unable to manage their schedule. The staff may need to set a timetable for finalizing scheduling plans for the year. The club and staff need time to prepare for and promote events. Often a club has such strong spectator appeal that a copy of its schedule should be posted at the facility or on a website. When scheduling an event with other clubs, each club should sign a written agreement. The agreement specifies the conditions that each club must fulfill and the purpose, date, time, and location of the event. A sample agreement is shown in Figure 10.11.

Before clubs use written agreements, they should examine legal liability. For example, under what conditions is the agency responsible if a club does not fulfill its obligations? Under what conditions is the agency responsible for injuries to representatives of visiting clubs? Must administrative or program staff sign the contract, or is the signature of a club officer sufficient? In settings where the agency closely supervises all club activity, the staff designs and approves the agreements. Club officers participate in a required review session with the program staff to ensure that each event is planned adequately and includes the appropriate safety precautions. After the event, the club should submit an evaluation that includes a financial statement and describes the outcome of the event, problems or accidents, and recommendations for improvements.

Use another written agreement for securing personnel to officiate or supervise the club event. The primary responsibility for obtaining such personnel rests with the club, although program staff may make referrals or assume responsibility for this task. Any agreement should include event particulars, rate of pay, and method of payment. An additional clause should indicate what will happen should someone not fulfill specified obligations. A sample agreement is presented in Figure 10.12.

Morale is damaged if a club hosts or travels to an event and another club does not uphold its agreement. Written agreements formalize responsibilities and serve as a more binding commitment than a verbal agreement, though there still is no guarantee that the event will happen as planned. Avoiding disappointment, loss of funds, and problems from failure to meet obligations requires realistic planning and an ability to anticipate difficulties. No agreement is valid unless the club demonstrates an ability to fulfill its obligations and has an approved plan for meeting them.

CLUB SPORT TRAVEL REQUEST

Date of trip _____ Destination _____

Duration of trip _____ Day _____ Overnight _____

Approximate time returning _____

Overnight Residence

Motel _____ Phone _____

Hotel _____ Phone _____

Campus _____ Phone _____

Other _____ Phone _____

Drivers _____

_____

Owners of vehicles _____

_____

_____

Vehicle registrations _____

_____

_____

Company insuring vehicles _____

_____

Number of people traveling _____ (attach list of names)

Purpose of trip _____

_____

Emergency numbers where safety officer or president can be reached _____

_____

Name _____ Date _____

Office _____

Approve _____ Reject _____

Figure 10.9. Club Travel Request. From *Recreational Sport Management* by Richard F. Mull, Kathryn G. Bayless, and Lynn M. Jamieson, 2005, Champaign, IL: Human Kinetics.

REQUEST FOR MOTOR VEHICLES

Name of organization _____ Account no. _____

Number of vehicles requested _____ Types _____

Purpose of trip _____

_____

Destination _____

Equipment to be carried _____

Date and time wanted _____

Date and time to be returned _____

Name of driver _____

Driver's license number and state of issue _____

Address _____ Phone/e-mail _____

Name of driver _____

Driver's license number and state of issue _____

Address _____ Phonc/c mail _____

Name of driver _____

Driver's license number and state of issue _____

Address _____ Phone/e-mail _____

List all passengers _____

_____

_____

_____

_____

_____

Approval

_____   _____
Director, motor vehicles   *Club sport staff*

_____   _____
Account manager   *Director, recreational sport*

Complete in quadruplicate.

Figure 10.10. Motor Vehicle Request. From *Recreational Sport Management* by Richard F. Mull, Kathryn G. Bayless, and Lynn M. Jamieson, 2005, Champaign, IL: Human Kinetics.

CLUB SPORT CONTEST AGREEMENT

This agreement, made and entered into this _____ day of _____ 20 ____, by and between the undersigned authorized representative of _____ and the undersigned authorized representative of _____ stipulates the following:

First, that the teams representing these named organizations or institutions agree to meet in _____ at

_____, _____
                    location of contest   *city and state*

on _____ 20 ____, at _____ o'clock _____ m., and at

_____, _____
                    location of contest   *city and state*

on _____ 20 ____, at _____ o'clock _____ m.

Second, that the consideration binding the two teams to play these contests shall be the appearance of each visiting team at the site of each home team in the aforesaid contests, or, as indicated in paragraph *nine,* if applicable.

Third, that the contests shall be played under _____ rules.

Fourth, that the officials are to be mutually agreed upon.

Fifth, that expenses of officials are to be borne by the home team.

Sixth, that the home management reserves the right to cancel the contest on account of inclement weather or other unavoidable cause, two hours before the visiting team leaves from its residence or the place of the previous game, notice of which time had been given at least three days before.

Seventh, that in case a contest is canceled after the arrival of the visiting team on account of inclement weather or other unavoidable cause, the home team shall pay the visiting team _____ dollars.

Eighth, that the day, time, and location of any of these contests shall not be changed without the written consent of the authorized representative of the visiting team.

Ninth _____

_____

_____

_____

In witness whereof, we have affixed our signature the day and year first above written.

For _____   For _____

By _____   By _____
              Authorized representative   *Authorized representative*

Return one copy of completed contract to _____

_____

Figure 10.11. Club Sport Contest Agreement. From *Recreational Sport Management* by Richard F. Mull, Kathryn G. Bayless, and Lynn M. Jamieson, 2005, Champaign, IL: Human Kinetics.

STATEMENT OF AGREEMENT FOR SPORT OFFICIAL

_____ of _____
                          (President)

_____ Club and _____
                                                                (Official)

hereby enter into the following assignment and terms for officiating:

1. Said official agrees to be present and officiate _____ contest(s) of
    _____ (sport) to be played at _____
    on the dates listed during the year 20 ___ - 20___.

Date	Day of week	Time	Clubs playing	Total payment

2. That in case of failure on the part of either one of the parties to fulfill the terms of this agreement, except by mutual consent, a forfeiture of $25.00 shall be paid by the offending party to the other party within five days after the date set for each game in this statement. It is understood that there is a moral obligation to be considered in the making and breaking of agreements. Where obligations are not mutually adjusted, _____ reserves the right to review the facts and determine what these adjustments should be.

3. This agreement is void if not returned on or before _____.

For club	**For contest official**
_____	_____
Signature of president	Signature
_____	_____
Club	Address
_____	_____
Address	Identification number
_____	_____
Date	Date
_____	_____
Telephone	Telephone

Names of other officials employed to work this contest (if available).

Name	Telephone	E-mail

Figure 10.12. Club Sport Officials' Agreement. From _Recreational Sport Management_ by Richard F. Mull, Kathryn G. Bayless, and Lynn M. Jamieson, 2005, Champaign, IL: Human Kinetics.

Instruction. Some degree of coaching and instruction occurs within any club. When a club desires qualified leadership, it may appoint or hire an instructor or coach. Program staff can assist clubs by discussing selection and hiring, reviewing job descriptions and contracts, handling or monitoring the payroll, approving club funds for employing personnel, and serving as a resource for club personnel. When providing such assistance, the recreational sport specialist needs to maintain a commitment to nondiscriminatory employment, understand whether the agency is liable for injuries sustained by club members performing activities designed by an approved instructor, and understand the consequences of any violation of a written agreement. Regardless of staff involvement in approving or hiring personnel, the clubs should perform certain tasks, including developing job descriptions, establishing minimum requirements, receiving membership approval for using funds, protecting funds allocated for employment purposes, using a reliable procedure for handling payroll, conducting an appropriate selection process, and documenting the conditions of appointment or employment. Because most club members want to learn more about their sport, selecting instructors is an important process. Consequently, program staff should be ready to assist clubs with personnel management.

Promotion. When clubs fall under the jurisdiction of an agency, their image reflects on the agency. Guidelines for club public relations and publicity reflect a common desire for a positive image. When the club bears full responsibility for promotion, staff should review the club's ideas. To allow time for revisions, require that plans gain approval in advance. If the club sport program provides resources or personnel to assist in club promotion, inform clubs how to take advantage of publicity opportunities, and coordinate deadlines for approving and implementing requests. To organize requests and eliminate mistakes in information or design, the club should submit its requests in writing and then review them with the appropriate staff members. An advantage in managing club promotional efforts is the opportunity to improve the quality of the projects. Proposals can be denied if the club submits them late or if they are unrealistic in terms of time, volume, or cost. Another aspect of promotion is the distribution of materials within the setting. Materials are often wasted and the setting cluttered with notices, resulting in a negative image of the club, agency, or institution.

Annual report. Each club ought to complete an annual report for historical reference and for planning future goals and objectives. From an administrative perspective, annual reports can update staff about club activities, identify participation trends, specify problems faced by clubs, and offer ideas for improving services to clubs. Establish deadlines for receiving the completed reports before election of officers and allocation of funds. In this way, current officers are responsible for documenting the information that will assist new officers. Finally, an annual report (see Figure 10.13) provides additional insight into a club's performance, which can be helpful when program staff are allocating funds.

Program assistance. The final subject covered in the club sport operational guidelines should explain the types of assistance each club may receive and how they may use this support. Assistance may include partial or complete provision for mail, telephone, a website, e-mail accounts, storage, duplicating, and office space. These services not only contribute to the success of club operations but also facilitate interaction and rapport among staff and club members.

Funding

One characteristic of club sport is financial self-support. Historically, clubs have sustained their activities through dues, donations, and fund-raising. Recently, clubs in some settings, particularly education, have received financial assistance from the agency that administers them. The amount of assistance depends on the budget and agency philosophy. Although such financial support may be useful, a greater dependence on and accountability to the agency is often the result.

Identifying the club's financial needs begins with a discussion about proposed activities. Strategies are established for securing the finances to meet club needs. Common sources include membership dues and fines, donations, fund-raising projects, and allocations from an agency. When seeking income sources, the club must follow certain procedures to avoid violating laws or policies of the setting. For example, clubs interested in soliciting donations through a door-to-door canvass should check city or state codes to be sure the approach is legal. The primary functions of club sport staff are to identify acceptable funding approaches, inform club officers of policies governing fund-raising, and establish a system to review club ideas for securing income.

ANNUAL REPORT

Club _____

Club officers	Fall	Spring	Fall (if elected)
President	_____	_____	_____
Vice president	_____	_____	_____
Secretary	_____	_____	_____
Treasurer	_____	_____	_____
Advisor	_____	_____	_____
Coach	_____	_____	_____
Council representative	_____	_____	_____
Instructor	_____	_____	_____

What is the total club membership? _____ Men _____ Women _____

How much are club dues per person? _____ Year or semester? _____

What was this year's total budget? _____

What is next year's projected budget? _____

Are you seeking money from the council? _____ How much? _____

What facilities did the club use on a regular or part-time basis? _____

_____

When were practice times? _____

_____

When and where did the club meet other than for practice or games (i.e., business meetings)?

_____

_____

How many competitive events were held against other clubs? List matches and results (away and home competition).

_____   _____

_____   _____

_____   _____

Where did the club travel? _____

cont.

Figure 10.13. Annual Report. From *Recreational Sport Management* by Richard F. Mull, Kathryn G. Bayless, and Lynn M. Jamieson, 2005, Champaign, IL: Human Kinetics.

Annual Report *(continued)*

What was the average personal expenditure for each club member not paid by the club?

Travel _____

Equipment _____

Entry fees in meets _____

Who can someone interested in joining the club contact? (Name and number if possible.)

_____

List any noteworthy accomplishments or awards received by the club.

_____

_____

_____

Write a paragraph explaining club activities (200 words maximum).

_____

_____

_____

_____

_____

_____

Briefly summarize the club's activities this past year. Include the club's short- and long-range goals.

_____

_____

_____

_____

Briefly state the club's goals and objectives for the coming year.

_____

_____

_____

List recommendations for improving club internal operations.

_____

_____

_____

_____

Figure 10.13. cont.

Annual Report *(continued)*

List recommendations for improving assistance to the club by the club sport staff.

_____

_____

_____

Report submitted by _____

Position _____

Date _____

Figure 10.13. cont.

Budget Preparation

A budget proposal is a helpful tool for projecting expenditures and income. It requires careful planning and organization and serves as a blueprint for the club. It also holds officers accountable for financial transactions. It is customary for the club officers or a treasurer to prepare a budget proposal for adoption by the membership. This proposal should include itemized expenditures and projected sources of income. Proposal categories include the following:

Income

- Membership dues
- Donations
- Grants or allocated funds
- Fund-raising projects

Expenses

- Equipment (club equipment not personally owned)
- Supplies and expenses (telephone, stamps, paper, posters, trophies)
- Hourly wages (payment for trainers, coaches, instructors, ticket takers)
- Travel (gas, food, lodging, entry fees)

Figure 10.14 is a sample budget, indicating club expenses and income for the current year to compare with the budget proposal for the following year. Before finalizing the budget proposal, the club should make sure it has reliable and acceptable sources of income and accurate estimates for projected expenditures. The club officers should be familiar with policies regarding budget preparation, particularly if the club is eligible for grants or an allocation from an agency.

Allocation Process

Club grants or allocations are based on a desire to support clubs as a vehicle for recreational sport participation. Without them, clubs struggle to provide consistent programming for their members, even when they have successful fund-raising activities. Financial support from an administrative agency, such as a club sport council, may also be beneficial in terms of administrative control because clubs tend to abide to certain standards in order to maintain access to funding. To ensure that all clubs receive equitable treatment in fund allocation, establish uniform requirements for funding requests and make these requirements known to all clubs. Explain the criteria for allocation decisions well before the allocation process. Knowing the criteria helps clubs in preparing proposals and aids decision making about the allocation request. Criteria also should indicate when a newly formed club is first eligible to request an allocation. For example, a club may be required to be operational and in good standing for a year before seeking an allocation, allowing the committee to better determine whether the club is well organized, stable, and responsible.

An allocation committee should comprise at least six and as many as 12 individuals familiar with the club sport program yet not directly involved with any club seeking an allocation. The committee may be appointed by the club sport staff and approved by a club sport council or selected by a club council of representatives. The first option may be more desirable because a professional staff member should not be biased in any way. The staff should not determine allocations because this invites conflict if a club is dissatisfied with its allocation. It is preferable for the staff to serve as a resource for clubs as they prepare a budget and presentation for the committee.

CLUB BUDGET

Item	Actual total Cost per × number	20__-20__	Projected total Cost per × number	20__-20__
Income				
Allocated money				
Membership dues				
Donations				
Movie ticket sales				
Benefit games				
Total income				
Expenditures				

Hourly wage
    Coaches
    Officials
    Trainers				

Equipment
    Balls
    Sticks
    Helmets
    Knee pads
    Nets				

Supplies and expenses
    Utilities
    Facility rental
    Stamps
    Phone
    Duplicating
    Stationery
    Trophies
    Newspaper ads
    Recognition banquet
    Insurance
    Laundry
    Bank charges				

Travel
    Gas
    Food
    Lodging
    Business trip
    Vehicle insurance				

Governing body Membership dues				
Total expenses				
_ Total income Total expenses				
Balance				

Figure 10.14. Club Budget. From *Recreational Sport Management* by Richard F. Mull, Kathryn G. Bayless, and Lynn M. Jamieson, 2005, Champaign, IL: Human Kinetics.

When seeking allocated funds, a club should prepare a budget proposal. It is helpful to use a standard budget format and to insist that clubs respect the deadline for submitting budget proposals. The staff may hold a special meeting on budget preparation and make appointments to meet with clubs individually. Such preparation reduces the time needed to make decisions and interpret budgets at the committee meeting. Next, provide a way for members of the committee to review the proposals ahead of time. Make copies of each budget for each member or establish a rotation system to review the originals. If committee members have questions about a club proposal or require further information, resolve these problems before the presentation. Hold a special training session for the committee members to answer questions about the budgets and the committee's duties. After the deadline for budget review has passed, each club requesting funds should present a brief oral proposal (10 to 20 minutes) to the assembled committee and respond to any questions. Before each presentation, a staff member or the executive officer of the club sport council should indicate how well the club has met its responsibilities for the year. The merits of each club's application should be judged on

- its explanation and justification of budgets,
- the nature of its expenses, and
- its fulfillment of duties to the granting agency.

These criteria and how they affect an administrative committee's decision to grant funds to club sport are examined in the following sections.

Budget presentation. Clubs should understand that they are required to do the following:

- include statements for the previous and current year as well as a proposed budget for the coming year;
- specify club expenses and revenues, indicating a balance; and
- estimate proposed needs as accurately as possible, based on their plans, justifiable expenses, and revenue.

Budget justification. Clubs must explain anticipated costs for the following:

Hourly wages. A club incurring expenses for instructors, coaches, officials, or athletic trainers should give detailed explanations (e.g., rate, hours, days, number of people needed).

Equipment. The administrative agency provides support only for equipment purchased for long-term use. This includes individual equipment (e.g., uniforms) necessary for club activities that the individual member is not expected to provide. The agency will consider expenses related to the club's current equipment and its necessary maintenance or replacement.

Supplies and other detailed expenses. A club incurring expenses for facility use should give a detailed breakdown of costs (rates, hours, days). Agencies should discourage a miscellaneous expenses category unless the club can provide an itemized breakdown.

Travel expenses. Travel is defined as moving to a location outside the agency setting for participation. A club should justify travel (e.g., to obtain competition at its own ability or to further opportunities for training or instruction). Clubs should attempt to combine matches in one geographical area into a single trip. Agencies should support the minimum number of players needed to participate. All expenses, such as food, gas, and lodging, need explanation.

Responsibilities. Allocation committees often consider factors less tangible than financial need. Such criteria reflect a club's dedication to its stated goals and those of the agency. Generally, no allocation is made to any club that has not met its financial responsibilities (payment of dues and fines, if any). Similarly, under a conservative model, no allocation is made to any club whose file with the external administration unit is not complete. A complete file includes the following:

- constitution or operating guidelines,
- budget request and annual report,
- general information sheet and membership roster,
- list of officers,
- minutes from business meetings,
- consent forms, and
- equipment inventory.

The committee will consider whether a club has met other responsibilities, such as attending meetings, keeping files current, and fulfilling obligations to committees. Failure to comply with these minimal standards subjects clubs to a reduction of the allocation. The committee should note instances in which the club council or agency levied fines against a club's current allocation when the club did not meet its responsibilities. Certain actions or gross neglect of responsibilities may warrant decreasing allocations for the following year. On the other hand, staff may institute an incentive plan to reward clubs for meeting established criteria. Determine appropriate incentives based on input from club officers and based on organization policies that govern the use of resources within the agency. Examples of incentives include monetary rewards, priority consideration in facility scheduling, free use of office equipment and supplies, availability of expertise from personnel to assist with club marketing and fund-raising, and reducing or waiving fees for facility use.

Distributing funds. Once the committee decides a need is justified, it can determine each club's percentage and total fund allocation through the following formulas:

Percentage of Allocation to Club A =

$$\frac{\text{Justified Need of Club A}}{\text{Total Justified Need of All Clubs}}$$

Allocation to Club A = Percentage of Allocation to Club A * Total Allocated Funds for all Clubs

Guidelines should explain how the club gains access to its allocated funds. The money may be provided in a direct payment to the club or retained in an account supervised by the club sport staff. A more conservative approach is taken when there are restrictions on how the club can spend the money and when documentation of club financial transactions is necessary. In this approach, a club makes a written request to the staff, justifying need, identifying potential vendors, and providing cost estimates. Using a request form (see Figure 10.15) assists bookkeeping and accounting. Regardless of the total amount, staff should make every attempt to eliminate opportunities for mishandling club funds. Such problems greatly damage the credibility of club sport and often form the grounds for serious legal or disciplinary action.

Fund-Raising

A club's allocation often falls short of its needs, so clubs should be encouraged to hold fund-raisers. Be sure the club conducts all fund-raising with the approval of the administrative agency (see Figure 10.16). After an event, the club should forward a summary to the agency (see Figure 10.17). Some fund-raising activities may be an integral part of a club's function, and administrative agencies should consider such activities when making allocation grants. Common fund-raising ideas for club sports are

- letter drives to family, friends, alumni, and local businesses;

- car wash (also boat or dog wash);
- rent an athlete;
- bingo night;
- garage sale;
- bake sale;
- sales of club sport apparel;
- providing parking arrangements for special events or sporting events;
- cow drop;
- raffle draws;
- 50–50 draws at sports games or special events; and
- golf tournaments or bowl-a-thons.

Following are examples of fund-raising criteria used in the allocation process:

- In its request, a club should not include fund-raising revenue, activities unrelated to the club's sport, or activities not needed by the sport community (e.g., activities for which the club is not the only source).

- A club should include fund-raising activities of the previous year or current year and activities related to the club's sport and needed by the sport community (e.g., a martial arts club serving as the only source for uniform sales or a volleyball club serving as the only source of officials for a community intramural tournament). In the committee's evaluation of justified need, it should deduct a club's expected fund-raising income from budgeted expenditures. However, the committee should not consider past fund-raising activities a credit or deduction applicable to the club's allocation.

Control

By providing standards of conduct for the club sport program, the recreational sport specialist promotes safety, acceptable social interaction, positive public relations, and accountability. Conduct expectations vary depending on the administrative philosophy (conservative or liberal). Procedures that guide conduct and provide recreational sport specialists with controls must also afford clubs a fair review. Specific statements addressing behavior and duties expected of members and officers should be part of each club's constitution.

REQUEST FOR FUNDS

Club _____ Date of request _____

Amount requested _____ Date needed _____

Justification of Need

Funds will be used for (e.g., equipment, hourly wages, etc.)

_____

_____

_____

_____

Specific information (e.g., size, quantity, color)

_____

_____

_____

_____

Projected cost per item

_____

_____

_____

_____

Suggested Vendors

1. _____

2. _____

3. _____

Submitted by _____, Treasurer

Amount approved _____ Remaining balance _____

Comments _____

_____

_____

_____

_____

Staff signature _____ Date _____

Figure 10.15. Request for Funds. From *Recreational Sport Management* by Richard F. Mull, Kathryn G. Bayless, and Lynn M. Jamieson, 2005, Champaign, IL: Human Kinetics.

FUND-RAISING PROJECT APPLICATION

Club _____

Date submitted _____

Project chairperson _____

Local address _____

Phone _____ E-mail _____

Project description _____

_____

_____

Date(s) of project _____

Location(s) _____

Time(s) _____

Income source(s) _____

Total anticipated income from project $ _____

Expense items _____

_____

_____

Total anticipated expenses from project $ _____

Total anticipated profit from project $ _____

Use of proceeds _____

_____

_____

Will the project be an annual event? _____

Does the organization have a local bank account?   Yes _____   No _____

The undersigned in connection with and as a part of this application for a fund-raising project certifies that he or she is a club member and that the information listed is correct to the best of his or her knowledge and belief.

Signature _____

Comments _____

_____

_____

Approved by _____

Date approved _____

Note: Please complete in duplicate and return to the club sport office. Depending on the event additional information may be required.

Figure 10.16. Fund-raising Project Application. From *Recreational Sport Management* by Richard F. Mull, Kathryn G. Bayless, and Lynn M. Jamieson, 2005, Champaign, IL: Human Kinetics.

FUND-RAISING PROJECT SUMMARY

To be submitted to the club sport office within one week following the fund-raising project.

Project _____

Sponsored by _____

Date of project _____

Location(s) _____

_____

_____

_____

_____

Total income received $ _____

Expenses listed by major items _____

_____

_____

_____

_____

_____

_____

Total expenses $ _____

Profit $ _____

Use of proceeds _____

_____

_____

Signature _____

Date _____

Figure 10.17. Fund-raising Project Summary. From *Recreational Sport Management* by Richard F. Mull, Kathryn G. Bayless, and Lynn M. Jamieson, 2005, Champaign, IL: Human Kinetics.

Addressing Violations

Penalties for violating a code of conduct are to be handled as an internal matter within the club. However, when the actions of a club or member violate agency policy, investigation and intervention may be warranted. Delineation of club and staff responsibility for disciplinary action is necessary for several reasons. First, a concept basic to club sport is self-governance. Staff intervention weakens this principle and results in club dependency on the staff for problem solving. Second, the role of staff in control is to make rulings that direct the club as a whole, not as individual members. The club is responsible for dealing with internal problems, while the staff holds the club accountable for this responsibility. Finally, the staff should not intervene in internal club problems before the officers have had a chance to deal with them. Premature intervention hinders the ability of the staff to hear an appeal objectively. Situations that may require disciplinary action, whether imposed by the club or staff, include the following:

- verbal or physical abuse by club members or club representatives,

- alcohol or substance abuse,

- damage to equipment or facilities,

- mishandling of funds, and

- violations of club or agency policies.

Review Process

Addressing alleged problems requires a commitment to fair treatment, a predetermined set of guidelines, and an informed club that recognizes its responsibilities and the consequences of failure to meet them. There are several models for review procedures. One model involves an initial investigation and ruling by the staff, allowing an appeal to a hearing board made up of club sport representatives, at least five and up to 10 club representatives trained to serve on an appeals committee. (See Chapter 9 for more about disciplinary boards.) The following material contains suggested policy guidelines that explain the grounds for disciplinary action, the investigation process, the appeal and hearing processes, and imposing and enforcing penalties. Following these models should help the recreational sport specialist reach fair and appropriate decisions. However, unless the staff is committed to due process, even the best model can turn into a mockery of justice. Take disciplinary measures when necessary to improve the club system, not to demonstrate power and authority. If the clubs view the process as fair, they will participate in resolving problems in the same fashion.

Grounds for action. Consider complaints against a club for any action that violates policy, whether committed by the club, club representatives, or individual members. Proven violations become grounds for penalties. Once the club sport staff has received a complaint for investigation and ruling, the staff should notify the club of the complaint, preferably in writing.

Staff investigation and ruling. When a complaint is referred to the club sport staff, obtain written statements from the plaintiff, accused club, witnesses, and other appropriate parties. In addition, conduct verbal conferences with the plaintiff, accused club, witnesses, other appropriate parties, and the executive committee. The club sport staff should make a ruling based on the evidence uncovered during the investigation. Finally, the staff should notify the club of the ruling in writing.

Appeal. If the club wishes to appeal the decision, it may do so through written notification either to the staff or to the club sport council president. The case may then be referred to a club sport hearing board. This board consists of five, six, or seven club representatives unrelated to any of the clubs involved. The council president customarily appoints these representatives, one of whom acts as a secretary, at the beginning of the year. Next, the club sport staff or council president arrange a time and place for the hearing that is convenient for all parties involved.

Hearing. At least three board members, including the chairperson and secretary, should be present throughout the hearing. Only these members may vote after the board's deliberation. The secretary should keep a record of the hearing, including a list of those present and the substance of all evidence and arguments. If possible, make a tape recording to avoid error. Following is a suggested procedure for the hearing:

- The chairperson states the purpose of the hearing.

- Opening statements proceed, first by a representative of the plaintiff and then by a representative of the accused club.

- The parties may then present additional evidence of any sort, subject to questions by those present.

- The parties make final statements.

- The board concludes with questions to any party.

Once the board begins its deliberation in private, no record needs to be kept. Afterward, the chairperson may entertain motions to increase or decrease penalties against the club, to sustain the club sport staff's rulings, or to exonerate the club. The decision should have the support of at least three members of the hearing board to lend legitimacy to the ruling. Within one week of the hearing, the decision and a rationale should be presented in writing to the club sport staff, to be forwarded to the club. The club may obtain a transcript of the hearing record, bearing the cost of its provision.

Penalties. Penalties imposed on a club should have administrative approval. Examples of penalties include fines, temporary loss of funding or facility privileges, suspension from specified facilities, probation for a specified period under certain conditions, or recommendation for continued review.

Enforcement. A staff member commonly is responsible for enforcing disciplinary rulings. In some instances, an administrator may overrule a decision if it can be shown that due process was violated or significant new evidence has arisen that could alter the decision. Administrative veto power may motivate the staff and hearing board to be more thorough and conscientious in their deliberations. If an administrator intervenes unnecessarily or frequently, however, the hearing board procedure becomes suspect.

Shining Example

Indiana University Club Sports

The Club Sports program at Indiana University is part of Campus Recreational Sports. It provides students, faculty, and members of the community with opportunities to participate in a wide variety of sports at both casual and competitive levels. Indiana University Club Sports also boasts the nation's largest martial arts program at an academic institution, second in size only to the program at West Point. The Club Sports program is governed by a Club Sport Federation, comprised of an executive board and representatives from each club.

Clientele:

Club Sports are open to anyone aged 18 years of age or older. There are over 1,900 participants in approximately 50 club sports. The majority of participants live in the university's home town of Bloomington, but some come from farther away to practice with clubs that offer activities that are unavailable elsewhere..

Facilities:

Indiana University Club Sports uses the space in the School of Public Health and Wildermuth Intramural Center, the Student Recreational Sports Center (SRSC), many of the university's athletic facilities, and some off-campus facilities (as in the case of the equestrian and ice hockey clubs)..

Program Details:

The student-run club sports, offer a wide range of opportunities for participants to keep fit, make new friends, and learn new sports. They also offer the chance to lead demonstrations, attend seminars, or compete at institutional, state, national, and even international levels. Some clubs (such as Men's and Women's Rugby) compete extensively with other collegiate teams, while others (such as Table Tennis and Ballroom Dance) are more socially oriented. There are several martial arts clubs, some of which are complimented by academic courses within the School of Public Health.

Budget:

The Club Sports budget is approximately $68,000 per year, and is used for club allocations and incentive programs. It does not include the staff salaries, which are paid by Campus Recreational Sports. Clubs also generate income through membership dues, fund-raising events, donations, and sponsorships.

Marketing:

Individual clubs are responsible for their own marketing, and many use flyers, sidewalk chalking, and apparel as primary methods. Many clubs host their own Web sites that are linked to the Campus Recreational Sports' Web site (www.recsports.indiana.edu). The division uses several methods of marketing for the Club Sports program, including tri-fold brochures, word-of-mouth, social networking, and sections in the division's in-house publications as well as the campus newspaper. They have also recently implemented the use of social networking and text notifications.

Affiliated Professional Organizations:

The staff in charge of the program belong to a variety of professional organizations, including the National Intramural and Recreational Sport Association (NIRSA) and student-activity related organizations.

Conclusion

Club sport programming is challenging yet rewarding. The challenges involve promoting diversity in sport interests and purposes; securing resources such as funding, facilities, and personnel; and maintaining appropriate operational guidelines. It is gratifying when a quality club program results from the combined efforts of members, officers, and staff. It is also rewarding to watch participants gain experience in decision making, time management, leadership, and social skills and find satisfaction in their involvement.

The purpose of this chapter was to differentiate the three purposes of club sport, describe the financial and administrative patterns in club sport, and identify control techniques for club sport. In so doing, this chapter discussed different club types (athletic, instructional and social) and administrative philosophies (formal vs. informal), organizational structure (external and internal including duties of the different club sports officers), and operational guidelines including different classification systems, club sports constitution, eligibility, event management, and funding including the allocation process.

Club sport in the United States will continue to be influenced by the state of the economy. In times of financial stress, clubs may experience cutbacks in activity. Sport programs that depend on an agency for financial support and staff direction, such as intramural, extramural, and athletic sport, may be sharply reduced or even eliminated. It is possible that maintenance of club sport programs may require the pooling of resources from members and commercial or corporate sponsors. Clearly, the recreational sport specialist is able to influence strategies for facilitating club sport. Although the challenges may be difficult, the recreational sport specialist must recognize that clubs are a distinctive, worthy avenue for sport participation.

Bibliography

Burwell, P., & Yeagle, S. (1990). Developing potential: The extramural sport clubs conference. In J. A. Clements (Ed.), *Management strategies in recreational sports* (pp. 207-213). Corvallis, OR: National Intramural–Recreational Sports Association.

Carlson, D. A. (1990). Sport clubs: From the classroom to the office: Academic and continuing career preparation. *National Intramural–Recreational Sports Association Journal, 14*(3), 35-37.

Cleave, S. (1994). Sport clubs: More than a solution to shrinking dollars and growing demands. *National Intramural–Recreational Sports Association Journal, 18*(3), 30, 32-33.

Dubord, R. R. (1987). Leadership training workshops for sport club officers. In National Intramural Recreational Sports Association (Ed.), *Cultivation of recreational sports programs*, (pp. 107-114). Corvallis, OR: National Intramural–Recreational Sports Association.

Matthews, D. O. (1987). *Managing collegiate sport clubs.* Champaign, IL: Human Kinetics.

Roberts, T. M. (2008). Sport clubs. In National Intramural–Recreational Sports Association (Ed.), *Campus recreation* (pp. 169-182). Champaign, IL: Human Kinetics.

Roberts, T. M., & Miller, T. (2003). *Sport clubs: A resource guide* (2nd ed.). Corvallis, OR: National Intramural–Recreational Sports Association.

Robinson, M. J. (2010). *Sport club management.* Champaign, IL: Human Kinetics.

Sawyer, T. H., & Smith, D. (1999). *The management of clubs, recreation, and sport: Concepts and applications.* Urbana, IL: Sagamore.

Stier, W. F. (1994). *Fundraising for sport and recreation.* Champaign, IL: Human Kinetics.

Part IV

RESOURCE CONNECTION

Part IV centers on key resources for a recreational sport specialist in order to integrate their role and responsibilities to overall management. Significant areas include employment and staffing, funding, facilities, and equipment, each with unique emphasis dependent on setting, agency, and the recreational sport specialist's assigned responsibilities. These key elements usually receive comprehensive attention through other curricular design and course content.

CHAPTER 11

Staffing

CHAPTER OBJECTIVES

After reading this chapter, you will understand the functions of staffing; understand the recruitment, selection, training, and supervision of staff; be able to identify levels of staff in recreational sport settings; understand customer service as it relates to staffing; and understand volunteer management.

KEY CONCEPTS

Organizational structure	**Hiring**
Recruitment	**Selection**
Training	**Orientation**
Rewards	**Performance evaluation**
Volunteer management	

Introduction

All recreational sport programs have staff involved in their delivery, meaning that in the recreational sport world, understanding how to manage staff is fundamental to what the recreational sport specialist does. Simply put, staffing (referred to as human resources management, personnel management, or leadership, in sport literature) relates to managing how the individuals in an agency work toward achieving agency goals. Depending on the size of the unit or department and available resources, the scope of staffing will vary; however, common functions are recruitment and selection, training and development, supervision, and rewards. Each of these functions is embedded in the workplace environment that a recreational sport specialist creates, reiterating the interrelatedness of these concepts.

Human resources as a theoretical concept has evolved over time. It was during the 1930s that managers began to appreciate a connection among productivity, employee relations, and group norms. The idea that an employee's well-being could translate into productivity as well as improve the individual's life became an important concept. Thus began research, knowledge, and development related to a more humanistic view of employees, which is still evident today through workplace initiatives such as employee wellness programs. While human resources was previously the responsibility of personnel departments, it is currently situated with individual managers because of their direct involvement with staff on a regular basis. As a result, most recreational sport specialists will be responsible for staffing.

The dynamic aspects of recreational sports attract individuals who are passionate about physical activity, health, and recreation and who have a desire to interact with people. These factors, as well as others, impact the success of staffing activities. Beyond the four common aspects of staffing (i.e., recruitment and selection, training, supervision, rewards), there are additional concepts that support staffing goals including organizational structure, volunteer management, and workplace culture, which will be discussed in this chapter.

Organizational Structure

There are different types of jobs in recreational sport settings (e.g., program leader, facility manager, fitness instructor). An organizational chart is used to visually orient individuals to the different roles and overall structure of an agency. Figure 11.1 is an example of a recreational sport department organizational chart. Even though organizational structure is determined by its sector (i.e., commercial, public, private not-for-profit), there are common elements seen in all organizational charts. The organizational chart illustrates job titles, chain of command, and departments or units, and a job analysis identifies specific responsibilities. The description of all jobs in an agency or department should also correspond to rewards and performance evaluation measures.

The purpose of the job analysis is to describe the roles and responsibilities that make up individual jobs including information related to the knowledge, skills, abilities, and other characteristics needed (sometimes referred to as KSAOs) (Busser, 2005). In completing a job analysis, it is useful to talk with current employees in the position as well as make observations. The results of a job analysis

- provide a description of the agency's jobs,

- form the basis for developing a pay structure that reflects levels of achievement,

- inform all job descriptions and job announcements, and

- should be consistent with rewards and performance evaluation measures.

As described, the organizational structure and supporting job analysis serve as the foundation of staff management.

Staffing Levels

In recreational sport settings, there are various types of positions that are needed to support service delivery. These positions are similar in that they are related to recreational sport delivery; however, they differ in their expected qualifications, roles, and level of responsibility.

Front-Line Staff

Front-line staff is any individual who has direct contact with participants in a recreational setting. Individuals in this category are extremely important because they represent the agency to its users. Examples of front-line positions include officials, lifeguards, fitness instructors, coaches, door attendants, front-desk attendants, playground leaders, weight room supervisors, and program leaders. With this staff level, ongoing training and effective performance evaluations are critical to ensure that service delivery is meeting its goals. Front-line personnel typically require an eagerness to work and a willingness to complete certifications such as first aid once employed.

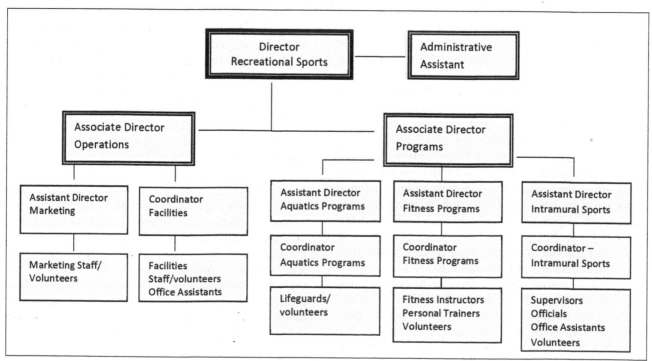

Figure 11.1. Recreational Sport Organizational Chart

Program Staff

Program staff refer to individuals who in a sense bridge front-line staff and management staff. This is where the recreational sport specialist is often found. The work performed by program staff is extremely varied and can include direct program delivery but also extends to include tasks such as marketing and public relations; purchasing and inventory-taking; staff recruitment, training, and supervision; program development; facility operations; and the implementation and evaluation of policies and procedures. It is assumed that program staff have more training, education, and experience than front-line staff.

Management Level Staff

Management level staff (e.g., directors) is responsible for steering the agency into a desired position by focusing on overall direction and management. Even though this level of personnel has very little direct delivery contact with participants through programs, surveys, comment cards, and approachability are strategies used to remain aware of the experiences of participants. Depending on the size of the agency, the number of individuals at this level will vary, especially in public recreational sport settings (e.g., municipal recreation departments). It is important to note that this individual also works with external groups, associations, and other departments in the achievement of agency goals. In addition to experience and qualifications, this individual will have seniority, meaning that he or she will have worked in the field five to 10 years.

Volunteers

A recreational sport specialist likely will work with volunteers. Extramural programs as well as other program areas rely heavily on volunteers due to the nature of their programming. As a group, volunteers need to be incorporated into an organization and made to feel as though they belong. There are numerous tasks that volunteers can perform in recreational sport settings across all three sectors including helping to organize and supervise events, serving as a board member, performing office work duties, coaching teams, and instructing programs. The strategies discussed near the end of this chapter highlight key areas to consider when working with volunteers; many of the tasks associated with staffing in an agency also relate to volunteers but in a slightly different manner.

Staff Recruitment and Selection

Employee recruitment and selection represents an important function of staffing because all the individuals in a workplace impact workplace culture, meaning the right individuals need to be recruited and selected. Determining the required numbers of staff is an important task. Information should be gathered from various sources including organizational structure, job analysis, and enrollment numbers from previous years. Throughout this work, it is important that individuals understand and adhere to policies and regulations developed and enforced by the U.S. Equal Employment Opportunity Commission. A job announcement is then crafted using information from the job description already existing in the agency. Figure 11.2 shows sample job announcements in a university recreational setting. All certifications and/or requirements identified in the job analysis (e.g., police check, university degree) must be included in the job announcement. Common certifications include first aid, CPR, High 5 training, Wilderness First Responder. To create consistency and ensure specific information is gathered, many agencies use standardized application forms to help in the selection process. Furthermore, it is common practice to have an application form on the department's or agency's website to attract a wide pool of applicants. Figure 11.3 is an example of a municipal recreation application form that is available electronically.

Determining when and where to advertise is important, and factors such as available budget, time frame, and level of the job will help answer this. In recreation, there will be times of the year when multiple staff positions need to be filled. For example, at the beginning of the swim season or ice-skating season and/or before summer holidays, additional part-time staff (e.g., lifeguards, rink supervisors, day camp leaders) are hired and are therefore advertised together. When deciding to hire, it is important to allow enough time to properly train individuals before it is the busiest time of work to ensure quality programs are delivered.

In terms of where to advertise, first be sure to create awareness about the job internally because current staff members may be eligible or know of interested candidates. In terms of recruitment, being known as a good employer with satisfied employees is helpful in attracting potential employees—current employees are the best assets in terms of securing others. Research suggests that recreation and sport agencies tend not to have difficulty in attracting employees because the market for recreational sport positions is competitive. In a university recreational sport setting, job announcements can be posted on the department's website, the university's human resources website, and in the student newspaper. Alternatively, a YMCA job or a municipal job should be advertised in a local community newspaper and on websites. If recruitment needs to be done on a

---

1. Intramural Sports Supervisors Job Announcement

General Information: Our intramural supervisors work throughout the school year in a variety of sports. Intramural supervisors oversee various intramural sports including but not limited to flag football, basketball, volleyball, soccer, softball, tennis, and other special events.

Specific Responsibilities: They work with participants by reporting games of the night as well as taking photos, and addressing concerns, incidents, and accidents that occur during intramural sports.

Qualifications: An ability to communicate and interact with participants is required. Good interpersonal skills and maturity strongly desired.

2. Member Services Hourly

General Information: Member Services Hourly serve as the front line office personnel. This is a part-time position averaging over 20 hours a week including days, evenings and weekends.

Specific Responsibilities: Customer Service; collection of program fees, assisting walk-in and phone customers by providing them with accurate and timely information regarding memberships, programs and policies.

Qualifications: Customer service skills; 2 years cash handling experience; excellent verbal and written communication skills; ability to work under limited supervision.

Figure 11.2. Sample Job Announcements

larger scale, advertising in professional magazines and journals as well as e-recruitment are options. E-recruitment is an online job board designed to match individuals with available jobs, internships, and so forth (e.g., http://www.jobsinsports.com/).

It is critical that individuals doing the hiring understand the jobs they are looking to fill. Breaking jobs down by task has been shown to be beneficial when hiring. For example, jobs that have high levels of contact with participants and low levels of routine (e.g., day camp leaders) will require individuals to have strong problem-solving skills. Conversely, jobs that have high levels of routine and low levels of contact with participants (e.g., bookkeeper) will require individuals to have attention to detail and an ability to work independently. The more clear a recreational sport agency can be when hiring, the greater the recruitment process will be.

Depending on the number of individuals to be hired and the job classifications, there are different approaches to selecting candidates. Group interviews may be an option if a number of front-line employees (e.g., officials) are being hired, whereas individual interviews are better suited for program staff positions or higher. The point of the interview is to learn more about individuals based on their application and/or résumé and determine if they have the skills and competencies to perform the necessary duties. Interviews can be formal and follow a scripted list of questions or can be informal and conversation driven. The difficulty with taking an informal approach is that important points of discussion may be missed and/or inappropriate questions asked (e.g., marital status, physical disabilities). Scenario-type questions (i.e., the individual is provided with a scenario likely to occur during the job and asked for a response) are useful during interviews. Additional points to cover during an interview include the following:

- **Commitment to the current position.** Many positions in recreational sport settings are part-time, so it is important to establish an individual's interest in the position and whether there is an interest in full-time work should it develop. When hiring students, it is important to determine how busy their schedule is and whether they actually have the time needed to complete the job. This is why it is so important that the interviewer understand the job and its requirements.

Vancouver Parks & Recreation
Application for Employment

Please complete this form accurately as it will become an important part of the assessment to determine your suitability for the position. As an equal opportunity employer, Vancouver Parks and Recreation values candidates who reflect the diversity of our community. We invite applications from all qualified candidates. You will need to:

- Complete a **separate application form** for **every position** for which you apply (attach your resume if you wish)
- Complete all required areas denoted by an asterisk (*)

* Date of Application	* Position Applied For	Type of Employment
		Seasonal ☐ Internal Posting ☐

Personal Information

To support your application for employment with the City of Vancouver we need to collect some personal information from you. This information is being collected under the authority of the *Freedom of Information and Protection of Privacy Act* (FOIPPA). It will only be released in accordance with the FOIPPA or as otherwise required by law. Questions about how the FOIPPA applies to this information may be directed to the Manager, Corporate Information and Privacy, City Clerk's Department, 453 West 12th Avenue, Vancouver, BC V5Y 1V4, Tel: 604.873.7999.

* Last Name	* First Name	Type of Application
		New Applicant ☐ Past Employee ☐

* Address: No.   Street   * City

* Province   * Postal Code   * Phone No. (day)   Phone No. (alternate)

E-mail Address   * Employee No. (current or past CoV employees only)

Education

What school grade have you completed?   Name of Institution

Work Experience with Vancouver Parks & Recreation and/or the City of Vancouver
Please start with your most recent position. Add an additional sheet if required.

Position Title	From	To	# of Months	Supervisor's Name	Key Duties

Other Previous Work Experience (please start with your most recent position)

Position Title	From	To	# of Months	Company Name	Key Duties

Vancouver Parks & Recreation, Attn: Human Resources, 2099 Beach Avenue, Vancouver, BC V6G 1Z4
Fax: 604.257.8185   VANCOUVER.CA/JOBS

Figure 11.3. Municipal Recreation Application Form. *Reprinted with permission.*

- **Career plans.** Sometimes individuals apply for recreational sport positions without having an understanding of its career potential and are focused on earning money or enhancing their résumé. In contrast, other individuals have a clear idea of their future career plans and see a recreational sport position as helping in that goal. Both individuals can be good employees, so it is useful information to know.

- **Background.** There are many aspects of an individual's background that can help in determining their suitability for a position including education, past work and volunteer experiences, previous and current recreational pursuits, and types of academic courses completed.

- **Potential scheduling conflicts.** While this represents more of a logistical concern, it is important to be aware of any overarching scheduling conflicts that may affect an agency's ability to hire an individual. For example, if a night supervisor is needed for a weight room, it is essential that the individual be available at night. Being very clear about the job details will help avoid scheduling conflicts in the future.

When making decisions about who to hire, clearly the level of the position being filled will impact the decision; however, for front-line staff, it is best to keep in mind that interpersonal skills are sometimes more important than other skills (e.g., the technical skills) because training will be provided. Research has found that entry-level staff (e.g., front-line) need to be able to communicate clearly, demonstrate an ability to listen, deal with the public, multitask, and act in a professional way (Hurd, 2005). Therefore, individuals who are eager to learn, show a willingness to take training courses, and show a strong work ethic in other spheres of their life are usually a good choice. When making final decisions, there are a number of factors that can help. These include interview response, references, examples of previous work (if applicable), education, qualifications, and past experiences. The hope is that a good decision is made; however, all employees operate under a 90-day probationary period where either employer or employee can decide it is not working out. This means that any employee may be terminated without going through the normal channels (e.g., written reprimands), which will be discussed later in the chapter.

Staff Training and Development

New Staff Training

Once individuals have been hired, the training begins. There are two parts to training: new staff training and ongoing training and development. Each is important to understand because each is tied to building a customer-focused workforce. Orientation is the first action to occur after hiring. An orientation includes providing new staff members with an overview of the mission and culture of the agency, the structure of the agency, and the role of staff within the overall agency. This verbal orientation should also include a physical orientation that involves a facility tour including offices and outdoor spaces. It is important that all staff be aware of the facility and its amenities (washrooms, exit doors, etc.). The purpose of new staff training is to communicate the way activities and tasks are completed, by focusing on both interpersonal skills and technical skills. The goal of new staff training is to socialize the individual into the workplace culture and familiarize them with the formal and informal processes and procedures in place.

At the end of new staff training, employees should

- have completed an orientation of the facility;

- understand the operations, policies, and procedures (e.g., health and safety, time-off procedures, scheduling);

- have completed all necessary documentation related to payroll;

- have shadowed relevant staff positions; and

- have met with the recreation directors and upper level management team members.

It is also valuable to provide staff with a phone number and e-mail contact list and a handbook for use throughout their time as an employee because initially learning all the necessary things at a new agency can be overwhelming. Figure 11.4 is a sample table of contents in an employee handbook. An agency may also have handbooks for emergency plans, officials' handbooks, supervisor handbooks, volunteer handbooks, and so forth. The key with handbooks is to make them up-to-date and user friendly so that procedures are easily adopted. Putting a manual on an agency's website is a strategy that reinforces its value, relevance, and importance.

Employee Handbook
Table of Contents

1. Welcoming remarks ....

2. Organizational structure
   2.1 Job titles and descriptions ....
   2.2 Contact information ....
   2.3 Department/agency background ....
   2.4 Mission Statement ....
   2.5 Goals ....

3. University/Agency Policies
   3.1 Equal employment opportunity/affirmative action policy statement ....
   3.2 Sexual harassment ....
   3.3 Drug free workplace ....

4. Policies and Procedures
   4.1 Dress code ....
   4.2 Evaluation/Performance ....
   4.3 Submitting hours/paychecks ....
   4.4. Scheduling ....
   4.5 Training and development ....
   4.6 Staff meetings ....
   4.7 Hiring process ....
   4.8 Employee of the month ....
   4.9 Disciplinary procedures ....
   4.10 Grievance procedures ....

5. Appendices
   5.1 Organizational Chart
   5.2 Facility Map

Figure 11.4. Employee Handbook Table of Contents

Ongoing Training and Development

Ongoing training is an activity that relates to all employees. Training has been shown to be so important that a lack of training can result in lower job satisfaction and organizational commitment among recreational professionals. For training to be effective, there are five criteria that must exist (Schneider & Bowen, 1995): (a) training must be valued by everyone in the agency because otherwise employees will not regard training as an activity to be taken seriously; (b) training must be ongoing because agencies represent evolving institutions; (c) training must be rewarded; (d) training must be available to all individuals in the agency; and (e) finally the practices, policies, and methods of evaluation must support training ideas.

Training can be facilitated by staff members or by outside consultants or other professionals within the professional leadership system. Training methods can include workshops, demonstrations, discussions, symposiums, seminars, hands-on learning, and online training modules. Topics should be focused with clear objectives for each session, such as team building, fostering organizational vision, situational leadership, aligning strategy, structure and culture, evaluating and managing stress in the workplace, employee wellness, motivating and mentoring others, interpersonal communications, giving and receiving constructive feedback, and service quality indicators. An agency can demonstrate its commitment allowing individuals to attend training during work hours.

If training is approached in this manner, it will not be something that is only done the first week of work. Rather, it will be part of everyone's job responsibility all the time, thus ensuring a commitment to service quality and customer satisfaction. Because so much of the work that is done in recreational sport settings relates to people and providing services, elements of service quality presented in Chapter 16 should be a primary focus of training. There are many reasons to invest in staff training, but some clear benefits of training include increased job satisfaction and morale, reduced staff turnover, better understanding of risk management issues, and improved efficiencies. So, while training requires resources, it should be regarded as an investment because it will contribute to greater levels of customer service.

Staff Supervision

Once staff are hired and trained, it is time for them to begin working. Supervision refers to the management of staff in ensuring the ongoing implementation of the agency's policies and procedures aimed at the goal of delivering a quality service. An agency's organizational structure will determine the degree of supervision; however, it can be assumed that the recreational sport specialist will be responsible for some amount of supervision, likely officials, part-time employees, and even volunteers (depending on the type of recreational sport agency).

Many recreational sport settings have extremely long hours. For instance, university recreational sport facilities and/or YMCAs may be open from 6 AM to midnight, therefore making it impossible to supervise employees at all times. Therefore, to ensure service quality, there are different strategies that can be used including the following:

- **Regular staff meetings.** Regular meetings allow a recreational sport specialist to stay aware of issues that are occurring between front-line staff and participants. Information shared at meetings can include updates by different program areas, service quality issues, and the introduction of any new policies or procedures.

- **Daily reports.** Requiring that staff complete daily reports at the end of their shifts helps to identify issues quickly.

- **Visibility.** Having program staff on-site and engaged in the supervision of staff allows improvements or suggestions to be made quickly.

- **Manuals, opening and closing procedures, and daily checklists.** These represent strategies that can help recreational sport specialists with their supervisory responsibilities. An example of an opening and closing checklist and a daily responsibility checklist is included in Figure 11.5.

- **Clear policies regarding acceptable behavior at work.** This is especially important around the use of personal radios, iPods, MP3 players, pagers, televisions, video games, cellular phones, magazines, and palm pilots.

Given that recreational sport settings are dynamic, staffing requirements can be demanding. Anticipating busier times and assigning more staff to those times is a strategy that can ensure quality service. As a courtesy to employees and to better serve participants, schedules should be posted on a monthly basis if possible. Providing a calendar or book of dates for staff to request a shift off can prevent scheduling difficulties. As well, having a protocol in place (which includes some form of documentation) for switching shifts will ensure all shifts are covered. Figure 11.6 is an example of a switch shift form. Depending on the size of the agency and/or complexity of scheduling, there is management software available that builds a schedule tailored to staff and their shift availability. One of the greatest staffing challenges for recreational sport specialists is the sheer number of staff, each with unique scheduling demands needing to be accommodated.

Opening Responsibilities Checklist
- Examine the facility (including washrooms)
  - Write up any maintenance problems and report them to the supervisor. Place 'OUT OF ORDER' signs on malfunctioning equipment/washrooms
- Count opening float and confirm it is allotted amount.
- Turn on computer/cash register
- Write up any signs that help direct participants
- Turn on the televisions (if applicable)
- See Chore Schedule for updates related to this shift.

Closing Responsibilities Checklist
- Tidy up facility
- Cash out and complete closing out procedures
- Deposit envelopes/ money into safe
- Make sure all participants have left the facility
- Lock the facility

Daily Responsibilities
- Greet each participant upon entrance / exit of facility.
- Let participants know rules and regulations, and the reasons for the rules and regulations.
- Check participants for proper attire
- Constantly walk around the facility checking for hazards, anything that needs to be cleaned, anyone who looks like they might hurt themselves, anyone who looks like they are unsure how to use a machine, etc.
- Record any comments/suggestions or maintenance issues patrons bring to you in the maintenance book.
- Finish task list duties for your shift and initial off on each one.

Figure 11.5. Responsibility Checklists

Another strategy that can help with staff supervision is the development of performance standards. Performance standards establish a level of service that is to be achieved by all staff. For example, standards in a recreational sport setting can include

- greeting individuals as soon as they enter the facility,

- answering the telephone within three rings,

- responding to e-mail questions within 24 hours, and

- offering a satisfaction guarantee for all programs.

To reinforce the importance of standards, they should be incorporated into performance evaluation procedures and reward structures. Supervision represents a large portion of what a recreational sport specialist will do on a daily basis, so it is important to develop realistic policies, procedures, and standards that reflect the agency's desire to deliver a quality recreational experience while at the same time contribute to the working environment of individuals.

Performance Evaluation

Included in supervision is staff performance evaluation. Performance evaluations tend to be approached with caution by some supervisors and even feared by some employees. However, that is not the point of performance evaluations; they need to be viewed as a mechanism for ensuring the agency's tasks are being accomplished and serve as an opportunity to provide feedback (both ways) ultimately improving service delivery.

Shift Change Requests

Please complete this form and give to your supervisor.

Shift changes can be made however, please make every effort to find someone to cover your shift before you request time off. Please make all arrangements **at least one week in advance** of the date of the change, including getting approval from your supervisor. (In the event of sickness or emergency, please call your supervisor as soon as possible.)

Please be sure you have received a response approving your request before you make arrangements to take the time off.

Name: _____

Shift in Question: Day: _____   Date: _____   Hours: _____

Reason for Request: _____

_____

_____

Proposed Change

☐   Trade with another employee

Employee Name: _____

Shift to be traded: _____

Approved by   Recreational Sports Supervisor _____

Date _____   **Schedule changed:** _____

Figure 11.6. Shift Change Request

When conducting evaluations, it is best to reiterate the purpose of the evaluation and explain the process. The advantages of conducting evaluations include determining which employees are ready for added responsibilities (i.e., promotions), determining which employees are not meeting expectations, making decisions about pay increases, being able to see where additional training is required, developing a plan for overall improved service delivery, and highlighting retention strategies. Therefore, it is clear that performance evaluations have many purposes and are a worthwhile task for all recreational sport specialists.

For a performance evaluation to be effective, the following must be adhered to:

- **Objective performance criteria must be used.** Staff must feel that they are being evaluated objectively with criteria such as those in the appraisal form in Figure 11.7.

- **Criteria must be clearly communicated.** All employees should be provided with a copy of the appraisal form (in the employee manual) to ensure they are aware of the criteria being used. The timing of evaluations is also something that should be communicated to employees (e.g., every 6 months).

- **Training should be provided.** To help communicate the evaluation process, both the staff member and the supervisor should receive training.

- **Written guidelines.** In addition to the overall purpose and process, it is necessary that clear guidelines related to disciplinary action be communicated to staff.

- **An opportunity for appeal.** A formal policy on what to do when a staff member is dissatisfied, unclear, or wants clarification with his/her evaluation should exist.

OAKVILLE RECREATION AND CULTURE DEPARTMENT
INTERMPART-TIME EMPLOYEE PERFORMANCE APPRAISAL LEADER
RECREATION SERVICES

FACTOR	BASE REQUIREMENT	EXCEEDING	MEETING	NOT MEETING	N/A
1. Punctuality & attendance	• Is always at location on time • Is prepared to start on time • Rarely uses substitutes	■			
2. Appearance	• Appearance is neat & tidy • Wears name tag &/or staff uniform as required	■			
3. Conduct	• Supports a positive, professional image • Adheres to policies & procedures of the job description				
4. Work with leaders & others	• Develops co-operation & teamwork • Keeps associates & supervisors informed • Establishes & maintains effective relations with others				
5. Drive & commitment	• Exhibits a positive attitude • Strives for personal improvement • Maintains a high energy level				
6. Judgment & decision making	• Identifies & evaluates issues • Reaches sound conclusions • Understands consequences				
7. Accept constructive direction	• Positive response to feedback • Follows up on feedback • Adapts to new ideas & procedures				
8. Program planning/lesson	• Is well prepared & varied • Is creative & innovative • Forecasts needs & sets priorities • Uses available materials & resources				
9. Rapport with participant	• Is respectful of the needs & individual differences of participant • Encourages participation • Adjusts practices to suit a changing environment				
10. Group control/class	• Has group under control • Takes appropriate steps to correct disruptive behaviours • Ensures all members of the group are involved				
11. Customer service	• Is polite & knowledgeable • Attends to detail • Demonstrates good verbal skills • Available to parents, public, & contract services				
12. Administrative skills	• Prepares forms clearly, concisely & accurately • Records, reports & assignments available & organized • Time deadlines are kept				

Figure 11.7. City of Oakville Recreation and Culture Department Part Time Employee Performance Appraisal Form. *Reprinted with permission.*

cont.

INTERM PART-TIME EMPLOYEE PERFORMANCE APPRAISAL
LEADER

RECREATION SERVICES

Employee's Strengths:

_____
_____
_____
_____

Areas for Improvement:

_____
_____
_____

General Comments:

_____
_____
_____

Employee's Comments:

_____
_____

Part Time Employee	Immediate Supervisor	Full Time Staff
Date	Date	Date

Figure 11.7. cont.

Once the evaluation tool is developed and communicated, a process needs to be established that will likely include the performance evaluation, a meeting between supervisor and staff, and follow-up. During the meeting, a supervisor will provide his or her assessment of a staff member and discuss different issues related to job performance. If an employee is performing well, this is where added responsibilities could be discussed. If the employee is struggling, it will be important for the supervisor to clearly state this and indicate ways to improve performance. At the end of the meeting, signatures will be required from both the supervisor and the employee confirming the evaluation was discussed. In recreational sport settings, sometimes the sheer number of staff can be staggering, making the performance evaluation process seem daunting. However, this task needs to be regarded as a tool to continually enhance service quality and be incorporated into the overall job of the recreational sport specialist.

Beyond a performance evaluation process, a procedure to deal with disciplinary issues should also exist. Examples of issues that should be dealt with promptly through a sequence of steps include inappropriate behavior at work, smoking or drinking at work, reporting late for work, stealing, refusing to perform duties outlined in the job description, and verbally abusing participants, among others. A clear policy needs to exist that explains the following:

- **Oral warning.** An oral warning represents the first in a series of potential attempts to deal with a problem caused by an employee at work. It is then up to the individual giving out the oral reprimand to decide whether to document the action in the employee's file.

- **Written warning.** After an employee has received at least one oral warning, additional problems should result in a written warning to be filed in an employee's file.

- **Dismissal.** If after both an oral warning and a written warning, an employee continues to disobey workplace policies and procedures, dismissal may be the only option. As long as previous incidents have been documented, a recreational sport specialist can show there is significant reason for the dismissal.

For the recreational sport specialist in a supervisory level position, it will be important to supervise staff in a fair and transparent manner. Furthermore, over the past decades, management literature and practice has shifted toward supervision being grounded in principles of leadership. In fact, many agencies now view emotional intelligence as a core competency of all managers. The definition of emotional intelligence is "the ability to understand and manage one's own moods and emotions and the moods and the emotions of other people" (Jones, George, & Langton, 2005, p. 256). Basic to all agency success is the idea that staff need to respect each other in the workplace. In recreational sport settings, staff members are always working with participants and other staff, and sometimes problems arise. However, if the recreational sport specialist has the necessary leadership skills to be able to manage these issues, the work of an agency will be enhanced.

Staff Reward Structure

In recreational sports, common benefits include a fun and dynamic work environment, opportunities to interact with other people, flexible hours, and convenient locations, especially if on campus. Rewards, then, are based on the idea of individuals benefiting from their engagement in an agency. As identified, these benefits are not related to financial incentives, suggesting that there are many types of rewards. Staff rewards represent an integral aspect of working in any type of setting. However, rewards are complex because individuals can be motivated by both intrinsic and extrinsic rewards at the same time. Examples of intrinsic rewards are feelings of satisfaction, increased self-esteem, a sense of belonging, whereas examples of extrinsic rewards are pay raises, promo-

tions, merchandise, and tangible items associated with performance. Furthermore, rewards combine elements of both intrinsic and extrinsic features; they are not equal and will vary from individual to individual.

A different reward structure will exist in a commercial setting (e.g., private golf club) versus a private not-for-profit setting (e.g., YMCA). Across all recreational sport settings, however, it is important to develop rewards that can be supported financially while accomplishing the necessary goal of reinforcing desired behavior. Rewards are used to recognize the work of staff or volunteers and show appreciation of an individual's contribution to an agency. Rewards can be financial or non-financial in nature and can include

- tuition reimbursements;

- time-off benefits (e.g., vacation, holidays);

- discount program registration fees;

- free memberships (if applicable);

- health and dental insurance;

- financial incentives including gift certificates;

- helping people connect through networking opportunities;

- providing practical work experiences that can strengthen résumés;

- implementing staff awards (e.g., staff member of the month), which can include a gift card to a local restaurant;

- letting staff members pick projects to work on that they are interested in; and

- providing resources to support career development (e.g., conference attendance, professional development, and/or learning sessions). In addition to supporting staff, this reward benefits the agency because of the increased knowledge exchanged.

Clearly, as shown with this list, there are numerous ways that staff can be rewarded for a job well done, and some reflect a creative approach to managing staff. When rewarding staff, it should be done in a genuine manner, which will contribute to the organizational culture of an agency.

Volunteer Management

At the beginning of this chapter, volunteers were briefly introduced for the substantial role they play in recreational sport settings. In fact, in some community recreational sport settings, volunteers are the drivers behind service delivery. Therefore, while staff tasks are relevant to volunteers, there are variations in the way they are implemented because volunteers and staff differ. For example, when recruiting volunteers, it is important to emphasize the benefits of volunteering with the agency rather than the actual work performed, because the list of tasks may vary as needed. As well, while in theory volunteers will undergo a volunteering screening process that includes applications, interviews, and reference checks, often times the number of positions exceeds the number of volunteers. Therefore, while the process may become a little less rigorous in the selection of volunteers, it is just as important to recruit the right volunteers as it is to hire the right staff because both contribute to workplace culture. Volunteers are a reflection of the agency and can positively or negatively impact program delivery.

As listed earlier, there are numerous tasks that volunteers can perform that help an agency deliver quality programs. Similarly, there are different ways that volunteers can be organized, ranging from informal to formal or individual to group based. Some volunteer programs encourage individuals to serve an agency on an individual basis where the capacity of individual volunteers ultimately determines the tasks. For example, a little league coach will work for the most part independently using his or her skills and abilities and will rely on the agency for support and resources only as needed. Alternatively, other volunteer programs are formalized and encourage volunteers to serve an agency in a group format through boards and councils. An agency will list positions that need to be filled (board of directors or a sports council representative), and a selection process will ensue. With this latter type of volunteer program, the roles and responsibilities of volunteers are clearly identified and communicated, and individuals are chosen who can best complete the identified tasks. The variety of ways volunteers can support an agency need to be understood so that opportunities that best match volunteers can be realized to ensure the agency and the volunteer remain satisfied.

Like training staff, training volunteers is crucial and must begin right away. Strong volunteer training programs have been shown to lead to more satisfied volunteers with a greater capacity to accomplish goals in an efficient manner, therefore making greater contributions to agency goals. Additionally, sometimes there is more training that is required for volunteers because they may not possess the skills and/or certifications that staff members bring to a position. Evaluation, while it will have different objectives, is also a function that should be considered when working with volunteers. It is important that volunteers and supervisors have opportunities to discuss the tasks being completed and determine if changes are needed. Rewards again are also a key ingredient when working with volunteers. For rewards to be relevant, they must be aligned with the motives of volunteers (which are different than staff motives) and can include recognition, name badges, free parking at events, opportunities to socialize with other volunteers, respect, feeling valued in the agency, a letter from higher management, public recognition (e.g., wall plaques), and/or job titles.

Shining Example

Texins Activity Centers

Texins is a corporate health, fitness, and recreation organization for the employees of Texas Instruments. The organization was established over 40 years ago as a nonprofit group. Texins started an annual Christmas party in 1953 and within five years, had expanded to serve over 2,000 Texas Instruments employees and their families, offering 17 clubs and athletic activities. Texins has a family philosophy and extends all services to the dependents of Texas Instruments employees.

Clientele:

Texins serves Texas Instruments employees, retirees, and contract. It boasts over 15,000 total members, with an average of 1,100 people using the facilities each day. The ages of the clientele range from 14 to over 75 years of age, with the majority falling between 25-45 years of age.

Facilities:

There are three Texas facilities in total, one at each corporate site in Dallas, Spring Creek, and Sherman. The Dallas facility includes a gymnasium, exercise area, a six lane pool, locker rooms, a kids room, a game room, a conferencing center, sand volleyball courts, tennis courts, a quarter mile track, an outdoor basketball court, a field area, group exercise rooms, an indoor walking track, and a cycling room. The newer Spring Creek Facility includes a large exercise area, a gymnasium, aerobic rooms, outdoor swimming pools, outdoor basketball and volleyball courts, and locker rooms. The Sherman facility has a large exercise area, group exercise rooms, outdoor tennis, basketball and volleyball courts, outdoor horseshoe pits, outdoor running track, cardio theatre, and locker rooms.

Program Details:

Texins offers a large amount of programs each month in areas such as health and wellness, fitness, youth programs (camps, childcare), aquatics, recreation, and massage services. In addition Texins offers recreational, intermediate, and power leagues for basketball, golf, and volleyball. Each of its facilities has extensive hours of operation to accommodate its employee work schedules and the Dallas facility has an outdoor team-building area as well.

Budget:

The budget for Texins is approximately $3.8 million.

Marketing:

Marketing and communication is handled by teams in respective program areas. Marketing mediums include electronic newsletters, posters, fliers, their Quarterly Texins Activity Center magazine and displays on the corporate campus. Information is also offered during new-hire orientation and in industry journals and at fairs. A Web site is also maintained: (https://www.texinsactivitycenters.com/).

Jobs and Careers:

The staff consists of 226 professionals who offer a diverse knowledge base in health, fitness, and recreation. Positions include executive director, operations manager, accounting and member services controller, marketing and business development manager, recreation manager, retail services manager, information services manager, site managers for remote locations, kids' room manager, coordinators for member services, fitness, aquatics, youth & intern programs, advertising, and communications. In addition, there are fitness specialists, group exercise instructors, personal trainers, a dietician, front desk attendants, guest relations personnel, retail services staff, and accounting specialists. In addition to career opportunities available within Texins, associates are eligible for opportunities nationwide through Health Fitness Corporation, its parent company.

Salary:

Salary ranges from $7-$32/hour for non-exempt employees, to $22,000-$63,000 per year for exempt employees.

Internship:

A few internships are available in spring, summer, and fall. They involve exposure to all areas of operation.

Affiliated Professional Organizations:

Professional organizations affiliated with the various staff positions include the American College of Sports Medicine (ACSM); Aerobics and Fitness association of America (AFAA); American Council on Exercise (ACE); and International Health, Racquet, and Sportsclub Association (IHRSA).

▶ **Computer Tip**

Organizational Chart Software

Organizational charts are ideal for managing information and planning in recreational sports. Software designed for organizational charting helps you create professional looking organizational charts quickly and easily. More important, software eliminates the manually drawn charts that are usually quickly out-of-date. Several software programs import data from the agency's human resource data files, which means that all recreational sport employees can have online access to the most current organizational chart. Microsoft Publisher is the most popular as it is a module of Microsoft Office that is installed as a basic program on most computers.

Since organizational charts can be viewed at an employee's desk, departments no longer have to distribute printed charts that can be outdated. Employees can view the latest agency structure, search the organizational chart by name, department, or relationship; and view or print specific charts.

Drawing a chart and connecting lines is simple and fast using toolbar buttons to click, drag, and drop employees' names, positions, and boxes anywhere in the chart. Most programs automatically position text and expand or shrink boxes as you type. You can also use simple menu selections to change box borders and fonts, apply shadows, and change the thickness and style of box lines.

Other special features of organizational chart software may allow you to

- search the agency for "who reports to whom," allowing you to locate names, departments, and position titles;

- print various organizational levels;

- use a "make it fit" command that can reduce charts to fit on one page or expand charts for multipage diagrams;

- import recreational sport agency logos and graphics;

- use special legend boxes; and

- use drawing tools to get the precise effects you want.

Conclusion

As a way to summarize the concept of staffing as it relates to recreational sports, it is useful to describe the idea of workplace culture, which is the result of staffing policies and procedures. Even though workplace culture is not tangible, it is powerful and influences staff and volunteers as well as the experiences of customers or participants. By recruiting, selecting, training, and then supervising the right individuals (staff and volunteer alike), agency goals are more likely to be realized. However, it is important to keep the right individuals in the organization; therefore, retention strategies are needed, which is where workplace culture comes into the picture. Policies that reflect fairness and compassion, ongoing commitment to training, and a work environment that values individuals as representatives of the agency all translate into workplace culture. When individuals like where they work, they are more likely to be loyal and satisfied with their job, which in turn can reduce staff turnover. Reduced staff turnover is the goal of every staffing strategy. There is much the recreational sport specialist can do to create a workplace culture that values its people (i.e., staff, volunteers, participants) and recognizes the role of individuals in delivering a quality recreational sport experience.

Bibliography

Ball, J., Simpson, S., Ardovino, P., & Skemp-Arit, K. (2008). Leadership competencies of university recreational directors in Wisconsin. *Recreational Sports Journal, 32*, 3-10.

Bartlett, K., & McKinney, W. (2004). A study of the role of professional development, job attitudes, and turnover among public park and recreation employees. *Journal of Park and Recreation Administration, 22*(4), 62-80.

Busser, J. (2005). Human resource management. In B. van der Smissen, M. Moiseichik, & V. Hartenburg (Eds.), *Management of park and recreation agencies* (pp. 437-467). Ashburn, VA: National Recreation and Park Association.

Cuskelly, G., Hoye, R., & Auld, C. (2006). *Working with volunteers in sport: Theory and practice.* London, England: Routledge.

Edginton, C., Hudson, S., Lankford, S., & Larsen, D. (2008). *Managing recreation, parks and leisure services: An introduction* (3rd ed.). Urbana, IL: Sagamore.

Hurd, A. (2005). Competency development for entry-level public parks and recreation professionals. *Journal of Park and Recreation Administration, 23*(3), 45-62.

Jones, G., George, J., & Langton, N. (2005). *Essentials of contemporary management* (1st Canadian ed.). Toronto, Canada: McGraw-Hill.

Robinson, L. (2004). *Managing public sport and leisure services.* London, England: Routledge.

Schneider, B. & Bowen, D. (1995). *Winning the serving game.* Boston, MA: Harvard Business School Press.

Schneider, R., Stier, W., Kampf, S., Haines, S., & Wilding, G. (2006). Characteristics, attributes, and competencies sought in new hires by campus recreation directors. *Recreational Sport Journal, 30*, 142-153.

Stier, W. (1999). *Managing sport, fitness, and recreation programs: Concepts and practices.* London, England: Allyn and Bacon.

Stier, W., Schneider, R., Kampf, S., & Gaskins, B. (2010). Job satisfaction for campus recreation professionals within NIRSA institutions. *Recreational Sports Journal, 34*, 78-94.

Taylor, T., Doherty, A., & McGraw, P. (2008). *Managing people in sport organizations: A strategic human resource management perspective.* New York, NY: Elsevier.

Torkildsen, G. (2005). *Leisure and recreation management* (5th ed.). London, England: Routledge.

CHAPTER 12

Funding

CHAPTER OBJECTIVES

After reading this chapter, you will understand the financial responsibility of recreational sport specialists, understand the budget process inherent in most recreational sport programs, know what is required to estimate and implement a budget plan, be able to identify the different costs with recreational sport offerings, and be able to identify revenue sources in recreational sport settings.

KEY CONCEPTS

Budget process	Purchasing
Budget formats	Bonds
Expenditures	Grants
Operating budget	Charitable giving
Taxes	Contractual income
Merchandise and product sales	Sponsorship
Pricing	Fixed costs
Capital budget	Variable costs
Fees	Contingency costs

Introduction

The importance of understanding fiscal matters cannot be stressed enough because oftentimes recreational sport specialists are consumed more with their programming responsibilities than with financial matters. For instance, all types of recreational agencies are pursuing the construction of large multipurpose facilities, and given that an average public community center (a pool, two arenas, meeting rooms) is estimated to cost $4 million, a professional sports facility such as the Safeco Field in Seattle $498 million, and some American university recreational complexes upwards of $35 million, a strong competence in financial solvency is required. Recreational sport represents a huge industry, and a firm grasp of the financial aspects is essential.

This chapter discusses the budgeting and financial basics for the recreational sport specialist. The information cannot replace experience and coursework in financial management, but it does provide an overview of the typical revenues and expenses associated with sport and recreational programs. When reading this chapter, it is important to recognize that fiscal matters vary greatly depending on factors such as agency size, type of funding support, and the economic environment.

Organizational Sector

Prior to discussing key concepts in funding, it is relevant to provide a brief discussion on the link between organizational sector and financial decision making. There are four program areas in recreational sports: instructional, informal, intramural and extramural, and club sports. There are three sectors of recreational sport: commercial, public, and private not-for-profit. Table 12.1 is adapted from an earlier chapter to illustrate the types of organizations that operate within each sector. Organizational sector will determine many financial decision making strategies such as profit orientation and profit goals.

Table 12.1

Settings/Sectors and Agencies for Recreational Sport

Sector	Examples of Settings
Public Sector Agencies for Recreational Sport	• Cities and communities (Chicago Parks and Recreation Department, South Bend Parks and Recreation Department) • Public golf courses • Publics schools (elementary and secondary schools, colleges, universities, military schools, junior colleges) • Military (army, navy, marines, air force, coast guard) • Correctional (jails, detention centers, penitentiaries) • State and National Parks (Yellowwood State Forest, Hoosier National Forest, Yellowstone National Park)
Private Not-for Profit Sector Agencies for Recreational Sport	• YMCAs • YWCAs • Boys and Girls Clubs • Boys Scouts • Girls Scouts • Churches
Commercial Sector Agencies for Recreational Sport	• Private schools • Private clubs (golf and country clubs, health clubs, boat clubs, riding clubs) • Private facilities (golf clubs, sky diving, bowling centers, ski hills) • Entertainment (resorts, theme parks, cruises)

Recreational sport is delivered by all three sectors, and each follows a different philosophy to fiscal management and consequently decision making. Within the commercial sector, decisions are made to maximize profits and success is determined by the willingness of investors and users to support programs. In this sector, profit must be generated to remain viable, so decisions are based on that premise.

Within the public sector, rather than a concern with maximizing profits, serving a social mandate and "the general good" are concepts that drive decision making. This sector relies heavily on government support, but increasingly a diversified revenue plan is necessary to ensure adequate funding levels. Proper accounting is extremely important in the public sector because so many programs and services are funded by taxes.

In the private, not-for-profit sector, a social mandate is apparent and decision making is based on an agency's mission of improving the lives of specific groups or individuals. In general, grants, donations, and fees keep this sector functioning; however, fi-

nancial uncertainty is characteristic of many agencies and financial objectives are often to simply break even.

While each sector is influenced by its mandates and objectives, collectively funding recreational sports is dependent upon planning, controlling, and monitoring financial resources combined with determining strategies to acquire funds. See Figure 12.1 for how these terms relate.

Planning: The Budget Process

A budget is a necessary document in any agency. To determine how recreational sport is funded, the recreational sport specialist must understand the budgeting process. Key terms include the following:

- **Budgeting**—a financial plan that identifies anticipated revenues and expenditures for an agency

- **Fiscal year**—a 12-month period (typically July 1–June 30 or January 1–December 31)

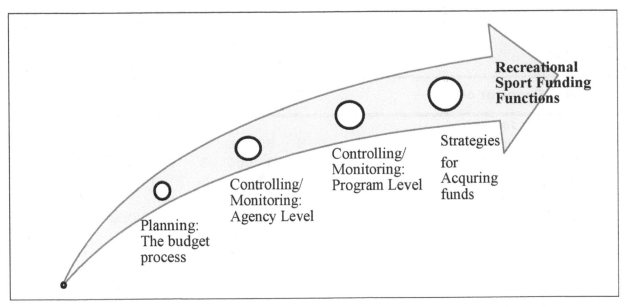

Figure 12.1. Understanding the Funding Functions in Recreational Sports Agencies

- **Budget**—a working document that guides an agency in meeting its financial goals

- **Revenues**—all money coming into an agency (tax support, fees, etc.)

- **Expenditures**—all money leaving an agency (salaries, utilities, etc.)

Beyond the fact that a budget is a necessary document for all agencies, there are many functions it serves including providing staff members with parameters for responsible program delivery, reinforcing an agency's strategic plan and planning objectives (see Chapter 15), helping to ensure decision making is sound and reflective of the agency's financial objectives, allowing program goals and objectives to be measured, and serving as a communication tool with stakeholders.

Operating and Capital Budgets

There are two types of budgets: an operating budget and a capital budget. An operating budget refers to the day-to-day fiscal operations and therefore includes all revenues and expenditures of an agency. Examples of revenues in an operating budget can include registration fees, membership dues, parking fees, tax support, charitable donations, and grant monies. These are discussed in more detail later in the chapter. Expenditures in an operating budget include personnel costs (e.g., salaries, wages, benefits), utilities (e.g., gas, water, electricity, telephone), and supplies (e.g., stationery, equipment, maintenance, repair).

A capital budget reflects non-recurring projects that have a life expectancy of at least 10 years such as new construction, major renovations to existing facilities, or large equipment purchases. There are two approaches for financing capital projects: "pay as you go" or "pay as you use" (Brayley & McLean, 2008). Pay as you go means that revenue is generated through current programs and services and then used to fund the future capital project. For example, students on university campuses are sometimes assessed a fee for a future building cost that they may likely never use. The second option, pay as you use, borrows money to fund new projects with the anticipation that future users will finance the project. Considering the number of agencies building multipurpose facilities, it is important to understand the difference between an operating and capital budget because they are managed and funded differently.

Budget Formats

There are different methods of recording revenues and expenditures that refer to budget formats. These include line-item, program, and performance. Each type of budget emphasizes different budgetary elements.

Line-item budget. Budget items are classified according to expenditure type for the fiscal year (previous year and/or anticipated can also be included). See Table 12.2 for an example of a line-item budget.

Table 12.2

Line-item Budget

Object Code	Description	Last Year Actual	This year anticipated
1000	*Personnel*		
1100	Full time salary	$ 85,000	$ 88,000
1200	Part-time salaries	$ 41,000	$ 42,000
1300	Benefits	$ 12,500	$ 13,000
2000	*Utilities*		
2100	Water	$ 9,769	$ 10,000
2200	*Electricity*	$ 8,800	$ 9,000
2300	*Telephone*	$ 1,200	$ 1,300
3000	*Supplies*		
3100	Paint	$ 100	$ 120
3200	Paper	$ 250	$ 280
3300	Towels	$ 1,100	$ 1,200
3400	Tennis balls	$ 5,000	$ 5,200
4000	*Properties*		
4100	Equipment	$ 3,000	$ 3,000
4200	Building renovations	$ 10,000	$ 10,000
4300	Taxes	$ 7,000	$ 7,500
	Total	$ 184,719	$ 190,600

Source: Fictitious data, for illustration purposes only

Budget items such as revenue, salaries, utilities, supplies, and so forth are assigned projected or estimated costs. This budget is popular because it is easy to develop and is easily understood across units and departments. However, the categories are sometimes too broad and prevent an in-depth analysis of expenditures. As well, this format tends to emphasize expenditures rather than the benefits of a program.

Program budget. This budget extends the line-item budget by grouping expenditures according to program units with corresponding costs. See Table 12.3 for an example of a program budget. See Figure 12.2 for an example of program budget goals and output measures.

This type of budget links expenditures with organizational policy, objectives, and impact. For example, aquatics, sports camps, fitness, special events, or adult programming budgets may all exist, each with some type of line-item classification. This type of budget allows for more flexibility in program delivery; however, it tends to highlight areas that may be considered to be underperforming in budgetary terms. The completion of program evaluations at the end of a program is recommended to justify any future budget modifications.

Performance budget. A third type of budget is a performance budget that links resources to the amount of work produced to outcomes (i.e., customer or program goals). The goal of this budget is to find efficiencies in work; so work that is easily measured is best suited for this type of budget.

For example, grass cutting, pool maintenance, or landscaping work are areas that can be easily measured and where efficiencies can be gained. This budget can highlight the savings incurred by cutting the grass every 8 days rather than 5 days. See Table 12.4 for an example of a performance budget.

Recreational Sport Specialist's Role in the Budget Process

Regardless of the budget type or format, there are two aspects of all budgets: revenues and expenditures. A recreational sport specialist will be required to submit a budget request based on program areas, estimating both the revenues and expenditures for the upcoming fiscal year. Once submitted, reviewed, and incorporated into the overall agency budget, budget deliberations and modifications begin. Depending on the size of the agency, the entire budget process can take months to develop. Once approved the budget serves as a working document.

Table 12.3

Program Budget

Program Area	Last Year Actual	This year anticipated
Fitness Programs		
Staff	$ 10,000	$ 11,000
Supplies	$ 500	$ 600
Marketing	$ 500	$ 600
Day camp		
Staff	$ 12,000	$ 13,000
Supplies	$ 700	$ 750
Marketing	$ 100	$ 150
Total	$ 23,800	$ 26,100

Source: Fictitious data, for illustration purposes only

Department of Recreational Sports

Goal of Department of Recreational Sports: To improve the health status of students

Program Area: Fitness

    Goal: To provide opportunities for students to engage in fitness training

Output Measures:

    Number of students that register for fitness classes
    Cost effectiveness of program

Figure 12.2. Accompanying Goals and Output Measures for Program Budget

Table 12.4

Performance Budget—Swimming Pool Maintenance Division-Community

Program Area MAINTENANCE	Last Year Actual	This year anticipated
Input		
Total budget	$10,000	$11,000
No. of employees	12	12
No. of pools	5	5
Output		
No. of worker hrs on pool maintenance/repairs	1,531	1,600
Efficiency		
Worker hrs per pool	120	125
Effectiveness		
Percentage decrease in work order requests at pools.	10%	10%

Recreational sport specialists should also consider the seasonal variances that occur in some program areas. During summer months, many agencies tend to offer additional instructional programs for children and youth because they are on summer break. Similarly, during the academic year on university and college campuses, there is an increase in intramural programming. Seasonal programs translate into increased revenues and expenditures during these times of the fiscal year.

Controlling and Monitoring Funding

While a budget theoretically allows a recreational sport specialist to perform his or her job, it is important to remember that budgets are forecasts and require control and monitoring to stay on track. Control and monitoring occurs at two levels: the overall agency level and the program level.

Agency Control and Monitoring

At the broadest level, agencies develop accountability procedures and policies to which all within the agency must adhere. Many agencies follow prescribed practices such as "Generally Accepted Accounting Practices" (GAAP) that outline procedures for managing agency finances. To ensure the budget and overall finances are properly managed, accountability control mechanisms are adopted both internally and externally based on these principles. In terms of external accounting, agencies have a responsibility to provide financial reports to investors or shareholders, members, or the general public. While accountability is extremely important across all sectors, in the public sector with its reliance on tax revenue,

transparency and proper accounting procedures are crucial. In all sectors, external audits performed by outside firms are used to ensure accountability.

In terms of internal accountability, each agency will use its own procedures to ensure straightforward monitoring of finances. Financial statements that reflect this effort can include balance sheets, income statements, and cash flow statements.

Balance sheets. Balance sheets take into consideration an agency's assets, liabilities, and equity to provide a snapshot of the agency's financial worth. Assets (everything the agency owns) include current (e.g., cash), fixed (e.g., land), and intangible (e.g., copyrights) assets. Liabilities refer to both current (e.g., debts to be paid within one year) and long-term liabilities (e.g., debts to be paid after one year). The last part of the equation, equity, is the balancing factor. As the name suggests, a balance sheet reflects an agency's assets in comparison to their liabilities and equity, so increases or decreases to one side of the sheet will be offset by the other side (Total assets = Total liabilities + Equity). It is likely that a balance sheet (see Figure 12.3) can be done on a fairly regular basis (e.g., at the end of each month).

Income statements. Income statements (see Figure 12.4) "compare expenses against revenue over a certain period of time to show the firm's net income or loss" (Scarborough & Zimmerer, 2003, p. 222). In other words, income statements identify income and expenditure changes between two points in time. Figure 12.4 is an example of a financial record typically done at the end of a fiscal year and will clearly contribute to an agency's budget preparation.

ASSETS		LIABILITIES	
Current assets		Current liabilities	
Cash	$3,500	Accounts payable	$15,500
Inventory	$6,000		
Accounts Receivables	$1,500		
Total current assets	$11,000	Total current liabilities	$15,500
FIXED ASSETS		LONG-TERM LIABILITIES	
Major Equipment	$50,000	General Obligation Bonds	$20,000
Land	$100,000		
Total Fixed Assets	$150,000	Equity	$125,500
TOTAL ASSETS	$161,000	**TOTAL LIABILITY AND EQUITY**	$161,000

Figure 12.3. Balance Sheet for a Public Recreational Sports Agency

September 1 - September 30, 2012			
REVENUE		**EXPENDITURES**	
Membership Sales	$9,500	Wages	$10,500
Pro Shop Merchandise	$1,500	Supplies	$500
Lesson Packages	$2,500	Advertising	$500
		Debt payment	$1,000
TOTAL REVENUE	**$13,500**	**TOTAL EXPENDITURES**	**$12,500**
Net Revenue (Loss)	**$1,000**		

Figure 12.4. Income Statement

Cash flow statements. Cash flow statements relate to the way an agency has used its cash over a specific period of time. Cash flow statements tend to provide complementary information to the income statements but are more common for agencies that rely heavily on cash exchanges.

Beyond the use of these financial statements, the sector, size of the agency, legal regulations, and accounting needs will determine the level of sophistication and degree of reporting that is needed. In addition to being able to interpret the previous statements, a recreational sport specialist will need to be well versed in using forms that reflect more ongoing financial procedures such as fee collection forms and payroll forms (e.g., time cards, punch clocks, sign-in sheets). Additionally, daily deposit forms may exist, depending on the agency's type of work.

Purchasing Procedures

Agencies also control and monitor finances through their purchasing procedures. There are three types of purchase procedures that routinely occur in all agencies. These include petty cash purchases, normal purchasing procedures, and formal bidding procedures (Sellers, Gladwell, & Pope, 2005).

Petty cash or business credit card purchases. If supplies purchased are small (the amount is determined by the agency's policy) and a matter of urgency, staff can use a fund called petty cash or a business credit card and then file original receipts with the accounting department. Petty cash purchases tend to be for amounts less than $75. Petty cash purchases are recorded on a voucher or a running petty cash list.

Normal purchasing. Normal purchases are for larger items and therefore require approval and authorization. With normal purchasing there are often arrangements with different approved contractors where purchases are commonly made. Administrators work with vendors for best pricing and develop an approved contractors database that guarantees set pricing for supplies. For example, paper products may come from a contract with an office supplier or sports equipment may be purchased through a specialized sports company with preapproved discounts. Depending on the sector, there are procedures in place where any items that need to be purchased over a certain amount will require quotes from at least two vendors prior to authorization. Normal purchasing is completed through a purchase order form. See Chapter 14 for an example of a purchase request form. The information required on a purchase order includes quantity, item description, cost of item, account numbers, and rationale for purchase. Approval is then given based on the paperwork (i.e., purchase order) completed.

Formal bid procedures. The third type of purchasing is a formal bid process that is similar to normal purchasing but reserved for larger and more expensive purchases such as office furniture, landscaping, refurbishing basketball courts, or large equipment. With formal bids, specific criteria and specifications are outlined by the agency with deadlines and procedures for submitting a quote. Once all bids are received, reviewed, and approved by the administration, a contract is awarded. This process is lengthy and, depending on the sector, requires different levels of approval. For instance, with public sector bids, it could be county councils who approve all bid contracts.

The intent of all these forms and procedures is to standardize revenues and expenditures so that money can be tracked throughout the fiscal year. By using standardized forms, agencies are able to make ongoing assessments regarding their financial situation.

Program Control and Monitoring

The second level of funding control and monitoring is at the program level where an understanding of program costs and pricing strategies is necessary. Recreational sport specialists provide programs and services to individuals; therefore, it is important to understand the costs involved in programming. There are three costs associated with programming (i.e., fixed, variable, and contingency costs).

Fixed costs. Fixed costs are costs that do not vary according to the number of participants in a program. There are two kinds of fixed costs associated with running recreational programs. First, direct fixed costs relate directly to the cost of running a program, meaning that if a program is canceled, the costs are not incurred. For example, with a yoga class the cost of the gym rental is a direct fixed cost. Second, indirect fixed costs refer to ongoing costs associated with recreational sport programs including staff salaries, debt payments, and insurance payments. These costs occur regardless of whether the program is offered.

Variable costs. Variable costs associated with running a recreational sport program fluctuate or vary based on the numbers of individuals participating. For example, the number of life jackets, basketballs, yoga mats, or facility space will be different based on the number of participants, and therefore the costs accordingly go up or down.

Contingency costs. Contingency costs relate to costs that cannot be anticipated. In other words, all programs should include an emergency fund to ensure there are financial resources available should a problem occur. For example, when a basketball backboard cracks during a three-on-three game, it will need replacing, and without a contingency fund, there may not be enough money to cover the costs.

To determine actual program costs, it is important to include all three costs into the following equation: $PC = ((F+V) + C (F+V)) / N$.

PC = program cost
F = fixed costs
V = variable costs
C = contingency costs
N = demand

PC represents a unit, which can be hourly, per session, or per person. This understanding plus using a standardized form (such as Figure 12.5) will help in determining different fee structures for participants and will allow the recreational sport specialist to compare the costs of running different programs at different levels.

City of Welland
Parks, Facilities, Recreation & Cultural Services

Program Fee Assessment - Youth Programs

PROGRAM: _____

INSTRUCTOR: _____

SESSION: ▢ Winter   ▢ Spring   ▢ Summer   ▢ Fall   YEAR: _____

DAYS: _____   TIME FRAME: _____

_____   _____

_____   _____

A) Class Hours: _____ weeks x _____ hours/week = _____ contact hours

B) Preparation time: _____ hours

C) Hourly rate: $ _____

D) Instruction cost: [(A) _____ + (B) _____] x (C) _____ = $ _____

E) Cost for instruction/student: (D) _____ = $ _____
          minimum # of students _____

F) Consumable supplies/student: $ _____

G) Building Supervision surcharge $1.00

H) Total fee/student:

        (E) _____ + (F) _____ + (G) _____ + 13% (HST) _____ = $ _____

Figure 12.5. Program Fee Assessment Worksheet

Clarity around the direct, indirect, and contingency costs of a program allows a recreational sport specialist to make more accurate estimates when submitting budget requests.

Pricing Strategies

In addition to the control and management of costs at the program level, pricing strategies are important to understand so that proper structures can be developed and implemented. In almost all recreational sport settings prices exist. Four types of pricing are described.

Arbitrary pricing. This refers to pricing a program or service simply because it sounds "right" and for no other reason. In arbitrary pricing no consideration is given to the actual costs required to offer a program. While this may seem rare, many program areas inadvertently adopt this approach, and actual prices are chosen that are easy to work into a budget request. This approach can negatively affect revenues because the cost of offering a program may be much higher, resulting in an unanticipated deficit.

Cost-recovery pricing. Unlike the previous strategy of pricing, cost-recovery pricing aims to recover some or all of the expenses associated with offering a program. To determine a price, it is necessary to know the fixed and variable costs as well as the break-even point of a program. Additionally, one must identify the percentage of costs that need to be recovered because many programs only run when full cost recovery is achieved (i.e., all costs are recovered). Traditionally, commercial agencies hope to recover more than their costs, private not-for-profit agencies hope to come close to their break-even point, and more and more public agencies need to recover their costs.

Competitive pricing. This approach to pricing refers to establishing fees and charges similar to other programs. For example, if a YMCA charges $50 for a set of swimming lessons, then the local parks and recreation department may charge $48 for their set of swimming lessons to remain competitive. However, it is important to make sure that other aspects of the programs are similar to warrant the competitive price (e.g., number of instructors, class size, type of course); otherwise, customer satisfaction may be affected.

Market pricing. Market pricing refers to setting fees and charges based on demand. The idea with this type of pricing is that the same program can be priced differently based on different factors (e.g., time) in relation to its value. Market pricing is commonly used by agencies that promote prime and non-prime times for participation. For example, ice arenas charge more for ice time between 3 p.m. and 7 p.m. than throughout the day when there are not as many participants (and therefore the ice is not as valued). This approach is very useful in encouraging use at times when use may not exist otherwise.

Determining fees and charges is an ongoing responsibility in recreational sports and implementing the proper pricing strategy can yield greater financial resources.

Recreational Sport Specialist's Role in Control and Monitoring

Even though control and monitoring occurs at two levels, a recreational sport specialist will be primarily involved with program control and monitoring. A recreational sport specialist can expect to be responsible for completing purchase orders for items related to their programs, monitoring hourly wage staff, and overseeing fee collection procedures (e.g., program registration, refunds, membership dues). An hourly wage worksheet is a form that collects information from electronic or paper time sheets generated by either the recreational sport specialist or the employee. On a weekly or biweekly basis, this information is then transferred to a payroll system in preparation for pay periods. As discussed, the use of forms will aid in the monitoring of these tasks. Furthermore, because fees are one of the most common sources of revenue for recreational sport programs, it is important to develop a straightforward process for collecting and managing all fee collections to allow for ease at overseeing this work. Steps should include

- the development of standard forms to be used in the collection of fees and charges;

- training and supervision of all staff on the collection of fees and especially cash register or point of sale functions, if applicable;

- the development of beginning shift procedures that include confirming starting drawer amounts as well as close out procedures where totals reconcile to sales;

- issuing tickets, permits, stamps, or whatever other mechanism has been instituted to indicate fees have been paid; and

- securing and depositing funds collected.

A final task that a recreational sport specialist will likely perform is monitoring the operating budget, which is typically done on a quarterly basis, but with personal computers and technology, more frequent monitoring is possible. Table 12.5 is an example of a quarterly budget report.

Table 12.5

Quarterly Budget Report–Program Area within Recreational Sports

OBJECT CODE	DESCRIPTION	BUDGET AMOUNT	YEAR TO DATE EXPENDED	ENCUMBRANCES/ REQUISITIONS	AVAILABLE BUDGET	% USED
1000	Personnel	$ 21,000	$ 11,000	$ -	$ 10,000	52%
3000	Supplies	$ 4,850	$ 3,000	$ 350	$ 1,500	69%
3100	Equipment replacement/ repair	$ 3,500	$ 500	$ 250	$ 2,750	21%
5000	Marketing	$ 2,000	$ 1,500	$ -	$ 500	75%

However, during registration periods for some programs, it may be prudent to monitor the budgets on a weekly basis so that a clearer status of actual revenues and expenditures exists. The skills with which program costs are established and pricing strategies are adopted will certainly influence an agency's ability to offer quality programs at reasonable prices.

Sources of Revenue

The previous section described the ways in which agencies and departments develop structures to support the financial activities that regularly occur, but one element that cannot be overlooked is the actual acquisition of funds in recreational sport settings. Organizational sector, financial skills, and competence will determine which revenue strategies are successfully pursued, but the following is a list of possible sources of revenue in recreational sports (see Figure 12.6).

Taxes

Federal, state, and local taxes represent a significant source of revenue for publicly funded recreational sport organizations. There are many different types of taxes that are paid by individuals and corporations, but this text will focus on some of the more common or relevant taxes in relation to recreational sport agencies.

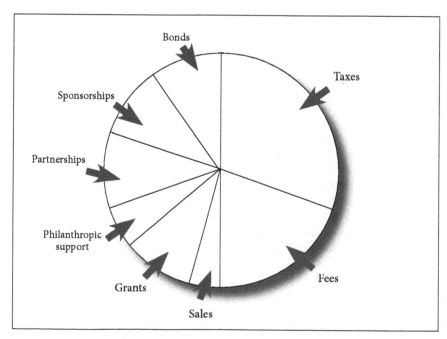

Figure 12.6. Sources of Revenue

Property taxes. Property taxes make up the largest portion of generated taxes for local government, and there are two types of property taxes: real property tax and personal property tax (Sellers et al., 2005). Personal property taxes (in 41 states) by their very nature (i.e., tangible and intangible property) are complex to assess and "only a few states allow local governments to tax the personal property of individuals" (Sellers et al., 2005, p. 505). However, when personal property is taxed, it is added to the second type of tax—real property tax. Real property tax, which is based on an assessed value of land and/or improvements, is collected across all states. These assessments are typically below market value and are used in combination with tax rates to determine the amount of taxes to be paid on an annual basis.

Sales tax. Sales tax represents the second greatest source of tax revenue for municipalities. Throughout the United States, there is variation in the tax rate applicable to the sale of products (i.e., not services) at the retail level. As of 2012, there are five states that do not impose a state sales tax (Alaska, Delaware, Montana, New Hampshire, and Oregon), and among the other states, sales tax rates vary from 2.9%–7.25%.

Excise tax. Excise taxes are added to certain items including gasoline, alcoholic beverages, and tobacco and services such as hotels and motels (i.e., lodging tax), rental cars, and restaurants. This tax can be applied at either the local or the state level.

Income tax. Income taxes are administered at each level of government (i.e., local, state, federal), and the two types of income taxes are personal and corporate. Similar to sales taxes, there is variation among states in both whether taxes are collected and according to what formula. For example, Alaska does not collect income tax and Oregon has a five bracket system whereby individuals are taxed more as their incomes increase.

While recreational sport specialists will not be directly involved in the administration of tax collection, it is beneficial to understand the different types of taxes that may support an agency's programs and services. Because almost all citizens are required to pay taxes, the idea is that, through taxation programs, services and facilities will exist for all to use. However, the reality is that often public institutions also require additional fees in order to maintain the desired levels of service.

Bonds

Bonds are used to fund capital budgets as opposed to operating budgets and are only a source of revenue for public agencies. Bonds are defined as "a promise by the borrower (the agency bond issuer) to pay back to the lender (the financial institution bond holder) a specific amount of money with interest within a specified period of time" (Crompton, 1999, p. 32). Bonds provide agencies with large amounts of borrowed money quickly, which would be impossible to generate otherwise. Depending on the type of bond, different levels of approval are required, but given the ballooning costs of new facility development in recreational sports, bonds are extremely relevant. The residents of South Bend, Indiana, in a referendum approved $4 million worth of local bonds to be used to build the first artificial white-water river in North America in 1982 (http://sbpark.org/parks/east-race-waterway/).

Two of the more common bonds used in recreational sport settings are general obligation bonds and revenue bonds.

General obligation bonds. These are used to fund projects that are intended for the entire community, and as a result, the retirement of its debt is spread across the entire community. These types of bonds are typically repaid through increases in real property taxes (Brayley & McLean, 2008); however, voter approval is required.

Revenue bonds. These bonds are used to finance revenue-producing facilities with the intention that the facility and its profits will retire the debt rather than the public. The drawback with this form of bond is that the facility must generate enough revenue to maintain the facility as well as retire the debt, which may be challenging. However, an advantage with this type of bond is that voter approval is not required.

Like the different forms of taxation among public agencies, bonds are an important concept to understand, but in terms of application, a recreational sport specialist will not be involved in either their acquisition or their management.

Fees

Fees represent a broad category of revenue generation ranging from program fees including instruction, entrance fees, registration fees, facility and equipment rental fees, and licenses and permits. Many recreational sport program areas tend to augment their core programs as a way to cover expenditures and generate needed revenue. For example, parking at extramural programs and child care services in club settings (e.g., YMCAs) are common fees that can positively impact an agency's operating budget. Instructional programs rely heavily on user fees. For example, fee structures at a tennis facility can be arranged around private, semiprivate, and group price levels.

Merchandise and Products Sales Through Concessions, Gift Shops, Pro Shops

A concept that originated in the commercial sector but is now seen across all three sectors is the idea that selling concessions and items such as drinks, t-shirts, and golf balls can result in large revenues when the right items are sold in the right setting, such as a pro shop. While in many of these examples resources are required to manage the sales (e.g., staff and inventory), simply having a self-serve vending machine can generate revenue while creating an added value for participants.

Grants

Grants represent a source of revenue for public and private not-for-profit recreational sport agencies. Local, state, and federal granting agencies exist to support agencies. For example, in Bloomington, Indiana, a local granting agency is the Community Foundation of Bloomington and Monroe County (http://www.cfbmc.org/), "which administers over 160 funds that produce grants" to local recipients. This foundation alone has been able to award more than $15 million in cumulative grants since its inception in 1990 with support from individuals such as former Bloomington North, Indiana University Basketball All-American and current New York Knicks forward Jared Jeffries who contributed to the Bloomington Park and Recreation Foundation's Olcott Youth Scholarship Fund.

In addition to granting agencies residing at different levels of government, there are different types of agencies ranging from corporations to private not-for-profit granting agencies that award money, services, equipment, and materials. For example, a private foundation such as the United Way is a well-known granting organization that raised $5.09 billion in 2010, making it the largest foundation in the world (http://www.unitedway.org/).

Skills in the development and writing of grants are a definite asset when seeking employment because the granting environment has become competitive and success can be difficult to achieve. It is also advantageous to begin writing smaller grants and build up to national level grants. However, a common aspect of all successful grant applications is a strong link between need, solutions, and long-term impact.

Sponsorships

Revenue generated through sponsorship agreements is on the rise globally, especially among sporting events. Sponsorship is the "acquisition of rights to affiliate or directly associate with a product or event for the purpose of deriving benefits related to that affiliation or association" (Brayley & McLean, 2008, p. 153). For a recreational sport agency, the advantage of sponsorship is that it generates revenues that may otherwise not exist. Reasons that organizations sponsor events include receiving event tickets; being highlighted in media guides, programs, scoreboards, and facility signage; and receiving special items (VIP room, luxury box, parking passes). Company names and logos on uniforms, in program guides, and around facilities are examples of sponsorship in recreational sport settings.

For a recreational sport specialist, it is advantageous to determine whether there are programs or services within the agency that are well suited for sponsorship. Similar to many other revenue generation strategies, it will require time and effort, but the benefits may be worth the work. However, with sponsorship, it is important to keep in mind that research has suggested that certain types of sponsorship are more acceptable than others when it comes to public park and recreation facilities, programs, and services (Mowen, Kyle, & Jackowski, 2007). For example, individuals tend to think sponsorship is less favorable when a sponsored program also has user fees and when the sponsor is not a local business. Assessing the form of sponsorship being desired, the venue, and the program must be considered so that a positive situation results from the agreement.

Philanthropic Support

Charitable donations. Donations are gifts of financial resources in exchange for benefits (e.g., tax deductions, VIP access) and represent a growing source of revenue for both public and private not-for-profit recreational sport agencies. As individual wealth continues to climb for the top 1% of Americans, the impact of charitable donations will continue to be felt, especially in university settings. Although the size of donations will vary greatly depending on numerous factors, maintaining contact with alumni or previous participants can be advantageous. For example, at Indiana University—like at many other institutions—alumni are quite active in supporting their alma mater, and as a result, many programs and services are directly supported by alumni. There are a number of specific strategies that can secure donations, but a small-scale example can include a gift catalog. A gift catalog identifies different items (e.g., tree = $250, park bench = $500) that can be purchased with the money being earmarked toward specific programs or services.

In-kind contributions. In-kind contributions occur when supplies, material, or equipment are donated to an agency. For instance, when running an extramural event, a local business may donate the refreshments at the event in exchange for publicity. While securing in-kind support requires some work on the part of the recreational sport specialist, this form of support can yield needed resources quickly at no cost.

Volunteers. Recreation and sport agencies are often one of the most highly supported agencies by volunteers. Many programs would not exist without the support of volunteers. For instance, baseball leagues are often coached and managed entirely by volunteers. Volunteers are discussed in Chapter 11 in more detail.

Partnerships

As agencies continue to face rising costs of doing business, partnerships are a reality for many. Partnerships occur when two or more agencies work together to achieve a common goal. Types of partnerships can range from joint programming to joint facility use to actual mergers. While the benefits of partnerships are numerous including the generation of resources (whether they are human or financial), it is important that recreational sport agencies find the right partners who share similar goals and missions.

As is shown with the diversity of revenue strategies available to recreational sport agencies, it is clear that financial understanding is no longer a function solely for the commercial sector or only for the finance department. Keep in mind that the more diversified an agency is with respect to revenue generation, the stronger their financial foundation will be.

Shining Example

Olympic Regional Development Authority

The New York State Olympic Regional Development Authority (ORDA) was created by the state legislature in 1982. It manages, operates, and promotes the Olympic venues in Lake Placid, New York, and hosts not only national and international sporting competitions and Olympic training, but also entertainment events. ORDA also works to promote awareness and youth participation in sport, as well as tourism in the Adirondack region.

Clientele:

ORDA serves over two million visitors at its collective venues each year.

Facilities:

The venues operated by ORDA include the Whiteface Mountain, Gore Mountain, the Olympic Ski Jumping Complex, the Olympic Center, the Olympic Sports Complex (including the sliding track and cross country track), and the Olympic Speed Skating Oval.

Program Details:

Each of the ORDA venues hosts a variety of programs and events for both recreational and Olympic athletes. In addition, ORDA promotes educational programs such as ORDA Sports Development, which encourages youth sport participation.

Budget:

ORDA's budget is over $26 million per year as of 2011.

Marketing:

ORDA employs a variety of marketing strategies, including flyers, brochures and other tourist information, Flame magazine, press packets, and a Website (http://www.orda.org/corporate/index.php). Recently the marketing department at ORDA has utilized the Whiteface Lake Placid Road Warriors (a team of enthusiastic promoters that attends New York events and uses social media), targeted elevator wraps in the Empire State Plaza, and banners strategically placed on ORDA facilities.

Salary:

Managerial salaries range from approximately $45,000-$65,000, depending upon experience.

Internships:

Due to housing restrictions, there are no internship opportunities.

Affiliated Professional Organizations

ORDA itself is a governing body that oversees the operation and management of sport venues and events.

▶ Computer Tip

Spreadsheets

Regardless of the size of the recreational sport program, most organizations use business and accounting software. The use of general ledgers, journals, payroll, and balance sheets have been replaced by even the simplest and least expensive accounting software. Budgeting, payroll, accounts receivable, accounts payable, forecasting, comparisons between income and expenditure allocations, and cost analysis are now standard features.

It is easy to be intimidated by the complex accounting software currently on the market. Spreadsheet programs are powerful tools for organizing, analyzing, and presenting the data that require the traditional row-and-column reports (such as budgets, payroll, and other record keeping files). Spreadsheets can perform both simple and complex calculations and can chart data in a number of formats. Anything once done with a pencil, a piece of paper, and calculations can be done by a spreadsheet program.

Most work in a spreadsheet program is done on a worksheet, which is the first thing you see when open the program. The worksheet is simply a large grid (up to 256 columns and 16,000 rows). To enter data, click on a cell, and enter the information. The real power of a spreadsheet comes from the ability of cells to store formulas and display the results, just as a calculator. For example, by conducting "what-if" analyses, all related or affected cells in the entire worksheet are re-calculated based on the given formula. Spreadsheets improve accuracy because they eliminate the necessity of re-working figures with calculators and pencils. With a spreadsheet, you don't have to worry about introducing errors because you don't manually erase and recalculate numbers.

Microsoft Excel is a very popular spreadsheet because it is a function of the Microsoft Office program that is installed on many computers as a basic computer software program. To calculate a budget for officials and supervisors for a sport, the recreational sport specialist would enter the projected number of officials and supervisors, hourly wages for the personnel, projected number of teams, league size, round-robin and play-off estimates of forfeits, number of officials and supervisors per game, and estimated percentage of work-study employees. Using this information, the spreadsheet program would immediately calculate the formula and present a total hourly wage budget figure, all in a matter of seconds. The formulas and other specifics for this can easily be modified to a specific program. Give it a try!

Conclusion

In summary, this chapter has discussed different aspects related to funding recreational sport programs across all three sectors. In particular, the budget process was explained followed by a description of the control and monitoring tasks that occur at both the agency and program level. A final section presented strategies that can be used to generate revenue in recreational settings. Throughout this chapter, the specifics of financial management were explained with an underlying message that financial competence is a requirement of all recreational sport specialists.

Bibliography

Brayley, R., & McLean, D. (2008). *Financial resource management: Sport, tourism, and leisure services.* Urbana, IL: Sagamore.

Carlson, M. (1995). *Winning grants step by step.* San Francisco, CA: Jossey-Bass.

Crompton, J. (1999). *Financing and acquiring park and recreation resources.* Champaign, IL: Human Kinetics.

DeSchriver, T., & Mahoney, D. (2003). Finance, economics, and budgeting in the sport industry. In J. Parks & J. Quarterman (Eds.), *Contemporary sport management* (pp. 231-254). Champaign, IL: Human Kinetics.

Edginton, C., Hudson, S., Lankford, S., & Larsen, D. (2008). *Managing recreation, parks, and leisure services: An introduction* (3rd ed.). Urbana, IL: Sagamore.

Hall, M., Lasby, D., Ayer, S., & Gibbons, W. D. (2009). *Caring Canadians, involved Canadians: Highlights from the 2007 Canada Survey of Giving, Volunteering and Participating.* Ottawa, Canada: Minister of Industry.

Havitz, M., & Glover, T. (2001). *Financing and acquiring park and recreation resources in Canada.* Champaign, IL: Human Kinetics.

Holdnak, A., & Mahoney, E., & Garges, J. (2005). Budgeting. In B. van der Smissen, M. Moiseichek, & V. Hartenberg (Eds.), *Management of park and recreation agencies* (pp. 537-591). Ashburn, VA: National Recreation and Park Association.

Kanters, M., Carter, D., & Pearson, B. (2001). A community based model for assessing the economic impact of sport and recreation services. *Journal of Park and Recreation Administration, 19*(2), 43-61.

McCarville, R. (1995). Pricing for public leisure services: An ethical dilemma? *Journal of Applied Recreation Research, 20*(2), 95-108.

Mowen, A., Kyle, G., & Jackowski, M. (2007). Citizen preferences for the corporate sponsorship of public-sector park and recreation organizations. *Journal of Nonprofit & Public Sector Marketing, 18*(2), 93-118.

Scarborough, N., & Zimmerer, T. (2003). *Effective small business management: An entrepreneurial approach* (7th ed.). Upper Saddle River, NJ: Prentice Hall.

Sellers, J., Gladwell, N., & Pope, M. (2005). Financial management. In B. van der Smissen, M. Moiseichek, & V. Hartenberg (Eds.), *Management of park and recreation agencies* (pp. 493-536). Ashburn, VA: National Recreation and Park Association.

Silverberg, K., Marshall, E., & Ellis, G. (2001). Measuring job satisfaction of volunteers in public parks and recreation. *Journal of Park and Recreation Administration, 19*(1), 79-92.

Stier, W. (1999). *Managing sport, fitness, and recreation programs: Concepts and practices.* London, England: Allyn and Bacon.

Stier, W., Schneider, R., Kampf, S., Wilding, G., & Haines, S. (2005). The financial and facility status of campus recreation programs at NIRSA colleges and universities. *Recreational Sports Journal, 29*, 127-142.

Warren, R., & Rae, P. (1998). Fee supported parks: Promoting success. *Parks and Recreation, 33*(1), 81-88.

Wiener, S., Toppe, C., Jalandoni, N., Kirsch, A., & Weitzman, M. (2002). *Giving and volunteering in the United States: Findings from a national survey.* Washington, DC: Independent Sector.

CHAPTER 13

Facilities

CHAPTER OBJECTIVES

After reading this chapter, you will appreciate the extensiveness of facilities in recreational sport, be able to discuss responsibilities that relate to facilities, be aware of the relevant aspects of facility coordination, understand facility scheduling techniques, recognize the importance of facility security, and realize the different stages of facility development.

KEY CONCEPTS

Extensiveness
Responsibilities
Coordination
Scheduling

Categories
Security
Facility development

Introduction

Facility management is a critical responsibility in recreational sport. Primary to the delivery of any kind of sport activity is marketing the space in which that sport takes place. Not only are facilities necessary to sport programming, but also their management has far-reaching implications for user satisfaction and safety.

Unfortunately, recreational sport specialists often lack full understanding of the important role facilities play in their professional responsibilities. This chapter concentrates on the context for sport facility management as well as scheduling options and considerations, security measures, and facility development.

Overview

Operating a facility where recreational sport is delivered is far more complex than the notion that the facility exists and is used. To the average participant, detailed information about facilities is not important, but to the recreational sport specialist, this knowledge is fundamentally important. The recreational sport specialist also needs to understand the role played by architects, engineers, and other positions specific to facility use and control. Many recreational sport agencies, especially those that are large and complex, rely on highly qualified personnel and sophisticated systems to attend to facilities. Developing greater awareness and appreciation of facilities means examining the importance of facility areas and space and responsibilities involved.

Extensiveness

Facilities take on prominence in recreational sport partly due to the diversity of sporting needs for space and equipment. Recreational sport facilities represent an extensiveness that is not easily comprehended. This extensiveness is observed in facility size (volume or square footage) and purpose (single-purpose facilities or multipurpose complexes). Extensiveness can also be observed by looking at different indoor and outdoor facilities, as illustrated in Figure 13.1.

Another way to understand the extensiveness of facilities is to examine the varied delivery functions of facilities, including requirements, conditions, and circumstances, as well as personnel, policies, procedures, equipment, safety standards, maintenance, rules, and regulations. None of these responsibilities are trivial, and some require knowledge of and experience with industry standards.

Indoor	Outdoor
Areas	*Areas*
Badminton courts	Archery range
Basketball courts	Baseball field
Billards	Disc Frisbee course
Bowling lanes	Driving range
Climbing wall	Football field
Dance studio	Horseback riding/trails
Gymnasium	Ice skating
Gymnastic room	In-line skate parks
Indoor track	Pool and diving well
Jogging track	Race track
Racquetball courts	Shooting range
Soccer	Sand volleyball court
Strength Conditioning	Soccer field
Swimming pool	Softball field
Table games	Tennis court
Volleyball court	Track and field
Yoga studio	Water front
Complexes	*Complexes*
Aquatic center	Aquatic center
Basketball arena	Climbing and Rappelling
Fieldhouse	Country Club
Football stadium	Golf Course
Health Club	Outdoor sport fields
Ice arena	Race track
Recreational sport center	Riding Stables
Tennis courts	Ski resort
	Sport camp
	Target facility

Figure 13.1. Types of Indoor and Outdoor Facilities

A final way to gain appreciation for the extensiveness of facilities relates to technological advancements. Technology has heightened the professional's role in facility use, requiring greater specialization and expertise. Examples of these advancements are cameras and surveillance systems; computer-controlled heating, air conditioning, and ventilation; photo-sensor lighting levels; sophisticated portable equipment; electromagnetic security systems; wireless communication systems; automated irrigation systems; specialized turf and court surfaces; hydraulic pool floors; and resilient gymnasium surfaces.

Responsibilities

One way of understanding the importance of facilities in recreational sport is to examine the responsibilities required in their use. Historically, these responsibilities may have been taken for granted, but in today's world, use requirements undertake special significance and attention.

Maximum use. Undesignated space in a facility is viewed as waste and is no longer acceptable. Today's administrative leadership is more involved than ever in the analysis and assignment of space to maximize its use. Efficiency of space as a meaningful contribution to productivity is critical to administrative plans. Recreational sport specialists are expected to contribute by identifying ways to maximize facility use.

Laws and codes. In almost all fields of management, human health, safety, and equal opportunity have been increasingly emphasized. Laws and codes have been written by state and federal governing bodies to protect the welfare of all facility users and personnel. Strict regulations pertaining to facilities include fire protection, chemical use in pools and cleaning, crowd control and capacity levels, weather-related standards, evacuation procedures, and so on. The interpretation and application of these regulations require special attention in order to represent and protect participants and administration. The recreational sport specialist shares in this responsibility to uphold laws and codes that relate to facilities.

Cost savings. Management has moved toward the idea that operations must reflect cost effectiveness and efficiency. Wasted assets result in lost income or profit, so all facility-related costs are scrutinized, including original construction, utilities, operations refinancing, capital savings, and maintenance. Cost analysis has become systematic and intentional and should be recognized by the recreational sport specialist as an essential responsibility.

Liability. Recreational sport facilities by their nature can be hazardous. There is always a potential for injury. Owners, administrators, and executives should be aware of the heightened liability for injuries attributed to facility misuse. Recreational sport specialists must attend to participant health and safety as a primary concern. This requires awareness and a capacity not only to see what is happening in a facility but also to ensure that the facility itself does not contribute to injury. Recreational sport specialists who are knowledgeable about facility liability can go a long way toward protecting participants and avoiding legal action.

In briefly covering the extensiveness and responsibilities of facilities, it is clear that little occurs in recreational sport that does not relate to a facility. This reality places the burden with the professional to make sure the facility does not negatively affect participant experience or profit potential.

Coordination

The scope of all that arises with the delivery of recreational sport magnifies the importance and challenges of coordinating facility use. The challenges intensify when facilities are shared by different groups such as varsity athletic teams, schools, corporations, and nonprofit organizations. Facility coordination involves creating and maintaining an effective system for arranging all aspects of facility use in a harmonious and timely fashion. Accomplishing this coordination can require a great deal of time and effort. Coordinating facilities requires integrating individual and group interests into an overall plan. The following are reasons why coordinating facility use is so important.

Value

Being effective and efficient in coordinating facilities is a critical consideration for overall operations because facilities are expensive to build and can be expensive to maintain. Coordinating maximum use demonstrates sound stewardship, which in turn reflects positively upon management.

Another value of sound coordination is the avoidance of problems such as having people in the wrong place at the wrong time, not having doors open on time, or not having an activity or event where it belongs. The absence of such problems enhances the experience for users. Sound coordination is linked to user satisfaction and loyalty, which are both valuable results.

Influences

To bring about proper facility coordination, important considerations that influence the management system need to be in place. One such consideration is the administration or leadership's overall belief about the importance of coordination. The preference is for a conviction that emphasizes the mission, goals, and objectives of program delivery above personalities or political agendas. Establishing sound principles of facility operation and coordination protects against inappropriate requests and unnecessary problems with facility arrangements.

Further influences on coordination are employee and participant personality, gender, race, social status, attitude, and motivation. These factors come into play when trying to work with varied individual preferences and forms of expression. Such influences can be positive or negative and should be anticipated in order to provide objective and positive coordination.

A common influence on facility coordination is the various time options that are available and whether some times are more desirable than others. For example, do users have expectations for access during certain hours of the day or days of the week? Do these expectations change according to season?

Finally, a significant influence on coordination is the availability of particular spaces and how circumstances and conditions can affect what will or can take place. Areas may have restrictions or warnings, limiting what can be coordinated. These restrictions may result from safety concerns, maintenance work, capacity limitations, or hazardous conditions. Such situations require proper attention to enhance coordination efforts.

Concerns

A number of concerns can be anticipated in coordinating facilities. One such concern is limited space. Most facilities do not have this problem when they are first constructed. Over time, however, participants may increase in number and cause crowding. The recreational sport specialist must keep abreast of use patterns and industry trends in order to recognize limited space and create solutions.

Another concern is the interests of potential users. Pressures for space are often the result of changes in interests. Due to the expense of facility development, outside user groups often seek access to existing facilities. These varied interests become conflicting interests when the demand exceeds the supply and when political persuasion is used to gain access to space for a particular activity or event.

Still another concern is unrealistic attitudes from individuals who are unfamiliar with the requirements of facility coordination. Some individuals are so passionate about their activity or event that they simply do not care about the process, view it as an obstruction, or oversimplify it. Conduct may range from unresponsive to demanding and abrasive behavior. In these situations, be patient and seek common ground or negotiate alternatives. In facility coordination, concerns of this nature are all too common, but dealing with negatives and making them positive is where training and expertise can assist the recreational sport specialist.

Necessities

There are two basic prerequisites to coordinating varied interests and retaining sufficient control. The first and most important is to have the established authority for creating or executing facility-use policies. This authority should extend to decisions that represent the best interests of management, all aspects of safety, protection of the facility and its equipment, and appropriate delivery of the sport activity or event. Without authority to keep things under control and flowing smoothly, problems can occur. The basis for and scope of authority should be planned, structured, and communicated so that all potential users are well informed and recognize their responsibility to management authority.

The second necessity is recognizing the importance of staff. One of the greatest mistakes made in facility coordination is not taking the staff's role seriously. Staff can easily become overworked, resulting in little attention to detail, low morale, and poor overall organization. Being aware of these tendencies is a necessity in facility coordination. The key to success in staffing considerations is being proactive, making sure that everyone's needs are addressed.

As generally understood in recreational sport, administrative leadership strives to create successful program delivery. In facility use, meeting that goal means applying facility coordination principles. Recreational sport specialists may or may not find themselves with direct responsibilities for facility use. Regardless, they will be involved in bringing sport activities and events to participants, and insight into the coordination process will be critical.

Scheduling

Scheduling is a large part of coordinating facilities. Scheduling is the actual act or process of assigning a specific time, place, and date for use of facilities or equipment in response to a formal request. Scheduling details can vary with agency management as well as with particular groups and facilities. The common functions of organizing, directing, and controlling are necessary to understand when it comes to facility scheduling. The following categories, procedures, policies, and techniques are presented to create insight into the details involved.

Categories

There are four categories requiring facility scheduling: users, personnel, areas, and events. Each of these categories has unique characteristics and overlapping implications for scheduling.

Users. User characteristics affect scheduling practices and principles. Users may come from within the agency (tax-paying citizens, members, identified clients), or they may come from outside the agency. Analyzing and understanding user data such as age, ability, gender, and health can be insightful and is recommended. In addition, social status, economic level, special interests and needs, ability and willingness to pay, product popularity, and user availability should be surveyed. Once such information is gathered and understood, users can be appropriately scheduled into a system that correlates user needs to area and equipment availability. Techniques for accomplishing such scheduling are discussed later in this chapter.

Personnel. Facility scheduling is affected by employees and volunteers who are involved with programming and maintenance. Scheduling these individuals to be in the right place at the right time can become difficult to arrange. Scheduling of workers requires insight into assignments, timing, and priorities so as not to create conflict with other workers or users in the facility.

Areas. Another scheduling category is arranging and controlling desired space. Whether it is a court, field, classroom, auditorium, park, or pool, an area has its own unique requirements. Available space may be large or small, indoor or outdoor, multipurpose or single purpose. Each area is intended for certain activities, and potential use must be reviewed carefully before scheduling.

Events. One of the most involved categories of scheduling stems from internal and external requests for major events and group activities. This type of scheduling usually requires large indoor or outdoor areas to host events of varying durations, such as concerts, sport extravaganzas, sport tournaments, club events, large dances, and lectures. This type of scheduling is demanding and requires special supervision and safety measures, not to mention event setup, takedown, and maintenance. Large events require a great deal of detail, preparation, and thought in order to meet expectations.

Understanding the categories involved in scheduling is just the beginning. Much is involved in facility scheduling, and because there are different applications from agency to agency, this chapter simply provides key concepts and principles. Recreational sport specialists should be prepared to modify information to conform to their particular responsibilities and requirements.

Procedures

Scheduling procedures may take two directions: (a) scheduling that involves participant space and (b) events or programs that require special arrangements. This section will first review tips for scheduling spaces. Initial arrangements for scheduling a facility begin with a contact person who has been designated to handle such requests. Depending on the extent of the agency, this position could range from an hourly receptionist to a full-time professional in charge of facility management. Area and space requests are submitted via a facility reservation form, as in Figure 13.2. This form is the first step in a system that links management to potential users.

FACILITY RESERVATION REQUEST

TO: COORDINATOR OF FACILITIES   DATE: _____

FROM:

Name_____

Organization _____

Address_____

_____

_____

This organization requests reservation for the following:

1.   Facility:_____
2.   Activity:_____
3.   Dates:_____
4.   Times:_____
5.   Number in group:_____
6.   Responsible person:_____

        Signed:_____

Note: Requests must be submitted in writing at least two weeks in advance of times and dates requested.

Figure 13.2. Facility Reservation Request

Procedures

Whether scheduling a sport team, specialized group, or organization, a system for *processing* requests is needed. These *procedures* are sequential steps designed to guide and control the arrangement process. The system should receive prior administrative attention and could incorporate several of the steps represented in Figure 13.3.

Depending on the nature of the request, certain responsibilities and related information should be carefully reviewed and established before scheduling the area. Suggested responsibilities are provided in Figure 13.4. This information should help guide the critical thought process involved in scheduling arrangements.

Policies

Participants and interested user groups need to understand the policies associated with facility requests. These policies should be established in advance and endorsed by the administration. Whether the request is for an hour, a day, a week, or more, Figure 13.5 describes the different policies that need to be formalized. Each policy helps establish sound communication and improve mutual understanding that is vital, especially if the request involves special considerations.

Announcements: Potential users need to be aware of what is available.

Letter/Form: Formalizes and shows a sincere interest and commitment.

Log: Recorded date and time received.

Review: Each request should be studied completely. Meet with representative of user group to clarify event purpose and assess feasibility.

Response: Management should respond in writing or in person in a timely fashion.

Appeal: If there is denial, an appeal helps to lessen the negative feelings of rejection.

Formal Agreement/Contract: Final understanding should be in writing establishing details of the arrangements.

Follow Up: Check area after use for items left behind, clean up, damage or theft.

Figure 13.3. Steps to Scheduling an Area

Set up/Clean up: Specifically decide who will set up and clean up.

Security: Determine what security is necessary and who will provide.

Supervision: Establish level of supervision and who will provide.

Equipment: Decide equipment needs and who will provide.

Safety: Assess activity and level judging potential liability.

Figure 13.4. Area Scheduling Responsibilities

Charges: Areas and time period related to a specific fee.

Deposit: Fee required to show intent and commitment.

Refunds: Specific considerations that allow for return of fees charged.

Timing: Statement requiring requests by a certain date and time.

Rescheduling: Statement allowing for rescheduling based on predetermined circumstances.

No Show: Penalty understanding for a no show.

Cancellation: Stated circumstances that allow for cancellation

Damage Policy: Understanding that reflects level of protection of the facility and equipment.

Figure 13.5. Policy Areas in Scheduling

Techniques

Different scheduling techniques exist to meet a variety of needs. Some practices are simply common sense and apply to all requests. Examples include having a reminder process to keep details from being forgotten, meeting with users to review details of the request, laying out time lines, and anticipating last-minute adjustments. However, there are more specific techniques that warrant explanation because they assist with organization and reliability of information that can lead to maximal use of space.

Master schedule. Few responsibilities in recreational sport are more complicated than keeping all scheduled use noted and organized. A master schedule that includes locations, dates, and time periods is used to keep track of scheduled use. The master schedule should be the assigned responsibility of an ongoing employee who takes pride in maintaining an accurate system. The master schedule should be kept available for planning and for reference, helping to maintain organization and avoid duplication and conflicts.

Types. Scheduling of areas varies, and each occurrence has unique variables that entail a great deal of information. See the computer tips for examples of the different types of scheduling that a recreational sport specialist might use.

Seasonal. In most places, seasons influence scheduling. In some geographical areas, winter requires a move indoors for some sports, signaling peak use of certain facilities. The return of warm weather often results in a switch to outdoor sports, requiring another seasonal adjustment. Seasonal scheduling coordinates the availability of facilities based on the seasons, making it easier to coordinate over an extended time such as 8, 10, or 12 weeks. When a seasonal schedule covers a long period, the effect of holidays should be considered. Figure 13.6 illustrates a seasonal scheduling pattern for the fall session at a municipal community center.

According to traditional scheduling practice, most major maintenance occurs before or after a season. Emergency or preventive maintenance occurs as required, little affected by seasonal demand.

Monthly or weekly. Monthly or weekly scheduling works well when there is a need to structure use, creating ongoing understanding so that users can establish a pattern. There may be different uses at different times, but scheduled activities take place regularly for the entire month. Figure 13.7 illustrates a typical week in the monthly schedule for a swimming pool.

Daily. Daily scheduling divides the day into general time periods: morning, afternoon, and evening. Each period indicates early morning, late morning, early afternoon, late afternoon, early evening, and late evening. This structure requires an understanding of participant lifestyles and interests so facility scheduling can be tailored for a particular activity or program. Each option creates a different use in the same area over an entire day. Figure 13.8 provides an example of a daily schedule, showing three areas with varied uses throughout the day from which participants can choose.

Sport	Day	Time	Fee	Weeks
Aquatics				
Age 3-5	Monday/Wednesday	3:45-4:15 pm	Free	4
	Tuesday/Thursday	5:30-6:00 pm	Free	4
	Saturday	9:00-9:30 am	Free	4
Age 6 and over	Tuesday/Thursday	6:00-6:30 pm	$2.00	4
(Basic)	Saturday	4:00-4:30 pm	$2.00	4
Family Swim	Friday/Saturday	7:30-9:30 pm	Free	6
	Sunday	1:30-3:30 pm	Free	6
Scuba	Tuesday	8:00-10:00 pm	$10.00	6
Tennis				
Beginning	Monday/Wednesday	7:00-8:30 pm	$4.00	6
Intermediate	Tuesday/Thursday	7:00-8:30 pm	$6.00	6
Volleyball				
A league				
(2nd session only)	Friday	8:00-10:00 pm	$6.00	6
B league				
(2nd session only)	Sunday	8:00-10:00 pm	$4.00	4
Karate	Monday/Wednesday	7:00-9:00 pm	$6.00	6

Figure 13.6. Season Program Schedule

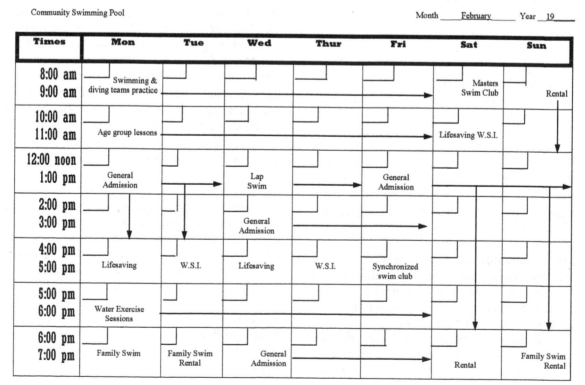

Community Swimming Pool   Month   February   Year   19

Figure 13.7. One Week of a Monthly Facility Schedule

Time	Free-weight room 092	Universal gym room 092A	Gym 095
7:00 am	Informal Sport	Athletic Sport	Instructional Sport
7:30 am	Informal Sport	Athletic Sport	Instructional Sport
8:00 am	Informal Sport	Athletic Sport	Instructional Sport
8:30 am	Informal Sport	Athletic Sport	Instructional Sport
9:00 am	Closed	Closed	Closed
9:30 am	Closed	Closed	Closed
10:00 am	Closed	Informal Sport	Informal Sport
10:30 am	Closed	Informal Sport	Informal Sport
11:00 am	Informal Sport	Informal Sport	Informal Sport
11:30 am	Informal Sport	Informal Sport	Informal Sport
12:00 noon	Informal Sport	Informal Sport	Informal Sport
12:30 pm	Informal Sport	Informal Sport	Aerobic Rhythm
1:00 pm	Informal Sport	Informal Sport	Group Exercise
1:30 pm	Informal Sport	Intramural Sport	Group Exercise
2:00 pm	Informal Sport	Intramural Sport	Stretch Fit
2:30 pm	Informal Sport	Intramural Sport	Stretch Fit
3:00 pm	Informal Sport	Informal Sport	Closed
3:30 pm	Informal Sport	Informal Sport	Judo Club
4:00 pm	Informal Sport	Informal Sport	Judo Club
4:30 pm	Informal Sport	Informal Sport	Judo Club
5:00 pm	Informal Sport	Informal Sport	Judo Club
5:30 pm	Informal Sport	Informal Sport	Judo Club
6:00 pm	Weight Club	Informal Sport	Hapkido Club
6:30 pm	Weight Club	Informal Sport	Hapkido Club
7:00 pm	Weight Club	Informal Sport	Hapkido Club
7:30 pm	Weight Club	Informal Sport	Hapkido Club
8:00 pm	Weight Club	Informal Sport	Aikido Club
8:30 pm	Weight Club	Informal Sport	Aikido Club
9:00 pm	Informal Sport	Informal Sport	Wrestling Club
9:30 pm	Informal Sport	Informal Sport	Wrestling Club
10:00 pm	Informal Sport	Informal Sport	Wrestling Club
10:30 pm	Informal Sport	Informal Sport	Wrestling Club
11:00 pm	Closed	Closed	Closed

Figure 13.8. Daily Facility Schedule

Hourly. Many recreational sport facilities have sport areas that are scheduled for a specific hour and possibly an hour and a half or even two hours. This is common practice in commercial recreational sport, where management depends on an hourly charge to generate income. This type of scheduling could be arranged where hours are established to allow for prime time. Charges are higher for prime time and lower for non-prime time. This type of scheduling usually limits when requests can be made, such as no more than a week in advance. Such scheduling practices can be observed at golf courses, tennis or racquetball facilities, and bowling alleys. It is also used for scheduling equipment for hourly use at a fitness-oriented facility. The hourly scheduling in Figure 13.9 shows the hours of the day as well as the courts in an eight-court tennis facility. Names can be written into the spaces to indicate a scheduled time and court.

Block. Block scheduling helps objectively address different interests in facility scheduling. Certain groups, programs, or special needs could have priority, arranged into a specific block of time during a day. Within the system, a particular interest is given facility use for a specific time of the day, and that use takes priority for an ongoing but specified period of time. Often these priorities receive administrative attention before the arrangements are made, creating equitable distribution of space to meet needs and interests. An example of such scheduling can be observed in Figure 13.10, which shows block scheduling for a large gymnasium. Note the very different purpose in use, including physical education; recreational sport that may involve informal, intramural, and club sport; and individual and team training. Block scheduling may be set to run on a weekly, monthly, seasonal, or even annual basis. Because block scheduling identifies regular time spans of facility use, it establishes order and permits staff and participants to have a routine in their use.

HOURLY COURT SCHEDULING

Day _____   Date _____

Time	Court 1	Court 2	Court 3	Court 4	Court 5	Court 6	Court 7	Court 8
7:00 am								
7:30 am								
8:00 am								
8:30 am								
9:00 am								
9:30 am								
10:00 am								
10:30 am								
11:00 am								
11:30 am								
12:00 pm								
12:30 pm								
1:00 pm								
1:30 pm								
2:00 pm								
2:30 pm								
3:00 pm								
3:30 pm								
4:00 pm								
4:30 pm								
5:00 pm								
5:30 pm								
6:00 pm								
6:30 pm								
7:00 pm								
7:30 pm								
8:00 pm								
8:30 pm								
9:00 pm								
9:30 pm								
10:00 pm								
10:30 pm								
11:00 pm								
11:30 pm								
12:00 am								

Figure 13.9. Hourly Court Scheduling

	Monday	Tuesday	Wednesday	Thursday	Friday	Saturday
8:00 am	Physical Education					
9:30 am						
11:00 am	Recreational Sport				Recreational Sport	
12:30 pm						
2:00 pm	Athletics					
3:30 pm	Physical Education					
5:00 pm						
6:30 pm	Recreational Sport					
8:00 pm						

Figure 13.10. Block Scheduling for a Large Gynmasium

Acknowledgment. A written document should detail user responsibilities, especially for groups, teams, and clubs. Management must ensure that users understand their responsibilities as outlined in the document. See Figure 13.11 for a statement of responsibility for facility use.

Events. Scheduling also involves making arrangements to bring an event to a facility. Event scheduling requires an expanded approach of the previously mentioned techniques, creating much greater responsibility in the overall process. Event scheduling can incorporate both internal and external groups, with each request requiring detailed attention to needs and conditions. These events can take place over any period of time but most often last between four and eight hours, usually requiring large spaces. Such arrangements should be taken seriously because there are many details that could create communication and logistical problems. Ex-

amples of events within recreational sport facilities could include a sport extravaganza, graduation ceremonies, a concert, club sport, and intramural and athletic team competition.

Event reservation request. A formal process is necessary for scheduling events, including a letter of inquiry and a detailed request form. Figure 13.12 illustrates the specific information that needs to be obtained before an event is scheduled. This information begins the process of making such arrangements.

Checklist. A critical event scheduling technique is a preplanned checklist of tasks. Because there are so many details, a checklist makes a major contribution to the effectiveness and efficiency of the process. Items that should be included in a checklist can be observed in Figure 13.13. As each task is accomplished, it is checked off, ensuring that everything is addressed.

STATEMENT OF RESPONSIBILITY FOR FACILITY USE

The user, or his/her sponsor if one is deemed necessary, shall be responsible for cleanup, damage, injuries, supervision, and any liability incurred curing the use of facilities requested in the application received by this office. The specific responsibilities are listed below:

A.   **Supervision.** The user agrees to supervise the use of the facility to ensure that there is no abuse to it nor any violation of the laws of the state or the rules and regulations of the agency. Assistance may be sought through the facility supervisors. Verification on reservation will be required (bring confirmation slip).

B.   **Injury.**   Any personal injury requiring immediate medical attention must be reported to facility supervisor or the ambulance service. A written report describing the circumstances must be completed and returned to this office or facility supervisor. Accident report forms are available from the facility supervisor or from this office.

C.   **Cleanup and damage.**   The facility will be inspected by a facility supervisor of this office before and after use. If cleanup is necessary it will be done by the following.

1)   The user assuming the physical action of the cleanup. This will again be subject to inspection.

2)   Placing a work order for its cleanup. The user will accept financial obligations for this action.

Any damage to the facility, its furnishings, or equipment must be reported in writing to this office. The user will be responsible for the cost of repair or replacement.

I, _____, acting as the responsible
Individual for _____ have read the above
statement and will ensure that these stipulations are followed.

Date _____
Signed_____

Note: This statement must be returned by _____

Figure 13.11. Statement of Responsibility for Facility Use

```
┌─────────────────────────────────────────────────────────────────────┐
│              FACILITY RESERVATION REQUEST FOR EVENTS                  │
│                                                                       │
│  Name _____ Phone _____      │
│  Address_____        │
│                                                                       │
│  Contact Person                                                       │
│  Name _____ Phone _____      │
│  Address _____        │
│  Organization _____        │
│                                                                       │
│    1.   Summarize previous facility reservations by your organization │
│         (include date, facility, time, event).                        │
│         _____          │
│         _____          │
│                                                                       │
│    2.   What kind of event is to be conducted (tournament, clinic,     │
│         etc)? Please Explain. _____          │
│         _____          │
│         _____          │
│                                                                       │
│    3.   How many individual or teams are expected to participate? ___ │
│    4.   Will there be any user fee? _____ Spectator admission     │
│         fee? _____                                                │
│         If yes, how much? _____ If yes, how much? _____      │
│    5.   What facilities are being requested? (Please List.) _____  │
│         _____          │
│                                                                       │
│    6.   When is the event to take place?   Dates:   1st Choice _____  │
│                                                     2nd Choice _____  │
│                                                                       │
│    7.   What special equipment or facility preparation might be        │
│         needed? (Please list.) _____         │
│         _____          │
│                                                                       │
│    8.   How many people will be assisting in the operation of the      │
│         event? _____        │
│                                                                       │
│    9.   Does anyone in the group have first aid or CPR certification?  │
│         _____ If yes, please indicate name                          │
│   10.   Are there any plans to have any type of concessions at the     │
│         event?  If yes please explain, _____                      │
│         _____          │
│                                                                       │
│   11.   Is there a need to have assistance by personnel from           │
│         recreational sport? If so how many, what functions, and how    │
│         do you plan to pay them? _____       │
│                                                                       │
│   12.   Additional comments _____        │
│         _____          │
│         _____          │
│         _____          │
│         _____          │
└─────────────────────────────────────────────────────────────────────┘
```

Figure 13.12. Event Reservation Request

Consultation and negotiations. Event scheduling can be time consuming, often requiring discussion and consultation. All previously noted procedures and policies need to be taken into account along with considerations unique to the event. Special communications take place to plan for potential problems, accidents, and emergencies. Information that is gained can be very important, especially in revealing costs that may challenge the arrangements. More often than not, management is interested in making such arrangements because events can produce income. Negotiation of details may be necessary, which means discussing and resolving differences between the interests and personalities involved. Figure 13.14 lists different topics that could require consultation or negotiation.

Written agreement. To confirm acceptance of the conditions, the event's representative is required to acknowledge outlined responsibilities. The detailed information found in an agreement or contract depends on the nature and scope of the event as well as the level of understanding and clarification required. Such documentation is critical, especially in detailing technical and logistical responsibility, including liability. Before the event, all written material and contracts should be reviewed and approved by the appropriate administrators as well as legal counsel.

All of the mentioned techniques for scheduling facilities are fundamental for the recreational sport specialist. Not everyone will have scheduling responsibilities. However, as a supportive member of a management team, a recreational sport specialist should understand the details involved in scheduling facilities.

EVENT SCHEDULING CHECKLIST

INITIAL REVIEW
    Request form completed
    Determine facility availability
    Initial response (informal)
    Deposit received

INITIAL FACILITY WALK THROUGH
    Assess areas – lighting, electrical, space functionality, etc.
    Equipment – what is available and what is needed?
    Auxiliary Support – parking, restroom, etc.

MEETING TO REVIEW EVENT
    Event needs: area preparation, equipment details, food service,
    special needs, capacity, etc.
    Management Requirements: policies, procedures, emergency measures,
    see consultation/negotiation topics, etc.

CONSULTATION AND NEGOTIATION MEETING

FINAL AGREEMENT/CONTRACT WRITTEN
    Sent   _____
    Received   _____

FINAL WALK THROUGH   _____

POST EVENT REVIEW
    Managements area assessments
    Groups evaluation received

Figure 13.13. Event Scheduling Checklist

Security

All recreational sport facilities assume some degree of security. The space and related equipment need to be free from trouble, personal injury, and property damage or loss as well as controlled for use by eligible participants. Security is the process of creating a safe, comfortable environment. Security measures are usually established during facility design and development. However, security systems can be developed and applied at any time, such as when incidents of negative behavior increase or facilities become outdated. To help the recreational sport specialist appreciate the security function, the following information describes how security systems are developed, what surveillance involves, and what access control involves.

Systems

Depending on the technological sophistication and complexity of the facility, security systems may be a demanding responsibility. Some facilities require little or no security while others use extensive systems that are intricate and costly. When security is necessary, attention needs to be paid to the different options available as well as the level of security needed. Developing a security system includes making a complete, detailed assessment of the facility and equipment; anticipating problems; doing comparative shopping; and considering expert assistance from consultants. Figure 13.15 is a list of points that can help with such a review. Some systems require expansive application that can be expensive. Whether it is a public or private facility, funding influences the level of security systems that can be applied. There should always be a balance between what is affordable and what is needed.

Surveillance

One application of security is a surveillance system where administration takes steps to keep a close watch over space, equipment, and users. Surveillance is the most common form of security in recreational sport facilities and is often built into job descriptions for area supervisors. The following information briefly describes three types of surveillance.

Fees and charges

Level and type of supervision

Specific equipment needs and when and who responsible

Timing and coordination details

Crowds or spectator numbers

Emergency action responsibilities

Medical requirements

Damage to facilities or equipment understanding

Insurance type and coverage

Set up/clean up arrangements

Food service arrangements

Access control specifics

Penalty for cancellations and/or no shows

Figure 13.14. Consultation and Negotiation Topics for Event Scheduling

Location of facility (rural or urban)

Facility design and layout

Product and facility attractions

Area and equipment protection needs

Level of access control

Activation level (use)

Liability conditions and potential

Maintenance requirements

Sport or event related concerns

Signage influence and control

Figure 13.15. Considerations for Security Development

Supervision and guarding. Few recreational sport facilities and related activities exist without a system in place to guard or supervise what is taking place. Depending on the situation, degree of risk, facility, equipment, and so on, formal observation may vary from volunteer to hourly employees. Typical security positions include supervisor, official, lifeguard, coach, and instructor, as well as formal security guards and police. Every precaution should be taken to make sure these individuals are trained to meet the circumstances of the facility and its programs. Individuals in these positions are expected to make careful observations, communicate information, take appropriate action, and when necessary fill out forms and report all relevant information to administration.

Lighting. Surveillance includes lighting systems that heighten visibility in both indoor and outdoor facilities. Obviously, lighting is most important where it creates the ability to observe what is going on in high- and low-use areas. There are areas in recreational sport facilities where emergency backup is usually required, such as stairwells, elevators, and locker rooms. In addition, certain locations may require special lighting, such as motion-sensor lighting, automated lighting, and special lighting for pathways, sidewalks, and parking lots. Lighting intensity can deter unwanted activity.

Cameras. Cameras and monitors are more efficient than supervisors or guards in certain situations. Such technology allows a single station to watch many different areas. Unruly behavior, theft, injury, and unwanted entry can be easily observed. The mere existence of cameras sometimes acts as a deterrent for inappropriate behavior. Systems exist that can be triggered when users walk through a door or across an area. Cameras may also be hidden or kept out of reach so as to not be tampered with.

Surveillance can be much more complicated than what has been described. The ability to watch and prevent unwanted behavior is enhanced by improving technology. In designing a surveillance system, much thought should be given to the facility's unique situation.

Access Control

Controlling access into a recreational sport facility is a common practice when there are limitations on who can enter. Where there are memberships, entry fees, and special use policies and procedures, access control is necessary. Each of the following applications contributes to restricting facility access.

Scheduling. As mentioned earlier, many techniques for scheduling influence who has access to a facility. The actual scheduling arrangement communicates what is taking place and who is involved. Through such arrangements, use restrictions can be determined and agreed upon.

Barriers. Often not considered as security but as part of a facility layout are barriers and fences that block and discourage access. There are natural barriers such as mounding, trees, bushes, and shrubs, and man-made barriers such as bars, chain-link fences, and even barbed-wire fences. More common in recreational sport are gate-and-door systems that have electrically automated mechanisms permitting entry. Turnstiles can also be used to take head counts and control access.

Entry checking. When recreational sport facilities are very popular, they may have a special entry-checking system. In this system, a person who desires access to a facility is identified by a picture ID, school ID, employee ID, or driver's license. Entry checking is often incorporated into facility supervision responsibilities and, in some cases, is assigned to specific control-center personnel. In some cases, IDs have a bar code for a scanning system that automatically allows entry, and in extreme situations, there may be specialized entry systems such as metal detectors, finger printing, retina scanning, trained canines, or chemical substance testing, which have become more common in recent years.

Door control. Another aspect of access control is lock systems. These systems may be padlocks and keys, combination locks, and in some cases electronic keypads. Standard keys and locks are often inadequate because they can be lost, stolen, or duplicated. Recent technology has introduced electronically programmed key cards and door systems that use hard plastics with coded magnetic stripes. These coded cards slide into a reader and an electronic device scans the card and then releases the lock. Although keys and locks are still used, where security is a serious concern more sophisticated systems are put to use.

Alarms. Entire facilities as well as individual areas may require systems that indicate something negative may be occurring. This is accomplished by using alarms that make a loud noise or send a message to a supervisor's station or an administrative office. Alarms most often signal inappropriate access, fire, and theft. Some alarms can be connected to a telephone line that alerts outside support such as fire departments, police, and security companies.

Whether an existing system is upgraded, a new one created, or security details implemented, such responsibilities must be based on the facility's circumstances. The information just presented should assist in the identification of basic concepts involved in facility security.

Development

One of the greatest opportunities for a recreational sport specialist is the opportunity to influence the development of a new facility or major renovation. This effort may involve many years and stages of development. The following information will prove useful when recreational sport specialists face a challenge of this nature. Conveying detailed information of what is involved represents a book in itself. The following is a synopsis of the different stages of facility development, from the initial assessment of limitations to the opening ceremonies.

Assessment

The first step in facility development is gaining an accurate idea of areas or spaces that affect program delivery. Whether existing facilities need improvement or no facility currently exists, certain factors can help to identify limitations and enhance progress. Such an effort is often referred to as a needs assessment or feasibility study and involves gathering information to demonstrate the need for construction or improvement. Facility limitations are used to create the list of needs.

Need factors. In conducting an assessment, certain factors should be taken into account to help determine the condition of and satisfaction with existing facilities or the interest for nonexistent facilities. Observe in Figure 13.16 the different assessment factors that can be involved in gathering assessment information. Each factor has varying degrees of importance depending on the nature of the recreational sport facility under consideration.

Influencing support. Once an assessment has been conducted and the results justify the need, the next step to moving the project forward is to gain appropriate administrative support using the techniques shown in Figure 13.17. These techniques can be used to gather information and data that demonstrate interest, commitment, and the potential for partial or full funding from administration or potential benefactors. Each technique should be carefully planned and applied. Take necessary precautions to build objectivity into the influencing process.

Another option that could be applied in the assessment stage is a final written proposal representing pertinent information that supports facility construction. This special proposal is described in more detail in Chapter 15. It has proven to be extremely effective when trying to influence busy administrators and potential supporters.

Safety: Does the facility meet safety requirements.

Satisfaction: Does the facility or lack of one negatively impact user fulfillment?

Participation: Does the facility negatively affect the number of participants that desire use?

Efficiency: How much more efficient would your sport activity be with a new or improved facility?

Comparison: Does your competition have a better facility?

Modernization: Does your outdated facility negatively affect success and what technological limitations exist?

Laws: Are there any laws or codes not being met or broken because of your facility?

Figure 13.16. Factors Used in Facility Assessment

Visitation: Take key administrators to see a successfully functioning facility to help them realize shortcomings back home.

Expressed Opinions: Document facility users and workers opinions which express problems and concerns that reflect the need for facility improvement.

Survey: Conduct a formal internal and/or external survey(s) to provide data that will objectively demonstrate comparative facts of support.

Opinion Poll: Solicit opinions about the need for a facility through interviews or phone calls and have an objective system for doing so.

Petitions: Have a statement of support for a facility and get signatures and phone numbers that demonstrate the validity and support of signer.

Figure 13.17. Techniques Used to Influence Support

Planning

Although the assessment stage is necessary to get started, nothing is more important than the actual planning. This stage is where ideas for solving the problems or limitations of the facility begin to take shape. Planning is systematic anticipation of all facility needs. This anticipation includes documentation that brings forward information that will eventually go into the project. The following section touches on key points in the planning stage.

Approaches. A great deal of planning for a facility is based on the nature of the agency as well as management's philosophy on how to solve problems. To help the recreational sport specialist understand what this means, two general approaches will be described. First is the *administrative* approach, observed in the private sector, in which key executives make all planning decisions. In this approach, subordinates may be involved, but high-level administrators address all technical information and priority decisions.

The second option is the *participant* approach, which is usually observed in public settings where tax dollars and mandatory fees are a critical part of fiscal support. In this process, a cross-section of users and nonusers is involved in the project in an advisory capacity. In public settings, user involvement is often required in obtaining support to sustain the project.

Planners. When it comes to facility planning, involving key user and management representatives can prove valuable. They are often highly motivated because they recognize limitations and problems, and in many cases, they bring a facility expertise that

is not otherwise available. Figure 13.18 provides a look at individuals commonly involved in a planning team.

Project statement. One of the vital elements produced by this planning team is a written project statement that describes specific information for the architect, giving direction about space needs and serving as a transitional document from planning to design. This document evolves from both the assessment and the early planning efforts and is the first formal step in facility development. The more detailed and clear this statement is, the easier it is for the architect to translate intention into the facility design. Figure 13.19 presents information that should be covered in a project statement.

Design

At the design stage, considerable information has been gathered, interests have been identified, and the idea of developing a facility has gained momentum. Relevant details are brought together and integrated into documents that diagram and describe what is to be developed. Understanding what takes place during the design stage is important for recreational sport specialists because most help can occur directly or indirectly with the facility design effort.

Design team. The design team usually evolves from the previously mentioned planning team to a formal group that stays with the project through completion. The data compiled during the planning stage will guide the design team in creating the design documents. Because design is so important, those involved have a tremendous responsibility not only to create a desired facility but also to meet legal and

Administrator/Owner: Individual involved with the big picture or master plan for the future and responsible for the ultimate cost.

Consultant: Outside expert that assists with providing concepts, ideas and alternatives plus helps with establishing cost and design priority decisions.

Sport Activity Representative: Employee (s) who is (are) specifically involved with day to day delivery and programming responsibilities.

User Representative: A person (s) very familiar with the facility as a user and enthusiastic supporter

Maintenance Representative: Person that is crucial but often left out in providing input on routine and non-routine maintenance needs as well as important space information.

Figure 13.18. Early Stage Project Planners

Objective: Description of the anticipated outcome of the facility to include the primary core product delivery areas and their ultimate benefits.

Basic Assumption: Statement citing how the facility will solve the problems and weaknesses that exist or present new opportunities

Trends: Statement that reflects how things in society are changing and how those changes affect demand for the sport activity(s).

Primary Space: List of names of the various spaces being planned, along with size of areas specific functions related to each.

Auxiliary Space: List of the name and sizes for the core product extension space including requirements for the area as well as specialized equipment.

Space Relations: Description of how all the areas of a facility will relate to each other that includes an explanation for flow and movement of users.

Environmental Necessities: Description of the general area or location and impact that the facility will have on the area and surrounding environment.

Figure 13.19. Project Statement Information

technical requirements. The design team is usually made up of an administrator, owner, program representative, or some combination thereof; a construction manager; a user representative; a maintenance representative; and a consultant, possibly carried forward from the planning process. New at this stage is the architect. The architect ultimately assumes all responsibilities for facility design. The design team works together in a cooperative and professional fashion to bring the project to reality under the leadership of the architect.

Administrative role. Recreational sport specialists might find themselves working with the administration to represent specific and critical information in the project design. Because the facility is being built for management, this representation is significant. As a member of the design team, the administrator makes many, if not all, of the key decisions. Figure 13.20 shows that the role of the administrator or representative carries many responsibilities.

Meetings: Attending many meetings, plus helping to organize and plan the agenda with the architect.

Commitment: Being dedicated to the project and demonstrating enthusiasm about its value.

Authority: Being in charge with a quality that requires listening to all interests and points of view so as to make fair and accurate judgments.

Coordination: Receiving and coordinate the varied users' interests and represent them in an objective fashion.

Timing: Monitoring everything from management's perspective to avoid unnecessary time loss that can cause problems and added expenses.

Detail Discussion: Having the ability to realize, analyze, and discuss the sport activity's (product) details as they relate to the facility.

Cost: Relating preliminary construction estimates to all the product design areas and related equipment.

Quality Control: Functioning as a "watch dog" to make sure that all assessment and planning information is properly incorporated in the design.

Figure 13.20. Administrator Role in the Design Team

Topics. During the design process, the design team discusses certain essential topics. Each team member should research the topics in advance as they look to give direction and guidance to the architect. Some of the discussions involve preliminary cost estimates, often referred to as ballpark figures, which are provided by the architect. The project statement is reviewed to make sure all details are accurate. The project schedule is discussed and a timetable established. Certain permits for the project must be obtained at this stage. Obtaining permits can be time consuming, especially when political problems and local interests complicate the process. Facility location influences major design discussions as well; items to be addressed include how the site works, the project's effect on the site, land preparations and area access, and utility availability and requirements. Structure needs have to be identified (size, shape, height, square footage), and the different types of materials to be used in the project, both interior and exterior, need to be reviewed. Mechanical systems must be discussed, including the expertise of architects and special engineers in making sure these systems are designed properly. At some point, discussions are held regarding equipment and furniture. Finally, finishes, signage, and acoustical considerations are discussed. All of these topics require tremendous attention to

detail and a willingness to make suggestions so that the best information is available for decision making.

Schematics. The design stage includes a preliminary representation of the project, a project statement, and site plans that reflect actual details and are presented by the architect in the form of a schematic drawing and a scale model. The schematic drawing is a sketch of the facility that shows its core product and core-product extensions with all areas diagrammed, including walls, rooms, stairwells, corridors, outside topography, landscaping, and access roads. This drawing represents only a few of the actual project details and is sometimes referred to as a footprint because it shows how the facility is laid out in the overall site.

With large projects, a scale model is built that shows the facility at the site. This tabletop model provides an accurate rendition of what the finished facility will look like. Schematics can prove valuable in creating support for the project and bringing insight to the design team's discussions.

Design Documents

Although facility projects can differ greatly in location, size, shape, and expense, all projects require design documents. These documents create a formal system of communication between the architect, the design team, and the construction contractor. They are expected to be accurate, providing detailed information. The following is an overview of the two common document systems: blueprints and specification books.

Blueprints. Blueprints serve as a road map, allowing the architect to communicate with the construction contractors. Blueprints act as a formal construction guide, detailing how the facility should be built. It is important for recreational sport specialists to learn how to read blueprints so they can help in the construction effort by giving detailed information about areas and space that architects often do not have. Understanding the specific components (title block, viewable sections, direction indicator, scale, notes, keys) that make up a blueprint can seem difficult at first, but with a little effort they become routine. Blueprints have varying degrees of detail depending on the extensiveness of the project. Figure 13.21 presents a list of different blueprints.

Specification books. Another way of communicating details to the contractors is through specification documents or "spec books," which are written details that describe everything contained within the blueprints. These documents are not always used, especially with small projects where all communication is through blueprints. Specifications are used

first in the bid process for forming cost estimates, and then they are used by primary contractors, subcontractors, and vendors because they spell out the details that represent the architect's and design team's expectations.

Codes and laws. One of the key responsibilities of the design process is making sure the design follows legal requirements. These requirements take the form of laws, codes, standards, and local ordinances that architects must be aware of and follow in the design of the facility. Specific information must be accurately incorporated into the design documents. If such information is missing or neglected, the architect and engineers can be held liable. Administrators and owners strongly depend on the expert advice of architects and engineers when dealing with code or law compliance issues.

Construction

After all the time spent on planning and design, nothing is more exciting than seeing these efforts come together in the final construction stage. It is a demanding stage requiring a great deal of coordination and effort to meet all design details. Demand increases with the size of the project under construction. There are two major parts to this stage that need explanation: funding and construction management.

Site: Represents the lay of the land, elevation, and everything about the area.

Demolition/Preparation: The design that will lead to the leveling of some land areas and raising of others for the site.

Structural: Main drawing that shows the specific areas and related detail that will house the core product and core product extensions.

Mechanical: Includes anything that is mechanical in the facility, including plumbing, heat air condition, ventilation, and drainage.

Electrical: The detailed diagram involving all electrical work

Landscape: Diagrams the detail on all exterior and ground surrounding a facility, including; lawn, trees, shrubs, etc.

Structural equipment: Shows all attached equipment necessary to the production of the product and auxiliary needs.

Finish Plan: Guide or chart that cites detailed finishes for all areas of the facility. Also known as the "finish schedule".

Figure 13.21. Design Blueprints

Funding. Funding is dealt with throughout the entire development process. It is necessary to have a sense of the cost of everything being designed. Funding is finalized in the construction stage. Construction cannot take place unless there is an understanding of the specific costs involved. Every aspect of the project relates to a dollar amount.

Sources. Because funding is so important, sources that finance the project are critical to project implementation. Administrators can draw from a variety of funding sources, depending on agency type, political support, priorities, and so on. Examples of sources are presented in Figure 13.22. Each of these options can be used exclusively or in combination to fund the total costs of construction.

Costs. Understanding the project cost, construction cost, and budget can be complicated and even confusing at first. Once recreational sport specialists understand the costs, however, they will be able to assist in budget decisions. Figure 13.23 illustrates the two areas involved in budgeting: hard costs and soft costs.

Bid process. Before construction begins, a contractor or company must be hired to build the facility. Special attention should go into finding the best company for the best price in order to end up with the best facility. In a private setting, a contractor can be chosen by the administration. However, it is recom-

mended in all settings and required in public settings that a bid process be followed to ensure equal opportunity for all interested parties to bid on a project. Usually, this process takes place over three to six weeks, with blueprints and specification books made available to all qualified contractors. The resulting bids and cost estimates are kept confidential so that each contractor bids independently. Bidding creates competition with pricing, also known as project quotes. The bid process entails a formal letting of the bid, an announced timetable, and a public opening of the bids with the lowest bidder almost always receiving the contract for the project. Construction quotes can be presented as a lump sum, a fixed price, separate bids, or special alternates (parts of the project that are bid separately for later inclusion if funding allows). The bid process should be fair, avoiding bias or conflict of interest.

Contract arrangements. After selecting the contractor, administrators, architects, and the contractor come together to work on the project costs and details. With a bond (a percentage of the project cost) in place to guarantee the contractor's commitment to the project, formal conversations, called value engineering, are held. These conversations ensure that all design details are interpreted properly. The design team works with the contractor to solve problems. During this time, all insurance and financing arrange-

---

Mandatory Fees: A fee charged to all individuals using the agencies and its product(s). A portion of it can be designed to fund a facility's new construction, renovation, or repair

Tax Levy: A portion of the tax dollars collected are used to fund a specific facility project. This type of funding requires community support and may take years to evolve.

User Fees: Source of funding which comes from patrons, customers, participants, etc., who pay for the facility's core product.

Bond Issue: Raising funds by issuing tax exempt bonds for the general public to buy with a return of the principle plus interest after a certain period of time.

Donations/ Contributions: Finding from supportive individuals who have special and/or invested interest resulting from a past involved with the agency.

In-Kind Gifts: Contractors provide labor and/or materials in exchange for a tax deduction or tax write-off.

Grants: Funds provided by the government, private, institutions, or foundation that usually requires a formal proposal prior to the award.

Sponsorships: Outside groups or administration will provide funds so that their company, corporation, or business receives special recognition.

Assessment: An arrangement to create funds based on a number of specific payments as it relates to the project cost.

Figure 13.22. Funding Sources for Facility Projects

Hard Costs: Expenses that represent fixed or permanent considerations and costs that are directly linked to the construction process.
Examples:

> **Construction** – Quantity of material 'x', quality of material & labor
> **Construction Management** – Team that oversees construction
> **Furniture** – All items to be placed in a facility (chairs, tables, desks, etc.)
> **Equipment** – Items/objects that are attached or not attached which contribute to all aspects of operation
> **Signage** – All attached directional indicators

Soft Costs: Expenses that are necessary to get a project started and designed properly, as well as meeting any extended or unexpected costs that might be encountered.
Examples:

> **Architectural Fees** – Contracted amount for architectural services
> **Engineering Fees** – Amount paid to engineers for review of design details
> **Consultant Fees** - Costs for those hired as part of the planning and design team for their extensive experience
> **Permit Fees** – Standard, pre-determined fees for local requirements that must be obtained prior to the construction.
> **Reimbursables** – Amount paid to architects, consultants, and engineers for any costs outside of the direct project costs.
> **Contingencies** – An amount set aside for potential problems, emergencies or unexpected/unplanned situations that develop.

Figure 13.23. Construction Costs

ments are reviewed. Some projects have special pricing arrangements, incentives, or maximum amounts, which all need to be understood due to fluctuations in the economy. Contract arrangements require the talent and ability of experts, especially when complicated projects are involved. When all parties realize their responsibilities, the signing of a formal contract takes place, which allows construction to commence.

Management. Because administrators and architects have limited expertise or trained ability when it comes to construction, acquiring formal assistance is a common practice and is recommended for extensive projects. Companies are available for hire that bring the expertise needed to oversee all aspects of a construction project from beginning to end. This process is called construction management, and it involves a contractual arrangement with a company that will protect the interests of the owner and the architect to ensure that all aspects of the project (supervision of contractors and subcontractors, project timetable, problems) and its requirements (codes, laws, standards) are accomplished in a timely and satisfactory fashion.

Responsibilities. With construction management taking over responsibility for the project, administrators and owners often find themselves in a position of observing and providing advice as needed. Construction managers have the knowledge to supervise, review, and control all aspects of construction. Figure 13.24 provides a brief summary of the details that are involved.

Final stage. The final stage of construction can be complicated because everyone is anxious not only to finish but also to make sure the end result is what was intended. This stage can be demanding due to the many details and finishing schedule requirements that are described in Figure 13.25. Each detail represents specialized work that requires timing and coordination between construction management, contractors, and vendors of finished materials.

As part of the final stage, construction management creates what is called a "punch list." This list documents all late work as well as work that must be completed before the project can be accepted. As corrections are made and work is completed, they are taken off the list, but only after formal inspection and final approval by construction management.

Ceremonies

Most facility projects involve two types of ceremonies. The first, the groundbreaking, takes place just before construction. This event provides public recognition for all those involved in getting the

Meetings: All aspects of the project are discussed and reviewed in detail, especially the examination of existing or potential problems.

Coordination: Special attention is given to make sure everything is done in a timely fashion, to keep things progressing as planned while avoiding conflicts.

Schedule: This effort reflects every phase of the project with specific dates.

Quality Check: Monitor contractor's work to identify poor workmanship and problems, and then take the necessary steps for correction.

Interpret Requirements: Interpret code and law details making sure everything is done accurately and meets specific design requirements.

Inspection: Work cooperatively with formal inspectors, recognizing that they could show up unannounced.

Changes: Coordinate any construction changes between contractors and architects with the administrators and design team.

Site Security: Help keep all areas safe with use of barriers, signs, and special guards if necessary.

Visitation: Organize and control special interests for visitation.

Owner/Operator Training: Organize training sessions to make sure administrators and management representatives learn what they need to know to operate certain facility areas as well as equipment.

Maintenance Manuals: Provide administrator/manager maintenance manuals that give details on how to care for certain areas of the facility and equipment.

Figure 13.24. Construction Management

Finishes: Represents the many details including; paint, light fixtures, doors, windows ceilings and floor coverings.

Keying: Securing facility from inappropriate access. May include keys and locks, combination locks, magnetic strip cards, bar code cards, etc.

Signage: Linking all facility areas to each other with visual directional signage.

Furniture/Equipment: All items that are brought to the facility are coordinated with the vendor and administrator by construction management in the most cooperative and effective way possible.

Security: Installing all protective equipment to include fire and door alarms, cameras and monitors, special lighting, etc.

Figure 13.25. Final Stages of Construction

project formally started and approved. The ceremony usually includes the actual act of shoveling dirt at the site to symbolize the start of construction. Ground-breaking ceremonies typically include speeches expressing the positive aspects of the project, donor or sponsor appreciation, and media coverage to keep members informed about the project.

At the completion of construction, another celebration, the opening ceremony, is conducted. This ceremony creates an opportunity for administrators and owners to publicly thank everyone involved as well as promote the facility. The opening ceremony includes speakers and a ribbon cutting. It also allows for media coverage, tours, and in some cases the presentation of commemorative gifts to those who played important roles in the project.

Facility development can be exciting and rewarding, but there are many details that need to be realized. To some extent, such tasks might entail a whole new career for a period of time. There may be plenty of help available from consultants, architects, engineers, and construction managers, but few will be more involved than the recreational sport specialist. This chapter provides a foundation from which recreational sport specialists can feel confident to deal with any facility development projects that may occur in their career.

Shining Example

RDV Sportsplex, Orlando, Florida

RDV Sportsplex is a large multi-sport complex located in Orlando, Florida. Its mission is to enhance the lives of individuals and families in our community through exercise, sports and recreation, by providing world-class service, facilities and programs all within an environment of active fun. In addition to providing facilities for recreational sports and fitness, RDV Sportsplex hosts the facilities for Orlando's professional basketball team, the Orlando Magic. In a joint venture with Florida Hospital, RDV Sportsplex offers rehabilitation and wellness services.

Clientele:

RDV Sportsplex serves approximately 1,000,000 participants per year (approximately 82,600 per month). That number includes members of the Sportsplex Athletic Club and participants at the Ice Den as well as customers from Florida Hospital and other, smaller entities within the Sportsplex. The Athletic Club membership is comprised primarily of individuals aged 18 years and older (55% male and 45% female). Approximately 10% is comprised of youth aged 13-18 (63% male and 37% female), and 20% is comprised of children aged 13 years of age or younger (57% male and 43% female). The last 5% of the membership is composed of individuals aged 60 years or older (44% male and 56% female).

Facilities:

The RDV Sportsplex is made up of many facilities. The Athletic Club contains over 450 pieces of strength-training and cardiovascular equipment, an Olympic sized pool, two NBA-sized basketball courts, four exercise studios, a multisport gym, Kid's Stuff (programming for kids), and a professional-athlete training room. In addition, it has men's and women's locker rooms, racquetball and squash courts, an outdoor volleyball court, a full-sized basketball court and a half-court, a tennis center, and an aquatics center. The Ice Den boasts two ice rinks (one NHL size and one Olympic-sized), along with a concession stand and skate rental. The latest addition to the RDV Sportsplex Athletic Club is the state-of-the-art Sports Performance Center. On site Florida Hospital facilities include Florida Hospital Rehabilitation and Sports Medicine, Jewett Orthopedic, Pediatrics, Central Care Executive Services and, Advanced Dental Wellness. In addition, there is a full-service salon and spa, three pro-shops, and facilities for the Orlando Magic basketball team.

Program Details:

In its pledge to offer a wide variety of activities and a fun environment for individuals, families, and professional athletes RDV Sportsplex offers many programs including personal training, fitness and wellness programs for children and adults, summer camps, public and private swimming and skating lessons, and rehabilitation and health care services. The new Sports Performance Center offers Parisi Speed School. This is a performance enhancing sports training program designed to maximize the physical and mental potential of athletes. Nationwide, the Parisi Speed School has trained more than 40,000 athletes.

Marketing:

Marketing for RDV Sportsplex is divided into four areas: Athletic Club marketing, Ice Den marketing, group sales and events marketing, and communications. The mediums used include direct mailings, radio sponsorship, television advertising, an annual 5K race, and a quarterly magazine produced in-house containing editorial and programming information. In addition, the RDV Sportsplex maintains several websites, such as www.rdvsportsplex.com.

Jobs and Careers:

The RDV Sportsplex has approximately 150 full- and part-time employees. The Orlando Magic corporate offices, which are housed within the Sportsplex, have approximately 300 employees and a separate human resources department. Job and career opportunities available at the Sportsplex include full- and part-time positions in all aspects of the facility from service desk to personal trainers to administration. Management positions include directors, managers, team leaders, coordinators.

Internship:

There are internship positions available through the Orlando Magic in areas such as marketing, game operations, media relations, community relations, and corporate sales.

Affiliated Professional Organizations:

Personal trainers at RDV Sportsplex hold certifications from the American College of Sports Medicine (ACSM), American Physical Therapy Association (APTA), National Academy of Sports Medicine (NASM), National Athletic Trainers Association (NATA), and the National Strength and Conditioning Association (NSCA).

▶ **Computer Tip**

Facility Reservation Software

Each agency has its own needs, constraints, facilities, and levels of staff and financial support. All of these factors must be taken into consideration before a reservation system can be effectively computerized. The goals of any facility reservation system should be identified to maximize the use of available facilities and to provide all staff with instant access to accurate information regarding site availability.

Facility reservation programs

* automatically assign a unique reservation confirmation number;
* allow reactivation of canceled reservations;
* track deposit transactions;
* allow overbooking of a site by a certain percentage by season or month ;
* calculate the estimated total charge for advanced reservations;
* allow for additions, changes, cancellations, report printing, and reactivation;
* duplicate user information from one reservation to another;
* accommodate special requests and comments for each reservation;
* print billing information by site and user;
* track complaint and problem maintenance for each site and track preventative maintenance performed by each site's supervisors and users;
* identify all resources needed to manage scheduled events or sessions, and
* accept facility and equipment reservations via the Internet.

Reservation modules should also have the ability to

* display sites available for booking during any range of dates,
* display a particular site,
* display user groups by summer or by details,
* block or unblock a site by user group,
* show all reservations assigned to a particular site,
* show all sites assigned to a specific reservation,
* display total sites reserved versus total sites available for any date,
* display the total number of sites reserved by user type per day,
* display all facilities reserved for a specific date and time, and
* forecast facility availability.

Finally, many recreational sport specialists who reserve facilities are often called upon to counsel inexperienced individuals using the facilities. Examples of counseling range from recommending how to conduct sport events to how to schedule tournaments. An effective computerized facility reservation system should provide ways to monitor facility counseling sessions and checklists. This not only protects you legally, but also allows users to have safe and enjoyable experiences at the facility.

Conclusion

Operating a facility is an expansive, important responsibility. The purpose of this chapter was to show the details involved in overseeing and developing facilities. Recreational sport specialists may only interact with facilities in the delivery of programs, with a small percentage of time spent on facility management and development. Understanding and appreciating the information presented in this chapter is the beginning of acquiring a wide range of interests that can serve to expand a recreational sport specialist's role. Some recreational sport complexes entrust recreational sport specialists with the responsibility of making sure that the facilities work properly.

Bibliography

Ammon, R., Southall, R. M., & Nagel, M. S. (2010). *Sport facility management: Organizing events and mitigating risks* (2nd ed.). Morgantown, WV: Fitness Information Technology.

Brauer, R. L. (1992). *Facilities planning: The user requirements method* (2nd ed.). New York, NY: American Management Association.

Brown, M. T. (2000). *Financial administration of sport facilities and programs*. North Chelmsford, MA: Courier Custom.

Cotts, D. G. (2010). *The facility management handbook* (2nd ed.). New York, NY: AMACOM.

Flynn, R. B. (1993). *Facility planning for physical education, recreation, and athletics*. Reston, VA: American Alliance for Health, Physical Education, Recreation, and Dance.

Fried, G., Shapiro, S. J., & DeSchriver, T. D. (2008). *Sport finance*. Champaign, IL: Human Kinetics.

Gil, F. (2010). *Managing sport facilities* (2nd ed.). Champaign, IL: Human Kinetics.

Mull, R. F., Beggs, B. A., & Renneisen, M. (2009). *Recreation facility management: Design, development, operations, and utilization*. Champaign, IL: Human Kinetics.

National Intramural–Recreational Sports Association. (2006). *Managing the collegiate recreational facility*. Champaign, IL: Human Kinetics.

Petersen, D. C. (1996). *Sports, convention, and entertainment facilities*. Washington, DC: Urban Land Institute.

Sawyer, T. H. (Ed.). (2002). *Facilities planning for health, fitness, physical activity, recreation and sports: Concepts and applications* (10th ed.). Urbana, IL: Sagamore.

Sayers, P. (1991). *Managing sport and leisure facilities: A guide to competitive tendering*. New York, NY: Routledge.

Walker, M. L., & Stotlar, D. K. (1997). *Sports facility management*. Champaign, IL: Human Kinetics.

CHAPTER 14

Equipment

CHAPTER OBJECTIVES

After reading this chapter, you will appreciate the importance and role of equipment; understand the equipment purchasing process; comprehend the stages of systemizing equipment; realize the ramifications of equipment storage, utilization, and maintenance; be able to identify the critical aspects of equipment checkout and rental services; and understand the continuance of equipment services in equipment sales.

KEY CONCEPTS

Research	**Receiving**
Special proposal	**Inventory**
Purchase request	**Storage**
Bid process	**Utilization**
Purchase order	**Maintenance**
Delivery	**Checkout and rental systems**
Invoice	**Sale**
Warranty	

Introduction

The use of equipment as a resource may seem simple at first, but nothing could be further from the truth. Equipment can involve staggering numbers and cost as well as sophisticated technology. Equipment acquisition, distribution, and stewardship are distinctive procedures that the recreational sport specialist needs to master. This chapter provides a descriptive overview of equipment, the purchasing process, its use and control, delivery options as a service, and the sale of equipment as a source of income.

Overview

Defining equipment can be challenging, especially as it relates to the numerous management settings and operating functions of recreational sport agencies. Equipment can best be described as items, mechanical and otherwise, that are necessary for all aspects of administrative and delivery operations. This description is a liberal approach that includes alternative items along with traditional equipment. This section will review the extensiveness of equipment by discussing challenges, alternative items, and how such variety can be classified.

Extensiveness

Equipment is extensive due to the unique purpose of all the different items. The role of equipment can be demonstrated in discussing a few of the challenges it offers as well as alternative items that incorporate equipment into the overall management process.

Challenges. Most equipment is easy to use, requiring little or no instruction or preparation before its use. However, other equipment is so complex that its use requires technical knowledge, placing greater responsibility with owners and users. Challenges include difficult instructions, warranty requirements, laws and codes that must be observed, a detailed purchasing process, distribution and control, and maintenance needs.

Another challenge that reflects the extensiveness of equipment is its actual use. Some equipment requires a great deal of training, even certification prior to use. Administration must be aware of such requirements because improper use can be dangerous, causing harm, injury, or even death. Every precaution should be taken to ensure that users of such equipment realize the potential danger through proper notification and training. The more dangerous the equipment, the greater the challenge it poses.

Equipment condition and location must be known at all times. Because equipment affects all elements of operations, a monitoring system should be in place. Someone not only needs to be responsible for condition and location but also must be attentive to equipment status. Items need to be available and functioning. This is a challenging responsibility for the recreational sport specialist who accepts the role of monitoring equipment.

Alternative items. If equipment is defined as all items, mechanical or otherwise, then there are other considerations that need to be mentioned. Such items are administrative and delivery equipment designed to serve overall production success. Although these particular items are in a category of their own, they are included in this overview to demonstrate that they require the same responsibilities as other traditionally recognized equipment.

Supplies. Supplies are an identity unto themselves. They are expendable items that include office supplies (paper, staples, paper clips, pens), maintenance supplies (toilet paper, paper towels, soap, trash liners), and any other items of short duration. Supplies exist in the same fashion as other equipment; however, they do not represent nearly the cost to the administration. Their existence parallels that of equipment as it relates to purchasing, receiving, inventorying, storing, use, and replacement, which will be explained in greater detail later in the chapter.

Keys. All recreational sport facilities need to be secured in order to prevent unwanted use, possible damage, theft, vandalism, and so on. This responsibility on the administration includes keys that have different styles, systems, and sizes. Looking at keys as equipment is easy to understand; their responsibility again parallels the responsibility required for other equipment. Whether it is a traditional key and lock or a bar-code system with plastic key cards,

there is a procedure for planning, designing, purchasing, and recording keys with regular monitoring to assess status. Keying can be a complicated process and involves special expertise. However, the objects themselves require similar responsibilities as other equipment.

Furniture. Still another alternative equipment consideration is furniture. Although furniture is usually purchased in the last stage of facility development or during a remodeling or replacement project, it still goes through the same sequence that brings other equipment to a facility. Such equipment includes office desks and chairs, conference tables, sofas, coffee tables, and end tables. Furniture may require maintenance or repair after abuse or overuse, just the same as regular equipment.

Protective items. Some recreational sport settings require equipment to protect employees and participants as well as the facility and its equipment. Such protective measures help with surveillance (cameras, lighting), access control (turnstiles, barriers, identification readers), and fire protection (alarms, exit doors, smoke detectors). Like all equipment, this protective equipment is assessed regularly and repaired and replaced. In many situations, protective equipment is a serious responsibility within overall operations.

Decorative items. Virtually all recreational facilities have decorative items that help make areas attractive. Plants, pictures, statues, flower arrangements, and other items energize the environment, creating a pleasantness that helps everyone feel comfortable. The responsibility involved in decorative equipment parallels that of all other equipment. Decorations, too, are brought to a facility, maintained, and replaced as necessary.

Signage. Another form of equipment is facility signage, which helps users know where they are and how to get where they want to go. Usually signage is created in the late stages of facility construction or renovation. However, signage can be changed and put through the equipment process at any time. Signage considerations include an overall plan for color scheme, design, lettering style, level, and location; purchasing; and installation. Examples of signage include freestanding directories, directional signs, floor and wall guides, individual room and area signs, and announcement systems. Like any other equipment, signage can be changed, repaired, or replaced in order to meet its intended application.

Clothing and uniforms. Finally, and least often considered as equipment, is clothing and uniforms. Almost everything about these items parallels traditionally recognized equipment. Clothing and uniforms necessitate a unique responsibility in dealing with size, color, style, design, and other details that require assistance from the manufacturer or vendor. Such items may be sold in a pro shop, checked out, or rented for seasonal use. Clothing and uniforms, like other equipment, contribute to the overall enhancement of the recreational sport effort.

Now that items not commonly considered as equipment have been introduced, the expansiveness of this resource area should be apparent. It is hoped that through this brief description the recreational sport specialist will recognize that these items are used much the same way as items that are more commonly thought of as equipment.

Classifications

Fundamental to understanding equipment as a resource is knowing how equipment is organized into a system. A sound system for organizing equipment prevents confusion and loss. Two general classifications for equipment are types and categories.

Types. There are three types of equipment in management operations. These types are a means to identify equipment and classify their function for budget purposes. The first type is *permanent equipment*, which has a cost of more than $500 and a life expectancy of two or more years. This type of equipment can be expensive and is also called capital equipment. It is not affixed or attached to the facility, but it is necessary for the core product and core-product extensions to operate. Because of the expense involved with this equipment, its use and financial planning should be given special attention before purchase. Permanent equipment almost always requires special maintenance because of initial and continual operational costs. Examples of this type of equipment include cash registers, court sweepers, typewriters, golf carts, computers, and ball machines.

The second type of equipment is *expendable equipment*. It requires periodic replacement, costs less than $500, and has a life expectancy of less than two years. Expendable equipment mostly relates to program delivery and is used with the expectation that it will be broken, worn out, or possibly lost within that 2-year period. This equipment requires a great deal of attention to its condition because when it breaks down, it may negatively affect the recreational sport experience. Examples of such equipment include balls, bats, rackets, kickboards, and whistles.

The final type of equipment is *fixed equipment.* These items are permanently attached or fixed as part of the structure and are usually installed during the construction phase. They are facility fixtures, and their removal can negatively affect the facility's appearance and functionality. Fixed equipment is designed as part of the overall environment and brings convenience and comfort for users and workers. It includes heating, ventilating, and air conditioning (HVAC) hardware, basketball backstops, tennis nets and posts, and volleyball posts and nets.

Categories

Another way of classifying equipment is to describe it as it relates to various categories in overall management. Equipment complements different areas and functions, allowing for a system that can help with identification, inventory, and location.

One category of equipment is *structural*. Structural equipment is not removable, and its elimination would negatively affect the design and functionality of facility operations. This category includes doors, windows, railings, permanent barriers, and permanent seating.

Another category is equipment used in the *operating systems* of an indoor or outdoor facility. These systems for indoor facilities include air conditioning, heating, lighting, and ventilation, and systems for outdoor facilities include irrigation systems, lighting, and sprinklers. This equipment creates functional efficiency for users, and it is usually installed during construction and requires special technical ability to operate and maintain.

Equipment that supports *administrative* and executive responsibilities is another category. This equipment is not involved with recreational sport participation unless it is related to interaction with administration through registration, sign-up, and promotion. Such equipment includes all office, lobby, and reception furniture, as well as computers, printers, telephone, file cabinets, cash registers, calculators, fax machines, copy machines, typewriters, brochures, audiovisual technology, literature stands, and displays.

Another category is *delivery* or *programming equipment* relating to specific sports. The recreational sport specialist is very involved with this equipment because it enhances program delivery. This equipment varies greatly, and some equipment requires special training and precautionary measures.

Finally, *maintenance* has its own category of equipment. This equipment includes those items outside the structural and operational categories that more specifically relate to maintenance. Some of its use requires specialized training and even certification for use. Such equipment includes vehicles, rakes, brooms, mops, shovels, chainsaws, leaf blowers, and more expensive equipment such as floor and court sweepers, machine scrubbers, buffing machines, and pool-cleaning robots.

The recreational sport specialist needs to recognize the importance of equipment because each piece represents a cost and responsibility. Its existence is extensive, requiring an appreciation of how it challenges responsibilities with inherent details and classification

Purchasing

Items have to be purchased before they can fulfill a function. The following material provides a description of the steps involved in the purchasing of equipment.

Research

Equipment under consideration for purchase may require advance review in order to determine the best option available. This process involves researching a piece of equipment, assessing its potential to meet predetermined expectations, and making sure it is within funding parameters. This is often a responsibility of recreational sport specialists because they have firsthand insight to equipment and what is needed. Figure 14.1 lists the points of information that should be considered during research. Research is a key stewardship responsibility, especially when a major purchase is involved.

Special Proposal

Decision making can be aided by a written proposal, especially with expensive equipment and large-quantity purchases where high costs are involved. This proposal presents supportive information that can help persuade administrators to recognize a purchase need. Never underestimate administrators' distractions and other priorities. By using this proposal concept, a recreational sport specialist could gain much-needed support. It is logical to use a system that presents meaningful and well-thought-out information to persuade others that equipment is needed. Figure 14.2 is a sample equipment-purchase proposal, including key headings and a brief description of what could be included in such a proposal. This same technique can also be used in obtaining support for a facility development project.

Purchase Request

In most cases, the purchase request is the most common way to obtain administrative attention regarding a request for equipment. This effort could follow a special proposal and may even be a requirement. Figure 14.3 shows the information found in a purchase request, including type, size, model, cost, quantity, vendor, and delivery timetable. This form could also be used for in-house purchases and requests for petty cash.

I. **STYLE**
    Name
    Model
    Size
    Color

II. **RELATED DETAILS**

    Demand for use (utilization)
    Use expectation
    Wear/tear (durability)
    Risk (liability)
    Safety concerns
    Instruction/training
    Warranty
    Maintenance
    Storage
    Resale

III. **FEASIBILITY**

    Facts to support
    Logical/reasoning to support
    Benefits

IV. **FISCAL IMPLICATIONS**

    Estimate
    Unit price
    Shipping/handling
    Maintenance cost
    Budget impact
    Affordability

V. **VENDOR REVIEW**

    Options
    History
    Reputation
    Delivery
    Timetable

VI. **SAVINGS POTENTIAL**

    Discount
    Quantity break
    Sales
    Financing
    Payment options
    Bidding

VII. **GENERAL CONSIDER-ATIONS**

    Luxury versus necessity
    Used versus new
    Rent versus lease

Figure 14.1. Research Inquiry Considerations

Need/Title – Identifies what is wanted or needed, including very specific name and brief statement.

Recommendation – Formal statement of what is wanted.

Introduction – Provide overview of what the document will contain and what is to be accomplished to create awareness of the forthcoming content.

Rationale – Logical points of information. Provide objective points to support the equipment purchase as well as fundamental reasons behind the need.

Justification – The statement of facts that demonstrates/illustrates data to support the purchase.

Funding – Provide implications from a fiscal point of view. Include income and expenditure figures showing how the purchase works as it relates to funding.

Impact – Share the potential outcome, effect, impression, result and future benefit resulting from the purchase.

Conclusion – Summary restating recommendation and most influential points to support the purchase.

Figure 14.2. Special Proposal Outline

Purchase Request Form

Requested by _____   Approved by _____

Date _____   Date _____

Date needed _____   Vendor suggested _____

Budget charged _____   Address _____

(Check one):   _____

( ) Purchase Order ( ) Online purchase   Phone _____

( ) Bookstore ( ) Printing Plant ( )Other; specify: _____

Quantity	Brief description of item to include vendor stock number, model Number, color, size, type, other distinguishing information	Unit Price	Total

Figure 14.3. Purchase Request Form

Bid Process

Not all equipment purchases need to go out on bid, and some private management systems can purchase items directly by working with a vendor. However, usually this is not the best approach, and to get the best prices it is recommended that expensive equipment be submitted to qualified vendors for bidding. This bid process is the same as the bid process for a construction project. Different vendors have an equal opportunity to submit a cost quote on the specified equipment. The bidding system eliminates favoritism and stimulates competitive pricing. After the deadline for submitting a bid or quote, the vendor is chosen. The vendor with the lowest bid usually gets the business unless previous experiences with the vendor have been problematic. In such situations, an adjustment may be made following a review of the circumstances.

Purchase Order

The form for placing purchase orders reflects information often used or required in public institutional purchases. Once a vendor is selected, a purchase order, as illustrated in Figure 14.4, is used to initiate the formal purchase. This form contains specific information, making sure there is no misunderstanding regarding the equipment to be purchased. The form represents a type of contract with the vendor, who receives and accepts the purchase order with expectations to meet all requirements as presented.

Delivery

In the purchasing process, delivery should receive special attention because the shipping and handling could entail unique circumstances, especially if the equipment is large or costly, requiring special arrangements and protective measures. Certain equipment might require area preparation, which includes scheduling a time, place, and personnel for special installation or training for use. It is the vendor's role to meet expressed delivery expectations by coordinating efforts and being as cooperative as possible. The recreational sport specialist should stay alert to delivery, preparing to receive, check, and inventory the equipment.

Invoice

During or shortly after delivery, a vendor sends an invoice or a bill requesting payment for the equipment. Often there are terms on the invoice to honor, such as payment by a particular date, a discount if paid by a certain date, and a penalty for late payment. Obviously, administrators should be sensitive to this responsibility, but they should be fully aware of the equipment status before making the payment. The payment process may be a responsibility of the recreational sport specialist, who should see that the payment is taken care of in a timely fashion in order to maintain a good working relationship with the vendor.

Warranty

Some equipment may require a period of time to demonstrate that it meets specifications. A guarantee or warranty by the vendor or manufacturer states that they will be responsible for the equipment's performance through that particular time. The warranty states that if the equipment does not function as intended, the vendor will replace, repair, exchange, or authorize a return, providing a full reimbursement. A warranty could also include installation, employee training, vendor services, or maintenance guarantees by a specific date, at which time the warranty expires and the agency assumes full responsibility for the equipment.

Purchasing and related responsibilities may be outside the daily role of a recreational sport specialist. However, understanding and appreciating the process that brings equipment to a facility is fundamental to the recreational sport specialist's role as part of the management team.

Systemizing

After the purchasing process is completed, a completely new process begins. From the time the equipment arrives to the day it is discarded or replaced, it passes through the steps of a complete system, including receiving, inventory, storage, utilization, and maintenance.

Receiving

As mentioned, the vendor is responsible for delivering the equipment. At delivery, an entirely different process begins to make sure that what has been delivered is in good condition and represents what was ordered. Far too often, vendors make mistakes in fulfilling the order or damages occur during shipping. In addition, other problematic conditions can be discovered during an inspection, and it is at this point that the equipment can be rejected and returned according to the vendor's terms. Accepting equipment that is unsatisfactory can create a whole new set of problems such as determining who or what caused the problem as well as when the problem may have occurred. Administration does not want to receive or accept equipment that cannot be used or does not meet expectations, so careful scrutiny should be applied, accepting only what passes a receiving inspection.

Company Logo

Primary Business Address

Phone: 555-555-5555
Fax: 555-555-5555
E-mail: xyz@aol.com

Purchase Order

Bill To:

Mailing Address

Ship To:

Shipping Address

PURCHASE ORDER
(use this number on all invoices and correspondence)

Date: **Vendor ID:**

Req By	Ship When	Ship Via	FOB	Buyer	Terms: 2% 10, net 30	Tax ID

Quantity	Item	Units	Description	Discount %	Taxable	Unit Price	Total
						Subtotal	
						Tax	
						Shipping	
						Miscellaneous	
						Balance Due	

Figure 14.4. Purchase Order Form

Inventory

When equipment arrives and meets expectations, it should be entered into an inventory system. This system creates an initial record and tracks both use and condition of the equipment. Logging equipment is usually a simple task, but a high volume of equipment makes the inventory process demanding and time consuming. Figure 14.5, a sample inventory form, shows the many details that are involved. Equipment should also be marked, numbered, or receive an electronic bar code that helps facilitate the inventory process. As a rule of thumb, at least once a year a physical count of all equipment should be conducted and reported to administration. An inventory system can prove to be a valuable step for administration in determining short- and long-range equipment needs as they relate to budgeting and resource management. The inventory process also provides an indication of stewardship and accountability.

Storage

After equipment has been identified and inventoried, it can then be entered into another system, called storage. Equipment storage is more than just putting items away. Depending on equipment requirements, storage can be very systemized and tied closely to receiving and inventory. Space may allow for purchases of large quantities, thus saving money. Racks, bins, closets, cabinets, lockers, and other structures can maximize storage potential. Certain equipment might require an environment where temperature, humidity, and sunlight are controlled so that the equipment does not deteriorate or lose its stability.

Unfortunately, storage space is not always appreciated and often given up for other uses. This is especially the case with new construction when assessing project costs. If budget cuts are needed, storage space is often the first to go. In recreational sport, there is hardly ever enough room for storage, and administration would be wise to protect any and all storage space.

Utilization

Once equipment is available, a system is needed for utilization. Equipment could be used in several applications including administrative, delivery, and maintenance. As this system is developed, employees as well as participants have to be identified so that their equipment needs can be realized. This system may be set up as a service so that employees, volunteers, or participants have access through a designed system

of control. Rules and regulations as well as policies and procedures can be established to guide equipment distribution and use. Later in this chapter, different systems for making equipment available will be described. However, a good principle to remember is that the more technical, expensive, and dangerous the equipment, the more precaution should be involved in making it available for use.

Maintenance

Equipment inevitably deteriorates, requiring some type of maintenance to keep it functioning as long as possible. This responsibility can be extensive, requiring special staff members to fix, repair, clean, adjust, or rotate items to defer new purchases until absolutely necessary. Preventative maintenance plays a critical role in keeping equipment from negatively affecting recreational sport. Proper care and preventive action can create tremendous cost savings. More maintenance details are covered in Chapter 17.

Renting and Leasing

Certain equipment may be needed for short durations or to meet a specific need, and a purchase may not be justifiable because of expense or lack of interest. In such circumstances, two options are available: renting or leasing. Renting or leasing equipment is a low-expense option when it comes to maintenance or breakdowns. There are advantages and disadvantages to having an outside business provide equipment. Renting is common for small management operations because it requires few arrangements and usually minimal expense. Local businesses provide rentals requiring some paperwork, a valid ID, a deposit (which is usually returned when the item is returned undamaged), and a rental fee for short-term use. Sometimes specialized equipment may be needed beyond the rental option in which case leasing could prove valuable. Certain companies lease equipment for a designated period of time with special arrangements and signed contracts stipulating an agreement between parties. There are many factors to consider in renting or leasing equipment, and the administration would be wise to fully research such options in trying to solve equipment needs.

Equipment requires specific control mechanisms that fulfill management's expectations for accountability. The goal of this information on systemizing equipment is to help the recreational sport specialist implement a system that accounts for the requirements of the management agency.

Equipment Inventory	Item		Location						
	Model #								
Vendor			Phone number						
Address			Contact						
Catalog Page			Unit Cost		Minimum Order		Minimum Inventory		

Date Of Transaction	Received		Disbursed		Balance				
	P.O. #	Amount	Amount	Who	Amount	C	D	L	S

Status
C = Consumed
D = Discarded/broken
L = Lost
S = Stolen

Figure 14.5. Equipment Inventory Form

Services

Where there is a sport facility, there is more than likely some type of equipment service in order to enhance the sport experience. Such services, or core-product extension, can be in the form of either a checkout system or a rental system. These systems are similar; the only difference is the charge for rentals. Both require planning, organization, and control to ensure that the equipment goes out and is returned properly. Poorly managed equipment operations can be unpopular and costly. Following is operational information to help the recreational sport specialist understand what these systems involve.

Distribution

Early in the distribution process, the acquisition of user information is key to any equipment checkout service. Note in Figure 14.6, the required information is name, address, telephone number, and state-issued ID number. Before equipment is distributed, identification should be required, such as a photo ID or credit card. Each piece of equipment, especially equipment that is expensive or could cause injury if used improperly, should be accompanied by instructions for proper use and user responsibilities. Every aspect of the distribution process should be completely thought out. Where a fee is involved, give careful consideration to user variables such as affordability, willingness to pay, deposit process, and income accountability.

Policy and Procedure

A critical need in equipment service is formally stated policies and procedures that are established before equipment distribution and made available to all users. Rental fees should be carefully determined, printed, and posted. Time periods need to be in place delineating the length of time items can be out. Another consideration is predetermined user requirements such as experience, age, and training. A policy should state the consequences of damaging, losing, or stealing equipment. Some operations might require a deposit to cover any damage.

Waiver

When recreational sport activities or equipment involve a safety risk, a waiver statement may be used to help communicate the potential hazard. Users are required to read the statement and sign it, showing they recognize what risks they are assuming in checking out or renting the equipment. Such a waiver (see Figure 14.7) does not necessarily relinquish management's responsibility, but it does show good intent and prudent care for users' well-being and safety. Detailed liability information is covered Chapter 18.

Insurance

When expensive equipment is distributed or an injury could occur, insurance coverage should be arranged. Costs to cover insurance could be built into a rental fee, with care taken to avoid putting too great a burden on the user making the arrangements.

Tracking

A system for tracking equipment location and status at all times is a necessity. This tracking could involve computer software that ties together the checkout form and the details of the arrangements. Regular inventory should be conducted to ensure that equipment has not been lost, damaged, or misplaced. Poor tracking can be expensive and reflect negatively on management. Take the necessary steps to ensure that all items rotate in and out of use in a systematic fashion.

An equipment checkout and rental operation is a delivery process in itself. Recreational sport specialists could find themselves supervising such a service outlet and all that it entails. It is a unique role that requires sensitivity to detail and monitoring, not to mention equipment maintenance and liability concerns.

Equipment Checkout Form

Date _____

Name _____ Telephone _____

Address _____

State issued ID # _____

Activity _____ Locker number _____

EQUIPMENT REQUESTED

Quantity	Description of item

Office use only

Out | In

Staff Initial _____   Actual Return _____

Date equipment needed _____   Condition _____

Initial/date Return _____

I hereby aggress to pay for any equipment damage or not returned. Failure to do so will result in legal action.

Signature _____

Figure 14.6. Equipment Checkout Form

I, for myself and any minor children for which I am parent, legal guardian or otherwise responsible, release the *recreational sport facility name*, it's agents, employees, respective affiliates, owner, directors, shareholders, and officers from any liability for damage or injury to myself or any person or property resulting from negligence, adjustment, selection or use of this equipment. I understand that recreational activities involve inherent and other risks of injury. I voluntarily agree to expressly assume all risks of injury that may result from use, or which relate in any way to the use of this equipment.

I accept for use, as is, the equipment in good condition and accept the full responsibility for care of the equipment while it is in my possession. I will be responsible for the prompt replacement at full retail value of all rental equipment, which is not returned or is returned   damaged.

I agree to return rental equipment by agreed date in clean condition to avoid additional charges. All instructions on the use of the rental equipment have been made clear to me and I understand the function of the equipment. I accept the terms of this agreement and accept responsibility for the above charges.

_____   _____
Signature   Date

Figure 14.7. Sample Waiver Statement

Sales

An alternative equipment service is a system where equipment is actually sold with the purpose of making a profit. Selling equipment is usually an auxiliary or extended management role. The same steps for purchasing equipment are taken to purchase equipment for sale. In many recreational sport agencies, selling equipment is an everyday practice. Common delivery operations include retail outlets, pro shops, specialty shops, and gift shops. They operate predominately in the private sector of recreational sport management, although they do exist in public settings as well. Equipment sales have merchandising considerations, which are discussed in the following material.

Sellable Items

There are two basic influences in a successful sales operation: the recreational sport activity itself and the different items to be sold. Such items need to be scrutinized to make sure they have the potential to generate a profit. Specific items need planning, research, and market analysis. Detailed information should be obtained on how the item sells regionally and nationally, opportunities for wholesale purchases, product trends and popularity, and vendor reputations and service. Awareness of similar outlets in the area could prove valuable in providing information on the equipment strengths and weaknesses as an indicator of profitability.

Customer Awareness

In creating an equipment sales outlet, it is critical to assess potential customers' ability and willingness to pay for the equipment for sale. Identify potential buyers and learn about their habits, desires, interests, and needs. Do not assume something will sell just because you personally think it will sell or because you like the product. Know the customers, accept them for who they are, and then help them to realize the opportunity they have to purchase your equipment.

Price

Pricing strategy is critical to selling merchandise. The goal is to set a cost that at a minimum will cover costs and ideally will generate profit. Set an affordable price that attracts rather than discourages the sale. Pricing should take into consideration staffing, marketing, theft, insurance, utilities, loan interest, and rent or mortgage. Pricing a piece of equipment takes research, experience, and, probably most important, sound business practices. Be careful in setting prices because pricing can make the difference between success and failure.

Location

In the business world, location is the place where equipment is sold. In many respects it is as important as pricing. Many businesses preach "location, location, location" because being out of sight means being out of mind. Customers must come into contact with the potential purchase item. In the recreational sport facility, the sales outlet should be located in an area with maximum visibility to users. Signage can also be designed and strategically placed to attract customer attention.

Staffing

One of the roles involved in selling equipment is that of the individual salesperson. Sales personnel make direct contact with customers as well as help supervise the area and equipment. Staff must be honest, knowledgeable, friendly, enthusiastic, and sincerely interested in the equipment and how it relates to the customer. It is one thing to hire and train sales employees, but the real key is to be aware of their motivation. Sometimes when sales operations are well established, enthusiasm drains and staff become bored. Equipment outlets require capable salespeople, ongoing supervision, and high motivation in order to ensure success.

Other Considerations

Make sure that equipment does not sit on the shelf or on the racks too long since unsold items represent tied-up money. Special sales can be helpful, allowing for discounted prices, quantity purchasing, and payment plans. Creativity with sales and promotion can make a difference in moving the equipment and meeting customers' needs.

Another consideration is the use of displays, which store items as well as attract customers. It is best to set displays up so that they create a flow of traffic that contributes to customer awareness and interest in making a purchase. Displays can be arranged to complement the recreational sport activities, placing an emphasis on equipment related to participation. Displays can also be placed close to a cash register for impulse purchases or at an entrance to create buyer awareness. Displays should be attractive and clean. They should also be changed, adjusted, and moved around to keep the environment from getting stagnant.

The sales counter where the transaction occurs should be recognized for its role in equipment sales. Counter activity usually involves the use of a cash register, point-of-sale system, credit-card machine, and computer system, all requiring special training. The design of the counter should take into consideration appearance, functionality, accessibility, security, supervision, and location.

Other extra efforts that could increase sales include gift wrapping, shipping arrangements, warranty considerations, open houses, a relaxed return policy, special delivery, and reminders such as notes and phone calls, all of which contribute to customer satisfaction. Also, success breeds success, so every effort should be put forth to recognize what works and keep it going. Anticipate change and monitor trends that could affect the product, adjusting as best as possible to keep things progressing in a positive direction.

▶ **Computer Tip**

....

Database Management Software

Recreational sport programs are no different from any other business in terms of organizing and tracking inventory of sport equipment, facility equipment, and office furniture and machinery. Staff needs to maintain accurate equipment inventory to ensure accountability and inventory control. The type of equipment inventory system that is developed and implemented depends primarily on the needs of the agency.

Since recreational sport programs are unique to each setting, there isn't one particular software package that is specific enough for every agency. However, using a database management program to develop an equipment inventory system customized just for your agency is very easy. A typical inventory application should allow for

- adding, changing, or deleting items through a menu-driven screen;

- linking various databases (such as linking the equipment database to the vendor, staff, and facility location databases);

- extensive and flexible reporting capabilities; and

- an automatic tag-numbering system in which each piece of equipment is given a tag number for identification purposes.

Database management programs are relatively easy to use, but they are still powerful programs that allow you to manage and manipulate data in many ways. A database is a collection of related information that is grouped together in some logical order. The information is generally arranged and stored in a file using rows and columns (similar to a spreadsheet, which is discussed in chapter 12).

Each row contains one record or complete set of information about the specific piece of equipment in the equipment database. Each column contains a separate field or type of information, such as the location, the date of purchase, the specific cost, or the current condition of the equipment.

Database management programs have several tools for managing data, such as forms, queries, and reports. Forms display data that are stored in a file or information retrieved as a result of a query. Database forms are very similar to the traditional paper forms. Forms are used for adding new data to the file and for displaying existing data, usually one record at a time.

Once the data has been entered into the file, you can query or "ask questions" about the data. Queries are used to find and display a specific record or records, such as certain pieces of equipment, all equipment purchased after a certain date, or all equipment located in a particular facility.

Customized reports are the result of selective queries and are what database management is all about. Detailed and sophisticated reports are easy to produce and can be designed to fit your needs. Include only the data you desire from the various fields of the database and print the results in the desired formats, such as inventory summary reports, valuation reports, mailing labels, or bar code labels.

Whether you are a computer novice or an expert, you will find that database management software allows you to link data in useful ways that make it easy to locate, manage, and share agency and program information.

Conclusion

As a resource, equipment requires a great deal of responsibility that ranges from understanding its existence and knowing how it is acquired and maintained to knowing how it is distributed for use and even sold as a product. It is often taken for granted, yet where equipment is neglected or mismanaged, costs could be incurred that pose a difficult situation for management. As a recreational sport specialists, take the time to enhance your insight into your agency's equipment system and requirements, making sure you know and fulfill your responsibilities.

Bibliography

Campbell, J. D., & Jardine, A. K. S. (2001). *Maintenance excellence: Optimizing equipment lifecycle decisions*. New York, NY: Marcel Dekker.

Mull, R. F., Beggs, B. A., & Renneisen, M. (2009). *Recreation facility management: Design, development, operations, and utilization*. Champaign, IL: Human Kinetics.

Occupational Safety and Health Administration. (2007). *Safeguarding equipment and protecting workers from amputations* (OSHA 3170-02R). Washington, DC: Author.

Olson, J. R. (1997). *Facility and equipment management for sport directors*. Champaign, IL: Human Kinetics.

Reese, C. D. (2009). *Industrial safety and health for people-oriented services*. Boca Raton, FL: Taylor and Francis.

Salesman's Guide Staff. (1997). *Sporting goods buyers 1998*. Richmond, VA: Douglas Publications.

Snyder, P., & Southwick, M. (2003). *Sporting goods and activewear buyers*. Richmond, VA: Douglas Publications.

Walker, M. L. (1993). *Sports equipment management*. Sudbury, MA: Jones and Bartlett.

Walker, M. L., & Stotlar, D. K. (1997). *Sports facility management*. Champaign, IL: Human Kinetics.

Part V

ADMINISTRATIVE INVOLVEMENT

Part V addresses select administrative subject areas considered vital to sport program delivery. Such information could impact recreational sport specialists, depending on their assigned responsibilities, including proactive planning, reaching potential markets, facility and equipment maintenance, legal issues and concerns, and professional career options and implications. Awareness and appreciation for these areas can take on greater meaning to overall staffing, responsibilities, coordination, and cooperation.

CHAPTER 15

Program Planning

CHAPTER OBJECTIVES

After reading this chapter, you will understand the Recreational Sport Program Planning Model, comprehend how to use mission and vision statements to understand the goals and objectives of recreational sport organizations, understand the importance of, and how to assess, participant needs and organizational capacity, become familiar with different program planning and design strategies, define goals and objectives, differentiate between implementation and outcome objectives, develop SMART objectives, understand how to use program logic models when planning recreational sport programs, become familiar with the different components of the program plan, identify the key program planning considerations for the four recreational sport program delivery areas, and understand how to evaluate recreational sport programs and make recommendations.

KEY CONCEPTS

Key Concepts	**Planning**
Evaluation	**Programming**
Goals and objectives	**Program logic models**
Participant needs	**Program plans**
Organizational capacity	**Recreational Sport Program Planning Model**

Introduction

Why does a campus recreational sport department offer opportunities to play drop-in or pickup basketball, intramural basketball, and basketball at the club sport level? Why does a community agency offering a youth soccer program have different goals based on the age of the participants? The answers to these questions are often the outcome of a process of program planning.

Chapter 3 described administrative and delivery operations as two components of management. The chapter also discussed the four different functions of administrative operations including planning and delivery operations along with production. Planning was defined in terms of anticipating and documenting all aspects (of recreational sport programs) that lead toward expected levels of success. Planning can be broken down based on either timing (i.e., short-

vs. long-term planning) or the type of planning (facility planning, equipment purchase planning, maintenance planning, budget planning, master or strategic planning, etc.). Following are brief explanations of the different types of planning as they relate to recreational sports.

Short-term Planning

Short-term planning consists of the day-to-day or week-to-week tasks and responsibilities for the recreational sport specialist to ensure smooth and successful program operations.

Long-term Planning

Long-term planning consists of longer term plans, typically 5 to 10 years, sometimes longer. Long-term planning is often referred to as master or strategic planning:

Master or strategic planning specifies future directions of an organization and makes recommendations related to operational priorities to achieve that future.

Maintenance Planning

Maintenance planning helps determine and anticipate routine and nonroutine needs, changes, and deteriorations in equipment and facilities.

Facility Planning

Facility planning is the systematic anticipation of all facility needs and provides details and justification for developing a new recreational sport facility that might have been identified as a priority in a master or strategic plan.

Equipment Planning

Equipment purchase planning is the systematic anticipation of equipment needs.

Why Plan?

While there are numerous types and timing of plans, why should the recreational sport specialist be so concerned with planning? Preparing plans, regardless of the type, ultimately guides decision making by providing justification for program choices and design and establishes priorities for resource allocation. By assessing community needs and deciding how to best meet those needs, recreational sport specialists can ensure desires and needs are met. Also, by systematically anticipating and planning for mistakes, recreational sport specialists can prevent bad decisions and costly errors, and they will be proactive rather than reactive, anticipating implications and impacts of decisions rather than fixing the problems after they've occurred. Planning

also establishes accountability for programs and the outcomes of participation in those programs and provides a framework for evaluation (Harper, 2009).

The production function of delivery operations, or programming as it is more commonly known, is set in motion by the administration and consists of contact efforts, out-front activities, daily tasks, and resources. When the staff perform these tasks, all details, knowledge, and resources are synthesized. The production function of delivery operations was illustrated in Part III of this text, which provided details regarding the program delivery areas of recreational sports including instructional, informal, intramural, extramural, and club sports. The goal of this chapter is to combine both the planning and the production (programming) function in an effort to describe the program planning process. While there are numerous definitions of program planning in the literature, the term is not as ambiguous as management and most definitions have numerous commonalities. Program planning, as it applies to the field of recreational sports, can be thought of as a continual/interactive process of planning (Steps 1 and 2), developing (Step 3), implementing (Step 4), and evaluating (Step 5) recreational sport experiences for individuals or groups.

Recreational Sport Program Planning Model

There are five steps the recreational sport specialist must go through when planning, developing, implementing, and evaluating recreational sport programs, as outlined in Figure 15.1.

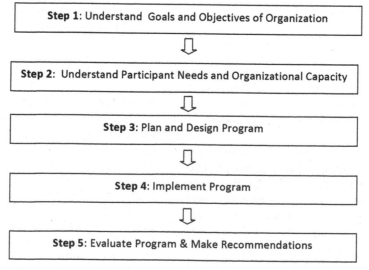

Figure 15.1. The Recreational Sport Program Planning Model

Although these steps are presented sequentially, this falsely conveys that program planning is a sequential or linear process when in fact it is an "iterative, interactive process requiring continued recycling of these steps until an operational program plan is completed" (Rossman & Schlatter, 2008, p. 97). Furthermore, the program format, duration, location, goals and objectives, and so forth vary based on the program delivery area; however, the process to plan, develop, implement, and evaluate the program is similar. There are also a lot of unique considerations for informal sports, instructional sports, intramural and extramural sports, and club sports when program planning, and these will be explained later in the chapter.

This chapter focuses on the production of recreational sport programs through program planning. Each step of the Recreational Sport Program Planning Model is described in detail throughout the remainder of this chapter.

Step 1: Understanding Goals and Objectives of Organization

In this first step, the recreational sport specialist needs to develop an understanding of the goals and objectives of the organization for which the programs are being developed. Organizational goals and objectives outline what the organization wants to accomplish or is trying to achieve, which provides an overall mandate for the organization. These goals and objectives can most commonly be found by examining the organization's mission and vision statements. In addition, three- to five-year plans or recent master plans can also be used to determine the direction for program development. Recreational sport specialists need to develop programs that are consistent with the goals and objectives of the organization and subsequently help the organization to achieve its mission, vision, and long-term strategic plans. Program planning begins with developing an understanding of the organization's goals and objectives, which should provide cues to the recreational sport specialist who is informing program direction and development. These goals and objectives are typically found in organizational mission and vision statements, which are defined below.

Mission statements declare an organization's purpose, reason for existence, and/or function in a community by specifying what they are trying to accomplish and for whom they are providing recreational sport programs. Mission statements should be found on organization's websites, promotional literature, and annual reports. See Table 15.1 for examples of mission statements from various recreational sport organizations.

Table 15.1

Sample Mission and Vision Statements

	Mission	Vision
Educational – Indiana University Campus Recreation	We connect, inform and inspire people to lead active, healthy lifestyles.	To be the leading recreational sports program in the country, offering the most comprehensive, inclusive and progressive programs and facilities that exceed participant expectations.
Military – U.S. Army Family and Morale, Welfare and Recreation	To support Army Force Generation by enabling all Commanders, Region Directors, and installations to provide family and MWR programs and services that result in a quality of life to Soldiers and Families commensurate with their sacrifice and service.	To be the driving force for programs and services that provide the foundation for the Army's home by increasing soldier and family resiliency, restoring balance, and enhancing recruitment, readiness and retention for soldiers and families.
Community – Welland Tennis Club	The Welland Tennis Club is a non-profit organization whose mission is to promote active living and enhance the social and physical well-being of its members by maintaining an excellent tennis facility and providing affordable tennis to all ages and play levels in a safe, friendly and sporting environment.	Not available.

When developing programs, the recreational sport specialist works from the mission statement of the agency or organization because the programs that he or she develops must contribute to helping the organization fulfill its purpose. If the mission is broad or general in scope (as in the case of the Campus Recreation department at Indiana University), then the recreational sport specialist will have considerable latitude and flexibility in developing programs that help the organization achieve its goals and objectives. If the mission statement is more focused and specific (such as the Welland Tennis Club), then the recreational sport specialist will be more confined and restricted in program development. In recreational sport programming, an understanding of the mission of the organization provides a starting point and direction for the development of recreational sport programs. The recreational sport specialist should also be aware that mission statements are often worded in the present and identify the organization's current purpose, what they are currently trying to accomplish, and whom they are currently serving. Recreational sport specialists also need to consider longer term directions of the organization, which are typically specified in vision statements.

Vision statements, unlike mission statements that are written for the present and specify what organizations are doing currently, provide direction for organizations and indicate "what an organization wants to become and where it wants to be in the future" (DeGraaf, Jordan, & DeGraaf, 2010, p. 67). In so doing, vision statements address questions such as the following:

• Whom does the recreational sport organization wish to serve?

• What core values, beliefs, or traditions does the organization want to instill?

• What individual and community beneficial outcomes will the organization strive to achieve?

• How does the organization plan on accomplishing these benefits (what resources will be needed)?

• What will the future look like? How does this future direction reflect organizational principles and philosophy?

• Why are these directions important to this organization?

See Table 15.1 for examples of vision statements from various recreational sport organizations. Note that most vision statements specify what the organization wants to accomplish in the future. When developing programs, recreational sport specialists need to consider the vision of the organization and develop and implement programs that are consistent with the direction that the organization is taking in order to help them achieve their vision. Many recreational sport organizations will also go through a master or strategic planning process once every 5 or 10 years, which will provide tangible recommendations in the areas of planning, programs, policies, personnel, facilities, and so forth for organizations to achieve their vision. Master and strategic plans are often completed using public input, so these plans should give the recreational sport specialist insight into the desires of the community for which he or she is developing recreational sport programs.

Public, private, and commercial agencies that deliver recreational sport programs will have different goals and objectives that will ultimately dictate the type of recreational sport being developed and why. While Chapter 2 identified common service goals (e.g., providing positive experiences and generating profits) and human development goals (e.g., involvement and leadership) for recreational sport, in order for programs to be successful, recreational sport specialists need to have a thorough understanding of the mission and vision of the specific organization for which they are developing programs. This will help ensure that the programs they develop, whether they are informal sports, instructional sports, intramural and extramural sports, or club sports, meet individual and community needs and ultimately help the organization achieve its goals and objectives.

Step 2: Understanding Participant Needs and Organizational Capacity

Participant needs. In order to ensure that programs are relevant and meeting the needs of participants, recreational sport specialists need to assess participant needs by obtaining input/feedback from them. A needs assessment is a systematic process of identifying the needs, wants, desires, and preferences of both current participants and prospective participants. Needs assessments are an essential part of the program planning and evaluation process and also provide the opportunity for recreational sport specialists to seek out participant input about programming ideas, attitudes, behaviors, and patterns of both participants and nonparticipants. The results from needs assessments allow the recreational sport specialist to set priorities and make decisions about programs and allocation of resources, and they provide the foundation for developing the program plan.

Needs represent an imbalance or discrepancy in a physical, psychological, emotional, spiritual, or social aspect of people's lives that determines their behavior. Maslow's (1943) Hierarchy of Needs has been most commonly used to understand various levels of needs (see Figure 15.2). According to Maslow, higher order needs (esteem, self-actualization) are ignored until other needs are met. These lower level needs are the driving force guiding behavior until they are satisfied. For example, if offering a summer sports camp for children from low-income families, recreational sport specialists may want to consider providing breakfast or meals to ensure that these physiological needs are met in order for children to be able to focus on fulfilling the higher order needs. Needs are considered necessary for sustaining life, whereas wants or desires involve a preference or a wish and are considered important for an acceptable quality of life but are not a necessity for life.

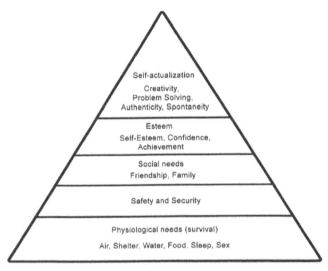

Figure 15.2. Maslow's Hierarchy of Needs

In addition to Maslow's (1943) Hierarchy of Needs, recreational sport specialists can also benefit from having an understanding of Self-Determination Theory (Deci & Ryan, 1985, 2000), which is based on the assumption that there are three innate psychological needs: (a) competence (sense of mastery and self-efficacy), (b) autonomy (perception that behaviors are freely chosen), and (c) relatedness (an interaction between and satisfaction with others and the social environment). Regardless of the specific needs, wants, desires, and preferences that are found from needs assessments, according to Self-Determination Theory recreational sport specialists should ensure that the programs they develop provide opportunities for (a) feeling competent by offering programs catering to different ability levels; (b) choice by offering a variety of program types, formats, times, and locations; and (c) feeling connected to others by paying attention to the social aspect of recreational sport programming.

While there are numerous reasons to conduct needs assessments, DeGraaf et al. (2010) have succinctly identified three overarching reasons with numerous sub-reasons, which are summarized in Table 15.2.

There are a variety of assessment procedures that the recreational sport specialist can use to determine the wants and needs of participants. While it is beyond the scope of this chapter to go into the logistics of executing each, the following should provide a brief summary of different methods available and the type of information the recreational sport specialist can expect to obtain:

- **Social indicators:** inventory of existing social conditions in a community such as the representation of groups, health, education, family structures, crime and unemployment rates, substance abuse, income, and so forth

- **Social surveys:** questionnaires or interviews of individuals regarding past participation, program preferences, desires, skill level, and so forth

- **Community group approaches:** public meetings and forums, focus groups, and nominal group and delphi techniques to help identify community consensus on programming issues

- **Advisory boards:** can be used to help determine needs by providing feedback that is useful during assessment, implementation, and evaluation. When soliciting information from advisory boards, be sure that responses are representative of participants and potential participants rather than reflecting personal opinions.

Once the recreational sport specialist has decided upon what type of information they want to collect and from whom, and after they have a sense of what the needs of participants or potential participants are, they also need to have an understanding of the ability of the organization to meet these needs through recreational sport programming, a concept also known as organizational capacity.

Organizational capacity. Once the needs of the participants have been identified, it is important for the recreational sport specialist to make sure they have a clear understanding of the capacity or capability of the organization to meet these needs. This began in the first step of the Recreational Sport Program Planning Model when developing an understanding of the goals and objectives of the organization. In addition, recreational sport specialists should know the answer to the following questions before designing and developing programs to meet the needs of participants:

Table 15.2

Why Conduct Needs Assessments?

---

1. Service Orientation/Participant Empowerment
- *Solicit constituent input*
  - ○ Help influence programming cycle about: Pricing, promotion, allocation of resources, facilities, activities, timing/schedules, format, etc...
- *Solicit responses to new ideas*
  - ○ Increase the diversity of ideas/viewpoints by asking questions about enhancing, changing or developing new programs
- *Ensure inclusion*
  - ○ Being inclusive of all people regardless of sex, age, physical abilities and qualities, sexual orientation, race/ethnicity, religion, education, SES, etc...
- *Meet real needs of constituents*
  - ○ Physiological – food, air, water
  - ○ Psychological – achievement, self-esteem, identity
  - ○ Socio-emotional – belonging, love, affection
  - ○ Spiritual – knowing a greater power than ourselves

2. Desire for Quality and Exceeding Expectations
- *Demonstrate professional commitment*
- *Appropriate resource allocation*
  - ○ Determine where to focus resources: increase staffing, facility maintenance, additional programs, etc...
- *Accountability*
  - ○ Being publicly responsible for actions/choices: use data to justify allocation of resources/programming decisions
- *Increase profits*
  - ○ As budgets continue to be cut and resources shrink, generating revenue in programs will become increasingly important: by planning and offering programs in which people intend to participate we can better ensure revenue generation.

3. Program Management
- *Manage duplication of services*
  - ○ Determine if needs are being met elsewhere.
- *Maintain and address safety issues*
  - ○ By asking questions that relate to how facilities, equipment, and programs are used, we can better understand where potential hazards might exist.
- *Help prioritize programming plans*
  - ○ Learn how many people want and need which type of program and respond accordingly.
- *Help design & implement wide variety of enjoyable programs*
  - ○ Because we have so many individuals involved in the programming process.
  - ○ Participant involvement in planning contributes to a sense of ownership in the program which often heightens fun and enjoyment.
- *Develop and meet individual goals*

Adapted from: DeGraaf, D.G., Jordan, D.J., & DeGraaf, K.H. (2010). *Programming for parks, recreation, and leisure services: A servant leadership approach* (3rd ed.). State College, PA: Venture Publishing Inc.

- How many staff are there? What are their skills?

- What programs currently exist that could meet the needs identified?

- What equipment, facilities, and supplies does the organization have access to?

- What is the budget situation like? (DeGraaf et al., 2010)

When developing programs, recreational sport specialists should systematically collect information about clients that will be useful in developing and revising programs so that organizational resources can be allocated to serving identified clients' needs. Needs assessments should precede the determination of the how, what, when, why, and where of recreational sport programming. Needs, in some combination and priority, will determine the rationale and intent of the program. Therefore, needs have some basis for deciding on the content of the program (i.e., what to include and focus on), the process (i.e., how to set up and organize the program), the conduct (i.e., expected behavior of both participants and program leaders), and outcomes of the program (i.e., what impact the program has on participants). Once these are identified from the needs assessment process, recreational sport specialists can then develop and specify program goals and objectives.

Step 3: Program Planning and Design

In this third step of the Recreational Sport Program Planning Model, the recreational sport specialist uses the information obtained from the needs assessment process to establish and identify the goals and objectives for a program. Once these goals and objectives are identified, the recreational sport specialist can decide on which of the four programming areas would be best given these goals and objectives and can begin to design the actual program by writing the program plan.

Goals and objectives defined. It is important for recreational sport specialists to develop goals and objectives based on the results of the needs assessment data in order to establish a clear understanding about what is to be planned, offered, and gained from the program for participants; facilitate program design (i.e., what it is that the recreational sport specialist needs to do and accomplish) and distribution of resources to meet identified needs; establish a basis for measurement and evaluation (i.e., evaluate program based on whether stated goals and objectives were achieved); and establish accountability for effort and results.

Program goals are a broad-based statement of intent regarding what the program is supposed to accomplish in general terms. For example, a goal of an instructional sport program might be to teach participants the skills, techniques, strategies, rules, regulations, etiquette, and so forth of a specific sport. Program objectives are specific operational statements derived from goals that describe how the goal will be accomplished. Program objectives are the measurement points of goals, describe the means by which the goals will be achieved, and consist of two types.

Implementation objectives. Implementation objectives specify the intentions for implementing the program and relate to inputs, activities, and outputs of the program logic model (see Figure 15.3).

Outcome objectives. Outcome objectives specify what the organization desires for participants, the community, or broader society. These objectives are typically participant centered and focus on the knowledge, behavior, experience, benefits, or achievement of the participant. Outcome objectives should address the following:

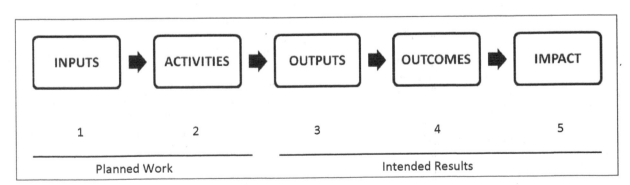

Figure 15.3. Program Logic Model. Adapted from W. K. Kellogg Foundation, 2004.

- Who: Who is involved in the behavior/action (e.g., program participants)?

- Behavior: What is involved in the behavior? How is the action to be displayed (e.g., writing, expressing, performing)?

- Condition: How they will do it?

- Timing: When is the behavior to occur?

- Degree: Means to measure if it was accomplished.

- Success: Standard of success or acceptable level of performance.

For example: At the end (timing) of the instructional clinic, each participant (who) in the basketball program will be able to do layups and jump shots (behavior). Acceptable performance will entail demonstration of the appropriate technique associated with each shot (condition) as judged by the instructor and the ability to make (success) a minimum of 6 out of 10 layups and 4 out of 10 jump shots (degree).

In addition to addressing the who, behavior, condition, timing, degree, and success when writing outcome objectives, recreational sport specialists should make sure their objectives are SMART. A SMART objective is an objective that is specific, measurable, attainable, relevant, and timely.

Specific: A SMART objective describes an observable action or behavior in a clear, concrete, and precise way.

Measurable: It defines the end result of the program in a way that can be objectively assessed and measured quantitatively or qualitatively.

Attainable: Objectives are realistically achievable provided participants have the necessary skills and resources.

Relevant: Objectives are relevant to the population and the needs identified and useful for program-related decisions. It also answers the question "what impact will achieving this objective have in relation to the goals of the program and the overall mandate of the organization?"

Timely: Objectives are provided a specific time frame for the achievement of the objective.

Recreational sport specialists can use the checklist in Table 15.3 to determine if the objectives they have developed are specific, measurable, attainable, relevant, and timely.

Program logic models. When writing implementation objectives, recreational sport specialists specify the intentions for implementing the program related to the inputs, activities, and outputs of the program logic model. Program logic models provide a visual method of outlining/describing the different components or elements of a recreational sport program. They offer the recreational sport specialist a way to

describe and share an understanding of relationships among elements necessary to operate a program or change effort. Logic models describe a bounded project or initiative: both what is planned (the doing) and what results are expected (the getting). They provide a clear roadmap to a specified end. The development of (logic) models provides an opportunity to review the strength of connection between activities and outcomes (Knowlton & Phillips, 2009, p. 5).

In its *Logic Model Development Guide*, the W. K. Kellogg Foundation (2004) defined logic models as a "systematic and visual way to present and share your understanding of the relationships among the resources you have to operate your program, the activities you plan, and the changes or results you hope to achieve" (p. 1). Recreational sport specialists should develop logic models for the programs they are designing as a way to better understand the totality of the program and how different elements of it are interconnected. While there are different types, the program logic model depicted in Figure 15.3 is the most common (albeit basic) and most applicable to recreational sport programs. This model consists of inputs (resources), activities, outputs, outcomes, and impacts. The inputs and activities represent the "Planned Work," which indicates the resources the recreational sport specialist may need to implement the program and what they intend to do. The outputs, outcomes, and impact represent the "Intended Results," which include all the desired or intended results of the program.

In their *Measuring Program Outcomes* manual, the United Way of America (1996) defined the different elements of the program logic model as follows:

Table 15.3

Assessing Whether or Not Objectives are SMART

Specific – what makes this particular objective specific? Is it:
- ☐ Clearly stated
- ☐ Describes a behavior to be performed
- ☐ Uses action verbs to describe what has to be done

Measurable – how is this objective measurable?
- ☐ Is it quantifiable
- ☐ Can it be observed
- ☐ Limits and parameters are defined

Attainable – is the objective within reach?
- ☐ Participants have the required degree of experience
- ☐ Participants have the necessary skills and knowledge

Relevant – how do you know the objective is relevant?
- ☐ Stemmed from the results of the needs assessment
- ☐ Related to overall goals of the program
- ☐ Will help organization fulfill its mission

Timely – what timeframes have been established for the achievement of the objective?
- ☐ It has a clearly defined completion date/time
- ☐ There is a clearly defined duration of the objective
- ☐ The frequency with which the objective must be performed is clearly defined

---

- **Inputs:** resources needed for the program (money, staff, volunteers, facilities, equipment and supplies, etc.).

- **Activities:** what the program does or entails.

- **Outputs:** products of program activities measured in terms of volume of work accomplished (number of participants, materials distributed, activities offered, etc.).

- **Outcomes:** benefits or changes for individuals during or after participation.

- **Impact:** the overall intended or unintended change in the organization, communities, or systems as a result of program activities within seven to 10 years.

Because logic models are visual by nature, they require the recreational sport specialist to think and plan in order to better describe their programs. Logic models also help the recreational sport specialist

better organize and systematize program planning, management, and evaluation efforts (W.K. Kellogg Foundation, 2004).

The program plan. Once the goals and objectives are established for the program, the recreational sport specialist can then design or develop the program in order to achieve these goals and objectives. This is where the recreational sport specialist will need to decide what program delivery area is best suited to achieve these goals and objectives. Once the program delivery area is decided upon, the recreational sport specialist will then need to make more detailed decisions regarding the program's specifications. These specifications should be outlined in a program plan. A program plan is a working document that a recreational sport specialist should develop when detailing all aspects of the program being developed. This plan serves as a blueprint for the development and implementation of the program. It should be sufficiently detailed so that someone other than the developer of the program could replicate the program based on the program plan alone. Recreational sport specialists should address the components of the Program Plan outlined in Table 15.4 and further add any additional details that may be unique to their particular program or that would be necessary for someone else to replicate it.

Table 15.4

Elements of a Recreational Sport Program Plan

1. Name, Mission, and Vision of Organization

2. Need for the Program
- *Why is this program needed and how was this need determined?*
- SWOT Analysis.
- After reading these first two sections it should be apparent why agency is developing/implementing this program.

3. Program Title and Brief Description
- Indicate the who, what, when, where, why, and how of the program.

4. Goals and Objectives of the Program
- Broad statements about what the program is supposed to accomplish (goals) and then specifically how it will be measured (objectives).

5. Operation Details
- This is akin to the coaches playbook and should include a detailed set of instructions regarding how the program is supposed to be implemented, operated, and evaluated.
- The recreational sport specialist should provide enough detail so that another programmer could reproduce the program. In so doing, a number of important features/elements of the program should be specified, such as:

  a. *Venue & special arrangements* - description of venue and any special arrangements required (i.e., transportation, entertainment, and/or concessions).
  b. *Inclusion plan* - ensure that all individuals regardless of gender, ethnicity, class standing, and ability can participate.
  c. *Equipment, supplies, and material needs.*
  d. *Promotion plan* – specifying target market, and how program will be promoted including types & distribution of promotional materials (see chapter 16).
  e. *Budget and pricing* – including a detailed account of related expenses, revenues, income projections, and how price was determined (see chapter 12).
  f. *Registration* - if required, how will this be done?
  g. *Staffing and staff orientation* - number and qualifications of staff needed to operate program. This section should also specify the roles and responsibilities of staff and volunteers when implementing the program.
  h. *Cancellation plan* - detail a course of action should the program be cancelled.
  i. *Set-up* - specify detailed plans for program set-up .
  j. *Risk management plan* – specifies how risk will be managed (see chapter 18).
  k. *Management plan* - details what needs to be done leading up to program implementation. Identify, sequentially order and prioritize tasks that must be completed. Gantt and PERT Charts are particularly useful for this. See Figures 15.4 and 15.5.
  l. *Lesson plan* - describes step-by-step, frame by frame, activity by activity, how participants will move through the program. The Social Recreation Curve (Ford, 1974) is particularly useful to the recreational sport specialist when designing the flow of the program.
  m. *Back-up plan* – detail a contingency plan based on different scenarios should any last minute adjustments or modifications to the program be needed that are beyond the recreational sports specialists' control.

6. Program Evaluation
- Approach and specific questions used to evaluate the program.

7. Recommendations
- Specifies what recommendations the recreational sports specialist has after evaluating the program.

Adapted from: Rossman, J., & Schlatter, B. (2008). *Recreation programming: designing leisure experiences* (5th ed.). Champaign, IL: Sagamore Publishing.

The Program (or Project) Evaluation Review Technique, otherwise known as PERT, is another example of a planning chart used to manage programs by representing the tasks (and timelines for completion) involved in developing, implementing, and evaluating programs. PERT charts (see Figure 15.4) provide more of a visual of the sequential flow of events from the development of the program idea to the program recommendations stemming from the evaluation of the program. PERT charts are particularly useful to the recreational sport specialist who is interested in conducting a process evaluation of the planning process, as PERT charts provide a detailed depiction of all of the program tasks and the progression of these tasks from program idea to evaluation.

A Gantt chart (named after Henry Gantt) is essentially a horizontal bar chart used to visually illustrate a project schedule or provide a timeline for tasks to be completed. These tasks relate to the development, implementation, and evaluation of a recreational sport program. Gantt charts (see Figure 15.5) are particularly useful for this aspect of the program plan, as they provide the recreational sport specialist a visual way of detailing the program-related tasks (what needs to be done and a timeline for completion) leading up to (and including) program implementation.

When designing and developing recreational sport programs, recreational sport specialists should consider using the "Social Recreation Curve" (Ford, 1974) as a way to manage the flow of the program. Ford observed that when planning programs, programmers should take note of a curve of action that typically characterizes program flow. She wrote,

In social activities, the pitch of excitement is at a natural quiet or low level as the participants arrive and start warming up to the activities and each other. The planner wants the group to leave the event calmly and quietly also. This means that the leader plans through the social events and socialization, that the high pitch of the event will be midway through the time of the program. (p. 90)

The social recreation curve provides a framework for managing the flow of a recreational sport program. Recreational sport specialists should incorporate the different stages of the social recreation curve into the design of their programs, as it has been successfully applied by leisure service programmers for years (Edington, Hudson, Dieser, & Edington, 2004).

In this third step of the Recreational Sports Program Planning Model, the recreational sport specialist uses the information obtained from the needs assessment process to establish and identify the goals and objectives for a program. Program goals were defined as a broad-based statement of intent regarding what the program is supposed to accomplish in general terms. Program objectives were defined as specific operational statements derived from goals that describe how the goal will be accomplished and serve as the measurement points of goals and consist of two types (implementation and outcome objectives). Once these goals and objectives are established, the recreational sport specialist can then begin to design the actual program and write the program plan.

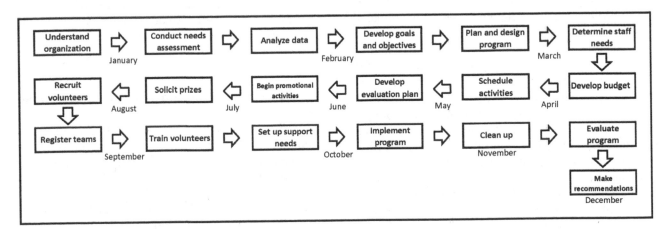

Figure 15.4. PERT Chart. Adapted from: DeGraaf, D. G., Jordan, D. J., & DeGraaf, K. H. (2010). *Programming for Parks, Recreation, and Leisure Services: A Servant Leadership Approach* (3rd ed.). State College, PA: Venture.

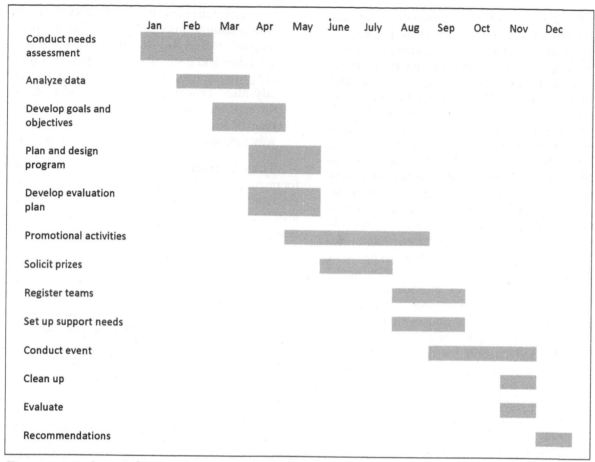

Figure 15.5. Gantt Chart. (Adapted from: DeGraaf, D. G., Jordan, D. J., & DeGraaf, K. H. (2010). *Programming for Parks, Recreation, and Leisure Services: A Servant Leadership Approach* (3rd ed.). State College, PA: Venture.

Step 4: Program Implementation

The fourth step of the Recreational Sport Program Planning Model involves actually implementing the program. This is how a program is animated or "set into motion" and also involves how this action is sustained throughout the duration of the program. This is going to vary greatly depending on the program delivery area, and specific program planning and program implementation details are best left for those chapters. However, there are unique program planning considerations for each program area, and those have been summarized in Table 15.5. In addition to these planning considerations for the different program delivery areas, the recreational sport specialist will also have different roles to play when implementing programs. For example, the recreational sport specialist will assume more of a facilitator role for club sports in which he or she may train individuals in the various leadership roles of a club sport and just help facilitate the club sport's operations. Whereas, the recreational sport specialist will assume more of a leadership role, taking direct

responsibility for the delivery and implementation of informal, intramural, and extramural sport offerings. Finally, the recreational sport specialist will be more of a broker who will organize other people in the community with the requisite skills, knowledge, and dispositions to teach or deliver instructional sport programs.

Step 5: Evaluate Program and Make Recommendations

This last step of the Recreational Sport Program Planning Model focuses on evaluating the program and making program recommendations. In order for recreational sport specialists to be able to successfully evaluate their programs, they need to develop a basic understanding of both the concept and the application of evaluation including understanding what evaluation is and why it's necessary; typical questions that program evaluation is designed to answer; general steps in evaluating a recreational sport program; and decisions required by recreational sport specialists in order to successfully conduct program evaluations.

Table 15.5

Key Program Planning Considerations for the Four Program Delivery Areas

	Recreational Sport Program Delivery Areas			
	Intramural and Extramural Sports	**Instructional Sports**	**Informal Sports**	**Club Sports**
Key Program Planning Considerations	Season or year event's calendar, training officials, tournament type, promotion, scheduling contests, emergency, supervision, facility/equipment arrangements, check-in and registration, etc...	What sports to teach, facility/equipment arrangements, instructional aids, instructor arrangements, evaluation system, season calendar for instruction, fee and charges schedule, payment arrangement, promotion, age limitations/categories, etc...	Supervision, facility hours, area scheduling/reservation system, fees collection (if any), emergency considerations, conveniences and auxiliaries, cleanliness, maintenance, etc...	Club type, organizational structure, administration, operational guidelines, legal liability considerations, constitutions, financial support and funding allocation process, provision of instructional or coaching personnel, equipment, facilities, travel and insurance, office & storage space, phone & computer access, clerical assistance, publicity, control and addressing violations, etc...

What is evaluation? Within the context of recreational sport, evaluation can be defined as the systematic collection and analysis of data in order to make judgments regarding the value or worth of a particular aspect of a recreational sport program. The particular aspect of the program may relate to the impact the program had on participants, the satisfaction of participants, the effectiveness of various marketing strategies, or anything to do with the inputs, activities, outputs, or outcomes of the program (i.e., the program logic model). Regardless of what is being evaluated, the goal is to systematically collect data that can then be used to make decisions. These decisions come in the form of both conclusions (i.e., interpretations stemming from the data analysis) as well as recommendations (i.e., proposed courses of action regarding what needs to be done or could be done based on the conclusions) that often suggest how the data might be applied in practice regarding the improvement of the program before offering it again.

Why is evaluation necessary? Evaluating recreational sport programs is important so that data-based decisions can be made regarding the merit, worth, value, or significance of the program, which subsequently allows the recreational sport specialist to make informed decisions before running the program again. Recreational sport specialists can also use evaluations to justify the allocation of resources and choose between competing programs. Furthermore, results from systematic evaluations are essential as recreational sport specialists are being increasingly held accountable for numerous aspects of recreational sport programs relating to the impact of the program on participants and cost efficiency (public sector) or the extent to which the program was profitable (private sector).

Evaluation can also identify and solve problems, find ways to improve management, determine the worth of the recreational sport program, measure success or failure, identify costs and benefits, identify and measure impacts, satisfy sponsors and authorities, or help the program gain acceptance, credibility, and support (Getz, 1997). In addition, Henderson and Bialeschki (2002) identified five purposes of evaluations:

Determine accountability. This involves establishing the extent to which the allocation of resources, revenue and expenses, marketing, promotion and sponsorship efforts, activities, and processes "effectively and efficiently accomplish the purposes for which [the recreational sport program] was developed" (Henderson & Bialeschki, 2002, p. 25).

Assess goals and objectives. Recreational sport programs can be evaluated in terms of whether the goals and objectives were met for the program. This may also help determine the appropriateness of the stated goals and objectives and if they need to be modified for future programs.

Ascertain outcomes and impact. The extent to which local, regional, national, or international recreational sport programs, tournaments, or events have encouraged tourism can be measured by the economic impact of the program through examining the direct and indirect financial benefits of tourist expenditures on a local economy.

Identify keys to success and failure. Evaluating recreational sport programs may also help to identify what worked well and why and what didn't work well, why it didn't work well, and how that could be avoided or improved upon in the future.

Improve and set a future course of action. Evaluations can also help identify ways that particular aspects of a recreational sport program can be improved as well as make decisions regarding the implementation, continuation, expansion, or termination of the program.

Regardless of the specific purpose, evaluation is a key component of the Recreational Sports Program Planning Model in which informed decisions regarding how to improve the program can be made as well as in which the recreational sport specialist can develop a better understanding of the factors and processes of the program, which either contributed to its success or were responsible for its failure.

Key evaluation questions. Somewhat related to the different reasons why evaluating recreational sport programs is necessary are the variety of questions that evaluations can be designed to answer. These questions typically fall into one of five recognizable types according to the issues that they address (Rossi, Freeman, & Lipsey, 1999):

Questions about the need for the program (needs assessment). Needs assessments are often used as a first step when determining the initial need for the recreational sport program or when designing and planning a new program or restructuring an established program (Step 2 of the Recreational Sports Program Planning Model).

Questions about program conceptualization or design (evaluating program theory). Evaluating the conceptualization or design of a program involves explicitly stating in written or graphic form the theo-

ry guiding the program and then measuring how appropriate it is. This is most important when planning brand new programs or when pilot testing programs in their early stages.

Questions about program operations, implementation, and service delivery (evaluating program processes). Process evaluation provides information for monitoring a specific procedure or strategy as it is being implemented so that what works can be preserved and what doesn't can be eliminated.

Questions about the outcomes and impact of the program (impact evaluation). Impact evaluation examines both the intended and unintended impacts/benefits of the recreational sport program.

Questions about program cost and cost-effectiveness (evaluating efficiency). Evaluating the efficiency of the recreational sport program involves examining the benefits of the program in relation to the costs incurred by the program. Cost benefit analysis can be used to evaluate the relationship between program costs and outcomes/impacts (benefits) by assigning monetary values to both costs and outcomes/impacts. Cost effectiveness analysis also uses program costs and outcomes but examines them in terms of the costs per unit of outcome achieved.

In summary, evaluating recreational sport programs can focus on the need for the program, the design of the program, the processes underlying the program, the impact of the program, and the efficiency of the program. Recreational sport specialists should be aware that basically any aspect of a recreational sport program can be evaluated including advertising, public relations, promotions, sponsorships, risk management, development and implementation of the event plan, financial aspects of the event, responsibilities and performance of staff or volunteers, facilities, supplies, equipment, logistics, technology, concessions, registration, scheduling, timing, venue, ticketing and entry, security, communications, information and signage, transportation, parking, and so forth. Before making any decisions with respect to the research design of the evaluation or even specific data collection strategies, the recreational sport specialist must clearly determine what is being evaluated, why it is being evaluated, and the criteria to be used to evaluate it.

Facilitating the process of evaluating a recreational sport program. In order to effectively facilitate and manage the evaluation process, there are a number of questions that the recreational sport specialist has to consider before undertaking such an endeavor. The following questions are adapted from McDavid and Hawthorn (2006) in order to better fit within the context of evaluating recreational sport programs:

- What type of recreational sport program, and where is the program at in the program life cycle?
- Who are the key stakeholders of the evaluation?
- What are the questions or issues driving the evaluation? That is, what is the goal or purpose of the evaluation?
- What resources are available to evaluate the program?
- Have any evaluations been conducted in prior years?
- What are the intended goals of the program?
- What kind of environment does the program operate in?
- Which research design strategies are suitable?
- What sources of evidence (data) are available or are appropriate given the evaluation issues, the program structure, and the environment in which the program operates?
- Should the evaluation be conducted?

General steps in evaluating a recreational sport program. The following are the five steps to evaluating a recreational sport program:

1. Determine what is being evaluated and specify the evaluation questions.
2. Identify sources of evidence; develop appropriate measures and data collection strategies.
3. Collect and analyze the data.
4. Prepare and disseminate the evaluation report.
5. Make decisions regarding the improvement of the program and modify as necessary.

In order to complete the fifth step, a number of decisions must be made. These decisions are outlined below.

Informal versus formal evaluations. Recreational sport specialists are so consumed by the design, development, and implementation of the program that they are continually evaluating aspects of the event informally. This may be through watching others or processes or through talking and listening to clients, participants, staff, or volunteers. While it is important for the recreational sport specialist to have a thumb on the pulse of the program, these types of informal evaluations do not result in systematic, reliable, and credible information that can be used as the only basis for improving the program. On the other

hand, formal evaluations based on systematically gathered data through planned observations, structured interview or focus group questions, or carefully developed questionnaires allow recreational sport specialists to make informed, data-based decisions that are reliable and can be used as the basis for improving the program.

Formative versus summative evaluations. Formative evaluations happen while the recreational sport program is still in progress and can be used to evaluate what is happening while the program is being implemented, whereas summative evaluations take place at the end of the program and typically examine the impact or effectiveness of the program (Scriven, 1972). The advantage of formative evaluations is that they can occur at any stage of the program and that feedback is provided while the program is still operating so that changes can be made on the go. From that standpoint, formative evaluations are intended to provide feedback about the processes of the program with the goal of improving those processes and their effectiveness while the program is still happening. Summative evaluations, on the other hand, focus on the "bottom line" and are often used for accountability purposes in terms of whether the event achieved its goals and objectives (McDavid & Hawthorn, 2006). Both formative and summative evaluations are important as the recreational sport specialist needs to make decisions during the design and development stages and during the implementation of the program as well as once the event has concluded in order to make decisions about how to improve it.

Quantitative versus qualitative evaluation. While there are considerable differences between quantitative and qualitative research methods, both have a place when evaluating recreational sport programs. Before making decisions with regard as to which to use, the recreational sport specialist should have a basic understanding of the differences and similarities between quantitative and qualitative approaches when it comes to evaluating programs. A quantitative approach is an "inquiry into a social or human problem, based on testing a theory made up of variables, measured with numbers, and analyzed with statistical procedures, in order to determine whether the predictive generalizations of the theory hold true" (Creswell, 1994, p. 3). Whereas, qualitative approaches are defined as "an inquiry process of understanding a social or human problem, based on building a complex, holistic picture, formed with words, reporting detailed views of informants, and conducted in a natural setting" (Creswell, 1994, pp. 2-3). Based on these definitions, recreational sport specialists should observe that quantitative approaches to evaluation typically emphasize measurement procedures that generate data in the form of numbers, whereas qualitative data is generally expressed in the form of words and provide a means for developing a deeper understanding of some aspect of the program. Recreational sport specialists need to decide what type of data will provide the necessary information to best answer their evaluation questions. Deciding whether the evaluation should be quantitative or qualitative should depend on the purpose of the evaluation as well as what is being evaluated.

Making program recommendations. After evaluating the program, the recreational sport specialist needs to make final recommendations regarding any changes that should be made to the program before running it again. These recommendations should be based on the data gathered from the evaluation. Rossman and Schlatter (2008) outline three choices that can be made when making program recommendations:

- operate program again with no changes,

- modify, or

- terminate.

If the recreational sport specialist recommends to offer the program again without making any changes, then he or she should explain why the program was so successful and support this with data from the evaluation of the program. If the recreational sport specialist recommends that modifications are necessary before offering the program again, then detailed recommendations regarding any aspects of the program plan or program logic should be offered, again grounded in data collected from the evaluation of the program. How difficult it will be for the recreational sport specialist to make these program modifications in the future will depend on both the degree of change (i.e., how much is to be modified or changed?) and the amount and type of information available about the advisability of change. Finally, the recreational sport specialist may choose to recommend that the program be terminated. If this is the recommendation, Rossman and Schlatter (2008) advise that recreational sport specialists establish specific criteria for termination that are agreed upon by the various stakeholders in the program. For example, termination decisions could be made from an economic standpoint (i.e., was the program profitable, or did it break even?) or whether the program met its goals and objectives. In order to avoid potential fallout from immediately terminating a program, recreational sport specialists might choose to gradually reduce program offerings or continue the program with reduced expenses, phased in over time, so that participants have time to find alternative programs to meet their needs.

This last step of the Recreational Sport Program Planning Model focused on providing recreational sport specialists with preliminary information and things they need to consider in order to successfully evaluate their program. In order for recreational sport specialists to be able to successfully evaluate their programs, they need to develop a basic understanding of both the concept and the application of evaluation including understanding what evaluation is and why it's necessary, typical questions that program evaluation is designed to answer, general steps in evaluating a recreational sport program, and decisions required by recreational sport specialists in order to successfully conduct program evaluations.

► **Computer Tip**

Project Management Software

Recreational sport specialists have turned to project management software to help them meet program goals and deadlines. In many cases, project management software can be the key to successful planning and evaluation. Whether you are a beginner or an experienced planner, project management software is a versatile management tool that can make you a more effective manager and help you set program goals, track projects, and manage the people, resources, and decisions necessary to reach your goals.

A project is simply a group of tasks, activities, or events with defined start and stop dates. Project management software provides visual tools and techniques for creating, scheduling, and controlling project plans; for communicating these plans to staff and for making necessary changes as they occur. Project management programs allow staff or project managers to easily understand their roles in the planning process.

Microsoft Project is an easy to use planning software available for Windows and Macintosh operating systems. It guides new users or project managers through the various phases of project planning by using familiar steps associated with the traditional planning process. Microsoft Project allows you to create a schedule that lists specific tasks that must be accomplished to complete the project, the approximate order in which the tasks will occur, and how long each task should take to complete. Tasks may be added, deleted, or modified as the project proceeds.

All project tasks are then organized by groupings and linked in sequence to create task relationships, showing you how long it ill take to finish the entire project. For example, some tasks may need to be finished before other tasks can begin, while there may be still other tasks that can be completed simultaneously. These differences in timing will affect the total time required to complete the project. Staff and equipment resources need to be assigned to the tasks once the tasks are appropriately grouped and in the proper sequence.

Project management software allows you to communicate and track project information clearly and effectively in a variety of ways. Most project management programs can print charts, reports, job assignments, equipment summaries, budgets, and other schedules. With this type of software, recreational sport specialists can plan event schedules, assign staff and equipment resources, and track the progress of events.

Conclusion

This chapter focused on the production of recreational sport programs through program planning. Proper program planning ensures that recreational sport programming decisions are based on identified needs of the population they are being designed to serve. The Recreational Sport Program Planning Model was introduced as a systematic way to develop, implement, and evaluate recreational sport programs. The model was described in detail in the chapter and consisted of five steps, including understanding goals and objectives of organizations (Step 1), understanding participant needs and organizational capacity (Step 2), planning and designing the program (Step 3), implementing the program (Step 4), and evaluating the program and making program recommendations (Step 5). While the program format, duration, location, goals and objectives, and so forth are going to vary based on the program delivery area (informal sports, instructional sports, intramural and extramural sports, and club sports), the process to plan, develop, implement, and evaluate the program is the same. It is important that recreational sport specialists develop the necessary competencies required for program planning, implementation, and evaluation. This chapter provided a starting point; the rest of the book should provide the recreational sport specialist with more details regarding the specific operational details of recreational sport programs.

Bibliography

Creswell, J. (1994). *Research design: Qualitative, quantitative, and mixed methods approaches* (2nd ed.). Thousand Oaks, CA: Sage Publications.

Deci, E., & Ryan, R. (1985). *Intrinsic motivation and self-determination in human behavior.* New York, NY: HarperCollins.

Deci, E., & Ryan, R. (2000). The "what" and "why" of goal pursuits: Human needs and the self-determination of behavior. *Psychological Inquiry, 11*(4), 227-268.

DeGraaf, D. G., Jordan, D. J., & DeGraaf, K. H. (2010). *Programming for parks, recreation, and leisure services: A servant leadership approach* (3rd ed.). State College, PA: Venture.

Edington, C. R., Hudson, S. D., Dieser, R. B., & Edington, S. R. (2004). *Leisure programming: A service-centered and benefits approach* (4th ed.). San Francisco, CA: McGraw-Hill.

Ford, P. M. (1974). *Informal recreational activities.* Bradford Woods, IN: American Camping Association.

Getz, D. (1997). *Event management and event tourism.* Elmsford, NY: Cognizant Communication Corporation.

Harper, J. (2009). *Planning for recreation and parks facilities: Predesign process, principles, and strategies.* State College, PA: Venture.

Henderson, K. A., & Bialeschki, M. D. (2002). *Evaluating leisure services: Making enlightened decisions* (2nd ed.). State College, PA: Venture.

Knowlton, L. W., & Phillips, C. C. (2009). *The logic model guidebook: Better strategies for great results.* Los Angeles, CA: Sage Publications.

Maslow, A. H. (1943). A theory of human motivation. *Psychological Review, 50*(4), 370-396.

McDavid, J. C., & Hawthorn, L. (2006). *Program evaluation and performance measurement: An introduction to practice.* Thousand Oaks, CA: Sage Publications.

Mull, R., Bayless, K., & Jamieson, L. (2005). *Recreational sport management* (4th ed.). Champaign, IL: Human Kinetics.

Rossi, P., Freeman, H., & Lipsey, M. (1999). *Evaluation: A systematic approach* (6th ed.). Thousand Oaks, CA: Sage Publications.

Rossman, J., & Schlatter, B. (2008). *Recreation programming: Designing leisure experiences* (5th ed.). Urbana, IL: Sagamore.

Scriven, M. (1972). Pros and cons about goal-free evaluation. *Evaluation Comment, 3*, 1-7.

United Way of America. (1996). *Measuring program outcomes: A practical approach.* Washington, DC: Author.

W. K. Kellogg Foundation. (2004). Logic model development guide. Retrieved from http://www.wkkf.org/Pubs/Tools/Evaluation/Pub3669.pdf

Wells, M., & Arthur-Banning, S. (2008). The logic of youth development: Constructing a logic model of youth development through sport. *Journal of Park and Recreation Administration, 26*(2), 189-202.

CHAPTER 16

Marketing

CHAPTER OBJECTIVES

After reading this chapter, you will understand services marketing, be able to identify marketing concepts, understand the importance of customers and their relation to agency success, and be able to identify promotional methods used in recreational sport.

KEY CONCEPTS

Market research
Services marketing
Product
Service quality
Place
Price

Promotion
Physical evidence
People
Process
Customer service
Market segmentation

Introduction

There are many different skills required of a recreational sport specialist throughout his or her job, and more and more one of those skills is marketing. Hiring recreational sport specialists with marketing abilities and skills has become essential. Marketing, or services marketing, relates to understanding and then meeting the needs of individuals through programming and services, which is what a recreational sport specialist primarily does. This chapter will describe services marketing, highlight how it differs from traditional/product marketing, and follow up with strategies for implementing the marketing mix (i.e., a plan) in various recreational sport settings. This chapter will begin by describing marketing concepts including market research, market segmentation, and service quality followed by a description of the "expanded marketing mix," which incorporates the four Ps (price, product, place, and promotion) of marketing and three additional Ps (people, process, and physical evidence) related to services marketing (Zeithaml, Bitner, & Gremler, 2009). Chapter 3 states, "In the field of recreational

sport, the core product is providing sport to create fun, learning, and fitness opportunities", and this understanding of recreational sport is consistent with the approach taken by services marketing.

The importance of marketing cannot be understated; it is critical that community members, participants, and staff be aware of what goes on in recreational sports. This awareness can contribute to a greater understanding of the benefits of recreational activity and help position recreational sport agencies as providers of well-being programs and help them to avoid severe budgetary cuts. Unlike financial decisions, which are impacted by sector (i.e., public, commercial, private not-for-profit) and their mandates (i.e., profit, social), services marketing principles and strategies are more universal in nature and cross sector boundaries. Furthermore, while in the past only commercial agencies tended to allocate resources to marketing, nowadays all three sectors engage in various aspects of what is known as marketing, or services marketing, because of its emphasis on understanding the customer and delivering a relevant program. Agency size, agency sector, and available resources will dictate the comprehensiveness of a marketing plan; however, some common activities will relate to determining appropriate prices, determining program locations, and maintaining Web-based promotions.

Why Services Marketing?

There are several reasons for framing this chapter around services marketing as opposed to goods marketing, or what has always been thought of as marketing. First and foremost, services marketing is more reflective of what actually occurs in recreational sport programming in that recreational sport specialists are providing experiences rather than products the majority of the time. Services marketing, as a concept, grew out of marketing for that simple fact—not all marketing was related to goods. As well, by understanding and adopting a services marketing approach, there are clearer links with service quality that can ultimately help agencies achieve higher levels of customer satisfaction. Four clear distinctions between products and services according to Parasuraman, Zeithaml, and Berry (1985) led to the development of services marketing and are discussed next.

Tangible vs. Intangible

Unlike products (e.g., golf clubs in a sporting goods store), services (e.g., instructional recreational sport programs such as golf lessons) are not objects that can be held or touched.

Nonperishable vs. Perishable

Likewise, services and products differ according to whether they are perishable. Services do not sit on a shelf and cannot be returned or saved for a later date, whereas products can be stockpiled, inventoried, and returned.

Standardized vs. Heterogeneous

One of the more important distinctions is that services are not exactly the same every time they are offered; however, all Callaway golf clubs are the same regardless of which store is selling the product. The greatest factor making experiences different is based on the employees delivering the service, which makes both service delivery and the marketing of service delivery challenging. For example, with instructional programming, it is accepted that different instructors will offer the same water aerobics course in a slightly different manner even though the actual content of the course is the same.

Production Separate From Consumption vs. Simultaneous Production and Consumption

Finally, unlike goods that follow a sequential pattern of production, purchase, and consumption, services begin with a purchase and then production and consumption occur at the same time. For example, a student may register for an intramural sport on a Monday and return to the gym on a Friday with his or her teammates for the first intramural game. Because consumption and production occur at the same time, customers affect both their own and others' experiences during service delivery.

In highlighting the differences between products and services, it becomes evident that a different approach is needed to market services. Furthermore, it is recognized that an intangible service is more difficult to market, which is why the seven Ps are all used to help make the service come alive and feel real to individuals. Specific strategies (i.e., the 7 Ps) related to making the service tangible are discussed later in the chapter.

Service Quality

Perceptions and *expectations* are two key terms related to service quality. Service quality is about meeting customer expectations during a service experience and underlies services marketing because of its close connection to customer satisfaction. In 2005, a specific instrument for recreational sports was developed to assess service quality (Ko & Pastore, 2005) based on the original work of Zeithaml, Parasuraman, and Berry (1990) (See Table 16.1).

Table 16.1

Subdimensions of Recreational Sport Service Quality

Range of program	Valence
Operating time	Sociability
Program information	Ambience
Client-employee interaction	Facility design
Inter-client interaction	Equipment
Physical change	

Source: Ko & Pastore, 2005

In recreational sports, customer satisfaction is important because it can translate into increased levels of customer retention (i.e., loyalty). If individuals are satisfied with an instructional program, they are more likely to participate in the future as well as register for additional programs. Furthermore, satisfied customers can provide positive word-of-mouth communications, which is a powerful method of promotion. In being committed to service quality, it is important that procedures and policies reflect this commitment. For example, recreational sport agencies may have a service commitment that tells customers what they can expect. Likewise, when things go wrong, it is important to have a good strategy in place for satisfying the customer.

Market Research

In services marketing, it is important to understand people because this information informs all seven Ps of the marketing mix. Through research, a recreational sport specialist is better able to answer the questions related to the seven Ps by understanding the consumers and therefore being able to provide services that best match the consumers' wants. This happens all the time in recreational sports. There are different degrees to which agencies engage in market research, but most recreational sport agencies will use direct and simple ways of measuring the expectations of customers. While it may seem a bit intimidating to be conducting research, it is not, especially for a recreational sport specialist who is involved in the delivery of services. Examples of market research questions are as follows: What percentage of the community knows about the new swimming program? Why did people stop at the Welcome Center, and what information did they obtain? What reasons do people have for participating in a softball league?

Often, a recreational sport specialist will know the participants in a program over time, and this informal communication enables the recreational sport specialist to ask questions about what is going on. Furthermore, because a recreational sport specialist is often engaged in the delivery, it is also easier to gauge the reactions of participants (this is an inherent aspect of the job). Staff are always concerned about the experiences of people during recreational sport programs. Because much of what recreational sport specialists do is related to understanding individuals, they are at a real advantage. Beyond this, while there

are many ways of collecting research, common approaches in recreational sport settings include

- solicited and unsolicited discussions with participants, staff, volunteers, and individuals outside of the agency;
- observations of programs both within and outside the agency, both planned and spontaneous;
- stakeholder meetings with participants, staff, volunteers, policy makers, and individuals outside of the agency;
- suggestion boxes;
- online feedback opportunities; and
- evaluation forms at a program's completion (see Figure 16.1).

There are different strategies that exist for ensuring feedback from participants. One example is the use of incentives in exchange for completing a questionnaire. Visibility is another way to "research" the market. For the recreational sport specialist, it is important to be visible within the organization (and have an office that is accessible to participants) so that unsolicited feedback can be gathered. Finally, it is important to convey to employees the importance of obtaining feedback. When all staff in a recreational sport agency, especially front-line staff with direct access to participants, feel engaged in soliciting feedback, greater insights will be gained. In summary, it is useful to think of market research as an ongoing part of the job, which will contribute to it becoming second nature.

Market Segmentation

Another task related to marketing is segmenting the market. When markets are too large to manage, segmenting the market, or breaking one large market into many smaller, more manageable groups, is advantageous. The result of market segmentation is a target market that describes a group of individuals who share one or more similar characteristics and have relatively similar service or program preferences. In recreational sports, the recreational sport specialist tends to concentrate on target markets because much of what he or she does is specialized. There are a number of ways that a market can be segmented, but some of the more common ways include the following: sociodemographics and lifestyle, needs, location, and loyalty.

Your Feedback is essential to ensure program quality and service variety. Complete your program evaluation and let your voice be heard!

Directions: Please place a check in the box that corresponds to your answer.

INSTRUCTOR EVALUATION	Very satisfied	Satisfied	Somewhat satisfied	Not satisfied	Unsure/ na
Was the instructor knowledgeable and professional?					
Did the program start on time?					
Did the instructor meet your expectations?					
Did the instructor create a welcoming environment?					
PROGRAM EVALUATION					
Was the number of participants suitable for the class?					
Was the length of the program suitable?					
Was the scheduled time for the program suitable?					
Was the content of the program what you expected?					
Was the program equipment suitable?					
Was safety considered in all aspects of program delivery?					
Were there levels of skill progression?					
COMMUNICATION/ REGISTRATION					
Was the registration process clear, and easy to complete?					
Did you receive a program confirmation in a timely manner?					
Were instructors clear in communicating program expectations?					
FACILITY					
Was the facility clean?					
Was the facility suitable for the program offered?					
If you have a special need, was the facility accessible?					
OVERALL					
Would you register for this program again?	Yes	No	Unsure		

Comments:

Figure 16.1. Program Evaluation Form

Sociodemographics and Lifestyle

Common tools for segmenting markets in recreational sport settings are sociodemographic and lifestyle indicators. Mass markets can be grouped according to age, gender, income level, professional associations, and religious affiliations. For example, swimming programs designed for specific age groups (children, youth, adults, seniors) are the result of segmenting a market based on age.

Needs

By segmenting a market further, the recreational sport specialist can focus on needs. Recreational sports are often segmented based on needs or benefits. For example, different strategies (marketing mix activities) can be developed based on instructional needs, informal needs, or extramural needs. In terms of understanding the benefits of recreational sports, younger adults may be looking for elements of socialization with their recreation choices, and by incorporating opportunities for socializing into young adult programs, their needs may be met.

Location

By grouping individuals based on a location, the recreational sport specialist can customize a program for that group. Students living in residences are an example of a market segment based on location, and once the recreational sport specialist is aware that this is the segment, decisions should be made accordingly. Similarly, the idea of location can be expanded to include facility use. For example, if part of a facilities inventory is a pool, a recreational sport specialist may target all the individuals who are current users of the pool.

Loyalty

The idea of grouping individuals based on loyalty is an idea that relates to service quality because essentially you want to reward the individuals that have been loyal to the agency. Research has found that participants tend to be loyal, especially to fitness programs. Understanding loyalty can be helpful, especially when there is direct competition with your programs and services. There is an 80/20 rule that relates to loyalty because 80% of revenues come from 20% of participants. Therefore, you want to be aware of the 20% of participants that are driving your programs and services. A strategy for rewarding loyalty can be tiered memberships where the highest memberships receive extra services. YMCAs use this strategy with their "membership plus" option in change rooms because, for an additional cost, members can access change rooms equipped with saunas, hot tubs, televisions, telephones, and comfortable seating. Loyalty can also be tied to levels of use, as is the case in Figure 16.2 where a golf club rewards frequent participation in a variety of golf-related activities.

Structural Constraints to Participation

By incorporating market research into ongoing job responsibilities potential structural constraints to participation can be addressed with subtle changes made to accommodate a wider set of individuals. There are numerous reasons why individuals do not or are unable to participate in recreational opportunities; however, one of the more commonly understood constraints is structural (Crawford & Godbey, 1987). Examples of structural constraints are a lack of time, a lack of money to register and purchase necessary equipment, not having a partner or team required for participation, and a lack of transportation to the program. By recognizing the relevance of structural constraints, efforts can be made to encourage greater participation. There are different strategies that can help minimize these structural constraints including the following:

Earn points just for playing golf, hitting range balls, purchasing equipment and even taking a golf lesson.

For every dollar you spend in the golf shop you earn points that you can redeem toward complimentary rounds of golf. Here's how it works:

Green Fees	1 point for every dollar
Multi-Play Cards	1/2 (.5) point for every dollar
Power & Push Carts	1/2 (.5) point for every dollar
Range Balls	1/2 (.5) point for every dollar
Golf Clubs, Balls & Bags	1/8 (.125) point for every dollar
Men's & Women's Wear	1/8 (.125) point for every dollar
Gloves, Hats, Shoes	1/8 (.125) point for every dollar
Golf Lessons	1/20 (.05) point for every dollar

300 points gets you a round of golf FREE!
That's only ten (10) rounds of golf to get one free! And all you have to do is sign up!

Sign up today to start earning points. **Please remind us you are member every time you make a purchase.**

Figure 16.2. Golf Course Loyalty Rewards Program *(Reprinted with permission.)*

- various price points of programs and services including free programming, if possible.

- varied program offerings. By offering programs and services at various times of the day and night, a greater portion of the population may be served. Programs need to be offered at a time when people are available to participate. As a recreational sport specialist, you may have developed the best program for a basketball league, but if it runs at a time that participants are not available (for any number of reasons), then it will not be a success.

- outreach programs to address accessibility issues. This means bringing programs and services to individuals who may not be able to get to the facility. For example, a university fitness program can be delivered once a week at a retirement home.

- program services such as tennis ladders or team sign-ups where individuals interested do not need to have a partner or be part of a team to participate.

Understanding service quality, market segmentation, and structural constraints to participation will help a recreational sport specialist meet the needs of individuals. Therefore, for recreational sport specialists, working through the marketing mix represents a strategy for accomplishing this.

Marketing Mix: Seven Ps – Strategies for Developing a Marketing Plan

In recognizing the fundamental differences between marketing a product and marketing a service, it makes sense that different strategies are required when developing a marketing plan. This section of the chapter deals with the aspects of a marketing mix that will inform strategies for a recreational sport specialist working in a recreational sport setting. When understanding marketing through a services marketing lens, there are three additional Ps that have been added to the standard four Ps of the marketing mix, which include people, physical evidence, and process (see Figure 16.3).

By working through these seven Ps, the end result is a marketing plan that outlines what activities should be pursued in meeting agency goals and ultimately satisfying people's needs. Even though a marketing plan is an extremely useful document in helping to achieve goals, a recent study found that

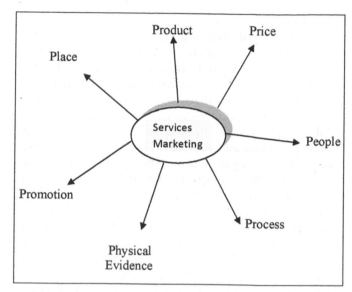

Figure 16.3. Seven Ps of Services Marketing

only 40% of campus recreation departments had a marketing plan (Kaltenbaugh, Molnar, Bonadio, Divito, & Roeder, 2011).

Product

Product is what is actually being offered to participants, and this is the most important P in the marketing mix. Without a product (e.g., recreational sport offering), there is nothing. As structured through the text, intramural and extramural, informal, club, and instructional make up the products that can be offered in recreational sport settings. However, there is more to it than that because what is important to understand about recreational sports is that it is actually the "benefits" that individuals are purchasing in recreational sports. For example, an intramural hockey league is selling "socialization, physical fitness, and skill development" in addition to hockey. See Figure 16.4 for examples of recreational sports programs.

Therefore, it must be positioned and communicated in that manner. Research on benefits of recreation began in the early 1990s and has grown so much that the National Recreation and Park Association developed a marketing campaign based on the idea that "the benefits are endless" in order to promote this concept. Similarly, in Canada, the National Benefits Hub is focused on the promotion of eight marketing messages designed to accomplish a similar goal (see Table 16.2).

**Municipal Recreation Department
Older Adult Fitness Class**

Older adults who are looking to improve their strength, flexibility, and cardiovascular fitness will enjoy this class for the socialization as well as the health benefits.

**Municipal Recreation Department
Preschool Basketball**

This program is designed to introduce youngsters to the game of basketball while learning skills such as socializing, teamwork and sportsmanship. Children will learn new skills and play basketball focused games.

YMCA Day Camp (available online)

YMCA camps emphasize participation, fair play, team spirit and leadership skills. Kids from all backgrounds and abilities participate in traditional sports, personal and team challenges and activities based on values such as caring, responsibility, respect, honesty and inclusiveness.

Figure 16.4. Examples of Program Descriptions

Table 16.2

Eight Marketing Messages Related to Benefits

Recreation, parks, sports, fitness, active living, arts and cultural services

- are essential to personal health and well-being;
- provide the key to balanced human development;
- provide a foundation for quality of life;
- reduce self-destructive and antisocial behavior;
- build strong families and healthy communities;
- reduce health care, social service and police/justice costs;
- are a significant economic generator; and
- provide green spaces that are essential to environmental and ecological well-being, even survival.

Source: http://benefitshub.ca/

Depending on the job, there may be a lot of "products" that the recreational sport specialist is responsible for offering. However, it is also likely that he or she will need to develop new programs and services. There are many reasons for developing new products (i.e., services), which include

- to replace programs that are not that well attended;
- to meet participant needs. For example, while informal sport may be offered at your organization, market research may suggest that an instructional program is desired; and
- to widen the range of programs offered. For example, YMCAs now offer all types of recreational programming discussed throughout this text. As well, an intramural division may continue to offer 6-week intramurals throughout the academic term but offer the occasional special 1-day tournament as an additional product during holidays, thus widening their program offerings.

Once a core product (i.e., service) is determined, it is relevant to decide on methods of augmenting this core product for many reasons. The first being that by augmenting a core service there is the potential to generate additional revenue for the recreational sport agency. Second, by augmenting core products, individuals may feel there is greater value associated with the service, resulting in greater levels of customer loyalty. For example, individuals may choose a workout facility based on the presence of a restaurant, child care, or well-equipped change rooms. Moreover, as a result of the additional services available, individuals may be willing to pay higher prices to gain access. Finally, by augmenting core products, the life of the original product can be extended.

Place

Moving along in the marketing mix is place. This is where the experience occurs, that is, a recreational sport setting. In Chapter 1, an overview of the numerous settings in which recreation can occur was presented. In terms of place, it is key that all facilities are accessible to the population being served. Furthermore, with new facility construction it is beneficial to incorporate principles of active transportation into the design. This means, in addition to traditional parking lots being accessible, adding features such as bike stands, bus stops, and adequate trails to and from the facility, thereby allowing more individuals to access a facility in a variety of ways. Being able to get to a recreational sport facility easily is paramount and for that reason place is critical. Often if a program is close and accessible, there is a greater chance of participation. For example, when students live on campus versus off campus, it is an easier decision to sign up for an intramural team because of the close "place."

Additionally, it is important to recognize that place can change. Outreach programs allow agencies to take their programs out of the facility and into the community. For example, when an agency holds a three-on-three basketball tournament in a downtown area or at a shopping mall parking lot, the program may have a wider reach. As well, with some club-based programs, reciprocal agreements exist among facilities, thus increasing the number of places an individual can participate. For example, YMCAs have developed this, whereby a membership includes access to any YMCA facility in the country, thus ensuring a place is always available.

Price

Price is instrumental in recreational sport programming. Price is very dependent on marketing because through promotion an agency has a chance to influence an individual's willingness to pay. There are many purposes that pricing serves. For example, pricing helps to recover the costs (indirect, direct, and contingency) associated with offering a specific program (see Funding chapter on cost-recovery pricing) and even generate resources.

Pricing can also be used to help establish value because when individuals pay for something, they tend to feel it is more valuable. It is important to remember that even nominal pricing can positively impact value. For instance, if a drop-in program of racquetball is really more about getting more people playing the sport than generating revenues, it will be considered more valuable to individuals if there is a small fee associated with it.

Finally, Pricing provides the recreational sport specialist with an opportunity to promote equity by making programs more accessible to all individuals. A recreational sport specialist may develop price structures where different markets (i.e., participants) pay different prices in order to ensure access for a greater population. For example, children's sport instruction programs tend to be less expensive than adult instruction programs, which is often an attempt by a recreational sport agency to achieve equity.

Once it has been determined that prices are necessary, there are considerations to remember when establishing prices. These include

- knowing the actual costs of the program or service including all direct and indirect costs. As simple as that sounds, there are often times when recreational sport specialists are left with deficits because the price failed to take into consideration all the costs;

- being aware of what other similar programs and services are charging;

- considering whether differential pricing will work for the program. For example, participant characteristics, time of program, and number of sessions, and so forth are all factors that may be well suited to differential pricing. For example, children and youth programs are less expensive than adult programs based on this concept; and

- understanding the psychological dimensions of pricing, especially in terms of adjusting prices, which inevitably happens. It is important to show participants the value they currently and in the future receive so that they are more willing to pay increased prices.

Overall, pricing is an important aspect of marketing, and it is important to remember that with all pricing activities, communication is key. Keeping individuals and staff members aware of costs, price adjustments, and value in a timely manner will lead to a more informed group of stakeholders willing to pay for quality programs and services.

Promotion

Promotion is the fourth P of traditional product marketing and sometimes is thought to represent all marketing, but as you can see, promotion is simply one (very visible) function of seven strategies related to services marketing. Promotion is essentially concerned with communicating programs and services to individuals. There are different objectives of communication, including to inform individuals about programs and services, to educate individuals about the benefits of recreational sport programming, and to persuade individuals to participate. Given the different functions of communications, it becomes evident that communications should be an ongoing part of a recreational sport specialist's job. As mentioned, due to several factors, services are more difficult to market, and the job of promotion in the marketing mix is to communicate and, in a sense, make the services tangible. There are several different ways to approach a discussion on promotion, but this text uses Lovelock's (2001) communication mix because it is based on services marketing ideas. This list is detailed next.

Personal communication. Personal communication is direct, face-to-face communication where a recreational sport specialist engages with individuals and informs them of the programs and services offered through the agency. Certain attributes that help a recreational sport specialist achieve the desired result include being well spoken, being passionate about programs and services, and being attentive. Personal communication is helpful when a service may be perceived to be complex so that questions can be answered and a service fully explained. Therefore, personal communication is best suited for new and novel services with which people may be unfamiliar. While traditionally personal communication can be labor intensive, incorporating aspects of customer service into one's job accomplishes the same goal but without so much emphasis on "selling."

Furthermore, it is not only the recreational sport specialist who can engage in personal communications because word of mouth is an example of personal communication that is very powerful because it is considered to be credible. However, it is important to recognize that word of mouth can also be negative. For the recreational sport specialist, it is important to remind participants about the importance of spreading the word about programs and services they enjoy. It is important to instill in participants the importance of communicating with staff when there is a problem (e.g., customer service) so that it can be dealt with.

Advertising. Advertising is a paid activity that is relatively inflexible and impersonal and aimed at reaching a large number of people. Examples of advertising "spots" can include billboards, newspapers, cinemas, the Internet, and buses. Because advertising is impersonal, it is beneficial to have a creative strategy for marketing services as well as for ensuring contact information is very visible. It is critical that individuals be aware of "who" the agency is behind the advertising. As well, due to the high cost of advertising, it is important to pick the right venue for reaching the target market.

Sales promotions. Sales promotions are made up of short-term incentives intended to encourage action and create excitement. Examples include samples and trials, coupons, price incentives, and gifts. For example, with renewed memberships, sometimes a recreational sport agency can offer a lock or a towel for the change rooms at no cost. Or early bird registrations can be used to reward individuals who commit early, which helps recreational sport specialists gain a better idea of their projected program enrollment numbers. Sales promotions are useful for a number of reasons including introducing new programs or services to individuals, attracting new participants, rewarding loyal participants, communicating value and the importance of recreation, and improving efficiencies (e.g., encouraging use at particular times, in particular facilities).

Publicity/public relations. Publicity deals with exposure not controlled by the agency, whereas public relations represents ongoing efforts (e.g., controlled exposure) by a recreational sport agency to create a positive image in the community. A one-page snapshot of the agency and its work is useful to have on hand to help with this endeavor. See Figure 16.5 for an example of a public relations one-page file.

A desired image is achieved by focusing on both internal and external efforts. Externally, it is important to continually work on achieving a desired position that can occur through various promotional campaigns including partnerships, speaking engagements, serving on boards and committees, and other activities that sustain an agency's presence in a community (however that community is defined). Internally, depending on the type of organization or unit, it is also important that other departments and units understand what recreational sport is and what function they are serving. For instance, in a university setting, it is important that administrators and decision makers across campus understand recreational sports. As well, it is important to keep participants aware of what a recreational sport agency is doing. Both old and new programs need promotion. Newsletters and bulletin boards are an effective way of keeping members and people in the organization aware of what is going on. Electronic newsletters, which accomplish the same thing as paper newsletters, are a good option when looking to save financial resources. The following are more specific examples of public relations.

Sponsorships. Sponsorships represent a nonverbal strategy aimed at a specific target market of participants, spectators, and the media. Traditionally, certain agencies and sectors have been more involved with sponsorship. For instance, pro sports organizations (i.e., commercial sector) have been able to generate a significant amount of revenue through sponsorships. However, increasingly more public agencies are allowing and, in fact, pursuing sponsorship for facilities (arenas, national park signage, etc.).

News releases. It is important to develop a relationship with the newspaper editors to help with marketing efforts. Tasks such as updating editors on upcoming events, being aware of submission policies and deadlines, and suggesting story ideas can make their jobs easier and boost the visibility of the agency. As well, regarding "letters to the editor" as an additional tool for communicating the agency's message is good to keep in mind.

RECREATIONAL SPORTS AGENCY

Who we are: State what programs and services are offered, state missions and goals.

Our goal is to provide quality skating lessons to children. We believe in parental involvement because it encourages a positive view of skill development

What we do: State what the program/service does

Our program is designed to provide children with the skills necessary to successfully transition from skating to hockey. Our focus is on the whole child, emphasizing each child's physical and mental skill development.

Impact: Provide some statistics on the agency's accomplishments as well as testimonials from participants

- We have been offering skating lessons to community members for 27 years
- We are one of the only programs still operating which emphasizes physical and mental skill development
- Over 150 children register annually with our programs
- Four current NHL'ers learned to skate with our instructors

"This skate program has been the best money we spent on lessons. Our son could not skate at the beginning of the lessons and by the third week, was able to skate independently and by the end of the session was competent" - testimonial

RECREATIONAL SPORTS AGENCY CONTACT INFORMATION
AGENCY WEBPAGE

Figure 16.5. One-page Information Sheet

Special events/open house. Having an open house, especially for member-based facilities, is an important promotional tool that allows individuals to see the facility and types of programs available in an informal, drop-in type format. Annual open houses can be tied to a program (e.g., registration time for instructional programs) or opening of a facility (e.g., outdoor pools opened after a winter season) or seasons (e.g., fall and the start of school). Having staff and volunteers in attendance at an open house is also a good idea so that there are enough people that can answer questions. In conjunction with an open house, sales promotions (e.g., giveaways) are used to ensure a large crowd attends. An open house can also be used as a strategy to reward members and current participants for their continued support, thus reinforcing elements of customer loyalty.

Speaking engagements/presentations. For the recreational sport specialist, it is important to serve a broader community and engage in different forms of public speaking/presentations. Speaking arrangements can range from local chamber of commerce monthly meetings to annual national conferences in recreation. Both opportunities provide the recreational sport specialist with a chance to promote what is going on with the agency and elevate the agency's role in the community.

Instructional materials. In recreational sport settings, emphasis is on the importance of developing instructional materials associated with services. Historically, examples have included fact sheets, newsletters (internal and external), brochures, flyers, posters, postcards, leisure guides, and pamphlets. However, now, a Web-based presence is also needed. See Figure 16.6 for an example of a website format. There are many advantages in developing and maintaining a website including increased accessibility for customers, improved methods of registrations, and enhanced communication. Even though other staff members will likely develop and maintain websites, the recreational sport specialist may be responsible for suggesting content.

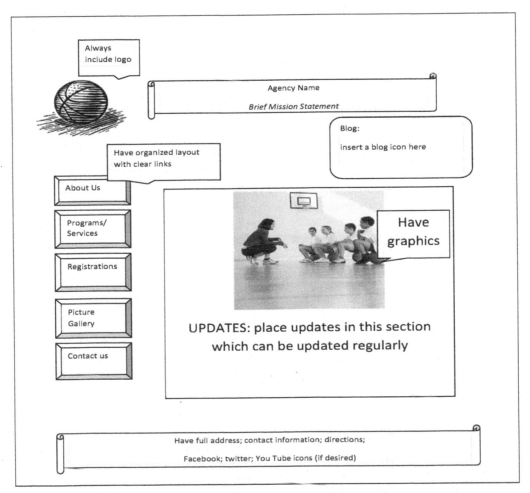

Figure 16.6. Sample Webpage Layout

As well, interfaces such as YouTube, Facebook, and MySpace are also worth considering as a vehicle for promoting the work of the agency. However, it is important to remember to develop a clear policy regarding social media and guidelines for content and material so that an agency's desired image is sustained throughout these additional outlets.

Corporate design. A last category of the communications mix according to Lovelock is corporate design and refers to things such as signage, vehicles, stationery, and uniforms needing to all have the same look. Once a logo is developed, it should appear on as many items as possible to remind individuals about the agency. These are all opportunities to continue to communicate with the public.

In developing a communications plan (i.e., promotion strategy) for a recreational sport agency, it will be important to use various components listed at various times.

Expanded Services Marketing Mix

People

There are numerous people that are involved in the delivery of recreational sport programming. Recruitment is an important part in accomplishing this (see Chapter 11 for more information on staffing). Once the right individuals (both staff and volunteers) have been recruited and hired, it is imperative that they are well trained because these people are working on behalf of the agency and impact a participant's view of a service. In recreational sport settings, interpersonal skills are paramount to the job because so much of the job relates to dealing with people. The importance of hiring the right individuals goes so far as to impact the culture of an agency. For instance, YMCAs have a strong culture of volunteerism where individuals share a passion for health and physical fitness, and this culture positively impacts a participant's experiences.

Physical Evidence

With this P of services marketing, it is the actual space where recreational programming occurs. People form impressions based on the appearance of a facility or program area. In addition to the actual aesthetics of the space, there is often a feel about a space that is important. A well-supervised area with staff present contributes to this feeling. Further examples of ways to use physical evidence to help with marketing efforts include uniforms, website design, furniture choice, bathrooms, change rooms, safety, parking accessibility, equipment, and facility design. These examples are developed more fully in other chapters and are important for contributing

to a participant's perception of a recreational sport setting, which impacts service quality.

Process

Finally, process refers to the systems that are in place that help deliver a service. In recreational sport settings there are a number of systems that impact service delivery. For example, how is registration handled? Is it Web-based, which may be easier for some but not for others? Is there a way of communicating cancellations or delays due to weather or other unforeseen circumstances? Some recreation agencies have a telephone hotline where updates can be provided to participants, whereas other agencies use the Internet as a communication tool. When the process is smooth, there is greater loyalty among participants.

Within this P is the development of an effective and efficient procedure for dealing with complaints. For example, front-line staff should have authority to make some decisions addressing and rectifying complaints. If that is not possible, the recreational sport specialist must deal with the scenario quickly. There will always be complaints, but it is how they are dealt with that individuals remember, and this response ultimately impacts a customer's service experience.

Role of the recreational sport specialist in services marketing. As shown throughout this chapter, a recreational sport specialist needs to be concerned with services marketing. To reiterate, services marketing is about knowing your participants and offering quality services that meet or exceed their needs. More specifically, while a recreational sport specialist will be engaged in all aspects of the seven Ps for their programs, there will be different Ps that benefit from more emphasis among different recreational sport programs. As a summary, each area of recreational sport is listed with specific examples to illustrate the concepts presented.

Informal sport. With informal sports, physical evidence is very important because informal sport is not dependent on instructors or staff. Therefore, the space in which it occurs must meet a participant's expectations. Furthermore, the physical evidence (e.g., facility, equipment, and aesthetics) may be what convinces an individual to participate, as opposed to other marketing mix activities. In developing promotional material related to informal sport, it is best to highlight the physical evidence through pictures with specific examples of equipment available.

Club sport. As with the others, product is an essential part of the marketing mix; however, when discussing club sport, it really is product that drives club sports. Therefore, promotional material should emphasize the quality of the sport being played, the opportunities available to members once they join, and the links with other clubs or associations.

Intramural. With intramural programs, it is relevant to discuss place because place is an integral aspect of intramurals. Often, but not always, intramurals occur on campuses and at elementary and secondary school settings, and for that reason, place is a key consideration. Intramurals provide individuals access and opportunity to participate in a recreational activity that may otherwise not exist. School settings and intramurals are a natural fit because all the individuals are there. Therefore, in developing promotional material for intramurals, creating awareness is critical, which can be done through on-campus or in-school bulletins, websites, or newsletters.

Extramural. By the very nature of extramural recreational sports and because there are always new participants, the process associated with its services are important because extramural programs are not ongoing and often need to be well orchestrated. For instance, if a dragon-boat racing championship is being organized, it must be easy to register, easy to find the location, and have ample parking; volunteers must be clearly identified on race days; and facilities must be clearly marked. When developing promotional material related to extramural events, it is key to highlight the effective and efficient process connected to the event.

Instructional. There are various manners in which instructional programs can be offered (e.g., private, group), but the common denominator is that people will influence the success of instructional programs. People refer to both staff as well as other participants in the program, so it is important that well-trained staff with qualifications teach more advanced types of instruction and that class sizes are kept low. Low group sizes are important because people signing up for instructional programs want to learn a skill, and this can be negatively impacted if the group size is too large. When developing promotional material for instructional programs, it is helpful to emphasize group size and staff qualifications.

Shining Example

Omni Amelia Island Plantation

Omni Amelia Island Plantation is an oceanfront resort located in northeastern Florida. It is unique in that it offers a variety of sports and recreation opportunities in addition to the typical resort amenities. In particular, the Omni Amelia Island Plantation offers the "Amelia Road Rally." This scavenger hunt event allows teams (families or company teams) to compete in a variety of sporting events, team building activities and trivia. Teamwork is mandatory, as all members of the team must contribute to their total score. Amelia Island offers a group recreation option which allows a business to plan sport activities around their conference agenda.

Organization:

The Omni Amelia Island Plantation is a resort and residential community that features beach, golf, tennis, and entertainment.

Clientele:

The Omni Amelia Island Plantation caters mostly to families for leisure business and over 80,000 square feet of meeting facilities allows for growing group business.

Facilities:

In addition to its golf courses, the Omni Amelia Island Plantation has several facilities devoted to tennis, volleyball, aquatics, shopping, dining, and special events.

Program Details:

The main focus of the resort is tennis and golf. It offers not only world-class tennis and championship golf courses, but also offers many educational lessons, clinics and camps. The resort offers many other activities as well, including family recreation programs (i.e. camps, movies), pools and beaches, nature programs, fishing, a luxury spa and salon, fitness classes, and more. The resort also offers bicycle and golf cart rental and Segway tours, as well as shopping and a variety of dining options.

Marketing:

The Omni Amelia Island Plantation markets itself toward families for leisure travel and group business. The recreation activities are promoted by weekly resort guides, which are available to the resort guests. The guide includes a calendar of events and a listing of recreation opportunities provided by the resort. Amelia Island also promotes its recreation programs with additional supplemental brochures, which accompany its resort accommodation guides, as well as through its website (http://www.omnihotels.com/Home/FindAHotel/AmeliaIsland/ResortActivities.aspx).

Jobs and Careers:

There are around 900 full- and part-time employees. Some of the many management positions include assistant golf course superintendent, recreation operations coordinator, program coordinator spa director and more.

Internship:

Omni Amelia Island Plantation offers several internship positions that encompass many area of operations, including golf, tennis, recreation, hospitality, and culinary arts.

Affiliated Professional Organizations:

Employees of the Omni Amelia Island Plantation may belong to various professional organizations related to the serves industry, such as the Resorts and Commercial Recreation Association (RCRA) and the American Hotel and Lodging Association (AHLA).

▶ Computer Tip

Desktop Publishing

As a recreational sport specialist, you will find yourself wearing many hats. You may do everything from personnel management to tournament scheduling to program marketing, publicity, and promotion. Unfortunately, you will have very little time to design advertising and marketing materials, program brochures, training manuals, and monthly volunteer newsletters. Fortunately, there are some easy-to-use desktop publishing programs currently on the market that will make these jobs much easier.

Desktop publishing programs are flexible, low-cost programs that help you quickly design your own ads, flyers, direct mail marketing, and forms. They are in-house marketing tools that will take your agency to a new level of professionalism and give you a promotional edge when attracting participants to your program. With desktop publishing programs, you can take advantage of the saying "A picture is worth a thousand words" and add sport pictures, seasonal photographs, graphics, clip art, and other appealing features to your publications.

Microsoft Publisher for Windows is a powerful desktop publishing program for novices. This program gives you control over text formatting, graphics importing, page numbering, dragging and dropping, and basic page formatting and layout without forcing you to learn complex concepts or techniques.

An attractive feature of Microsoft Publisher for Windows is that it includes many point-and-click options, including the popular Wizards function that is available in all Microsoft products. PageWizard takes the guesswork out of the process by walking you through the creation of nearly 250 different documents using preexisting templates for newsletters, calendars, flyers, brochures, tables, and common business forms.

PageWizard provides multiple templates for use in designing flyers. It will ask you questions regarding the desired final product, such as whether it is a logo, brochure, or newsletter. The program then creates the layout and design template, leaving you to fill in the blanks.

If you need further assistance, Microsoft Publisher for Windows also provides Cue Cards, which are prompts that pop onto the screen when needed and provide answers to common questions related to the document you are creating.

Although developing your own sport publications may sound intimidating at first, desktop publishing programs make it easy and allow you to create professional-looking printed material without becoming a professional designer.

Conclusion

In conclusion, this chapter has discussed services marketing as it relates to recreational sport specialists and their job responsibilities. As suggested with this chapter, services marketing provides a better framework for developing a marketing plan in recreational sports because it recognizes the importance of the experience and its interdependence with people. As such, marketing must be thought of as an ongoing part of a recreational sport specialist's job and requires focusing on different aspects of the marketing mix at different times. What is consistent is that services marketing and its ideas must occur both internally and externally to help establish and maintain a solid position as a reputable recreational sport setting. Market research and market segmentation are concepts that can aid a recreational sport specialist in understanding the participants who access recreation programs so that an optimal experience can be achieved. Many different promotional tools were presented so that a recreational sport specialist has the ability to align the program with an appropriate promotion.

Bibliography

Clark, J. (2005). Sport marketing. In A. Gillentine & B. Crow (Eds.), *Foundations of sport management* (pp. 83-94). Morgantown, VW: Fitness Information Technology.

Crawford, D.W., & Godbey, G.C. (1987). Reconceptualizing barriers to family leisure. *Leisure Sciences, 9*, 119-127.

Fisk, R., Grove, S., & John, J. (2008). *Interactive services marketing* (3rd ed.). New York: Houghton Mifflin.

Gladden, J., & Sutton, W. (2005). Marketing principles applied to sport management. In L. Masteralexis, C. Barr, & M. Hums (Eds.), *Principles and practices of sport management* (2nd ed.) (pp. 36-52). Boston, MA: Jones and Bartlett.

Howard, D., Edginton, C., & Selin, S. (1988). Determinants of program loyalty. *Journal of Park and Recreation Administration, 6*(4), 41-51.

Kaltenbaugh, L., Molnar, J., Bonadio, W., Divito, K., & Roeder, J. (2011). Impact of marketing strategies on campus recreational sports departments. *Recreational Sports Journal, 35*, 86-94.

Ko, Y., & Pastore, D. (2004). Current issues and conceptualizations of service quality in the recreation sport industry. *Sport Marketing Quarterly, 13*, 158-166.

Ko, Y., & Pastore, D. (2005). A hierarchical model of service quality for the recreational sport industry. *Sport Marketing Quarterly, 14*, 84-97.

Lagrosen, S., & Lagrosen, Y. (2007). Exploring service quality in the health and fitness industry. *Managing Service Quality, 17*(1), 41-53.

Lovelock, C. (2001). *Services marketing. People, technology, strategy* (4th ed.). Upper Saddle River, NJ: Prentice Hall.

McCarville, R. (2002). *Improving leisure services through marketing action.* Urbana, IL: Sagamore.

Parasuraman, A., Zeithaml, V. A., & Berry, L. (1985). A conceptual model of service quality and its implications for future research. *Journal of Marketing, 49*(4), pp. 41-50.

Shonk, D., Carr, J., & De Michele, P. (2010). Service quality and satisfaction within campus recreation: The moderate role of identification. *Recreational Sports Journal, 34*, 9-23.

Zeithaml, V., Bitner, M., & Gremler, D. (2009). *Services marketing: Integrating customer focus across the firm.* Boston, MA: McGraw-Hill.

Zeithaml, V., Parasuraman, A., & Berry, L. (1990). *Delivering quality service: Balancing customer perceptions and expectations.* New York: Free Press.

CHAPTER 17

Maintenance

CHAPTER OBJECTIVES

After reading this chapter, you will recognize the importance of maintenance; be aware of the three basic maintenance categories; understand the difference between routine and nonroutine maintenance; appreciate the value of maintenance planning; identify aspects of work arrangements and assignments; realize the ramifications of maintenance control; and understand the importance of manuals, storage areas, relations, and inspections.

KEY CONCEPTS

Functions

Categories

Routine maintenance

Nonroutine maintenance

Planning

Work arrangements

Work assignments

Control

Manuals

Storage

Relations

Inspections

Introduction

In recreational sport, clean and fully functioning sport facilities are paramount to creating a positive environment. To accomplish this, a sound maintenance system is necessary and should be recognized as a fundamental function that is critical to program participation. Maintenance is a support service that keeps facilities and equipment in clean and good working condition. An effective maintenance system includes cleaning, repairing, preventing, protecting, and preserving equipment and facilities, as well as preventive measures. Maintenance should be a priority, performed properly and in a timely fashion. This chapter focuses on maintenance's significance as a management function, a classification system for identifying divisions of maintenance responsibilities, a systemization process for work, and related considerations.

Significance

In some recreational sport agencies, maintenance is regarded as a secondary responsibility. This is unfortunate because poor maintenance has a counterproductive effect on user satisfaction, program success, and participant safety. Sport facilities and equipment should be clean, sanitary, safe, and functioning as intended. If this is not the case, it negatively reflects on management. The following information is intended to build awareness and demonstrate how good maintenance practices help make the recreational sport experience a positive one.

Functions

With few exceptions, maintenance is viewed as an indirect function because maintenance tasks seldom occur during participation. Administrators should strive to keep maintenance tasks out of sight, scheduling them outside of operational hours or at a designated time. This indirect approach may be more extensive and demanding in complex facilities.

When areas and equipment are dirty, broken, or shut down, they slow or halt participation. Poor maintenance affects comfort and causes unpleasant conditions that discourage ongoing user participation. Such circumstances are unacceptable, and management must create a proper environment for product or sport activity success.

Safety

One of the paramount responsibilities of a recreational sport specialist is to create and maintain a safe environment. Maintenance workers play an important role in this effort. It is natural for facilities and equipment to deteriorate or break, creating hazardous conditions. Such developments can have negative implications, even to the point of legal action. A nail sticking out of the floor, broken security equipment, a hole in a playing field, or a blocked emergency exit all affect the safety of a participant. In addition, many facility and equipment codes, laws, and standards exist to ensure management's compliance with safety requirements. Maintenance workers, along with the programming staff, are usually in the best position to observe and correct problems. Their role can be invaluable in keeping the recreational sport experience free from serious emergencies.

As a recreational sport specialist, your role is to cooperate with the maintenance staff, coordinating your tasks with theirs so that such an important responsibility can be accomplished with as little interruption as possible on the users' recreational sport experience.

Classification

At first glance, the maintenance concept is simple to understand: Maintenance keeps facilities and equipment functioning as intended. Such an undertaking is not commonly viewed as demanding. Yet maintenance is much more involved than it seems.

Categories

Maintenance can be observed to operate within three broad categories: buildings, grounds, and equipment. These categories identify the major work areas that lead to specific task assignments.

Buildings. In recreational sport, buildings represent the structure in which the core product and core-product extension are programmed and produced. Facilities vary tremendously, but they share common maintenance tasks that become more demanding in larger structures. Indoor sport facilities have rooms, corridors, stairways, lobbies, lounges, offices, courts, pools, arenas, gyms, auditoriums, and so on. These areas are then broken down into pieces, such as floors, walls, ceilings, electrical outlets, and lighting. All building areas have unique maintenance requirements. The building category is broad and easy to recognize, but the details in its maintenance far exceed this brief description.

Grounds. The second general category of maintenance is the area exterior to the facility, or grounds. Grounds maintenance attends to entrances, sidewalks, parking lots, building exteriors, landscaping, lawn care, tree pruning, grassy areas (fields, fairways), and hard surfaces (cement, asphalt). Other outdoor maintenance applications include irrigation systems, pest and insect control, fertilizing, snow and leaf removal, mowing, and picking up trash. In some recreational sport agencies, individuals are specifically trained to maintain grounds.

Equipment. The final maintenance category encompasses all indoor and outdoor equipment, or items that support both administrative and delivery operations of recreational sports. There is sport equipment for participation; building-efficiency equipment for heat, air conditioning, and ventilation; and maintenance equipment such as court sweepers, ice-resurfacing machines, vehicles, leaf blowers, mops, and so on. Equipment as a maintenance category is easy to conceptualize, but the process of maintaining this equipment requires special competencies.

Types

Within each of the three categories of maintenance (building, grounds, and equipment), there are two distinct types of maintenance: routine and nonroutine. These two types of maintenance require technical and practical knowledge that influences the recreational sport specialist's role.

Routine maintenance. Routine maintenance attends to building, grounds, and equipment by keeping them in proper condition on a daily basis. Much of this maintenance has to do with keeping things attractive, clean, functional, and available. Routine maintenance usually takes place outside of the delivery of recreational sport. This type of maintenance should not be interrupted because delays or lack of attention can negatively affect operations. Routine maintenance requires supervised, organized, and coordinated systems of workers attending to the following types of tasks.

Cleaning. Almost all recreational sport facilities and equipment require some form of cleaning on a daily basis in order to keep everything in good working order. Maintenance workers who take care of such responsibilities are often called janitors or custodians. They do everything from sweeping and dusting to washing, mopping, and vacuuming. As mentioned, keeping areas and equipment clean can be critical because user satisfaction is a high priority in recreational sport.

Trash removal. No indoor or outdoor recreational sport facility is ever used without some type of trash buildup occurring from program delivery and administrative operations. Part of routine maintenance is removing all trash from the facility or premises. There are garbage cans and dispensers of all sizes and shapes, and there are even designated areas where garbage is picked up and removed from the site. Recent years have seen a trend in specialized waste care and removal such as recycling of paper, glass, and plastic. Recycling may represent a community interest that requires management's knowledge and support. Each recreational sport facility has its own trash-removal responsibilities that must be addressed in daily routine maintenance.

Sanitizing. Part of regular maintenance is ensuring facilities are free of germs and bacteria by sanitizing areas and equipment. Sanitizing substances include chemicals and cleaning fluids that need to be properly studied and labeled for safety purposes. Certain areas in the recreational sport facility require sanitation, including showers, toilets, sinks, fitness equipment, food preparation and service areas, and child care areas. Record keeping of such efforts is often required to demonstrate that these responsibilities have been fulfilled. Depending on the nature of the facilities and equipment, everything can be monitored and inspected by internal and external parties, making sure both workers and users are protected from germs and bacteria.

Orderliness. Another type of routine maintenance is keeping all furniture and equipment aligned, arranged, and properly stored so that optimal usage can occur. Equipment and furniture can get into a state of disarray or can even end up in an entirely different location. This responsibility involves returning these items to their designated positions. The following day's delivery of recreational sport may be negatively affected if things are out of order and not appropriately located. This responsibility is usually part of the cleaning process and thus is incorporated into the custodial responsibilities.

Nonroutine maintenance. Not all maintenance is on an ongoing or regular basis. Nonroutine maintenance results from needs that develop unexpectedly, including emergencies. Nonroutine maintenance usually requires the attention of trained maintenance workers or specialized craftsmen who can quickly and properly resolve the unexpected problem. The following information is presented to help you identify nonroutine situations that may occur within the three categories of the recreational sport environment.

Unforeseen. No matter how vigilant the effort, damage and wear occur at unpredictable times. Buildings, grounds, and equipment can reach a state where they no longer function as intended, requiring immediate attention. Maintenance of this type should be addressed by a system for such unexpected occurrences. The recreational sport specialist should handle unforeseen developments in one of two ways: as an *emergency*, which means taking care of all needs as soon as possible, or as part of a formal process that addresses needs as resources allow. *Unforeseen* emergencies may include water leaks, insufficient or damaged lighting, overflowing toilets, and failed HVAC systems. Unforeseen maintenance needs that may not require immediate attention include broken locks, vehicles not starting, broken windows, equipment damage, and any type of damage that can be scheduled for repair or replacement at a future time.

Prevention. Preventive maintenance anticipates what needs to be done to extend the life of facilities and equipment. This nonroutine maintenance is usually planned in advance and is most often applied based on predetermined requirements or assessments that determine the need based on the level of use and wear. Preventive maintenance helps prevent hazardous conditions or major breakdowns from occurring. Breakdowns and hazardous conditions can cause serious problems, such as high costs and legal action. Preventive maintenance includes changing vehicle oil, rotating tires, caring for equipment, trimming trees around electrical wires and buildings, controlling insects and pests, refurbishing wooden floors, painting and treating surfaces, and checking drainage systems.

Cyclical. Cyclical maintenance involves a complete set of tasks that fulfills a need. This type of nonroutine maintenance uses progressive steps that complete a full process over a period of time. An example of cyclical maintenance is turf management, which requires seeding, fertilizing, watering, mowing, and aerating. This process occurs in cycles with the seasons. Recreational sport specialists must pay attention to make sure cyclical maintenance is completed in a timely fashion.

Extra help. Most staff involved in program delivery have little time or interest to work outside of their programs, but sometimes they need outside help in delivering a program. For example, a maintenance worker may be needed to bring in, set up, and take down equipment for program delivery. Smooth transitions of these tasks will promote positive experiences for the participant, so the recreational sport specialist must anticipate the participant's needs and coordinate with the maintenance staff in a timely fashion.

Systemizing

Recreational sport specialists must recognize maintenance as a critical function that supports administrative and delivery operations. The recreational sport specialist will rarely be responsible for maintenance; however, he or she will interact with maintenance staff and tasks. Hence, the remainder of this chapter is devoted to details of the maintenance system and activities.

Recreational sport participants should not have to tolerate poor maintenance or unforeseen facility conditions that deter their participation. Their participation, whether it is at an indoor or outdoor facility, should not be affected by maintenance problems. As best as possible, all operational staff should anticipate all maintenance needs and problems. The following steps have been designed to systemize routine and nonroutine maintenance.

Planning

Fundamental to a sound maintenance system is advance planning. Everything about a facility and its equipment must be addressed, which can be an expensive and time-consuming undertaking. Figure 17.1 lists various indoor and outdoor facility considerations, indicating the detailed nature of the planning process.

Maintenance planning should incorporate both a short-range (monthly or yearly) and long-range (5, 10, or more years) plan. The key to this process is the proactive determination of needs, changes, deteriorations, and breakdowns. Anticipation is a demanding responsibility that is especially challenging when it comes to unexpected, nonroutine developments. Plans must be evaluated regularly and modified as necessary. The following areas should be systematically built into a total maintenance-planning process.

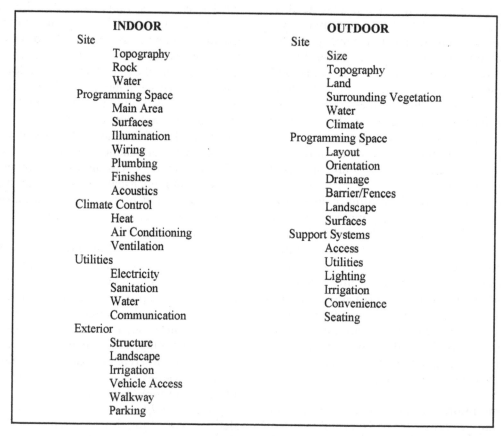

INDOOR	OUTDOOR
Site	Site
Topography	Size
Rock	Topography
Water	Land
Programming Space	Surrounding Vegetation
Main Area	Water
Surfaces	Climate
Illumination	Programming Space
Wiring	Layout
Plumbing	Orientation
Finishes	Drainage
Acoustics	Barrier/Fences
Climate Control	Landscape
Heat	Surfaces
Air Conditioning	Support Systems
Ventilation	Access
Utilities	Utilities
Electricity	Lighting
Sanitation	Irrigation
Water	Convenience
Communication	Seating
Exterior	
Structure	
Landscape	
Irrigation	
Vehicle Access	
Walkway	
Parking	

Figure 17.1. Facility Planning Considerations

Inventory. At the foundation of all maintenance is planning, a systematic inventory of everything that exists in an agency's total environment. Such an effort results in precise records that may be used as a reference in planning routine and nonroutine maintenance tasks. Information may be gathered and classified to reflect relevant factors including quality, quantity, condition, model, serial number, size, type, cost, and age. Figure 17.2 is a sample form used for such purposes. Categorizing this information is important because it aids administrative work such as budgeting, prioritizing, determining future needs, designing program activity, and staffing.

Assessing. The next likely step in maintenance planning is assessment, or routinely observing buildings, grounds, and equipment to ensure proper functioning and stability. This task occurs on an ongoing basis with complete and thorough assessments scheduled throughout the year. Assessing identifies structural problems, safety hazards, efficiency weaknesses, and potential emergencies. Formal feasibility studies, risk-management plans, and special-needs assessments must be interfaced with maintenance assessment. Assessment is a proactive effort that contributes to the planning process by discovering problems before they affect the recreational sport operations.

		Facility Items	Condition:	Location of Problem:	Comments:
General	Sport Activity Areas	Pool #1			
		Pool #2			
		Basketball Ct #1			
		Basketball Ct #2			
		Racquetball Ct. #1			
		Racquetball Ct. #2			
		Exercise/ Weight Room			
	Office Areas	Office #1			
		Office #2			
		Office #3			
		Break/Meeting Room			
		Reception/Lobby Area			
	Locker and Storage Areas	Locker Room #1 (women's)			
		Locker Room #2 (men's)			
		Storage Area #1			
		Storage Area #2			
	Safety	Fire Alarm System			
		Security System			
		Sprinkler System			
		Back-up Generators			
Structural	Interior	Ceiling			
		Floor			
		Walls			
		Windows			
		Doors			
	Exterior	Roof			
		Gutter and Downspouts			
		Wall Treatment			
		Windows			
		Doors			
Utilities	Water/Sewer	Water Lines			
		Sewer Lines			
		Water Heaters			
		Water Treatment Systems			
		Sink and Shower Fixtures			
		Toilets			
		Drinking Fountains			
	Electric/ Gas	Electric Lines			
		Gas Lines			
		HVAC Systems			
		Electrical Fixtures			
Grounds	Veget-ation	Trees and Shrubs			
		Grass			
	Parking and Walkways	Parking Lot #1 (asphalt)			
		Parking Lot #2 (gravel)			
		Sidewalk #1			
		Sidewalk #2			
		Mulch Path			

Conditions: S = satisfactory condition
H = hazardous condition exists
R = routine maintenance needed
M = large scale maintenance needed (> $500)
m = small scale maintenance needed (les than $500)

Figure 17.2. Facility Maintenance Inventory Form

Identifying tasks. Several maintenance tasks have been described so far. Each task has its own requirements, but the identification of each as part of the overall planning process demonstrates its nature and importance. For maintenance, especially nonroutine maintenance, to be addressed, such conditions must be identified through feedback. Feedback can originate from different sources including maintenance workers, recreational sport staff, and participants. Feedback can be presented through verbal or written complaints or comments citing a problem that needs attention. This input is important because it reveals information that can negatively affect delivery operations and success. Once maintenance situations are identified, they can be put into a work-order system that addresses all types of requests.

With so much depending on sound maintenance, administration cannot underestimate the importance of ongoing planning. The recreational sport specialist will play a key role in gathering and interpreting such information due to his or her insight into all facets of facilities and equipment.

Work-Order System

A number of maintenance needs develop in both indoor and outdoor recreational sport facilities. Once identified, these needs require an action system to analyze the situation, make a judgment, prioritize tasks against other needs, and assign workers to solve the problem. This responsibility can be demanding, especially at agencies with extensive facilities and specialized equipment. For this reason, formal arrangements for repair are made through a work-order system involving the following stages and areas of application.

Request form. Documentation is the first step of the work-order system and usually involves filling out a request form. Figure 17.3, a sample work-order request, includes information that identifies the category of work by citing the location, nature, and status (emergency or nonemergency) of the problem. If an emergency status is determined, predetermined arrangements are initiated to speed up communication and thus expedite the process. Before request forms are considered complete, a staff member is required to sign them, ensuring that follow-up information such as telephone number and e-mail address is included, along with a detailed description of the maintenance need. The work-order request begins a process that entails both administrative and maintenance time and effort.

Control center. The second stage of the work-order system is administrative in nature and involves the authority who receives and reviews all aspects of potential work. The request form is sent to a central location most often referred to as a control center. Administrative judgment prioritizes work, assesses costs, and assigns workers. The control center is also responsible for overseeing the work and keeping accurate, permanent records of all tasks in progress and completed.

WORK ORDER REQUEST

Date: _____   Contact: _____   Telephone: _____

Priority Level: ☐ High (emergency) ☐ Normal ☐ Medium ☐ Low

Was an "out of order" sign posted on equipment?   ☐ Yes   ☐ No

Was a "closed" sign posted at the facility site?   ☐ Yes   ☐ No

Program area: _____   Equipment: _____   Equipment ID#: _____

Specific location: _____

Description of work requested: _____

_____

_____

Submitted by/telephone/e-mail:_____
                  (signature)/   telephone   /   e-mail

Figure 17.3. Work Order Request

Job form. The control center uses a job form that represents the actual work to be done. Figure 17.4, a request for repairs, includes a description of the work along with a job number that serves as an identification code for the particular work. This number is easy to put into a computer database that keeps accurate records that can be easily accessed and compared as needed. The job form authorizes and assigns a task to a specific maintenance worker or team for completion. So that all parties can be apprised of the work, copies are made available to the requesting person or unit and the maintenance worker. The original copy is kept at the control center for further administrative purposes.

Accomplishing Tasks

After a work order has been issued, the next step is to proceed to the task. This requires administration to look at the extent of the work and the availability and ability of workers and then make a judgment relative to cost. Administration projects their influence to ensure the work will be done correctly and in a timely fashion. This is an important stage in agencies with limited funds or access to workers. In these agencies, administration may have to be resourceful in considering different options. In any case, work first has to be assigned and then controlled.

REQUEST FOR REPAIRS
JOB NUMBER_____

Date _____ Building _____ Room # _____

Priority Level: ☐ High (emergency) ☐ Normal ☐ Medium ☐ Low

☐ Classroom ☐ Office ☐ Storage ☐ Restroom: ____ Ladies ____ Mens ☐ Other

Specific Location _____

Contact Person _____

☐ Electric
- ___ Light
- ___ Ballasts
- ___ Wall Outlets
- ___ Lenses/Covers
- ___ Switches
- ___ Elevators
- ___ Broken Connectors
- ___ Wiring
- ___ Other

☐ Plumbing
- ___ Lavatories
- ___ Shower Area
- ___ D. Fountains
- ___ Stools
- ___ Drains
- ___ Stoppages
- ___ Urinals
- ___ Leaks
- ___ Other

☐ Heat/A.C.
- ___ Too Hot
- ___ Thermostats
- ___ Too Cold
- ___ Radiators
- ___ A/C Drains
- ___ Other

☐ Carpentry
- ___ Doors
- ___ Door Knobs
- ___ Locks
- ___ Door Closures
- ___ Panic Bars
- ___ Baseboards
- ___ Wall Repairs
- ___ Broken Glass
- ___ Stair Treads
- ___ Handrails
- ___ Carpets
- ___ Floor Tile
- ___ Venetian Blinds
- ___ Window Shades
- ___ Classroom Desks
- ___ Classroom Tables
- ___ Classroom Chalkboards
- ___ Other

☐ Moving & Set Up ___ Furniture   ___ Other

☐ Sheet Metal   ___ Roof Leak   ___ Other

☐ Equipment   Type: _____   ID: _____

Description of Problem: _____
_____
_____
_____

Job Started ___/___/___   Job Completed ___/___/___
Person Assigned _____   Actual Hours _____
                Signature _____

Figure 17.4. Request for Repairs

Assigning work. The control center or maintenance administration can address tasks in a variety of ways. Much of the discussions depend on the agency, resources, and ability to get things done. Following are three options for accomplishing maintenance tasks.

Unit. The unit option is an internal system that represents an agency's ability to accomplish tasks in-house. This system takes care of work specific to a facility and its equipment and grounds, with staffed workers who are familiar with everything that needs to be done. The advantage of a unit system is that workers are familiar with the equipment and facility, which in turn eases administrative decisions. It also breeds a high level of loyalty. The disadvantage to this approach is that workers must be trained in a variety of jobs. Supervisors usually oversee training, and often this effort is not the most efficient use of resources.

Specialized crews. Certain agencies have specialized crews or individuals who are experienced, trained, or certified, such as tree surgeons, mechanics, carpenters, locksmiths, plumbers, and electricians. These crews may be the only ones capable of performing particular tasks. Larger agencies usually have plenty of specialty work to keep these staff members busy. Special crews are extremely proficient in their work, providing the best use of expensive equipment and reducing accidents through quality work based on experience, skill, and knowledge. Disadvantages of specialized crews are idle time and costly travel between jobs.

Contracting out. Due to a lack of in-house expertise, some maintenance will need to be done externally. Arrangements can be made with outside help; such arrangements should always be preceded by a formal written agreement. Special attention should be given to the written agreement or contract to ensure that what is needed is thoroughly described so there is no miscommunication. Agency administration should orchestrate supervision to ensure that what is contracted is actually accomplished. Contracting is frequently used by agencies that cannot accomplish the task on their own. Advantages of this approach include no capital investment in equipment, well-trained and skilled workers, a shift of liability to contractors, and decreased work for internal maintenance staff. On the other hand, some disadvantages include limited control over how work is completed, higher costs, workers with little personal interest in the facility, and possible difficulty in coordinating a contractor's time with the facility use.

Controlling work. Controlling work is a critical task that requires constant attention to assess and correct workers' efforts. The following information should help you understand what takes place as the actual work progresses.

Coordination. The larger the agency, the greater the demand for coordination and oversight to ensure that work is done properly. Ideally, workers' efforts occur outside of administrative and delivery hours so that they do not disturb operations. This coordination requires attention given to the actual work request as it relates to time of completion. Coordination also requires insight into the work itself, including details such as job length, type and extent of work, potential delays, unforeseen obstacles, number and ability of workers, and prioritization. Coordination of all these components can be challenging, especially when tasks stimulate a great deal of administrative interest.

Supervision. Whether you are working with units, specialized crews, or outside contractors, administration needs to have a system of supervision. Maintenance personnel often vary in work ethic and style and require direction and control. Some workers may work hard, while others may goof off. Work should be routinely monitored, especially in important or specialized maintenance efforts. This type of supervision is not easy. Special care and tact are high priorities, especially when work requires high quality and a demanding time schedule. Supervision is essential for satisfactory final results because faulty work can prove expensive and can lead to greater problems including additional work.

Records. Records of assigned work should be kept in order to document all aspects of the work and provide a means to correlate the work to cost as it pertains to labor, time, material, and overhead. Such records help with budgeting, maintenance accountability, and proof of work, especially in cases where legal action might be involved. Detailed records can also help with scheduling subsequent projects and workers, especially when requests are similar.

For the recreational sport specialist, the idea of systemizing maintenance responsibilities can appear overwhelming at first. Each agency has its own way of addressing these needs, and what has been presented here is a generally recognized sequence. Wherever you are employed, you should research the stages involved and how administration addresses maintenance. It is your role to be involved, identify tasks, and where appropriate report concerns and progress as necessary.

Special Considerations

Because recreational sport requires a wide array of maintenance, there are a few other relevant points that need to be covered. Each point contributes to the overall maintenance system, and your awareness of these roles will prove helpful.

Manuals

Maintenance manuals are instructional documents that provide written descriptions, photos, and diagrams that explain exactly what is required in the care of facilities and equipment. These manuals are especially useful in specialized or highly technical facilities, providing specific guidelines for maintenance requirements and step-by-step checklists or systems. The recreational sport specialist should appreciate these manuals, especially when he or she is supervising the task. Manuals serve as formal guidelines, directing workers and addressing concerns such as preventative, cyclical, and daily maintenance. Maintenance manuals should be maintained and periodically updated to avoid any misunderstanding of the contents and the responsibility involved in performing a task.

Storage

One of the greatest problems in recreational sport is lack of storage space. Storage is often part of the maintenance function. Storage areas are spaces that secure maintenance items, equipment, bulk supplies, and spare parts. These areas are often managed by the control center for appropriate supervision and distribution. Specialty storage areas are necessary for storing items that require special protection or climate control such as chemicals, flammable material, paint, gasoline, fertilizer, and paper goods. In some instances, bulk items can be kept in storage areas, including grass seed, light bulbs, toilet paper, soap, and hand towels. Recreational sport management must have a full understanding of storage limitations so they can maximize space.

Relations

In some recreational sport agencies, the maintenance workers' attire, attitude, and conduct can make a difference and affect the success of program delivery. Maintenance workers can be an important link to user opinion and satisfaction, and some agencies take steps to ensure that these workers leave a positive impression, especially when high emphasis is placed on customer satisfaction as well as when children and teenagers are involved. For some agencies a top priority is making sure that both space and equipment are maintained at the highest level, leaving the most positive impression as possible. Maintenance relations can be beneficial in marketing recreational sport and should be applied carefully.

Inspections

A major focus of maintenance is keeping facilities and equipment safe for users and workers. Any number of conditions can develop, negatively influencing delivery operations. Laws, codes, rules, and regulations are legislated by local, state, and federal governing bodies and must be enforced. Outside certified or qualified inspectors should periodically conduct formal reviews and write reports to reflect the safety status of a facility, including problems. These problems can be serious, requiring immediate corrective action. Citations, fines, and facility closure might result if requirements are not met. Maintenance staff should understand facility requirements and ensure compliance by performing proper preventative measures. Regular inspections should be conducted and documented by internal maintenance staff to make sure the following are being maintained properly: fire codes, electrical wiring, plumbing, area capacities, and ventilation. Understanding the inspection process is an important responsibility in the maintenance process.

Each of these special maintenance considerations bears its own role in recreational sport, and the recreational sport specialist should realize his or her potential and incorporate them whenever necessary.

Conclusion

With facilities and equipment at the center of all aspects of operations, it seems obvious that maintenance should be a significant priority. Administrative and delivery operations should not be negatively affected by poor maintenance, and everything should be planned, organized, and systemized to ensure sport activity is not interrupted. The information presented in this chapter is fundamental for recreational sport specialists. You will be involved with maintenance responsibilities and workers, so be sure to recognize its importance so you can fulfill your role effectively.

Bibliography

Brown, D. W. (1996). *Facility maintenance: The manager's practical guide and handbook*. New York: American Management Association.

Campbell, J. D. (1995). *Uptime: Strategies for excellence in maintenance management*. New York: Productivity Press.

Campbell, J. D., & Reyes-Picknell, J. V. (2006). *Uptime: Strategies for excellence in maintenance management* (2nd ed.). New York: Productivity Press.

Hall, S. (2010). Impact of facility maintenance on campus recreational sports departments at public universities in the United States. *Recreational Sports Journal, 34*, 103-111.

Hurd, A. R., & Anderson, D. M. (2011). *The park and recreation professional's handbook*. Champaign, IL: Human Kinetics.

Lamke, G. (1985). Facility supervision: A vital function in overall facility management. *National Intramural–Recreational Sports Association Journal, 9*(3), 42-46.

Levitt, J. (2009). *Handbook of maintenance management.* New York, NY: Industrial Press.

Magee, G. H. (1988). *Facilities maintenance management.* Kingston, MA: R. S. Means.

Mull, R.F., Beggs, B.A., & Renneisen, M. (2009). *Recreation facility management: Design, development, operations, and utilization.* Champaign, IL: Human Kinetics.

National Park and Recreation Association. (2002). *25 keys to maintenance.* Springfield, MA: Pantera.

Palmer, R. D. (2005). *Maintenance planning and scheduling handbook* (2nd ed.). New York: McGraw-Hill Professional.

Payant, R. P., & Lewis, B. T. (2007). *Facility managers maintenance handbook* (2nd ed.). New York: McGraw-Hill.

Schneider, R. C., Stier, W. F., Kampf, S., Haines, S., & Gaskins, B. (2008). Factors affecting risk management of indoor campus recreation facilities. *Recreational Sports Journal, 32,* 114-133.

Wireman, T. (2005). *Developing performance indicators for management maintenance* (2nd ed.). New York, NY: Industrial Press.

Young, S. J., Fields, S. K., & Powell, G. M. (2007). Risk perceptions versus legal realities in campus recreational sport programs. *Recreational Sports Journal, 31,* 131-145.

CHAPTER 18

Legal Concerns

CHAPTER OBJECTIVES

After reading this chapter, you will understand the basic concepts of tort law, be familiar with risk management principles, understand standard of care requirements, understand principles of negligence, understand personal and agency liability, comprehend the importance of public security, know how to create a successful risk management program, and know how to accomplish risk management.

KEY CONCEPTS

Allegation	**Negligence**
Appeal	**Nuisance**
Cause of action	**Plaintiff**
Comparative negligence	**Property loss**
Contract	**Proximate cause**
Contributory negligence	**Risk**
Discretionary duty	**Sovereign immunity**
Fidelity	**Statute of limitations**
Foreseeability	**Tort**
Liability	**Waiver**
Litigation	

Introduction

This chapter is intended to be a primer in tort liability, negligence, and safety for persons working or studying in the recreational sport field. It does not cover OSHA standards or EPA regulations, and it does not cover every legal nuance or situation. It is intended to provide broad guidance on legal liability, safety, and risk management. When confronted with legal issues, consult your legal counsel.

The basic principles of law expressed in this chapter apply to all recreational sport providers. There may be a few local exceptions because all providers are subject to the laws of the individual states. Each organization and jurisdiction has rules and regulations related to legal liability, safety, and risk management. Seek copies of these documents and read them.

The purpose of this chapter is to create awareness of the legal liability that exists when agencies provide recreational sport and to encourage agency personnel to aggressively manage their legal risk by pursuing policy that leads to safe recreational sport experiences. There are two somewhat contradictory axioms to be considered when establishing management practices:

- *A good recreational sport safety program is good public policy.* Safety programs should concentrate on the participant's interest (risks) and not the interest (financial risks) of the organization. Sports organizations should offer a quality program with maximum protection for the participants and adequate safeguards that protect the organization from unnecessary litigation.

- *Recreational sport without some risk is uninteresting and monotonous.* Most people engaged in recreational sports are to some extent risk takers. To eliminate risk entirely is to eliminate fun. Even a small child in a playground swing enjoys the dangers of movement and height. Risk should be managed, participants warned of dangers, extreme dangers eliminated; however, all risks cannot and should not be eliminated. If risk were entirely eliminated, facilities would have to close.

Risk Management

Each year the number of sports-related civil lawsuits increases. Most of these cases seek money damages for personal injury or damage to property that occurs as a result of occupying and using sport facilities. The trend to litigate and sue over rather trivial matters makes this chapter particularly important for recreational sport specialists. Regardless of safety efforts and risk management, accidents will occur. Accidents result in claims and lawsuits with high costs of both time and funds. A good risk management program reduces the number of accidents and reduces the plaintiff's chances to successfully pursue a lawsuit. Employees should recognize their responsibility in protecting the public from accidents and property loss while at the same time protecting their agency from unnecessary litigation.

This chapter attempts to avoid technical legal language; however, in order to understand the context of this information, the recreational sport specialist needs to understand a few words or phrases:

- *Allegation*—An assertion of a fact that the person making it intends to prove

- *Appeal*—An application to a high court to correct or modify the judgment of the lower court

- *Cause of Action*—A legal right that includes right to sue

- *Comparative negligence*—The degree (percentage) of negligence assigned to the plaintiff and defendant. Damages are awarded on a basis of each party's relative carelessness.

- *Contract*—An agreement between two or more people that results in an obligation among the parties

- *Contributory negligence*—Conduct on the part of the plaintiff falling below that required for his protection that contributes to the plaintiff's injury

- *Discretionary duty* (referred to as *governmental immunity*)—An administrative duty carried out by a public official that is not subject to civil litigation

- *Fidelity*—Faithfulness to something; one is bound by faith or contract

- *Foreseeability*—An occurrence that a reasonable and prudent person would perceive and anticipate under normal and existing conditions

- *Liability*—A legal responsibility, duty, or obligation

- *Litigation*—A lawsuit

- *Negligence*—Conduct falling below the standard of care exercised by a reasonable and prudent person

- *Nuisance*—An act that causes a substantial and unreasonable interference with a person's use and enjoyment

- *Plaintiff*—The party who institutes the lawsuit

- *Property loss*—Involves injury or damage to property, real or personal

- *Proximate cause*—Something that produces a result (accident) without which the result (injury) could not have occurred

- *Risk*—A specific eventuality, hazard, or peril

- *Sovereign immunity*—A rule of law that a nation, state, or local unit of government cannot be sued without its consent. Generally considered as outdated legal concept or modified doctrine

- *Statute of limitations*—Statutes of the federal and state governments setting maximum time periods for the filing of lawsuits

- *Tort*—Any civil wrong not arising from breach of contract

- *Waiver*—An intentional release of a known legal right

Public and employee safety should be the concern of everyone in an organization. Unfortunately, risk management is often in conflict with the status quo or administrative freedoms enjoyed by some in the organization. Some organizations need to adopt new safety attitudes. Financial losses due to a lawsuit can be caused by any employee, so everyone in the agency must support the goals of the risk management program. All employees should respond to unsafe situations and take upon themselves the responsibility to take action when they see unsafe conditions or programs. Someone should coordinate and oversee the risk management efforts, but everyone should take personal responsibility.

The objectives of a safety and risk management program should include

- reduction in lost workdays from injuries (employees);

- reduction in number of injuries per 1,000 work hours (employees and participants);

- reduction in injury and property loss claims against an organization (employees and participants);

- reduction in the number of motor vehicle accidents per 1,000 miles (employees);

- adequate warnings for all known significant hazards (employees and participants);

- provision of a safe work environment (employees);

- provision of a safe recreational sport environment (participants); and

- empowerment of all employees as "safety officers" (employees).

Risk Principles

Risk management is neither complex nor costly. Risk management is simply common sense and a feeling of ownership in your organization's safety program. The goal of a risk management program is to provide a safe environment for visitors and employees. A viable risk management program also reduces successful claims and lawsuits brought against an organization (Roos, Nestor, & Berber, 1968). A single lawsuit can result in the expenditure of hundreds of hours of time investigating, documenting, and testifying.

Risk management encompasses four different elements: identification, evaluation, treatment, and implementation. The 2012 training program for the Insurance Institute of America, Chicago, Illinois has a training course referred to as ARM 54 – Risk Assessment. This introduction to risk management focuses on the first four steps in the risk management decision making process: identifying loss exposures and analyzing them, evaluating alternative techniques for treating these exposures, and selecting the most promising techniques.

Identification

Recreational sport specialists cannot identify all sources of risk on something as complex as a sport environment. Professionals must follow the adage that "we can only do what we can do." The successful identification of risk depends on the attitude of employees toward safety for their fellow employees as well as for the public. Recreational sport specialists should focus on meeting the public's recreational needs in a safe environment. An agency may be responsible for the actions of the participants, spectators, concessionaires, permittees, and contractors. Identification of risk may go beyond the immediate purview of the organization. An agency also must ensure that those who are permitted or licensed to carry out organizational objectives meet safety standards. Recreational sport providers can be exposed to several legal categories of risk. While the biggest concern is risks in tort, other financial risks include contracts, property loss, and fidelity (employees or others stealing cash, using equipment when unauthorized to do so, or stealing organization owned property).

As an example of risk identification, consider a beach volleyball court used for recreational volleyball. The site includes a steep, poorly maintained trail down a cliff from a parking lot to the beach. There are three areas to identify risk: the parking area with its entry onto a busy highway; the trail itself; and the beach area with its waterfront, volleyball equipment, and unlit restrooms.

There is a tendency to believe that safety is someone else's responsibility and someone else will see to it. Many believe that a safety hazard is the responsibility of the maintenance workers or the safety officer. Thoughtful risk managers will personalize their work by keeping in mind that their family may be the next ones at the scene of the hazard. They will ask themselves, "What can be done to make my own family's recreational sport experience safe?"

Evaluation

When a risk is identified, it needs to be evaluated according to its severity and frequency. Thinking back to the volleyball court, the trail is steep and there is a chance that people could fall and be killed or severely injured. The trail does not have a guardrail. While injuries on the trail would be infrequent, they would likely result in severe injury or even death. On the volleyball court, the accident rate would be relatively high, but the severity would be relatively low. Thus, the initial risk management effort should be directed toward trail safety because of the severity of the risk.

Treatment

When the risk has been evaluated, it is time to determine the best way to reduce losses. Treatment is the determination of a course of action. There are four major options for treating a risk: avoidance, reduction, retention, and transference.

Avoidance. Using the example of the volleyball court, the existing trail could be closed to all use or relocated. This would avoid the issue. Many recreational sport activities are by nature high-risk activities. Activities should not be eliminated simply because there is a chance that an accident may occur. An organization has to accept a certain level of risk in many of its activities; however, that does not mean that recreational sport specialists should not warn participants of the risks involved.

Reduction. Constructing a warning sign describing the dangers of being too close to the cliff edge or of slipping when the trail is wet will reduce the possibility of accidents. If the area is frequented by minors unaccompanied by parents, the construction of a guardrail may be necessary to avoid serious accidents. Warning notices (signs, verbal warnings, and brochures) provide the agency with an excellent defense against suits arising from inherently dangerous activities. Signs must be well maintained and located where their message is readily available to users. Other methods of reducing risk include developing safety rules for a particular site or activity; conducting periodic safety inspections of sites and activities using different members of the safety review team each visit; ensuring that the proper maintenance is scheduled and completed; and making certain that all employees are trained in risk management, first aid, and emergency procedures. The most important safety tool for a risk management program is a knowledgeable workforce.

Retention. Many times after an accident has been scrutinized, it is determined that the accident was the result of the complete carelessness of the individual involved or was an "act of God." The facilities, program design, maintenance, and supervisor had nothing to do with the accident. Examples of acts of God are lightning strikes or sudden winds causing a building to collapse. Nothing can be done about foolish acts that cause accidents and nothing can be done about acts of God. The organization would not be required to take any actions to prevent further accidents.

Transference. The management of the trail and beach facilities can be transferred to another agency or private operation, simply shifting the responsibility to someone else. The usual context of the term *transfer* relates to obtaining liability insurance. Many large public agencies are self-insured. In the private sector, insurance is the most common method of avoiding financial losses resulting from negligence suits. A good insurance underwriter should significantly reduce the cost of insurance when a sound risk management program is implemented. The cost of insurance is an important economic factor for permit-

tee or concessionaire operations, as more and more people are willing to sue.

Implementation

There are many tools for implementing a risk management program, including physical changes, signs, notices, brochures, spot announcements, news releases, and personal contact.

Easily understood, well-placed warning notices are an excellent way to communicate a safety hazard. A zealous administrator looking to avoid all possibilities of negligence suits could install an excessive number of warning signs. However, having more than five signs in one location or a long list of safety considerations makes them less noticeable to the visitor as well as distracts from the primary purpose and enjoyment of the area. Signs need to be maintained to be effective. Recreational sport participants, as well as the courts, expect a public or private agency to warn of any danger that is not obvious *(Van Gordon v. Portland General Electric Company, 1985; Butler v. United States, 1984; Davis v. United States, 1983)*.

When an area is known to attract young children or adults who do not speak or read English, special precautions are necessary. Young children cannot read signs or brochures, so physical barriers or parent involvement is necessary. In appropriate situations, those who are unable to read English need messages in their language. Many international safety signs bridge language barriers.

Warnings on signs, permits, maps, and brochures are the most common way to warn spectators and participants of dangers involved in recreational sport activities. While notices on bulletin boards and at offices are desirable, not all visitors stop at those facilities. Personal contact between employees and visitors continues to be an effective way to provide for public safety. Personal contact with law enforcement personnel provides a means by which the spectator/participant is warned and establishes an initial nonconfrontational environment of cooperation.

Bulletin boards provide a place to list emergency telephone numbers and special conditions or requirements that will help spectators and participants have a more enjoyable and safer recreational sport experience. Bulletin boards in offices and sport facilities are seldom read by the average visitor. It is still important, however, to post safety messages in locations accessible to the public, including bulletin boards. A wise manager will place safety and warning materials in areas that are frequented by the public. An ideal place to post safety material is on the back doors of restroom stalls. The restroom visitor usually has the time to read longer safety messages.

Mass media such as newspapers, radio, and television can also help disseminate risk-related information to the public. While mass media normally cannot be used for routine information, they can be utilized for special circumstances such as when there is danger of heatstroke, hypothermia, dehydration, or other dangers that are seasonal or one-time events. Television features reach a broad audience, especially when they are part of an evening newscast.

Standard of Care

The standard of care, or legal duty, owed to a visitor on a public recreational sport site is determined by the statutes of the visitor, applicable laws, regulations, written internal standards (manuals, handbooks, letters of direction), and common practices. The standard of care is a legal obligation to conform to a certain standard of conduct and protect others against unreasonable risks (Restatement, Second, of Torts, Paragraph 281; *Mudrich v. Standard Oil Co.*, 1949).

When individuals are injured while participating in public or private recreational sport activities, the plaintiff's legal counsel will want to know the agency's written standards related to management of activities and maintenance, design, and construction of the facility. The plaintiff's attorneys will also want to know if other accidents have occurred on the specific site involved in the accident or at similar sites. The managing agency must meet its own standards. Risk managers should check their agency's written instructions to make certain they are meeting those standards. If those standards are not being met, the written instructions should be changed or documentation filed as to why they choose to violate their own instructions. Failure to meet the standards or failure to justify the reasons the standards were not met can jeopardize the defense during litigation. Visitors are normally separated into three categories: invitee, licensee, and trespasser.

Invitee

An invitee is someone who is invited to participate in an activity, usually paying a fee for the services or use of the facilities. An invitee is either a public invitee or a business invitee.

- A public invitee is a person who is invited to enter or remain on land as a member of the public for specific recreational sport purposes, such as Little League or city soccer programs.

- A business invitee is a person who is invited to enter or remain on land for a purpose directly or indirectly connected with the business dealings with the possessor of the land. (Restatement, Second, of Torts, Section 332)

In the case of invitee, the owner, operators, and managers have a duty to ensure reasonable care has been taken to prepare the premises and make them safe for visitors. This includes protection from injury due to conditions of the land, facilities, and equipment or by injury from third parties. The owner, operator, or manager must inspect the premises and remove or warn of potential hazards and in general exercise reasonable care to protect users.

The following describes the duties that recreational sport providers or landowners owe the invitee (Kaiser, 1986):

- keep the premises in safe repair,

- inspect the premises to discover hidden hazards,

- remove the known hazards or warn of their presence,

- anticipate foreseeable uses and activities by invitee and take reasonable precautions to protect invitee from foreseeable dangers, and

- conduct operations with reasonable care for the safety of the invitee.

The prudent recreational sport specialist who complies with these five duties and keeps a written record of periodic inspections and repairs will be able to provide an excellent defense against potential legal action.

Licensee

The licensee user is owed a duty of care by the recreational sport provider. There is not a distinct dividing line among the three categories, and a great deal of gray area exists between classifications. The licensee is someone who has permission or consent, expressed or implied, to go on the land for his or her own purpose (Black, Nolan, & Connolly, 1979). In most jurisdictions the recreational sport provider owes the licensee reasonable or due care (*Mounsey v. Elland*). The licensee may go on the provider's land to conduct business or to the mutual advantage of the licensee and owner or occupant (*Samuel E. Pentecost Construction Company v. O'Donnell*).

An example may be a mail carrier, a gas meter reader, or a contractor who is injured in a fall due to an icy sidewalk on the premises. Each is classified a licensee, with implied consent to enter the property without specific permission. There is a distinction between a licensee whose presence is merely tolerated and a licensee who is expressly invited or a social guest. Although social guests may be invited and even urged to come, they are not an invitee within the legal meaning of the term. A social guest is no more than a licensee who is expected to accept the premises as the owner uses them (Restatement, Second, of Torts, Section 330).

Trespasser

A trespasser, or nonpaying user, is defined as someone who intentionally or without consent or privilege enters another's property (Black et al., 1979.). The word *trespasser* is commonly used for anyone falling under that definition and does not necessarily imply any illegal act. A person who goes on publicly owned land to enjoy a sport activity, such as tennis in a city park, has not committed a criminal act of trespass, but is still defined as a trespasser.

Owners, operators, and managers owe adult trespassers a duty of care less than that of a licensee or invitee. They have no duty to make their property or facilities reasonably safe or to warn of dangerous conditions. They only have a duty to avoid injury by gross conduct, intentional recklessness, or wanton misconduct.

There may be a question as to the status of the visitor who enters a public park to view a sport activity, play ball, or participate in a non-competitive sport activity. Essentially the visitor was invited, enticed, or attracted to the facility or activity. While these persons are technical trespassers, they have an in-between status and the courts will consider other standards as they relate to the care owed to a visitor. Visitors in this special category are sometimes defined as public invitee or simply non-paying visitors who are on the premises at the invitation of the owner.

Attractive Nuisance

Children are by nature curious and have very little sense of potential danger. Children trespass upon property because interesting or unusual attractions exist. The attractive nuisance laws provide for the protection of the mischievous child seeking a place to hide or play. Warning signs have no effect on the non-reader, and fences are meant to be climbed in the eyes of children, so in the case of trespassing children, the attractive nuisance doctrine applies. Essentially, owners who create artificial conditions where common sense indicates that children may trespass or owners who possess land containing features that may be expected to attract children are obligated to provide care such as a reasonable, prudent person would take to prevent injury. These provisions usually do not apply to natural conditions, only to artificial conditions. The phrase *attractive nuisance* is seldom used now, having been replaced by the foreseeable doctrine, but the principle remains. Children fit into a separate category when it comes to trespass visitors.

The courts vary considerably in holding parents responsible for the negligent actions of their children; however, parents can be held liable for negligently allowing their children to use inherently dangerous objects such as baseball bats. Proof of a child's inclination toward dangerous conduct usually has to be proven (*Patterson v. Weatherspoon*, 1976*)*. Parents can be held liable for the negligent acts of their minor children, particularly when there is willful or wanton intent. Courts have sent a mixed message when the children reach their teens.

Negligence

Negligence has been defined a person's failure to exercise the degree of care than someone of ordinary prudence would have exercised in the same circumstances. (Bryan A. Garner, *Black's Law Dictionary*, Thomson/West Publishing, 1990.) Negligence is also defined as "the omission to do something which a reasonable man, guided by those ordinary considerations...would do, or the doing of something which a reasonable and prudent man would not do" Whether negligence exists depends upon the circumstances of each case. The laws and court decisions are complex; so few generalities apply. Certain elements of negligence must be proven in order to have a viable court case:

- The plaintiff must prove that the defendant has a legal duty of care (i.e., is legally responsible to the plaintiff).

- The plaintiff must prove there was failure to perform a required task or there was a breach of duty.

- There must be some direct connection between the damages and the actions or lack of actions by the defendant. Simply stated, the plaintiff must prove that the breach of duty was the cause of the injury or property loss. This is commonly called *proximate cause*.

- The plaintiff must prove that he or she suffered damages (e.g., physical injury, mental anguish, or financial loss).

Legal Duty

Whether or not there is a legal duty in negligence cases is a question of law. Legal duty is determined by the judge, not the jury. The court decides whether the level of conduct was sufficient to present unreasonable risk. Once the duty has been established by the court, it is the jury or judge's responsibility to determine whether the defendant conformed to a standard of care of reasonable prudence and foresight sufficient to protect the plaintiff against unreasonable risk.

Reasonable man doctrine. The reasonable man doctrine compares the actions of a leader, teacher, supervisor, or coach with a reasonable person in the same or similar circumstances. The conduct of this hypothetical prudent person will vary somewhat and likely combine both objective and subjective elements, including physical attributes, mental capacity, and skills.

Regarding physical attributes, the reasonable person should possess characteristics typical of his or her circumstances. For example, if the person is mute, blind, or deaf or has another disability, the agency must act as reasonably knowing the circumstances and limitations. Such persons are entitled to live in the world and to have allowances made for their disabilities (Americans with Disabilities Act of 1990).

The recreational sport manager must make allowances for the type of participants and spectators they may reasonably expect. For instance, if a recreational sport event attracts very young children, a physical barrier such as a fence, rather than warning signs that a child cannot read, is needed between the child visitor and the potential danger. Wise recreational sport specialists hold parent–child sport events rather than youth sport events. The distinct difference is the parents' understanding that they are part of the recreational sport experience with the responsibility of supervising their own children. Sport equipment must be designed to safely facilitate its use by participants of all sizes and weights.

When considering mental capacity, no allowance is made for minor mental deficiencies. Defendants will be held to the test of reasonable conduct in the same manner as the prudent and careful person. Yet, if mental capacity is a reflection of minds that, because of immaturity or other mental limitations, are unable to comprehend danger or respond to written warning, special attention must be given to the situation.

Some recreational sport activities are relatively high risk such as skiing, football, soccer, rugby, and lacrosse. The question to ask is "What type of skills and equipment are needed to reduce the risk of the activities?" A certification system should be used to determine the competency of the user or guide high-risk activities. Leaders of certain high-risk recreational sports need a minimum amount of training under a certified instructor as well as specialized equipment. Waivers, releases, and agreements to participate may help reduce litigation for adults engaged in high-risk activities.

Rule of seven. A recreational sport provider is expected to give children greater care than adults. The courts recognize that, depending on the age of the child, children are held to various degrees of responsibility for their own actions. This is sometimes referred to as the "Rule of Seven." The four age categories are as follows:

- Children under age 7 are not responsible for their own welfare. A child under 7 normally cannot recognize dangerous situations or read warning signs. The recreational sport provider's greatest responsibility for supervision lies with this age group.

- Children between ages 7 and 14 are considered partially responsible for their own welfare. They can understand most warning signs and can comprehend some dangerous situations.

- Youths 14 through 18 years of age are mostly responsible for their own actions. They have the experience to make many good decisions related to their personal danger.

- Adults are considered responsible for their own behavior.

It is important to note that the courts have been known to change the Rule of Seven when special circumstances warrant modification.

Foreseeability. Like many aspects of legal liability, certain doctrines are difficult to understand. There are many interpretations and opinions on what is foreseeable and what is not foreseeable. The ability of a person to foresee a danger depends on the individual's training and experience. Foreseeability is the ability to see in advance that there is a reasonable likelihood that harm or injury may result because of certain acts or omissions: "As a necessary element of proximate cause this means that the wrongdoer is not responsible for consequences which are merely possible, but is responsible only for consequences which are probable according to ordinary and usual experience" (Black et al., 1979). In other words, the courts do not demand that the recreational sport specialist be able to read minds, but they do expect reasonable anticipation of risk.

Breach of Duty

Once a standard of care is established, the second element of negligence comes into play, that of failure to conform to the duty. Negligent conduct may occur because a person did something that was dangerous or because a person failed to do something. What is important from a legal viewpoint is that a defendant was somehow involved in an activity that resulted in an accident (van der Smissen, 1968).

Three words describe the type of breach involved with a negligent act: nonfeasance, misfeasance, and malfeasance (Black et al., 1979). They are crucial in determining the severity of the breach of duty and therefore the liability of the defendant:

- *Nonfeasance*—The nonperformance of some act that ought to be performed, omission to perform a required duty or total neglect of duty

- *Misfeasance*—The improper performance of some act that a person may lawfully do

- *Malfeasance*—Doing evil, ill conduct, the commission of some act that is positively unlawful

Res ipsa loquitur. There is a legal principle called *res ipsa loquitur* that translates into English as "the thing speaks for itself." The rule represents an evidence principle that the fact the accident occurred is indicative of the fault of the defendant. To apply this doctrine two things must be true:

- The accident or damage would not have occurred if reasonable care had been used.

- All the elements of the circumstances surrounding the accident were under the control of the defendant.

As an example, if tennis player 1 hits tennis player 2 with a tennis racket that has slipped out of player 1's hands, it is difficult to blame the injury on the injured player. Tennis player 1 should settle the claim and not try to litigate the matter in the courts (Prosser & Keaton, 1984).

Proximate cause. To prove negligence, the plaintiff must prove that there was a relationship between the plaintiff's accident or danger and an act or omission by the defendant. Proximate cause is a complex problem made up of a number of smaller problems that are not distinguished clearly by the law. That is why trials are conducted. A defendant can always point to someone or something else as the actual cause of the accident. Legal responsibility for an accident is limited to those causes that are closely connected with the results and of such significance that the law is justified in imposing liability (Prosser, 1980).

Injury and damages. There can be no negligence without injury to persons or property. The word *damage* refers to loss, injury, or deterioration caused by negligence. Damage can involve physical or mental harm or damage to property. Damages can be compensatory, punitive, or consequential (Black et al., 1979).

Compensatory damages. Damages awarded to a person as compensation, indemnity, or restitution for harm sustained

Punitive damages. Damages awarded to a person to punish other litigants because of their outrageous conduct

Consequential damages. Damages awarded a person for suffering because of the act of another even though the act was not directed toward the first person specifically and the damages did not occur immediately

Affirmative Defenses

Conforming to professional standards of reasonable care, following manual and handbook guidelines, using accepted standards of maintenance, and conducting activities in a competent manner help establish an individual or organization as reasonable and prudent. In addition to the absence of negligence, the law recognizes other defenses against legal liability. The following are considered defenses to negligence, though there are some variations among state tort laws:

Contributory negligence. This is conduct on the part of the plaintiff contributing as a legal cause of the harm they have suffered, which falls below the standard to which they are required to perform for their own protection (Prosser, 1980). The "Last Clear Chance" doctrine is an exception to the general rule that contributory negligence bars the plaintiff from recovery of damages. This doctrine allows a plaintiff to recover if the defendant, immediately before the injury, had an opportunity to prevent the injury but failed to do so.

Comparative negligence. Plaintiffs may only be awarded a percentage of their damages if they in some degree contributed to the accident. If a plaintiff is 40% responsible for an accident, he or she can only collect 60% of the court judgment. Most states do not allow awards to plaintiffs if their actions contributed more than 50% to the accident (Prosser, 1980).

Assumption of risk. A plaintiff who by contract or otherwise expressly agrees to accept a risk of harm arising from the defendant's negligence or reckless conduct cannot recover damages unless the agreement is invalid because it is contrary to public policy. A football player cannot claim the coach did not warn him that he might be blocked or tackled. The football player assumed a certain amount of risk by the very nature of the game (Prosser, 1980, pp. 439–457; Restatement, Second, of Torts, Section 496).

Government immunity (Prosser, 1980). Some actions by federal employees are governmental functions (planning, financing, and other discretionary activities), and they retain an immunity status. Those actions concerning day-to-day maintenance and operations are proprietary and generally are not protected from litigation. A considerable amount of protection is afforded to public employees (Federal Employee Liability Reform and Tort Compensation Act, 1988; Federal Tort Claims Act, 1946).

Statute of limitation. There is a fixed period of time to file a lawsuit. The period depends on the jurisdiction and the circumstances.

Notice of claim. State and federal laws require those who are making claims to file a claim within a given period after the cause of action, using proper procedures. If a party waits too long to file a claim, the claim is not accepted, no matter how legitimate. If injured persons are unable to make a claim because their condition or circumstances did not allow it or because the severity of the loss or injury was delayed, the notice of claim requirement is not a defense. Claims usually need to be made in writing.

Failure of proof. A plaintiff must prove that the standard of care was breached by the agency. If the plaintiff does not meet the burden of proof, the lawsuit will be rejected by the court *(Breslin-Griffitt Carpet Co. v. Asadorian; Muesenfechter v. St. Louis Car Co.)*.

Waiver or liability release. A written statement by the plaintiff stating that the plaintiff assumed all risks and released the agency from liability may provide a defense. These written releases are known as waivers, permission slips, consent forms, or agreements to participate. One should use this defense with some caution. The laws, regulations, and court cases provide the framework, and waivers cannot be used to change public policy. Releases must be written properly and signed by adult participants (*Schnackenberg v. Towle*, 1961). Releases are not valid if

- they are contrary to public policy (e.g., a waiver would be invalid if an intoxicated bus driver had a vehicle accident with the team on board);

- they are ambiguous, making it difficult to determine the extent of rights waived and to understand the exact hazards and conditions related to the recreational sport activity; and

- minors or their parents sign the release on their behalf.

In Loco Parentis is a legal term meaning "in place of the parent." Coaches and others supervising youth sports assume parent's role and the responsibility while the child is under their supervision. Those who supervise children should minimize the *in loco parntis* doctrine by encouraging the parents to attend competitions and practices. Encourage and enable parents to take action to safeguard their child as they deem necessary. Parents in the pool while their children are learning to swim is a good practice, particularly in regards to young children.

Waivers do not apply to minors, other than to inform the participants and their parents that there is some danger involved in the activity; recreational sport providers should have parents sign agreements to participate or informed consent forms rather than waivers or releases. The agreement to participate should be specific enough for the parent to understand the possible harm that may occur to their child as a result of the activity. While waivers may not be valid in all jurisdictions they provide a means by which an organization can inform the parent or guardian of the dangers associated with an activity. The typical parent defense to an injury that they "did not know about the danger" will not be effective.

Liability

The concept of sovereign immunity originated with the divine rights of kings, that is, "The King can do no wrong." This concept carried over to government at all levels in the United States. In the United States' early history, a court was established called the "Court of Claims" to hear claims against governmental entities. As demand increased with population growth the court proved awkward, expensive, and limited in accessibility to the general public.

Tort Claim Acts

In 1946 Congress passed the Federal Tort Claims Act *(29 U.S.C.A. Sections 1346, 1402, 2110, 2401, 2402, 2411, 2412, 2671–2680)*, which makes the United States liable for torts that include the negligent or wrongful acts or omissions of federal employees or agencies. *Federal liability is determined under the laws of the state where the wrong occurred.* Every state has legislation that is similar to the federal act and that allows its citizens to file suit against governmental entities.

The tort claim acts generally allow suits against recreational sport providers and their employees or agents in the same manner that suits are allowed against private companies and employees (28 U.S.C.A. Sections 1346(b), 2674). When public employees are working within the scope of their employment, they do not have to personally defend themselves; rather, the agency's legal counsel will represent their interest in any litigation *(Federal

Employees Liability Reform and Tort Compensation Act, 1988).

In all states, consent has been given to sue the state and local government under tort (Leflar & Kantrowitz, 1954). In most cases the statutes favor the state rather than the people of the state. There is an excellent list of the major elements of each state's tort claims act and government sovereign immunity in van der Smissen's book *Legal Liability and Risk Management for Public and Private Entities* (1990, pp. 179–195).

Recreation Land Use Liability Statutes

All states, with the exception of Alaska and North Carolina, have enacted recreation land use liability statutes. Recreation land use statutes protect public and private property owners from suits by non-paying individuals who use their property for recreation. As a general rule, the claimant must prove at least gross negligence in order to establish a basis for suit under the recreation use liability statutes. Gross negligence is determined when the defendant knows or should know the results of his or her acts.

The words *simple, ordinary, gross, willful, wanton,* and *reckless* are used to describe the degree of negligence in most courts. The following are the most commonly used terms.

Ordinary negligence. This is the failure to exercise care such as would be expected by the majority of people under like circumstances.

Gross negligence. This refers to the disregard of life and property of others, or great negligence. It consists of conscious acts of negligence.

Willful or wanton negligence. The conduct complained of was so gross as to have something of a criminal character or to be deemed equivalent to an evil intent, wantonness, or recklessness indicative of malice (West Publishing, 1971, pp. 447–448).

Under a recreation land use liability statute, the landowner owes no duty to care for those engaged in recreational sport or to guard or warn against known or discoverable hazards on the premises. The protection from suits found under these statutes is lost when a fee is charged for the use of the premises or when the landowner is guilty of gross or willful and wanton misconduct. Unlike mere carelessness, willful and wanton misconduct is more outrageous behavior, demonstrating an utter disregard for the physical well-being of others. Willful and wanton negligence has a strong element of an intentional action by a defendant that is so obvious that the defendant must be aware of it. It is usually accompanied by conscious

indifference to the consequences amounting almost to willingness (Kozlowski, 1986).

A careful analysis of your state's recreation use statutes would be a prudent exercise. Some states have liability immunity statutes specifically written for their state-owned public lands (e.g., Indiana Code Annotated Paragraph 14-2-6-3 and 4-16-3-1 to 3Q). At this time most of the recreation use liability statutes apply to all public lands (local, county, state, and federal) as well as private lands in the state.

Who Is Liable?

If an accident due to personal negligence occurs, you or your organization may be liable for damages. Employees, volunteers, members of boards, supervisors, commissions, and officers of private agencies are not personally liable for their actions as long as they are working within the scope of their duties. Supervisors and administrators could be held personally liable in the following three circumstances:

- if the administrator or supervisor participated in or in any way knowingly directed, ratified, or condoned the negligent act of the employee.

- if the administrator or supervisor has unsuitable employment or notification procedures. These may consist of the following:

  - incompetent hiring practices,
  - failure to fire a person when circumstances warrant the dismissal,
  - inadequate documentation of firing,
  - inaccurate or incomplete job descriptions,
  - insufficient training of staff,
  - unclear establishment/enforcement of safety rules and regulations,
  - failure to remedy dangerous conditions,
  - failure to study and comply with statutory and/or agency requirements, and
  - failure to give notice to others of known unsafe conditions.

- if there are violations of a person's civil (Constitutional) rights. They include infringements on

  - religion, race, creed, color, gender, or age;
  - rights of privacy;
  - rights against illegal search and seizure;
  - free speech;
  - rights of assembly;
  - due process; and
  - freedom of association.

Just because a person may not be personally liable does not diminish the fact that suits are exceptionally expensive, both in time and money to the organization. Every individual in an organization must recognize personal responsibility to reduce the organization's exposure to suits. If persons working within the scope of their duties are named in a civil suit where they are indemnified (held harmless) by policy or statute, the legal counsel for the organization will represent them if necessary and the damages will be paid by the agency.

Volunteers

Special attention should be paid to the volunteers because most public agencies use them in a variety of ways. While their time and effort is not recognized with monetary rewards, each supervisor should consider them as employees from a legal liability standpoint. Each volunteer working within the scope of the volunteer assignment subjects the organization to the same type of liability as full-time employees. An injured volunteer can also sue the organization for any damages sustained due to a negligent act of another. Recreational sport specialists should be extremely careful in recruiting, selecting, training, and supervising volunteers.

Strict Liability

Some categories of activities are so inherently dangerous, or ultra-hazardous, that liability is imposed on one who performs them if harm results, regardless of the degree of care (Stern & Ladden, 1971). The American Law Institute has eliminated the term *ultra-hazardous* in favor of *abnormally dangerous* and has stated six factors to be considered, one of which is whether the activity is inappropriate to the place where it is carried on. This was applied in *Yommer v. McKenzie* (1969), where gasoline was stored in dangerous proximity to the plaintiff's well.

Suits involving strict liability have not been a major problem in public agencies. The clearest examples of strict liability would be the known use of defective field equipment, allowing the public to use an unsafe playing field, and injury resulting from the use of dangerous or defective sports equipment. For example, if a football helmet is not manufactured and maintained in accordance with established safety standards (Consumer Product Safety Commission) and results in an injury, the manufacturer or agency may be held liable.

The Public and Security

Public safety and security are primary concerns of recreational sport specialists. While some will falsely recommend that a warning not be given when there are known hazards because it admits to knowledge of the problem, it is far better to warn the public of known hazards. Staff should be more concerned with public safety than they are with protecting the agency.

There is evidence of increasing spectator and participant violence in sport-related activities. For example some Little League parents have become legendary for their unacceptable, boorish behavior. Faced with this reality, the recreational sport specialist must try to anticipate the behavior of both the participant and the spectator.

Having uniformed officers present at recreational sport events provides a sense of well-being and security. In areas of high crime and in activities with a history of problems, patrols by agency personnel and local law enforcement officers should be made on a scheduled basis.

Releases, Waivers, and Agreements to Participate

Waivers, releases, and agreements to participate are not normally considered tools for the recreational sport agency; however, they need to be considered due to a litigious society. Recreational sport activities tend to be riskier than other forms of recreation. Releases and waivers justify, excuse, or clear the agency from fault in an accident or damages. Verbal waivers are too challengeable to be useful. Written waivers and releases are contracts. The court's response to waivers and releases has varied with individual judges and jurisdictions. Because minors are unable to contract, the use of waivers and releases with them is considered improper. Releases and waivers are invalid if they are

- signed by minors (children and youth under legal age cannot be a party to a contract),

- signed on behalf of minors by their parents or guardians (adults cannot sign away the legal rights of their children),

- not specific (ambiguity in the content of the waiver makes it difficult to determine the extent of the rights waived), or

- waiving rights contrary to public policy (i.e., negligent behavior). (Kaiser, 1986)

Waivers and releases have a higher likelihood of being validated by the courts if they are specific and are related to high-risk activities such as white-water rafting, mountain climbing, and spelunking.

Even with the limitations of waivers and releases, recreational sport providers should not be hesitant to use them with adult participants. When the documents are specific, they provide a strong reminder to the participant of the dangers involved in the activity. That reminder, accompanied by a signature, forms a basis whereby a specific waiver or release invokes the "assumption of risk" defense.

The best instrument for limiting the liability for minors is the "agreement to participate." This document must be specifically worded to cover in detail the risks involved in the activity. It also must include all the rules of conduct so that minors and their parents or guardians understand what is expected of them. The agreement to participate documents the fact the parents understand the dangers involved and agreed to tell their children to abide by the rules (van der Smissen, 1985).

An effective agreement to participate also triggers the assumption of risk defense to negligence. For the assumption of risk defense to hold in court, the risk of any activity must be described in some detail.

A public employee should be able to conclude that it is less risky to provide recreational sport activities for adult participants than for young participants. However, public agencies have an ethical and legal obligation to serve young people, even though that segment of the population is most vulnerable to accidents and needs the most protection from harm.

Intentional Torts

Recreational sport provides an environment where there is constant contact among players and between players and recreational sport specialists. For a number of reasons, including fatigue, alcohol, drugs, and personality characteristics, conflicts occur and people argue, fight, steal, trespass, defame, and commit other crimes and torts. These crimes are controlled by the criminal justice system. The negligence tort is usually involuntary in nature and can be described as an accident or incident caused by an act of negligence, whereas a voluntary tort, such as assault and battery, occurs through a deliberate and intentional act (Kaiser, 1986).

While public employees are somewhat protected from personal suits, the agency is not protected from suit and the embarrassment caused when employees commit personal torts. This category of tort includes, but is not limited to, assault, battery, defamation, invasion of privacy, false imprisonment, intentional infliction of extreme emotional distress, trespass to land, trespass to chattel, and conversion (Prosser, 1980).

While intentional tort cases are somewhat rare in recreational sport, they do occur. Recreational sport specialists should take action when participants commit intentional torts against their employees. Two of the most commonly occurring torts in a sport setting are assault and battery.

When a recreational sport organization violates a person's constitutional rights, it is difficult for the individual employees involved to be protected by immunity and to be assisted by governmental representation. A right is guaranteed to citizens by the constitution and so guaranteed as to prevent legislative interference of those guaranteed rights (Black et al., 1979). The U.S. Constitution guarantees that each citizen is to be protected from excessive governmental control of due process and discrimination because of race, religion, gender, age, and national origin, and each citizen is to be guaranteed the right to reputation and privacy, religious practices, freedom of speech, liberty, ownership of property, and civil rights. Certainly, when exercising a constitutional right violates another person's rights, action must be taken to protect the public's interest. For instance, one cannot yell "Fire!" in a crowded auditorium under the guise of exercising free speech.

Risk Management

Risk management is accomplished through employees and their administrators. Everyone in the organization should take personal responsibility to ensure that activities and property are safe for both the user and the employee.

Practical Guidelines

How can an organization reduce its susceptibility to lawsuits? The following are three ways for recreational sport specialists to take action to reduce the chances of a successful lawsuit:

- Investigate and take action where accidents have previously occurred. In such cases the agency is already "on notice" of the dangers and should apprise the public accordingly. All accidents and incidents should be investigated and reported (see Figures 18.1 and 18.2), but preventive actions are not necessary in all cases. Some situations or incidents occur as the result of individual carelessness and not at any fault of the agency.

- Concentrate on areas of high use. The statistical probability of an accident or incident arises with the intensity of use. A prudent recreational sport specialist will concentrate risk efforts in areas where the most people are involved rather than in areas with little activity.

- Warn people about conditions that pose extraordinary danger due to unknown or unrecognized hazards that an ordinary, prudent person might not anticipate, such as sharp edges on outfield fences or extreme weather conditions that increase the possibility of hyperthermia or heatstroke.

ACCIDENT REPORT FORM

A. Report data	Date: _____ Time of injury:_____a.m./p.m.
B. Personal data	Name of injured: _____ Gender: ❑ Female ❑ Male Age: _____

Local address: _____ Phone: _____ E-mail: _____

City, state, zip: _____

Classification: ❑ Student ❑ Faculty ❑ Staff ❑ Public ❑ Other _____

C. Injury data	Body fluid spill? ❑ Yes ❑ No (Did employees practice Universal Precautions?) ❑ Yes ❑ No

Part of body injured:

❑ Abdomen   ❑ Chest   ❑ Neck   ❑ Pelvis
❑ Back   ❑ Head   ❑ Nose   ❑ Other _____

R L   R L   R L   R L

❑ Ankle   ❑ Foot   ❑ Knee   ❑ Toe
❑ Calf   ❑ Forearm   ❑ Quadriceps ❑ Upper arm
❑ Elbow   ❑ Groin   ❑ Ribs   ❑ Wrist
❑ Eye   ❑ Hand   ❑ Shin   ❑ Other part _____
❑ Finger   ❑ Hamstring ❑ Shoulder

Nature of possible injury:

❑ Bruise
❑ Cut
❑ Dislocation
❑ Fracture
❑ Sprain
❑ Other _____

What action(s) taken:
❑ EMS called but victim not transported
❑ First aid (describe): _____
❑ First aid supplies used: _____
Victim transported to: ❑ Hospital ❑ Health center ❑ Home ❑ Other _____
Method of transport: ❑ Ambulance ❑ Private auto ❑ Police ❑ Other _____
(*Note:* The organization is not responsible for any medical and/or transport fees associated with injuries to participants.)

Time EMS called _____ a.m./p.m.	Time EMT arrived _____ a.m./p.m. EMT name(s) _____

Location of accident:

Figure 18.1. Accident Report Form. From *Recreational Sport Management* by Richard Mull, Kathryn G. Bayless, and Lynn M. Jamieson, 2005, Champaign, IL: Human Kinetics.

Accident Report Form *(continued)*

D. Program data	Activity

D. Program data

❏ Aquatics
❏ Fitness/wellness
❏ Informal sports
❏ Club sports _____
❏ Intramural sports _____
❏ Special events _____
❏ Other_____

Activity

❏ Babminton ❏ Flag football ❏ Softball ❏ Volleyball
❏ Basketball ❏ Racquetball ❏ Squash ❏ Wallyball
❏ Cycling ❏ Running ❏ Strength and conditioning
❏ Diving ❏ Soccer ❏ Swimming
❏ Group exercise _____ ❏ Martial arts _____
❏ Speciel event _____ ❏ Other _____

Employee #1 - narrative

State factual information, not opinions. Never diagnose injuries. (Interview the victim. Report the *who, what, when, where, how* and what you did surrounding the accident.) Use additional paper if necessary.

Employee name: _____ E-mail: _____

_____

_____

_____

_____

_____

Were you the only employee who responded to the accident? _____
If not, begin employee #2 narrative.

Employee #2 - narrative

Employee name: _____ E-mail: _____

_____

_____

_____

_____

E. Signatures

Injured participant: _____ _____
(if care provided)   *(Injured person's signature)*   *(Printed name)*
[Examples of care include: assistance with any of our first aid supplies, curbside assistance to a vehicle outside one of our facilities, calling for advanced medical assistance.]

Refusing attention signature: I, _____
_____, have been advised that I may have a medical condition(s) which may require an examination by a doctor, and I refuse such medical care and/or advice as has been rendered by the recreational sport personnel. Or, I do not believe a medical emergency exists and I require no further assistance.

Signature: _____ Date: _____ Time: _____

Report completed by: _____ _____ _____
         (Employee signature)   *(Name printed)*   *(E-mail)*

Figure 18.1 cont.

Accident Report Form *(continued)*

F. Witness info	(What did you see happen? [*who, what, when, where, how*] Use additional paper if necessary. Report names, times, and what you did related to the events surrounding the accident.)

Witness # 1
(*Note:* to be completed by a witness who saw the accident—*not* a recreational sport employee or the injured participant.)
Name of witness: _____ Phone: _____ E-mail: _____
Statement:

_____

_____

_____

_____

_____

_____

_____

_____

_____

_____

_____

_____

Signature of witness: _____ Date and time: _____

Additional witnesses
(*Note:* to be completed by witness(es) who saw the accident—not a recreational sport employee)
Record your statement, name, contact information, date, time and signature on a separate sheet of paper. Remember to include as many details in the statement as factually recollected.

G. Office date	Date of follow-up: _____ Staff person:_____ Follow-up comments:

_____

_____

_____

Figure 18.1 cont.

INCIDENT REPORT FORM

Date of incident: _____

Date of report: _____

Time of incident: _____ a.m./p.m.

Time of report: _____ a.m./p.m.

| Type of incident: | ❑ Theft | ❑ ID Violation | ❑ Verbal abuse/ unsportsman- like conduct | ❑ Fight/ physical Abuse | ❑ Dunking | ❑ Other (describe) _____ _____ |

| Program area: | ❑ Aquatics | ❑ Club sports (please name) _____ | | ❑ Fitness | ❑ Informal |

❑ Intramurals   ❑ Special event or exclusive use _____
(name of event)   ❑ Member services

Location of incident: _____

| Police called: | ❑ Yes | ❑ No | Officer name and badge number: _____ |

Name of employee taking report: _____   Position: _____

E-mail: _____   Phone: _____

| Did you, the employee observe the incident? | ❑ Yes | ❑ No | If yes, please describe: |

| Was participant/player cooperative after the incident? | ❑ Yes | ❑ No | If no, please describe: |

Involved participant #1:	Involved participant #2:
Name:	Name:
E-mail:	E-mail:
Phone:	Phone:
Status: ❑ Student ❑ Staff ❑ Public	Status: ❑ Student ❑ Staff ❑ Public
Description of Person #1 Involved:	Description of Person #2 Involved:
Gender: M /F Race: Age: Height:	Gender: M /F Race: Age: Height:
Hair color: Distinct feature:	Hair color: Distinct feature:

Figure 18.2. Incident Report Form. From *Recreational Sport Management* by Richard Mull, Kathryn G. Bayless, and Lynn M. Jamieson, 2005, Champaign, IL: Human Kinetics

Incident Report Form *(continued)*

	IM participant #1 additional info:		IM participant #2 additional info:	
Intramural only	Team name:		Team name:	
	Captain name		Captain name:	
	Captain e-mail:		Captain e-mail:	
	Captain phone:		Captain phone:	

Witness #1:		Witness #2:	
Name:		Name:	
E-mail:		E-mail:	
Phone:		Phone:	

Witness #3:	
Name:	
E-mail:	
Phone:	

Recreational sport employee narrative of incident (i.e., theft, list property taken):

_____

_____

_____

_____

_____

Was the player cooperative after ejection or removal?

_____

Figure 18.2 cont.

Witness Statement

Using direct quotations if possible, please address the following in your statements:

Why was the player/participant asked to leave the game or facility?

Please describe in detail what happened.

Please be objective in describing the situation and person(s) involved. Refrain from using your opinion.

Witness #1 (print name) _____ Signature _____

_____

_____

_____

_____

_____

_____

Witness #2 (print name) _____ Signature _____

_____

_____

_____

_____

_____

_____

Witness #3 (print name) _____ Signature _____

_____

_____

_____

_____

_____

_____

❑ Witness Statement is written by the witness and must be signed.

❑ If able to get participant statement please use comment card or blank sheet of paper and attach to incident form.

Figure 18.2 cont.

Incident Report Form *(continued)*

Participant Statement

Participant name:_____ Date:_____

_____
_____
_____
_____
_____
_____
_____
_____
_____
_____
_____
_____
_____
_____
_____
_____
_____
_____
_____
_____
_____
_____
_____
_____
_____
_____
_____
_____
_____
_____
_____
_____
_____
_____
_____
_____
_____

Figure 18.2 cont.

Documentation

Documentation of risk and safety inspections is critical to risk management. When a hazard analysis is made of fields or other facilities, findings must be documented and filed. If a recreational sport specialist decides not to make the scheduled safety inspection (a discretionary function) because of budget limitations or some other extenuating circumstance, he or she must document the reasons for that decision. This documentation is needed to limit the success of any future litigation problems should an accident occur. If the area does not have a history of safety problems and if there are no known existing dangers, a manager can make a decision not to inspect if the decision is based on good faith (*Christly v. United States*, 1985; *Duchy v. United States*, 1983; *Scheiler v. United States*, 1986). Any decision related to risk that intentionally changes written direction must be documented and filed. Part of the document should include the recreational sport specialist's rationale for the decision.

Legitimate Claims

If an injured person files a claim that is clearly the fault of the agency or private provider, the claim should be honored and expeditiously processed and paid. The principle of *res ipsa loquitur* ("the thing speaks for itself") is a rule of evidence that the negligence is inferred from the fact that the accident happened. To see if this doctrine applies to a specific situation and thus damages should be paid, the recreational sport specialist must determine if

- the accident or damage would not have occurred if reasonable care had been used and

- all the elements of the circumstances surrounding the accident were under the control of the defendant.

The doctrine can be further applied when there is no direct evidence to show cause or injury and when the detailed circumstantial evidence indicates that the negligence of the defendant is the most logical explanation for the injury (Prosser & Keaton, 1984).

Post-September 11 and Other Considerations

Since the terrorist attacks of September 11, 2001, people have been more sensitive to their personal safety. Large sport crowds could be the targets of a terrorist act. The 1996 Atlanta Olympics bombing is an example of the random possibilities that may draw a terrorist attack. Attacks by extremists may be perpetrated by international agents, domestic malcontents, the mentally ill, or individuals looking for notoriety. Trying to rationalize the reasons or target of terrorist rage may be folly; however, recreational sport specialists should consider a concentration of people to be a possible target and take adequate actions to safeguard the public. Before September 11, security was usually considered too much of an inconvenience for the participant and fan. However, people have come to expect and even want to have security checks as part of the sport event.

Recreational sport specialists have historically made safety decisions for participants and fans related to weather, such as rain, snow, cold, heat, lightning, winds, and flooding. Chemicals (insecticides and pesticides) on turf can be considered a health hazard when applied in non-compliance of label instructions. Due to situations that have occurred during the past two decades, security measures must now be taken in relation to fan riots, player fights, protection of officials, and even parent assaults on their own or other children participating in sports.

Investigation

Recreational sport specialists should be notified when an accident has occurred that may lead to litigation. The organization's legal counsel should also be notified as soon as possible. An investigation of any incident involving people or property must be made immediately after the accident while evidence and recall are fresh. (Each agency has its own investigation procedure. An example is the Forest Service USDA's procedures, contained in the policy section of the *Forest Service Manual and the Health and Safety Program Handbook*, FSH 6709.12, Amendment 1-32.1-5, dated April 1987, and in Investigations, Chapter 70 (6507.11K) in the *Forest Service Handbook*.) Preferably the investigation team includes recreational sport specialists as well as professional investigators. Do not expect the local law enforcement (state police, sheriff's department) to conduct an investigation that will meet your litigation needs.

If there is any indication that drugs or alcohol is involved in the accident, a request should be made for the necessary medical tests. This is particularly important in cases of serious injuries, death, or high property damage. Many times the recreational sport specialist is not aware that an accident has occurred until a claim or lawsuit has been filed. In such cases the investigation should occur upon receiving a formal claim or suit.

All investigation reports should be marked: *Attorney Work Product–Prepared in Anticipation of Litigation–Confidential*. This caption means that the investigative report cannot be given to anyone outside the agency without approval of legal counsel.

All claims against an agency should be handled efficiently and courteously regardless of the merits of the claim. Employees have no authority to agree to pay medical expenses or property damage; however, they should render as much assistance as possible to help save life, reduce pain and suffering, comfort family members, and limit property damage. Help, courtesy, and compassion can be generous without obligating the agency.

Accomplishing Risk Management

Personal commitment, rule enforcement, and emergency care are three components for successful risk management. By focusing on these components as part of a risk management plan, the recreational sport specialist will help the recreational sport program meet the objectives of a safety and risk management program mentioned at the beginning of the chapter.

Personal Commitment

A recreational sport specialist cannot provide effective risk management alone. The only way to implement an effective plan is to ingrain the concept of personal commitment in the minds of all employees. This can be done with threats, incentives, and numerous other psychological manipulations. However, experience has proven that force simply does not work when it comes to safety and risk management. Personal example is likely to be the best means of communicating commitment. A recreational sport specialist stooping down and wiping up a wet spot on a playing floor is an indelible memory for all who witnessed this commitment to a safe facility. Nothing had to be said; the deed was enough to communicate the message. The recreational sport specialist's example will result in other employees looking for wet spots on playing floors.

Rule Enforcement

Most recreational sport specialists choose their public contact personnel with a great deal of care. Especially important are the individuals in charge of sport rule enforcement. Astute recreational sport specialists will be wary of individuals who enthusiastically want a rule enforcement assignment. Some of the best enforcement personnel are interested in working with people first. Rule enforcement should

- protect individuals from each other,

- protect the facilities from abusive individuals, and

- protect individuals from dangers within a facility.

Overall, people should feel safe in a recreational sport setting.

Emergency Care

Because recreational sport may involve special locations and situations, emergency care may not be immediately available; thus the first care may be provided by organization personnel who are usually first on the scene of an accident. In many cases ambulance service and emergency medical technicians may be several minutes away. Agency personnel trained in first aid can save lives, so recreational sport personnel should receive first aid training on a regular basis.

Some people are hesitant to render assistance because of the possibility of lawsuits if after the assistance is rendered the recipient of the treatment believes he or she was not treated properly at the accident scene. All but two states have emergency care statutes that limit the liability of persons providing emergency assistance. The two states that are the exception, Alabama and Colorado, have case precedents that essentially accomplish the same thing.

Recreational sport specialists do not need to consult legal counsel every time there is an accident. They do need to prepare and train their personnel to adhere to professional standards, have adequate supplies and equipment to aid accident victims, be able to perform the most updated methods of first aid, keep records of the accident, and conduct a thorough investigation. There is no magic formula that provides immunity from suit. Agencies should not hesitate to provide recreational sport opportunities for the public, even though there is an element of risk in the activity. Participants in high-risk sports should be fully informed of the dangers involved, and efforts should be made to minimize that danger through training, certification, and proper equipment.

Some personnel may understandably be uncomfortable coming into contact with the families of individuals who were severely injured or killed in an accident. Personnel may even experience some animosity from the victims and their families. It is extremely important that cordial contact be maintained between agency personnel and victims of accidents. Organization personnel should not admit any guilt or offer to pay medical expenses; however, they should be generous with comfort and compassion.

Conclusion

Recreational sport specialists have a responsibility to protect the interests of three well-defined groups: the athlete, the fan, and the organization. They must be ready to take immediate action when significant risk is identified. Those who identify legal liability issues should be thanked, not condemned. This chapter provides a broad background in identifying and taking actions to reduce legal liability. When significant legal questions arise, consult with your organization's legal counsel or obtain legal counsel if none is provided by the organization.

Bibliography

Black, H. C., Nolan, J. R., & Connolly, M. J. (1979). *Blacks law dictionary* (5ᵗʰ ed.). Eagan, MN: West.

Breslin-Griffitt Carpet Co. v. Asadorian, Mo. App., 145 S.W.2d 494.

Butler v. United States, 726 F.2d 1057 (1984).

Christly v. United States, 20 F. Supp. 285 (D.C.S.C. 1985).

Davis v. United States, 716 F.2d 418 (1983).

Duchy v. United States, 713 F.2d 504 (1983).

Federal Employee Liability Reform Tort Compensation Act of 1988, Pub. L. No. 100-694.

Federal Tort Claims Act of 1946, 28 U.S.C. § 1346(b).

Kaiser, R. A. (1986). *Liability and law in recreation, parks, and sports.* Englewood Cliffs, NJ: Prentice-Hall.

Kozlowski, J. C. (1986). Recreation use laws applies to public lands in NY, NE, ID, OH, WA. *Parks and Recreation,* p. 22.

Leflar, R., & Kantrowitz, B. (1954). *Tort liability of the states, 29* N.Y.U.L. Rev 1363.

Mounsey v. Elland, 363 Mass. 693; 297 N.E.2d 43.

Mudrich v. Standard Oil Co., 1949, 87 Ohio App. 8, N.E. 2d 324, affirmed, 1950, 153 Ohio St. 31, 90 N.E.2d 859.

Muesenfechter v. St. Louis Car Co., Mo. App. 139 S.W.2d 1102.

Patterson v. Weatherspoon, 29 N.Car. App. 711, 225 S.E. 2d 634 (1976).

Prosser, W. L. (1980). *Law of torts.* St. Paul, MN: West.

Prosser, W. L., & Keaton, W. (1984). *Prosser & Keeton on torts.* St. Paul, MN: West.

Restatement (Second) of Torts, 1982, 1984, 1986.

Roos, Nestor, & Berber, J. (1968). *Governmental risk management manual.* Tucson, AZ: Risk Management Publishing.

Samuel E. Pentecost Construction Company v. O'Donnell, 112 Ind. App. 47; 39 N.E. 2d 812.

Scheiler v. United States, 642 F.Supp.2d 1210 (.D. Cal 1986).

Schnackenberg v. Towle, 123 N.E. 2d 925 (NY 1961).

Stern, S. T., & Ladden, C. S. (1971). *Civil litigation.* St. Paul, MN: West.

U. S. Consumer Product Safety Commission. (Year). *A handbook for public playground safety.* Washington, DC: Author.

van der Smissen, B. (1968). *Legal liability of cities and schools for injuries in recreation and parks.* Cincinnati, OH: W. H. Anderson.

van der Smissen, B. (1985). *National Safety Network Newsletter, 1*(4).

van der Smissen, B. (1990). *Legal liability and risk management for public and private entities.* Cincinnati, OH: W. H. Anderson.

Van Gordon v. Portland General Electric Company, 693 P.2d 1285 (Oregon 1985).

West Publishing. (1971). *American jurisprudence* (2nd ed.). St. Paul, MN: Author.

Yommer v. McKenzie, (1969) 225 Md. 220, 257 A.2d 138.

CHAPTER 19

Career Implications

CHAPTER OBJECTIVES

After reading this chapter, you will understand the implications of professionalism in recreational sport; be familiar with existing professional leadership systems and their contributions to recreational sport; recognize the importance of involvement in career development; identify career-advancement attributes; be aware of career options in training, setting, and stages of development; be able to formulate your marketability; and be able to analyze job offers.

KEY CONCEPTS

Professionalism
Career setting
Leadership systems
Career stages
Association
Marketability

Specialty organization
Career development
Trade group
Individual attributes
Training

Introduction

Careers in recreational sport are diverse, are challenging, and hold the potential for individual growth and community benefit. Realizing this potential is as fundamental as learning basic information about recreational sport. Recreational sport specialists must have professional goals in mind and then determine the best course of action in achieving those goals. Such an effort requires special attention, guidance, and perseverance as well as insight into career information. This chapter reviews key points that will help a recreational sport specialist realize what it means to have a professional career by emphasizing the importance of planning ahead for career development. It also discusses what a profession encompasses and strategies for pursuing possible employment opportunities.

Professionalism

In understanding a career, it is important to also understand the professional leadership system in which careers are embedded. This system reflects the overall meaning of a profession, and it represents the characteristics of the profession and its people as they fulfill their responsibilities in bringing a product or service into society. This section reviews the basic meaning of a profession, the leadership systems that support professionals, and how decisions made related to professional involvement can enhance a career.

Professional Basics

It has already been noted that recreational sport is a specialization within leisure, recreation, and sport. It is important for individuals in the field to understand what that specialization means to them because it can mean many things. Additionally, this means understanding the profession and its defining criteria. Although there are various approaches to defining a profession, there are three basic indicators: (a) global impact, (b) knowledge, and (c) control.

Global impact. All professions (law, medicine, education, engineering, etc.) perform a social function and as a result aim to meet a significant need, both locally and globally. A profession delivers products and/or services to individuals and in doing so represents a significant organizational structure with ongoing responsibilities. Leisure, recreation, and sport, in their broadest and most basic existence, impact the lives of individuals and ultimately have the potential to improve the quality of life around the globe. As such, recreational sport is a significant field that delivers a unique, popular product with its basic principles and practices being sport for all, with fun, enjoyment, and personal development as the incentives and benefits.

Knowledge. All professions also have unique information that has been developed specifically for academic preparation or training in the profession. This training must take place prior to individuals being endorsed or certified by their professional body. Profession-specific information combines both practical and theoretical concepts, representing an entire system that is often referred to as the profession's body of knowledge. This body of knowledge is continually studied and researched to stay relevant for its members. Colleges and universities are a large producer of professional bodies of knowledge, but there are additional institutions that promote the creation and development of professional knowledge such as government research organizations.

Control. The final and most critical indicator of a profession is control, which encompasses strategies to assess and oversee the activities of the profession. Such strategies allow professional regulatory bodies to observe, monitor, limit, guide, and test members, ensuring quality control measures are in place across the profession. This control can be implemented in different ways to maintain and protect the profession and its role in society. One example is professional preparation involving formal curricula and accreditation systems that help guide training (i.e., universities, colleges). Also, professions have established codes of ethics and conduct, which are written statements that communicate mission, integrity, and characteristics of the profession to those within and outside of the profession.

Perhaps most important to professional control is the leadership system that formally acts as keeper of the profession. These professional organizations provide affiliations and opportunities for involvement for all individuals in the profession. As such, these organizations provide a great amount of influence in both determining and then reinforcing the profession's mission and guiding norms.

Viewing recreational sport as a profession is rooted in the reality that such responsibilities are not only societal but also cross-cultural, serving individuals globally. The field has a body of knowledge that is complex, involving many administrative and delivery details. Professionally managing such knowledge protects it and provides a positive, safe leisure experience, which is a core value of recreational sport.

Leadership Systems

As noted, critical to any profession is its leadership and the norms that guide all those involved. Leisure, recreation, and sport have varied leadership systems that influence the field throughout the world, especially in the United States. Professional associations, specialty organizations, and trade groups each operate independently to support sport specialist professionals, among others.

Professional associations. True professions are organized by formal associations or societies, which vary depending on the scope and nature of the profession. An example of a professional association in recreation is the National Recreation and Park Association (http://www.nrpa.org/). To the layperson, such systems can seem complicated and irrelevant, but for the professional sport specialist they are fundamental and necessary to understand for career development. Being affiliated and an active member in such associations is a career responsibility. Associations are founded on formal protocols and procedures that are intended to support the work of its members. For example, leaders are typically elected at annual general meetings, and their activities are then guided by established constitutions and bylaws intended to advance the cause of the profession. In the case of recreational sport, the cause could be increasing sport opportunities or enhancing sport experiences.

In recreational sport, several related associations represent the field. In many respects, recreational sport is still evolving as a profession, and its true identity in society has yet to be fully realized. While this is unfortunate for many reasons, it is understandable due to the field's extensiveness and confused existence as explained in Chapter 1. There are varied interpretations of recreational sport's nature as a discipline. In an effort to reflect this diversity, Figure 19.1 identifies different associations that incorporate recreational sports and provides accompanying website information for further review.

American Alliance for Health, Physical Education, Recreation, and Dance
www.aahperd.org

American Association for Leisure and Recreation
www.aahperd.org/aalr/

International Association of Athletics Federations
www.iaaf.org

**National Intramural-Recreational
Sports Association**
www.nirsa.org

National Recreation and Park Association
www.nrpa.org

North American Society for Sport Management
www.nassm.com

**National Association for Sport and
Physical Education (NASPE)**
www.aahperd.org/naspe/

Figure 19.1. Associations that Incorporate Recreational Sports

Specialty organizations. Leisure, recreation, and sport activity is so expansive, popular, and complicated that there are all kinds of specialty organizations devoted to addressing its needs and thus supporting the profession. Although these organizations practice professionalism, they do not represent the full meaning of a profession and corresponding responsibility because they are usually focused on a specific activity. It is important to note that the motivation for such organizations varies and may not solely revolve around recreational sport. The list of specialty organizations is lengthy, but Figure 19.2 provides examples of current organizations that incorporate recreational sport.

Trade groups. Still another form of leadership that is intended to bolster a profession is the trade group, which positions itself to serve (and benefit from) a profession. Trade groups play an important professional role meeting varied needs by selling products and services as well as providing expert assistance through consultation and advising. Their trade shows and attendance at national conferences provide the recreational sport specialist with valuable professional interaction because of their current knowledge, relevant facts, and information that can enhance the delivery of recreational sport. Although trade groups do not have professional memberships,

they do provide a much-needed service that may not be available otherwise. The international recognition of some of the trade groups listed in Figure 19.3 demonstrates the nature and importance of these professional leadership supports.

Thus far this chapter has discussed three different professional leadership systems that will likely be a part of one's career in recreational sport; however, awareness of such systems is only the beginning. Being involved in and benefiting from these systems is fundamental to being a professional. For the recreational sport specialist there are ample reasons to become the best professional possible, including being on the cutting edge of the profession and taking advantage of what leadership systems have to offer.

Involvement

In order to get the most out of a professional leadership system, involvement is key. Involvement in a professional leadership system often occurs in a state system, a specialty organization, or a national association. Becoming involved allows individuals the opportunity to make a contribution to the profession while at the same time receive personal and professional benefits. Before considering the benefits that are derived from professional involvement, a recreational sport specialist needs to decide how to get involved.

Aerobics and Fitness Association of America www.afaa.com	**National Strength and Conditioning Association** www.nsca-lift.org
Amateur Athletic Union www.aausports.org	**Professional Bowlers Association** www.pba.org
Association of Volleyball Professionals www.avp.com	**Professional Golf Association** www.pga.org
Boy Scouts of America www.scouting.org	**United States Air Force** www.airforce.com
Boys & Girls Clubs www.bgca.org	**United States Amateur Baseball Association** www.usaba.com
Girl Scouts of America www.girlscouts.org	**United States Army Recreation** www.armymwr.com
International Amateur Boxing Association www.aiba.net	**United States Navy Recreation** www.navy.mil
International Health, Racquet, and Sportsclub Association www.ihrsa.com	**United States Racquetball Association** www.usra.org
International Water Ski Federation www.iwsf.com	**United States Tennis Association** www.usta.com
Gus Macker Basketball Association www.macker.com	**United States Water Fitness Association** www.uswfa.com
National Alliance for Youth Sports www.nays.org	**YMCA** www.ymca.net
National Collegiate Athletic Association www.ncaa.org	**U.S. Youth Soccer Association** www.usysa.org

Figure 19.2. Specialty Organizations that Incorporate Recreational Sport

Selection. First, it is necessary to research the available options. By assessing each system's strengths and weaknesses, you can decide which one best serves your career aspirations. In the beginning you should start locally with professionals who have related experience and can provide assistance and direction with your everyday work. Such groups include citizen organizations, clubs, and committees that focus on an interest related to your career.

As this initial involvement increases over time, it becomes important to decide on the level of desired involvement. Examples of involvement include serving on a committee, making presentations, attending conferences and special workshops, and accepting leadership roles, all of which will help you understand the needs and concerns of the profession. This understanding then can be used to enhance your ongoing work as a recreational sport specialist. This effort should lead you in the direction that best serves your interests and ability and is consistent with career expectations. Selecting a path and degree of involvement should not be taken lightly because your career will be defined by not only what you do but also the benefits (e.g., networking, knowledge, opportunities) that you gain through professional affiliations.

Athletic Business Magazine www.athleticbusiness.com	**Ping Golf** www.pinggolf.com
Daiwa Sport Fishing Tackle www.daiwa.com	**REI Sporting Goods** www.rei.com
Eastbay Online www.eastbay.com	**Runner's World Magazine** www.runnersworld.com
Fitness Magazine www.fitnessmagazine.com	**Speedo** www.speedo.com
Kawasaki Motor Sports www.kawasaki.com	**Sport Court Game Courts** www.sportcrt.com
Life Fitness Equipment www.lifefitness.com	**Timeless Technologies Software** http://www.timelesstech.com
Nike www.nike.com	**Trek Bicycle Equipment** www.trekbikes.com
Outside Magazine http://outsidemag.com	**Wilson Sporting Goods** www.wilson.com

Figure 19.3. Trade Groups and Recreational Sports

Benefits. Being associated with one or two professional leadership systems can translate into many benefits. The most important aspect of leadership systems is their role as advocate for the profession. This means they can develop, foster, and provide accurate information; lobby government and decision makers when and where it is necessary; support interests and concerns; and perpetuate the meaning and significance of a profession. Involvement can lead to varied educational opportunities such as academic credit through continuing education, conferences with speeches and work sessions, special workshops, and seminars. These opportunities expose a recreational sport specialist to product demonstrations and methods by focusing on the latest innovations of the profession. Such affiliations also create and maintain communication systems (electronic messages, magazines, newsletters) and networking systems (problem solving, supporting one another, relationships) that will prove invaluable throughout one's career.

Additionally, leaders work to create and foster positive professional behavior and activity through written standards, a code of ethics, and guidelines. Such leadership also recognizes positive and meaningful contributions and provides incentives for members to practice professionalism and pursue excellence. Still another important benefit to becoming involved in professional activities is access to information relevant to recreational sports, including formal research, survey data, assessments, and critical work resulting from scholarly activity.

With this basic insight into professionalism, it is hoped that as a recreational sport specialist, you have come to realize your future role and responsibility as a professional. Competence in daily tasks is expected; however, going beyond the minimum requirements and becoming involved with other professionals on a local, regional, or national level can add to your value as a recreational sport specialist and ultimately enhance your career development.

Individual Attributes

Professional involvement and commitment to a career can only be fully realized if you accept the idea of professionalism and align it with your ongoing employment activities. Finding a suitable position that brings career satisfaction can be challenging and in some respects complex, especially because the field of recreational sport can be competitive, with many individuals seeking the same employment opportunities. When asked about desired competencies, campus recreation directors indicated that strong language/speaking skills and writing skills were essential in most recreational sport settings. It is wise to review your capacities and create a plan for obtaining your desired employment. To help create this plan, the first step is realizing what kind of background traits employers look for in potential employees.

Background

No matter where you are in your career, your background continues to grow, week to week, month to month, and year to year. Everything you do that relates to recreational sport (and beyond) can and will make a difference in how far you advance in your career or how good of a professional you become. There are three aspects of background that will be discussed: (a) education, (b) experience, and (c) attitude.

Education. As you pursue your career, your employers will consider certain knowledge a basic necessity for a job. Education, training, and overall career development are fundamental to one's career. One of the most important aspects of a professional career as a recreational sport specialist is formal study at a college or university that offers a degree in leisure, recreational, or sport management with an emphasis in recreational sport. Completing such a degree program demonstrates your understanding of required knowledge and communicates this to prospective employers. In making decisions about which degree program to complete, know that an ac-

credited program is more valuable than an unaccredited program because there is a guarantee that certain competencies are delivered. Figure 19.4 lists some colleges and universities that are recognized as leaders in professional preparation of recreational sport specialists.

Another example of education a recreational sport specialist may possess is certifications. A list of certifications is listed in Figure 19.5; all of them represent special training that may parallel an interest you might have. Note that some are specific to sport while others deal with safety and care of participants. All will contribute to your development as a professional.

Experience. Another critical foundation of career background is hands-on experiences because so much about recreational sport needs to be experienced to be understood. Pursuing meaningful experiences that contribute to your career cannot be overemphasized, whether such experiences occur during college and university studies, through internships or part-time jobs, or during summer work as an official, coach, supervisor, lifeguard, ranger, instructor, or program assistant. Many campus recreational sport directors began their careers as officials or swim instructors. Even working outside of the field as a waiter or waitress, parking attendant, or construction worker demonstrates a work ethic that can impact one's professional skills.

Central Michigan University
www.cmich.edu

Georgia Southern University
www.georgiasouthern.edu

Indiana University Bloomington
www.iub.edu

Indiana State University
www.indstate.edu

Kent State University
www.kent.edu

North Carolina State University
www.ncsu.edu

Temple University
www.temple.edu

Texas Tech University
www.ttu.edu

University of Arkansas
www.uark.edu

University of Idaho
www.uidaho.edu

University of Illinois at Urbana-Champaign
www.uiuc.edu

University of Iowa
www.uiowa.edu

University of Minnesota
www.umn.edu

University of Mississippi
www.olemiss.edu

Figure 19.4. Top Colleges and Universities Offering Recreational Sport Programs

---

Health and Safety Certifications

- Cardiopulmonary resuscitation (CPR)
- Automated external defibrillators (AED)
- First aid
- Lifeguard
- Water safety instructor

All of these certifications can be found at www.redcross.org.

Sport Certifications

- Referee and official
- Coach
- Instructor
- Tennis
- Aquatics
- Martial arts
- Ski patrol

Fitness Certifications

- Aerobics instructor
- Personal training

All of the fitness certifications can be found at www.acefitness.org (America Council on Exercise).

Figure 19.5. Examples of Special Training in Recreational Sports

In addition to paid experiences, volunteer experiences should contribute to the recreational sport specialist's career development. Volunteering in community activities such as Boys and Girls Clubs, 4-H, and youth sports or serving as a student leader or officer of a student organization suggests leadership traits that speak volumes. These are real-life situations that complement classroom learning and help supplement one's recreational sport career. Seeking out as many opportunities as possible and considering how each one ultimately contributes to one's career is a worthwhile activity.

Attitude. As a recreational sport specialist develops an awareness of his or her background, it is critical to realize the importance of attitude. Attitude is reflected in personality and style of expression and is only as good as how one feels and acts in different situations. Having a positive attitude can go a long way in a career, especially in recreational sport where challenging situations are often regular occurrences. Do not underestimate the importance of attitude. This is especially important when supervising staff and volunteers so that a negative work environment does not develop.

Education, experience, and attitude are three career attributes that should be taken seriously. As a recreational sport specialist, you should make every effort to build each one as they relate to your career because each will definitely come into the picture as potential employers assess your background and career potential.

Traits

Professional traits parallel background. These traits exist in everyone and can be valuable if recognized and applied in a professional manner properly. Professional traits can be universal because they are widespread among all professionals, especially successful professionals. As you pursue your career, you should build professional traits to reflect the unique package that is you. These traits are listed in alphabetical order to emphasize that they are equally important.

Ethics. Ethics are so important to professions that they are incorporated into a leadership system in the form of a code of conduct. Career-minded professionals must practice ethical behavior. Ethical behavior includes being honest, having integrity, being accountable, and being moral at all times. While often not a significant part of university or college curricula, professional associations, workplaces, and peers can provide guidance with respect to knowing what is right and wrong in the workplace.

Fairness. Everyone likes to be treated fairly without undue stress, misrepresentation, or deceit. Unfortunately, management sometimes creates situations where individuals lose sight of being fair to others. Often goals become too important, overriding all other concerns and causing individuals to lose sight of how decisions affect individuals (whether they are participants or employees). Good professionals are careful to avoid such situations, practicing fairness through objectivity, cooperation, decency, and being attentive and reasonable to all individuals engaged in an agency.

Focus. Professionals can be described as those who are focused, committed to their work, and interested in contributing to the overall agency goals and mission. Often professionals take on additional responsibilities and accomplish tasks in a positive and even progressive fashion. Such individuals are valuable to employers because their productivity helps management goals to be met and product delivery to be successful. The traits of a focused professional include being hard working, well organized, timely, good at problem solving, and dedicated.

Image. Reputation results from performance and how recreational sport specialists present themselves (i.e., their image). Image may or may not be openly discussed, but it should not be taken for granted. As a professional, you should project a professional image to enhance your career. All examples of images are important, so take into consideration things such as appearance, style, tidiness, speaking, and listening.

Loyalty. Loyalty is an interesting concept as it relates to career development. Loyalty can exist at an individual level between supervisor and subordinate, administration and employees, and anywhere that recognition and support of authority is important. Working in a recreational sport environment requires teamwork and cannot be accomplished without loyalty to leadership and established mission and goals—in other words, loyalty to the agency. Aspects of loyalty include commitment and devotion to leadership, adherence to principles of operation, dedication, trustworthiness, respecting policies and procedures, and not talking negatively about colleagues and superiors.

Sensitivity. In this day and age, sensitivity is crucial. Sensitivity can be thought of as thoughtfulness to all individuals and a lack of bias or discrimination of any type. Insensitivity can have legal implications that may negatively affect a recreational sport specialist's reputation. Always treat others as you would like to be treated: with fairness, kindness, thoughtfulness, and appreciation. Emotional intelligence as discussed in Chapter 11 explores this idea more fully.

There may be other traits valuable to a career-minded person, but those just discussed are relevant to anyone entering recreational sports. Each should be included in the day-to-day work of all recreational sport specialists.

Options and Decisions

At some point, all professionals need to review their options and make a choice about the direction their career is headed. Because recreational sport is a major part of the leisure, recreation, and sport industry, a career path as a recreational sport specialist has great potential and a number of opportunities. Determining when and where to apply learned competencies requires special attention. Certain questions can help with this decision-making process:

- What are my career options?
- In what area should I specialize?
- What fits my abilities and interests?
- What will bring me the greatest career satisfaction?

The following section on specialty areas and common career paths should help in addressing these questions and create some clarity regarding individual career paths.

Specialty Areas

Job opportunities within the field of recreational sport can essentially be divided into two specialty areas: jobs that emphasize programming and jobs that emphasize sport. There are many similarities between programming and sport-related areas. For instance, both areas approach programming by using unique methods to meet participants' needs and interests; both are influenced by the agency's scope, size, and structure; and both are prerequisites for career advancement into higher level administrative roles. As careers progress, a recreational sport specialist will tend to take on greater leadership and management responsibilities while lessening their direct involvement with programming.

Program emphasis. The first specialty area (program) is heavily based on learned competencies across the different recreational sport delivery areas, such as instructional sport, informal sport, intramural and extramural sport, club sport, and special events. Training or education can occur as part of a higher education curriculum in recreation or sport management where academic course content is applicable to agencies across the three sectors such as military bases, city or community agencies, correctional institutes, college and university campuses, YMCAs, Boys and Girls Clubs, and commercial settings such as Disneyland. Training material is quite comprehensive and covers all program areas and techniques that address participation for large populations; a variety of sports, facilities, and equipment; and program staffing.

Program emphasis is a complex area of study that requires a broad spectrum of skills and abilities. For example, a recreational sport specialist needs to be competent in providing sport instruction to large numbers of individuals, organizing tournaments of varying interests, and serving as an adviser of clubs and youth groups of particular sports. Furthermore, a recreational sport specialist with a programming emphasis type job may also supervise large facilities, oversee several hourly employees and volunteers, coordinate and schedule sport activities and facilities, and supervise maintenance tasks.

Sport emphasis. The second specialty area in recreational sport represents a job with more specific training in one particular sport. Employment opportunities are usually in sport-specific facilities (e.g., golf course) requiring trained and certified experts (e.g., golf professional) to deliver the activity. Delivery and programming usually include sport instruction, tournament arrangements, reservation system management, and special event planning. While programming strategies are often similar to those in the previous specialty area (program), the application is different in part because participation numbers are fewer due to the single-sport interest. Emphasis on a single sport is less common in recreational sport, but it does exist and may interest those who have a special sport skill and/or aptitude.

Sport-emphasized positions usually require certification as a prerequisite to employment. Examples of sport-emphasized employment include golf course management, aquatic and waterfront management, ski slope management, and marina management. Facilities can be independently operated or connected to much larger recreation management systems such as resorts, independent businesses, and country clubs. Sport-specific facilities include tennis courts, bowling centers, racquetball courts, and horseback-riding farms or parks.

After considering these two specialty areas, it is important to determine how one's background, education, and experience contribute to a likely choice and help determine a future career choice.

Career Paths

In recreational sport there are three general career paths based on the organizational sector discussed throughout this text: public sectors, private not-for-profit sectors, and commercial sectors. As previously discussed all have their own management philosophy, purpose, and structure. Although the product, sport activity, may be the same, employment requirements, standards, principles, and so on are very different.

Public sector careers. Recreational sport opportunities in public settings represent an extensive area of employment including local, state, and federal governmental systems. For example, within most municipalities, there is a recreation department, of which opportunities exist for a recreational sport specialist to gain employment. There may be multiple agencies within each of these management systems that deliver recreational sport as part of their total service. Local governments are influenced by legislation, policies, districting, and other factors that require specific knowledge and training. The same is true of state systems, such as state parks, vacation areas, and water space for public use.

The federal management system is also a public setting that offers a variety of career paths. This career option tends to focus on, but is not limited to, outdoor recreation with the majority of the duties being sports related. Management systems include the National Park Service and related services, the Fish and Wildlife Service, and the Bureau of Land Management, which all provide opportunities for the public to incorporate recreational sport into their outdoor experiences.

Private not-for-profit sector careers. The second career path available to a recreational sport specialist is the private not-for-profit sector and represents a substantial number of opportunities at local, state, and national levels. Jobs at settings such as YMCAs, Boys & Girls Clubs, and amateur sport organizations can provide wonderful opportunities for applying knowledge gained through education, training, and experience. It is important to note that many individuals are able to begin developing their career through voluntary experiences in this sector because of its heavy reliance on volunteers.

Commercial sector career. A third career path is the commercial sector, which is almost always founded on an entrepreneurial spirit. Management systems of this nature are designed to sell a sport activity as a product in order to generate a profit. These recreational sport agencies may include sole proprietorships, partnerships, or corporations, all of which deliver sport activities and services to clients, customers, and members. Further examples of settings related to recreational sports are retail outlets or sport pro shops, sport product manufacturing and wholesaling, sport travel, and tourism businesses. Recreational sport specialists who choose to work in private settings need specific business skills and knowledge particularly in budgeting, accounting, and marketing.

Although the three settings offering recreational sport employment opportunities differ in many respects, parallels do exist in the value they place on sport participation and activity, which allows for moving between sectors. With training and self-awareness, a recreational sport specialist will be able to select a setting that optimizes his or her career potential.

Career Stages

As presented in Chapter 11, employment in recreational sport settings can be categorized around three stages. As professionals move through these stages, additional knowledge is gained and experiences are expanded, which adds to a professional's development and potential to move. These stages can be broken down into three segments: early or entry, middle, and late, each with defining characteristics.

Early career stage. Entry-level or early career employment usually lasts from one to six years and primarily consists of positions involving the direct delivery of sport activity to participants. This role gives inexperienced professionals an opportunity to familiarize themselves with the recreational sport environment. Salaries are usually low, and benefits are not always included. It is during this stage that a recreational sport specialist should strive to demonstrate work ethic and positive attitude, displaying a willingness to be productive and contribute to upper management efforts. While entry-level positions may only be part time or seasonal, they provide incredible experiences that include direct contact with participants. Entry-level work can be characterized by long hours, challenging situations that require the understanding and application of basic techniques. These responsibilities are an excellent opportunity for young or inexperienced professionals to develop their skills by implementing the basic concepts and principles of recreational sport management.

Middle career stage. Middle-management positions usually last from five to 15 years, depending on the agency, organizational structure, and career development opportunities. During this stage, a professional may be responsible for other employees, which entails various management strategies. Even though these positions involve program planning and organization, middle-management staff is not responsible for direct delivery. A sport program coordinator usually delivers the programming. Middle stage can be characterized by autonomous work, the coordination of specialty areas of recreational sport (e.g., program, sport), management of facilities and equipment, program management, staff supervision, and the marketing of programs and services. If performance is judged positively, administration may assign individuals to positions that allow for more significant leadership. Middle-management positions include titles such as assistant director, associate director, head professional, and club manager.

Late career stage. Late or upper management career stage represents the executive, administrative effort of recreational services. Such opportunities are usually associated with years of experience, specialized skills, and professional activity. Reputation and credentials play a major part in securing these coveted positions. Senior positions include directors, executive directors, executive officers, and division heads, with the primary responsibility relating to overall administration, leadership, and supervision. These professionals are responsible for determining the overall direction of the department and rely on others to make sure program delivery goes as planned. Increasingly, this role has become more complex, especially in campus settings, as the field has grown and diversified in its mission. Specific duties include goal and mission development, long-range planning, budgeting, facility development, personnel, public relations, and maintaining standards of operations. At this level, a professional has the greatest ability to serve the profession through committee work, executive leadership, presentations at conferences, and significant involvement at national organizations.

This overview of the different management levels is intended to explain another consideration in planning your career. Increasing responsibilities, advancing positions, and changing assignments will all affect career progression. Be patient, and most important, be professional. Do the best you can in order to make the next level a real option for career growth.

Pursuing Aspirations

Now that the concept of a profession has been discussed, including individual attributes and different career options, specific strategies related to achieving career goals merit discussion including self-marketing and judging potential employment opportunities.

Self-Marketing

No matter what stage a recreational sport specialist may be at in his or her career, the goal of moving upward is consistent with being a professional. Because recreational sport is a viable entry-level and middle-management career path, this text shares basic information on marketing oneself. Whether it is a lateral or upward move, new opportunities and career growth should be your goals. There are specific activities for you to do in order to market yourself and plan for career progression, which are now discussed.

Portfolio. Early on you should be thinking about a portfolio or a documentation system that represents an ongoing reflection of your career. This may seem burdensome and time consuming, but it is well worth the effort. As time passes, it is important to have a system in place that helps you recall career activities in an organized manner. The following items should be included in a portfolio, along with anything else that demonstrates your career progress:

- college transcript,
- certifications,
- recognition letters,
- photos,
- written evaluations,
- résumé,
- publications,
- speeches,
- letters of recommendation,
- summary of work responsibilities,
- project involvement,
- job description,
- attendance at seminars and workshops, and
- creative activity.

A portfolio may not be requested by an employer; its value lies in its convenience for quick reference and availability. In fact, portfolios are rarely requested with job applications, but such documentation is an excellent resource, especially during the middle and later stages of your career.

Résumé. The most common document in self-marketing is a professional résumé and accompanying cover letter. This document is almost always required by potential employers and is the primary way you present yourself. A résumé briefly summarizes career stages and other pertinent information, giving an impression of your work and professional activity. Résumé styles can vary greatly, but Figure 19.6 is a style that is received well by employers. As you can see, the résumé highlights important elements about you and your career, including education, professional experience, certifications, technical skills, career aspirations, and references. It is important that your résumé is current, taking into account early, middle, and late career information that positions you with a job opportunity that matches your potential. When applying for positions, it is important to always tailor your cover letter to the position announcement and highlight how your résumé aligns with the position.

Recommendation letter. Letters of recommendation commonly accompany a résumé. Letters of recommendation are usually written by past supervisors and colleagues. Such letters may be asked for during the search and screen process, and you should take special care in determining who will provide the most supportive and positive recommendations. Your relationship with these individuals can and should be nurtured, even to the point where you might advise them of their importance to you and ask them to serve as a reference. Take into consideration their experience, job title, and career success because their prestige and reputation will be noted as they share their thoughts regarding your performance, work ethic, attitude, and potential to do the job. These letters should be thought of as formal documents that are confidential between the reference and the potential employer.

Search options. The next step in marketing yourself occurs when you are looking for a new position. In searching for a new position, there are many approaches that can yield success, which include

- reviewing professional publications, journals, and job announcements. These announcements usually cite the job title, provide a brief description, and list applicant requirements.
- networking with colleagues, peers, mentors, and alumni where information about other work options is shared in a more informal manner. Attending alumni events is always a useful strategy when looking for employment.

Full name:_____ E-mail Address:_____
     (First, middle initial, last)

Current address:_____
                (Where you currently reside)
Permanent address:_____
                (Address where future (up to 1 year) correspondence can be sent)

A campus address for a student_____
                         (Not necessary if the same as permanent)

Career Objective
- Brief statement that reflects career aspirations.

Education
- List high school and college degrees and dates attended.

Skills and Certifications
- List specialized training beyond degrees.
- List applicable certifications (CPR, lifeguard, first aid)

Work Experience
- List work positions held.
- Include job title, time period, and brief description of primary responsibilities.

Volunteer Experience
- List positions and program activities where you donated your time.

Affiliations
- List memberships in national and state professional organizations, local groups, honor societies, and so on.

Honors and Awards
- List honors and awards received academic honors, scholarships, philanthropic honors, competition awards)

References
- List the names of previous supervisors, college professors, or specialized trainers who can vouch for your character, work ethic, and potential as an employee (include an address, telephone number, and e-mail address).

Figure 19.6. Resume Format

- searching the Internet where there are services that help connect employees with potential employers. As well, visiting the actual websites of organizations that offer recreational sport programs and services is a useful activity.

Personal contact. As you market yourself, you will eventually make contact with potential employers. At this point, everything you have done in your career along with your self-marketing system will come together to represent who you are as a professional. You will be assessed and compared to other individuals who are vying for the same job. The critical part of this contact is the planned interview, which consists of inquiries that allow potential employers to interact with you regarding your experience, communication skills, attitude, appearance, and professional contributions. It is important to be professional and realize that you are being judged, but you must also assess what the potential employer has to offer.

Judging Offers
Once you receive a job offer, you must determine whether to accept or reject that offer. Depending on

where you are in your career, offers can be reviewed with colleagues as well as family members. The following points should be given serious thought as you make your decision: job description, employer beliefs and attitudes, salary and benefits, and potential career growth.

Job description. When a potential employer initiates a formal search for a particular job, they usually make a job announcement that is based on a formal job description. Most job descriptions include agency title and address, job title, position summary, administrative reporting line, and job functions. Such information should be studied carefully since this document can eventually serve as a contract. Specific job functions can reveal a great deal about employer expectations. Ask questions about job expectations, including office hours, level of responsibility, job flexibility, weekend and evening work, and so on. The job description provides an excellent example about the actual work and the many details that are involved.

Employer beliefs and attitude. The basic beliefs and attitudes of your potential employer are critical in judging a potential employment opportunity. So much about a work environment is influenced by the administration and its leadership style. It is important to take the time to reflect on how the employer's beliefs and attitudes compare to your own. Often these characteristics are revealed during the interview when you ask questions or make observations about how they approach problems, motivate, and give direction. Interviewers are usually future supervisors who you will be required to interact with frequently, and it is imperative that you feel comfortable working with them.

Salaries and benefits. No matter where you are in your career, employee compensation for work responsibilities should receive special attention. Because recreational sport often has certain needs requiring work beyond the call of duty, salary is very important. Fair compensation for work should be discussed and even negotiated where appropriate. Factors include cost of living (housing, food, taxes, insurances, and utilities), salary, and benefits (health insurance, vacation, and sick leave). Such compensations for your services should be adequate and parallel to what you bring to your employer through education and experience.

Potential growth. The steps in a career that enhance professional growth are critical, so whenever it comes time to judge a job opportunity, determine its potential to enhance your expertise, knowledge, and experience. For example, does the job offer creative activities, time for professional development, and involvement in leadership systems that can bring professional exposure not only for you but also for the agency? You will need to determine whether a potential job is an upgrade that will add to your portfolio and résumé and that will lead to meaningful career growth. Judging an employment opportunity can be challenging, but it is critical. You will be making a professional decision that can take you to the next stage of your career as well as affect your personal life because of the changes it brings. The better prepared you are to handle such situations, the better your chances are of dealing with it in the best interests of you and those close to you.

Shining Example

The Ohio State University Department of Recreational Sports

The Ohio State University (OSU) Department of Recreational Sports is an example of a comprehensive recreational sports program at a large university. It boasts a large number of indoor and outdoor sport and fitness facilities as well as programming in many different areas.

Clientele:

The OSU Department of Recreational Sports served over three million participants in its programs and facilities yearly. These participants include students, faculty, and staff at the university, as well as members of the community.

Facilities:

The department manages 14 facilities. The 5 indoor facilities consist of a main recreation center; two smaller centers with multipurpose courts, free weights, climbing wall, and cardio equipment; a tennis center; and two new centers, including an Adventure Recreation Center. The outdoor facilities consist of basketball courts, baseball diamonds, jogging paths, disk golf fields, and sand volleyball court, a roller hockey rink, and sports fields

Program Details:

The Department of Recreational Sports offers a variety of programs and activities including class instruction, aquatics, adventure trips, climbing, drop-in fitness and recreation, intramural sports, sport clubs, massage therapy, personal training, disc golf, skateboarding, roller hockey, and many other activities.

Budget:

The department's budget is approximately $2.4 million per year.

Marketing:

Several marketing strategies are used, including the departmental Web site (http://recsports.osu.edu/), display cases on campus, tours, outreach events, and information in orientation guides. In addition, there are marketing programs for residence halls and Greek and other student organizations. Other modes of marketing include comprehensive print brochures, advertising in campus and community newspapers, and word-of-mouth direct communications. The department also utilizes social networking in its marketing strategies (i.e. YouTube, Facebook, etc.).

Jobs and Careers:

There is over 60 full-time and over 750 student staff. The staff in higher level positions includes a director, 4 associate directors, 10 assistant directors, a business manager, a human resources director, 5 program coordinators, and 18 graduate students; as well as various departmental specialists and office associates

Affiliated Professional Organizations:

Employees of the Department of Recreational Sports belong to many professional organizations including the National Intramural and Recreational Sports Association (NIRSA), National Recreation and Park Association (NRPA), American Council on Exercise (ACE), International Dance Exercise Association (IDEA), and the National Academy of Sports Medicine (NASM). In addition, employees belong to regional associations, including the Ohio Recreational Sports Association, Central Ohio Football Officials Association, and the Ohio Parks and Recreation Association.

Internships:

Internships are available in several areas including adapted recreational sports specialized, administrative positions, aquatics, camps, competitive sports, development and fundraising, event management, facilities, marketing and graphic design, outdoor recreation, research, and scheduling.

Awards and Recognition:

Members of the Department of Recreational Sports at Ohio State University have received many awards from national and state professional organizations, including merit and service awards from NIRSA and honor awards from the Ohio Recreational Sports Association. In addition, several members of the staff have received grants or held executive positions within those organizations.

Conclusion

Working in the field of recreational sport is exciting and rewarding because it has a tremendous potential to enhance the recreation and sport profession. Realizing the responsibility of preparing for a professional career is fundamental for all recreational sport specialists. Serious attention should be given to this endeavor, including sound planning and decision making. It is important to focus on a specific direction in recreational sport, looking to the future for answers on how and what you are doing. In an attempt to help you do so, this chapter looked at the basic criteria of a profession and the leadership systems that will impact your career. It also reviewed how involvement as a professional can provide advantages. It described individual attributes that are important in everyday work and career development, and it discussed different career options in recreational sport. Finally, it covered points to help you market yourself and make decisions in considering job offers. The valuable information in this chapter will contribute to your future in the field of recreational sport.

Bibliography

Adair, J. E., & Allen, M. (2003). *The concise: Time management and personal development.* London, England: Thorogood.

Ball, J., Simpson, S., Ardovino, P., & Skept-Arlt, K. (2008). Leadership competencies of university recreational directors in Wisconsin. *Recreational Sports Journal, 32,* 3-10.

Chelladurai, P. (2006). *Human resource management in sport and recreation (*2nd ed.). Champaign, IL: Human Kinetics.

Hoff, K., Kroll, J., & Parks, J. (2003). *Developing a professional perspective.* In J. Parks & J. Quarterman (Eds.), *Contemporary sport management* (2nd ed.) (pp. 23-40). Urbana, IL: Sagamore.

Hums, M., & Goldsbury, V. (2005). *Strategies for career success.* In L. Masteralexis, C. Barr, & M. Hums (Eds.), *Principles and practice of sport management* (pp. 436-449). Boston, MA: Jones and Bartlett.

Kjeldsen, E. M. (1990). Sport management careers: A descriptive analysis. *Journal of Sport Management, 4*(2), 121-132.

Parks, J. B., & Zanger, B. R. (1990). *Sport and fitness management: Career strategies and professional content.* Champaign, IL: Human Kinetics.

Ross, C., & Schurger, T. (2007). Career paths of campus recreational sport directors. *Recreational Sports Journal, 31,* 146-155.

Rowh, M. (2001). Sports careers: Not just for athletes. *Career World, 29*(4), 6-12.

Schneider, R., Stier, W., Kampf, S., Haines, S., & Wilding, G. (2006). Characteristics, attributes, and competencies sought in new hires by campus recreation directors. *Recreational Sports Journal, 30,* 142-153.

Shivers, J. S. (1993). *Introduction to recreational service.* Springfield, IL: Charles C. Thomas.

Index